LIBRARIES, BOOKS & CULTURE

LIBRARIES, BOOKS & CULTURE

Proceedings of
Library History Seminar VII
6–8 March 1985
Chapel Hill, North Carolina

Edited by
Donald G. Davis, Jr.

Graduate School of Library And Information Science
The University of Texas at Austin
1986

Library of Congress Cataloging in Publication Data

Library History Seminar (7th : 1985 : Chapel Hill, N.C.)
Libraries, books & culture.

"Reprinted from Journal of Library History, volume 21, numbers 1 & 2."
Includes bibliographies and index.
1. Libraries—History—Congresses.
I. Davis, Donald G. II. Journal of library history (University of Texas at Austin) III. Title.
Z672.5.L53 1985 027 86-14821
ISBN 0-938729-00-4

Printed in the United States of America

Contents

Foreword

This volume documents the formal content, though little of the excitement and intellectual ferment, that characterized Library History Seminar VII, "Libraries, Books & Culture," held at Chapel Hill on 6–8 March 1985. The second such conference to be held on a now-established pattern of the fifth and final years of each decade, this seminar marked the first time that the library schools of two major institutions—the University of Texas at Austin and the University of North Carolina at Chapel Hill—cooperated closely in its execution. Support for the Seminar came from the National Endowment for the Humanities, the Library History Round Table of the American Library Association, and more than 120 alumni and friends of the University of North Carolina at Chapel Hill School of Library Science.

Nearly 160 people from 29 states and several foreign countries attended the Seminar. Many commented on the consistently high quality of the presentations and discussions, the ample hospitality of the host school, and the opportunity to converse with knowledgeable colleagues. The attendance was over half again as many as that of the Austin meeting of 1980 and nearly 10 times the 17 in attendance at the first gathering at Tallahassee in 1961. A brief report of the Seminar appeared in the Fall 1985 issue (20/4) of *JLH*.

As the planning for this Seminar began in early 1983, the Advisory Committee, consisting of John Y. Cole, Phyllis Dain, Donald G. Davis, Jr., Edward G. Holley, and Arthur P. Young, agreed that the call for papers should be as broad as possible, but that four invited guest speakers should address specific aspects of book and library history as integrated fields, as well as other important related subjects, thus modifying the emphasis of the 1980 Austin meeting. From the eighty prospectuses submitted, the Committee selected twenty-four for presentation. These promised to provide diversity in subject content, treatment, and experience brought to the topic, as well as a good balance with other contributions. Together, they provided an interdisciplinary array and their authors represented historians, library educators, bibliographers, literary scholars, librarians, and library administrators—some veterans in their fields, others just beginning their careers.

As with any collection of conference papers with the breadth that this one embraces, this volume of proceedings stands on its own. Although the contributors and the editor have striven for accuracy and clarity, benefiting from the lively discussions at the Seminar, each author writes from a unique perspective, with a unique approach, and in a unique style. These features remain intact. Differences in scope, methodology, and conclusions will be inevitable; but the craft of library history will benefit if these papers provoke others to intellectual action, productive study, and shared results. Readers of the *Journal of Library History* form a natural audience for continuing discussion and the *JLH* "Communications" column provides a convenient initial medium.

While this short introduction cannot adequately set the tone for the papers that follow, omission of thanks to those who helped bring this Seminar to pass would be unpardonable. Besides the speakers and conveners, Edward G. Holley and his assistant, James V. Carmichael, Jr., and their staff at Chapel Hill gave their best efforts. In Austin, Dean Ronald E. Wyllys offered every encouragement; the Coordinator's assistants, Jim Patterson and Noelle Hendricks Barron, and the library school staff helped at every opportunity. Special thanks go to Mary Kingsbury and Boyd Rayward for reading papers on short notice for speakers who were unable to be present. Marilyn Kuehlem and Janet Fisher of the University of Texas Press, Journals Department, have been supportive from the first stages of planning and Bette Oliver, *JLH* editorial assistant, has helped copyedit these proceedings through the summer. *Vox audita perit, littera scripta manet.*

Donald G. Davis, Jr.
Seminar Coordinator
and Editor
Journal of Library History

Fall 1985

Haynes McMullen

Honoring Haynes McMullen

Edward G. Holley

In the last thirteen years, I have often said that one of the most important actions I have taken as dean was to lure Haynes McMullen from Indiana University to Chapel Hill. True, he was ready to leave Indiana for new challenges. True also that I promised him the opportunities for a less burdensome course load and *no summer school teaching*. True also that I promised to encourage him in his efforts to complete his massive studies of American libraries before 1876. So he came to us in the fall, 1972, and ever since has made significant contributions to this school. As the Beta Phi Mu Award citation in 1981 noted, he has "exerted a profound influence upon the lives of his students and colleagues. He is a demanding scholar, careful researcher, wise counselor, and patient mentor."

All of these characteristics I had heard about in 1972. I knew he was one of the most respected library historians among us, that his encouragement of doctoral students at Indiana had resulted in a number who were beginning to make their own contributions in the American library history field, and that he was a member of that vanishing breed, the gentleman scholar. What I had yet to experience personally was how accurate the descriptions were. In the past thirteen years Haynes McMullen has not only contributed to the rising distinction of the University of North Carolina School of Library Science; he has also been, as the Seminar program describes him, a friend, teacher, and colleague.

Haynes McMullen is a quiet scholar, albeit one with a fine sense of humor and a balanced view of the world. As a brash new dean, I had a firm conviction about how library schools should be run, as well as a fairly strong view of how poorly they had been run. Haynes was a good mentor not only for the faculty, but also for the students and the dean. After all, he had been a faculty or staff member at three of the nation's great universities and an acting director of one library school. He had a sure sense of faculty prerogatives and a sensitivity to their needs.

Edward G. Holley *formerly dean, is now professor, School of Library Science, University of North Carolina at Chapel Hill.*

I well remember, early in his tenure with us, a few times after faculty meetings, when Haynes would appear at my office about 9 a.m. the next morning (he always came to work early), and say, "Now Ed, I know you didn't mean to do this yesterday, but the faculty think. . . ." A real contribution to "shaping up the dean." He always did it with such directness and simplicity that it was impossible not to take his advice. He also had a suggestion about how a potentially difficult situation might be defused. Moreover, he was invariably right. Yet he is such a gracious person and his suggestions were couched in such a friendly manner that no one could possibly take offense.

There were faculty members then, and there are faculty members now, who are not reluctant to give advice to the dean, but their sense of righteousness was often a put-off rather than a contribution to the dean's education. Not so with Haynes McMullen. When he makes a suggestion, a dean had jolly well better listen.

Another contribution Haynes makes to the faculty and dean are remarks at faculty meetings. Having sat through such meetings for many years, he knows when our discussions are becoming unproductive. We know we have reached the outer limits when Haynes says, "Well, we don't have to settle *that* now."

One more comment before I laud his contributions to library history. Haynes has been a splendid model for junior faculty. A scholar himself, he prizes scholarship, is generous with his time in its advancement, and has always been willing to read manuscripts before they are sent off to the publisher. He is ruthless on misplaced pronouns, on sloppy syntax, on subjects and verbs that do not agree. His ability to detect poor logic, inadequate outlines, and nonsupportive references is legendary. At one AALS meeting several years ago he read a delightful paper on hackneyed phrases that appear in research articles. I was standing by one of his former students who is noted for such use and he visibly winced as Haynes skewered some of his favorite phrases. This ability to help improve his colleagues' prose is a characteristic he shares with his friend, Les Asheim. Both junior *and* senior faculty have benefited from his assistance with what we believe to be our deathless prose. The literature of our profession owes much to his skillful editing, even though his name may not appear on the articles.

For example, when the massive *Dictionary of American Library Biography* was nearing completion, McMullen was one of the handful of scholars who undertook to rewrite a number of the biographical essays to meet the high standards of the managing editor. His name, of course, does not appear on some of these essays, though the rewriting was substantial.

Let me now turn to Haynes's many other contributions to library history. Because he has always been interested in the place of books and libraries in American history, Haynes has produced many journal articles. They have been published in magazines as diverse as the *Papers of the Bibliographical Society of America, Pennsylvania History*, the *Journal of Academic Librarianship* and *Wilson Library Bulletin*, and, of course, in that major publication, the *Journal of Library History*. A few of the topics illustrate the breadth of his interest: "College Libraries in Ante-Bellum Kentucky," "Ralph Waldo Emerson and Libraries," and "The History of Charging for Services in American Libraries That Have Traditionally Been Free." He has more entries to his credit in the Harris and Davis *American Library History: A Bibliography* (1978) than any other author. His essay "American Librarianship and the Pursuit of Happiness" became the theme of the 1981 American Library Association conference. In that essay, McMullen argued that libraries should be as concerned with the emotional needs of their users as they are with their informational needs.

McMullen's major interest has been books and libraries in America before 1876. As is true of the real scholar, he has not been content to accept the received wisdom. For years he has been working on two projects: an annotated bibliography of all references to libraries in American periodicals before 1876 and a statistical analysis of library development in various sections of the country before 1876. In May 1983 McFarland and Company brought forth his *Libraries in American Periodicals before 1876: A Bibliography with Abstracts and an Index*.

The main entry in LC gives the credit for this work to Larry Barr, one of Haynes's former students and now a faculty member at Appalachian State University. A number of us tried to get Haynes to list himself as the major compiler of that bibliography because, as we pointed out to him, no one would be in doubt about the senior author of that work. He would not hear of it. The original idea and much of the work was Larry Barr's and he deserved the credit, even though by McMullen's own estimate, at least 60 percent of the work was done by Haynes. He also insisted that his UNC student, Steven Leach, be listed on the title page because Leach had done so much to advance the bibliography. He did allow himself to be listed as the "editor," but library historians will not be fooled; the bibliography was, is, and forever more will be the "McMullen bibliography." Its usefulness can only increase in the next hundred years as younger scholars mine those resources for articles that will assure a more accurate history of the library profession. But I point out this facet of Haynes's career not to denigrate the contributions made by his former students, but rather to indicate again his basic humility and his insistence that his students receive full credit for their contributions. There are a lot of persons in our profession who appear to be humble; Haynes McMullen is one of the truly humble.

Articles are continuing to flow from Haynes's pen. The *Library Quarterly* will soon publish his "The Very Slow Decline of the American Social Library" (55 [April 1985]: 207–225). Within the next year he expects to complete his work on the emergence of libraries in the various regions of the United States before 1876. Thus his lifelong work and major contributions will have been completed.

When the Advisory Committee for Library History Seminar VII first met to consider where we should hold this meeting, I suggested that Haynes McMullen would be retiring this year. Therefore, Carolina would be an especially appropriate place for our meeting. The Seminar would also provide an opportunity to honor the McMullen contributions to library and book history. My colleagues immediately agreed. We, therefore, decided to dedicate Library History Seminar VII to Haynes McMullen. We also planned for this occasion to be a surprise. I am well enough aware of Haynes's reluctance about such ventures to realize that if I had told him ahead of time, he probably would have vetoed the idea. We have successfully kept him in the dark about this portion of our Seminar until today. We rejoice that such a large group of Haynes's friends and colleagues has joined us on this occasion.

And now, on behalf of the Advisory Committee, the faculty, and the students of the School of Library Science at the University of North Carolina at Chapel Hill, I am privileged to dedicate this Library History Seminar VII to one of our nation's distinguished library historians, Haynes McMullen.

The Cover

The development of social libraries in New England during the eighteenth century survived a lull during the Revolutionary War to continue with renewed vigor in the 1780s. The spirit of nationalism that produced the Constitution of 1787 also fostered a general interest in educating citizens for the new republic. Both schools and social libraries were already strong traditions in Connecticut. Citizens of New Haven had discussed a town library as early as 1664, when they established the Hopkins Grammar School; by 1797 the town had several common district schools, one named after Noah Webster, who, after graduating from Yale College, had settled in New Haven to teach and to write a spelling book.

Higher education for adults was firmly established with the first building of Yale College in 1717. However, the New Englanders found industry, as well as education, a route to prosperity. By 1790 New Haven was one of the largest manufacturing towns in Connecticut; nearby was one of the first cotton cloth factories in the state. In 1798 Eli Whitney, another Yale man, grew tired of cotton-ginning and built a munitions factory about two miles from New Haven.

Feeling strongly that "the establishment of a public library in the City of New Haven, would advance useful knowledge and Literature," a group of men met at the State House on 5 February 1793 to read and ratify the *Constitution* of the Mechanic Library Society of New Haven. Evidently the Library was organized informally the year before; the original bookplate is dated 1792, and Sabin's *Bibliotheca Americana* lists the "Constitution of the Mechanic Library Society and Catalogue of Books" with a date of 1792. However, the earliest document extant that relates to the Library (containing the above quotation) is *The Constitution and Bye-Laws of the Mechanic Library Society of New-Haven, With a Catalogue of Books and List of the Proprietors*, printed in New Haven by Abel Morse, 1793 (available in the Readex Microprint series of *Early American Imprints*).

The Constitution and Bye-Laws of 1793 sets forth in detail subscription rights and rules for administration and operation of the Library, including selection and purchase of books. Supported through the sale of shares (9 shillings) and annual dues (one half dollar annually for five years, then one fourth dollar annually), the Library seems to have been a combination of the two main forms of eighteenth-century social libraries, proprietary (joint-stock ownership) and subscription. In 1793 hours were set from 5 to 9 o'clock on Monday afternoons, when the librarian or his substitute was to be present to record all books "delivered" out and returned. Overdue fines were prescribed, and all books were to be returned by the first Mondays of January and July for an inventory of the collection.

In June 1794 the Library gained a new member, the president of Yale College, Ezra Stiles, who noted in his diary that he had bought a four-dollar share in the 430-volume library. Stiles's diary note indicates active acquisition during the Library's first year, a considerable increase over the 204 volumes listed in the *Catalogue* of 1793. Like the first, subsequent catalogues are alphabetical, with the addition of numbers showing that the inventories were carried out. Inventory numbers from a catalogue of about 1812 show over 900 volumes.

The bulk of the 1793 collection consisted of history, biography, travel, literature, and fiction; nine volumes could be classed as theology, and only one as science. This profile seems to have changed little as the holdings increased. The small portion of science books is rather surprising, considering that the name "Mechanic" suggests an early example of the mechanics' institutes movement, also germinating in Great Britain, where it would flourish in the next century. Apprentices' libraries were perhaps more numerous in the United States, and the lyceum movement was stronger, but the New Haven society was one of the earliest organizations on either side of the Atlantic to call itself "Mechanic."

Both of the principal conditions that motivated founders of the English institutes were present in New Haven: industry demanding new skills and a growing interest in science, both philosophical and practical. Ezra Stiles, in addition to his qualifications as lawyer, minister, linguist, and college president, was also an amateur scientist, who tried some of the first electrical experiments in New England on electrical apparatus sent to Yale by Benjamin Franklin in 1749. With the books of Yale College at his disposal, it seems unlikely that such a scholar would have cared to own stock in a mechanic library, unless perhaps its other members shared his interests.

If the bookplate shown on the cover reflects the vision of the Library's founders, the title "Mechanic" surely represents an attempt to involve manufacturers and workingmen of New Haven in the advancement of "knowledge and Literature" and maybe a little science. The design features two muscular cherubs diligently hammering away at tongs on an anvil, under the motto "Improve the Moment," resounding a theme of self-education for the average citizen. This industrious scene is set in a roundel surrounded by an ornate floral frame, crowned by a radiant stack of nine well-bound volumes in three graduated sizes. Originals of the plate, which measures 3 1/2 by 4 1/4 inches, are held by Yale University, the American Antiquarian Society, and the present Institute Library in New Haven. The copy on the cover is reproduced from *A Treasury of Bookplates* (Dover, 1977); another reproduction is in Shera's *Foundations of the Public Library* (Chicago, 1949), plate XIII.

The signature identifies the artist as Amos Doolittle, a New Haven engraver known for his 1775 scene "The Battle of Lexington," one of the first copper engravings done in New England. Doolittle's early training as a silversmith may have inspired his design of the miniature smiths; his design of 1804 is a refinement of the more earthly scene on an earlier bookplate by an unknown artist (see next page). Doolittle, "delineator et sculptor," designer and engraver, made silver eagles and engraved music as well as bookplates, illustrations, maps, and portraits of notable Americans, including Ezra Stiles.

Through mergers and metamorphoses, the Library has continued to the present day. In 1815 the Mechanic Library united with the Social

Library Company, begun in 1808 and incorporated in 1810. Three officers named in the 1793 document are among the subscribers of the Social Library Company in 1815, a list that also includes the name of Eli Whitney. Inventory numbers from the catalogue representing the combined collections show well over 1,600 volumes, and the cherubs on the new Doolittle bookplate hold a scroll instead of hammers.

In 1826 an Apprentices' Literary Association was started by eight young workingmen for the purposes of discussion and debate as well as keeping a library. By 1828 they called themselves the Young Mechanics' Institute and offered classes in several subjects, such as grammar and bookkeeping. As membership grew (remaining largely working-class), lectures on politics and practical science became more popular than classes and continued into the Civil War period. Women were admitted to certain classes and lectures.

In 1840 the Institute purchased the most valuable of the books remaining in the Social Library Company and changed its name to the present corporate form; in 1841 the Young Men's Institute Library was chartered by the General Assembly. The large circulating library (over 7,000 volumes in the mid-1850s) proved the most enduring function. The Institute Library, as it is now called, with about 250 subscribers (membership by recommendation and invitation), is located at 847 Chapel Street in the building erected by the Institute in 1878. Unfortunately, none of the original volumes remain, but a collection of over 38,000 volumes emphasizes current fiction and nonfiction. The librarian, Doris K. Hendricks, kindly provided information needed for this sketch, including reproductions of the earlier (1792) bookplate now used once more by the Library.

Courtesy of American Antiquarian Society (reduction)

Beth Hogan
University of the South
Sewanee, Tennessee

The Book in History and the History of the Book

John P. Feather

The history of books is made up of many elements. The book historian has to analyze the size and composition of the reading public, the availability of books, the technical history of book production, the economic history of the book trade, and the legal and political aspects of publishing. The history of libraries, librarianship, and library education is part of this wider subject and is a matter of great interest to the book historian, especially when it puts these matters into a wider societal context. Book history itself is of fundamental importance to understanding the essentially book-based culture of the West.[1]

Daniel J. Boorstin wrote recently that "our democracy is based on books and reading." While it is not my purpose to discuss this statement in detail, it is a useful reminder of the significance that is attached to books, far beyond their functional role as containers of texts. In the National Museum of Ireland in Dublin there are some exquisite boxes, encrusted in jewels and gold, that at first glance appear to be reliquaries. In a sense this is exactly what they are, but they were actually made to contain books. Some of these books still survive and are among the greatest ever made; the Book of Kells is only the most famous of a group of manuscripts from the golden age of Celtic Irish culture. These manuscripts and their reliquary-like boxes are another reminder of the symbolic significance that has been attached to books at various times and in various places, not merely as texts but as objects. In a very different society, William Morris saw the "book beautiful" as the most powerful physical representation of the ideal medieval world of free craftsmen, which he claimed to be reviving and which he had actually invented. Bibliophiles venerate certain books not for their contents, but for their physical form. How many of us have read, or would wish to read, or would even dare to read, a book in a Grolier binding? In the spring of

John P. Feather *is senior lecturer, Department of Library and Information Studies, Loughborough University, England.*

1985, the British Museum mounted an exhibition entitled "The Golden Age of Anglo-Saxon Art." On display were artifacts of all kinds, including some superb manuscripts. Most of the latter were elaborately decorated or illuminated, but in one case were four rather ordinary looking books that were attracting very little attention. They had no rubrications, no drawings, no glistening gold leaf; they were the unique manuscripts of *The Wanderer*, *The Battle of Maldon*, Wulfstan's *Sermon to the English*, and *Beowulf*, four of the masterpieces of Old English literature. As an historical and cultural phenomenon, the book can only be fully understood when we recognize that it is more than merely a vehicle for a text.

The relationship between text and object is a complex one, which has rarely been considered, and yet it could be argued that our understanding of a text is ultimately influenced by the physical form of its presentation. Consider, for example, the meticulously edited texts in which we can now read many, if not yet all, of the major British and American authors. The ideal is that the assiduous editor should not only print the actual words that the author intended us to read, but should do so with the spelling and punctuation that the author used or approved. Yet even in the very rare cases where this ideal can be fully achieved, it is not, in one crucial sense, what the author intended. An example will illustrate the point. It is well known that John Milton, despite his blindness, succeeded in exercising a minute control over the text and orthography of *Paradise Lost*. Yet the modern editor who follows this, as one must, does not reproduce what Milton's first readers saw, or what he knew that they would see: an octavo, well printed by the standards of late-seventeenth-century London, but printed on handmade paper in hand-cast and hand-set type of the design and quality that English printers of the period accepted without question. Whether the appearance of the modern edition on clean white paper in neatly photoset typography affects our reading of the poem is a question for the literary critic to answer; indeed, it would be agreeable if the question were even to be asked. I will only venture to suggest that it does so by giving a false air of contemporaneity. My principal point is a rather different one: that authors can only envisage the dissemination of their works in the physical form that is the normal product of the techniques available at the time of writing. When the techniques or the forms undergo major changes, such as those from the scroll to the codex, or from manuscript to print, or from print to VDU, the text itself may be the same, but the reader's perception of it is profoundly different.

The historian cannot ignore these fundamental physical characteristics of the form in which a text reaches its audience. Elizabeth Eisenstein has properly emphasized the uniformity that printing imposed on the presentation of texts and the far-reaching effects of this wholly new phenomenon in the fifteenth and sixteenth centuries. The dissemination of the printed book, and of the art of printing itself, is, of course, one of the most important phenomena in our history, but when we attempt to analyze its consequences, and to draw specific conclusions about them, we are faced with great difficulties. How do we assess the influence of books or of a book? The literary critic may be able to determine that one author was "influenced" by another. At one level it may be very general, as in the case of Shakespeare's influence on Keats; at another, it may be far more diverse, as Lowes found when he looked at how Coleridge's reading had helped to create *Kubla Khan*. When we move away from the individual work or the individual author, the problem is a more complex one. Most people would agree that three of the greatest influences on twentieth-century Western civilization are Darwin, Marx, and Freud, who for good or ill have substantially created the mental climate in which we all live. All of us have some idea of what they said, but how many of us have actually read *On the Origin of Species*, or the works of Freud, or *Das Kapital*? Project that question back into history. It seems probable that few of the Minute Men were intimately acquainted with Locke's *Second Essay on Civil Government*, any more than the *sans culottes* could quote at length from *L'esprit des lois* or *Le contrat social*. In short, when we speak of the influence of the book, we are speaking, so far as direct influence is concerned, of the reactions of a small intellectual elite, through whom knowledge and concepts are transmitted, often transmuted, to the mass of the people.

It follows from this that the first concern of the book historian is to define the size and constitution of the audience for books. Such a task cannot be undertaken without some knowledge of the extent of literacy and of the means of acquiring it. The book historian is, therefore, vitally interested in the history of education and of literacy, and while the formal history of educational provision is a well-ploughed field, historical studies of literacy, despite all the advances of recent years, are still in their infancy. From my own studies of the book in eighteenth-century England I conclude that literacy was far more widespread than has often been supposed, although in other parts of Europe, especially in the Catholic south, it was far less common among the lower and lower-middle classes. Mere statistics, however, tell us little. We need to know who the literates actually were. We can assume that professional men were literate, and, certainly in eighteenth-century England, so were the tradesmen. But what of the tradesman's wife or his servant? Too often the answer is that we do not know, and yet the historian who seeks to analyze the penetration of society by ideas embodied in print needs to know as precisely as possible who were the potential recipients of those ideas.

At the same time, the book historian has his or her own unique contribution to make to this study. We know, for example, that in England in the eighteenth century, in communities throughout the country, groups of professional men and tradesmen came together to form book clubs and subscription libraries. In many of these communities there were also bookshops, or at least shops that sold books; by 1800 there were not fewer than 1,000 of them in England outside London, serving a population of fewer than 8 million. When we know the names of the members of the book clubs, or of the customers of the booksellers, we can put some flesh on the bones of the literacy statistics and begin to understand just how deeply a print-based culture has penetrated into that society.

Another source of great value for such studies, and one that has been increasingly exploited in recent years, is to be found in the lists of purchasers printed in books published by subscription. These lists need to be used with care. They do not tell us who read a book. They do, however, tell us who was sufficiently interested in a book to make a direct financial contribution to its publication, although even that assumption needs to be handled carefully, since some people subscribed from social or political considerations, rather than from intellectual or literary interest. Nevertheless, subscription lists are very valuable to the historian, and indeed to the literary critic. They can help us to delineate a book's audience by occupation, by social status, and by place of residence. There is, for example, a consistent pattern in eighteenth-century England of subscriptions from some parts of the country, but not from others, to works by Methodist and other dissenting theologians, and Pat Rogers showed some years ago how a well-defined group of social and political colleagues and allies formed the main body of Pope's subscribers.

If we can make some advance in assessing the potential readership of printed matter in general, or of particular groups of books, or even of specific titles, we then confront another series of equally difficult questions. What books were available? How did people obtain them?

To discover what books were available is, in one sense, a comparatively simple task, although enumerative bibliographers may disagree with the use of the word "simple." Thanks to the work of generations of bibliographers, we have lists of English and American books down to the end of the seventeenth century; the record for the eighteenth century is nearing completion; and that for the nineteenth century is well advanced. Even though the various short-title catalogs are based only on extant copies found in libraries, we can supplement this information from the book lists that were issued by printers, publishers, and booksellers in increasing numbers from the beginning of the sixteenth century.

To know that a book exists, or has existed, is, however, only the first stage in a study of its availability to contemporaries. At the most basic level, we need to know how many copies were printed, and since we usually lack the documentary evidence that would give us a definitive answer to that question, the book historian has to consider the history of both the printing industry itself and the retail and wholesale trades through which books were sold. If the history of the book is not firmly based in the inky reality of the printing house, it can too easily become a string of vague hypotheses and unjustifiable generalizations. A knowledge of the processes involved in papermaking, typesetting, printing, and binding is as essential to the book historian as is a knowledge of human anatomy to the physician. It cannot be said too often that historical bibliography and the history of the book are not two subjects but one, two parts of a unified whole. Indeed, the tendency of some book historians to ignore or dismiss the technical history of printing has led to the neglect of many important issues in book history. I should like to deal briefly with two of them.

The first is a deceptively simple question. Why was printing invented at all? Successful technological innovation is more than merely a demonstration of the inherent cleverness of inventors. It is a response to social, economic, and political demand. The principles of steam power, for example, were known for decades before economic imperatives made it a viable source of energy for industry and inspired James Watt to develop a more efficient steam engine. The same was true of printing. All the basic principles and techniques had been known and used for generations before the middle of the fifteenth century. Leaving aside the possibility of Oriental influence, we know that woodcuts were probably impressed on paper in western Europe before the invention of typographic printing. The press itself, without the sophistications of the lever mechanism and the hanging platen, had been in use for centuries for pressing grapes in wine-making, and indeed by bookbinders. Engraved metal tools, including letterforms, were also used by medieval binders, as well as by goldsmiths and silversmiths. It is not enough to argue that all of these were brought together by the genius of one man.

In fifteenth-century Europe, the literacy rate was increasing, partly because of the gradual secularization of society, and partly because the plagues, wars, and famines of the previous hundred years had had their most devastating effects on the illiterate classes. On the political front, the three great monarchies of western Europe were all striving for a greater centralization of government. In the economic sphere, Europe's trade was becoming more complex, both internally and in its rapidly developing relations with Asia and Africa. Gutenberg may have been aware of some, or all, or none of this, but, in a sense, that is irrelevant. All his genius, for he was indeed a brilliant innovator, might have been wasted if these conditions had not existed. Even so, Gutenberg might be argued to have anticipated the emergence of the demand for printing, for he was not only the first printer; he was also the first printer to go bankrupt. It was not until the 1480s that printing was established on a sound commercial and financial basis. Printing was ultimately successful not simply because it represented a technical advance on copying by scribes, but because it became available at a time and in a place where it was economically, socially, and politically desirable. Merely to accept the appearance of printing in late-fifteenth-century Europe, as if it were some newly discovered natural phenomenon, is to miss the point: the printing press was an agent of change because it was able to play an important role in the society in which it was invented, and from whose needs it had been developed.

The second important issue that has been neglected concerns a later period, the late eighteenth and early nineteenth centuries. From about 1780 onward, a series of technical innovations transformed the printing craft into an industry. The landmarks are familiar to all students of the subject: the building of the first iron press by Stanhope in 1800 and, in the following decade, the commercial exploitation of the papermaking machine by the Fourdriniers and of stereotyping by Andrew Wilson, followed, in 1814, by König's first steam press, built for *The* (London) *Times*. These great developments made books and newspapers both cheaper and more plentiful than they had ever been before. None of them, however, came out of the blue.

Experiments with papermaking, and with the improvement of the common press, had been taking place for many years before Robert and Stanhope set to work; stereotyping had been not only invented, but actually used in one or two isolated instances, before 1750, and then abandoned and forgotten. Why then were these revolutionary changes made when they were? Partly because of other technological developments, which had, for example, brought machine tools to a point at which a metal platen could be perfectly planed, or, in another field, made it possible for steam or water power to be used to drive a Fourdrinier machine. Yet these developments, important as they are, are not the true explanation. Again, the rate of literacy was rapidly increasing, as indeed was the population as a whole. The French Revolution, and the reaction to it in Britain by both its supporters and its opponents, created a huge new demand for books, much of it from people who had never read books before. Hannah More and other evangelicals started the Sunday Schools with the intention of strengthening the moral fiber of the lower classes by teaching them to read their Bible and other improving literature; some did, and as many more read Paine's *Rights of Man*. Above all, this was an age of great technological change in a wide range of economic activities as Britain rushed headlong into its Industrial Revolution.

Against this background, the changes in the printing industry in the late eighteenth and early nineteenth centuries not only become more comprehensible, but also more significant. We can see printing as only one of many trades that were transformed by new equipment and new techniques. At the same time, we can see it responding to society's needs and demands, not only economically, but also in the cultural and political spheres. Book historians cannot ignore the technical changes that made possible the proliferation of cheap books in the early nineteenth century, because these changes themselves, and the chronology of them, tell us a great deal about the underlying causes of the revolution in English reading habits between about 1790 and 1830.

I have deliberately chosen two monumental examples of the intimate relationship between the technical and cultural history of the book. On a lesser scale, however, technical history, the traditional province of the bibliographer, can inform the book historian at every point. How many copies of a book were printed? How much did a copy cost? How did a potential reader discover that a book existed? How did one actually obtain a copy of a book one wanted to read? None of these questions can be ignored if we are to trace the influence of a book, or the penetration of a print-based culture into a society.

The economic history of the book, like its technical history, has certainly not been ignored, although it has only too rarely been related to the broader issues of which it is a part. In particular, although the history of publishing is now a flourishing and well-established field of study, the history of the selling of books is a sadly neglected topic. Compared with the printing house or even the publisher's office, the bookshop is dull and uninviting; in the last analysis it is, after all, just a shop. Yet without the bookshop, at least before the development of mail-order bookselling in the last hundred years, there would have been no book trade, and the great majority of the population who had no access to libraries would have had no access to books. There can be no doubt that an important factor in the general increase in edition sizes in England in the eighteenth century was the development of a vigorous bookselling trade outside London, in response to the growing demand for books, and the same is true, at other times, of other countries. Publishers' catalogs, book advertisements in newspapers and periodicals, and book reviews in magazines were all vital factors in spreading a knowledge of books and in stimulating the desire to own and to read them. Some excellent work has been done on the history of catalogs, but there is still no adequate history of newspaper advertising, and very little on book reviewing before the beginning of the nineteenth century. These vast gaps in our knowledge (and I have not even mentioned such matters as wholesaling, distribution, and the international trade in books) can only be remedied when we take a view of the history of the book that looks at more than the minutiae of its production or, at the other end of the scale, its alleged societal consequences.

There is one other aspect of the economic history of the book that deserves our attention, that of authorship. The author is strangely absent from most histories of the book, yet there were authors before there was a book trade, and without authors there would be no books. Only a tiny minority of authors write for simple and single reasons. Their motivations are very much the concern of the book historian, whether that motivation is political influence, artistic expression, academic reputation, or money. It is realistic rather than cynical to suggest that it is the last of these that has been predominant during the last two centuries.

A good deal of progress has been made in this field in recent years. We no longer execrate Milton's publisher for paying him what was, by contemporary standards, a perfectly reasonable fee for *Paradise Lost.* We recognize that if hacks did indeed live in garrets, they did so of choice, and that few, if any, starved. By the middle of the eighteenth century, and in some cases earlier, authorship was an established, if not entirely respectable, profession in which it was possible to make a reasonable living. Yet a whole series of questions remains unanswered. We know less than we should and less than we could about the relationships, both personal and financial, between authors and publishers before the nineteenth century. Most of what we do know is about the major literary writers who, however important we may judge their works to be, were neither the majority nor typical of the majority. Reverting to the early days of printing, it would be interesting to know who was the first author to write a book with the specific intention that it should be circulated as a *printed* book. This is an inquiry of more than merely antiquarian interest, for the answer to it would tell us a good deal about the acceptance of the printed book and the recognition of its importance as a cultural phenomenon.

The economic and social conditions of authors are integral to the history of the book, as indeed are the legal aspects of the author's work. In the most liberal societies authors must take account of the laws of libel, privacy, and official security. All of those are matters of concern to the book historian, as are the moral constraints on authorship whether by social pressures or the law of the land. In less liberal societies than our own, that is, the great majority whether in the past or at the present time, the insidious hand of the censor can never be ignored; nor can the multitude of ingenious and often entertaining ways in which authors and publishers have evaded his attentions.

Yet another part of the law that impinges deeply on book history is that of copyright. Indeed, copyright is an issue of central importance to authors and publishers alike. It is well known that the first copyright law was that passed in England in 1710, and the modern concept of "intellectual property" was evolved, not without some difficulty, over the next sixty years. The history of copyright leads the book historian into all sorts of matters that might superficially be thought remote. By an historical accident, copyright laws are generally associatd with the compulsory deposit of books in certain libraries, so that we have to consider the development of the concept of the comprehensive archival research library. The purchase of copyrights is the most important investment a publisher ever makes, so that we cannot understand the economics of publishing without a knowledge of copyright law. For the author, as for the publisher, it is copyright law that protects his or her investment, in the author's case of time and intellectual effort. Indeed, one reason why authorship did become a viable profession in eighteenth-century England was precisely that the interpretation of the 1710 Act, and the development, in a series of judicial decisions, of the concept of "intellectual property," gave the author a lever to use against the publisher. As the relationship between author and publisher became more overtly commercial, we find parallel development in commissioning, in contracts, and in methods of payment. These mundane financial matters are integral to a full understanding of the history of the book.

The political dimension of book history has already been mentioned, but it is important enough to deserve some further consideration. One of the many unforeseen consequences of the dissemination of printing in the fifteenth century was the development throughout Europe of a more stringent control over what could be written and circulated. By the end of the sixteenth century, prepublication censorship was enforced throughout the continent by a combination of secular and ecclesiastical authorities, and continued to be so for centuries. In England there was limited press freedom after 1695, but it was not finally established, and then by practice rather than by law, until the 1830s. In France, it was not until 1870 that the press was finally released from its chains. In what is now West Germany, freedom of the press, save for the brief interlude of the Weimar Republic, was unknown until after World War II. The First Amendment was uniquely enlightened in the guarantees that it offered, and was for decades the only light of freedom shining over the enslaved press of the world.

The speed with which bishops and princes reacted to the growth of printing in the fifteenth and sixteenth centuries is in itself an eloquent testimony to its perceived importance. Yet the reactions of the authorities of western Europe were not wholly negative. Strong kings like Henry VIII of England and Philip II of Spain recognized that the power of the press, which could be so damaging to their interests, could also be turned into their servant. Laws and proclamations could be widely and unambiguously circulated throughout a monarch's dominions, so that no subject could plead ignorance of the law as an excuse for breaking it. The arguments of a monarch or a church or, later, of a political party, could be circulated far more widely than ever before. Propaganda, like censorship, was one of the growth industries of the age of the printed book.

By the middle of the eighteenth century, the newspaper was beginning to displace the pamphlet as the principal organ of propaganda, at least for the great mass of literate people outside the political elite. At the same time, print was becoming ubiquitous in every sphere of life. It is, indeed, tempting to argue that it was not until the eighteenth century that the full force of the printing press as an agent of change was felt by the societies of western Europe. Certainly the intellectual movements of the sixteenth and seventeenth centuries were ultimately dependent upon the availability of the printed book. It is also true that the effects of these movements, like the influence of Darwin, Freud, and Marx, were felt far outside the circles of those who were directly concerned with them or were even consciously aware of them. It was not, however, until the eighteenth century that print became truly ubiquitous in western Europe and in those parts of North America that had been settled by Europeans. Until literacy was comparatively widespread, it was inevitable that news was disseminated and information was gathered by word of mouth. Indeed, oral transmission remained common for centuries after the invention of printing. There is evidence to suggest that in rural areas of England literate people would read the newspapers aloud to their illiterate neighbors, while the ballad-singer continued to be a familiar figure at country fairs until the middle of the nineteenth century. Increasingly, however, illiterates were at a disadvantage both socially and economically. It is believed that in mid-eighteenth-century England, after a change in the law required that the bride and bridegroom should sign or mark the marriage register, young couples learned to write their names so as to avoid the stigma of illiteracy on their wedding day.

In economic life, literacy was more than a social convenience; as the pace of industrialization quickened, it became a necessity. The pages of Samuel Smiles are full of uplifting stories of poor boys who learned to read from spelling books propped up on a loom or a lathe. The most famous product of what would seem to have been a remarkably dangerous form of autodidacticism was George Stephenson, the pioneer railroad engineer of the 1820s and 1830s. The ubiquity of print was, however, fully established half a century before young George learned his ABCs. By the third quarter of the eighteenth century, the presses of Europe were producing advertisements, catalogs, packaging material, headed stationery, tickets, and blank forms at the rate of hundreds of thousands a year. Some material of this kind had always been produced. There is a famous example of a book advertisement printed by Caxton, and the STC lists sixteenth- and seventeenth-century Visitation Articles, which are, in fact, questionnaires. In the eighteenth century, however, there were few areas of economic life that were untouched by the proliferation of printed material of this kind. When, after decades of wrangling between religious factions, primary education in England at last became both free and compulsory in 1870, the effect of the law was to do little more than mop up the last few remaining pockets of rural illiteracy. The great bulk of town dwellers had been literate, of necessity, for two generations.

If the imperatives to attain literacy were social and economic, the consequences were, in part, political. The radicalization of the urban working class, and the contemporary conversion of the capitalists to *laissez-faire* liberalism, between about 1800 and 1840, were both achieved largely by the printed word, although the public meeting also played an important part, not least, of course, through the reports of such meetings that were printed at great length in the newspapers. Something was said earlier of the technological changes in the printing industry that resulted from this increased demand for the written word. At the same time political change on this scale created still further demands for print and underlay the continuing and increasingly rapid changes in printing technology during the rest of the nineteenth century, with the rotary press, the web-fed press, and mechanized typesetting and bookbinding.

As it is portrayed here, book history is a vast, indeed all-embracing, subject. The book historian has something to learn and something to teach at every point at which the printed word impinges on the organization of society or on economic activity. Most difficult of all, however, is the very topic with which we began, the perception of the book, and its force as a cultural symbol.

In one very important sense, our entire culture is based on a book, or rather a collection of books. Christians, Jews, and Muslims have so many ideas and moral standards in common because from the earliest days of Judaism the basic concepts of religion and the behavioral inferences drawn from them were transmitted by the written word. In all three religions the book is treated with great veneration and plays a central part in acts of communal worship. The objects themselves were created to be masterpieces of the bookmaker's art; it is no accident that Western illuminators and Arabic calligraphers reached the highest points of artistic achievement in manuscripts of the Bible and the Qur'an. The text is also treated with special respect. Although the revival of the art of textual criticism in the fifteenth and sixteenth centuries was initially associated with the Greek and Latin classics, it was in the establishment of the text of the Bible, and especially of the Greek New Testament, that it reached its apogée. In Islamic tradition, the text of the Qur'an was treated with such respect that fear of error delayed the introduction of printing into the Muslim world by two and a half centuries, and even today a devout Muslim will read the Qur'an only in Arabic, to avoid the dangers of silent interpretation implicit in the act of translation. In this sense, all the "people of the book" have a very special relationship with it as more than merely an object and more than merely a text: it is a symbol of the most deeply held beliefs, and even among those who no longer adhere to those beliefs the symbolic significance of the book has substantially survived.

The respect that we accord to books has spread far from religion. The anthropologists tell us that in illiterate societies learned people, whether priestesses, medicine men, or witch doctors, were accorded special respect because of their knowledge. They stood outside the hierarchy of warriors and farmers and were not only the advisers of the chiefs but sometimes even treated as their equals. In literate societies the book becomes the symbol of the knowledge that it contains. In medieval and renaissance iconography, the fathers of the Church are portrayed reading or writing or sitting in their studies surrounded by books. Even today books in the home are a far more potent status symbol than phonograph records or videotapes. When children go to school they learn to read before they learn anything else. In the developing countries, vast resources are being poured into primary education programs to reach the goal of a literate society.

In part, all of this is a recognition that our society is print-dependent, but it is also an implicit acknowledgment of the primacy of the printed word. It is, therefore, all the more strange that historians have been so neglectful of this central phenomenon of our culture. A change of attitudes is, at last, beginning to appear. From the beginning of this century the history of books was, for more than fifty years, almost entirely the province of bibliographers and their uneasy and sometimes unwelcome companions, textual critics. The great advances in bibliographical scholarship that began with Bradshaw's studies of fifteenth-century typography in the middle of the last century reached their climax in the work of Greg and Bowers a hundred years later. The achievements of that century of effort laid the foundations upon which the superstructure of the history of the book can now be built. We know how books were made; we know how to identify technical difficulties in their making; and we know something of the effects of technical processes on texts.

It was said earlier that the history of the book must be firmly based in the reality of the printing house. No apology is needed for repeating the point: book historians who are not at least aware of bibliographical techniques are ill equipped for their task, and it could be forcefully argued that a knowledge of historical bibliography should be the basis of their training as scholars. We should also, however, venture outside the confined space of the printing house into the world in which its products were used. The transition is indeed inevitable. When Pollard studied the "bad" quartos of Shakespeare, he also laid the foundations of our knowledge of the Elizabethan book trade. More recently, Robert Darnton's work on the *Encyclopédie* has taken the reader from the activities of the Société Typographie de Neuchâtel, through the inadequacies of the European papermaking industry, to the alleged reading habits of the provincial bourgeoisie during the last years of the *ancien régime*.

The historian of libraries also has a unique contribution to make to this history of books. Like the history of the book, the history of libraries has been transformed in recent years by a more general historical awareness and a broader social and cultural approach. Library history is no longer a tedious catalog of the good deeds of benefactors, the enacting of laws, and the opening of buildings. One of the finest examples of the new style of library history is Phyllis Dain's history of the New York Public Library, not merely offering a chronicle of the formative years of one of the world's great libraries, but also giving fascinating insights into the political and social history of New York and showing how the early history of NYPL is inseparable from that of the city and the people it was intended to serve.

There is one aspect of library history that can be particularly informative to the historian of the book: the study of the use of libraries. It was suggested earlier that the book historian needs to know something about who read books, and, although borrowing a book from a library is no more a guarantee of reading it than buying it from a bookshop, it does suggest at least some minimal interest in, or need for, a book on a particular subject. Studies of the loan records of libraries, in those few cases where they survive, can be very illuminating. If we turn again to eighteenth-century England we find that there is, for example, a consistent pattern of interest in historical and geographical literature by library users. This interest is also attested by the catalogs and inventories of bookshops, and some explanation for it needs to be offered. One tentative suggestion might be that, as Britain became a world power, its people became more interested both in their own history and in the world beyond the seas that was becoming so important to their destiny. It would be interesting to know whether a similar phenomenon was observable in the United States when it stepped onto the world stage during and after World War II.

Libraries and the history of libraries are important to the historian of the book in another crucial sense. The history of the book must indeed rest on a sound basis of the technical history of book production, but the theoretical study of the history of printing, even when it is supplemented by practical work as enlightening as it is entertaining, is in itself inadequate. The historian of books, like the bibliographer, is concerned with the books themselves not only as tools, like all scholars, but as primary evidence. Library collections are similarly valuable evidence, for the history of their development, use, and perhaps ultimate dispersal can give important insights into the more general history of books. British examples that come to mind are the parochial libraries established under the auspices of Dr. Bray and his associates at the end of the seventeenth century, and the Miners' Libraries that proliferated in mining communities in Scotland a hundred years later.

The history of the library as a collection is, however, more than merely the story of the accumulation of books. The historian has to study who was selecting the books, the basis on which the selection was made, and, once again, how the books were obtained from booksellers or publishers. During the last hundred years, librarians have become the most important single group of customers for the book trade, and a history of libraries that ignores that trade and its relationship to library history is as blinkered as a history of the trade that ignores libraries.

Because the book historian is concerned with all aspects of the historical role of the book in society, it follows that he or she also is interested in all of those people who were active in the world of books. It was suggested earlier that the history of bookselling has been neglected; so too, until very recently, has been the history of librarianship and of education for librarianship. John Richardson's recently published history of the Graduate School of Library and Information Science at Chicago will, we must hope, inspire other scholars on both sides of the Atlantic to look more closely at the history of the library profession and those who have worked in it.

It should now be clear that the history of libraries is not only a worthwhile study in itself, but also a part of the larger subject of book history, never more so than when the book historian ventures, as is often necessary, into the history of scholarship and education. Indeed, the distinction between the history of the book and the history of libraries, so often embalmed in library science curricula, is a false one, and the two subjects should be studied and taught together as a unified whole. They are, in effect, dependent upon each other, for the books whose history the book historian seeks to study are very largely the books that have been preserved by generations of collectors and librarians, while the library historian cannot ignore the books that are, after all, the *raison d'être* of the library itself. Just as the history of the book is a vital part of the history of our culture, so the history of libraries is a vital part of the history of the book.

The history of the book is built up, like all social history, with bricks, each complete in itself, but each fulfilling its true role only when it is linked with others. If it is indeed true that the book, and the written or printed word that it contains, is central to our history, then it follows that it is also central to the study and writing of history. Our understanding of the past, which is the ultimate objective of all history, will be severely impaired if we do not recognize this crucial fact. It has been said truthfully that textual criticism will never prove that Hamlet was a woman or that *King Lear* is a comedy; nor will it, but textual critics properly argue that if words matter, then all words matter, and we should grant authors the respect of reading what they actually wrote. Similarly, the history of books will not show that the American Revolution began in 1777 or that the Bastille was stormed in 1790, but it may help us to understand these events, by illuminating the intellectual and spiritual world of the men and women who participated in them. The perimeters of book history are defined by the perimeters of the printed word itself, and if we accept, as surely we must, that we live in a culture whose development has been based on the transmission and understanding of words, then the history of the book is as fundamental to history as is the book itself to the culture whose history we seek to learn.

Note

This paper was written in response to a request to put library history into the context of recent developments in book history in general. Without having seen the other papers that were to be presented at the Seminar, I found that I had anticipated both the philosophy and the methodology that underlay many of them. Readers who are unfamiliar with the ongoing debate to which this paper is, in part, a contribution are referred to G. Thomas Tanselle's Hanes Lecture entitled *The History of Books as a Field of Study* (1981), and my review of it in *JLH*, 17 (1982): 463–7.

The History of the Book: New Questions? New Answers?

David D. Hall

The history of the book is a traditional field of study that has recently gained a new importance and undertaken new tasks. This essay reports on a conference on "Needs and Opportunities in the History of the Book in American Culture" held in 1984 at the American Antiquarian Society in Worcester, Massachusetts. The report focuses on four topics or problems that seem particularly important to the "new" history of the book: the history of reading, the history of popular culture, the role of bibliographical techniques in studying the transmission of texts, and the relationship between social history and the history of the book.

Some years ago a *New Yorker* cartoon mysteriously appeared on the bulletin board outside the office of the American Studies Program at an Ivy League university. It showed a group of Indians circling around a campfire. Underneath, someone had replaced the original caption with these words: "American Studies in search of a method."

This gentle putdown came to mind as I began anew to reflect on another academic field that has yet to achieve clear definition, the history of the book. I am not fond of the words "method" and "theory," two words that get bandied about among the good folk who do American Studies, and I will not use them in describing the tasks or the opportunities of the history of the book: there is no *one* method or one theory that works in all cases, or even works well most of the time. Better, I think, to assume that certain questions come to characterize a discipline or field of study. We know who we are by the questions we ask. What I propose to describe is the agenda of topics or questions that seem to define the history of the book. Let me observe that this field of inquiry is just emerging from its infancy—and at this point I am reminded of the French witticism that America is the only culture to pass from adolescence to decadence without ever experiencing maturity. The future of book history is more promising, though its passage to maturity will

David D. Hall *is professor of history at Boston University.*

surely not occur without hard work and some rough going. It was to aid this passage that an international group of book historians met in Worcester, Massachusetts, on 1–3 November 1984 to consider "needs and opportunities in the history of the book in American Culture."

The starting point for the Worcester conference was the tried and true assumption that we find out where we want to go and what we should accomplish by studying what we have accomplished in the past. We reflect on the strengths and limitations of our predecessors as a means of understanding ourselves, and of imagining alternatives. Thus it was urged on all contributors to the Worcester conference that they "review the literature." In the next breath, contributors were encouraged to reappraise the standard framework, the prevailing categories. We were seeking critical essays that, in summing up the past, would throw light upon the future.

The sponsor of the conference was the American Antiquarian Society through its Program in the History of the Book in American Culture. The Program came into being in 1983 with a statement of purpose that was widely circulated in the United States. Invoking the scholarship of (among others) Lucien Febvre, Henri-Jean Martin, Robert Darnton, and Elizabeth Eisenstein, the statement of purpose suggested that the history of the book "may be likened to a crossroads" at which several lines of inquiry converge. A more recent version of this statement declares that the history of the book requires or makes possible certain "shifts of perspective."

> Every book is an economic commodity that passes through a cycle of production and consumption as it makes its way from the mind of the author, to the printing office, and finally to the reader. The history of the book thus recasts the history of ideas, as Robert Darnton has demonstrated in his studies of the spread of the Enlightenment. It recasts literary history by restoring to it the social history of writers and readers. It re-energizes the history of popular belief by paying close attention to the cheapest and most widely circulating forms of print and to the milieu in which they travelled. Most importantly, the history of the book enlarges our understanding of authority—social, cultural, and political.

This broad conception of book history stood behind the Worcester conference; and I should add at this point that "book" in Worcester parlance encompasses the entire range of printed matter, though I suspect that we shall never have too much to say about railway timetables and restaurant menus, highly interesting though these items be!

Eleven persons presented papers at the conference, on subjects that ranged from the history of printing and the book trades to reading, popular culture, journalism, and bibliography. I say with some embarrassment that none of the papers took up the history of libraries as its main focus; nor did any paper deal with authors, the history of censorship, schoolbooks and education, government publications, or particular literary genres. But let me emphasize the cup half full. Collectively these papers furnished a systematic and imaginative summing up and rethinking. What new questions emerged, and what new answers? I propose to focus on four topics that coincide with my own competency or curiosity: popular culture, reading, the relationship between the history of the book and social history, and the transmittal of texts.

First, however, two observations. Just about everyone at this conference remarked on the highly specialized kinds of research that predominate in the various fields that make up the history of the book: on printers and publishers, libraries and book ownership, newspapers and magazines. If the strength of this research is what we learn about the trees, the weakness is a limited angle of vision that obscures the interconnections, the woods. Thus it was pointed out that studies of the great journalists and newspaper editors must be supplemented by broadly conceived investigations of patronage, audience, and emerging professonalism, all of them subjects that may say more about the nineteenth-century newspaper than the personality of a Greeley or a Pulitzer. The blessing of American scholarship is also its curse, the great abundance of local studies, or those of individual books and individual persons.

The other side of this question is to ask, how can we improve on our stock of generalizations, many of which seem blandly to ignore the rich, complex texture of American society. Speaking on the topic of book distribution, James Gilreath observed in his paper for the conference that the New England we encounter in studies of seventeenth-century libraries and booksellers "is a seamless web of readers in which books appeared magically and circulated without regard to class, region, profession, or any other variable," that is, without regard to context. Gilreath extended this criticism to two historians of literary culture in the south, Louis B. Wright and Richard Beale Davis, noting that "both writers think of books as being uniformly distributed throughout Southern culture without regard to social class or geography." Quoting a passage from Davis's *Intellectual Life in the Colonial South*, in which Davis weaves "together all classes of readers into a southern seemless web," Gilreath concluded that "students of the American book could benefit from some methodological hand-wringing about distribution and readership similar to that found among general cultural historians during the 1970s regarding the possibility of profiling a national character." We need, in other words to invoke something more specific than "Americans'' in general, even though we also need to avoid the extremes of empiricist detail.

Let me pass from these two observations to the heart of the matter, the questions that provide a core or center for the history of the book: the history of reading; the history of popular culture; the history of ''authority,'' to borrow a word that was employed at the conference; and the history of texts and their transmittal.

I have said elsewhere,[1] and I wish to reiterate, that the history of the book departs from histories of printing, publishing, and the book trade because of its concern with readers and the act of reading. In its modern guise, the history of the book builds on what may be referred to as the ''new'' history of reading, in contrast to an ''old'' history that has been with us for many years. We have always been curious to know what books people owned or encountered in libraries and bookstores. The difference between old and new is that the act of reading has emerged as a subject of concern; that is, not merely the what, but the how, or process of reading. We have come to realize that modes of using and understanding print changed over time.

In olden times—I refer to the centuries between 1500 and 1800—many persons could not read. Many others did possess this skill. Some readers owned many books—perhaps as many as two or three hundred. But it seems likely that most persons who could read owned very few titles—less than ten, and perhaps no more than one or two. As for the act of reading, the rise of ''silent reading'' in the late Middle Ages seems to mark a decisive shift in the relationship between text and reader. For many centuries, reading was communal, public, and bound up with speech or recitation. Afterwards, reading became personal and private, and the printed page acquired an authority on its own. The transition from one mode to another took place slowly, though perhaps the pace of change accelerated in the late Middle Ages, as Paul Saenger has argued. In colonial America, the process of learning to read remained rooted in recitation and memorization; children became literate by hearing certain texts read aloud, or by repeating words and phrases others spoke to them. The history of reading in early America remained linked with older patterns.[2]

A second major transition occurred between the seventeenth century and the end of the nineteenth, the transition from limited to universal literacy. As I write, the history of literacy is in a modest state of turmoil arising out of doubts about the methods used to measure the extent of literacy in past societies. The most significant objection to the method of counting signatures on wills or other documents is that learning to write and learning to read were taught separately, not together. We must assume, therefore, that some persons could read but not write, though not necessarily the reverse. Margaret Spufford was perhaps the first historian to remind us of the fact that, in sixteenth- and seventeenth-century England (and, it now seems, generally throughout Europe and America in these centuries), reading was taught first, and writing second;[3] reading was taught in households and informal schools, in a manner that enabled children to acquire the skill at an early age, and without much expense of time. On the other hand, the skill of writing was taught mainly in a formalized setting, and with an eye to its occupational significance. Hence many more men than women learned to write. Can we conclude that women were substantially literate, meaning they could read? It may be also that the transition from limited to universal literacy occurred earlier in some regions, and later in others. France is one of the regions where it came late: asking who could sing the Marseillaise, one historian has reminded us that in 1800 many peasants still did not know French.[4]

A broader argument for change revolves around the concept of a "reading revolution." William Gilmore gave a paper at the Worcester conference that focused on this revolution. Taking the concept from the German historian Rolf Engelsing,[5] who argued that the German reader underwent a major change of habits between the middle of the eighteenth and the middle of the nineteenth centuries, Gilmore drew on his own research on the upper Connecticut Valley to document a transition in American reading and American print culture. Literacy became nearly universal; local printers and booksellers multiplied; and the quantity of books and periodicals in circulation increased dramatically to the point where, for Americans, reading had become a "necessity of life," no longer incidental or peripheral but part of the daily routine, and an essential vehicle of information.

There is much evidence as well as other scholarship to sustain this concept of a reading revolution. We may turn, for example, to the autobiographies of two American publishers and writers, Joseph Buckingham and Samuel Goodrich. Recalling the Connecticut of his youth, Buckingham remembered that farmers in the late eighteenth century owned a mere handful of books: "The Bible and Dr. Watts's Psalms and Hymns were indispensable in every family. . . . There was also, on the book shelf, a volume or two of sermons, Doddridge's 'Rise and Progress of Religion,' and a very few other books and pamphlets, chiefly of a religious character." Goodrich was emphatic that few books circulated in *his* corner of Connecticut; he could remember the thrill of encountering, as a young boy, a small collection of children's books his father brought home from Hartford, and his evocation of a Broadway (New York) bookstore of the mid-nineteenth century, with its teeming abundance of books, some of them his own creation, pointed up the contrast between the old age and the new.[6] His is impressive testimony in support of a "reading revolution," as is the evidence for a new national system of distribution, the changing price structure of print, the increase in formal schooling, and the rise of cheap newspapers. Yet there are also significant difficulties with the argument that Gilmore presented. One is the problematic role of literacy as cause; if we locate the onset of near-universal literacy in the northern states in the middle or late decades of the eighteenth century, then the increase in literacy operated slowly, at best, to produce a revolution. A second difficulty arises from the perception, recently signaled by Joseph Kett, that nineteenth-century proclamations that reading had become universal—that contemporaries were living in a new era—were self-serving and promotional, and cannot be taken at face value. Kett and his fellow investigator came to this conclusion after an extensive study of surviving probate inventories in late-eighteenth- and early-nineteenth-century Virginia. To their surprise—or should it not be a surprise?—they found that many inventories contained no books and many others but one or two, circumstances that did not change with time. Nor was there a pronounced shift to fiction, as is usually suggested by those who argue for a reading revolution. The taste of readers in post-independence Virginia was decidedly traditional, the range of reading limited.[7] Elizabeth Cometti came to these same conclusions in her study of a North Carolina bookstore; when the proprietor offered for sale books by Laurence Sterne, Oliver Goldsmith, and Henry Fielding, his customers passed them up and purchased Bibles, Bunyan's *Pilgrim's Progress*, and other religious tracts in quantity.[8]

Readers may have remained traditional in their tastes, in ways that qualify the argument for a "revolution." It also may be possible to discern moments of extraordinary ferment—veritable explosions of print—in the centuries that precede the coming of the steam press, the cheap newspaper, and the novel. Could we apply the term "revolution" to the surge of imprints in continental Europe, and especially Germany, in the early sixteenth century? In the 1520s book production leaped 300 percent as people rushed to buy up Bibles, psalmbooks, and catechisms in the vernacular, and to participate in the great controversies between Catholic and Protestant. The period of the Civil War in England offers another example of print becoming commonplace and accessible, as any glance at the Thomason Collection makes obvious. Or we might wish to turn our attention to the late seventeenth century, when English printers turned out as many as 400,000 copies of almanacs a year, along with remarkable quantities of chapbooks and, increasingly, a devotional literature written by Protestant evangelicals, most of whom were indifferent to doctrinal and ecclesiological issues that had divided the Protestant community during the first half of the century. We do have to wait until the nineteenth century before we encounter a reading public large enough to buy 70,000 copies of Joseph Alleine's *Alarm to the Unconverted* within a few years of its publication in 1673.

The historian of reading must somehow reconcile two, or perhaps three, distinct tendencies: the very real phenomena associated with the "reading revolution," and especially the enormous increase in the quantity of newspapers; large-scale publishing during times like the English Civil War, or the evangelical campaigns of the late seventeenth century; and the persistence of old-fashioned styles of reading and old books even after literacy became universal and fiction surged in popularity. A copy of Joseph Alleine's *Alarm* that I picked up in Maine some years ago proved to be an edition published for the use and benefit of Methodist Sunday Schools in the fourth decade of the nineteenth century!

A second characteristic of the history of the book is a concern with popular culture. The Worcester conference had the benefit of David Grimsted's masterful critique of popular culture studies in America, and a thoughtful commentary by Roger Chartier, speaking from the perspective of the social historian of early modern Europe.[9] Chartier and Grimsted both argued that the historian of popular culture must avoid two facile extremes: the one of denouncing the "popular" as inferior, degraded, or escapist, and the other of embracing the popular as though it were genuinely democratic or "of the people." Enthusiasm and snobbery are equally useless. Grimsted devoted much of his essay to demonstrating that popular texts embody complexities of various kinds. He called attention to certain theories of culture, or theories of the relationship between society and culture, that had brought new energy to the field, and at the same time, new difficulties, as in the effort to separate the culture of the working class from that of the employer. Indeed, Grimsted and Chartier were both uneasy with the assumption that social level dictates the kind of culture that one has. As Chartier made clear in his essays on the *bibliothèque bleue*, the cheap books that began to appear in seventeenth-century France, certain items deemed "popular" circulated widely, finding readers among the bourgeoisie and the peasants, the urban classes and the rural. If a narrowly defined social history does not provide an organizing framework for understanding popular culture, as Chartier insisted, neither does a narrowly based aesthetics, as Grimsted made evident.

What seems clear is that historians of the book must embrace the outcasts—and there are always outcasts to reclaim and rediscover. No form of print is too lowly to deserve attention. In saying this I do not mean to espouse a simplistic populism. The historian of "outcast" books must acknowledge the politics that constantly function to exclude and include, a politics that can arouse radical anger among those groups that feel pushed to the margins. Anger and conflict thrust their way into the history of popular culture. So does the politics of domination as one group seeks to impose its values on another: the tract societies of the nineteenth century come immediately to mind. What may be most difficult to understand and live with is the realization that popular culture is playful. Its mode is often one of inversion, that is, taking the stock wisdom, the "serious" beliefs of a society, and subjecting them to laughter. The great ritual of "carnival"—a world turned upside down—had its echoes in print culture. I think especially of the fictiveness of certain genres, like those broadsides that contain the dying words of a criminal, the real authors being the printers themselves (sometimes in competition with *other* contrived versions). Almanacs thrived on playfulness. So did melodrama, as Grimsted has demonstrated in his excellent book on the genre. In sum, popular culture is no trivial subject. It belongs at the center of the history of the book and, as conceived by Grimsted and Chartier, transforms the history of the book into a broad scrutiny of the relationship between culture and society.

A third characteristic of the history of the book is its concern with this very relationship. The French phrase "livre et société," the book *and* society, reminds us that, when Lucien Febvre issued his famous call for a new kind of book history, he intended to ground this new history in social, economic, and intellectual contexts. What he feared was a "literary" book history that focused on texts in isolation from the worlds of printers, publishers, networks of diffusion, and readers. Books, he insisted, were commodities in the workplace.

Robert Gross (Amherst College) concluded the Worcester conference with an essay on social history and the book. How, he asked, can the different fields that make up the history of the book contribute to an understanding of social and cultural history? John Foxe, the great English martyrologist, had celebrated the invention of printing as God's instrument for liberating the Word from the clutches of Catholicism. In our own day, Elizabeth Eisenstein has proposed far-reaching connections between printing and intellectual and religious movements.[10] If not always on so broad a scale, such connections surely exist.

Robert Gross sought to elucidate the connections between structures of power and the structure of book history. He observed that American historians have sketched three very different frameworks in the colonial period. First he singled out Daniel Boorstin's chapters on printers and printing in *The Americans: The Colonial Experience*, in which Boorstin argued that printers in America functioned in a very different manner from printers in Europe: here there was no Paris or London, that is, no cosmopolitan center; here, too, there was no strong central state or aristocracy. Printers had to look elsewhere for patrons, a search that left them responsive to local needs and not to centralized authority. To quote

Boorstin, in early America "print lost its exalted status as the companion of privilege, adapted to necessity, and took on a more pragmatic, democratic purpose as a community-oriented vehicle of useful information."[11] The history of printing thus expressed Boorstin's larger theme, the process of Americanization, or the emergence of a democratic people accustomed to a freedom and a flexibility unlike what was possible in Europe.

The theme of democracy had its counterpoint, Gross argued, in two other interpretations. One of these he extracted from essays of my own in which I have argued that elite and popular belief in early New England really were not very different. Gross viewed me (and others) as suggesting that printing (Bibles, catechisms, primers, almanacs and the like) "sustained a deeply conservative social order, where consensus on fundamental values held sway."[12] But in *The Transformation of Virginia*, a recent prize-winning study of eighteenth-century Virginia, Gross found the argument that books belonged to the privileged few and were emblems of hierarchy. By contrast, ordinary people remained within an oral culture that was relatively indifferent to print. Isaac extended this contrast into an interpretation of the evangelical revivals of the mid-eighteenth century; for him, the upsurge of evangelical preaching was akin to a revolt against the gentry and their books. In effect, Isaac was arguing that print was an instrument of control whereas speech promoted spontaneous, unstructured, democratic politics.

Gross found that historians of nineteenth-century America also disagreed on the significance of books and reading. Some argued that culture became democratized as literacy rose and production flourished. Others—and here he cited in particular Ann Douglas's *The Feminization of American Culture*—have proposed that the ethos of competitive capitalism permeated book culture to such an extent that few, if any, alternatives could be sustained. For Douglas, the history of books and readers provides the illusion of choice and the reality of domination.

Since Professor Gross is transforming his essay into a book on the "authority of the word," we may leave to him the task of reconciling these divergent interpretations. To add a little spice to his dish, I would like to call attention to one other paper presented at the conference, a co-authored essay on "Forms of Expertise" by Steven Botein (Michigan State University) and David Jaffee (Smithsonian Institution). Botein contributed a section of this paper on lawyers and their expertise, an expertise they gained (in the early nineteenth century) chiefly by devoting themselves to close study of Blackstone's *Commentaries*. Here is a social history—or so it seems—of a group of persons who assume a powerful role on the basis of mastering a body of knowledge. But, as Botein observed, the book that was the means of acquiring authority was widely published in America, and often in editions that provided reading aids for the less learned. Printing history, in this case the history of American versions of Blackstone, suggests that expertise was not so very "expert" after all, much less an exclusive commodity.

My fourth and final topic is that deceptively simple word, the text. Deceptively simple, because, as every bibliographer has discovered, any text contains within itself a myriad of questions and answers. The physical form is made up of many different elements, each with a history to it. As for the contents, that is to say, the "text" as we conventionally employ this word, the naive reader can scarcely comprehend the skepticism that the bibliographer or textual critic brings to bear upon the evidence. Is what we see before us exactly what the author intended? What is the *history* of transmittal, and especially of the changes that this process seems inevitably to impose upon a text?

Addressing these issues, Thomas Tanselle (Guggenheim Foundation) presented a paper at the Worcester conference in which he criticized historians for their indifference to the history of texts, and bibliographers for not providing adequate detail in their collations. The thrust of Tanselle's presentation was to emphasize the strong possibility of variants—and as he reminded us, variants occur not only between *editions* but within a single *printing* of a given text. Were the community of bibliographers to follow his advice on how to perform signature collations, the result would be a vastly greater knowledge of variants—to which, presumably, historians would pay increasing attention.

Yet there was skepticism of another sort among those listening to this argument. Granting the existence of variants, the counterargument ran, so what? The task of taking all of them into account was impossible to accomplish; in any event, was it not the case that significant variants would turn up as, in time, different groups or persons read or put to use the same text in different manners? To turn this point around, was it not true that the essentials of most texts seemed to persist from one edition to the next?

At this distance of time from the discussion that occurred at the conference, I can put the issue in two different ways: what does it mean to search for an authentic text, when authors, printers, publishers, and readers in past times have *not* perplexed themselves with this issue? What can we learn about levels of culture from the process by which texts are transmitted and, as happens in so many cases, modified in one direction or another? Let me speak briefly about the latter of these questions, and its promise for historians of the book. I take my cue from Roger Chartier and other French students of popular culture, who in studying the texts that make up the *bibliothèque bleue* have illuminated a fascinating process of abridgment and rearrangement. Some of these French texts descend from longer literary works that circulated in the late Middle

Ages. Squeezed into the format of the chapbook, these texts lost their integrity, lost perhaps their complex structure, gained perhaps a quality of folklore or at least participated in some shift of level. So at least the comparison of different editions seems to suggest. In this activity lies, I think, a promising avenue of approach to the formation of popular culture, and to the role of certain cultural intermediaries. A book I called attention to above, Alleine's *Alarm*, went through a savage process of abridgment before it ended up in the hands of Methodist children in the early nineteenth century. Yet we know nothing about this process. It ill behooves cultural or religious historians to assume that the Alleine they may know from the seventeenth century is the same Alleine available to nineteenth-century readers. The point has wide application. In this regard we must heed any plea to study texts and their transmittal, even though we may also take a commonsense approach to the sum total of the process.

In sketching for you some of the questions that arose at the Worcester conference, I have spoken candidly about their strengths and limitations. It is a sign of health that argument can occur, and disagreement; it is also a sign of health that persons from so many different fields—literary, social, and intellectual history, the history of printing and publishing, the practice of bibliography, to name the more obvious specialties—find that the history of the book brings them together. As at this very conference on the history of libraries, so at Worcester the progress was visible amidst debate and discussion.

Notes

1. David D. Hall, *On Native Ground: From the History of Printing to the History of the Book* (Worcester, Mass.: American Antiquarian Society, 1984), pp. 23–25.
2. Paul Saenger, "Silent Reading: Its Impact on Late Medieval Script and Society," *Viator* 13 (1982): 367–414. See also David D. Hall, "The Uses of Literacy in New England, 1600–1850," in William L. Joyce et al. (eds.), *Printing and Society in Early America* (Worcester, Mass.: American Antiquarian Society, 1983), pp. 1–47.
3. Margaret Spufford, "First Steps in Literacy: The Reading and Writing Experiences of the Humblest Seventeenth-Century Spiritual Autobiographers," in Harvey J. Graff (eds.), *Literacy and Social Development in the West, A Reader* (Cambridge: Cambridge University Press, 1981), pp. 125–150.
4. Eugen Weber, "Who Sang the Marseillaise?" in Jacques Beauroy et al. (eds.), *The Wolf and the Lamb: Popular Culture in France* (Saratoga, Cal.: Anima Libri, 1977), pp. 161–173.
5. Rolf Engelsing, *Der Bürger als Leser: Lesergeschichte in Deutschland 1500–1800* (Stuttgart: J. B. Metzler, 1974).
6. Hall, "The Uses of Literacy," pp. 1–2.
7. Joseph F. Kett and Patricia A. McClung, "Book Culture in Post-Revolutionary Virginia," *Proceedings of the American Antiquarian Society* 94 (1984): 97–147.

8. Elizabeth Cometti, "Some Early Bestsellers in Piedmont North Carolina," *North Carolina Historical Review* 16 (1950): 324–337.

9. David Grimsted, "Books and Culture: Canned, Canonized, and Neglected," *Proceedings of the American Antiquarian Society* 94 (1984): 297–335.

10. Elizabeth Eisenstein, *The Printing Press as an Agent of Change,* 2 vols. (Cambridge: Cambridge University Press, 1979), part 3.

11. Daniel Boorstin, *The Americans: the Colonial Experience* (New York: Random House, 1958), book 3, parts 11–12.

12. G. Thomas Tanselle, "The Bibliography and Textual Study of American Books," *Proceedings of the American Antiquarian Society* 95 (1985): 113–151; Norman Fiering, "A Comment on Mr. Tanselle's Paper," ibid., 152–160.

Women and the History of Scientific Communication

Margaret W. Rossiter

Recent work on the history of women in science has led to increased interest in the history of scientific librarians, libraries, and books (including textbooks, reference works, journals, and abstracts). These seem to be neglected subjects, despite assertions by sociologists and others of the centrality of communication to science. Like most of "women's work," much of scientific communication has been so invisible to outsiders that it has been taken for granted, and its importance is often minimized. When more attention is paid to the history of scientific communication, especially to women's roles therein, truer assessments of the relative value of various types of scientific work may be possible.

I'm glad to have the opportunity to be here and both to meet so many people interested in library history and to have a reason to focus on and develop systematically some ideas I've been playing with sporadically for some time now. I presume I was invited because John Cole, whom I met years ago at a meeting on the history of knowledge in America,[1] and Phyllis Dain, who had good things to say about my recent book on the history of women scientists,[2] were on the program committee. It was in writing that book that I came across the subject of the history of librarianship, for not only were some of my women scientists librarians (or editors or bibliographers), but much of the vocational guidance literature of the 1930s addressed to women in science (chemistry especially) urged them to become librarians or abstractors. This was intriguing, but I was unable to find out much more about the topic at the time; the best I could do then (c. 1980 and 1981) was to suggest in a footnote that others take up the history of scientific libraries and librarianship.[3] By now (1985), however, I've taught a course on the history of women in science from antiquity to the present and done more research on the

Margaret W. Rossiter *is visiting scholar, department of the History of Science, Harvard University.* *This essay is dedicated to the memory of Derek J. de Solla Price (1922–1983). Part of the expenses of this project were paid by NSF grant SES-83-2161.*

decades after 1940, when "science information" becomes a field in itself. This has caused me to ponder more systematically than before what the history of the book, library history, and, in its most general form, the history of communication look like to a historian of science interested in gender issues and women's history.

My first reaction to the phrase "the history of the book" is the territorially defensive one that historians of science have been doing this in their own way for decades, though under the guise of what is called the "internal" history of science. In the early days of the field, textual analysis was perhaps the most rigorous work that was done, as shown in now-classic editions and studies of Euclid's *Elements*, Galen's *On the Usefulness of the Parts*, Copernicus's *De Revolutionibus*, Harvey's *De Motu Cordis*, and Newton's *Principia Mathematica.* Since then the notebooks of some scientists, such as Charles Lyell and Charles Darwin, have begun to be published, as has Robert Stauffer's edition of the long, unpublished early version of Darwin's *Origin of Species*. Behind such studies are a reverence for the text and a belief that unless one has the texts right one can never know what the scientific thoughts were, let alone how they changed over time. But though central to the history of ideas, such textual analysis can seem limited and lacking in any sense of social context. Nor will it lead to the discovery of many women in science.

More recently, especially since the late 1960s, historians of science have worked on the transmission as well as development of scientific ideas, be it through the successive copyings of medieval manuscripts or via the numerous printings and editions of printed works. I myself wrote a dissertation on the spread of the ideas of Justus Liebig, a German organic chemist, to America in the nineteenth century. Here it was standard procedure to trace the numerous German, English, and American editions of Liebig's several works in order to show when his controversial and ever-changing ideas came to the United States.[4] This task might have been easier had a bibliography that appeared in 1969 included more American editions,[5] or had the Library of Congress's *National Union Catalog of Pre-1956 Imprints* reached Liebig a few years earlier.[6] In any case, intellectual agendas were broadening in the late 1960s, moving beyond textual analysis and into the new social history just as major research tools, themselves the result of decades of effort toward bibliographic control, were coming to completion.[7] These new tools were to make more of this social history, including the pursuit of women in science, possible.

It's in the transmission rather than the creation of science that one begins to glimpse more than a few women in science. (This is not surprising, since they were excluded from the universities from their formation in the twelfth and thirteenth centuries until the end of the nineteenth in most countries.) Thus one finds nuns as well as monks copying manuscripts in the Middle Ages,[8] and it was Madame du Chatelet in France in the eighteenth century who was the first to perform the towering intellectual feat of translating Newton's *Principia* into French.[9] Later in the nineteenth century it was the Scotswoman Mary Somerville who performed the reverse feat of translating Laplace's work on celestial mechanics into English, and then in 1862 Clemence Royer of France who translated Darwin's *Origin of Species* into French.[10] This kind of work is one part of what historians of science have called, pejoratively until lately, the mere "popularization" of science. This term would lump together the readership of important books, the publication of popular books, attendance at public lectures or natural history museums, the rise of scientific magazines (such as *Scientific American* or *Popular Science Monthly*), newspaper coverage or science journalism, and, for the twentieth century, other media such as radio, television, and movies. Besides such "informal" channels, "popularization" would also include certain more formal forms such as the curricula and textbooks of science education.

When one is pursuing the history of women in science, science textbooks gain new interest, for starting in the mid-eighteenth century, some were designated as especially "for the ladies." The first of this genre was Francesco Algarotti's *Il newtonianismo per le dame* (Naples, 1737), which Elizabeth Carter translated into English two years later. In the 1750s came Robert Heath's *Truth Triumphant, or Fluxions for the Ladies* (London, 1752) in mathematics and Benjamin Martin's *Young Gentlemen and Lady's Philosophy* (London, 1759) in natural science. Several other textbooks "for ladies" later in the century were by women authors.[11] The best known and most prolific of this group was Jane Marcet, the wife of a scientist at the Royal Institution in London. She supplemented her wifely duties by attending the Institution's public lectures on science and entertaining its staff and visiting scientists. After hearing about their latest discoveries (such as the element chlorine), she described them in her series of textbooks, the most popular of which was her *Conversations on Chemistry*, which went through at least fifteen English editions and many abroad. (The Edgar Fahs Smith Collection at the Van Pelt Library of the University of Pennsylvania has, for example, thirty-three copies of her works.)[12] The social message conveyed by the appearance and wide sale of such books (since, of course, girls could read other textbooks without "ladies" in the title, if their parents permitted) was that now, even before seminaries and academies existed, let alone public schools with formal curricula, it was acceptable for women to study elementary science. Ann Shteir of York University in Canada is doing very interesting work on the early botanical works for ladies, including especially those by the British author Priscilla Wakefield.[13]

Another kind of "book" already somewhat studied by historians of science, but given new interest by the recently detected involvement of women, is the whole realm of science periodicals. David Kronick's classic history of such works includes a few with the term "ladies" in their title. The longest-lasting of this group was the *Ladies' Diary, or the Woman's Almanack, Containing Many Delightful and Entertaining Particulars Peculiarly Adapted for the Use and Diversion of the Fair Sex*, which appeared from 1704 until 1840, when it merged with the *Gentleman's Diary, or Mathematical Repository* (started in 1741) to become the *Ladies' and Gentlemen's Diary*, which lasted into the 1870s.[14] Two studies of the contributors to the *Ladies' Diary* have shown that, despite the title and many exhortations to women to send in their puzzles and/or solutions, most of the contributors were men, including some (like the prolific "Ann Nichols") who used female pseudonyms. Nevertheless, such popular magazines offer one chance to estimate the extent of mathematical literacy (or numeracy, as Patricia Cline Cohen has termed it recently) in eighteenth- and nineteenth-century England.[15] Other scholars have determined when the first scientific articles by women were published in various journals: 1834 in the *American Journal of Science*, 1878 in the *Proceedings of the American Association for the Advancement of Science*, and 1883 in *Science*.[16] Two other scholars have now gone beyond this public realm to give a glimpse of another side of the scientific journal, the makeup of its staff. The prevailing notion (largely because unexamined) seems to be the naive one that the editor alone, and heroically, put out "his" journal.[17] But now Ann Shteir and Dorinda Outram have shown that, at least in British botany and French paleontology, scientific publishing could be a family affair. The Hooker family dominated British botany for most of the nineteenth century, as father and son successively held major posts at Kew Gardens. Yet when Shteir looked behind the scenes she found Maria Hooker, wife of Sir W. J. Hooker, who, to quote a dictionary, served for fifty years, "as her husband's helpmeet and amanuensis, and to her the successive series of the *Journal of Botany*, the *Botanical Miscellany* and other of Sir William's publications, owe much of their literary style and typographical accuracy."[18]

Other intelligent and largely home-educated wives and daughters of botanists helped out with the scientific works as illustrators (drawing lessons were, after all, part of a cultivated lady's education), editors and clerks or label-writers (good penmanship was another ladylike accomplishment). Similarly, when Dorinda Outram recently scrutinized the career of Georges Cuvier, the famed French paleontologist, she found his step-daughter Sophie Duvaucel, an unpaid illustrator on one of "his" many publications (which included an encyclopedia).[19] Thus though a man's name might be the only one on the title page, there were women behind the scenes in scientific publishing, long before propriety or scientific "norms" would allow them the public credit and recognition for their efforts. Since then, of course, scientific publishing has expanded greatly, but the old pattern of male editors, all-male editorial boards, and partially feminized staffs remains. The chief difference today would be that there would be some women on the editorial boards and the names of all would be printed on the title page, as in a recent issue of *Science*, which listed four male editors and deputy editors (100 percent), twelve men of fourteen persons on the editorial board (86 percent), and twenty-nine of thirty-five on a "board of reviewing editors" (83 percent). As for the staff, however, men are only twelve of the forty-five names listed (27 percent) and only one of the (seemingly) top five (20 percent).[20]

One step beyond the world of scientific journals per se is that of scientific abstracts, a field or genre that Bruce Manzer dates back to the 1790s but that has grown explosively in the United States since the 1920s.[21] Many women have worked in this largely invisible and anonymous area from the lowest levels (Nellie Payne, a National Research Council fellow of the 1920s, at *Biological Abstracts*),[22] to the middle management (Margaret Schindler, who oversaw the U.S. Department of Agriculture's *Bibliography of Agriculture*),[23] to top management (Phyllis Parkins at *Biological Abstracts* in the difficult 1960s),[24] and conception and organization (physicist Kay Way of *Nuclear Sciences Abstracts* at Oak Ridge National Laboratory after World War II).[25] Women seem to have done least well hierarchically at the oldest and largest of these information services, *Chemical Abstracts* of Columbus, Ohio, started in 1907.[26]

Many women have worked on the preparation of scientific reference books over the years, though again anonymously (at least I haven't found one named for a woman yet). At the Harvard College Observatory many women worked for several decades on the "Henry Draper Star Catalog," named by its donor for her deceased husband. This project was directed by Edward C. Pickering, director of the Observatory, with the able assistance of Williamina P. Fleming, his former maid, who oversaw the work of up to ten women "computers" at a time. The status of these women interested me: their salaries were a pittance (as low as the traffic would bear), yet their collective efforts were praised as useful or even essential to the advance of astrophysics. In the end the university and the Observatory gained the prestige of their collective labors

Yet these Harvard women were not totally anonymous, as the limited recognition given Fleming and some of her associates indicates. Her name appeared on the title page of some of the last Draper volumes she "edited," and she and her successor, Annie Jump Cannon, were voted stars in the *American Men of Science* by their fellow astronomers. (Their colleagues Henrietta Leavitt, once nominated for a Nobel Prize, and Antonia Maury were not, however.) But despite this honor, given to 4 women and 137 men in astronomy between 1903 and 1943, neither woman was elected to the more prestigious National Academy of Sciences. Thus heroic lifelong labors on a major reference book in one's science might lead to one level of recognition but not to the very highest.[27]

Yet the Harvard astronomers were just one part (the most visible tip) of a wider phenomenon, which brings me to my "comparable worth" stage. A while ago on a visit to the Harvard University Achives (where I had been many times before), aided this time by an entry in Andrea Hinding's massive directory of manuscript sources for women's history, I looked up the obituary of Mary Day, a librarian, or rather bibliographer, for three decades at the Gray Herbarium (1893–1924). Though she was listed in no scientific directories and received no honors in her lifetime, she was in her own way the equal of Mrs. Fleming and Miss Cannon in astronomy. According to this obituary by Herbarium director B. L. Robinson, she had come to Harvard after several years of study at Lancaster Academy in Massachusetts, seven years of school-teaching and six years in a public library, where as first assistant she had also picked up some experience as an accountant. Though her predecessor at Harvard, a graduate of the Albany Library School, had left in disgust at the library's cramped conditions and her lack of freedom to rearrange the shelves, Miss Day thrived at the Herbarium. Despite what Robinson admits was a "lamentably small" salary, her first task was the verification of about 5,000 bibliographical references to the *Synoptical Flora of North America*, one of the Herbarium's ongoing projects then being prepared for the press. She thrived on this detail, plowing "through this task conscientiously and with great patience and good humor, quickly recognizing errors when called to her attention and not rarely suggesting improvements in the citations." She became a good proofreader and quickly learned how to keep the Herbarium's statistical records and even its budget. She joined the New England Botanical Club and for many years prepared the annual index, at first gratis, of its journal *Rhodora*. But this was only the beginning. When the Herbarium staff then devoted nearly ten years to revising and rewriting *Gray's Manual* (prepared earlier by the great Harvard botanist Asa Gray), Miss Day undertook, as Robinson terms it, "no end of bibliographical work" with the verification and proofreading "on the side." When this was complete and the Herbarium moved over a period of six years into a new and larger building, Miss Day "showed much executive capacity." Though delighted that the library's books could now be shelved properly, Miss Day soon realized that the whole catalog should also be made over and accordingly did so. On top of all this she also prepared a major reference work of her own: in 1903 she took over from Josephine Clark of the U.S. Department of Agriculture the preparation of the "Card Index of New Genera, Species and Varieties of American Plants." This involved indexing every page of more than 130 scientific journals and monographs in many languages for citations to American plants. Each quarter, therefore, she prepared 1,000 to 2,500 new cards, which were sold in duplicate sets to eighteen other botanical libraries around the world. As the index grew, it came to be regarded as "a well nigh indispensable feature" of research on American botany. And yet, according to the director, "this great work," which was named for the Herbarium and not for her, "was merely incidental in Miss Day's routine, a species of knitting work, carried on in the intervals between many other duties." She also remembered everybody in the field and had a wide correspondence with botanists everywhere who called upon her for bibliographical and even personal advice. (One out West wanted her to send him a wife!)[28]

Upon reading this one begins to get a little angry (the Harvard Archives can be a radicalizing place!) and to wonder why, if Miss Day's work was as important as her director realized after her death, she hadn't been appreciated more and paid better in her lifetime. Though she was probably quite modest and self-effacing, Miss Day's virtues should have been noticed long before. I wondered also, if this was how she spent her time, what were the other persons on the staff, including the director himself, doing that was presumably more important and better rewarded and recognized? What is the status of people who, paid or unpaid, devote decades to the preparation of reference works?[29] Is it low if they are staff women paid a pittance but high if they are already renowned professors at the top of the scale (often aided by women like Miss Day)? Shouldn't quality or accuracy or coverage enter the calculation? How does one evaluate such contributions when writing the history of a science, as, here, of botanical classification? Should one, as is generally the case, praise the Gray Herbarium and its staff of (male) botanists and directors, leaving the "literature" and contributors like Miss Day anonymous or in the footnotes? It was only by studying women scientists that one found her at all and began to penetrate the invisibility that has heretofore surrounded such people and such types of work.

This pondering on the status of reference books and their authors then led me to consider the history of the sites of their labors—specialized scientific libraries. These institutions, especially those at herbaria, observatories, museums, and marine biology stations, have often fostered long careers in scientific literature or bibliography, because they are physically separate from larger libraries, separately endowed (initially at least), and thus perhaps imbued with certain traditions, dominant personalities, and strong commitment to their clientele. (In this regard one might think of the libraries at the Museum of Comparative Zoology at Harvard, at the Harvard College Observatory, and at the Marine Biological Laboratory at Woods Hole.)[30] Departmental libraries, though also somewhat specialized and chronically underfunded, seem to have had less of a long-term commitment to complete collections or an experienced librarian/bibliographer, hiring short-term student help instead. They also seem to have been more closely integrated into the bureaucracy of the main library (either physically, as a room in the main building, or budgetarily). (In this regard one can point to the mathematics and physics libraries at Harvard University, for examples.)[31] This niggardliness seems to have limited the autonomy and willingness of the many potential "Miss Days" of this world to take on literature chores, develop their specialty, and build up a clientele (often far beyond their own university).

Beyond the universities and the separate research institutions there have been a few other important private or independent scientific libraries, but with seemingly fewer women bibliographers of note. (At least the libraries' published histories do not mention them.) Of these institutions the earliest would be the American Philosophical Society in Philadelphia, whose collections were heavily concentrated in science. The largest would be the John Crerar Library in Chicago, established in the 1890s and long employing women catalogers, printers, and assistants on its staff. The youngest might be the Linda Hall Library in Kansas City, Missouri, started in the 1940s with a $10 million endowment.[32] In city government the first metropolitan library to have a science and technology division (opening in 1889) was the Carnegie Library in Pittsburgh, but few of these institutions, which must have employed many women, apparently had any worth writing about in their science divisions. At New York Public, separate science and technology divisions were created to coincide with the opening of the new main building in 1911, but they were consolidated into one department in 1918. The Detroit Public Library started its Technology Division in 1917 (hiring a staff member from the John Crerar to head it), though its science and technology collections, including the voluminous records of the U.S. Patent Office, went back long before that (and had been so heavily used by the young inventors Thomas Alva Edison and Henry Ford that the library's historian considers the collections as "in a sense, the poor man's college of engineering").[33]

At higher governmental levels the state libraries may have had science collections or departments, but more interesting, especially to one wishing to see the knowledge in action *in situ*, are the agency libraries. At the New York State Department of Health, long the largest and most important state science agency nationwide, libraries were taken so seriously (according to the historian of one division, herself its former librarian) that its building was arranged so that each office or laboratory opened onto the library, which was at its center.[34]

At the federal level of the United States government, female science librarians and bibliographers seem to have made more visible contributions at the agency libraries than in the science divisions of the major national libraries. The Smithsonian Institution, for example, started its library early but soon (1857) gave up the ambition for a comprehensive library and concentrated instead on its "international exchange system" of publications among scientific societies and public institutions.[35] The Smithsonian was quickly overtaken in science by the Army Medical Museum (later the National Library of Medicine) and the Library of Congress, which had been acquiring books on science since about 1815, when, after a fire during the War of 1812, Congress purchased Thomas Jefferson's personal library. Since then it has, of course, created a series of scientific divisions (aeronautics in 1929, technical information in 1947, and science in 1949, which merged with technical information in 1958 to form one unit) and performed much bibliographic and technical work for particular agencies on a contract basis: on space for NASA, Antarctica for NSF, and air pollution for the U.S. Public Health Service. In 1962 it also set up a National Referral Center for Science and Technology, supported by a grant from the National Science Foundation. But again, though one suspects there were many female minds involved in this work, none are "important" enough to appear in the published histories.[36]

Besides these well-known libraries of the federal government, almost every agency has had its own, which in the case of the more scientific agencies, such as the U.S. Department of Agriculture, U.S. Geological Survey, and Naval Research Laboratory, have been quite notable in their fields. At some of these agency libraries, women have made important contributions, though (except for agriculture) less as bibliographers than as administrators. At the USDA, whose large decentralized library system has since become the National Library of Agriculture in Beltsville, Maryland, there was, besides the bibliographers Josephine A. Clark and Margaret Schindler mentioned above, a woman chief librarian, Claribel Barnett, who served from 1907 to 1940.[37] Similarly, at the Naval Research Laboratory, Ruth Hutchison Hooker created and directed its library for over thirty years. Coming in 1930 after three years of teaching physics at Hood College, she served until 1965. In

1975 her portrait was hung in the library where she had labored so long, and the library was named in her honor, a very rare event in any government agency.[38]

To a certain extent this pattern of women's involvement in scientific agency libraries continues outside the United States (though I'm not trying in this short talk to be comprehensive!). In Canada, for example, Margaret S. Gill was for many years (1928–1957) chief librarian at the government-sponsored National Research Council in Ottawa. She was also for decades a major force behind the move for expanded library service throughout the nation and especially the establishment of a National Library of Canada in 1953.[39] In Britain, however, where the British Library was created in 1972 out of several preexisting units (including the Science Reference Library, which had grown out of the old Patent Office Library founded in 1855, and the Science Museum Library, which went back even further to 1843 when Henry de la Beche, the first director of the British Geological Survey, left it his books), there is no mention of prominent women librarians or bibliographers. One can hope, however, that there were some toiling diligently behind the scenes.[40]

Although basic to any broader understanding of the history of scientific communication (including chronology and possible periodization, for starters), this institutional history of science libraries can become repetitious and celebratory, as administrators and trustees of each one face and fight similar battles more or less successfully. Their constraints reflect the real world of ever-growing collections, inadequate buildings, staff shortages, rising costs, and the like. There is very little contemplation in this literature of such philosophical concerns as the cumulative value of all this reference work or its place in the larger world of science education or research. Everyone is busy, straining to the utmost to get the information organized and into the hands of the user, but to what end? One place in which such questions might be raised (if not actually answered) would be in the professional societies of specialists, particularly the Special Libraries Association, established in the United States in 1909. In 1923 it formed under the enthusiastic leadership of George Lee of Stone and Webster of Boston, a science and technology group. Always one of the Association's largest divisions, it provided many later presidents of the Association, including several women, such as Betty Joy Cole, a former chemist of the American Cyanamid Company, Ruth H. Hooker of the Naval Research Laboratory, and Margaret H. Fuller of the American Iron and Steel Institute. Over the years this division also had many useful projects including running symposia, issuing a newsletter (*Sci-Tech News*), preparing many exhibits, initiating the *Technical Book Review Index*, and, perhaps most ambitiously, preparing a guide to the organization and management of scientific and technical libraries. This work first appeared in 1951 and has since gone through a major revision (1964) and second edition (1972).[41] It would be interesting to pursue the activities and goals of this group, which offer a way to focus on the people most heavily involved in running science libraries and in articulating their needs and goals.

But around 1960 there comes a great discontinuity in what is written about science libraries and bibliographies. Suddenly the scene shifts outside the library, and the literature is dominated by the broader concepts of "information" and more optimistically "communication," which turn out to have their own brand of sexual politics. Although the Royal Society of London had held a conference on "scientific information" in 1948 and the new National Science Foundation had been charged with concern for it in its organic act of 1950, the whole "STINFO" movement, as it came to be called, mushroomed as a result of the Soviet launching of Sputnik I in October 1957. Suddenly, competing with and beating the Russians, who had also just set up a menacingly large science abstracting system (VINITI), became such a high American priority that it could no longer be left to mere librarians and abstractors, who, it seemed, had let the country down. A panel of the newly formed President's Science Advisory Committee published the first of a series of reports on science information in December 1958. (These panels were not composed of science abstractors or special librarians but of prestigious science administrators—all men—who, like W. O. Baker, vice-president of Bell Laboratories, or Alvin Weinberg, director of the Oak Ridge National Laboratory, could command political attention.) Their panels urged, in the frenzied tones and rhetoric of the Cold War, that an information explosion was upon us, and urgent steps were necessary. At the very least the NSF should increase its commitment in this area, expand its Office of Scientific Information into one of Science Information Service with a greatly increased budget that would allow it to support worthwhile projects, either old ones that had been stalled for lack of funds before Sputnik or new experimental ones.[42]

Because this was about the time when machine translations (from Russian especially) began to seem possible and when the major abstracting services were becoming increasingly automated, one good way to spend a lot of money quickly was to help them out. *Chemical Abstracts* was a major recipient of this new largesse, having taken some $23 million for "automation research and development" work from NSF by 1975.[43] Among the new projects were the documentation research project at the American Institute of Physics, the National Referral Center for Science and Technology at the Library of Congress (mentioned above), and the expansion of the Bio-Sciences Information Exchange at the Smithsonian Institution into the Science Information Exchange in 1960.[44]

Though some of these projects created jobs and even careers in the new "information science" for a few women (such as Pauline Atherton, later of Syracuse University, and Rita G. Lerner, who both worked at the AIP in the 1960s), the new money and importance placed on this field also led to a certain eclipse (early resignations, some embarrassment, and modest protest) for some other women who were already in administrative positions. For example, Helen Brownson, who had been at NSF since it opened and had been the program director for science documentation since 1954, was not promoted to head the Office, whose budget was growing so rapidly; instead Burton W. Adkinson, director of the reference department at the Library of Congress, was appointed and stayed until his retirement in 1971. In another case, Stella Deignan had been director of the Office of Exchange of Information at the National Institutes of Health until 1950, when she moved to the National Research Council to head the new Medical Sciences Information Exchange. Although she proved so successful at this that it was expanded in 1953 to cover all the biosciences and some parts of psychology, when it was to be expanded again to cover all of science in 1959, she resigned to take a job at the World Health Organization. When in 1964 Miles Conrad, the longtime head of *Biological Abstracts*, died unexpectedly at age 53, there was a long seven-month delay while the all-male trustees searched the world for a suitable successor. In April 1965, when the organization was trying to plan a future full of profits rather than government grants, the trustees turned to Phyllis Parkins, Conrad's longtime assistant director, to salvage the company. (She later became the second president of the National Federation of Abstracting and Information Services [in 1966–1968] after Carolyn Flanagan of *Engineering Index* [in 1965–1966].)[45] Finally Kay Way, mentioned earlier as physicist and director of the Nuclear Data Project at Oak Ridge National Laboratory and editor of *Nuclear Data*, complained in a 1968 article in *Science* that compilers of reference works needed more money and perhaps some financial aids or incentives, but that they did not need any more (all-male) advisory committees; if scientists did not need committees of experts to tell them what research to do, neither did reference-work compilers. Generally they knew best and could be trusted without all the committees and panels that had proliferated in recent years.[46]

Meanwhile the "information explosion" attracted some new analysts, such as Derek J. de Solla Price, my late professor, who gained much fame by publicizing his ideas on the exponential growth rate of knowledge (be it number of journals, number of articles, or number of pages in journals), and his friend Eugene Garfield, who built a whole business in Philadelphia on the idea of "citation analysis." If their work was a little abstract (leaving out not only libraries but also people!), William D. Garvey, a psychologist at Johns Hopkins, took up one of Pauline Atherton's suggestions and published many articles and a book on scientific communication, the latter expressly for librarians. Yet this, in a way, undercut the whole STINFO justification, for it spelled out for all to see the weak conceptual underpinning of all the "formal" means of communication everyone was working so hard to perfect. To a social scientist the *least* interesting (and perhaps least important) communication going on in science was in the library or through the journals, however well and expensively organized, indexed, and abstracted. The key information for those at the research front (or in the so-called invisible colleges) was in the preprints and conversations with colleagues at meetings and over the phone about the latest work and results. The only persons who would go to a library to find out information would be students (to the postdoctoral level) or scientists outside the select inner circles.[47] In this view, libraries and abstracts might be full of "information," but they were well-nigh superfluous to much, perhaps the most important, scientific "communication."

By this time (the 1970s), moreover, some feminists had been complaining that women were ignored at scientific meetings, and, being excluded from these very select channels of information, could not hope to compete equally. Evidently the much-vaunted "communication networks," "invisible colleges," and even "citation analysis" were not as sex-blind or neutral as a generation of male experts had blandly assumed. Perhaps it was time (and the women's perspective offered a chance) for a fresh look at this elusive but reportedly essential "informal communication."[48]

One place to start would be the notorious *Double Helix* by James D. Watson, which can be praised at least for the honesty with which it describes how he interacted (or failed to communicate) with other scientists racing for the Nobel Prize. Another starting point would be an ethnographic survey of daily or weekly life of a group of scientists, as recently done in Bruno Latour and Steve Woolgar's *Laboratory Life.*[49] These would suggest the importance of scientific meetings and of scientific entertaining and friendships. As for meetings (on which W. D. Garvey has also published some papers), Margaret Mead published with Paul Byers in 1968 a book, *The Small Conference, An Innovation in Communication,* that summarized two decades of "human dynamics" and "human relations" research on meetings and included many photographs of three particular ones along with a running commentary of what was being said. Similarly, Peter Woodford's history of the Ciba Foundation of London, which made a specialty in the 1950s and 1960s of running just such small meetings of emerging "invisible colleges," has several chapters on its experience in picking topics and participants and tries to evaluate why some of their 200 conferences succeeded better than others.[50] (Woodford thought that "possibly the least successful" was the one held in November 1966 on the very topic "Communication in Science." It had failed, he felt, because the participants were librarians and information scientists rather than bench scientists and their papers revealed little that was new. He cited a reviewer of the published proceedings who had claimed that their authors' thinking was "so woolly and wordy that their papers are virtually unreadable.")[51]

As for scientific entertaining and hospitality, the role of the "scientific hostess" remains to be analyzed. In a few cases this job has been a professional (or at least paid) one, as in the case of Bettye Athanasiou, a private secretary, "seismic secretary" and "hard-working public affairs specialist" for the Society of Exploration Geophysicists as well as a succession of oil exploration companies in Houston. In some ways her outstanding achievements remind one of Mary Day at the Harvard Herbarium (can we call it the "Day syndrome" or "phenomenon"?), or to cite a recent history of the field:

> Based in Houston, she has edited three company magazines . . . and operated scores of hospitality suites for the thirsty explorationists throughout the world during the past three decades. Graced with near total recall, she knows by face (and generally by name) perhaps some 6,000 geophysicists not only from attendance at innumerable conventions and exhibits, but also by visits to the field, some of which have taken her far north of the Arctic Circle. While on visits to such remote outposts of the geophysical profession, she listens to everyone's hopes and frustrations, takes their picture [of which she has since published an album], and writes down urgent errands she can perform for them once she returns to civilization. For these unique efforts as "Den Mother" to an entire profession, the Society of Exploration Geophysicists made her a "Life Member" in 1978, and the Houston Geophysical Society followed with a similar award a year later.[52]

Less dramatically and more privately, many scientific wives (some of whom were also scientists) have put on innumerable dinner parties and other kinds of social activities designed to enhance the desired "informal communication" and perhaps to build political alliances. The importance of such entertaining can hardly be questioned, though to my knowledge it has never been analyzed or explored in any systematic way. Perhaps the time is ripe. One place to start might be the growing literature of autobiographies by women in science, some of whom were wives and such efficient helpmeets to their scientific husbands that formal entertaining was just the beginning of their useful services to them and to science.[53]

At this point, having exceeded my allotted time and space I must briefly conclude: evidence is showing increasingly that women have been in science, and especially in scientific communication, for centuries; the prevailing methods of the history of science are beginning to change and broaden, and in so doing, to find more and more women in places and roles formerly overlooked. This trend is promising, for, if future historians do take women into consideration, they will find a new view not only of the history of science but also of the history of books (including textbooks, journals, and bibliographies), libraries (including the administration of government ones), and communication down to its most informal levels. Much remains to be done; we're beginning rather than concluding!

Notes

1. John Y. Cole, "Storehouses and Workshops: American Libraries and the Uses of Knowledge," in Alexandra Oleson and John Voss, (eds.), *The Organization of Knowledge in Modern America, 1860–1920* (Baltimore: Johns Hopkins University Press, 1979), pp. 364–385, and Margaret W. Rossiter, "The Organization of the Agricultural Sciences," in *ibid.*, pp. 211–248.

2. Phyllis Dain, "Women's Studies in American Library History: Some Critical Reflections," *Journal of Library History* 18 (1983): 454, 458, and 461; see also the review by Suzanne Hildenbrand in the same issue, a special one on women, pp. 478–481.

3. Margaret W. Rossiter, *Women Scientists in America, Struggles and Strategies to 1940* (Baltimore: Johns Hopkins University Press, 1982; paperback, 1984), pp. 60, 253–254, 259–263 passim, 337*n*23 and 387*n*34.

4. Margaret W. Rossiter, "Justus Liebig and the Americans: A Study in the Transit of Science, 1840–1880" (Yale University Ph.D. dissertation, 1971), published as *The Emergence of Agricultural Science, Justus Liebig and the Americans, 1840–1880* (New Haven: Yale University Press, 1975), appendix 1, esp. pp. 178–183.

5. Carlo Paoloni (comp.), *Justus von Liebig, Eine Bibliographie sämtlicher Veröffentlichungen* (Heidelberg: Carl Winter, Universitätsverlag, 1968).

6. *National Union Catalog, Pre-1956 Imprints* (London: Mansell, 1968–1980), vol. 332 (1974).

7. Gordon R. Williams, "History of the National Union Catalog, Pre-1956 Imprints," in *ibid.*, vol. 1 (1968), pp. vii–x.

8. Hildegard of Bingen (1098–1179) was one of the few women scientists of the Middle Ages. She prepared herbals and wrote on nature and medicine as well as being an abbess of a convent in Rupertsberg, Germany. It is tempting to extrapolate from one of her experiences that many more medieval manuscripts might have survived if they had been placed in such convents run by women rather than in monasteries run by male monks: in 1163, when Frederick Barba-

rossa, the Holy Roman Emperor, was battling his enemies and devastating much of the Rheingau, she sought and he gave her an imperial letter of protection, which both sides honored, and spared her convent (Walter Pagel, "Hildegard of Bingen," *Dictionary of Scientific Biography* [New York City: Charles Scribner's Sons, 1970–1980], VI: 396; hereafter cited as *DSB*).

9. René Taton, "Chatelet, Gabrielle-Emilie," *DSB* III: 215–217.

10. Elizabeth C. Patterson, *Mary Somerville and the Cultivation of Science, 1815–1840* (The Hague: Martinus Nijhoff, 1983). Another autodidact who took on the task of translating Laplace's *Mécanique céleste*, perhaps as a way to show he was the equal or better than college-educated persons, was the American Nathaniel Bowditch (Nathan Reingold, "Nathaniel Bowditch," *DSB* II: 368–369).

11. Judit Brody, "Select List of Early 19th Century Popular Science Books Written by Women [in Britain]," unpublished list distributed at the International Conference on the Role of Women in the History of Science, Technology and Medicine in the 19th and 20th Centuries, 15–19 August 1983, Veszprem, Hungary.

12. Eva V. Armstrong, "Jane Marcet and Her 'Conversations on Chemistry,'" *Journal of Chemical Education* 15 (1938): 53–57; John K. Crellin, "Mrs. Marcet's 'Conversations on Chemistry,'" *Journal of Chemical Education* 56 (1979): 459–460; George D. Tselos (E. F. Smith Collection) to author, 26 March 1984.

13. Ann Shteir, "Priscilla Wakefield (1751–1832): Author, Philanthropist, 'Respectable Person,'" unpublished paper, c. 1981; Ann Shteir, "'With Bliss Botanic': Women and Plant Sexuality," paper presented at session on "Women and Gardens in Theory and Practice," at American Society for Eighteenth-Century Studies, San Francisco, April 1980; and Ann Shteir, "Women and Plants—A Fruitful Topic," *Atlantis* 6 (1981): 114–122.

14. David A. Kronick, *A History of Scientific and Technical Periodicals, The Origins and Development of the Scientific and Technical Press, 1665–1790*, 2nd ed. (Metuchen, N.J.: Scarecrow Press, 1976), p. 245.

15. Teri Perl, "The Ladies' Diary or Woman's Almanack, 1704–1841," *Historia Mathematica* 6 (1979): 36–53; Teri Hoch Perl, "Women and Mathematics in the Late 18th Century: A Query," *Historia Mathematica* 7 (1980): 188–189; Ruth and Peter Wallis, "Female Philomaths," *Historia Mathematica* 7 (1980): 57–64; Patricia Cline Cohen, *A Calculating People: The Spread of Numeracy in Early America* (Chicago: University of Chicago Press, 1983).

16. Rossiter, *Women Scientists in America*, pp. 322*n*22, 79, and 334*n*53.

17. Oftentimes the early editors owned the journal themselves and paid its deficit out of their own pockets. Sometimes this ownership and editorial control was reflected, if not in the journal's official name (such as *American Journal of Science*), then in its informal one ("Silliman's Journal"). In later years the name of a former editor (and owner?) was sometimes made part of the official name of the journal, such as *Liebig's Annalen* or *Virchow's Archiv*. (I thank Joy Harvey for this example.) It is not clear what the advantage of such eponymy would be —authority? presitige? marketing advantage? An active scientist would not need to be told who had once edited which journal, and any journal that needed such support and buttressing might be in danger of being accused of living off its past glories.

18. Ann B. Shteir, "Linnaeus's Daughters: Women and British Botany," in Barbara J. Harris and JoAnn K. McNamara (eds.), *Women and the Structure of Society: Selected Research from the Fifth Berkshire Conference on the History of Women* (Durham, N.C.: Duke University Press, 1984), pp. 67–73 and 261–263; quotation on p. 70.

19. Dorinda Outram, *Georges Cuvier: Vocation, Science, and Authority in Post-Revolutionary France* (Manchester: Manchester University Press, 1984), p. 172.
20. *Science* 229 (5 July 1985): 9.
21. Bruce M. Manzer, *The Abstract Journal, 1790–1920: Origin, Development and Diffusion* (Metuchen, N.J.: Scarecrow Press, 1977).
22. Nellie Payne, in *American Men and Women of Science*, 12th ed. (1972), p. 4819. Some of her private correspondence, describing her activities at *Biological Abstracts* and distaste for it, is in the Division of Entomology and Economic Zoology Files at the University of Minnesota Archives.
23. Margaret C. Schindler, "The Preparation of the *Bibliography of Agriculture*," in Jesse H. Shera and Margaret E. Egan (eds.), *Bibliographic Organization* (Chicago: University of Chicago Press, 1951), pp. 226–235, describes her yearly work cycle.
24. William Campbell Steere, with the collaboration of Phyllis V. Parkins and Hazel A. Philson, *Biological Abstracts/BIOSIS, The First Fifty Years, The Evolution of a Major Science Information Service* (New York: Plenum Press, 1976), esp. introduction and pp. 123–139.
25. Katharine Way, in *American Men and Women of Science*, 14th ed. (1979), p. 5396; clippings in Physics Department file, Duke University Archives; Burton W. Adkinson, *Two Centuries of Federal Information* (Stroudsburg, Pa.: Dowden, Hutchinson and Ross, 1978), pp. 43–48.
26. Mary Magill, in *American Men and Women of Science*, 12th ed. (1972), p. 4023; F. W. Adams, "Opportunities for Women as Research Bibliographers," *Journal of Chemical Education* 16 (1939): 581–583, reprinted in Roy I. Grady and John W. Chittum (eds.), *The Chemist at Work* (Easton, Pa.: *Journal of Chemical Education*, 1940); Janet D. Scott, "My Work with *Chemical Abstracts*," *ibid.*, pp. 79–91; Charles A. Browne and Mary Elvira Weeks, *A History of the American Chemical Society: Seventy-Five Grateful Years* (Washington, D.C.: American Chemical Society, 1952), pp. 336–367; D. B. Baker, J. W. Horiszny, and W. V. Metanomski, "History of Abstracting at Chemical Abstracts Service," *Journal of Chemical Information and Computer Science* 20 (November 1980): 193–201; and Herman Skolnik and Kenneth M. Reese (eds.), *A Century of Chemistry, The Role of Chemists and the American Chemical Society* (Washington, D.C.: American Chemical Society, 1976), pp. 126–143.
27. Dorrit Hoffleit, "Annie Jump Cannon" and "Williamina P. S. Fleming," *DSB* III: 49–50, and V: 33–34, and in *Notable American Women*, I: 281–283 and 628–630, and Rossiter, *Women Scientists in America*, pp. 53–57, 293, and 350*n*16. For more details on who got stars in *American Men of Science*, see Stephen S. Visher, *Scientists Starred, 1903–1943, in "American Men of Science"* (Baltimore: John Hopkins University Press, 1947).

Cannon's case offers the additional interesting twist that apparently her boss, Harlow Shapley, successor to Fleming's Pickering, disagreed sufficiently with the fairness of the university's restriction on her status to go out of his way to solicit outside honors for her (such as an honorary Sc.D. from Oxford University in 1925 and the Draper Medal of the National Academy of Science in 1931). Perhaps he hoped in this way to create such a status inconsistency—how could Harvard continue to treat this world-renowned astronomer like a nonperson?—that President Abbott Lawrence Lowell might relent and grant her higher, possibly even faculty, status. But if such was Shapley's plan (and few other directors nominated their women assistants for outside honors), it had no visible success at Harvard.
28. B. L. Robinson, "Miss Day," *Rhodora* 26 (1924): 41–47; see also B. L. Robinson and Lesley C. Wilcox, "The Gray Herbarium Card Index," *Science* 71

(1930): 253–256; and Elizabeth A. Shaw, "The Gray Herbarium Card Index," *Taxon* 20 (1971): 333–336. Urged on by a questioner at the Chapel Hill conference to find out what happened after Miss Day retired, I visited the Harvard Herbarium library to discover that her spirit did live on, especially in successor Lazella Schwarten, who served from 1944 to 1967 (after thirteen years at the New York Botanical Garden). She too personified the service ideal, performing selflessly on the job (as when combining the Gray and Arnold Arboretum libraries in the late 1950s) and preparing reference works, seemingly in her spare time ("Mrs. Lazella Schwarten Retires as Librarian of the Arnold Arboretum," *Arnoldia* 27/8 [25 August 1967]: 68; and Richard A. Howard, "Lazella Harenberg Schwarten," *Journal of the Arnold-Arboretum* 54 (1973): 419–421, and Herbaria Archives Guide, vol. III). Like Miss Day decades before, Mrs. Schwarten had no college or library school training, just Hunter High School in New York City (1914–1918). She started as a typist at the New York Botanical Garden in the 1930s when she was widowed and left with two children to support.

29. There is a brief discussion of the status of bibliographers (i.e., the "widespread" belief that it "lacks intellectual dignity") in D. W. Krummel, *Bibliographies, Their Aims and Methods* (London: Mansell Publishing Limited, 1984), pp. 10–12 and 147–148, and of indexes and abstractors in Sidney Passman, *Scientific and Technological Communication* (Oxford: Pergamon Press, 1969), p. 73.

30. Dorrit Hoffleit, "The Library of the Harvard College Observatory," *Harvard Library Bulletin* 5 (1951): 102–111; Robert L. Work, "Ninety Years of Professor Agassiz's Natural History Library," *Harvard Library Bulletin* 6 (1952): 202–218; and Sandra E. Belanger, "History of the Library of the Marine Biological Laboratory, 1888–1973," *Journal of Library History* 10 (1975): 255–263. I have no particular favoritism for science libraries in Massachusetts; these are just the ones in the Harris and Davis bibliography in 33 below.

31. Garrett Birkhoff, "The George David Birkhoff Mathematical Library," *Harvard Library Bulletin* 9 (1955): 282–284; Roger W. Hickman, "The Physics Libraries of Harvard University," *Harvard Library Bulletin* 10 (1956): 356–366. For a general discussion of the inadequacies of departmental (versus central university) libraries, see Lawrence Thompson, "The Historical Background of Departmental and Collegiate Libraries," *Library Quarterly* 12 (1942): 49–74, which looks back to days before the consolidations into large central buildings in the 1910s and 1920s, a movement that the science libraries often did not join. See, for example, the recent history of Widener Library by William Bentinck-Smith, *Building a Great Library: The Coolidge Years at Harvard* (Cambridge: Harvard University Library, 1976). See also Connie R. Dunlap, "Organizational Patterns in Academic Libraries, 1876–1976," *College and Research Libraries* 37 (1976): 395–407, reprinted in Richard D. Johnson (ed.), *Libraries for Teaching, Libraries for Research, Essays for a Century* (Chicago: American Library Association, 1977), pp. 102–114.

32. Murphy D. Smith, *Oak from an Acorn, A History of the American Philosophical Society Library, 1770–1803* (Wilmington, Del.: Scholarly Resources, 1976); *The John Crerar Library, 1895–1944, An Historical Report Prepared under the Authority of the Board of Directors, by the Librarian* (J. Christian Bay) (Chicago: John Crerar Library, 1945); Joseph C. Shipman, "Linda Hall Library," *College and Research Libraries* 16 (1955): 138–141 and 163. See also William S. Budington, "'To Enlarge the Sphere of Human Knowledge': The Role of the Independent Research Library," *College and Research Libraries* 37 (1976): 299–315, reprinted in Johnson (ed.), *Libraries for Teaching*, pp. 168–184.

33. Elizabeth W. Stone, *American Library Development, 1600–1899* (New York:

H. W. Wilson, 1977), p. 177; Phyllis Dain, *The New York Public Library, A History of Its Founding and Early Years* (New York: New York Public Library, 1972), pp. 327 and 328; Frank B. Woodford, *Parnassus on Main Street, A History of the Detroit Public Library* (Detroit: Wayne State University Press, 1965), pp. 334–341; quotation on p. 335. Very helpful in locating such items (especially periodical ones) were Michael Harris and Donald G. Davis, Jr., *American Library History, A Bibliography* (Austin: University of Texas Press, 1978), and, particularly for non-U.S. libraries, Elmer D. Johnson and Michael H. Harris, *History of Libraries in the Western World*, 3rd ed. rev. (Metuchen, N.J.: Scarecrow Press, 1976). Since some of the earliest science libraries hired their staffs from each other (Crerar's first librarian, C. W. Clements, had come from the Massachusetts Institute of Technology, where he had been a chemist with library duties on the side), it might be possible to trace the early days of the emerging specialty in terms of the careers of a few key persons. Most such mobile persons would be men, however, for the women mentioned most often seem to have spent very long careers (decades) at one institution.

34. Anna M. Sexton, *A Chronicle of the Division of Laboratories and Research, New York State Department of Health, The First Fifty Years: 1914–1964* (Lunenburg, Vt.: Stinehour Press, 1967). I have, on the whole, however, omitted both medical and technical libraries and bibliographies from this paper, as possibly different in important respects.

35. Johnson and Harris, *History of Libraries in the Western World*, p. 214; Stone, *American Library Development, 1600–1899*, pp. 74 and 75.

36. Mary E. Corning and Martin M. Cummings, "Biomedical Communications," in John Z. Bowers and Elizabeth F. Purcell (eds.), *Advances in American Medicine, Essays at the Bicentennial* (New York: Josiah Macy Foundation, 1976), II: 748–750; Wyndham D. Miles, *A History of the National Library of Medicine, The Nation's Treasury of Medical Knowledge* (Washington, D.C.: Government Printing Office, 1982). On LC, see Dwight E. Gray, "Science, Technology, and the Library of Congress," *Physics Today* 18 (June 1965): 44–46 and 48; see also note 44 below.

37. Foster E. Mohrhardt, "The Library of the United States Department of Agriculture," *Library Quarterly* 27 (1957): 61–82. Obituaries of Barnett are in *Agricultural History* 25 (1951): 143, and *Journal of the Washington Academy of Sciences* 42 (1952): 167–168. U.S.G.S. Library is mentioned in Paul Howard, "The Department of the Interior Library System," *Library Quarterly* 27 (1957): 38–46.

38. Ruth Hooker, in *Who's Who of American Women*, 11th ed. (1979–1980), p. 382. In general, academic libraries seem to have received much more attention from historians and others than government libraries.

39. Sister F. Dolores Donnelly, *The National Library of Canada* (Ottawa: Canadian Library Association, 1973); John Y. Cole, "The National Libraries of the United States and Canada," in Sidney L. Jackson, Eleanor B. Herling, and E. J. Josey (eds.), *A Century of Service, Librarianship in the United States and Canada* (Chicago: American Library Association, 1976), pp. 243–259; Margaret Gill, in *Canadian Who's Who*, 12th ed. (1970–1972), p. 403.

40. M. W. Hill, "The Science Reference Library," in W. L. Saunders (ed.), *British Librarianship Today* (London: Library Association, 1976), pp. 73–74; Maurice B. Line, "The British Library Lending Division," in ibid., p. 87; Bernard Houghton, *Out of the Dinosaurs: The Evolution of the National Lending Library for Science and Technology* (London: Clive Bingley, 1972); L. R. Day, "Resources for the History of Science in the Science Museum Library," *British Journal for the*

History of Science 18 (1985): 71–72. See also H. Philip Spratt, *Libraries for Scientific Research in Europe and America* (London: Grafton, 1936), which describes pleasantly an extensive tour in the 1930s, and for Germany only Fritz Meyen, *Die technisch-wissenschaftlichen Bibliotheken, Ihre Enstehung und Entwicklung* (Braunschweig: Georg Westermann Verlag, 1949). Despite its title, K. G. B. Bakewell's *Industrial Libraries throughout the World* (Oxford: Pergamon Press, 1969) has material on science libraries, such as the projected National Science Library of India, pp. 109–110.

41. Alma Clarvoe Mitchill, *Special Libraries Association, Its First Fifty Years, 1909–1959* (New York: Special Libraries Association, 1959), esp. pp. 99–105; on Lee, see Richard S. Huleatt, "The Stone & Webster Library, 1900–1970, Seventy Years of Special Library Service," *Special Libraries* 61 (1970): 374–376; Betty Joy Cole, in *Who Was Who in America*, 5th ed. (1969–1973), p. 142; Margaret Fuller, in *Who's Who of American Women*, 8th ed. (1974–1975), p. 320; Lucille Jackson (ed.), *Technical Libraries, Their Organization and Management* (New York: Special Libraries Association, 1951); Lucille J. Strauss, Irene M. Strieby, and Alberta L. Brown, *Scientific and Technical Libraries, Their Organization and Management* (New York: Interscience Publishers, 1964; 2nd ed., Becker and Hayes, 1972). See also Angelina Martinez, "Service to Special Clienteles," in Jackson et al., *A Century of Service*, pp. 110–128, and Ada Winifred Johns, *Special Libraries, Development of the Concept, Their Organizations, and Their Services* (Metuchen, N.J.: Scarecrow Press, 1968). The British equivalent of the American SLA is ASLIB (Association of Specialized Libraries and Information Bureaux), which was started in 1924 and in 1949 merged with the British Society for International Bibliography.

42. Ralph R. Shaw, "Royal Society Scientific Information Conference," *Science* 108 (1948): 148–151. The best summary of the STINFO movement is a government document, Library of Congress, Congressional Research Service, *Federal Management of Scientific and Technical Information (STINFO) Activities: The Role of the National Science Foundation*, Prepared for the Special Subcommittee on the National Science Foundation of the Committee on Labor and Public Welfare, United States Senate, 94th Congress, 1st session, Committee Print (Washington, D.C.: U.S. Government Printing Office, 1975). See also Adkinson (formerly of NSF), *Two Centuries of Federal Information*, and Harvey A. Averch (also of NSF), *A Strategic Analysis of Science and Technology Policy* (Baltimore: Johns Hopkins University Press, 1985), chap. 5.

43. Skolnik and Reese, *A Century of Chemistry*, p. 149.

44. John F. Stearns, "National Referral Center for Science and Technology," *Special Libraries* 54 (1963): 45–46; idem, "National Referral Center's First Year," *Special Libraries* 55 (1964): 20–23; M. W. McFarland, "The National Referral Center: Science and Technology in the Library of Congress," *ASLIB Proceedings* 16 (1964): 258–268 (which is broader than its title); and William H. Fitzpatrick and Monroe E. Freeman, "The Science Information Exchange: The Evolution of a Unique Information Storage and Retrieval System," *Libri* 15 (1965): 127–137.

45. Pauline Atherton, in *Who's Who of American Women*, 7th ed. (1972–1973), p. 27; Rita Lerner, in *American Men and Women of Science*, 15th ed. (1982), p. 688; Helen Brownson, in *Who's Who of American Women*, 4th ed. (1966–1967), p. 155; Adkinson, in his *Two Centuries of Federal Information*, p. 156; Deignan, in ibid., p. 158; Parkins, in William Campbell Steere, *Biological Abstracts*, pp. 122–124; K. Way, "Free Enterprise in Data Compilation," *Science* 159 (1968): 280–282.

46. Malcolm Rigby, "The History of NFAIS, 1958–71," in M. Lynne Neufeld, Martha Cornog, and Inez L. Sperr (eds.), *Abstracting and Indexing Services in Perspective: Miles Conrad Memorial Lectures, 1969–1983, Commemorating the Twenty-fifth Anniversary of the National Federation of Abstracting and Information Services* (Arlington, Va.: Information Resource Press, 1983), p. 12.

47. Derek J. de Solla Price, *Science since Babylon* (New Haven: Yale University Press, 1961); Derek J. de Solla Price, *Little Science, Big Science* (New York: Columbia University Press, 1963); Eugene Garfield, *Citation Indexing—Its Theory and Application in Science, Technology, and Humanities* (New York: John Wiley and Sons, 1979); William D. Garvey, *Communication: The Essence of Science* (Oxford: Pergamon Press, 1979), p. x; this volume includes many of his previously published articles. Sidney Passman, *Scientific and Technological Communication* (Oxford: Pergamon Press, 1969), is also useful.

48. Martha S. White, "Psychological and Social Barriers to Women in Science," *Science* 170 (1970): 413–416; Margaret Rossiter, "Fair Enough?" (Essay review of Jonathan Cole's *Fair Science, Women in the Scientific Community* [New York: Free Press, 1979]), *Isis* 72 (1981): 99–103.

49. James D. Watson, *The Double Helix, A Personal Account of the Discovery of the Structure of DNA* (New York: Atheneum, 1968); and Bruno Latour and Steve Woolgar, *Laboratory Life, The Social Construction of Scientific Facts* (Beverly Hills: Sage Publications, 1979). I thank Henry Etzkowitz, a sociologist at SUNY-Purchase, for the suggestion of an ethnographic survey.

50. Garvey, *Communication*, see index; Margaret Mead and Paul Byers, *The Small Conference, An Innovation in Communication* (Paris: Mouton, 1968), which has a lengthy bibliography; F. Peter Woodford, *The Ciba Foundation: An Analytic History, 1949–1974* (Amsterdam: Elsevier, 1974).

51. Ibid., pp. 109–110.

52. Charles C. Bates, Thomas F. Gaskell, and Robert B. Rice, *Geophysics in the Affairs of Man* (New York: Pergamon Press, 1982), pp. 247–248; Bettye Athansiou in *Who's Who of American Women*, 10th ed. (1977–1978), p. 29.

53. My favorites among those who are also wives of scientists and helpful assistants, especially in difficult fieldwork, include Edith S. Clements, *Adventures in Ecology* (New York: Hafner, 1960); Frances Hamerstrom, *Strictly for the Chickens* (poultry wildlife studies) (Ames: Iowa State University Press, 1980); and Margaret Murie, *Two in the Far North* (Alaska) (New York: Knopf, 1962).

Autobiographies by wives who were more independent in their science and consequently more visible include Margaret Mead, *Blackberry Winter, My Earlier Years* (New York: Simon and Schuster, 1972); and Margaret Morse Nice, *Research Is a Passion with Me* (Toronto: Consolidated Amethyst Communications, 1979). Alma Smith Payne, *Partners in Science* (Cleveland: World Publishing, 1968), is for juveniles, and Angelo Hall, *An Astronomer's Wife: The Biography of Angeline Hall* (wife of Asaph Hall) (Baltimore: Nunn, 1908), is also disappointing.

The American Academic Library Building, 1870–1890

David Kaser

The academic library buildings constructed on this continent prior to 1870 had almost the single purpose of providing secure protection for the books that they housed. By that year, however, college study had become too complex to be accommodated any longer in such simple library buildings, and architects and librarians alike began seeking more adequate structures. Their first efforts resulted in the tripartitioning of space among readers, books, and staff, but by 1883 it was clear that even that was insufficient and that further partitioning was needed to allow for such additional activities as reserve collections, seminars, special collections, periodical collections, and map rooms.

The first academic library buildings constructed on this continent, those of the period 1840 to 1870, were simple, essentially single-function buildings modeled almost entirely upon the eighteenth-century alcoved book rooms of Britain. During the two decades following 1870, however, they suddenly relinquished entirely these traditional roots and took on vastly more complex forms clearly predictive of the full-fledged university library buildings of the present century. This paper reviews the causes of this dramatic and rapid change, documents its evolution, identifies the architectural modifications that resulted, and points out their significance to library practice during subsequent decades.

Given the circumscribed purpose of American higher education up to 1870, it is not surprising that college libraries were at best of limited importance. Operating in most cases totally without funding, accreting only gifts of charity to their very small collections, administered by a lone professor assigned part-time as library custodian, open only one or two hours a week so that an occasional faculty member or upper classman could withdraw a book, these libraries were even less stimulating of intellectual vigor than were their parent institutions.[1]

David Kaser *is professor of library science, Indiana University. He is preparing a monograph on the evolution of American academic library buildings from 1840 to 1980.*

Understandably, libraries with such restricted obligations could be operated in very small amounts of space laid out in very simple designs. By far the major part of a library's function was simply to house and protect the books owned by the college. To be sure, some libraries also provided a few tables and chairs in case someone wished to consult a reference on site or so that the librarian would have a place to sit while he inscribed a new acquisition into the catalogue. But those tables and chairs, if indeed they were needed at all, could be fitted in almost anywhere; their infrequent use did not require any particular location. Thus the single function of book storage determined the configuration of space within the library.

Libraries with such limited functional requirements could be housed very effectively in buildings patterned upon both Greek temples and Gothic chapels. The narthex provided a sheltered entry; the nave accommodated tables and chairs; books were shelved in alcoves in the aisles, usually with one or two galleries above. The bookshelves were lighted by lancet windows between the buttresses, and the nave was lighted by clerestory windows. Some, such as Gore Hall, had transepts, while others even had apses. Unless one considers Thomas Jefferson a librarian when he designed the rotunda at the University of Virginia, and with the exception of Lawrence Hall at Williams College, no library erected before 1870 benefited from input by librarians.

By 1870, however, rapid developments in American higher education were beginning to impact heavily upon library operations. Small collections of a few good books were no longer enough. Large collections, embracing poor books as well as good books, were now required. Pamphlets and periodicals were becoming important for the first time, as were newspapers, documents, and unpublished papers. Also for the first time, libraries had to be open many hours daily, and their new and more extensive responsibilities required much larger and better-trained staffs.[2]

It was soon apparent that the simple, single-function buildings that had previously housed academic libraries were no longer adequate. A significant amount of book storage space was now needed, and extensive accommodations were required for numerous readers. Special rooms were now needed that could be devoted to periodicals or to documents, or could be used by staff for library administration, or could house reserve books or seminar collections. None of the pre-1870 buildings had these capabilities.

Concurrent with these changing needs were two other circumstances that would contribute to these new kinds of academic library buildings. One was the professional awakening of librarians. Clearly bespeaking this development, of course, was the founding in the 1870s of the American Library Association. The other was a similar professional awakening on the part of architects. Although the American Institute of Architects had been established in 1857, the nation's first school of architecture was opened only in 1866, and a new era of profound change was about to commence in American architecture. Libraries would no longer be expected simply to inhabit Greek temples or Christian basilicas; instead they would reflect hereafter a merging of the professional tencts of two distinct vocations: librarianship and architecture.

This brief but significant period from 1870 to 1890 in academic library-building design can be divided into two parts. During the first part, from 1870 to 1885, efforts were made to meet the new functional needs of libraries by what has been called "tripartitioning," that is the allocation of interior space to three separate library purposes: book storage, reader accommodations, and staff work areas.

Some modest concessions had been made, even before 1870, to the need to divide up library space rather than simply assign it all to the single function of book storage. As early as 1846 Williams College had allocated some of the ground floor of Lawrence hall to staff activities and to a periodical facility. This building was designed by Thomas Tefft of Providence, who sought and received considerable counsel from Charles Coffin Jewett. The Chancellor Green building, constructed at Princeton in 1873, was modestly tripartitioned, with the center of its octagon occupied by the librarian's station, reading tables arrayed in a concentric circle around it, and radial stacks extending thence to the building's perimeter. Here again it was a librarian's involvement, in this case that of Frederic Vinton, that gained this improvement. Neither of these buildings, however, fully attained the degree of separation needed for these distinct functions.

The first completely tripartitioned academic library in this country, and the first to make a frank separation of books from readers, was constructed at Lehigh University in 1877. This so-called Venetian style structure located its reader tables in a rectangular space at one end of the building and its books in a three-level, semicircular stack, comprising columns of iron but shelves and floors of wood, at the other end.[3] Some space was also designated for library staff, completing its tripartitioning. This building, twice enlarged, still serves Lehigh as the Linderman Library.

At almost the same time, 1878, Brown University opened its first separate library building, and it also represented a completely tripartitioned plan. Although technically this Venetian Gothic building was designed by architect William A. Walker of Providence, the plans were based almost entirely upon sketches prepared by librarian Reuben Guild after studying the new Chancellor Green library at Princeton. In the form of a Greek cross, Brown's building placed its reader stations in a central

Reading Room and Stack, Lehigh University, 1877
(Courtesy Lehigh University Archives)

rotunda that was lighted from clerestory windows in the lantern above, while galleries of bookstacks occupied semioctagonal termini in three of the arms.[4] Lehigh and Brown represented innovations, however, only in their separation of books and readers; the strong influence of the alcoved book room may still be seen in them.

Two other simply tripartitioned buildings of this era were those at the University of Vermont and at Dartmouth, both opened in 1885. Billings Hall at Vermont was the only academic library designed by the great innovator Henry H. Richardson. He wrote of the building, one of the last he designed before his untimely death, that "it is the best thing I have yet done."[5] Typical of his candid Romanesque style, its several separate gross functions are clearly adumbrated in its massive facade, with book room to the left, reading room ahead, and staff space in one of the two towers;[6] in detailing the interior, however, Richardson appears to have been largely oblivious of the rapidly changing functional requirements of libraries. Both the rectangular book room and a special collection room were simply traditional galleried alcoves, heavily imitative of the earlier period. This building is now being renovated to serve as a student center.

The exterior of Dartmouth University's library, Wilson Hall, is clearly influenced by Richardson's Romanesque style. In its interior appoint-

Billings Library, University of Vermont, 1885
(*New England Magazine* [December 1897]: 428)

ments, however, this building, which was designed by Samuel J. F. Thayer of Boston, displays greater sensitivity to changing library function than did the building at Burlington. Rather than copying the earlier alcove arrangement, this three-level book room was clearly patterned upon the multi-tier structural stack that had been introduced to this continent eight years earlier in the wing added to Gore Hall at Harvard.[7] Featuring floors, stairs, uprights, and shelves all made entirely of iron, this kind of book storage space was about to become a standard feature of American academic libraries right up until World War II. Meanwhile, Wilson Hall served as Dartmouth's library until 1928, when the Baker building was built, and today it is the home of the University's drama and film studies department.

Tripartitioning, however, did not take library-building planning far enough to meet its rapidly evolving functional requirements. It was abundantly evident to the University of Michigan, when it began in the early 1880s to plan its first library building, that extensive multipartitioning was called for. President Charles Kendall Adams retained Justin Winsor's architect friend and neighbor, Henry Van Brunt, to design this building. Van Brunt had planned the 1877 wing on Gore Hall and, with Winsor to guide him, was probably the best-informed academic library architect in the country. The resulting building, which merged the academic concerns of President Adams, the library acumen of both Justin Winsor and Michigan's Raymond Cazallis Davis, and the architectural expertise of Henry Van Brunt, represented the state of the art when it was opened in 1883.

University of Michigan Library, 1883
(*New England Magazine* [December 1897]: 431)

This library at Michigan contained a large reading room and administrative areas at its entry level; seminar, reference, and research facilities at the second level; an art gallery on the third level; and a three-level, multi-tier structural steel stack to its rear. There was also a lecture hall. This building, therefore, was the first to incorporate all or most of the special as well as general facilities requisite to good twentieth-century university library service.[8]

It appears that Van Brunt was influenced in massing the building at Michigan by the library opened six years earlier at Lehigh, although he reversed its principal elements and used a rectangular stack and semicircular reading room rather than Lehigh's rectangular reading room and semicircular stack. He also borrowed the twin towers from Lehigh; since Michigan was a coeducational institution (perhaps the first to construct a library), he used the towers to provide separate entrances for men and women. Regrettably, however, these alterations diminished the building's grace, making it look faintly like a sitting hen with two heads.

Van Brunt himself said that the "apse-like form [of the reading room] suggests a rear and not a front." It was also difficult to designate it as of any particular architectural style; President Adams called it Norman Gothic, but library historian Jackson Towne perhaps more appropriately denominated it "Ann Arbor Victorian."[9] At any rate, all but its stack-tower was razed in 1918 so that Michigan's present Harlan Hatcher Library could be built on the site.

In 1889 Syracuse University opened its Von Ranke Library, a Romanesque structure fashioned by local architect Archimedes Russell. While this building contained all of the elements of a modern university library, they were less well articulated here than they had been at Michigan or than they would be in the remaining three buildings of the decade. The principal novelty of the Von Ranke building was that its three-level structural stack was erected in two sections, one on each side of a large room, with reading tables arrayed between them, resulting in a configuration quite similar to the earlier alcoved book room.[10] This building served only briefly as a library. In 1907 its services and contents were removed to the University's new Carnegie Library, and the structure was remodeled as an administration building, a function it still serves today.

Three more academic libraries were constructed in this country in the closing years of the 1880s, and all three of them were good, serviceable, carefully planned, multifunctional designs. Each of the three was conceptualized sufficiently in tune with modern library and educational needs to be able to serve adequately for some three score years and ten as its parent institution's only central library building. These buildings were at Pennsylvania, Colgate, and Cornell, all three of which were dedicated within a few months of each other in 1891.

The library at the University of Pennsylvania was the work of the somewhat eccentric but brilliant architect Frank Furness. Called French Gothic in style, its exterior incorporated both military components such as its crenellated tower and ecclesiastical elements like its apse-like northern terminus. The tower, however, housed the stair, and the apse or ambulatory created six curvilinear chapel-like alcoves in which were located subject reference or reserve collections. The building contained a large reading room, ample staff work space, seminar and lecture rooms, map and file room, and a three-level stack constructed entirely of fireproof materials, all configured in a manner consistent with modern library operations. In distributing these many functional spaces, the architect benefited from extensive advice given by Justin Winsor, Melvil Dewey, and University of Pennsylvania librarian Talcott Williams.[11] Much of the building was roofed entirely in glass, especially above the stack and the apse, and the stack floors were also of glass, all used to increase natural illumination in these areas.[12] The Furness building remained the University's central library until the construction of the Van Pelt building in 1964, and today it houses the School of Architecture.

In Hamilton, New York, meanwhile, philanthropist James B. Colgate had committed himself to providing a library building for the institution that now bears his name. After reviewing several schemes that had been submitted in an architectural competition, however, he rejected them all because, in his words, "there was too much architect, and but little library." Working thereafter with his next door neighbor in Yonkers, architect Edwin A. Quick, Colgate set out to acquaint himself with contemporary library needs. He wrote:

> With him I began a course of inquiry. We consulted librarians, and visited libraries. When we commenced, our conception of a library was an immense building arranged with galleries and step ladders, and with books piled to the third heaven. That was our idea; but it ended in something very different. We went on consulting librarians, and found it was necessary to have a stack room, so arranged that the books should not be exposed to either heat or dampness, for these destroy bindings. Then it was necessary to have a good reading-room, librarian's room, a cataloguing room, a repairing room, and a reception room. Mr. Quick pursued this idea with a great deal of pertinacity, and after writing, consulting, and seeing plans innumerable, we at last produced something.[13]

Colgate University Library, 1890
(Courtesy Colgate University Archives)

He might have added that the building also had reference, periodical, document, and seminar rooms, for so it did. He denominated its architectural style "Romanesque American"—presumably meaning that it was not simply a slavish copy of an eleventh-century original—and that is perhaps as good a description as any. Cruciform in shape, it featured a three-level fireproof bookstack with a reading room above,[14] rather in the fashion of the Bibliothèque Ste. Geneviève and anticipating the New York Public Library of later date. The institution finally moved its library out of this building in 1958, and since that time it has been occupied by Colgate's central administration.

When Cornell University needed its first library building in 1884, President Andrew Dickson White had just visited and greatly admired the library building that Henry Van Brunt had designed for the University of Michigan. White even made a sketch of what he felt would be an appropriate library structure for Cornell, and its facade is clearly copied from the Ann Arbor building. In the following year, moreover, following White's resignation, Charles Kendall Adams left the presidency at Michigan to assume that office at Cornell, and his new appointment seemed to assure that Van Brunt would be selected as the architect for Cornell's new library. Adams, White, and Van Brunt proceeded in the subsequent two years to make many studies and sketches preparatory

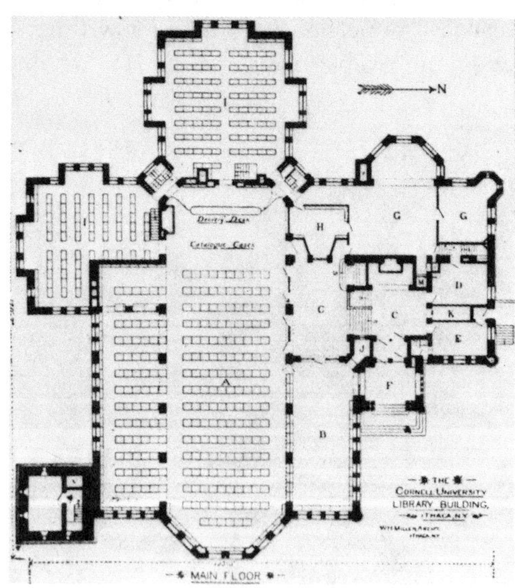

Main Floor, Cornell University Library, 1890: A—reading room; B—periodical room; C—lobby; D—men's cloak room; E—women's cloak room; F—vestibule; G—technical services; H—administration; I—stacks.
(*Library Journal* [April 1889]: 122)

to the actual designing of the building, and as a result more bibliothecal and scholarly thought, as well as architectural deliberation, probably went into this library than had gone into any that had been built previously.[15]

Ultimately, however, the donor demurred, and the architectural contract for Cornell's library went not to Van Brunt but to William H. Miller of Ithaca. Miller did follow faithfully all of the functional requirements identified by Presidents White and Adams, and he used much of the massing of the building as sketched by Van Brunt. With a cruciform basilica reminiscent of, but not all copied from, the earlier alcoved book rooms, the new library featured a large reading room in the nave and in one aisle, while periodical and entry rooms occupied the other aisle, a five-level structural stack in one transept and a seven-level stack in a rectangular apse, with fully seven seminar rooms, staff work space, separate cloak rooms for men and women, and special facilities for the Andrew Dickson White collection in the other transept.[16] This was Cornell's only library building until the Olin Library was occupied in 1961, and it is today the University's Undergraduate Library. Called "Square Romanesque" by some,[17] this building was probably the best academic library built to that time.

In summary, then, beginning about 1870 a number of factors rendered simple, single-function college library buildings inadequate. Principal among these factors was the sudden need for more space for books, readers, and library staff to accommodate recent changes in higher education. The newly established professions of architecture and librarianship first attempted to meet these new needs by allocating separate space to each, but within the same temples and basilicas that had been used before. When it became apparent that such simple cosmetic changes would not suffice, architects and librarians alike began seriously to seek a distribution of materials, services, and staff facilities appropriate to twentieth-century library needs.

Librarians for the first time began to rationalize their recently enlarged responsibilities in an attempt to conceptualize proper spatial requirements and interrelationships to meet these new needs. Architects sought new construction materials, techniques, and forms, and they imported the multi-tier structural stack from Europe, in order to meet these new expectations. Both worked together, and in concert with the professoriate, to effect a new kind of library building, one with a functional integrity of its own, a library *qua* library capable of fulfilling the multiplicity of book- and study-related requirements of modern higher education.

As a result of this cooperation, several good new functional buildings were built by 1890 that helped immeasurably to recast the intellectual ambience of the American college. Their extensive facilities for advanced study made them the nation's first libraries that were hospitable havens for productive researchers. They and their emulators were for the first time able to accommodate the great book collections that came to be attracted to them—those of the aforementioned Andrew Dickson White, Henry C. Lea, Hubert Howe Bancroft, and Jared Sparks. Such libraries rightly deserved the epithets of "scholar's workshop" and "humanist's laboratory" that were applied to them. They hastened the shift from the anti-intellectual aura that pervaded the mid-century campus to a *fin-de-siècle* environment that was conducive to modern research and study. These buildings were destined to serve as the only models for American university library-building planning for the next fifty years.

Notes

1. Howard Clayton, "The American College Library: 1800–1860," *Journal of Library History* 3 (April 1968): 120–137.
2. Edward G. Holley, "Academic Libraries in 1876," *College & Research Libraries* 37 (January 1976): 15–47.
3. *Harper's Weekly* 32 (1 September 1888): 657–658.
4. John J. Boll, "Library Architecture 1800–1875: A Comparison of Theory and Buildings" (Ph.D. dissertation, University of Illinois, 1961), pp. 379–397.
5. Ashton R. Willard, "College Libraries in the United States," *New England Magazine* n.s. 17 (December 1897): 433.
6. Jeffrey K. Ochsner, *H. H. Richardson: Complete Architectural Works* (Cambridge: Massachusetts Institute of Technology, 1983), pp. 300–305; Laurel Ginter, "Building Billings," *Vermont* (Winter 1984): 2–7.
7. Willard, "College Libraries," pp. 434–435.
8. John C. Abbot, "Raymond Cazallis Davis and the University of Michigan Library 1877–1905" (Ph.D. dissertation, University of Michigan, 1957), pp. 96–134.
9. Jackson E. Towne, "Charles Kendall Adams and the First University Library Building," *Michigan History* 37 (1953): 140.
10. Addison Van Name, "Report on Architecture," *Library Journal* 14 (January 1889): 173; W. Freeman Galpin, *Syracuse University: The Pioneer Days* (Syracuse University Press, 1952), p. 95.
11. Talcott Williams, "Plans for the Library Building of the University of Pennsylvania," *Library Journal* 13 (August 1888): 237–242; 14 (May–June 1889): 171.
12. James F. O'Gorman, *The Architecture of Frank Furness* (Philadelphia: Museum of Art, 1973), pp. 164–167.
13. Arthur Meggett, "The James B. Colgate Library," *Philobiblon* (February 1964): 1–9; Howard D. Williams, *History of Colgate University 1819–1969* (New York: Van Nostrand, 1969), pp. 184–186.
14. F. S. Retan, "Colgate Library Building," *Madisonensis* 21 (18 May 1889): 209–212.
15. Kermit C. Parsons, *The Cornell Campus: A History of Its Planning and Development* (Ithaca, N.Y.: Cornell University Press, 1968), pp. 152–172.

16. George W. Harris, "The New Library Building of Cornell University," *Library Journal* 14 (April 1889): 121–124.

17. Parsons, *The Cornell Campus*, p. 168.

Books in Artisan Homes of Sixteenth-Century Germany

Michael Hackenberg

One definite result of Lutheran educational reforms during the first half of the sixteenth century was the rise of the private household library among German artisans. Postmortem property inventories of artisan households in northern Braunschweig, central Schwäbisch Hall, and Heilbronn, and in the Tyrolian Catholic town of Hall, show a discernible increase in vernacular book collections among artisan families after mid-century. Regional variations do, however, appear, as Protestant artisans of northern Germany more often owned books than did their southern counterparts in lower Germany and Austria. By the end of the century, new vernacular readers in German-language areas included substantial numbers of artisans, whose books fulfilled their private devotional, occupational, and (in some cases) entertainment needs.

Not only did sixteenth-century German artisans share in the exhilaration that "city air brings freedom," but they also took enormous pride in the hard-won political and economic status that they had successfully been acquiring since the thirteenth century. Strengthened by elaborately protective guild structures and strategically positioned upon the city councils alongside their merchant and patrician compatriots, such artisans exerted powerful influence within urban life. While the Nürnberg cobbler and minnesinger Hans Sachs today is perhaps overly immortalized through the work of Richard Wagner, his descriptive rhymes and the accompanying powerful woodcuts by Jost Amman in the 1568 Frankfurt edition *Eygentliche Beschreibung aller Stände auff Erden*, which depict daily scenes of German artisans at work in their urban environment, provide even more convincing evidence of the pivotal roles played by German artisans of the era.[1]

The printed word certainly played a major part in shaping artisan consciousness in the cities, and a not inconsequential amount of vernacu-

Michael Hackenberg *is assistant professor at the Graduate Library School, University of Chicago.*

lar literature was clearly directed at urban artisans. Educational reforms under Philip Melanchthon and his colleagues during the 1530s and 1540s brought artisans into literacy in substantial numbers, as new urban elementary schools for both boys and girls stressed reading for both religious and practical purposes. Indeed, the rise of the "new" lay reader in sixteenth-century German areas was fundamentally the rise of the vernacular artisan reader. Each decade of the century witnessed an ever-increasing flood of vernacular titles aimed at the semiliterate and newly literate in the cities.[2] Books in the home became the norm for thousands of artisans who previously had not read or bothered to own books. By 1581 the Augsburg minnesinger Daniel Holzman could claim as an already established proverb throughout German lands that "he is but a half-man who cannot read or write."[3] Private household libraries among most of the urban classes were so commonplace by the end of the century that the Frankfurt pastor Konrad Lautenbach could report in his 1597 *Marckschiffer Gespräch*:

> Dem Teutschland mans zu dancken hat,
> Wie sichs befindt selbs in der That,
> Dass jeder ihm jetzt leicht kan zeugen,
> Ein Liberey, dass ers hab eigen:
> Die man fande vor alten Zeiten
> Nur bey gross Herrn, reichen Leuthen.[4]

To understand what such household book collections contained, and, indirectly, what titles urban book owners preferred to read, necessary "windows" into the private lives of sixteenth-century German artisan households need to be employed. One source has, to date, remained relatively unexplored for German-language areas of the sixteenth century, namely the postmortem property inventory (*Nachlassinventar* or *Verlassungschaftsinventar*).[5] With the rapid development of urban merchants and artisans through upward social mobility in the fifteenth and sixteenth centuries, and the concomitant interest in property, wealth, and social status, there arose the frequent need for assessing the value of estates, houses, and shops of deceased owners in order that local courts might settle property claims among the numerous and often contentious heirs. Municipal notaries were frequently called upon to record with witnesses present all the possessions of the deceased. These property inventories, whose completeness no doubt depended upon the ability of the heirs to pay for the service, were, nevertheless, generally thorough to the point of tedium, but are often very reliable documents illustrating lifestyles and household items from the period.[6] Those from three German archives and one Austrian, plus selected inventories from other

German cities that have appeared in secondary German source material, serve as the basis for much of the following analysis.[7]

Relatively unbroken series of archival postmortem property inventories remain extant from the period of about 1520 until well into the seventeenth century. During the century between 1520 and 1620, a significant increase in the ratio of urban inventories listing books compared with the total number of inventories extant can be seen from archival records at Braunschweig in northern Germany, at the two neighboring German cities of Heilbronn and Schwäbisch Hall, and at the Tyrolian salt and shipping center of Hall (see table 1).

TABLE 1
Ratio of Inventories Mentioning Books to Total Inventories

Inventories at	pre-1521	1521–1530	1531–1540	1541–1550	1551–1560	1561–1570	1571–1580	1581–1590	1591–1600	1601–1610	1611–1620
Braunschweig	0 / 15 0%	1 / 7 14%	3 / 31 10%	2 / 23 9%	0 / 35 0%	9 / 55 16%	10 / 33 30%	22 / 38 58%	16 / 29 55%	28 / 37 76%	8 / 14 57%
Schwäbish Hall	2 / 5 40%	1 / 8 12.5%	0 / 4 0%	2 / 9 22%	3 / 15 20%	3 / 8 37.5%	14 / 53 26%	10 / 50 20%	6 / 48 12.5%	16 / 71 22.5%	34 / 130 26%
Heilbronn	0 / 12 0%	0 / 13 0%	0 / 18 0%	2 / 25 8%	1 / 17 6%	1 / 15 7%	0 / 4 0%	3 / 12 25%	4 / 14 29%	2 / 18 11%	14 / 49 29%
Hall/Tirol	– / – –	– / – –	0 / 3 0%	1 / 4 25%	1 / 6 17%	1 / 7 14%	0 / 2 0%	1 / 17 6%	1 / 43 2%	23 / 248 9%	36 / 324 11%
Total	2 / 32 6%	2 / 28 7%	3 / 56 5%	7 / 61 11%	5 / 73 7%	14 / 85 16%	24 / 92 26%	36 / 117 32%	27 / 134 19%	69 / 374 18%	92 / 517 18%
Total (excluding Hall/Tirol)	2 / 32 6%	2 / 28 7%	3 / 53 6%	6 / 57 10.5%	4 / 57 7%	13 / 78 17%	24 / 90 27%	35 / 100 35%	26 / 91 27%	46 / 126 36.5%	56 / 193 29%

About 95 percent of the 280 inventories listing books in the homes of the deceased were prepared *after* mid-century, and there is a noticeable increase during the sixty-year period from 1560 up through the second decade of the seventeenth century. During those six decades the average ratio of book owners to the total adult number of persons whose possessions were inventoried leveled off at about 21.5 percent (or 28.6 percent, if the figures for Austrian Hall are excluded). But if one looks at each city separately for the sixty years, more variation becomes readily apparent. Proportionally more book owners existed in northern Braunschweig than in the two Württemberg towns of Schwäbisch Hall and Heilbronn, while relatively fewer were to be found in the Tyrolian center of Hall (decadal averages for the period of 1561–1620: Braunschweig 49 percent, Schwäbisch Hall 24 percent, Heilbronn 19 percent, and Hall/Tirol 7.3 percent). From a quantifiable viewpoint there existed, then, clear regional differences in book ownership patterns during the sixteenth century.

What one is seeing here is the rise of new categories of readers, because of increased book supplies and the impact of vernacular educational reforms coming in the wake of school reorganization in the 1520s and 1530s. By 1527 Schwäbisch Hall had adapted Johannes Brenz's vernacular catechism for training pupils; in 1531 Heilbronn began teaching its elementary school students (both boys and girls) in the vernacular. In Braunschweig, the local reformed superintendent and confidant of Luther, Johannes Bugenhagen (Pomeranus), had introduced the Reformation by 1529, quickly bringing not only Lutheran-oriented Latin middle schools but also elementary schools for the vernacular teaching of reading, writing, and mathematics, including no fewer than four schools for training girls. Only Catholic Hall, because of the anti-Lutheran stance of its Habsburg protectors, possessed no vernacular foundation to its school program until after the 1571 establishment of the Jesuits there under Petrus Canisius.[8] If one bears in mind an average life expectancy of 30–40 years for urban dwellers during the century, the significance of those vernacular educational changes during the 1530s and 1540s clearly connects with the already observed post-1560 increase in the percentage of book owners among urban populations.[9]

Artisan inventories account for a large segment of that increase in household book collections—a fact not surprising since by far the majority of German urban dwellers were engaged in the myriads of both skilled and unskilled trades that supported the daily life of the cities. If one includes the lower echelons of the nonuniversity-trained medical professions (i.e., the apothecaries, barber surgeons, and bath personnel) among the artisans, that increase can be seen as charted by decades in table 2:

Table 2
Book Inventories by Occupation

Occupations	pre-1521	1521–1530	1531–1540	1541–1550	1551–1560	1561–1570	1571–1580	1581–1590	1591–1600	1601–1610	1611–1620
Medical Practitioners	–	–	–	1	–	2	1	3	2	3	6
Artisans	2	2	1	6	9	12	22	22	18	28	47

Unlike the often sizable book collections of learned readers and even differing from the private libraries of some of the urban patricians and wealthier merchants of German cities, artisan book collections were, however, generally small and usually fulfilled the simple devotional and (often) occupational needs of their owners.

Table 3
Size of Book Collection by Occupation

Occupations	Total Inventories	1–10 Books	% of Total Inventories	11–50 Books	% of Total Inventories	51–100 Books	% of Total Inventories	101–200 Books	% of Total Inventories	Over 200	% of Total Inventories
Medical Practitioners	17	4	24%	12	71%	-	-	-	-	1	6%
Artisans	159	104	65%	47	30%	5	3%	2	1.3%	1	0.6%

Nearly two-thirds of the sixteenth-century artisans or day laborers had small numbers of books in their households. Table 3 shows that 104 artisan inventories (or 65 percent of the total) fall into this category. Nearly all of the remaining third owned between eleven and fifty titles. Only 8 of the identifiable 159 artisans possessed more than fifty titles. These were certainly the newer readers of the period, and the development of book ownership among them can be chronologically charted, such that the majority of the artisan inventories mentioning books were prepared after 1560. This trend is clear in nearly all geographical areas of Germany, although the growth of private libraries among Catholic artisans may have occurred somewhat later in the century. In Austrian Hall, only one artisan inventory (that of 1587) can be dated to the sixteenth century, while a series of twenty-two were prepared there between 1602 and 1619. Heilbronn, a Lutheran town, however, also exhibited a late appearance of books among its artisan community, with six book collections mentioned in inventories between 1588 and 1619.

Forty kilometers due east of Heilbronn, only seven artisan book inventories were compiled in Schwäbisch Hall before 1560 out of a total of sixty-one still extant; an amazing twenty-two, however, were prepared during the decade 1611–1620. A similar tendency can be observed in Braunschweig, where only one artisan book inventory was written before 1560 out of a total of thirty-one in the city. Braunschweig artisans did, however, own more books than their southern counterparts. A total of 527 titles was itemized in artisan inventories in that city between 1521 and 1613, for an average of about 17.6 books per inventory (or 20.6 books if one omits the figures for the pre-1581 artisans). Heilbronn artisans between 1588 and 1619 owned only about 7.6 books each, and the twenty-three Catholic artisans in Hall possessed a total of only 171 books between 1587 and 1619, for an average of 7.4 titles per person. Schwäbisch Hall artisan inventories between 1581 and 1620 mention 349 books, for an average of about 8.8 titles per owner.

Only under exceptional circumstances did sixteenth-century German artisans own more than fifty titles. Tradesmen connected with such book-related industries as printing and binding often fell into that category. The inventory for the Basel printer Sebastian Franck's house and shop listed 112 titles in 1542; in a later 1606 inventory, the Braunschweig bookbinder Benedix Gerssner left 364 books in his household bindery, along with hundreds of other titles in an adjoining bookshop. In both cases it remains unclear how many books represented personal books or stock for their clientele.[10] Hans Sachs's seventy-four mostly popular German titles, which were inventoried in 1562, were certainly uncommon, but Sachs himself was no ordinary cobbler.[11] Four other artisan book collections of more than fifty books are known. A Schemnitz (modern Czech Stiavnica) lead distributor owned much popular vernacular literature and ten books on accounting among his fifty-six books in 1585 (although he was more a supervisor than a craftsman).[12] A 1609 Hall goldsmith's inventory mentions sixty-one "large and small, German and Latin printed books" (unfortunately with no titles).[13] Finally, both a wealthy Braunschweig tinsmith with one hundred and twenty-two Latin and German titles in 1609 and a Mährisch-Trübau (now also in Czechoslovakia) clothcutter and city mayor in 1612 with fifty-one Lutheran and humanistic titles were a bit exceptional, as they both had received some university training.[14]

German artisans were upwardly mobile, both within their professions and within their political and social environments. The above-mentioned Sebastian Franck began his career as a soapmaker and ended it as a distinguished humanist printer in Basel. To appreciate fully the nature of private book collections among such socially conscious urban residents of sixteenth-century Germany, we need to ascend through the various social strata of the artisans and discuss a few representative book inventories from the era.

Even in the homes of laborers and the lower segments of the artisan classes, popular devotional and other literature could be found. The public executioner in Heilbronn (generally, a socially ostracized individual in most cities) owned seven vernacular books, which included no complete Lutheran Bible, but rather the *Biblischer Auszug oder Historien mit Bildern* by the Frankfurt pastor Hartmann Beyer; he also owned a small hymnal, a Gospel book (in Latin), and a commentary upon the Gospels. Secular titles included Adam Lonicer's *Kreuterbuch* and the popular cookbook *Koch- und Kellermeisterei*. A decade earlier a Heilbronn pensioner and his wife died, leaving four devotional books plus the knightly tales of *Fortunatus* and *Ritter Ludwig*, as well as an old *Modelbuch* (a manual on sewing or pattern design). Even simple barge operators in Heilbronn and Austrian Hall left five religious books in 1615, while a Freiburg guesthouse waiter owned four at his death in 1578, including the history of Johannes Schleidanus and a *Kalendertafel.*[15]

Most artisans with distinctly manual skills owned at least a few books, often religious in nature. Two carpenters at Schwäbisch hall died with but two books in their homes.[16] An early Strassburg inventory of 1536 mentions five German books including Johannes Pauli's *Schimpf und Ernst* (a collection of popular stories) found in a mason's home, while the 1597 Braunschweig mason Balzer Kircher owned a folio "Historien boeck" and both folio and quarto editions of two unidentified "Kunstbücher" (design or pattern books).[17] A glassmaker at Schwäbisch Hall had "several old books" in 1563; his fellow townsman, a tilemaker, left behind six books in a trunk of clothes in 1572.[18] A rather wealthy potter in 1585 Braunschweig owned ten devotional books, and a 1609 potter's inventory in Schwäbisch Hall mentioned eleven folio books in one of the rooms.[19] One ropemaker there left over fifteen unspecified titles in 1556, while another turned over to his son in 1618 only a German psalter and a collection of sermons for the home. Hans Hueber, a wealthy ropemaker in Catholic Hall, left behind in 1613 a sermon collection, a history book, and a copy of Tyrolian legal regulations.[20]

Most woodworkers had small book collections. In 1573 at Schwäbisch Hall, a furnituremaker left only four books, but ten years later a joiner and woodcarver at Braunschweig gave up a more substantial library of twenty-eight titles, mostly Lutheran devotional titles in Low German, although the presence of two "papistische büechere," one octavo medical "pocketbook," an accounting book of a local scrivener, and Bernhart Herzog's *Schildwacht* (a collection of droll tales) was also noted.[21] In 1605 master cooper Paul Maurer left behind at Hall an unidentified chronicle and eight "old books not worth appraising," while three years later another master of the same guild possessed at home only a sermon collection for young children.[22]

Among artisans in the more technically demanding clothing trades, books could also be found. Two cloth dyers (father and son) in Schwäbisch Hall each owned only a single copy of the Lutheran *Hauspostill*, however, and a weaver in the same city had fourteen "small books" in his living room in 1600.[23] Three tailors from Freiburg (1552), Frankfurt/Main (1572), and Heilbronn (1590) possessed, respectively, book collections of five, twenty-three, and seven titles.[24] Only the Frankfurt library of Hans Schilling (who was also a furniture dealer) is partially itemized. Besides a Basel edition of Sebastian Münster's *Cosmographie* and a Jena Bible, he owned a folio edition of some of Hans Sachs's works and a folio edition of the treaty uniting the Swabian League. Sebastian Krauss, a Schwäbisch Hall clothcutter and city councilman between 1521 and 1552, left behind thirteen mostly German books at his death in 1561. His seven devotional books were editions of Scripture and the local church regulations, but he lacked controversial literature. One title, "der heiligen legennt," was in fact Catholic—Jacopo de Voragine's *Lives of the Saints*. Krauss also owned a copy of Terence, the legal compendium *Laienspiegel*, an herbal, two vernacular medical guides, and a "buch vonn phrauewen" (possibly Johann Pfeiffelmann's 1533 excerpts from Eusebius and Plutarch on famous women or a midwifery manual).[25] David Stadtmann died in the same town in 1615, leaving a huge estate valued at 22,000 gulden but only a paltry nine books, among which were a 1580 edition of the Lutheran *Konkordienformel*, Frankfurt editions of histories by Johannes Schleidanus and Philip Melanchthon, and a 1585 Frankfurt edition of Luther's Bible. A ribbon or lace cutter in the same town left behind fifteen prayerbooks at his death in 1619.[26]

Most post-1565 book inventories for leatherworkers appear in Protestant towns. Eleven book collections among tanners dated between 1571 and 1615 have been discovered, and seven among leather cutters and trimmers, dated between 1565 and 1610. About six books constituted the average library for these occupations. Among the tanners Protestant devotional literature predominated; indeed, several of these leatherworkers owned only a single psalter or a *Hauspostille.*[27] A 1599 Braunschweig tanner did own, however, fifteen books, including Hieronymus Bock's herbal, the local police regulations, and a *Thaler und Münzbuch* for evaluating the diverse coinage circulating at the end of the century. Also of note is the 1615 property division of a Schwäbisch Hall tanner, who willed his heirs one *Hauspostille* and a book on devils and all types of sins.[28] Among the leather cutters and tailors similar book collections were present, with all but one to be found in Schwäbisch Hall. Those inventories of Schwäbisch Hall unfortunately list only the quantities of books (two libraries of 1576 and 1610 included, respectively, fifteen and twenty books). An interesting single-page inventory of March 1582, which describes the clothing and six weapons from the estate of Jörg Moser, a former city councilman who had been removed from this post in 1573 on a charge of usury, lists only two books, a "Notariat buch" and Johannes Brenz's catechism, but it is possible many of Moser's possessions had been disposed of earlier (he died in 1575).[29]

Interestingly, sixteenth-century cobblers averaged more books in their private collections than did other leatherworkers. Even if the large library of Hans Sachs should be excluded as somewhat nonrepresentative, the remaining eight book inventories of German cobblers between 1575 and 1614 averaged over seventeen books per inventory. All but one cobbler resided in Protestant towns, that exception being a Freiburg shoemaker, who owned a bound copy of that city's legal code and an old German history book in 1583.[30] Several cobblers in Schwäbisch Hall owned a considerable number of books, with some larger inventories there citing nineteen, twenty, and even twenty-seven titles. In the 1612 property division of the possessions of Hans and Margretha Hermann at Schwäbisch Hall, four children divided up the nineteen, mostly devotional, books, although daughter Apolonia received the family copy of Münster's *Cosmographie* and son Joseph a quarto copy of the *Koch und Kellermeisterei*. In 1613 the twenty books of Hans Schart at Mährisch-Trübau included ten religious books, plus four German law books (one against the counterfeiting of coinage), one quarto tablature for the lute, four popular medical books (including two midwifery manuals), the *Der alten Weisen Exempelbuch*, quarto and octavo editions of an unidentified *Steinbüchlein*, and an intriguing but likewise unidentifiable book cursorily entitled *Von den Bezauberten, Verunreinigten und Verblendeten*. The substantial 1596 book inventory of the Braunschweig cobbler Peter Crüger suggests that its owner attended a middle-level Latin school or possibly a university. Humanistic literature (including Dasypodius's *Dictionarium latino-*

germanicum and two Greek works) was present, as well as an old accounting book, the printed guild regulations for leather workers, local legal codes, a German edition of Albertus Magnus (his well-known book on women's hygiene), a *Confutatio Alcorani* (possibly the work of the Spanish humanist Juan Luis Vives), a chivalric *Ritterbüchlein*, and Johannes Coler's handbook on domestic household economy.[31]

A laboring-class group unique to the city of Schwäbisch Hall was formed by the saltworks laborers. An independent guild organization of these workers flourished during the century with its own court, four guild masters, and official secretary. Thus, the *Salzsieder* (in actuality, those who toiled firing the furnaces for the evaporation process) exercised considerable political importance in the city during the sixteenth century.[32] Although much of their work consisted of heavy manual labor, these workers did, somewhat surprisingly, own private book collections. One saltworker owned an "Evangelij buch" as early as 1516, but the remaining five book inventories of the saltworkers, who were also some of the "newer" book owners in the wake of the reformed pedagogy of the 1520s and 1530s, are dated between 1572 and 1620. The wife of the guild secretary owned "several small books" in 1572, and one of the guild masters had only the Old and New Testament in his home in 1574. Hans Dötschmann's inventory of 1607 mentions (without titles) four folio and "several" octavo volumes. In 1620 the younger Michel Botz, who was on the city council, owned seven folios, three quartos, and three octavos. That same year, Anna Reitz, whose deceased husband Georg had worked in the saltworks and probably attended a Latin middle school, died, and her property was divided among the heirs. One son received a Latin book, while a second child (the gender of this heir was not specified) inherited the remaining twenty titles—Latin and Greek schoolbooks, Johannes Scapula's Greek-Latin dictionary, and eleven undescribed Latin and German titles.[33]

Urban metalworkers also owned books during the sixteenth century. Five inventories of German blacksmiths are dated between 1550 and 1619 —all from Protestant towns. In Schwäbisch Hall, Ursula Eisenmenger, wife of the smithy Sixt Conrad, owned twenty-two books in 1550, but Georg Knopf, a weapons-maker and city gatekeeper, left behind only "two large books and several prayerbooks" in 1618. At Braunschweig a cannon-forger had only his copy of the Bible in 1566, whereas Anne Linden, whose husband was probably a blacksmith, owned eleven German devotional titles. A Heilbronn horseshoe maker owned sixteen books at his death in 1619, nearly all of which were popular theological titles, with the exception of the 1541 edition of the city's statutes and reformed regulations. One of the ideological titles included a response of a local Lutheran pastor to a religious tract of the Jesuit writer Georg am Ende.[34]

That seven tinsmiths of the period had book collections is attested by inventories at Braunschweig and Schwäbisch Hall, all dated late. The number of books in those inventories between 1586 and 1614 ranges from two to fifteen titles with an average of about nine. Excluded from that average are the one hundred and twenty-two books of Jacob Goes, probably a university graduate, whose inventory at Braunschweig was mentioned earlier. Two other tinsmiths at Braunschweig owned books. Jürgen Understal, in addition to numerous tools in his house and over four hundredweight of lead in the cellar, left a folio Bible and Luther's *Hauspostille* at his death in 1590. Gertrudt Storing, widow of Zacharias Boiling (who also served terms as the city's mayor), owned fourteen German religious books and a bound quarto edition of a German translation of the original Spanish epic *Hystorien von Amadiss auss Frankreich*, a series of which began pouring off the presses of Sigismund Feyerabend in Frankfurt in 1569. In Schwäbisch Hall a poor tinsmith of 1599 owned four folio volumes, and another, Hans Hofmann, left eighteen books "large and small" in 1611. In the 1614 property division of Hofmann's widow Anna, one son received one old medical book, three sermons of Luther, and an old prayerbook, while another prayerbook went to a surviving daughter. The September 1614 inventory of the Schwäbisch Hall tinsmith and city gatekeeper Nathaniel Niet mentions (without titles) five books, but a later property division of December in that same year awards a Bible, a collection of household sermons, and eight quarto and octavo books to his son.[35]

A bell-founder in Catholic Freiburg owned but a solitary book of fables in 1584. In 1616 a Schwäbisch Hall locksmith left behind eighteen books, which the notary simply noted as a Bible and a copy of the *Hauspostille* (of Luther?), with the remainder described as "very small," suggesting the presence of ephemeral pamphlets. An intriguing inventory at Schwäbisch Hall in 1596 for Marx Walther, a gunpowder-maker who certainly would have known metalworking technology, mentions sixteen books "gross unnd klein allerly Matheria," unfortunately with no further description.[36]

Goldsmiths and others dealing in precious metals definitely would have needed reading skills for dealing with pattern books and technical manuals on assaying and similar processes. All eleven book inventories of goldsmiths are dated between 1569 and 1613, except that of a Braunschweig craftsman who owned a book of the Gospels, a book on the Passion, and a chronicle at his death in 1522.[37] Interestingly, most goldsmiths generally owned few books during the period. Two at Freiburg had only a single book in their households, although a *Guldenschreiber* (an artisan doing gold lettering) there left "all sorts of large and small books worth twenty gulden" upstairs in 1591. Property divisions of the estates of two goldsmiths (one at Schwäbisch Hall in 1604 and the other at Braunschweig in 1613) mention only a single book. Another Schwäbisch Hall goldsmith had but a Bible and a *Hauspostille* in 1613, and a contemporary at Austrian Hall possessed a folio edition of the local police regulations and a bound herbal. The sixty-one unspecified books of the 1609 Hall goldsmith have already been mentioned.[38] Perhaps most useful is the 1611 inventory of books owned by Jost Rosenhagen, a Braunschweig goldsmith and member of the city financial council. The twenty-seven books included a 1561 Wittenberg Bible, a Saxon-dialect New Testament, and several sermons and theological works by local pastors. Devotional works included Basilius Faber's *Christliche nötige und nützliche Unterrichtungen von den letzten Hendeln der Welt* (on Lutheran notions of the Last Judgment), Johannes Matthesius's tract, *Vorgiss mein nicht* (found in the living room), an octavo *Teufelbuch* by Jodocus Hocker, entitled *Der Teufel selbst, von den Teuffeln*, and a sermon collection that juxtaposed Lutheran and Catholic dogma on opposite pages. Also in the library were a German edition of Josephus, two works on the political situation with the city's ducal overlords, Heinrich Bünting's history of Braunschweig, Johann Baumgart's history of nearby Magdeburg, and a book of Hans Sachs's comedies.[39]

Books appear in inventories of various urban foodstuffs provisioners, although a lone copy of Euripides's tragedies in the possession of a cook in 1549 Freiburg must surely be an anomaly. Two millers owned books at Schwäbisch Hall—the wife of one having "several books" at the very early date of 1500, while Paul Speltacher owned "eleven books large and small" in 1604. A Freiburg vineyard worker with ten books in 1553, including a copy of Terence, Dasypodius's Latin-German lexicon, and a grammar by Cyriakus Spangenberg, may have attended a Latin middle school. One year later in the same city the estate of the widow of a cellarmaster included thirteen books in a trunk. By 1585 a probable brewmaster at Braunschweig had forty-seven books in his living room, although the notary listed only five larger religious books, an herbal, and another medical book, and simply noted the remainder as "small."[40]

Four butchers from Schwäbisch Hall and one in Freiburg had books. In the latter city, Hans Ziblin owned three books at his death in 1565. Butchers' estates in Schwäbisch Hall in 1524 and 1585 list but a single devotional book each, but later estates there in 1613 and 1614 mention (without itemization) twenty-four and twenty-eight books, respectively. Four slaughterhouse operators in Braunschweig possessed very small book collections of religious titles between 1578 and 1613, all having five or fewer books, except for the 1613 library of the widow of Kilian Haverland, which totaled twenty-four religious books with no less than three Lutheran Bibles in folio, quarto, and octavo formats.[41]

Crucial to the provisioning of German cities were the bakers, since they prepared the daily stocks of bread, which the city governments tightly regulated. Most cities instituted elaborate bread regulations, specifying ingredients, loaf weights, prices, and distribution methods. Indeed, a 1619 barber-surgeon's inventory at Graudenz (in modern Poland) specifically listed the 1616 Leipzig edition of Sebald Müller's *Bericht vom Brodtbacken*, which itemized the bread regulations of the cities of Königsberg and Leipzig. Reading knowledge would have been essential for bakers subject to such municipal bureaucratic control.[42] Book inventories among bakers appear relatively late. Although an early one appears at Freiburg in 1564 (with two books), the remaining seven were written between 1599 and 1620. The average size of those book collections was about ten titles per inventory. In the Baltic coastal town of Wismar, a baker owned six Lutheran titles in 1599, and two baker housholds in 1608 Braunschweig included small libraries of ten and twelve titles—with the exception of one Latin dictionary, all of them also Lutheran religious books. The wife of a gingerbread-maker in 1615 Schwäbisch Hall left a German Bible, Michael Bock's Christian consolation book known as the *Würzgärtlein*, and fifteen small books not identified by title. Two Austrian bakers in the Protestant towns of Linz and Wels owned twenty-seven and five books, respectively, in 1615 and 1619. Among the eight books of a Schwäbisch Hall baker's inventory in April of 1620 were a Hungarian chronicle (possibly a German edition of Anthonius Bonfinius), an "old Anabaptist book," and a "Türkisch Raissbuch."[43]

Practitioners of popular medicine abounded in German cities to treat all manner of health and cosmetological needs. Among the nonuniversity trained were the barber-surgeons, masters of the baths, bone-menders, midwives, and apothecaries, who practiced their trades under the eyes of either municipal authorities (as with the midwives or bath personnel) or of guild officials (as with the barbers). Since they too needed information on anatomy, elementary chemistry, medicinal plants, and therapy techniques for purging, bone-setting, and other treatments, their need for literature in those areas is clear. Their inventories (which often itemize their shop equipment and medical paraphernalia) indeed confirm the presence of substantial book stocks.[44] Furthermore, it is among these practitioners that the greatest correlation between books present and books necessary for the trade of the owners can be found. Eighteen book inventories of popular medical practitioners are dated between 1550 and 1619 and can be found in both Protestant and Catholic cities of the period. Although the number of books listed in each inventory ranges from 2 to 241 titles, an average of about 20 titles was observable in those libraries.[45]

In 1572 at Schwäbisch Hall the tools of a barber's trade "with several books'' were noted in a locked trunk of Gabriel Schill, who had enlisted as a soldier.[46] A still extant, composite volume of thirteen medical tracts owned by the 1550 Danzig barber Simon Willenberg can be found in the library of the Polish Academy of Science in Gdansk. Although Willenberg probably owned additional books, the extant titles are all in German and cover such topics as analysis of urine specimens and of kidney stones, dentistry, bloodletting, pregnancy, syphilis, and several booklets on various plagues (including one on the so-called English sweat).[47] In a June 1603 inventory of Hans Feichtmayr at Austrian Hall are listed two herbals (one of Hieronymus Bock) and a medical book each of Christoph Wirsung and a certain Baltherus Schiff, plus twenty-four books ''of all types, small and large.'' Two masters of the baths had small libraries in Hall, with the titles unspecified in the inventories. Melchoir Schlegl, in November of 1570, willed to relatives his two herbals, a *Feldbuch* (a book for treating military injuries), two manuscript medical books, and two other books. Also unspecified were the eight ''Arztney und Distelier Piecher'' in the house of the bathmaster and barber Hans Edlman in 1618.[48]

At Schwäbisch Hall, the 1615 property division of the bathmaster, Caspar Neubeck, awarded to his son and daughter twelve books, including four religious titles, a copy of Aesop's *Fables*, Michael Neander's collection of Greek poetry, and five booklets of ''all types of songs,'' but not a single medical work. In addition to a large amount of barbering equipment, the son of the barber Zacharias Werlin received in 1619 his father's own handwritten medical book in quarto and his folio edition of Münster's *Cosmographia.*[49]

In Braunschweig, David Grefe (Greve), a healer of wounds, left twenty titles in his home in 1593. Grefe was apparently esteemed as a bone-mender and oculist, and had been feted by the city council in 1581 for at least forty successful recoveries, including eighteen settings of fractures. In addition to religious books, three histories, and the folio *Deutscher Process* of Abraham Saur, Grefe owned an apothecary's *Confect Buch*, seven herbals or practical medical handbooks (an edition of Wirsung is mentioned, as is the 1564 large herbal printed at Frankfurt by the heirs of Christian Egenolff), and editions of Paracelsus's *Labyrinthus* and the occult-laden *Archidoxa* (a book of the secrets of nature).[50]

Two Braunschweig barber-surgeon inventories are extant, one dated 1567 and the other 1583. Twenty-seven of the thirty-one books owned by Joachim Wittenheder were medical books, including eight books of Paracelsus, three of Walter Ryff, individual herbals or medical manuals of Eucharius Röslin, Hieronymus Bock, and Lorenz Fries, a book of metals, six manuscript ''kunstboke'' (perhaps alchemical in nature), and an unidentified work of the fourteenth-century Spanish ecclesiastic and philosopher Ramon Lull. In the 1583 inventory of Bernd Rottendorf were noted ten medical volumes out of a total of twenty-eight books—the remaining books nearly all of a popular devotional nature, except for a collection of 300 common proverbs by Johannes Agricola. Among the medical books were a handbook on various diseases by the Nürnberg *Wundarzt* Franz Renner, a book by Paracelsus, an unidentified title on diseases of the chest, one distillation manual, three manuscript "Kunstbücher," and a manuscript book on scurvy.[51]

Smaller libraries were to be found in the homes of Braunschweig masters of the baths. Caspar Kreutzberg, who owned a house and courtyard with a public bath in 1585, left sixteen titles and numerous tin implements and containers. Six books were of medical content—two were manuscript copies. Nearly all are simply described as "medical books" without the name of the author. One was, however, an herbal. A generation later in 1616, Bartold Nisch, whose bathing establishment was near St. Peter, left twelve titles, of which two were medical—one herbal and a German translation of the *I secreti . . . appartenenti a ogni gran signora* by Isabella Cortese.[52]

Sixteenth-century German artisans became book buyers in the wake of vernacular educational reforms during the 1530s and 1540s. In general, however, they bought only those books essential for their private devotional and (less often) occupational needs. It ought not to surprise one today that their reading tastes appeared narrowly defined and limited to titles that might be frequently consulted for reasons of spiritual support, domestic household operation, and occasional entertainment. This was an era of intensive rereading of selected books; the development of extensive middle-class libraries of seldomly reread books would not receive its impetus until the eighteenth-century rise of the novel.[53] When the sixteenth century began, artisans were still generally excluded from the world of books; when the century ended, a significant number of them (especially in northern Germany) could indeed show off their small household book collections. Indeed, readership tastes were already in flux, and it is appropriate to end this discussion with the complete list of books from a 1595 Braunschweig inventory, which perhaps best represents changing readership tastes among the urban middle class.[54]

Of Anton Weidenteich little is presently known, except for the information from his 1595 Braunschweig property inventory. He was apparently a renter; a large amount of gold jewelry and two assayist's scales and weights suggest he might have been a goldsmith, although the notary also found a clavicord, four lutes, and several other stringed instruments, suggesting Weidenteich might have been a musician. In a cupboard were found the following books:

Ein Kunstbuch In gelb pergament gebunden
Antomia Vesalij In slecht pergament gebunden
Die Bibel In folio
Hausspostilla Lutheri
Examen concilij tridentini D. Chemnitij
Ein papistisch legenden buch
Zehen Tomi operum lutheri deutsch
Flavius Josephus, deutsch
Der Bienen Korb
Ein hauffen alter Almanach

Betbuch Lutheri
Hortulus animae
Die lautere warheit
Experiment büchlein
Beschreibung der wilden leute, in America
Artzeney spiegel
Trostschrift M. Friderici Petri
Ein buch in Reussischer Sprach
Rechenbuch Adam Risen
Ein Reisebuch ritter Ludewichs
Ein Buch darin rein papir gebundenn
Zwey Leichtpredigtenn

Anthonij Weitenteichs Rechenbuch Inn weiss pergament gebundenn
Zwey newe Romische chartenn
Inn einem kleinen kestlein
Vier lautenbücher, in folio
Einn klein lautenbuch so Paulus rhemnilius? gehabt

Einn kleinn kestlein
darein
Alte Zeitung undt lieder

Weidenteich's books most aptly point out the new reading tastes of the sixteenth century. Among his personal religious books appear a folio Bible, Luther's *Hauspostille*, and ten volumes of the reformer's collected works in the vernacular. Devotional manuals included Luther's prayer-book, the *Hortulus animae* (despite its title, a *vernacular* devotional book), the consolatory manual of Friedrich Petrus, and two funeral orations. But he also possessed a "popish" book on legends (probably that of Jacopo de Voragine), the caustic denunciation of the Council of Trent by Martin Chemnitz (Braunschweig's Lutheran superintendent from 1567 to 1584), and the extremely vitriolic satire against the Roman Church *Der Bienenkorb*, written by Philip van Marnix, a Dutch Calvinist theologian. But secular literature also occupied a place in Weidenteich's collection. An "Experiment büchlein" and one "Kunstbuch" were probably alchemical books, while a popular medical manual (Lorenz Fries's *Spiegel der Artzney*) and one of the two German editions (1551 or 1575) of Vesalius supplied him with medical information.

Practical bookkeeping was aided by a copy of Adam Riese's popular arithmetic, as well as by Weidenteich's own personal household ledger. Assisting his interest in music were five books of lute scores, and the notary also discovered in a small chest "an old news-sheet" and printed songs. Two new maps of Rome were also in the apartment, and a stack of old almanacs attested to ephemeral reading habits. A German edition of Josephus and the chivalric epic of the *Ritter Ludwig* provided some popular diversion. Two remaining titles point to *new* reading areas not common to artisan libraries from the earlier part of the century. What is one to make of the notary's itemization of "Ein buch in Reussischer Sprach"? Certainly, Russian imprints were available after about 1564, but it remains enigmatic why this artisan should have owned a Cyrillic book. More intriguing is the "Beschreibung der wilden Leute in America," probably one of the several Frankfurt editions of the 1590s, which Theodore de Bry edited and published in the wake of various voyages to the New World. Clearly, world horizons of even a simple Braunschweig citizen were being affected by the proliferation of vernacular literature into artisan households during the second half of the sixteenth century. Further systematic study of other book inventories from additional German cities might do much to expand our knowledge of that literature and its pervasive influence in the daily lives of German artisans and other urban residents of the period.

Notes

Abbreviations used in the notes include *inv.* for inventory and *StadtA* for Stadtarchiv.

2. Hans Sachs, *Eygentliche Beschreibung aller Stände auff Erden* (Frankfurt: bey G. Raben, in Verlegung S. Feyerabents, 1568). A good survey of German artisan life is Ernest Mummenhoff's *Der Handwerker in der deutschen Vergangenheit* (Leipzig: E. Diederichs, 1901). See also Ernst Walter Zeeden, *Deutsche Kultur in der frühen Neuzeit* (Frankfurt: Akademische Verlagsgesellschaft Athenaion, 1968), pp. 126–135.

2. The rise of the new lay reader is discussed by Rudolf Hirsch, *Printing, Selling and Reading 1450–1550*, 2nd printing (Wiesbaden: O. Harrassowitz, 1974), pp. 147–149, and Rolf Engelsing, *Analphabetentum und Lektüre; zur Sozialgeschichte des Lesens in Deutschland zwischen feudaler und industrieller Gesellschaft* (Stuttgart: J. B. Metzlersche Verlagsbuchhandlung, 1973), chap. 7. The more than fourfold

increase in the annual production of German-language titles during the century is traced by Friedrich Kapp, *Geschichte des deutschen Buchhandels bis in das siebzehnte Jahrhundert* (Leipzig: Verlag des Börsenvereins der Deutschen Buchhändler, 1886), pp. 786–809.

3. Engelsing, *Analphabetentum*, p. 33.

4. Lautenbach (1534–1597) sets the phrase into a hypothetical dialogue between a student and a marketplace vendor of reading glasses. It is quoted by Fried Lübbecke, *Fünfhundert Jahre Buch und Druck in Frankfurt am Main* (Frankfurt: H. Cobet, 1948), p. 56.

5. Dresden inventories have recently been studied by Christian Alschner, "Der Buchbesitz Dresdener Bürger im 15./16. Jahrhundert," *Beiträge zur Inkunabelkunde* 3/Folge 8 (1983): 144–161. For work from French-language areas of the sixteenth century, see the discussion of Albert Labarre, "L'étude des bibliothèques privées anciennes," in *Refugium animae bibliotheca; Festschrift für Albert Kolb* (Wiesbaden: Pressler, 1969), pp. 294–302, and his exemplary study of private libraries in Amiens, *Le livre dans la vie amiénoise du seizième siècle; l'enseignement des inventaires après décès 1503–1576* (Paris, Louvain: B. Nauwelaerts, 1971).

6. "Les inventaires après décès, documents de verité," according to Fernand Braudel, *Civilisation matérielle et capitalisme (XVe–XVIIIe siècle)* (Paris: A. Colin, 1967), 1: 212.

7. This paper is drawn from segments of my "Private Book Ownership in Sixteenth-Century German-Language Areas" (Ph.D. dissertation, University of California, Berkeley, 1983).

8. On Bugenhagen's reformed curricula in Braunschweig, see Werner Spiess, *Geschichte der Stadt Braunschweig im Nachmittelalter vom Ausgang des Mittelalters bis zum Ende der Stadtfreiheit (1491–1671)* (Braunschweig: Waisenhaus, 1966), pp. 670–680; on Brenz in Schwäbisch Hall, see Ernst Iserloh, Josef Glazik, and Hubert Jedin, *Reformation, katholische Reform und Gegenreformation* (Freiburg, Basel, Wien: Herder, 1967), p. 245; on the Heilbronn reorganization, see Friedrich Dürr, *Heilbronner Chronik* (Heilbronn: E. Salzer, 1895), pp. 94–95. The Jesuit appearance in Hall was aided by duchess Margareta, daughter of Ferdinand I. Protestant pastors were ordered out of the city, and Lutheran books were burned. See Ernst Tomek, *Kirchengeschichte Österreichs* (Innsbruck-Wien: Tyrolia-Verlag, 1949), 2: 458–460, and Hans Hochenegg, *Kulturbilder aus Solbad Hall und Umgebung* (Innsbruck: Österreichische Kommissionsbuchhandlung, 1970), pp. 23–24. Even after the Jesuit reforms, book ownership remained considerably limited in Hall, and even some well-to-do citizens possessed only a single book as late as the 1640s. See, especially, Lore Berger, "Wohnkultur des Haller Bürgertums von 1550 bis 1650" (dissertation, Innsbruck, 1948), p. 117.

9. On life expectancy in sixteenth-century German cities, see Zeeden, *Deutsche Kultur*, pp. 286–288.

10. Anton Bruckner, "Verzeichnis der hinterlassenen Bücher Sebastian Francks," *Zentralblatt für Bibliothekswesen* 54 (1937): 286–289; Michael Hackenberg, "The Shop Inventory of Benedix Gerssner, Bookbinder of Braunschweig," *The Library* 6th ser., 2 (1980): 413–429.

11. Karl Goedeke, "Die Büchersammlung des Hans Sachs," in his *Gesammelte Schriften; Buchkunde—Bibliophilie, Literatur—Kunst u.a.* (Frankfurt: für den Verfasser gedruckt, 1927), pp. 260–263

12. Adalbert Baker, "Beiträge zum Geistesleben der Schemnitzer Waldbürger im XV.–XVII. Jahrhundert," *Karpathenland* 9 (1936): 9–16, 41–49, 67–72.

13. Inv., Peter Peitschger (StadtA Hall, 1609).

14. Inv., Jacob Goes, 1619 (StadtA Braunschweig AI4 J7), and Moritz Grolig,

"Büchersammlungen des 17. Jahrhunderts in Mähr.-Trübau," *Mitteilungen des Österreichischen Vereins für Bibliothekswesen* 9 (1905): 57–64.

15. Inv., Balthus Knapp, executioner (StadtA Heilbronn K1); bargemen Hans Premberger (StadtA Heilbronn Pl) and Wolfgang Strasser (cf. Gilbert Trathnigg, "Beiträge zur Welser Kulturgeschichte des 16. Jahrhunderts; der Buch- und Kunstbesitz nach den Inventaren im Stadtarchiv," *Jahrbuch des Musealvereines Wels* 6 [1959–1960]: 106–151). The books of the Freiburg waiter are mentioned by Josef Rest, "Freiburger Bibliotheken und Buchhandlungen im 15. und 16. Jahrhundert," in *Aus der Werkstatt, den deutschen Bibliothekaren zu ihrer Tagung in Freiburg, Pfingsten MCMXXV, dargebracht von der Universitätsbibliothek* (Freiburg: C. A. Wagner Buchdruckerei, 1925), p. 48.

16. StadtA Schwäbisch Hall, Inv. 31 (1555) and Inv. 303 (1611).

17. The Strassburg books of Agnes Götz, wife of a mason, are mentioned in Edmund Ungerer, *Elsässische Altertümer im Burg und Haus, in Kloster und Kirche; Inventare vom Ausgang des Mittelalters bis zum Dreissigjährigen Kriege aus Stadt und Bistum Strassburg* (Strassburg: K. J. Trübner, 1911–1917), 2: 90–91. Inv., Balzar Kircher, 1597 (StadtA Braunschweig AI4 J6).

18. StadtA Schwäbisch Hall Inv. 45 and 58.

19. StadtA Braunschweig AI4 J4 and StadtA Schwäbisch Hall Inv. 283.

20. StadtA Schwäbisch Hall Inv. 35 and 383; inv., Hans Hueber, 1613 (StadtA Hall).

21. StadtA Schwäbisch Hall Inv. 61; inv., Hans Seeck, 1583 (StadtA Braunschweig AI4 J4).

22. Inventories of Paul Maurer (1605) and Hans Riedmayr (1608) in StadtA Hall.

23. StadtA Schwäbisch Hall Inv. 363, 373 (father and son), and 291 (Heinrich Franck, a weaver).

24. Inv., Jacob Herb, 1552 (see Rest, "Freiburger Bibliotheken," p. 50); inv., Hans Franck, 1590 (StadtA Heilbronn Fl). Hans Schilling's books were itemized by Friedrich Bothe, *Frankfurter Patriziervermögen im 16. Jahrhundert; ein Beitrag zur Charakteristik der bürgerlichen Vermögen und der bürgerlichen Kultur* (Berlin: A. Duncker, 1908).

25. StadtA Schwäbisch Hall, Inv. 44.

26. StadtA Schwäbisch Hall, Inv. 347 and 407.

27. For the lengthy list of the sources, see Hackenberg, "Private Book Ownership," p. 109*n*1.

28. Inv., Margaret Meier, wife of Peter Wilcken, 1599 (StadtA Braunschweig AI4 J6) and Hans Weinmar, 1615 (StadtA Schwäbisch Hall, Inv. 361).

29. StadtA Schwäbisch Hall, Inv. 90, 132, and 287.

30. Hackenberg, "Private Book Ownership," p. 111*n*1.

31. Forty-one titles are listed in the 1596 inventory of Peter Crüger (StadtA Braunschweig AI4 J6).

32. On the laborers and their guild structure at the Schwäbisch Hall saltworks, see the discussion by Gerhard Wunder, *Die Bürgerschaft der Reichsstadt Hall von 1395 bis 1600* (Stuttgart, Köln: W. Kohlhammer Verlag, 1956), pp. 9, 36, 63–71.

33. Books among the saltworkers: StadtA Schwäbisch Hall, Inv. 7, 57, 72, 266, 415, and 421.

34. Book inventories of metal workers: StadtA Schwäbisch Hall, Inv. 27 and 389; inv. of Hinrick Slachmann, 1566 (StadtA Braunschweig, Sachsche Sammlung HV Bd. 157, pp. 223–242) and of the wife of Gregor Meizen, 1597 (StadtA Braunschweig AI4 J6); inv. of Martin Zier, 1619 (StadtA Heilbronn Z1).

35. Tinsmiths at Braunschweig: Gertrude Storing, wife of a metalworker, 1586 (StadtA Braunschweig AI4 J4); Jürgen Understal, 1590 (StadtA Braunschweig

AI4 J5); and wife of Jacob Goes, 1609 (StadtA Braunschweig AI4 J7). Tinsmiths at Schwäbisch Hall (StadtA Schwäbisch Hall, Inv. 216, 297, 336, and 344).

36. Rest, "Freiburger Bibliotheken," p. 52, mentions the book of Hans Sternecker, the Freiburg bell-founder. The other inventories are those of Casper Geutner (StadtA Schwäbisch Hall, Inv. 369) and of Walther, who actually died in a gunpowder explosion (StadtA Schwäbisch Hall, Inv. 185).

37. On goldsmith inventories, see Hackenberg, "Private Book Ownership," p. 117*n*1.

38. See note 13 above.

39. The twenty-seven books of Rosenhagen appear in StadtA Braunschweig AI4 J8. An excellent discussion of the vernacular genre of *Teufelbücher* is given by Heinrich Grimm, "Die deutschen 'Teufelbücher' des 16. Jahrhunderts; ihre Rolle im Buchwesen und ihre Bedeutung," *Archiv für Geschichte des Buchwesens* 2 (1969): 513-570.

40. See the list of inventories in Hackenberg, "Private Book Ownership," pp. 119-120*n*2.

41. Ibid., pp. 120-121.

42. On the essential role of the bakers in the policing of foodstuffs, see Zeeden, *Deutsche Kultur*, p. 129. The Müller book appears in the inventory of the Graudenz barber-surgeon Johannes Rettelius (see X. Froelich, "Bürgerliches Leben in Graudenz während der ersten Hälfte des 17. Jahrhunderts," *Altpreussische Monatsschrift* n.F. 5 [1868]: 41).

43. Sources for the eight inventories in Hackenberg, "Private Book Ownership," p. 124*n*1.

44. For good treatments of popular medical facilities and personnel, see Zeeden, *Deutsche Kultur*, p. 282-307, and Hermann Peters, *Der Arzt und die Heilkunst in der deutschen Vergangenheit* (Leipzig: E. Diederichs, 1900). The medical situation in sixteenth-century Braunschweig was carefully analyzed by Franz Fuhse in his two articles "Hygiene und Heilkunst in der Stadt Braunschweig während des 16. Jahrhunderts," *Niederdeutsche Zeitschrift für Volkskunde* 4 (1926): 23-33, and "Die Bader und Barbiere in der Stadt Braunschweig während des 16. Jahrhunderts," *Unsere Heimat Niedersachsen* 1924: 30-36.

45. Hackenberg, "Private Book Ownership," p. 125.

46. StadtA Schwäbisch Hall, Inv. 56.

47. Stanislaw Sokól, "Die Bibliothek eines Barbiers aus dem Jahre 1550," *Centaurus; International Magazine of the History of Science and Medicine* 7 (1961): 197-206.

48. Books of Feichtmayr are mentioned in two inventories of 1603 and 1614 (StadtA Hall). The inventories of Schlegl (1570) and Edlman (1618) are also extant in the StadtA Hall.

49. StadtA Schwäbisch Hall, Inv. 340 and 352.

50. StadtA Braunschweig AI4 J5. Details on Grefe's successful practice are given by Spiess, 567.

51. Wittenheder, 1567 (StadtA Braunschweig A14 J2, Nr. 157) and Rottendorf, 1583 (StadtA Braunschweig AI4 J8).

52. StadtA Braunschweig AI4 J4 and AI4 J8.

53. This differentiation between *intensive* as opposed to *extensive* reading was first adumbrated by Rolf Engelsing, "Die perioden der Lesergeschichte in der Neuzeit," *Archiv für Geschichte des Buchwesens* 10 (1970): 945-1002.

54. Books of Anton Weidenteich, 1595 (StadtA Braunschweig AI4 J5, pp. 1241-1245.

Books as Totems in Seventeenth-Century England and New England

David Cressy

Books in seventeenth-century England and New England enjoyed a cultural significance that extended beyond their textual content. The Bible in particular was employed as a magical talisman, as an aid to divination, as medicine, and as a device for social display. In New England in 1642 contesting Puritans carried a Bible atop a pole during a community affray. Understanding this episode requires examination of other occasions when people made unorthodox, nonliterary, or symbolic use of books.

When John Osgood of Andover, Massachusetts, made his will on 12 April 1650, he assigned eighteen shillings to the meeting house of Newbury "to buy a cushion for the minister to lay his book upon."[1] This provision of a luxurious material, a soft padding for the heavy word of God, reminds us of the extraordinary reverence with which the Bible was treated in the seventeenth century. Valued for its content, as Holy Scripture, the book was also venerated as a sacred artefact, as a Puritan totem, and as the touchstone of the Protestant Reformation. Even in austere New England, in a religious culture set firm against superstition, the physical bound volume possessed some of the attributes of a religious icon or talisman. John Osgood's will, providing an eighteen-shilling cushion for a five-shilling book, reminds us that the Bible was worthy of unusual handling, devout care, and special public presentation. The Bible cushion was, perhaps, the Puritan successor to the elaborately embellished lectern of Old World religion.

Books, of course, have always had a cultural significance that extends beyond their mere textual content. Intellectual historians in particular may need to be reminded that a book is a physical object with weight, bulk, and dimensions. Regardless of the quality of its content, a book has basic properties in common with other books—type printed on paper, squared edges, sewn fascicles, and usually some kind of binding. It can

David Cressy *is associate professor of history, California State University, Long Beach.*

be held in the hand, clasped to the breast, stuffed in a pocket, stacked on a shelf, laid on a table, or tossed in the air; it can be purchased, lent, stolen, given away, or burned.[2] While librarians and physical bibliographers are familiar with this notion, historians, whose interest in books is largely confined to the *ideas* they contain, may find it arresting.

My concern here is the deployment of books as magical talismans, as aids to divination, as devices for social display, and for other nonliterary purposes, in England and New England in the seventeenth century. I shall also be citing some examples from earlier and later periods. In a culture that venerates the book, where religious ideology is shaped by the book, it should not be surprising to find irregular and nonliterary uses of the books alongside more orthodox applications. By studying what people did with books, especially Bibles, and how they *handled* them in ritually sensitive settings, we may gain insight into some of the lesser-known workings of early modern culture. Behavior, in some contexts, may prove to be more informative than text, just as folk wisdom knows that actions speak louder than words.

Seventeenth-century almanacs, chapbooks, pamphlets, periodicals, and other ephemeral publications were pressed into service for a variety of uses after their primary textual purpose had expired. Indeed, their versatile serviceability may partly explain why so few of them have survived. We find printed paper being used as draught excluders, for stuffing cracks in chimneys and windows, as lining for boxes, and as spills to light a fire or a pipe. Old books were useful in the kitchen, where their pages could serve as foundations for a pie or as wrapping for spice. Countless sheets of printed paper must have gone into privies, employed as toilet paper.[3] Cheap secular books, it seems, had no more residual value than scraps of paper, too soiled to write on but serviceable for menial household tasks. No reverence was attached to the chapbook text, and there was none of the Chinese reverence for written characters that deserved a solemn cremation. The English displayed, rather, an unsentimental, utilitarian attitude toward ordinary books. We find this attitude revealed in such seventeenth-century probate inventory notations as "his books and other trash."[4]

The Bible, by contrast, was normally exempt from these destructive and practical applications. As a sacred text, the Bible would not usually be found in the privy, or as a fireside commodity in the kitchen. As the word of God, as the fundamental text of Protestant Christendom, the Bible enjoyed a special reverence that no other book could claim. It was the most commonly owned book in the seventeenth century, in England and New England, and could even be found in households where nobody could read.[5]

But because of its special religious significance, the Bible, more than any other book, was subject to a multitude of irregular uses. It was sometimes deployed in circumstances other than those for which it was intended and for purposes quite alien to its scriptural content. For example, the Bible served for swearing oaths, registering births, curing the sick, making decisions, predicting the future, and warding off devils. It could be imagined as a shield or a weapon, or used as a talisman or totem.[6] In seventeenth-century New England we even find townsmen carrying a Bible on a pole, like a legionary standard, when they went to dispute with their reprobate neighbors. The Bible, held aloft, served as an inspirational emblem and as a weapon, even without the necessity of being opened. This episode deserves close attention.

Early in 1642 Thomas Lechford, a lawyer, resettled in London after four unhappy years in America and wrote a critical account of conditions in New England. His work was published in 1642 as *Plain Dealing, or News from New England* and was revised and reissued two years later as *New Englands Advice to Old England.* The book set out to warn against the "anarchy and confusion" that followed when congregational independency was adopted in place of orderly episcopal government. Lechford tells the following story, which climaxes with the martial display of a book on a pole, like a military standard carried into battle:

> At Northam, alias Piscataqua, is master Larkham pastor. One master H.K. was also lately minister there, with master Larkham. They two fell out about baptising children, receiving of members, burial of the dead; and the contention was so sharp that master K. and his party rose up and excommunicated master Larkham and some that held with him. And further, master Larkham flying to the magistrates, master K. and a captain raised arms, and expected help from the Bay; master K. *going before the troop with a Bible upon a pole's top*, and he or some of his party giving out that their side were the Scots, and the other English.[7]

What was going on? We have two issues to untangle; first, the background to this extraordinary story, and second, the significance of displaying the Bible as a battle standard, brandished on a pole. As is often the case with such anecdotes, a brief remark in an historical source points to a telling episode, but what it "tells" is likely to be hidden beneath the surface.

The Piscataqua River cuts Maine from New Hampshire, some eighteen miles northeast of the Massachusetts border. Outside of the strict jurisdiction of the Bay Colony, and neglected by the proprietary government at Strawberry Bank, places like Northam (later renamed Dover, New

Hampshire) became rowdy frontier settlements, notorious for their drunkenness, ill discipline, and irreligion. The early 1630s saw a violent clash along the Piscataqua between a trading party from Plymouth Colony and Lord Seye's men, which left several people dead. Religious dissidents from Massachusetts migrated to this area of lax ecclesiastical administration. Piscataqua received religious incendiaries like John Wheelwright, the antinomian, and crypto-Laudians and sensualists like George Burdet. By 1639 Dover (also known as Northam and Piscataqua) was "a scene of confusion and trouble, both civil and ecclesiastical," and its religious community was rent with "factions and strange confusions."

Into this troubled town came Hanserd Knollys, the "master H.K." of Lechford's narrative, soon to be joined by his nemesis Thomas Larkham. Knollys, an English cleric, arrived in New England in 1636 already tainted with suspicions of religious unorthodoxy. The Bay Colony refused him permission to settle, on account of his sympathy for Wheelwright and the antinomians, so Knollys moved north to New Hampshire. By 1639 he was installed as minister at Dover, trying to achieve a godly reformation, criticizing and then ingratiating himself with the colonial leadership at Boston, and at the same time conspiring with Captain John Underhill of Dover to bring the Piscataqua township under the jurisdiction of Massachusetts.

Thomas Larkham joined the Dover church in 1640 and became Knollys's pastoral assistant. Being himself "a preacher of good talents," Larkham soon eclipsed Knollys, "raised a party" of his own, and had Knollys excommunicated. The Dover Christians split into factions. Driven by a narrow and idiosyncratic interpretation of Scripture, closer to Wheelwright and the antinomians than to the Massachusetts Puritans, Knollys restricted baptism, burial, and church membership to a tested elect. Larkham, by contrast, "baptized all the children of the town, making no distinction between a parish and a gathered church." Here, on the northern frontier, the protagonists were battling over one of the central theological controversies of the seventeenth century.

From the beginning Knollys appears to have been impetuous and unstable, the kind of man who was likely to enter a religious affray with a Bible on a pole. An extravagant letter he wrote to friends in England "greatly scandalized the church and civil state." Apologizing to John Winthrop, he turned the blame on "the Devil," who had "caused my wretched heart to conceive, nourish and bring forth such a monstrous imp so like himself, to wit, an accusation of the brethren." In his dispute with Larkham, Knollys produced a twenty two point testimony of disagreement, based on points from the Bible, and led his followers in violent disruptions of church meetings. In his own account of events,

Larkham cast doubt on Knollys's sanity, citing "his wild and weak and pope-like carriage in this church, and odd phrases in sermons, unwarrantable and unpatterned expositions of Scripture, and other absurd yet impudent practices." Both preachers accused the other of moral misconduct, and evidence surfaced to prove each of them right. "The revelation of Larkham's scandalous private life led to Knollys' reinstatement, but the night after Larkham had been excommunicated for moral misconduct (he had made a widow big with child) Knollys himself was discovered in the bed of his maid."

The affair came to a climax in the scene described by Thomas Lechford. Knollys had publicly assaulted Larkham, who in turn sought assistance from the local magistrates. In a state of righteous agitation, the Knollys faction gathered their forces "and so marched out to meet Mr. Larkham, one carrying a Bible on a halberd for an ensign, Mr. Knollys being armed with a pistol." Perhaps awed by their opponents' firepower, perhaps taking account of the political as well as the physical risks of combat, and no doubt awed by the mighty biblical standard, the Larkham forces withdrew. The tables were soon turned, however, when the governor sent reinforcements from Strawberry Bank (Portsmouth, N.H.). Knollys's house was besieged (nobody mentions whether the halberded Bible was still on display), and he and his supporters were punished. Both ministers soon returned to England, Knollys in 1641, Larkham in 1642. (Both became chaplains in the Parliamentary army, serving with neither happiness nor distinction.)

The affair reveals an unstable community polarized and shaken by religious dispute. Closely associated was the constitutional and jurisdictional issue of whether Dover should submit to New Hampshire or Massachusetts. And, if the records were adequate, we would probably see a social and economic division involving migration patterns, livelihoods, and landownership too. The aborted battle of Northam may have been a forerunner of the kind of intense community dispute that later did so much damage at Salem.[8]

But for present purposes, we must return to the book. Knollys, or one of his supporters, brandished the Bible above the heads of the mob, "mounted on an halberd, for an ensign." Like a legionary standard, like regimental colors, the book provided a visual focus for the disputants as well as talismanic protection. Who could prevail against the Book of God? And lo, their enemies scattered! Held aloft, the Bible served as an inspirational emblem and as a weapon, even without being opened. Knollys's dispute with Larkham hinged on biblical exegesis—hence his twenty-two articles—and the physical bound volume symbolized this textual and theological contest. Knollys's pole-top Bible was almost certainly a Geneva Bible, loaded (larded?) with Calvinist commentary, which waged symbolic battle against the Authorized (King James) version used by Larkham.[9] It was probably a quarto volume, in black-letter rather than roman type, and it would be interesting to learn how it was attached to the pole. Finally, we learn from Lechford that as the Knollys forces paraded into Dover, led by the Bible, they represented themselves as "Scots" and their opponents as "English." This can only refer to recent events in England, when the Scottish armies invaded to protest the imposition of the Anglican prayer book. It is worth remembering that the Scots revolt in 1638 began with the tossing of a book, the hated English *Book of Common Prayer*, across the aisles of Edinburgh Cathedral. By identifying with the Scots, who drew their inspiration from one book (the Geneva Bible) in defiance of another book (the English *Book of Common Prayer*), the dissidents at Dover cast their opponents as Laudians and as enemies of True Scripture. The Bible was an appropriate physical symbol for this contest, as well as for control of the Piscataqua congregation.[10]

To further understand this episode we must place it in the context of other symbolic or unorthodox uses of the Bible in early-modern England. The potency of the book on the pole makes more sense when we understand how people deployed the Bible in other circumstances. I shall describe two totemic uses: one in which the book was treated as a sacred object, and did not have to be opened to have its effect, and another in which some reading was required, although not of the sort that the church fathers intended.

An incident from the sixteenth century provides a convenient point of reference. In 1559, while Queen Elizabeth was in procession through the streets of London on her way to her coronation, she passed beneath an allegorical tableau on which a Bible was displayed. "A Bible in English, richly covered, was let down to her by a silk lace from a child that represented Truth. She kissed both her hands, with both her hands she received it, then she kissed it, afterwards applied it to her breast, and lastly held it up, thanking the City especially for that gift, and promising to be a diligent reader thereof."[11]

A full explication of this episode would require comment on Elizabeth's birth as a precipitant of the English Reformation, on her accession as a deliverance from Marian Catholicism, and on the earlier history of the English Bible, which Elizabeth's father had introduced into every parish. The silk thread from on high might be connected to the breath of God or the workings of a *deus ex machina*, while the Truth-child could be associated with Renaissance putti. More significant is Elizabeth's reaction, a ritual performance in several stages. First she kissed her hands (a purifying gesture?), then reverently took the book (as one might take the body of Christ at communion?), formally kissed it (an intimate transaction involving her own breath?), embraced it to her breast (more intimacy?), then held it high for all to see (as the priest might elevate the host?). When the book was proffered, the queen evidently knew exactly what to do, and the crowd and chronicler knew just what to observe. This episode only makes sense if we understand the "richly covered" volume as a sacred *object*, something like a totem or fetish fraught with ancestral, religious, and communal meaning.

Kissing the book was an important part of seventeenth-century court proceedings. A defendant not only swore to speak truth, "his hand upon the book," but also "must kiss the book, in testimony that he sweareth." Witnesses had to "lay their hands upon a Bible or Testament," then, having taken the oath, they "are to kiss the said book."[12] (One wonders, parenthetically, whether these books ever wore out from the repeated pressure of lips, or whether the constant kissing was a means of transmitting disease.) Swearing on a book was, in fact, in direct descent from the medieval practice of swearing on holy relics. The procedure did not require *opening* the book, and certainly needed no literacy. What was important was the public acknowledgment of the power of the volume to amplify and sanctify an oath.

Nor were courts of law unique in this regard. Dozens of incidents are known in which individuals made use of the Bible for magical, talismanic, or curative purposes. The holy book was credited with medicinal powers, as a universal specific, a remedy for ailments of all sorts. Some people believed that the holy pages had healing properties, quite apart from the text that was printed on them. The Bible might, for example, be invaluable in child-bearing, or be laid on the head of a restless patient in order to induce sleep. Seventeenth-century reformers attacked this practice—"surely God's word should rather awake men than cast them into a sleep," challenged the Puritan Barten Holyday—but it was not one they could easily eradicate. In other applications the Bible might be made a pillow, placed under the head, as a restorative, or simply be brought into the sickroom as an aid to health.[13]

On the eve of the English civil war the Royalist rector of Finningham, Suffolk, Edmund Taylor, told his parishioners that "a Bible in a house would keep the devil out." The mere presence of the book would ward off evil spirits. Since many diseases were thought to have spiritual or diabolic dimensions, such a device could be especially useful. It may be significant that in probate inventories that show the location of possessions room by room, the Bible was often found in the bedchamber, where it was available for use by the sick or dying.[14]

In 1703 an English traveler described primitive biblio-medicine as practiced in Scotland, "My landlord having one of his family sick of a fever, asked my book as a singular favour for a few moments: I was not a little surprised at the honest man's request, *he being illiterate*, and when he told me the reason of it I was no less amazed, for it was to fan the patient's face with the leaves of the Book; and this he did at night. He sought the book again next morning, and again in the evening, and then he thanked me for so great a favour, and told me the sick person was much better for it; and thus I understood that they had an ancient custom of fanning the face of the sick with the leaves of the Bible.'' Martin Martin, the Augustan Englishman who tells this story, cites it as an example of ''heathenism and pagan superstition'' found in the Western Isles. But he could have found similar instances closer to home.[15]

He could also have read in St. Augustine how the Gospel of St. John was laid on the heads of those suffering with fever, or recalled the ancient ceremony for consecrating a bishop, in which a Bible was laid on his head, ''as the means of communicating the Spirit and Christ's indwelling.'' And he would surely have been aware of those stories from the English civil war involving ''the marvellous preservation of soldiers by Bibles in their pockets which have received the bullets.''[16] The implication in all these cases is that the power of the Bible lay not simply in its text, to be unlocked by rigorous exegesis, but rather in its ineffable holiness, its sacred magic. The Bible as an object, symbolizing and encapsulating the word of God, was believed to do duty comparable to or superior to the Scripture as text.

Nor were such beliefs confined to remote areas or to the pre-industrial epoch. They are not unknown in modern Britain and modern America and may well have had credence in colonial New England. From old Hampshire, England, at the end of the nineteenth century, comes the extraordinary story of the woman who ''ate a New Testament, day by day and leaf by leaf, between two sides of bread and butter, as a remedy for fits.''[17] This may have provided excellent roughage, good for the digestion, but the physiological benefits were surely secondary to the psychological. Ingesting the word of God, and systematically destroying a book in the process, swept aside the need for conventional, and literary, religious practices. It places this Victorian countrywoman in the same tradition as those in the fifteenth century who employed communion bread as a poultice for boils or who wore scraps of paper with holy phrases as amulets to cure disease or as security for good health.

Literate and sophisticated people also found multifarious uses for the Bible. For many centuries men of letters had resorted to the *Iliad* or the *Aeneid* to help them resolve a crisis. Random opening of the text would display a phrase or passage that could then be interpreted as a guide to immediate action. This ancient practice, the *sortes Virgilianae*, survived into the modern era, with the printed Bible substituting for the pagan epic. In each case the primary book of the age, the most venerable writings of the culture, were brought to bear as implements for making decisions. Bibliomancy of this sort was widely used in seventeenth-century England, despite the misgivings of some Puritan divines. Some preachers disapproved of this undisciplined use of the Bible, quoting Deuteronomy 18 to the effect that divination is an abomination to the Lord. And since "to foreknow man's purpose or lot is God's prerogative," not ours, any attempt to guess the future is tainted with blasphemy.[18] Yet devout Christians, Puritans included, fell back on the *sortes Biblicae* when otherwise frustrated or lost.

Young John Dane, for example, was "utterly forlorn in . . . spirit and knew not what to do," before it occurred to him to go to New England in the early 1630s. The Bible, randomly opened, not only confirmed Dane's decision to emigrate but turned his parents from opponents to supporters of the venture. This is John Dane's story from "A declaration of remarkable providences in the course of my life." "I sat close by a table where there lay a Bible. I hastily took up the Bible, and told my father if where I opened the Bible there I met with any thing either to encourage or discourage, that should settle me. I opening of it, not knowing no more than the child in the womb, the first I cast my eyes on was: 'come out from among them, touch no unclean thing, and I will be your god and you shall be my people.'" That clinched the matter. "My father and mother never more opposed me, but furthered me in the thing, and hastened after me as soon as they could." By 1636 the Danes were settled at Roxbury, Massachusetts.[19]

It could be objected, of course, that Dane had fixed the book, or had so often studied the passage in question that it naturally fell open, or even that he made up the whole story to embellish his autobiography. But that would be beside the point. Dane and many of his contemporaries evidently believed in the power of the randomly opened book and sought meaning and guidance from phrases and verses culled quite separately from their scriptural context. A guiding message sprang out from the book on the table, like a voice from heaven or a *deus ex machina*. A few more examples will illustrate this practice of bibliomancy.

Arise Evans, a visionary preacher of the 1630s and 1640s, was launched on his career by a voice that told him, "Go to thy book." The voice alone, good enough for the likes of Joan of Arc, directed Evans to a superior source of wisdom, the holy text. "I suddenly started up," he relates, "and to the table went where my Bible lay open, immediately fastening mine eyes upon Ephesians 5.14, being these words . . . 'Awake thou that sleepest . . . and Christ shall give thee light.'" It might be argued that this was not strictly a *sortes Biblicae* since the book already lay open, perhaps where Evans had left off reading. But at other times, Arise Evans made deliberate and explicit use of the Bible as a source of random instruction and inspiration. In a state of religious frenzy, coupled with paralyzing indecision, "I opened the book three times suddenly, not caring where, and fastened mine eyes upon the place that first presented itself to me." This time the Bible gave him passages from Isaiah and from Joel, to the effect of "Awake ye drunkards" and "I have called him." Taken out of context, as personal messages, these stray verses gave Arise Evans the confidence and inspiration for his mission. Believing that God had called him to deliver a personal message of prophecy and warning to the king, Evans steeled himself for this task by once again employing a *sortes Biblicae.* "With much fear I opened the Book the fourth time, and the place was in Exodus . . . 'Behold I send an angel before thee.' " That was enough! Evans was on his way.[20]

The king himself, the target of Arise Evans's prophecies, is said to have employed books for predictive or divinatory purposes. One writer claims that Charles I resorted to a *sortes Biblicae* to help him decide whether to support or abandon the Earl of Strafford, and that another time he tried his fate with a copy of Virgil in the Bodleian Library. These stories are probably apocryphal, since Charles was the least superstitious of monarchs, but their circulation attests to the presumed power and efficacy of the book-opening process.[2]

In 1660 we find Lord George Berkeley, "being sick, and under some dejection of spirit, opening my Bible to see what place I could first light upon which might administer comfort." Berkeley's finger fell on the line in Hosea, "come, let us return unto the Lord," and at once he commenced a spiritual as well as medical recovery. Berkeley, a moralist of refinement and scholarship, felt sheepish in using such an unsophisticated practice, and so offers this apology: "I am willing to decline superstition upon all occasions, yet think myself obliged to make this use of such a providential place of scripture"[22] Providence supplied the key. The book had power, which could be released and focused through blind stabbing at a randomly opened page. God would so work it that an appropriate message would come to the fore.

Practices of this sort continued on both sides of the Atlantic long after the seventeenth century, testifying to the security people found in the book, as well as to their unschooled and irregular use of the text. An oracular fragment, randomly discovered, might be more serviceable than the underlying message of the Scriptures, and, of course, reading it took much less time and effort. As the most commonly available book in most households, and as the book invested with the most sacred power, the Bible was uniquely suited to this purpose. The Bible, the good book, contains hundreds of thousands of verses, which, like fortune cookies or readings from the *I Ching*, could be taken as counsels of comfort, incitements to action, or guides to the future. In America a widespread custom was to make a wish, and if the Bible opened at the words "it came to pass" the wish would come true.[23]

In Victorian Oxfordshire "it was customary to dip into the Bible before twelve o'clock on New Year's Day, and the first verse that meets the eye indicates the good or bad fortune of the enquirers through the ensuing year." We hear, for example, of the distress of a woman who remembered that she had not yet "dipped" in the Bible. "Last year," she reported, "I opened on *Job*; and sure enough, I have had nought but trouble since."[24]

As late as 1900 English folklorists could report that Bible "dipping" on New Year's Day "is a superstitious practice observed in some parts of the country, and much credit is attached to it. It is usually set about with some little ceremony on the morning, before breakfast, as it must be done fasting. The Bible is laid on the table unopened, and the parties who wish to consult it are then to open it at random. Wherever this may happen to be, the inquirer is to place his finger on the chapter contained in the two pages, but without any previous perusal or examination. It is believed that the good or ill fortune, the happiness or misery of the consulting party, during the ensuing year, will be in some way or other described and foreshown by the contents of the chapter."[25]

The *sortes Biblicae* involved reading, if only a single verse, but another popular practice made use of the Bible without any immediate connection to its text. The ritual of the book and key, as a sure guide to thief detection, was widely known in England from the Middle Ages to the modern period. Examples survive from before the Reformation; a writer in Lancashire in 1907 acknowledged that the practice "may not be even now entirely obsolete."[26]

William Newport, vicar of St. Owens, Gloucester, in 1551, used his Bible in the following manner. First he "inserted the key and tied the book up with string. He then invoked the Father, the Son and Holy Ghost, bidding the key to turn when he reached the name of the guilty party. It turned when he pronounced the name of Margaret Greenhill; and the participants left the chancel of the church, where the ritual had been carried out, to search the suspect's straw bed for the missing objects."[27] William Barckseale of Fareham, Hampshire, employed the book and key ceremony with similar success in the seventeenth century to identify some robbers. Examined in 1632 about "what art or meanes he used to discover those parties, saith he used no magical art or communication but only a key and a Bible."[28] In an eighteenth-century account, "a Bible having a key fastened in the middle, and being held between the two forefingers of two persons, will turn round after some words said, as, if one wishes to find a thief, a certain verse taken out of a Psalm is to be repeated, and those who are suspected nominated, and if they are guilty the Book and key will turn, else not.''[29]

Divination by book and key was reportedly ''very prevalent'' in Victorian England, especially in country areas. Nineteenth-century villagers in Surrey made use of the Bible for detecting a thief, in the ancient manner. With a key placed in the book of Ruth, chapter 1, verse 16, and the book tight shut with a string, ''the Bible falls to the ground'' when the name of the guilty party is pronounced. The same ''ordeal of the key and Bible'' was used to ensnare a thief on the Welsh borderlands in 1871. By then, however, the ancient practice had lost its power, so a supplementary test was made to find the criminal. In this case the thief-finders boiled a live toad inside a ball of clay, expecting the toad to scratch the name of the guilty party in the clay before it died.[30]

A variant of the ritual was in use in Victorian Lancashire, where the book and key were used to divine the name of a future lover rather than the name of a thief. A girl tied up the key in the Bible, again inserting the key at the book of Ruth. The key verse read ''whither thou goest I will go,'' and taken out of context it could be used in either courtship or thief detection rituals. ''Holding the Bible suspended by joining the ends of her little fingers inserted under the handle of the key,'' the girl recited the names of prospective suitors. When the right name was mentioned the book miraculously turned and the identification was made.[31]

The Lancashire girls had evidently mixed up two quite separate traditions regarding the nonliterary employment of the Bible. Besides the technique for identifying criminals, the Bible was also used, with naive irreverence, for forecasting the names of future lovers. '' 'Tis a custom among Country Girls to put the Bible under their pillows at night, with sixpence clapt in the Book of Ruth, in order to dream of the men destined to be their husbands,'' explains the eighteenth-century antiquarian John Brand.[32]

Reports of such practices provide valuable illumination of the darkest areas of social and cultural history. They indicate ways in which people made use of the tools at their disposal, Bibles in particular, to gain control over uncertainty or to rally to a common symbol. They also serve as a corrective to the view that books were simply conveyors of ideas and information, and that analysis of their text is enough.

Notes

1. *The Probate Records of Essex County, Massachusetts, vol. I, 1635–1664* (Salem, 1916), p. 141.

2. Natalie Zemon Davis, ''Beyond the Market: Books as Gifts in Sixteenth-Century France,'' *Transactions of the Royal Historical Society*, 5th ser., 33 (1983):

69–88. For examples of charitable distribution of books, see Richard Baxter, *Reliquiae Baxterianae* (London, 1696), p. 89; and "Diary of Cotton Mather," *Massachusetts Historical Society Collections*, ser. 7, 7 (1911): 54, 65. For theft of Bibles, possibly for superstitious purposes, see John Cordy Jeaffreson (ed.), *Middlesex County Records* (Clerkenwell, 1888), III: 24, 36. Professor D. W. Krummel reminds me of Sir Walter Greg's insistence that bibliography is "the study of books as physical objects, irrespective of their contents."

3. Joseph Addison, *The Spectator* 367 (1 May 1712); Holbrook Jackson, *The Anatomy of Bibliomania* (London: Soncino Press, 1930–1931), pp. 156–157; Margaret Spufford, *Small Books and Pleasant Histories: Popular Fiction and Its Readership in Seventeenth-Century England* (Athens: University of Georgia Press, 1982), pp. 48–50.

4. See, for example, Francis Steer (ed.), *Farm and Cottage Inventories of Mid-Essex 1635–1749*, 2nd ed. (London: Phillimore, 1969); Margaret Spufford, *Contrasting Communities: English Villagers in the Sixteenth and Seventeenth Centuries* (London: Cambridge University Press, 1974), p. 211.

5. For Bible ownership in England, see Peter Clark, "The Ownership of Books in England, 1560–1640: The Example of Some Kentish Townsfolk," in Lawrence Stone (ed.), *Schooling and Society* (Baltimore: Johns Hopkins University Press 1976), pp. 95–111; Norwich Survey Unit, University of East Anglia, files on "Probate Inventories and Book Ownership." For Bibles in New England probate inventories, see William B. Traske (ed.), *Suffolk County Wills* (Baltimore: Genealogical Publishing, 1984), and *Probate Records of Essex County* (Salem: Essex Institute, 1916).

6. See, for example, the striking depiction of Protestant Bibles as a battering ram, a shield, and a projectile against Papism, in Natalie Zemon Davis, "The Sacred and the Body Social in Sixteenth-Century Lyon," *Past and Present* 90 (1901): facing p. 57. The great Dr. Johnson is said to have used an Elizabethan folio edition of the Greek Bible to strike down a bookseller (Jackson, *Anatomy of Bibliomania*, p. 167).

7. Thomas Lechford, *New Englands Advice to Old England* (London, 1644), Sig.A3v, 44, my emphasis. Other versions of the story appear in James Kendall Hosmer (ed.), *Winthrop's Journal, "History of New England" 1630–1649* (New York: C. Scribner's Sons, 1908), II: 27–28; Jeremy Belknap, *The History of New Hampshire* (Boston, 1792), I: 34–51; Nathaniel Bouton (ed.), *Provincial Papers: Documents and Records Relating to the Province of New Hampshire* (Concord, N.H., 1867), I: 120–123. Modern commentators include Charles E. Clark, *The Eastern Frontier: The Settlement of Northern New England 1610–1763* (New York: Knopf, 1970), pp. 39–41; and Francis J. Bremer, *The Puritan Experiment* (New York: St. Martin's Press, 1976), p. 87. The account that follows is based on these sources, supplemented by Massachusetts Historical Society, *Winthrop Papers, Vol. 4, 1638–1644* (Boston: Massachusetts Historical Society, 1944), pp. 143–144, 176–179, 317–319; Everett Emerson (ed.), *Letters from New England* (Amherst: University of Massachusetts Press, 1976), pp. 229*n*, 180; David D. Hall, *The Faithful Shepherd: A History of the New England Ministry in the Seventeenth Century* (New York: Norton, 1974), p. 97; "Hansard Knollys," *New England Historical and Genealogical Register* 19 (1865): 131–132; William L. Sachse, *The Colonial American in Britain* (Madison: University of Wisconsin Press, 1956), pp. 135, 139; *Dictionary of National Biography, sub.* "Knollys," "Larkham."

8. Paul Boyer and Stephen Nissenbaum, *Salem Possessed: The Social Origins of Witchcraft* (Cambridge, Mass.: Harvard University Press, 1974).

9. Harry S. Stout, "Word and Order in Colonial New England," in Nathan O. Hatch and Mark A. Noll (eds.), *The Bible in America: Essays in Cultural History* (New York: Oxford University Press, 1982), pp. 31, 38.

10. For modern accounts of the English background, see Kevin Sharpe, "The Personal Rule of Charles I," in Howard Tomlinson (ed.), *Before the English Civil War* (London: Macmillan, 1983), pp. 53–78; and J. Sears McGee, "William Laud and the Outward Face of Religion," in Richard L. DeMolen (ed.), *Leaders of the Reformation* (London: Susquehanna University Press, 1984), pp. 318–344.

11. John Hayward, *Annals of the First Four Years of the Reign of Queen Elizabeth* (Camden Society, London, 1841), p. 17. For the context of this Elizabethan entry, see Sydney Anglo, *Spectacle, Pageantry and Early Tudor Policy* (Oxford: Clarendon Press, 1969), pp. 350–351.

12. H. Conset, *Practice of the Spiritual or Ecclesiastical Courts* (London, 1685), pp. 99, 100, 113.

13. Keith Thomas, *Religion and the Decline of Magic* (New York: Scribner, 1971), p. 45; Barten Holyday, *Motives to a Good Life* (Oxford, 1657), pp. 129–130; Jackson, *Anatomy of Bibliomania*, p. 170.

14. A. G. Matthews, *Walker Revised* (Oxford: Clarendon Press, 1948), p. 339.

15. Martin Martin, *A Description of the Western Islands of Scotland* (London, 1703), p. 248.

16. James Hastings (ed.), *Encyclopaedia of Religion and Ethics* (New York: Charles Scribner's Sons, 1926), II: 611; Baxter, *Reliquiae*, p. 46; W. H. D. Longstaffe (ed.), *Memoirs of Mr. Ambrose Barnes* (Durham: Surtees Society, 1867), p. 107; Jackson, *Anatomy of Bibliomania*, p. 166.

17. *Notes and Queries*, 9th ser., 8 (1901): 103. Ritual use of the Bible to cure nose bleeds, warts, and ganglions is recorded in modern America, in Wayland D. Hand, Anna Casetta, and Sondra B. Thiederman (eds.), *Popular Beliefs and Superstitions: A Compendium of American Folklore from the Ohio Collection of Newbell Niles Puckett* (Boston: G. K. Hall, 1981), pp. 1638–1639. I am grateful to Roger Abrahams for introducing me to American Bible folklore.

18. Thomas, *Religion and the Decline of Magic*, p. 118; Holyday, *Motives to a Good Life*, p. 128.

19. John Dane, "A Declaration of Remarkabell Provedenses in the Corse of my Lyfe," *New England Historical and Genealogical Register* 8 (1854): 152–154.

20. Arise (Rhys) Evans, *An Eccho to the Book Called a Voyce from Heaven* (London, 1653), pp. 10–15.

21. William E. A. Axon, "Divination by Books," *Manchester Quarterly* 26 (1907): 27; James Welwood, *Memoirs of the Most Material Transactions in England*, 3rd ed. (London, 1700), p. 106; Jackson, *Anatomy of Bibliomania*, pp. 179–181.

22. George Berkeley, *Historical Applications and Occasional Meditations* (London, 1670), p. 90.

23. See, for example, Vance Randolph, *Ozark Superstitions* (New York: Columbia University Press, 1947), p. 336; and J. D. Clark, "North Carolina Superstitions," *North Carolina Folklore* 14 (1966): 18.

24. *Notes and Queries*, 2nd ser., 12 (1861): 303.

25. T. F. Thiselton Dyer, *British Popular Customs* (London, 1876), p. 5.

26. Thomas, *Religion and the Decline of Magic*, p. 214; Axon, "Divination by Books," pp. 31, 32.

27. *Transactions of the Bristol and Gloucestershire Archaeological Society* 60 (1938): 120–121.

28. R. C. Anderson (ed.), *The Book of Examinations and Depositions, 1622–1644* (Southampton: Cox and Sharlands, 1931), II: 108.

29. John Brand, *Observations on Popular Antiquities* (London, 1813), II: 641.

30. *Notes and Queries*, 1st ser. (1850): 413; William Plover (ed.), *Kilvert's Diary 1870–71* (London: J. Cape, 1938), p. 301.

31. *Notes and Queries*, 1st ser. (1850): 5.

32. Brand, *Observations on Popular Antiquities*, II: 469, quoting from "Poems by Nobody" (1770).

Foundation for Service: The 1896 Hearings on the Library of Congress

Jane A. Rosenberg

The impending move to a new building and difficulties in Library operations led to a Congressional inquiry regarding the "condition of the Library of Congress" in 1896. Leaders of the American Library Association were unable to get the organization to endorse representation at the hearings. They obtained invitations to testify as individuals and presented their own agenda for the Library: national library services, a professionalized staff, and continuing ALA involvement through a board of visitors. Their requests were heard, but not granted. Similarly, Congress did not accept most of the expert advice regarding Library operations, concentrating instead upon replacing Librarian Ainsworth Rand Spofford and otherwise maintaining the status quo. Members rejected a proposal from the Joint Committee on the Library to assume control over Library appointments and regulations. Finally, they endorsed the wide span of control for the Librarian that had been the norm during Spofford's tenure. Congressmen and senators also retained their traditional access to Library patronage by giving the Librarian the power of appointment. The hearings are considered significant because they led to statutory endorsement of the powers of the Librarian, but the ALA leaders' testimony laid the foundations for the expansion of LC services.

On 5 May 1896 the U.S. Senate passed a concurrent resolution authorizing the Joint Committee on the Library of Congress (LC) "to sit in Washington, District of Columbia, during the recess of Congress, for the purpose of inquiring into the condition of the Library of Congress, and to report upon the same at the next session of Congress, with such recommendations as may be deemed advisable; also to report a plan for the organization, custody, and management of the new Library building and

Jane A. Rosenberg *is program associate, Council on Library Resources, Washington, D.C.* *The author wishes to thank John Y. Cole, Ronald Powell, Maris Vinovskis, Catherine Whitaker, and Wayne Wiegand for their comments on an earlier version of this paper. Thanks also to Wayne Wiegand for copies of several items cited in the notes.*

the Library of Congress."[1] This action signified two things: first, that a decade after it had been authorized, the mammoth seven-million-dollar building that towered over First Street, Southeast, was finally to be occupied; and second, that members anticipated that the move to the new Library would include more than a transfer of staff and books. Congress had spent a huge sum, much of it during hard economic times, for a monument that would rival the great European national libraries and symbolize the cultural aspirations of the nation. The size and magnificence of the building helped prompt more congressional attention to the Library's organization and services. Their interests included the patronage opportunities implied by the expansion of staff, encouraging more businesslike methods and economical operation, and improving the administration of the Library.[2] To obtain expert advice on the latter, they enlisted the help of leaders of the American Library Association (ALA), who seized the opportunity to urge the organization of American library services on the national level. This article analyzes congressional action and the initiatives taken by ALA leaders to influence that action and promote a new agenda for LC.

Librarian Ainsworth Rand Spofford and his small staff were no less interested in the progress of the new building than the members of Congress. The seventy-year-old Spofford had devoted his thirty-two years as Librarian to expanding the collections, lobbying for a new building, and obtaining recognition of LC as the national library of the United States. The first endeavor had led to the second: to insure comprehensive coverage of U.S. imprints, the Librarian had secured passage of a copyright deposit law in 1870, which built Library collections rapidly, but simultaneously resulted in severe space problems in LC's Capitol building quarters.[3] In 1877 *Library Journal* reported: "of the 315,000 volumes it [the Library] now numbers, 60,000 are piled about the floors"—"stacked up like cordwood," as William Frederick Poole added acidly.[4] Congress had authorized a new building in 1886, but disputes over design and construction had delayed the work. By 1896 only 400,000 of the Library's 740,000 volumes could be accommodated on shelves.[5]

Congressional attention to Library matters had focused mostly on the new building. Although Spofford was nominally responsible to the Joint Committee on the Library, in practice he controlled virtually all LC functions, albeit on a perpetually meager budget. Because Congress viewed copyright deposits as the major source of acquisitions, the Library's funds for books and subscriptions were limited to $11,000 per year—less, Spofford noted, "than is expended by twenty or thirty different moderate-sized libraries in the country." Neither had there been support for adequate staffing. When the Librarian requested $10,000 in

1894/95 for additional staff to handle copyright receipts, the economy-minded congressmen and senators appropriated only $6,800.[6]

By the mid-1890s, it was evident that the Library of Congress fell below contemporary standards of administrative efficiency. Many of the problems resulted from shortages of space and money, but some difficulties were traceable to the need for new leadership. Spofford's strengths were collection-building, speech-writing, fact-finding, and scholarship. He controlled the collections primarily by exercising a memory that contemporaries agreed was legendary, but his talents did not extend to large-scale organization and administration.[7] Moreover, fully three-fourths of his time was spent on copyright correspondence, records, and certificates rather than on the Library itself.[8] Two episodes revealed to Congress—and others—the extent of the difficulties. First, in 1895 the Treasury Department noted discrepancies in the copyright and payroll accounts, and at the President's request, investigated Spofford's book-keeping practices.[9] Then, in 1896, two Library employees stole manuscripts, including the diary of George Washington, from Spofford's office. The crime went undetected until a suspicious New York manuscript dealer raised the alarm. Although exonerated of wrongdoing, the Librarian was greatly embarrassed by both incidents.[10]

In anticipation of the move to the new building, the Appropriations Committee included in the March 1895 Appropriatons Act (for fiscal 1896) the requirement that the Librarian make a full report "touching a complete reorganization of the Library of Congress." Spofford's report, transmitted in December 1896, urged creation of nine separate departments: printed books, periodicals, manuscripts, maps and charts, works of art, catalog, binding, copyright, and superintendent of the building, with the law library and a reference library for Congress to remain in the Capitol. Included in his plans were the creation of the separate post of register of copyrights, and a staff of 97, including 39 for the copyright section; the Librarian noted that, in size, the current staff of 42 (of which 24 were assigned to copyright work) compared unfavorably with libraries of national stature that possessed fewer volumes and no copyright registration responsibilities: the British Museum, the national library of France, the Royal Library of Prussia, and, in the United States, the Boston Public Library.[11]

The responsibility for providing funds for the move rested with the Appropriations Committee, but the Joint Committee on the Library also planned its own special inquiry. When Rep. Lemuel Quigg (R-N.Y.) presented the Joint Committee's plan to the House, he cited completion of the building, the need for special legislation to accomplish the move, and "other matters related to the removal" as the primary justifications.

He also mentioned Congress's need for information regarding the custody and management of the building and "the space the library is to occupy." Undoubtedly thinking of Spofford's difficulties, Rep. Nicholas N. Cox (D-Tenn.) then asked whether the inquiry involved "the question of the Librarian." Quigg replied, "It does not," and Rep. Henry Bingham (R-Pa.), a member of the Appropriations Committee, added, "Not in any way." No such questions were raised in the Senate, where Library Committee chair Henry C. Hansbrough (R-N.D.) and Sen. William E. Chandler (R-N.H.) explained that the Joint Committee's task was to prepare recommendations for the Appropriations Committee.[12]

Having approved the inquiry, Congress decided to delay action on Spofford's request for additional staff since the building was not expected to be ready until early 1897. Members also rejected on 21 May 1896 a provision in the Appropriations conference report that would have allowed the Joint Committee to select a register of copyrights who might also function as general disbursing officer for the Library. Without questioning the need for such an officer, several senators voiced doubts about the constitutionality of the measure since Congress lacked the power to appoint executive officers of the government. All action on Library problems thus awaited the Joint Committee hearings.[13]

Postponing the task until after the tumultuous campaign of 1896, the Joint Committee scheduled its inquiry just before the new session was to begin. Sen. George Peabody Wetmore (R-R.I.) gaveled the Committee to order on 20 November. The list of witnesses included Bernard Green, who had charge of construction of the new building; Librarian Spofford; Dr. William T. Harris, commissioner of education; Samuel P. Langley, secretary of the Smithsonian Institution; and Dr. Cyrus Adler, its librarian. In addition to its accustomed informants, the Committee had also invited several "gentlemen of experience in library management," all of them members of the American Library Association.[14]

The Library of Congress and the ALA

The librarians' appearance before a congressional committee was an unprecedented occurrence. Before 1896 LC, as represented by Spofford, had observed merely those relations with ALA that professional courtesy demanded.[15] The story of intermittent ALA-LC contacts is chronicled in the pages of *Library Journal*, which reported the progress of the new building, and occasionally deplored Congress's failure to provide adequate support for the Library. The Association had provided assistance for Spofford in the form of resolutions and expressions of support for his building and staffing requests, and on two occasions had met in the Washington, D.C., area—in 1881, specifically to help the Librarian convince the Congress to build a new Library. Moreover, the Association accorded Spofford, both as a colleague and as Librarian of Congress, a position of respect aptly described by President Justin Winsor's phrase, "the official father of us all." There was also ample evidence that members thought they had a special stake in what many thought of as the national library.[16] As William Frederick Poole declared:

> Our interest in the Library of Congress arises not simply from the fact that it is one of the two great libraries of the country, but largely from the other fact, that it is a National Library, and that our citizenship gives us proprietary interest in it. We have, therefore, a right to meddle with its concerns, and to give our advice when we think it is needed. As individuals, and as an Association of American Librarians, there are duties which we owe to that library. We can serve it by getting the ears of the Senators and Representatives from our own States, and influencing them in its favor. As an Association, we can, by our united action, strengthen the hands of our worthy colleague, its chief executive officer, who asks for our advice and support.[17]

There were indications that ALA members wanted the Library of Congress to assume a more active role within the library community. Among the new functions they proposed for LC were the provision of space for the handling and distribution of public documents, initiation of interlibrary loans, and a separate copyright department.[18] Another proposal was that the Library operate a centralized cataloging service. Melvil Dewey, the most prominent advocate of the idea, had asked in 1876 whether it might not be practical for LC to catalog for the whole country, and others had occasionally voiced similar hopes. However, during the first ALA convention in 1876, an appeal to Spofford evidently proved fruitless. Advocates of cooperative cataloging had subsequently witnessed the failure of several schemes to provide subscribers with printed cards.[19] The Library remained a desirable place for such a project, however, since it received all U.S. imprints via copyright deposit and could provide both an established institutional base and the needed facilities.

The main obstacle to a wider role for the Library of Congress was obtaining the support of the Librarian. Spofford's limited acquaintance with the American library world was probably due as much to his own predilections as to his heavy workload, because cooperation with other libraries and librarians was not part of his conception of the role of the Library of Congress. In his view, a U.S. national library should be completely independent of other institutions, on the model of European national libraries. Although Spofford firmly believed that libraries should be used, and had pressed the Joint Committee on the Library to extend services to noncongressional users, the idea of LC as part of a national network of libraries was foreign to him. Thus, with the largest library collection in the country, the Library of Congress stood at the head of a rapidly growing list of public and institutional libraries, but, having developed independently, LC had never assumed—or aspired to—a position of leadership in the library world.[20]

Whether Congress would approve a more active LC role was unknown, but by the mid-1890s a foundation had been laid that might support approval of national library services. First, the Library had been opened to the public; and Congress had not contradicted Spofford's frequent assertion of national library status. Second, the value of libraries had been demonstrated through the use of tax dollars for their support, and precedents for government action and aid had been established by states through state libraries and library commissions. Finally, many librarians, educators, and congressmen had emphasized the importance of libraries in the educational enterprise. Publicly funded support for library services, therefore, would be a natural accompaniment to the ongoing expansion of educational opportunities.[21]

The ALA and Congress

Richard Rogers Bowker sounded a call to action in the August 1896 *Library Journal*. In an article titled "The American National Library," he stressed the importance of having the library community represented in the Joint Committee's inquiry, noted the likelihood that Congress would be receptive, and proposed that a special committee be appointed at the 1896 ALA meetings. A longtime member and chair of the ALA Committee on Public Documents, and also an experienced politician, Bowker saw the hearings as a means of bringing together the library community with a natural ally, if not leader, and he hoped that the inquiry might help to achieve statutory recognition of LC as the national library.[22] As *Library Journal* pointed out, the physical details of the removal of the books could "scarcely be discussed without developing in the course of the discussion the large scheme on which the national library must be administered in the future, if it is to be really the national library."[23]

However, in proposing to influence Congress directly, Bowker departed from ALA tradition. The role of the Association, as defined by its founders and maintained by a homogeneous leadership group, had been to provide a means of communication and a congenial annual meeting that served as both renewal and reward. This conception of the ALA's role had meant, in practice, resistance to having the Association make judgments on professional matters. It was assumed, for example, that individual libraries and librarians should retain autonomy with respect to the choice of methods for their own institutions. Early efforts to standardize and codify library processes encountered objections; and the ALA cooperative projects that were most successful were those that did not encroach upon the prerogatives of individual libraries. Proposals to impose sanctions or provide endorsements similarly encountered opposition; for example, the organization initially declined to take formal responsibility for as basic a professional matter as the education of practitioners.[24]

Previous ALA efforts to influence congressional action had been confined to urging individuals to contact their representatives or passing resolutions on such topics as federal documents distribution and the new building for the Library of Congress.[25] In 1882, when William Frederick Poole objected to plans for the new Library, he was exasperated enough to propose that the Association "be heard by the committee when the subject next comes up for consideration in Congress." But others resisted the attempt to influence Congress directly—partly because they were willing to accept Spofford's judgment, but also because they resisted any stronger expression of the Association's position.[26]

Melvil Dewey also had urged more active efforts to influence Congress. In 1890, speaking of the need for better distribution of public documents, he noted that the Association's work for such legislation spanned fifteen years and stated: "I don't believe we are going to accomplish much by passing general resolutions. The right thing to do would be to pick out the right man and send him to Washington to find members of Congress and senators who would follow this up. . . . Our old way is like trying to drive a tenpenny nail with a shingle."[27] Samuel Swett Green reported that Superintendent of Documents John G. Ames had recommended that librarians go to Washington and testify before committees, but added that he thought the suggestion impractical. Members of the Association's Public Documents Committee did occasionally visit their representatives in Washington, but confined their efforts to explaining libraries' needs.[28]

The early character of the ALA—ceremonial and social, deferential to individual opinions and practices, and reluctant to commit the membership to either standardization or discipline—was similar to at least one other contemporary professional organization. Thomas Haskell has described the rise and demise of the American Social Science Association (ASSA) as an early and ultimately inadequate response to the challenges posed by a modernizing society to social scientists who were students of that society.[29] Unlike the ALA, the ASSA was superseded by several major professional social science organizations—the American Historical

Association, the American Economic Association, and the American Political Science Association. During the years before 1890, the ASSA was "an aggregate of individuals." Members adhered to what Haskell characterizes as old habits of thought: self-reliance, individualism, and independence. As time passed, however, the Association's character and leadership changed.

Haskell found that what differentiated the old ASSA members from the new was a concept that he calls "interdependence." Recognition of interdependence entailed consciousness of new social linkages: a "tendency of social integration and consolidation whereby action in one part of society is transmitted in the form of direct or indirect consequences to other parts of society with accelerating rapidity, widening scope, and increasing intensity."[30] This consciousness differentiated the old ASSA members from the younger men who eventually founded separate professional organizations. It also linked the social scientists' world of ideas with contemporary society, for interdependence was a fact of socioeconomic life during the late nineteenth century, manifested in occupational specialization, improved transportation and communication, and the growth of the marketplace.[31]

Similar differences in views divided the old from the younger leaders in the American Library Association. In the library field, new leaders hoped to replace the old individualism with standardized methods and cooperative endeavors. Melvil Dewey's interest in cooperation and uniformity of practice encountered resistance in the early years. But when Dewey became ALA president in 1893, he was chosen as the result of a shift in membership and leadership from the old guard that had founded the Association and dominated it since 1876, to a new group that included individuals from libraries located outside the northeastern United States, more women librarians, and a growing number of library school graduates. Between 1892 and 1897, with the exception of Dewey, the ALA presidency was occupied by chief executives of large public libraries. Like other large library administrators in the 1890s, they were interested in acquiring materials rapidly and administering growing collections; and hence, seeking ways to achieve efficiency and economy—particularly in the labor-intensive work of cataloging and classification. Rather than devising new local schemes, they favored adoption of standardized methods that could guide large and small libraries alike, and also the employment of library school graduates trained in those methods.[32]

Dewey, Bowker, and other library leaders of the 1890s also had a different conception of the role of the ALA, and indeed, of the library profession, than men such as Justin Winsor, Ainsworth Rand Spofford, William Frederick Poole, William I. Fletcher, and others who had led the Association during the earlier decades. For example, the new leaders envisioned extending professional ties. Concerned to keep the increasingly diverse groups within the library community united, Dewey proposed that the various library clubs and organizations that had sprung up nationwide be affiliated with the ALA. He and others also were active in disseminating library influence in other groups such as the National Education Association, which, under the influence of John Cotton Dana, formed a librarians' section in 1896 that elected Dewey as its first president. The concern with the Library of Congress arose as part of a confluence of several endeavors congenial to the changing ALA membership and leadership: outreach and organization, cooperation, and harnessing interest in the national library to ideas for development of the entire library community.[33]

At the September 1896 ALA conference in Cleveland, Bowker introduced a resolution to appoint a seven-member committee "to represent this Association in relation to the reorganization of the National Library in preparation for the occupancy of the new building, and to take such steps as may promote the future development of the National Library on a more modern and most comprehensive plan." He added,

> We know that there have been certain difficulties in connection with the Library of Congress, and that perhaps it is not in all respects up to the time, and we have reason to suppose that this congressional committee will give hearings and will be glad to hear from this national Association. Perhaps if the committee is not of its own motion desirous of hearing the views of librarians, it is not less worth while that this national Association should put itself on record as being ready to offer suggestions to the congressional committee.[34]

Opposition to the resolution came almost entirely from Cyrus Adler, librarian of the Smithsonian Institution, who argued that the ALA should not intrude upon congressional matters without an invitation and protested the criticism of the Library and of Spofford implied by the formation of a committee. Insisting that reorganization of the Library was not intended to be part of the inquiry, Adler proposed leaving ALA action to the president and the council. With no recorded support for Bowker, the question was tabled until the next day, when Samuel Swett Green introduced a substitute resolution that had been composed by Herbert Putnam, director of the Boston Public Library, and approved by both Bowker and Adler. It specified that upon receipt of a Joint Committee request for "information or counsel," ALA President William Howard

Brett would appoint a six-member committee, led by himself, to furnish such information and counsel "as seems to them to represent justly the views of this Association." The substitute resolution was approved.[35]

The Inquiry

With the possibility for aggressive ALA action lost, the initiative passed to the Joint Committee. Probably due to Bowker's urging, the congressmen decided to ask President Brett to select some witnesses, and invited others. The list included Brett himself, director of the Cleveland Public Library; Melvil Dewey, secretary of the University of the State of New York, and director of the New York State Library; Herbert Putnam, director of the Boston Public Library; William I. Fletcher, librarian of Amherst College; George H. Baker, librarian of Columbia University; Charles C. Soule, trustee of the Brookline, Massachusetts, Public Library, and Rutherford P. Hayes, ALA secretary, and an Ohio state library commissioner and public library trustee. Among the witnesses, only Fletcher represented the old ALA leaders. Dewey, Hayes, and Baker all had advocated cooperative work. Putnam, although new to his position, had a reputation as an innovator, and was understood to be interested in organization and administration, as was Soule, who had visited nearly every large library in the United States and in England.[36]

During its first sessions, the committee heard testimony on the new building and the status of the Library. The chief questioner, Rep. Lemuel Quigg, had Superintendent Green provide a physical description of the building, and later Spofford led a tour through the new Library, describing his plans for the assignment of space. Beginning on 21 November and continuing through 26 November, the Librarian recited details of every aspect of library operations, ranging from ages and experience of the staff to the subjects and difficulties of every chapter in the classification scheme, pausing only to allow Langley and Adler to answer questions regarding the relationship of the Smithsonian Institution to the Library.

Although Spofford was the principal witness, just over half of the hearing transcript consists of the other librarians' testimony, with Dewey and Putnam providing the longest statements. The ALA members had little or no time to prepare statements or anticipate questions, but they dwelled, at Quigg's direction, on possibilities for the future and on issues of organization and administration. Although representing a variety of institutions and perspectives, the librarians voiced remarkably similar opinions on the scope and organization of the Library of Congress.[37]

Rep. Quigg's questions to Melvil Dewey began with the statement that the committee wanted to know "what the Congressional Library can acomplish for the country." Dewey responded directly, going to the heart of what he and others had hoped: "we shall never accomplish our best results in librarianship until we have at the National Library in Washington a center to which the libraries of the whole country can turn for inspiration, guidance, and practical help, which can be rendered so economically and efficiently in no other possible way."[38] Emphasizing that the Library would not meet "the modern ideal" until a catalog was prepared, Dewey pointed out the benefits of having cataloging done for the entire country at LC:

> We have perhaps 4,000 public libraries in the country of 1,000 volumes or more. If a book is published that 500 of these libraries will buy, where can you think of a greater waste than that every one of the 500 should have to undertake, each for itself, with, in most cases, limited bibliographic machinery and insufficient force, to catalogue that book when it has been already catalogued in the National Library by the most expert staff in the country, having at their disposal every known resource? Printing is very cheap. Any library willing to pay the cost of paper and postage could have a copy of these cards furnished without extra expense to the Government which has already paid for making its own cards. This distribution of printed catalogue cards has long been the dream of librarians. . . . It would mark an era when the National Library was ready to do this incalculable service to the libraries and students of the country.[39]

The other witnesses endorsed Dewey's request. Fletcher recommended merely that the Library be involved in cooperative ventures, but Putnam stressed that by providing a uniform system, the Library might influence other institutions to adopt proper practices. Others emphasized the need for national support for library activities such as interlibrary loan, reference and bibliographic services, a union catalog, public documents distribution, and the exchange of research materials.[40]

In connection with their interest in having LC undertake new responsibilities, all of the witnesses expressed the hope that the Library of Congress would be recognized as the national library. Baker and Hayes suggested that Congress make the national library an independent department, while Dewey noted that a Capitol branch library should be sufficient for congressional use, while LC, as the national library, engaged in activities that had nothing to do with Congress. He also advocated that the national library gather in "whatever the nation wishes to preserve or exhibit in connection with literature, art, science and history." Drawing a comparison with the State University of New York, he asserted that the Library ought to be united with the Bureau of Education and the National Museum in a "single national educational department," including a museum of fine arts. However, Putnam, Brett, and Baker dissented. Putnam in particular emphasized that without unlimited funds, "a library universal in scope is not practicable"; in his view it was the bibliographic and cataloging work that the Library of Congress was best fitted to adopt on a large scale and only a certain amount of work could expediently be undertaken.[41]

The Joint Committee, however, wanted more from the librarians than ideas for a national library. The Committee, Quigg said, had called in experts for specific purposes: one was to obtain information about other libraries' operations, and the other, to receive practical advice regarding the Library of Congress's needs for the legislative appropriations bill. Spofford had addressed a 42-item questionnaire to the officials of three national libraries—those of Great Britain, France, and Germany, and the answers documented the comparative lack of resources provided to LC. Several of the ALA members pointed out that LC's budget and staff also were less than in the largest libraries in the United States, and they declared that Spofford's estimates of future needs were too small. The Librarian had requested that the staff be more than doubled, and he wanted a 50 percent increase in copyright staff. But Spofford had requested only eight catalogers; Dewey told Quigg that twenty were needed. Soule endorsed Dewey's estimate, but Putnam, whose Boston Public Library staff totaled 112, thought that even twenty was too few. At Boston, the librarian commented, sixteen catalogers were able to keep up with accessions of 30,000 volumes per year, but only due to the presence of eighteen additional employees in the shelf list and ordering departments. Putnam, who also employed forty-four staff members in the reading room and stacks, thought that the new Library of Congress would require 250 employees.[42]

Dewey had called attention to libraries' need for trained staff, and his description introduced the subject of LC appointments. On 6 May 1896 President Cleveland had added 30,000 positions to the civil service, thus increasing the number of federal workers on the merit system by more than one-third. It was the largest proportional increase in the service ever mandated, and congressmen and senators had protested the president's action. Members were understandably disinclined to concede any additional patronage prerogatives, and Republicans were particularly insistent upon this point, since the election of William McKinley made it certain that they, as the majority party, would again receive their full share of offices. It was not an auspicious time to urge inclusion of the Library in the civil service system, and when Quigg began his questions on the topic of staffing, he noted that congressional employees traditionally were controlled by Congress, a policy against which "this committee does not, perhaps, feel it can wisely undertake to make a fight."

Since the Committee intended to retain congressional control over LC employees, the librarians emphasized the need for experience and library school training for the technical and administrative positions. In general, they favored the civil service system. But because library directors' enthusiasm for civil service arose primarily from the wish to prevent political control of library employment, they were open to discussing suitable alternatives to the merit system. Dewey readily accepted Quigg's suggestion of special competitive examinations conducted by librarians for the Committee as being "much the same thing" as civil service; and under the congressman's prodding, most of the witnesses admitted that they preferred a "rather elastic" system such as that of the Boston Public Library, where the librarian examined and selected his own employees.[43]

With regard to one appointment, however, there was a clear consensus. Although the library world had been reluctant to criticize Spofford, the witnesses obviously felt that other competencies were needed to manage an institution of the Library's status. As *Library Journal* put it: "Mr. Spofford has been so busy with the mass of detail which he has undertaken to handle that he has not trained himself as an executive for this kind of work, nor been able to keep in touch with the modern developments of library organization and practice." Putnam, more tactfully, stated the belief that it was necessary "to render the Library more independent of the physical limitations of any one man or set of men; in other words, that the time has come when Mr. Spofford's amazing knowledge of the Library shall be embodied in some form which shall be capable of rendering a service which Mr. Spofford as one man and mortal can not be expected to render."[44]

The "modern developments" that the witnesses felt were most urgent were to organize and fully catalog the LC collections. To this end, several of them alluded to the desirability of transferring business and copyright affairs to other officials, but others noted that more than technical knowledge and a new job description were needed. Dewey, Fletcher, and Putnam all thought that the chief administrator ought to exemplify "superior executive ability and efficiency," but it was Putnam who emphasized these qualities most. He opted for an administrator as opposed to a bookman, noting that the officer need not be "a profound bibliographer or need to know the most of all the persons in the library, as to what the library contains."[45] He compared the position to that of the president of a university:

I presume that the modern college president considers that his

> chief function is to secure the best men for each department, and to administer on a large scale this business, and see that the business is conducted properly, and to secure great efficiency, and more especially at the beginning, to consider and determine the scope of the work to be undertaken, to form plans on a large scale. . . . I don't say a knowledge of specialties, in addition to these capacities, would be inconsistent with them, but it seems to me that those capacities are undoubtedly necessary, and that the chief executive must have them preeminently.[46]

Putnam's sketch of the Librarian as administrator, planner, and efficiency expert fitted well with the congressional desire for good management and economy in Library operations. However, after the inquiry, the Boston librarian decided that he had failed to balance his portrait of the chief executive as administrator with that of the chief as a professional able to appreciate the needs of the specialized departments. He wrote the Committee a supplementary letter to that effect. Summarizing the ALA members' testimony, Putnam pointed out their essential agreement, and underscored the consensus on the necessity of introducing "mechanical aids" while retaining "personal mediation between the reader and the books."[47]

Results of the Hearings: The ALA

The implications of the librarians' testimony were clear: it was time to provide the Library of Congress with the technical expertise and adherence to the principles of modern librarianship that its collection and status deserved. It was also time for the Library to assume a leadership role and to provide national library services to the growing library community. The January 1897 issue of *Library Journal* announced that "the future of the national library in its new home is really *the* library question of the year," because "that this library will ultimately become in name as it is in fact the national library is beyond doubt, and the failure to recognize now this manifest destiny and to provide now on the large scale which this implies will be nothing short of a national misfortune."[48]

A second "library question of the year" was what additional action the ALA would take. President Brett had disclaimed any desire to "intrude advice" upon the Congress. However, it appeared possible that the congressional request for expert testimony might set a precedent for a future advisory role. Spofford testified that he had thought that a board of trustees might provide "closer and more constant supervision" for the Library, and, with the exception of Fletcher, the librarians agreed on the need for a supervisory group. Dewey suggested "a board of the most eminent citizens of the country'' for the national library, and Baker had proposed two committees, one consisting of librarians and the other, of scholars. After hearing Baker's ideas, Rep. Quigg had suggested that the ALA reincorporate under U.S. law, an act that would permit the Association to offer advice to LC through a formal board of visitors.[49]

This proposal seemed advantageous in several respects. Prospects appeared favorable for increasing cooperative activities with LC, and even, perhaps, for obtaining government assistance for establishing an ALA headquarters and hiring a staff member. There might also be a means of expanding the publishing program if Congress authorized government printing of ALA manuscripts—as it had for the American Historical Association and the National Academy of Science, both of which had federal charters. The official recognition also would enhance the ALA's status as the national professional library organization.[50]

Putnam, Dewey, Fletcher, and Baker petitioned the ALA board to consider Quigg's offer to introduce a bill for reincorporation, and the board passed unanimously a resolution stating the desirability of reincorporating and locating an ALA headquarters in Washington. Hoping to act quickly, before Congress lost interest, Dewey urged Putnam to ask for a special membership meeting on the question. At the meeting, held in New York City on 6 February 1897, a committee composed of Putnam, Dewey, and Bowker presented a resolution authorizing the executive board to proceed with reincorporation. However, a substitute motion that merely asked the board to consider the matter and report at the next annual conference was adopted instead. *Library Journal* explained that reincorporation had not been accepted because ''It did not seem advisable under the circumstances of the present Congress . . . it was the general opinion that the time was not yet ripe for this act, and that any action toward this end should be taken in full conference.'' In the absence of assurances that the Joint Committee was ready to secure passage of the reincorporation bill, and also without an invitation from Congress to constitute a board of visitors, members thought that ''the Association certainly could not afford to put itself in the position of seeking aggrandizement for itself by a crusade in its own behalf.'' Those present at the special meeting had been unanimous in their verdict—and Putnam, Bowker, and Hayes made a public statement declaring their agreement with the decision to defer action.

None of them, however, had changed their minds on the visitation issue. ''I did not and do not see,'' wrote Putnam to *Library Journal*, ''why the Association should decline to render such a service, provided the Library of Congress be a national library, whose administration is a matter of national concern, and provided the A.L.A. be the best representative of the experience and judgment of the library profession of the

United States and of the interests represented in the libraries of the United States.'' Tying the reincorporation decision to the board of visitors proposal had caused the difficulties: Putnam explained that he had become aware that ''certain prominent members of the A.L.A.'' felt that the ulterior motive of visitation would underlie any application for a charter. In fact, it was old guard leaders such as Justin Winsor and John Shaw Billings who had voiced objections to any ALA alliance with LC. When the reincorporation question was raised again at the 1897 conference in Philadelphia, discussion was postponed—as it turned out, permanently.[51]

Results of the Inquiry: The Library

The reorganization of the Library did not await the report of the Joint Committee, which was not published until March 1897. Instead, the day after the inquiry ended, Spofford was called to testify at the Appropriations Committee's hearings, which had begun unusually early in the session. On 12 December Quigg, Hansbrough, and Harmer also appeared, to provide information on the Joint Committee inquiry.

The House took up the appropriations bill immediately. When debate on the Library portions occurred on 17, 19, and 21 December, it became evident that the bill the Appropriations Committee had approved nullified most of the Joint Committee's authority over LC, and, thus, any advice it might offer concerning reorganization. The issue on which the two committees disagreed was the future control of the Library. The Joint Committee proposed that the Library be administered by a library director appointed by the President, under whom the Librarian and Register of Copyrights would serve. Every staff member except the director would be appointed by the Joint Committee, which would thereby assume responsibility for greater control over LC. In contrast, the Appropriations Committee bill made no change in the position of Librarian. Its plan empowered the Librarian to make all LC appointments on the basis of ''special aptitude for library work,'' and in accordance with whatever rules he elected to impose, in effect, endorsing the power that Spofford had exercised. The two committees agreed on the personnel estimates that Spofford had revised after the Joint Committee inquiry, but the Appropriations Committee declined to increase funds for the purchase of materials.[52]

Joint Committee members were displeased that they had completed a lengthy inquiry only to be denied influence over legislation. During the debate, Quigg consequently offered the Committee's proposal as a substitute motion. Disclaiming any desire to concentrate Library patronage in the hands of Committee members, Quigg explained that examinations would be required for certain Library positions. Committee members, he said, had found the librarians' information both interesting and important; they would continue to seek advice from the profession. But in planning for the Library's future, the majority of the Committee had concluded that:

> Large powers under the law as it exists today seem to devolve upon the Joint Committee on the Library; and yet the law is so worded that while the powers of the committee seem to be ample, there are many respects in which the committee would not care to act without specific instruction from Congress. The legislation which we propose here is submitted for the purpose of obtaining from Congress either a release from all administrative functions or such clear direction and such ample authority as will warrant the committee in assuming the responsibilities which already the law implies.[53]

Members of the Appropriations Committee Joseph G. Cannon (R-Ill.), William A. Stone (R-Pa.), and Alexander M. Dockery (D-Mo.) attacked the substitute motion on the grounds that vesting power of appointment in the Committee was unconstitutional and that a national library required an executive with the power of appointment and removal. The proposal to retain patronage received extended and sometimes humorous attention, as representatives inquired about the availability of places on the Joint Committee. But, "in organizing this great library in that gorgeous new building," Dockery pleaded, "let us not make the grave mistake of also organizing a scramble for 187 offices to be disposed of under the direction and control of the joint Committee of the two Houses, to the detriment of public service." With a choice between control of appointments to the Library staff by their colleagues or by the Librarian, members obviously preferred the old system, in which they dealt with Spofford rather than with peers. After a number of amendments had been offered and defeated, including a proposal to place the Library under civil service, the Joint Committee substitute was defeated by an overwhelming majority, 85 to 27.

The Appropriations Committee bill directed the President to name a Librarian when the law went into effect—a broad hint that a new man was needed. Dockery explained that "the national library should be in charge of a management fully abreast of the progress of the times," and should perhaps employ a graduate of one of the new library schools "whose sole function, I am advised, is to equip gentlemen for the discharge of the duties of librarian."[54] Having decided to ask the President to appoint a new Librarian, the Appropriations Committee apparently thought that there would be no need for an outside supervisory group. When, in the Senate, a question was raised regarding the need for a board of regents, Sen. Cullom (R-Ill.), who had charge of the bill, replied that the Committee had decided to adopt the arrangement stated as a tentative one, hoping that in the future they "might get the way clear for a better arrangement later on if it shall seem necessary to provide for one." Since not even the Joint Committee proposal had included such a board, it appears that its members had rejected the idea very soon after the inquiry.[55]

Because Congress had decided to retain sole control over its Library, independent national library status was not considered either in the Appropriations Committee hearings or in floor debate. Passed on 18 February 1897, the appropriations bill endorsed the Librarian's virtually complete control over the Library proper, including making rules and regulations and selecting and dismissing staff. A Senate amendment to enhance its control over LC by requiring confirmation of the President's appointments of Librarian and Superintendent was accepted by the conference committee.[56]

The appropriations bill provided the librarians with few consolations. National library status had not been enacted, and the new law incorporated little of the expert advice offered by ALA members. In place of the twenty or more catalogers they had recommended, the act included only nine; there was no increase in the appropriation for books; and rather than a mandate to provide national library services, the bill replicated the Librarian's report of 1895 by enumerating departments to be included in the new building. Although both a separate register of copyrights and a superintendent of building and grounds were included, the idea of a board of visitors had been discarded.

Perhaps the most encouraging provision was the stipulation that qualified personnel be selected for the Library service; but subsequent events proved that the new law did not eliminate political pressures. The burden of satisfying both the provisions of the law and congressional requests remained with the Librarian, who himself remained essentially a political appointee, although subject to Senate confirmation. After making unsuccessful efforts to recruit both Putnam and Dewey, President McKinley nominated his old friend, journalist and diplomat John Russell Young, as Librarian. Upon taking office on 1 July 1897, Young, with an ample file of congressional requests, began to select new staff. *Library Journal*, stating that Spofford's retirement as Librarian came as no surprise, regretted the appointment as a signal "that the Library had been turned over as a fair field for the spoilsmen."[57]

Conclusion

By 1896 the American Library Association had been in existence for twenty years, and its continuing activity had helped foster the visibility of library work as an occupation. Through its meetings, members had encouraged the development of systems of classification and cataloging, and other technical advances; they had observed the growth of professional education programs, and they had formed an organizational community to exchange information and formulate cooperation projects that had potential for improving the field as a whole. At first, the ALA did not contribute much more than this to professional organization, since members valued their independence and individuality more than a strong association.

Whether those interested in standardized methods and cooperative work could find ways to get the Association to accept their views was a crucial question. Well into the 1890s, it seemed that some of their enterprises had made little progress, although the organization itself was becoming more diverse in membership and new leaders were more interested in uniform methods. The opportunity, in 1896, to influence the Congress's thinking about the future role and status of the Library of Congress—or as many librarians considered it, the national library—was unexpected. The subject was one of considerable interest to the membership, even though the Association had not engaged in more than rudimentary political activity. In the views of at least some ALA leaders, participation in the hearings provided an important opportunity to influence prospects for services to the entire library community, and to obtain a continuing voice in the affairs of a national library. When the ALA failed to approve action, individual members and officers testified instead, thereby establishing precedents for professional involvement with the Library of Congress, and for organizing the library community around a set of goals for a national institution. Librarians had already achieved the formation of a professional community organized around mutual concerns. Congress's recognition of that community provided public acknowledgment of librarians' professional credibility.[58]

On the surface, ALA influence on Congress appeared negligible. However, even though the 1896 inquiry is usually remembered most for helping to establish the unique powers of the Librarian of Congress, the event also marked the beginning of a wider role for the Library. The ALA members presented the idea of a professional library community linked by services provided by a central facility: the national library. Their desire for businesslike administrative practices and uniformity in methods was congenial to legislators who had similar interests during a period when efficiency was becoming a national concern. And the Library of Congress's need for both efficient administration and the technical knowledge of cataloging and classification that librarians had developed during the decades preceding the mid-1890s was evident. The Library could both provide assistance to and profit from the community the ALA represented. In effect, articulating the logical professional interdependence of the Library of Congress and other libraries provided a foundation for service—a foundation that was to be useful two and one-half years later when Herbert Putnam, with ALA support, became Librarian of Congress and proceeded to fulfill many of the hopes librarians had voiced in 1896.

Notes

1. The original resolution, passed 23 March 1896, provided for the chairmen of the House and Senate Committees on the Library of Congress and one other member of each committee (to be chosen by each chair) to constitute a Joint Special Committee to sit during the recess; and it had been intended to include the Botanic Garden. This was modified, first by the Senate Committee to Audit and Control the Contingent Expenses of the Senate, which struck out the reference to the Botanic Garden, and, on referral to the House, by Rep. Quigg's amendment to have both full committees sit in order to provide for minority representation. *Congressional Record*, 54th Cong., 1st sess., 1895–1896: 3072, 4367, 4791 (hereafter cited as *Cong. Rec.*).

2. John Y. Cole, "A National Monument for a National Library: Ainsworth Rand Spofford and the New Library of Congress, 1871–1897," *Records of the Columbia Historical Society of Washington, D.C.* 48 (1971–1972): 479–495, 505; *Cong. Rec.*, 47th Cong., 2nd sess., 1882–1883: 221; 50th Cong., 1st sess., 1887–1888: 5392–5393; 54th Cong., 2nd sess., 1896–1897: 319, 2714; *Library Journal* 22 (1897): 1–2 (hereafter cited as *LJ*); Beverly Lynn Elson, "The Library of Congress" (Ph.D. dissertation, University of Maryland, 1981), pp. 55–75, 177–179.

Congressional interest in reviewing administrative efficiency and economy had been most recently manifested in the work of the Dockery-Cockrell Commission, during 1893–1895. See Leonard D. White, *The Republican Era, 1869–1901* (New York: Macmillan, 1958), pp. 66–68, 84–92.

3. See John Y. Cole, "Of Copyright, Men, and a National Library," *Quarterly Journal of the Library of Congress* 28 (1971): 123–136.

4. *LJ* 2 (1877): 82; William Frederick Poole, "Progress of Library Architecture," *LJ* 7 (1882): 131.

5. U.S. Congress, Joint Committee on the Library, *Condition of the Library of Congress*, 3 March 1897, 54th Cong., 2nd sess. Senate Report 1573 (Washington, D.C.: Government Printing Office, 1897), p. 28 (hereafter cited as *Condition of the Library of Congress*).

6. Joint Committee on the Library, Extracts from Minutes, 1861–1898, Library of Congress Archives, Manuscript Division, Library of Congress; John Y. Cole, *For Congress and the Nation: A Chronological History of the Library of Congress* (Washington, D.C.: Library of Congress, 1979), pp. 29–51; *Condition of the Library of Congress*, pp. 29–32, 47–48, 112–113; *Cong. Rec.*, 53rd Cong., 2nd sess., 1894–1895: 3937, 4310–4311; U.S. Congress, House of Representatives, Committee on Appropriations, *Hearings on the Legislative, Executive and Judicial Appropriations Bill for 1897*, 54th Cong., 2nd sess., 1896 (Washington, D.C.: Government Printing Office, 1897), pp. 114–115 (hereafter cited as *Appropriations Committee Hearings, 1897*); Stephen Skowronek, *Building a New American State: The Expansion*

of National Administrative Capacities, 1877-1920 (Cambridge: Cambridge University Press, 1982), p. 50; White, *The Republican Era*, pp. 66-68, 84-92.

7. *LJ* 19 (1894): 309; 20 (1895): 301-302; 21 (1896): 4, 22; *Condition of the Library of Congress*, p. 228; Richard R. Bowker, ''Seed Time and Harvest: The Story of the ALA,'' *ALA Bulletin* 20 (1926): 305; *New York Tribune*, 6 December 1896, 21 December 1896.

8. In the 1890s alone, copyright deposits had increased from 48,908 in 1891 to over 70,000 in 1896. And Spofford, in spite of the fact that he was not legally required to do so, signed every certificate himself, *Condition of the Library of Congress*, pp. 127-129.

9. The Ainsworth Rand Spofford Papers, Manuscript Division, Library of Congress, contain letters of sympathy and support, and a letter of 29 June 1897 confirming an appointment with the President; see also Grover Cleveland to Spofford, 15 June 1895, Grover Cleveland Papers, Manuscript Division, Library of Congress; *LJ* 20 (1895): 265, 288, 301-302, 325; *Evening Star* (Washington, D.C.), 10 July 1895, 21 August 1895.

10. *Evening Star* (Washington, D.C.), 23 April through 1 May 1897; *Washington Post*, 10 December 1897; *New York Tribune*, 12 February 1897, 30 March 1897, 11 December 1897;Fred Shelley, ''Manuscripts in the Library of Congress, 1800 1900,'' *American Archivist* 11 (1948): 11-14; *LJ* 22 (1897): 160, 274, 364.

11. Spofford's report essentially extended ideas expressed in his annual reports as early as 1872. U.S. Congress, Joint Committee on the Library, *Special Report of the Librarian of Congress*, 3 December 1897, 54th Cong., 2nd sess., 1896-1897, Senate Document 7 (Washington, D.C.: Government Printing Office, 1895); 28 Stat 764; *LJ* 21 (1896): 18-19; *Condition of the Library of Congress*, p. 47.

12. *Cong. Rec.*, 54th Cong., 1st sess,, 1895-1896: 4791, 4821.

13. *Cong. Rec.*, 54th Cong., 1st sess., 1895-1896: 4821-4822, 5496-5507; 2nd sess., 1896-1897: 265; 29 Stat 140.

14. *Condition of the Library of Congress*, p. ii; *LJ* 21 (1896): 471.

15. LC histories of the period generally omit reference to LC-ALA relations. See, for example, David C. Mearns, *The Story Up to Now* (Washington, D.C.: Library of Congress, 1947). Frederick W. Ashley's draft history of the Library (in the Library of Congress Archives, Manuscript Division) jumps from the organization of ALA in 1876 to 1899, when Herbert Putnam became Librarian, and William Dawson Johnston's fragmentary notes for a second volume of his history of the Library (William Dawson Johnston Papers, Manuscript Division) contain little that is relevant. A useful secondary account is John Y. Cole, ''LC and ALA, 1876-1901,'' *LJ* 98 (1973): 2965 2970.

16. *American Library Journal* 1 (1876): 139; *LJ* 4 (1879): 48; ''Papers and Proceedings of the American Library Association,'' *LJ* 4 (1879): 224, 281-282, 303

17. Poole, ''Progress,'' p. 131.

18. *LJ* 4 (1879): 48, 303; 8 (1881): 203; 8 (1882): 278; ''Papers and Proceedings of the American Library Association,'' *LJ* 21 (1896): 358; Ernest C. Richardson, ''Cooperation in Lending among College and Reference Libraries,'' *LJ* 15 (1890): 32-36.

19. The fact that Dewey was the inventor of a new classification system that he hoped would be widely adopted did not diminish his interest in standardizing library cataloging. See Wayne Wiegand, ''Melvil Dewey and the American Library Association,'' in Gordon Stevenson and Judith Kramer-Greene (eds.), *Melvil Dewey: The Man and the Classification* (Albany: Forest Press, 1983), pp. 114-115; ''Cooperative Cataloging,'' *American Library Journal* 1 (1876): 171;

"B.C.," "A National Library System with a Universal Catalogue," *American Library Journal* 1 (1876): 369–371; *American Library Journal* 1 (1876): 120, 290–291; *LJ* 21 (1896): 440, 463.

20. Ainsworth Rand Spofford, "The Function of a National Library," in Herbert Small (ed.), *Handbook of the New Library of Congress* (Boston: Curtis and Cameron, 1899), pp. 123–128; John Y. Cole, *Ainsworth Rand Spofford, Bookman and Librarian* (Littleton, Colo.: Libraries Unlimited, 1975), pp. 26, 38–41; *Condition of the Library of Congress*, p. 74; Cole, "Ainsworth Rand Spofford, The Valiant and Persistent Librarian of Congress," in *Librarians of Congress, 1802–1974* (Washington, D.C.: Library of Congress, 1977), p. 120.

By 1896 Spofford had attended only two ALA conferences in addition to the two held in Washington, D.C., although he occasionally assisted with ALA committee work and cooperative bibliographic projects.

21. Melvil Dewey, "The Library and the State," *LJ* 15 (1890): 135–136; *LJ* 21 (1890): 131; John Y. Cole, "Ainsworth Spofford and the 'National Library'" (Ph.D. dissertation, George Washington University, 1971), p. 144; Cole, "A National Monument," pp. 482–483.

22. R. R. Bowker, "The American National Library," *LJ* 21 (1896) 357–358; *LJ* 21 (1896): 439; E. McClung Fleming, *R. R. Bowker, Militant Liberal* (Norman: University of Oklahoma Press, 1952).

23. *LJ* 21 (1896): 439.

24. Francis Miksa, "Charles Ammi Cutter: Nineteenth Century Systematizer of Libraries" (Ph.D. dissertation, University of Chicago, 1974), pp. 684–689; George Watson Cole, "The Future of Cataloging," *LJ* 15 (1890): 172–176; Lewis H. Steiner, "Should Uniformity Mark the Arrangement and Administration of Our Public Libraries, or Should Individuality be Permitted to Assert Itself in Each?" *LJ* 16 (1891): 57–61; *LJ* 14 (1889): 284–285; *Condition of the Library of Congress*, p. 49; Sarah K. Vann, *Training for Librarianship before 1923* (Chicago: American Library Association, 1961), pp. 22–38; "Papers and Proceedings of the American Library Association," *LJ* 16 (1891): 112–113.

25. "Report of the Committee on Public Documents," *LJ* 15 (1890): 96–98; see also note 19 above.

26. *LJ* 6 (1881): 203; Poole, "Progress," pp. 130–134; *LJ* 8 (1883): 269–275, 278.

27. *LJ* 15 (1890): 104–105.

28. "Report of the Committee on Public Documents," *LJ* 15 (1890): 97–98; 17 (1892): 77–79; 18 (1893): 52–53; 19 (1894): 126–127; 20 (1895): 79–80.

29. Thomas Haskell, *The Emergence of Professional Social Science: The American Social Science Association and the Nineteenth-Century Crisis of Authority* (Urbana: University of Illinois Press, 1977).

30. Ibid., pp. 28–29.

31. Ibid., pp. 14, 43–44. Haskell echoes the shift that other historians have indicated, from a series of isolated communities to an urbanized, industrialized, more highly interactive society. See John Higham, "The Reorientation of American Culture in the 1890's," in his *Writing American History: Essays of Modern Scholarship* (Bloomington, Indiana University Press, 1970); Samuel P. Hays, *The Response to Industrialism, 1885–1914* (Chicago: University of Chicago Press, 1957), and "The New Organizational Society," in Jerry Israel (ed.), *Building the Organizational Society: Essays on Associational Activities in Modern America* (New York: Free Press, 1972); Robert Wiebe, *The Search for Order, 1877–1920* (New York: Hill and Wang, 1967); R. Jackson Wilson, *In Quest of Community: Social Philosophy in the United States, 1860–1920* (London: Oxford University Press, 1968); Morton

White, *Social Thought in America: The Revolt against Formalism* (Boston: Beacon, 1957). He also acknowledges a debt to Thomas Kuhn's *The Structure of Scientific Revolutions*, 2nd ed. (Chicago: University of Chicago Press, 1970).

32. Wiegand, "Melvil Dewey and the American Library Association," pp. 113–121; Wiegand, "View from the Top: The Library Administrator's Changing Perspective on Standardization Schemes and Cataloging Practices in American Libraries, 1891–1901," *Reference Librarian* 9 (1983): 11–27; Francis Miksa, *The Subject in the Dictionary Catalog* (Chicago: American Library Association, 1983), p. 164; *LJ* 15 (1890): 323; 18 (1892): 371.

33. *LJ* 20 (1895): 58–61; 22 (1897): 3.

34. "Papers and Proceedings of the American Library Association," *LJ* 21 (1896): 81.

35. Ibid., pp. 82–83. Because the Smithsonian Deposit was part of the Library of Congress, Adler was closely associated with Spofford. The 1896 ALA Conference was the first he had ever attended. See *Condition of the Library of Congress*, pp. 42–43, 50–54, 94–96; *LJ* 21 (1896): 112–113.

36. R. R. Bowker to Lemuel E. Quigg, 18 November 1896, and Bowker to Rutherford P. Hayes, 24 November 1896, R. R. Bowker Papers, New York Public Library; Cole, "LC and ALA," p. 2967; *Condition of the Library of Congress*, pp. 138, 169, 228, 267; *LJ* 17 (1892): 4–5; 21 (1896): 455–456, 463; 22 (1897): 4, 14; "Papers and Proceedings of the American Library Association," *LJ* 21 (1896): 79.

37. William I. Fletcher to R. R. Bowker, Bowker Papers, New York Public Library; *Condition of the Library of Congress*, pp. 170, 228, 266.

38. Ibid., p. 142.

39. Ibid., p. 145.

40. Ibid., pp. 145–149, 169–170, 188–189, 206, 230–232, 242–243, 266.

41. Ibid., pp. 143, 161–167, 189, 206–207, 222–227, 234, 244, 262; "A Congressional Library or a National Library?" *LJ* 22 (1897): 7–9.

42. *Cong. Rec.*, 54th Cong., 2nd sess., 1896–1897, p. 417; *Condition of the Library of Congress*, pp. 154–159, 171–173, 189–202, 211, 220, 264–265; U.S. Congress, House of Representatives, Committee on Appropriations, *Hearings before Subcommittee on House Committee on Appropriations: Legislative, Executive and Judicial Appropriations Bill for 1898* (Washington, D.C.: Government Printing Office, 1896), pp. 84–89 (hereafter cited as *Appropriations Committee Hearings, 1898*).

43. The number of positions available at LC was small compared to the 92,000 workers still outside the examination system, but even so, congressmen apparently felt they could not afford to relinquish any opportunities to assist job-seekers. Melvil Dewey to John Shaw Billings, 9 December 1896, John Shaw Billings Papers, New York Public Library; Paul Van Riper, *History of the United States Civil Service* (Evanston, Ill.: Row, Peterson, 1958); Skowronek, *Building a New American State*, pp. 68–74; *Condition of the Library of Congress*, pp. 169–179, 181–184, 201–204, 214–216, 224–225, 235, 242–243, 247–249, 264.

44. Edith Clark to William Howard Brett, 13 October 1896, William Howard Brett Papers, Cleveland Public Library; *LJ* 22 (1897): 4.

45. *Condition of the Library of Congress*, pp. 148–158, 221–239

46. Ibid., p. 221.

47. Ibid., pp. 225–228.

48. Ibid.; *LJ* 22 (1897): 3–4.

49. *Condition of the Library of Congress*, pp. 112–113, 143, 162–163, 207–213, 267–268.

50. David D. Van Tassel, "From Learned Society to Professional Organiza-

tion: The American Historical Association, 1884-1900,'' *American Historical Review* 89 (October 1984): 940-941; *LJ* 22 (1897): 92; Wayne Wiegand, *The Politics of an Emerging Profession: The American Library Association, 1896-1917* (forthcoming).

51. R. R. Bowker to Herbert Putnam, 24 December 1896, and Herbert Putnam to Bowker, 29 December 1896, Bowker Papers, New York Public Library; *Condition of the Library of Congress*, pp. 212-213; *LJ* 22 (1897): 91-92; Wiegand, *The Politics of an Emerging Profession.*

In fact, just after the Joint Committee ended, it was evident that Congress would not support the idea of a board of visitors; see discussion below.

52. Mearns, *The Story Up to Now*, p. 126; John Y. Cole, ''Herbert Putnam and the National Library,'' in Harold Goldstein (ed.), *Milestones to the Present*, Fifth Library History Seminar (Syracuse, N.Y.: Gaylord Professional Publications, 1978), p. 112; *Condition of the Library of Congress*, pp. i-ii; *Appropriations Committee Hearings, 1898*, pp. 82-89, 109-113; *Cong. Rec.*, 54th Cong., 1st sess., 1895-1896: 4791.

53. *Cong. Rec.*, 54th Cong., 2nd sess., 1896-1897: 314.

54. ''Method of Appointments in the Library: The Debate of 1896 (Dec. 17, 18, 21) in the House of Representatives,'' typescript, Library of Congress Archives; U.S. Library of Congress, *Use of the Congressional Library, Statement of Mr. Spofford, Librarian of Congress, January 18, 1897*, 54th Cong., 2nd sess., 1897, Senate Document 65 (Washington, D.C.: Government Printing Office, 1897); *Cong. Rec.*, 54th Cong., 2nd sess., 1896-1897: 377-391, 1945-1947; *Appropriations Committee Hearings, 1897*; *New York Tribune*, 18 December 1896; *Evening Star* (Washington, D.C.), 16 December 1896; *New York Times*, 22 December 1896; *Washington Post*, 16 December 1896.

55. *Cong. Rec.*, 54th Cong., 2nd sess., 1896-1897: 977.

56. *Cong. Rec.*, 54th Cong., 2nd sess., 1896-1897: 975-977, 1945-1947; *Washington Post*, 16 December 1896; 29 Stat 538.

57. *LJ* 22 (1897): 340, 366; undated typescript memo regarding 1897 LC appointments, and ''Thirty-three Years a Bureau Chief,'' typescript, Thorvald Solberg Papers, Manuscript Division, Library of Congress; James C. M. Hanson, ''The Library of Congress and Its New Catalogue: Some Unwritten History,'' in William Warner Bishop and Andrew Keogh (eds.), *Essays Offered to Herbert Putnam* (New Haven: Yale University Press, 1929), pp. 178-194; *Cong. Rec.*, 54th Cong., 2nd sess., 1896-1897: 1947.

58. Haskell, *The Emergence of Professional Social Science*, p. 19.

Library Politics and the Organization of the Bibliographical Society of America

Wayne A. Wiegand

When the American Library Association turned most of its attention to improving practice and technique in American public libraries shortly before the turn of the century, a number of ALA members located primarily in large academic and privately endowed research libraries became disenchanted. At first, they organized the Bibliographical Society of Chicago in 1899; later they replaced it with the nationally based Bibliographical Society of America in 1904. The desire to identify scholarly and research bibliography as a separate research province constituted the major reason for organizing the BSA outside the library profession.

In November 1858 *Historical Magazine* published a letter to the editor from "A Student of American Bibliography" who, after noting the recent organization of several professional associations, cited the need for "an American Bibliographical Society."[1] Forty-six years later organizers met at an American Library Association (ALA) conference in St. Louis on 18 October 1904 to establish the Bibliographical Society of America (BSA). Why did it take nearly a half-century for people interested in bibliography to answer the student's call? Two authors have provided a skeletal chronology of events leading to BSA's formation in 1904,[2] but to date no one has explored existing primary source materials in which the foundation for a more comprehensive, detailed, analytical history resides. This paper is an attempt to provide that analytical account. Tracing historical threads connecting the two events involves close analysis of complex issues that surface from a series of movements and pressures within the library community. The story that emerges from this research shows that the BSA was founded by privately endowed research and academic library employees whose self-perceived needs ran counter to the direction in which ALA was taking the nation's library community.

Wayne A. Wiegand *is associate professor of library and information science, University of Kentucky.*

The author would like to thank the University of Kentucky Research Foundation for travel funds necessary to complete the research on this article.

On 6 October 1876 the centennial conference of librarians agreed to form the American Library Association "for the purpose of promoting the library interests of the country, and of increasing reciprocity of intelligence and goodwill among librarians and all interested in library economy and bibliographic studies."[3] That ALA founders saw fit to add these last three words is significant. In 1876 librarianship was in its professional infancy. Librarians had not yet forged a professional identity, and, in their efforts to make themselves attractive to as wide a group as possible, ALA founders also courted those interested in bibliographic studies. Besides, many of the nation's most prominent librarians—Boston Public Library superintendent Justin Winsor, Chicago Public Library director William Frederick Poole, Boston Athenaeum director Charles Ammi Cutter, and Librarian of Congress Ainsworth Rand Spofford, to name but a few—were also bibliographers. The tie seemed natural; librarians engaged in bibliographical work.

Over the next thirty years, ALA's constitution underwent several changes as the Association struggled to keep pace with changing times and increased demands upon the profession. A "public library movement" gained momentum in the 1890s, and ALA, heavily influenced by New York State Library director Melvil Dewey's call for efficiency and standardization, responded in kind. As Andrew Carnegie accelerated his multimillion-dollar benefactions to erect hundreds of public libraries across the nation, ALA assumed the role of advocate of the public library as the "people's university." From that role ALA developed a distinct profile: the Association addressed itself primarily to the public library community and advocated the publication of practical bibliographies to serve the needs of the ever-increasing numbers of library employees (the vast majority of whom were women) in small public libraries. The ALA *Handbook* for January 1897 declared on its front page: "The Association seeks in every *practicable* way to develop and strengthen *the public library* as an essential part of the American educational system" (emphasis mine). By 1897 ALA even dropped the words "bibliographic studies" from its constitution and substituted the vague terminology "others engaged in library or allied educational work." A draft of a revised constitution considered at the 1899 conference simply stated that ALA's object "shall be to promote the welfare of librarians in America."

The Association's publishing section, organized in 1886, had most success selling practical bibliographies and bibliographic aids like *Reading for the Young* (1890; supplement, 1896), *List of Subject Headings for Use in Dictionary Catalogs* (1895), and *List of Books for Girls and Women and Their Clubs* (1897). Likewise, *Public Libraries* (*PL*) and *Library Journal* (*LJ*), the profession's two major journals, emphasized public librarianship and practical bibliography. In addition, by the turn of the century, four library schools enrolled over 200 students, each of whom passed through a technical curriculum emphasizing the efficiency, standardization, and mechanics that Dewey advocated for librarianship. It was no coincidence that Dewey organized and ran the nation's first library school and that heads of the other three (Drexel, Pratt, and Armour in Chicago) were graduates of his curriculum. Finally, in 1900, nineteen states had their own state library associations; sixteen elected public library employees as association presidents.[4]

One group remained within the Association, however, that occasionally addressed the needs of the individuals interested in scholarly and research bibliography. The College Section organized in 1889 to discuss concerns of common interest not being considered in general meetings at ALA conferences. For a time bibliographers employed in libraries found an occasional forum for their interests here. But two late-nineteenth-century developments—one in philanthropy, the other in higher education—worked against this loose relationship. In the last quarter of the nineteenth century several wealthy individuals left sizable estates specifying the establishment of privately endowed research libraries. While the Lenox, Astor, and Tilden trusts funded the research arm of the New York Public Library in the nation's metropolis, half a continent away the newly founded Newberry and Crerar Libraries likewise created a need for staff with a more sophisticated working knowledge of research and scholarly bibliography. This new group of professionals had needs the ALA's College Section was hard-pressed to meet. The latter concentrated on the more practical problems of the academic library administrator, an emphasis in which the former had little interest. In addition, academic librarians at large prestigious universities became increasingly aware of their institutions' demands for research production. Seeking an area of endeavor that better fit this environment, they seized upon scholarly bibliography as a research province they could call their own, with which they could identify, and which promised to augment their status within the scholarly research communities on campus and within the nation. This new breed of librarian was dedicated to the "advanced" stage (or what they called "the higher departments") of library work.[5]

Although all these developments served as a nexus for the formation of a bibliographical society, like other organizations the BSA still required the energy and persistence of one individual who willingly assumed the role of catalyst. That self-assumed resonsibility fell to Askel Gustav Solomon Josephson, a Swedish immigrant. Josephson had worked as librarian of Uppsalás Verlandes Arbeitarbibliothek in the early 1890s, but in the summer of 1893 he emigrated to the United States to enroll in the New York State Library School in Albany that fall. He withdrew before completing the program; if attitudes he subsequently expressed about library education are any indication of his reasons for leaving, he probably disliked Dewey's emphasis on technique and preferred the more scholarly training expected of European librarians. Whatever his reasons, however, he did bibliographic work for *Publisher's Weekly* for a while, then became a cataloger at the Lenox Library in New York City. In 1896 he accepted a position as chief cataloger of the recently founded John Crerar Library in Chicago, where he labored for the remainder of his professional life. Josephson was an ambitious fellow eager to make a contribution to his profession, which he thought sadly lacked emphasis on bibliographic scholarship.

With this in mind he called together several Chicago library colleagues in the summer of 1899 to consider plans for a local bibliographical society. Besides himself, librarians attending included Charles H. Hastings of the University of Chicago Library, Juul Dieserud of the Field Columbian Museum, Streingrimur Steffanson of the Newberry Library, and Carl B. Roden of the Chicago Public Library. The mix is significant; of the five, three were ALA members, but only one an academic librarian; three were immigrant research library employees who had firsthand knowledge of the nature of European librarianship. After two more informal meetings, the group appointed a temporary organizing committee consisting of Josephson (chair), Hastings, Mabel McIlvaine of the Newberry, and Professor Frederick Ives Carpenter of the University of Chicago, and charged the committee to draft a constitution and issue a call for membership in a Bibliographical Society of Chicago. *LJ* announced in its August issue that the organizers "proposed to combine, if possible, the interests of the practical, scientific bibliographer and that of the lover and collector of books, although those who have originated the movement have the former interest most at heart." Eleven pages prior to this announcement *LJ* reprinted Josephson's letter to the editor lamenting ALA's lack of emphasis on bibliography. "Until the [ALA] executive board has perfected the plan for preventing duplication of bibliographic work," he wrote, "I would suggest that the *Library Journal* be made a medium of information on the subject."[6] *LJ* ignored his suggestion.

And an air of discontent stirred elsewhere. On 11 October 1899 librarian William Warner Bishop of the Polytechnic Preparatory School in Brooklyn forewarned ALA secretary Henry J. Carr that academic librarians within the ALA were getting restless. "They are beginning to realize that they cannot combine their work with that of the public libraries, and the ones of their number who have some spirit of independence and progress are stirring up the others." Bishop did not elaborate. Twelve days later the Bibliographical Society of Chicago formally organized "1, to encourage and promote bibliographical study and research; 2, to compile and publish special bibliographies''; and ''3, to arouse interest in the history of books and libraries.'' Officers elected included Hastings as president, McIlvaine as vice-president, and Josephson as secretary. At its inaugural meeting on 8 December 1899, the society voted to compile a report on valuable libraries in the Chicago area, to provide bibliographic descriptions of rare and valuable books in these libraries, and to list incunabula and forward it to John Thomson of the Free Library of Philadelphia, who was compiling an incunabula bibliography in American libraries. Thus the society wasted no time distinguishing its self-assigned responsibilities from ALA, and especially from the latter's Publishing and College sections. By its first annual meeting on 19 April 1900, Josephson reported that the society boasted ninety-six members, including forty-nine librarians, eight booksellers, and eleven university professors. He also noted that fourteen members did not even reside in the Chicago area.[7]

Josephson was active on two other fronts that spring. He recommended to William Coolidge Lane, Harvard College librarian and chairman of the ALA Publishing Section, that ALA undertake the preparation of a general bibliography of American literature. Then on 12 April 1900 he read a paper before the Chicago Library Club entitled ''Preparation for Librarianship.'' In it he lamented that curriculum emphasis on developing skills in methods in library schools came at the expense of developing skills in scholarship. ''But there must be a real scholarship behind the method,'' he implored his listeners; ''otherwise the schools will produce mere technical workers without appreciation of or acquaintance with the aims of scholarly activity.'' He went on to advocate a two-year curriculum for library schools, the first year devoted to method, the second year ''entirely devoted to professional studies,'' the ''top and crown'' of which would be a thesis that would ''very often take the form of a bibliography.'' Such a system would allocate the same importance to scholarship that German librarians insisted upon, ''and there is no reason why we in America should be behind in this respect.'' Overtones of ''advanced'' and ''higher departments'' of library work rang in his concluding remarks. ''We must keep above our work lest we sink below it. In all intellectual, as in other organic life, stagnation means retrogression and death. The only condition of life is conscious progress.''[8]

In the meantime, the ALA Publishing Section was having problems. Since organizing in 1886 the section had been controlled by Ivy League college library directors who advocated the publication of special bibliographies, indexes, and aids primarily to serve the library user. The ALA *Index* was perhaps the best example. But ALA members representing small public libraries being built largely in the Midwest by Carnegie money argued that the Publishing Section had misplaced priorities. Most of these smaller libraries did not even subscribe to the magazines and periodicals covered by the *Index*. Instead, they called for a "tracts" series designed to assist the largely untrained librarians in charge of these libraries. Although the publishing section acquiesced to the pressure, individual numbers in the series experienced delays.

In April 1900 Frank Hutchins, secretary of the Wisconsin Free Library Commission, wrote Reuben G. Thwaites, the director of the Wisconsin State Historical Society, who was also ALA president for that year, to discover reasons for the delays. Thwaites then wrote Carr, who responded on 18 April 1900 that the "hitch" was Lane. Apparently, Carr said, the section chairman complained that several of the tracts were "not quite up to the *Harvard standard.*" Carr also reminded Thwaites of Lane's "disposition to disregard and belittle anything done by or emanating from women."[9] He did not have to remind Thwaites that by 1900 a majority of ALA members were female, as were several tracts authors. Thwaites, Carr, and Hutchins eventually won their point, but Lane could not have been satisfied with the direction in which ALA was forcing him to take the Publishing Section. Philosophically and professionally, he found his interests more in tune with the objectives of the Bibliographical Society of Chicago.

While Thwaites would brook no attempt to thwart the will of a vocal majority on the direction of the Publishing Section, on another issue he took a minority position. On 22 November 1899 he asked Springfield (Mass.) Public Library director John Cotton Dana to chair the ALA committee on library schools. He complained that in the past the committee reports had been "rather perfunctory, being mere synopses of the official reports of the schools themselves. Let us have a different sort this year." Josephson agreed. He urged Dana to change the committee's name to reflect an expanded thrust he thought extremely important. Call it a "committee on instruction in librarianship and bibliography," he argued, which would hold library schools to the high quality standards he had already outlined in his 12 April address to the Chicago Library Club. He also suggested that the committee visit all library schools at least once a year at ALA expense. Dana thanked him for his suggestions, but noted ALA could not afford his scheme without the revenue generated by a substantial increase in membership. Josephson disagreed. Not more members, he argued, but a large endowment was needed

> to carry out the work that it [ALA] properly should do. The only solution that I can see at present is to interest some millionaire to endow the association. But then, the association must first show that it is trying to do something which is worth paying for. For instance, the ALA should publish the Library Journal, and edit it

> through its paid secretary. It should offer a course of instruction in really advanced bibliography and librarianship, [and] it should offer scholarships to young progressive librarians so as to enable them to pursue some special studies, either at home or abroad. Among other things, it should stand up for the profession, try to get the profession recognized as such by higher salaries, for instance, or by shorter hours, which would enable librarians and library assistants to undertake some bibliographic work or some serious studies. And at last, it should try to induce more *first class men* to take up library work.

Josephson's comments are revealing. He obviously thought ALA a weak organization unwilling or unable to lead librarianship to a higher status within the community of scholars. Like Lane, he was also uneasy about the growing feminization of librarianship and its impact on the profession. Dana agreed that ALA ought to publish its own organ, but, concerning his recommendations for courses in scholarly or advanced librarianship and bibliography, said, ''I presume you are right, though personally I am more interested in somewhat different movements on the Association's part.''[10]

Because Josephson could find no allies on Dana's library school committee, or apparently even within ALA, he turned to another forum. On 16 July he published a paper in *Dial* magazine entitled ''Wanted—A Bibliographical Institute.'' In it he cited the need for such extensive bibliographical undertakings as cooperative cataloging, a national bibliography, and a critical bibliography of bibliographies, but he noted at the same time that such monumental tasks ''cannot be attempted except by a specially founded Bibliography Institute,'' with a large endowment and a competent staff of bibliographers and scientific men. ''An endowment for one institution of this kind,'' he continued, ''would be of as much value as the endowment of ten public libraries.''[11] The appeal to Carnegie's philanthropy was unmistakable; if ALA would not go after the steel magnate's millions, Josephson implied that he would. What he did not know, however, was that several privately circulating plans for bibliographic work already had their sights set on Carnegie's fortune. Only later would these become public.

In the meantime, the Bibliographic Society of Chicago continued to hold regular meetings. On 1 November members cited the need for an annually updated bibliography of English literature that would do for that genre what Germany's *Jahresbericht* did for German literature. In January 1901 society members discussed the recommendations for a bibliographical institute that Josephson had made in *Dial*. In March the society issued the first number of its ''Contributions to Bibliography'' series—*Bibliography of Bibliographies: Chronologically Arranged, With Occasional Notes and an Index* by Aksel G. S. Josephson. In April it published a yearbook reprinting papers read before the society.[12]

But Josephson was not the only ALA member who wanted to increase emphasis on bibliography within the Association. In September 1900 the Librarian of Congress, Herbert Putnam, had appointed William Dawson Johnston to the Library's division of bibliography. Putnam had been Librarian for only 17 months, but during that short period he had made it clear to the nation's library community that he wanted the Library to assume a leadership role in library affairs. He was already working on a scheme with members of ALA's Publishing Section to issue and market prepared catalog cards of recently issued published titles. Because Putnam's aggressive leadership filtered down to his staff, it was not surprising that Johnston began advocating the formation of a bibliographical section within the ALA that could issue through its Publishing Section a bibliographical yearbook based on the work of his division. He asked advice from Boston Public Library director James L. Whitney, who suggested Johnston contact Josephson. The latter responded quickly and eagerly, but his response was so ambitious Johnston decided to show Josephson's letter to George Parker Winship, director of the John Carter Brown Library in Providence, Rhode Island.

Winship knew Josephson and cautioned Johnston against allowing the BSC secretary too much control in the organization of an ALA bibliographical section. "Josephson's a hustler," Winship remarked, "with national peculiarities which would unfit him for leadership. But he would do most of the work on anything he went into, and do it well." When the BSC acknowledged at its 4 April 1901 meeting that a bibliographical institute was beyond its means, it also directed Josephson to contact LC's bibliographical division. Josephson took his case directly to Johnston. "In order to do really important work," Josephson said, BSC "needs a larger constituency, and if we go along as we have a couple of years more, and enlist in our membership bibliographers not only in Chicago but from all over the country, we might some time be in shape to take up something of a larger scope. We have already over twenty non-resident members." Josephson did not even mention ALA as a possible vehicle for expansion.[13]

Nor did the BSC secretary tell Johnston of his plans for the forthcoming ALA meeting in Waukesha, Wisconsin, 3–10 July 1901. Josephson was scheduled to chair an informal round table meeting on "Professional Instruction in Bibliography." To prepare his case better, and perhaps to lay the groundwork for subsequent action, Josephson asked U.S. commissioner of education William T. Harris on 27 May for his views on a postgraduate training program in bibliography, which perhaps could be located in the nation's capital. Harris replied on 2 July that he liked Josephson's ideas, but he suggested any advanced school of bibliography in the Washington area ought to have some formal connection with the Library of Congress, and he was not at liberty to speak for Putnam.[14] Josephson had to go to Waukesha without the commissioner's endorsement.

Before the scheduled round table meeting, however, Josephson attended two other conference sessions. At a College and Reference Section meeting held 4 July, he suggested a bibliography of university theses. He also nominated Oberlin College Library director Azariah Smith Root as section chairman for the next year. Root was subsequently elected. That same day Josephson attended a BSC meeting held for members present at the ALA conference. Crerar director Clement W. Andrews presided. First order of business was a paper by John Thomson entitled "A Bibliographical Society of America," read in his absence by Carl Roden. Thomson, like Josephson not enamored of ALA's direction toward efficiency and standardization and away from scholarship and bibliography, suggested the BSC ought to develop a national body with a headquarters and paid officers—perhaps at the Library of Congress—who would collect current and past bibliographical works. At first BSC members balked at Thomson's bold suggestion. William Beer of the Howard Memorial Library in New Orleans called instead for a union list of bibliographies. William I. Fletcher of the Amherst College Library said the Library of Congress was already collecting bibliographical works soon to be available on interlibrary loan. Josephson himself thought local bibliographical societies ought to be formed and eventually organize into a federated national council. Andrews recommended that the BSC continue for at least another year, issue a few more publications, and, when non-Chicagoans outnumbered residents among the membership, the society should consider forming a national organization. Fletcher's motion to appoint a committee to consider Thomson's suggestions and report at a future BSC meeting passed.[15]

Six days later Josephson called to order a round table discussion on professional instruction in bibliography. He began with a formal presentation entitled "A Post-Graduate School of Bibliography." The word "bibliography," he argued, had two general definitions—one narrow, one broad. The former defined bibliography as a science of the book that provides the means for finding information in book sources and formed the foundation of contemporary formal library education that emphasized "the technical side" of library work. The latter, which he preferred because it also concentrated on the book's subject matter, its intellectual description, and its appropriate classification, would take library education much further by fostering the development of "solid bibliographic scholarship.'' This could only be accomplished, however, if professional schools attached themselves to large research or university libraries and offered courses in bibliography similar to those taught by Professor Karl Dziatzko at the University of Göttingen.

In the discussion that followed, Root described his bibliography courses at Oberlin; Andrew Keogh elaborated on the course he taught at Yale; and George W. Harris recounted the substance of his lectures on bibliography at Cornell. Other participants included Walter M. Smith of the University of Wisconsin library, J. I. Wyer of the University of Nebraska library, and W. Stetson Merrill of the Newberry. All agreed with Josephson's call for more ''solid bibliographic scholarship,'' and most regarded the scholarship evident in European librarianship as a model that Americans should emulate. Although round table participants moved no particular actions to improve the situation, their discussions were published in the conference proceedings. Analysis of the proceedings shows that those who participated were mostly men in prominent academic and research libraries who felt the need to raise the status of their profession through bibliographical scholarship, and to create broad awareness of the value of such scholarship among academic faculty and students.[16] The Waukesha conference had brought them together to share concerns and make plans for the future. Some of the ideas Josephson had been espousing for two years had finally found a sympathetic audience within ALA.

After the conference Josephson forged ahead. In October he published a letter to the editor of the *Library Journal* advocating the appointment of a ''commissioner of bibliography'' for the St. Louis World's Fair, scheduled for 1904. Among other duties, the commissioner ''should arrange a bibliographical exhibit, as comprehensive as possible, not only of American endeavors, but of European and international productions as well.'' On 22 November the BSC met in the John Crerar Library, drafted a committee to survey nonresident members about a national bibliographical society, and endorsed Josephson's call for a commissioner of bibliography. Ironically, that same day ALA president John Shaw Billings, director of the New York Public Library, told *LJ* editor R. R. Bowker that he would approach Carnegie about a publication endowment fund, the interest from which would be used to publish general purpose library aids like *Poole's Index to Periodical Literature*. Billings said he liked the idea, but suggested it would be unwise to combine that request with one for a permanent ALA headquarters, or one for establishing a bibliographical institute. The latter two had been advocated by other sectors within the ALA membership, he said, ''but the thing that I wish immediately to talk to Mr. Carnegie about is the publication fund.'' All negotiations, however, were to be kept confidential.[17]

Perhaps because Herbert Putnam saw potential conflict between a national bibliographical society and the Library of Congress's Division of Bibliography, W. Dawson Johnston asked Bowker if he could run a regular bibliography column in the *Library Journal* based on the work of his LC division. Bowker turned him down, citing too many problems in editorial arrangement with regular outside contributors. If Bowker would not help, Johnston surmised, would some sort of "library institute," perhaps attached to the "Carnegie University" rumored for the Washington area, be more appropriate? Johnston approached George Iles, an independently wealthy ALA member who had personally funded J. N. Larned's *Guide to the Literature of American History* (1902). Johnston wondered whether Iles might not ask Billings to speak to Carnegie on the matter. "My conviction is that the suggested Library Institute had best be a foundation by itself, not part of the Carnegie University soon to be established," Iles replied. "Dr. Billings knows every fact and suggestion in the case; he would properly resent any nudging from me as uncalled for and unnecessary."[18] Once again advocates of increased bibliographical scholarship had been spurned by ALA leaders.

By the February 1902 BSC meeting, Merrill reported that results of the survey of nonresidents concerning the foundation of a national bibliographical society were already coming in. Of the forty-three replies, he said, thirty-two approved Andrews's plan to organize after nonresidents outnumbered residents in BSC membership. He then suggested that BSC make a concerted effort to increase its nonresident membership. Josephson made another plea for "a central institute where bibliographical research will be carried out in the interest of productive scholarship"; in the discussion that followed, BSC vice-president James W. Thompson, a professor of history at the University of Chicago, suggested that the Carnegie Institute in Washington might be interested in such a plan.

By this time more details of the new Carnegie Institute were beginning to surface. In December 1901 Carnegie had transferred $10,000,000 worth of U.S. Steel Corporation bonds to control of a board of trustees he had appointed for the new Institute. He gave them one overriding mandate—promote original research. During the spring of 1902 the new board solicited suggestions for specific research that the institute might undertake. But if Josephson and the other members of the BSC thought bibliography would receive a high priority, their hopes were quickly but decisively dashed when John Shaw Billings, who dominated the executive committee of the Institute's board of trustees, responded to Merrill's BSC survey on 3 March 1902. "I believe in strengthening existing institutions and avoiding the creating of new ones wherever possible," he wrote. He said that people interested in bibliographical work should work within ALA. Melvil Dewey echoed Billings's sentiments. The New York State Librarian thought Josephson "was simply breaking into the distinct field of ALA and its Publishing Board."[19]

Despite Billings's ability to block Josephson and the bibliographical community from direct access to Carnegie's millions, the ALA president still worried about the formation of a national bibliographical society outside of the Association. It came as no surprise, then, when the ALA program committee for the forthcoming conference asked Josephson in late February to sponsor part of a general session to discuss the "question" of a bibliographical institute and the formation of a national bibliographical society. Although BSC accepted the committee's invitation, members were keenly aware of ALA's intentions. "I do not believe there should be anything more than a cooperative connection between it [a bibliographical society] and the ALA," Azariah S. Root wrote Josephson on 11 March. "I am not greatly enamored of ALA and think it is largely run by a certain set for the promotion of mutual interests."

On 14 March Billings formally asked Carnegie to donate $100,000 to ALA for a "special fund, the income of which is to be applied to the preparation and publication of such reading lists, indexes, and other bibliographical and library aids which will be especially useful in the circulating libraries of this country." He never used the words "scholarship" or "research" in his letter. On 26 March he told Josephson that the BSC should work toward establishing a bibliographic section within ALA. Then, on 5 April, Billings seemed to contradict himself. On that day he acted for the ALA executive committee and petitioned the appropriations committees of both houses of Congress for a $100,000 appropriation "to enable the Smithsonian Institute to prepare a catalogue of scientific literature of the United States." This action hardly suggested that ALA planned to consolidate bibliographical work in one institution or agency. It certainly did nothing to endear BSC members to ALA, nor to convince them that ALA had the best interests of the bibliographical community at heart. At the society's 25 April meeting, Josephson announced that 20 new members had joined since the first of the year, bringing the total to 107, 41 of whom were nonresidents.[20] The movement toward a national bibliographical society was building momentum.

The forthcoming ALA conference at Magnolia, Massachusetts, promised to be a watershed event for both ALA and BSC. In early June, Johnston, who was preparing a paper entitled "The Work of the Division of Bibliography, Library of Congress" for the session sponsored by BSC, submitted a draft of the paper to Putnam for comment. The Librarian of Congress, who, like Billings, also served on the Carnegie Institute's board of trustees, urged Johnston to make more specific the things the bibliographical division was already doing that Josephson was proposing for a bibliographical institute. "Josephson has put on paper various projects that independently undertaken would involve an elaborate organization. They are most of them to be undertaken in ordinary course by L. of C.," Putnam wrote. "I should like this to appear from your paper. Do not mention Josephson, as I cannot accept him nor be associated with his projects as his projects."[21]

Billings did not deliver his presidential address to the Association until the conference's third general session, held on 17 June. At the end of his address he announced Carnegie's $100,000 gift and the stipulations under which it was given. When ALA Publishing Board chairman Fletcher elaborated on the significance of the gift for ALA's publishing program several days later, he noted the distinction between the type of bibliographical aids ALA published and the type of research orientation the Carnegie Institute had under consideration. He then continued, ". . . the scheme for an American Bibliographical Society might be held in suspense until, in case the Carnegie Institution enters at all the bibliographical field, it shall be seen what ground remains for such a society to work in between the Carnegie Institution on the one hand and the Board on the other."

It was probably not a coincidence that Fletcher's report followed an afternoon BSC meeting introduced by two papers: Azariah Root's "The Scope of an American Bibliographical Society," and John Thomson's "A Plan for an American Bibliographical Society." What should the object of an American Bbliographical Society be? Root asked rhetorically. It would have to be founded on the broad definition of the word "bibliography" because the preparation of guides for readers, such as those undertaken by the ALA publishing board, would only attract the "average librarian. . . . it would probably be found exceedingly difficult to interest the scholars of the country, who ought to be brought into the membership of such an organization, in merely popular compilations." Who would join such an organization? "A considerable number" of professionals "in all the great libraries of the country" (here Root mentioned specifically the Boston and New York Public, the Library of Congress, and the Newberry and John Crerar), university professors, professional and amateur bibliographers, book collectors and book-lovers in general, a group Root estimated was large enough to sustain a national organization. What relationship should it have to ALA? The Oberlin College librarian argued against locating the organization within the Association. An ALA bibliographical section would appeal only "to those who are interested in bibliography as a practical aid," while an independent national society would appeal to the larger number "who are interested in bibliography as a serious study." What should an American Bibliographical Society do? Concentrate on American bibliography, on general, national, and special bibliographies, and on the history of printing in America. Root ended his speech by not answering his final question: "Shall such a society be organized?"

After Thomson's remarks, which reiterated points in his paper at the previous ALA conference, Dartmouth College librarian Marvin Bisbee recommended contacting the Carnegie Institute for support. C. Alex Nelson of the Columbia University Library argued that the new organization should be affiliated with but not be a part of ALA. Billings spoke as a Carnegie Institute trustee and told the group the institute expected "*results* first." Society members would have to look elsewhere for financial assistance. After Billings finished, the BSC committee assigned to survey the membership and nonmember bibliographers reported its findings. Of the eighty-seven respondents, eighty favored a national organization, and sixty-seven of these advocated that it grow out of the BSC. When the society endorsed Thomson's recommendation to appoint a committee to draft a "tentative" set of "rules and regulations for the government of the American Bibliographical Society" and confer with both ALA and BSC, it set in motion a movement that would not stop until a national society was organized.

The general session on bibliography sponsored by the BSC later that evening was anticlimactic. Roden opened the session with a paper describing efforts in international bibliography. Josephson followed with a description of his plan for organizing an institute for bibliographical research, but had to conclude "the only way to establish it must be by a large endowment and by utilizing existing institutions in all ways possible." When ALA president Billings shortly thereafter called the general session back to order, he eliminated any discussion of Roden's or Josephson's paper. Instead, conferees listened to Johnston, who predictably emphasized the past bibliographical accomplishments of the ALA Publishing Board (the section had changed its name the previous year), and the present plans for the Division of Bibliography of the Library of Congress, including: "(1) . . . keeping a record of all bibliographical work, past and present; (2) . . . preparing lists of references upon all popular questions"; and "(3) . . . preparing and publishing [through the Catalogue Division] a bibliographical record of every book which should find a place on the shelves of the national library, that is, on the shelves of the libraries of the United States." Johnston concluded by saying any other work depended on "the needs and wishes of students of the United States, and their representation in Congress assembled, and especially upon the wishes and advice of the members of the Association." His words probably did not find a sympathetic response among members of the BSC, who found little discussion of "scholarship."[22]

After the Magnolia Conference, contact between the BSC, on the one hand, and ALA and Carnegie Institute, on the other, consisted of little more than professional niceties. Josephson surmised he could count on neither for assistance in pushing the profession toward the scholarly and research bibliography he was convinced librarianship needed to raise its status in the community of emerging research professions. He was right. On 1 September Billings wrote Putnam, "I do not think [Josephson's] scheme of the work to be done by such an institution is a good one." The Carnegie Institute's Advisory Committee on Bibliography (consisting of Putnam [chair], Billings, and Cyrus Adler of the Smithsonian Institution) recommended that the Institute should revive publication of *Index Medicus*, a classified record of medical literature Billings started in 1879, which ceased publication in 1899. On 5 January several weeks after the Institute's executive board accepted the committee's recommendation, Putnam made further suggestions. He advised against undertaking a universal bibliography. "The field is too vast, the expense too great, the utility of the results, in the only form which they could be secured, too doubtful." He also rejected a national bibliography, because the Library of Congress was already issuing printed cards of its own collections and had on deposit copies of the card catalogs of the Harvard University and the Boston and New York public libraries. Finally, he discouraged any grants for any bibliographical "undertaking which is isolated or fragmentary, which is not likely to be continuing nor practically exclusive within its field," and he especially discouraged the funding of retrospective bibliographies. He concluded that the best service the Institute could provide in the field of bibliography was gathering information about coordinating existing projects in order to minimize duplication of effort and expenditures. Putnam's recommendation struck at the heart of what Josephson had in mind for a bibliographical institute. In effect, it imposed strict parameters on what a national bibliographical society could accomplish. The *Library Journal* commented on Putnam's report in an April editorial: "This will be a disappointment to some; but in the end the conservative and guarded attitude indicated in the committee's report cannot fail to exert a wholesome influence upon bibliographical endeavors in the country."[23]

When the Bibliographical Society of Chicago met on 29 January 1903, members appointed Harvard librarian William Coolidge Lane to replace Thomson as chair of the committee on organizing an American bibliographical society and authorized him "to appoint two additional members to be taken from among bibliographers not directly connected with libraries." At its 30 April meeting Josephson admonished his fellow BSC members to increase their numbers, especially those outside the Chicago area, and to augment the variety of BSC publications. He also criticized the procrastination of the committee on organizing a national society and urged it to move forward. At the end of the meeting, he was elected BSC president for the forthcoming year.

At the BSC meeting held in conjunction with the ALA conference in Niagara Falls on 22 June, Josephson pushed even harder. Lane's committee recommended that the Chicago society continue to expand its nonresident membership, and to enlist more "book collectors and scholars . . . to give the new society a more representative character at the start." The movement seemed to be gaining momentum as it found more specific direction. At its 5 November meeting, Josephson announced that 1,500 copies of a circular on the possible organization of an American bibliographical society would be sent to members of learned societies throughout the country. Although he did not say so, Josephson had asked Bowker for an *LJ* subscription list to facilitate the meeting. Bowker refused. At its 3 December meeting, the BSC council advised against any amendment to existing society bylaws, "pending the formation of the American Bibliographical Society."[24] Thus the society was poised for quick movement.

The circular, which went out in early December, reprinted a proposed constitution that specified that the object of the "American Bibliographical Society . . . shall be to promote bibliographical study and research." A cover letter invited response from interested parties willing to join a national society that

> should offer at its meetings opportunity for the discussion of bibliographical plans and problems, and in its publication, works of scholarly character especially in American bibliography, but without neglecting other branches of the subject; it should collect and make known information about bibliographical undertakings in progress or in preparation in this and other countries; it should try to arouse the interest of book collectors in scholarly research, and endeavor to persuade them to make their treasures available to the student and scientific worker and thus to take an active part in the promotion of learning; it should finally have for its chief object the establishment of an Institute for bibliographical research where large national undertakings could be planned and executed, and which could represent this country in an efficient way in such international undertakings as are sure to be proposed in a more and more increasing degree. The possibility of an international bibliographical congress at St. Louis in connection with the World's Fair makes the present time especially propitious for the formation of a society representative of American bibliography.

Significantly, the words "library" and "librarians" were not used in the circular. That same month the society published its second yearbook, and at its 23 April meeting the following spring, the BSC appointed a committee on permanent organization and voted to terminate its existence upon the organization of a national society.[25]

Action at the 1904 St. Louis ALA conference in the fall was predictable, almost choreographed. On 18 October the Bibliographical Society of America held its first meeting, routinely adopted a constitution, and voted a list of officers including Lane as president, Putnam and Thwaites as first and second vice-presidents, C. A. Nelson as secretary, and Roden as treasurer. Josephson was elected a member of council. Members also voted to hold annual meetings coterminously with ALA conferences; however, they chose not to affiliate with the Library Association.[26] The new organization was off to an inauspicious beginning. Members had sensed a need to organize to a common purpose, but were still unsure what that purpose was.

Because the public library, practical service, and technique-oriented direction the increasingly feminized American Library Association was taking did not serve their immediate professional interests, advocates of scholarly and research bibliography decided to organize outside the library profession, where they could forge their own identity and not have to fight perceptions of the library profession emerging from ALA's impact.[27] By establishing the Bibliographical Society of America in 1904, BSA founders finally gave scholarly and research bibliography the professional identity that had been called for by "a student of American bibliography" as early as 1858. As this essay demonstrates, BSA origins can be found in the activities of a group of librarians employed in university and privately endowed research libraries who wanted to harness scholarly bibliography—however ill-defined that area of endeavor remained—as a special research province to win them status in a developing community of scholarly professions.

Appendix

If the BSA sought to divorce itself from the image ALA was creating for the library profession, how clean was the break in reality?

Table 1 gives a profile of the membership for three years for which lists were easily available: 1905, 1908, and 1914. Males dominated the membership in all three years; females decreased to just 5 percent of the membership by 1914; while the percentage of institutional memberships increased more than fivefold in nine years. Employees of academic and/or research libraries generally comprised half of the membership, and public library employees no more than one-fifth, while "other" (the category into which the author placed professional bibliographers,

Table 1
BSA Membership: 1905, 1908, and 1914

VARIABLE NAME	YEAR OF MEMBERSHIP					
	1905 Total Membership: 147		*1908* Total Membership: 196		*1914* Total Membership: 135	
	No.	(%)	No.	(%)	No.	(%)
A. Member by Type:						
1. Male	121	(82)	149	(76)	87	(64)
		(94)		(88)		(69)
2. Female	17	(12)	24	(12)	6	(5)
3. Institutional	9	(6)	23	(12)	42	(31)
B. Member Employed By:						
1. Academic/ Research Library	68	(46)	96	(49)	72	(53)
2. Public Library	22	(15)	36	(18)	27	(20)
3. Other	57	(39)	64	(33)	36	(27)
C. Employer Located in:						
1. East	81	(55)	124	(63)	78	(58)
2. Midwest/West	54	(37)	57	(29)	46	(34)
3. South	4	(3)	5	(3)	3	(2)
4. Foreign	8	(5)	10	(5)	8	(6)
D. BSA Members Who Were Also ALA Members by Type:						
1. Personal	67	(46)	115	(66)	69	(74)
2. Institutional	6	(67)	14	(61)	38	(90)
3. Total	73	(50)	129	(66)	107	(80)

book sellers, book collectors, etc.) actually decreased from two-fifths to one-fourth of the total. Although the BSA grew out of the Bibliographical Society of Chicago, for the three years isolated here, members from the East always held a comfortable majority. Finally, comparing BSA with ALA membership lists for these three years reveals a definite trend. From its beginnings, almost half of the BSA members, whether personal or institutional, were also ALA members. In fact, by 1914 four-fifths of BSA membership were ALA members. In sum, table 1 shows that the "typical" BSA member was a male employee of an academic or research library located in the East who was also a member of ALA.

Table 2 compares the executive boards of BSC/BSA with the ALA for the years 1903–1907.[28] The statistics perhaps reveal more about what happened when the Bibliographical Society of Chicago became the Bibliographical Society of America than they reveal about the BSC/BSA and ALA executive board members. All BSC and BSA executives were male. Seven of ten ALA executives were male, but this figure is deceptive because of an unwritten rule that reserved the second vice-presidency for females.[29] Forty percent of the BSC executives were first-generation immigrants; all of the BSA and ALA executives were born to families who had lived in the United States four generations or more. Every one of the officers from all three groups came from families with origins in Northwest Europe, and, with the slight exception of BSA executives, the large majority was Protestant. All three groups were dominated by library employees, but perhaps most surprising is the 100 percent of the BSA members, seven-eighths of whom were employed in academic and/or research libraries. Only one-fourth of the ALA officers were academic/research librarians during this period. While all BSC board members were employed in the Midwest, three of four BSA board members were employed in the East, and nearly that many ALA members. Sixty percent of BSC executives belonged to ALA; 88 percent of BSA executives did. Like the ALA, BSA executives were mostly born in the Northeast. For the most part BSC and BSA officers were a better educated group than their ALA counterparts and their degrees came primarily from northeastern institutions. No BSA executives had formal library science training; BSC and ALA compare much more closely here. In sum, then, our typical BSC executive was a white Anglo-Saxon Protestant male ALA member with roots in Northwest Europe. He was also employed in a Midwest library, although he received his higher education in the Northeast and had some library training. Our "typical" BSA officer was a white Anglo-Saxon Protestant male ALA member whose family had emigrated from Northwest Europe more than four generations previously. He was employed in an academic and/or research library located in the East, where he received his higher education but

Table 2
BSC/BSA and ALA Executive Board Membership, 1903–1907

VARIABLE NAME	BSC, 1903–1904 (5 Ex. Bd. Members)		BSA, 1904–1907 (8 Ex. Bd. Members)		BSC/BSA, 1903–1907 (12 Ex. Bd. Members)		ALA, 1903–1907 (17 Ex. Bd. Members)
	No.	(%)	No.	(%)	No.	(%)	(%)
A. Sex							
1. Male	5	(100)	8	(100)	12	(100)	(70)
B. No. of Family Generations in U.S.							
1. First	2	(40)			2	(17)	
2. Fourth or more	3	(60)	8	(100)	10	(83)	(100)
C. Family's Country of Origin							
1. Northwest Europe	5	(100)	8	(100)	12	(100)	(100)
D. Religion							
1. Unknown/ Unaffiliated	1	(20)	4	(50)	5	(42)	(35)
2. Protestant	4	(80)	4	(50)	7	(58)	(65)

Table 2 (continued)

VARIABLE NAME	BSC, 1903–1904 (5 Ex. Bd. Members) No.	(%)	BSA, 1904–1907 (8 Ex. Bd. Members) No.	(%)	BSC/BSA, 1903–1907 (12 Ex. Bd. Members) No.	(%)	ALA, 1903–1907 (17 Ex. Bd. Members) (%)
E. Employed in Library While Holding Ex. Bd. Position							
1. Yes	3	(60)	8	(100)	10	(83)	(100)
2. No	2	(40)			2	(17)	
F. Type of Library at Which Board Member Employed							
1. Academic/Research	2	(40)	7	(88)	9	(75)	(25)
2. Public	1	(20)	1	(12)	1	(8)	(29)
3. Other							(46)
4. None	2	(40)			2	(17)	
G. Location of Position							
1. East			6	(75)	6	(50)	(65)
2. Midwest	5	(100)	2	(25)	6	(50)	(29)

Table 2 (continued)

VARIABLE NAME	BSC, 1903–1904 (5 Ex. Bd. Members)		BSA, 1904–1907 (8 Ex. Bd. Members)		BSC/BSA, 1903–1907 (12 Ex. Bd. Members)		ALA, 1903–1907 (17 Ex. Bd. Members)
	No.	(%)	No.	(%)	No.	(%)	(%)
H. Membership in ALA							
1. Yes	3	(60)	7	(88)	9	(75)	
2. No	2	(40)	1	(12)	3	(25)	
I. Birthplace							
1. Northeast	1	(20)	7	(88)	8	(67)	(70)
2. Midwest	2	(40)	1	(12)	2	(17)	(30)
3. Foreign	2	(40)			2	(17)	
J. Highest Degree Earned							
1. Ph.D	2	(40)			2	(17)	(6)
2. Law	1	(20)	1	(12)	1	(8)	
3. Divinity							(12)
4. Master's	1	(20)	3	(38)	4	(34)	(12)
5. Bachelor's	1	(20)	2	(25)	3	(25)	(35)
6. High School or Less			2	(25)	2	(17)	(35)

Table 2 (continued)

VARIABLE NAME	BSC, 1903–1904 (5 Ex. Bd. Members) No.	(%)	BSA, 1904–1907 (8 Ex. Bd. Members) No.	(%)	BSC/BSA, 1903–1907 (12 Ex. Bd. Members) No.	(%)	ALA, 1903–1907 (17 Ex. Bd. Members) (%)
K. Location of Schools at Which Undergraduate Degrees Earned							
1. No Undergraduate Degree			2	(25)	2	(17)	(35)
2. Northeast	3	(60)	5	(63)	7	(58)	(47)
3. Midwest	1	(20)	1	(12)	2	(17)	(12)
4. Foreign	1	(20)			1	(8)	
5. Other							(6)
L. Library Science Education							
1. None	3	(60)	8	(100)	10	(83)	(65)
2. BLS Program	2	(40)			2	(17)	(23)
3. Non-Degree Certificate							(12)
M. Library School Attended							
1. None	3	(60)	8	(100)	10	(83)	(65)
2. NY State Lib. School	2	(40)			2	(17)	(35)

no library science training. Our "typical" ALA board member was a white Anglo-Saxon Protestant male whose family had emigrated from Northwest Europe more than four generations previously. He had only one in four chances of being an academic and/or research librarian, but he was employed in the East, where he received his higher education. The collective profile shows a homogeneous group representative of the dominant culture of the Progressive Era. Minor differences do exist, however. With the exception of the type of library in which he was employed and library science training, the BSA executive board member resembled his ALA counterpart more than he resembled his BSC predecessor.

The statistics tend to support the hypotheses identified in the narrative. The BSA was founded by academic/research librarians who wanted scholarly bibliography to distinguish them from the rest of the pack. Even though ALA periodically hinted for BSA to join in affiliate status, BSA chose to maintain its independence and exclusivity. By 1909, as BSA became increasingly dominated by eastern, academic, and research librarians and the ALA came under the control of midwestern public librarians, some came to argue BSA had become too exclusive. When an ALA constitutional change was enacted in 1909 to push unaffiliated groups closer to ALA, Lane objected. BSA membership should be "a very exclusive thing," he said, "—the names to be very selective and passed upon by a very exclusive committee." Root bristled at the elitism in Lane's words. He wrote Josephson on 16 September, "This is not my idea at all."[30] But BSA had developed a momentum of its own by this time that carried it even further away from its BSC origins.

Notes

1. "American Bibliographic Association," *Historical Magazine* 2 (November 1858): 355.

2. Henry B. Van Hoesen, "The Bibliographical Society of America—Its Leaders and Activities, 1904–1939," *Papers of the Bibliographical Society of America* 35 (1941): 177–202; J. M. Edelstein, "The Bibliographical Society of America, 1904–1979," *Publications of the Bibliographical Society of America* 73 (1979): 389–433.

3. *American Library Journal* 1 (November 1876): 90.

4. Copy of 1897 ALA *Handbook* found in Melvil Dewey Papers, Special Collections, Columbia University Library (hereafter cited as Dewey Mss., CU). The explanation of ALA's status at the turn of the century is developed more fully in my forthcoming book *Politics of an Emerging Profession: The American Library Association, 1876–1917.*

5. See Orvin Lee Shiflett, *Origins of American Academic Librarianship* (Norwood, N.J.: Ablex Publishing Corporation, 1981), for a more comprehensive account of this development, although he argues academic librarians looked to the American Library Institute as the most appropriate vehicle to push specialized bibliography. See also Charles Edward Hale, "The Origins and Development of

the Association of College and Research Libraries, 1889-1960'' (Ph.D. dissertation, Indiana University, 1976), especially chapter III, ''The College Library Section, 1889-1923,'' pp. 33-71; *Proceedings of the American Library Association, 1897* (bound into *Library Journal* 22 [1897]: 159 and 172) for a College Section discussion and response to the need for more Association attention to ''advanced library work''; and David Kaser, ''A Century of Academic Librarianship as Reflected in Its Literature,'' in Richard Johnson (ed.), *Libraries for Teaching, Libraries for Research: Essays for a Century* (Chicago: American Library Association, 1977), pp. 219-236, for a closer look at what early library literature suggests were the major concerns among academic librarians.

6. *Library Journal* 24 (August 1899): 472, 483. See also Carl B. Roden, ''Aksel G. S. Josephson, 1860-1944,'' *News Sheet of the BSA* 66 (1 June 1945): 3. See also Josephson to William Stetson Merrill, 16 April and 30 May 1899, William Stetson Merrill Papers, Special Collections Department, Newberry Library, Chicago (hereafter cited as Merrill Mss., Newberry).

7. Bishop to Carr, 11 October 1899, Henry J. Carr Papers, American Library Association Archives, University of Illinois Library, Urbana, Illinois (hereafter cited as Carr Mss., ALA Archives); *Library Journal* 24 (December 1899): 677; 25 (January 1900): 26, (May 1900): 239-240.

8. Lane to ''Robert,'' 9 March 1900, William Coolidge Lane Papers, Harvard University Archives, Cambridge, Massachusetts; Aksel G. S. Josephson, ''Preparation for Librarianship,'' *Library Journal* 25 (May 1900): 226-228. See also Josephson to Merrill, 17 June 1901, Merrill Mss., Newberry, for more of Josephson's opinions of contemporary library education.

9. Carr to Thwaites, 18 April 1900; Thwaites to Carr, 21 April 1900, Carr Mss., ALA Archives. See also Lane to ''Members of the A.L.A. Publishing Section,'' 12 February 1900, Publishing Services, Associate Executive Director, Treasurer's Correspondence, 1899-1901, American Library Association Archives, University of Illinois Library, Urbana, Illinois.

10. Thwaites to Dana, 20 November 1899; Josephson to Dana, 11 May 1900; Dana to Josephson, 17 May 1900; Josephson to Dana, 22 May 1900; John Cotton Dana Papers, Archives, Springfield Public Library, Springfield, Massachusetts.

11. Aksel G. S. Josephson, ''Wanted—A Bibliographical Institute,'' *Dial* 29 (16 July 1900): 48.

12. *Library Journal* 25 (December 1900): 750-752; 26 (February 1901): 84-85; (March 1901): 167-168.

13. Whitney to Johnston, 31 December 1900; Winship to Johnston, 29 January 1901; Josephson to Johnston, 9 April 1901. W. Dawson Johnston Papers, Manuscripts Division, Library of Congress, Washington, D.C. (hereafter cited as Johnston Mss., LC); *Library Journal* 26 (May 1901): 280-281. For a brief summary of the cooperative ventures between LC and the ALA publishing section, see *Library Journal* 26 (January 1901): 4. Formal agreement on the cooperative cataloging scheme came at ALA's annual conference in July 1901. For another indication of Josephson's ''peculiarities,'' see William Warner Bishop, ''Some Chicago Librarians of the Nineties: Fragments of Autobiography,'' *Library Quarterly* 14 (October 1944): 348.

14. Harris to Josephson, 2 July 1901, Records of the Bureau of Education, Department of Interior; Letters sent by the Commissioner of Education, 1870-1901; Microcopy No. 635, National Archives, Washington, D.C.

15. *Proceedings, 1901*, p. 144; *Library Journal* 26 (July 1901): 405-406.

16. *Proceedings, 1901*, pp. 197–205. For a comprehensive account of bibliographic instruction in academic libraries before World War I, see Peter Hernon, "Instruction in the Use of Academic Libraries: A Preliminary Study of the Early Years as Based on Selective Extant Materials," *Journal of Library History* 17 (Winter 1982): 16–38. To trace the connection between academic libraries and libraries offering courses in bibliography and the origins of the Bibliographic Society of America, I checked the eighteen institutions Hernon identified against a 1905 BSA membership list. All but five were represented on the latter, some institutions (like Harvard and Cornell) by as many as five members each.

17. *Library Journal* 26 (October 1901): 730; 27 (January 1902): 34–35; Billings to Bowker, 22 November 1901, R. R. Bowker Papers, Special Collections, New York Public Library, New York City (hereafter cited as Bowker Mss., NYPL).

18. Bowker to Johnston, 30 December 1901; Iles to Johnston, 12 January 1902, Johnston Mss., LC.

19. *Library Journal* 27 (February 1902): 89–90; Billings to Merrill, 3 March 1902, John Shaw Billings Papers, Special Collections, New York Public Library, New York City (hereafter cited as Billings Mss., NYPL); Dewey to "Members of the ALA Committee on the St. Louis Exhibit," 14 January 1902, Dewey Mss., LC. At the time of this writing, the best account of the founding of the Carnegie Institute is Nathan Reingold, "National Science Policy in a Private Foundation: The Carnegie Institute of Washington," in Alexandra Oleson and John Voss (eds.), *The Organization of Knowledge in Modern America, 1860–1920* (Baltimore: Johns Hopkins University Press, 1979), pp. 313–341.

20. *Library Journal* 27 (March 1902): 146; Root to Josephson, 11 March 1902, Azariah Smith Root Papers, Archives, Oberlin College, Oberlin, Ohio (hereafter cited as Root Mss., OC); Billings to Carnegie, 14 March 1902; Billings to Josephson, 26 March 1902; Billings to Rep. Joseph G. Cannon (chairman of the House Appropriations Committee) and Senator William O. Allison (chairman of the Senate Appropriations Committee), 5 April 1902, Billings Mss., NYPL; *Library Journal* 27 (May 1902): 279.

21. Putnam to Johnston, 11 June 1902, Johnston Mss., LC.

22. *Proceedings, 1902*, pp. 8–9, 61–147, 150, 757–762; *Library Journal* 27 (August 1902): 774–775. Root's advocacy of a national bibliographical society is consistent with his own scholarly interests. For a discussion of the latter, see John Mark Tucker, "Azariah Smith Root and Social Reform at Oberlin College," *Journal of Library History* 16 (Spring 1981): 280–291.

23. Billings to Putnam, 1 September 1902, Herbert Putnam Papers, Library of Congress Archives, Central Services Division, Library of Congress, Washington, D.C.; *Library Journal* 28 (January 1903): 37; (April 1903): 155–156.

24. *LJ* 28 (March 1903): 18; (June 1903): 299, 300–301; (August 1903): 618, 619; (December 1903): 832;29 (February 1904): 80. See also Bowker to Josephson, 20 January 1904, Bowker Mss., NYPL.

25. *LJ* 29 (January 1904): 24–25; (June 1904): 310. See also Carl B. Roden, "Historical Sketch," *Bibliographical Society of America Proceedings and Papers* 1 (1904): 19–23.

26. *Proceedings, 1904*, pp. 252–253.

27. The concept of "community" in the Progressive Era is developed in R. Jackson Wilson, *In Quest of Community: Social Philosophy in the United States, 1860–1920* (London: Oxford University Press, 1968). More recently, T. Jackson Lears has explored turn-of-the-century strains of antimodernism that resisted the dominant cultural trends, yet ultimately provided a means to facilitate accommodations. See T. Jackson Lears, *No Place of Grace: Antimodernism and the Transformation*

of American Culture, 1880-1920 (New York: Pantheon Books, 1981). Closer analysis of the origins of other learned societies at this time may reflect similar patterns of reaction and accommodation. See Neil Harris, "Cultural Institutions and American Modernization," *Journal of Library History* 16 (Winter 1981): 39-41; and Hugh Hawkins, "University Identity: The Teaching and Research Functions," in Oleson and Voss (eds.), *The Organization of Knowledge in Modern America, 1860-1920* (Baltimore: Johns Hopkins University Press, 1979), pp. 285-312.

28. Statistics for the ALA executive board taken from Wayne A. Wiegand, "American Library Association Executive Board Members, 1876-1917: A Collective Profile," *Libri* 31 (August 1981): 153-166.

29. Ibid., p. 160. That the BSA executive board remained totally male until 1936, over three decades after its founding, lends credence to the hypothesis that BSA founders may have sought organization outside ALA in part because of the feminization of the latter. For a list of BSA officers to 1939, see Van Hoesen, "The Bibliographical Society of America," pp. 199-202.

30. *Library Journal* 35 (February 1910): 71-73; Root to Josephson, 16 September 1909, Root Mss., OC.

The Fire Company Library Associations of Baltimore, 1838–1858

John Calvin Colson

In Baltimore the three decades before the Civil War were a period of vigorous library development. More than fifty different library organizations were created in a variety of parent associations: churches, fraternal organizations, civic groups, and others. At least fifteen library associations were created within the volunteer fire companies of Baltimore. The fire companies were well-established civic organizations, largely within neighborhood communities, and their libraries appear to have been established to improve educational opportunities for those communities; they showed signs of developing into communal public libraries.

The fire companies also were sources of a considerable public disorder, and thus of great concern to the citizens of Baltimore. Technological change in fire-fighting—the introduction of steam fire engines in 1858—provided the basis for a radical reorganization of the Baltimore fire department (then known as the Baltimore United Fire Department) into a municipal, professional organization under the direct control of the City. The volunteer fire companies went out of existence, as did their library associations. One, the Library Association of the Mechanical Fire Company, established in 1838, managed to survive until 1871; the others vanished.

Baltimore had no poet to call it the city of the big shoulders, but in the decades before our Civil War it would have been an appropriate nickname. This maker of steel and railroad locomotives, of clipper ships and fire engines, of pianos and prefabricated hotels and houses, was one of the most vivid, vibrant cities in America, every bit as dynamic as its sisters and competitors, Boston, New York, and Philadelphia; and nothing else came close.[1]

The first English settlers came there in 1729, and their numbers in-

John Calvin Colson *is a printer scholar and library consultant and member of the faculty of Columbia Pacific University, San Rafael, California.*

Special thanks to Richard A. Erney, director, and Ellen Burke, of the State Historical Society of Wisconsin, for their extraordinary courtesy in lending microfilms of the Baltimore Sun. *Thanks are given also to the Maryland Historical Society for lending microfilms of the* Baltimore American.

creased slowly during the rest of the century; in 1790 only 13,503 persons lived in "Baltimore Town and precincts"—the small central city and surrounding area. Only seven decades later their numbers were 212,418 and increasing. During the period focused on in this paper, 1838-1858, the city's population more than doubled, for the third time in the century; a small city was turning into a major metropolitan area, with changes of scale that were unprecedented in the experience of Baltimoreans, new and old, accompanied by similar changes in the culture of the city.[2]

The people of the new Baltimore were an increasingly diverse group. Originally Anglo-Irish to an overwhelming degree, they became increasingly polyglot, increasingly diverse in religion, and increasingly diverse in ethnicity. For example, Germans of all varieties (Prussians, Bavarians, Hanoverians, etc.) began to emigrate to Baltimore in the 1840s, and in increasing numbers after the German revolutions of 1848. Baltimore has had the reputation of being a strongly Catholic city, but in 1830-1860 Roman Catholics appear to have been a minority there. In 1853 there were 122 places of worship in Baltimore: 105 were Protestant, 15 were Catholic, and 3 were Jewish. The distribution of churches was: Methodist—46; Methodist Episcopal—37; Protestant Episcopal—15; Roman Catholic—15; Jewish—3; Others—6. The total number included 8 Afro-American churches.[3]

Maryland was a slave state, but even by 1830 the number of "free colored persons" in Baltimore was 14,783, compared to 4,124 slaves. During the next three decades the numbers of free Afro-Americans continued to increase, despite repressive state laws and determined efforts to persuade free blacks to migrate to Liberia. They and their co-residents—English, Welsh, Irish, Scottish, German, French, Italian, and others—made the city a rich ethnic broth, bubbling dangerously close to the boiling point.

Baltimore's government was an anachronism in the America of Jacksonian Democracy. In form it was a municipal corporation, chartered by the state legislature in 1796, but closely subordinate to it. The mayor was elected directly by the resident voters—white males over the age of twenty-one. The City Council was bicameral, with first and second branches; and only property-owners could serve on the Council. During the 1830s-1850s the property requirements were $300 for the first branch and $500 for the second. The first branch contained two members from each ward, and the second branch, one. Despite its anachronistic qualities, the municipal government could not be called oppressive, except toward slaves, free blacks, and women. The City had very limited authority, and large measures of self-government were the rule for white citizens, in principle, at least. Nevertheless, the property requirements for election to the City Council foreclosed most of the city's workers from effective participation in the municipal government. Add in the disfranchised Afro-Americans and women, and you have a dangerously unrepresentative government.[4]

It is difficult even for a student of nineteenth-century America to peer back through the haze of history and understand the course of development in a major city. History tends to have been written by winners, or by historians sympathetic to the winners, or by historians convinced of the inevitability of events; and our vision seems to have been obscured by a veil of determinism, or by a shade of objectivity. We tend to know very little—and to feel less—about the course of events in, say, Baltimore, 1838–1858. Perhaps the best corrective for this condition is a course of close and extensive reading of the city's newspapers. It makes fresh the progress of development, unfolding as it goes. In a very real sense such a program of research amounts to a time-lapse motion picture of the past.[5]

The Baltimoreans of 1838–1858 lived in an urban conglomerate that for nearly all of them was not a part of their cultural heritage: their roots were agrarian, but they lived in one of the most rapidly developing cities in America; their occupational backgrounds were largely those of farmers or farm-related craftsmen, but by the 1850s many of them were workers in giant new factories and more or less remote from their employers;[6] their cultural memories were of close and closed horizons, but the steamship, the railroad, and the cheap daily newspaper had begun to expand those horizons toward infinity;[7] their communications networks were attuned to a slow, rural pace, but the express post and the telegraph were quickening the news and their responses to it;[8] the hurrying course of invention and urban-industrial development amazed and disturbed them.[9]

Fear also was a constant factor in their lives. The years considered here were not "the good old days." Crime, disease, and violence were steady companions of life in the city. Cholera was an annual scourge of summer.[10] Burglary, arson, and other crimes against property were common, and much of it was committed by young men;[11] but violent assaults against people were the despair of Baltimore's press and its readers.[12] It may be argued, from the record, that industrialism, immigration, and racism were the principal sources of violence in Baltimore, and of its other social ills as well.[13] It is possible to argue also that the ills were symptoms of a more complex problem: Baltimore was of a new kind of entity in the American political domain, and it lacked the institutional processes necessary to the control of "social problems." The older institutions—church, family, and state, especially—were inadequate to the kind of polity developing in Baltimore. The doctrines and ideals attributed to Cincinnatus were not adequate to the development of an industrial, urban society.[14] Industrial work and urban living required new responses to social problems, and new forms of social organization. Much of urban development in nineteenth-century America appears to have been experimentation toward the achievement of those forms.[15] There was a great fascination with the organizational possibilities apparent in the new machines becoming so pervasive in life.[16] At the same time, the ideas emanating from Europe, especially in the wake of the 1848 revolutions, were a source of disturbance. Socialism, for example, may have been the "offspring of a terrible necessity in Europe," but here there was no need for it.[17] Even the "joint stock" principle of corporate organization was seen as an unnecessary intrusion of socialism.[18] Individualism, tempered by a sense of civic responsibility, would be adequate to our needs. The "progress of half of a century" had created intolerable conditions, and had caused "many to abandon their faith in the stability of our democratic institutions" and the belief also that universal suffrage was "incompatible with sound administration of our large cities."[19] Reform, however, was perceived as the appropriate solution to the problems.

For all of the social diseases afflicting Baltimore during 1830–1860, it was subjected to a much greater, older terror—fire, which was the great natural enemy of cities. During the first forty-five years of its existence Baltimore appears to have relied upon the traditional fire defense: the bucket brigade of neighbors. By the 1760s an increasing population and density of buildings began to make apparent the need for a better system; and some Baltimoreans followed the example of their municipal neighbor to the north, Philadelphia, and organized the "Ancient and Honorable" Mechanical Company.[20]

The Mechanical Fire Company appears to have been organized in 1763, as a club or society for fire-fighting, flood control, and military purposes. In 1769 the Company bought the city's first "fire engine"—a ship's pump—and built a frame lodge and engine house. From that point the fire companies assumed an increasingly important role in Baltimore;[21] and from 1769 to 1855, twenty-five more of them were organized there. (A roster of the companies is appended to this paper.) Most became substantial neighborhood organizations; in 1843 the seventeen companies had a combined membership of 4,724 (4.6 percent of the city's population).[22] Also, the companies appear to have accumulated substantial amounts of property. In 1858 the real property of seven companies had the following values, according to the city comptroller: Friendship—$3,500; Independent—$8,000; Mechanical—$10,000; Mount Vernon—$3,000; Pioneer—$2,000; Union—$5,000; and United—$5,000.[23] Some image of the fire company establishments can be gained from a description of the Independent's house, a two-story building with a bell and clock tower nearly 110 feet high. The first floor contained the company's three "engines" and other fire-fighting equipment, and the offices of the Company. The second floor was an auditorium, with a seating capacity of nearly three hundred persons. An adjoining building housed the Library Association and Library of the Company.[24] The Patapsco's new house, built in 1849, was a three-story building, of Gothic design, and described as "really an ornament to the city."[25]

Their buildings illustrate the fire companies' importance in and to the city. They were much more than fire departments, and their houses were much more than fire stations. As early as 1819 the Independent rented its second-floor room for a day-school.[26] In 1828–1829 the Columbian, Deptford, and Franklin companies occupied one house, and its second-floor rooms were used as a school; this was especially pleasing to the mayor, because the school rent paid the interest on the money the City had spent to assist in building the house.[27] The Watchman's new house, built in 1848, was to be used for "public assemblies, parties, balls, and various other purposes required by the prosperous and increasing population in the southern section of the city."[28] The Patapsco's new building, in 1849, even constituted a sort of "urban renewal": it was built on a lot "formerly occupied by a number of mean-looking and dilapidated hovels," the destruction of which was much desired in "the respectable neighborhood."[29] At the same time the LaFayette was asking for a City appropriation to assist in building a new house, in a neighborhood without a fire company. The *Sun*, with support from the people of the neighborhood, endorsed the request, as it would both extend the influence of the company and "advance the interests of the property-holders."[30] Other organizations used the fire houses as well; in December 1856 the Women's Guild of the Fells' Point Mission held their week-long fair and festival in the Columbian Engine House.[31]

There were other indicators of the social importance of the fire companies, dating back at least to the American Revolution. The Mechanical was prominent in it, and operated Baltimore's Committee of Correspondence. The British Colonial governor considered the Company "the most rebellious and mischievous organization in the Province."[32] There was nothing new in that situation; in 103 A.D. Emperor Trajan warned Pliny (the Younger) against the organization of fire companies in his province: "Whatever name we give them, and for whatever purpose they may be instituted, they will not fail to form themselves into factious assemblies, however short their meetings may be."[33]

The apprehensions of emperor and governor were reconfirmed in Baltimore; the fire companies became among the most powerful political organizations in the city. During 1830–1860 at least three mayors of Baltimore, a Speaker of the State House of Delegates, a sheriff, and several members of the City Council and state legislature came from the ranks of the fire companies. The companies in their very nature were political organizations involved in most of the facets of the city's life. Their ranks included doctors and lawyers, school teachers and laborers, bankers and manufacturers. In a Baltimore that lacked most of the urban institutions of the twentieth century, the fire companies were major centers of communication and interaction. As another example, at least two insurance companies were organized by the several fire companies, whose members elected the directors of the insurance companies.[34] The fire companies were also intensely democratic, rather than administrative: their officers stood for election every year, rather than being appointed by municipal boards. Finally, the fire companies appear to have been a major base for the military power of the state, in an era when the national army was miniscule and an intense localism permeated the states' militias. Fire-fighting then was a "low-tech," labor intensive activity, and the fire companies' leaders appear to have been among the few persons with experience in the organization and control of large companies of men. The companies were active in raising militia companies in the War of 1812, and again in the Mexican War.[35] Also, during the 1840s and 1850s, several members of the Baltimore fire companies were battalion and regimental commanders and general officers in the Maryland Militia.[36] Clearly, the fire companies were significant sources of social and executive leadership in Baltimore.

Nothing is perfect, however, and if news is defined as stories of misfortune and catastrophe, the fire companies were a major source of news. The title "fireman" was definitely associated with violence: "Riots, turbulence, disgraceful conduct, and personal violence have repeatedly occurred. The name of a fireman has almost ceased to be respectable, and the badge . . . has almost become a badge of obloquy and an emblem of disorder."[37] The official historian of the Baltimore Fire Department wrote of the "gross excesses, culminating in riot and bloodshed," and of the department's "dark record of bloody street fights . . . riots . . . murders . . . destruction . . . zeal run mad."[38] The riots attendant to fire-fighting were frequent. In February 1849, for example, six were reported in the *Baltimore Sun*.[39] The number was not untypical, and a fire was not necessary to their genesis. In that month two of the riots resulted from false alarms, apparently made for the purpose of inciting riots. Worse, arson—then called "incendiarism"—often was committed to draw firemen out for a melee.[40] What Forrest called the "turbulent spirit" of the fire companies was prevalent throughout the years; and the editor of the *American* may have spoken for the entire city when he wrote in 1858: "We have always held the opinion that there are radical evils connected with our present department."[41]

The riots and the tumults rose within and without the fire companies: intercompany rivalries and competition, street gangs, and other factors contributed to the condition, which was of long standing. Even so, for more than half-a-century there was little systematic response to the situation. Regulations for the behavior of firemen and fire-watchers were adopted; criminal statutes were enacted; and both internal discipline and law enforcement failed to curb the "pugnacious propensities" of the firemen. Even the suspension of several companies by the mayor and the padlocking of their engine houses and equipment proved an ineffective measure. The "fire riots" were a constant burden on the city; and in the mid-1840s Baltimoreans began to consider alternatives.[42]

The *Sun* complained of judges' failures to impose "full sentences" on "fire rioters" and of the "inefficiency" of the courts, and called for reform.[43] The mayor proposed a hierarchy of "good conduct medals" or some other "appropriate mark of public approbation."[44] Individual companies began to tighten their own standards of behavior.[45] The most significant proposal came from a member of the City Council: for a full-time municipal fire department.[46] It did not flourish, and the *status quo ante* was undisturbed for another decade, during which technological development began to provide the basis for a municipal department.

The first steam fire engine was introduced in Cincinnati in 1853. It proved very effective, and in May 1858 the First Baltimore Company acquired the first steam engine in the city. It arrived on 18 May and was given a trial on the 19th, which was reported as a "complete success," although it was noted that eighty men were required to draw the engine on the run to the test site at the harbor.[47] By December steam engines were also owned by the Vigilant and Washington companies, and were on order by Mechanical and Patapsco. It was known then, however, that the steam engines would have to be horse-drawn, for the more effective use of both steam power and manpower; that the horses and engines would be owned by the City and the firemen would be City employees; and finally that only seven companies were necessary to make effective use of the new engines.

Even as the various companies were contemplating the purchase of steam engines, Mayor Thomas Swann was contemplating the abolition of the volunteer fire department; in his annual message to the Council, on 18 January 1858, he asked for the appointment of a commission on reorganization of the fire department.[48] The commission was appointed, and drafted an ordinance proposing a mixed fire department—volunteer companies organized around a core of City employees (engineers and hostlers)—and the Council passed the ordinance. The mayor vetoed it and urged a single department.[49] The Council capitulated and passed an ordinance establishing a municipal institution; the mayor approved it and began immediate implementation, on 10 December 1858.[50] There was a brief transition period during which several fire companies maintained their services until the City Fire Department was organized fully, but the era of *laissez-faire* fire protection was gone from Baltimore.

At the demise of the Baltimore United Fire Department (the umbrella under which the volunteer companies operated), there were twenty-two volunteer companies; fifteen of them had some form of library association. Before turning to those it seems appropriate to sketch briefly the general development of libraries in Baltimore, as there has been no comprehensive study of the subject. The quarter-century before the Civil War was a period of extensive and vigorous development of libraries in Baltimore, in the sense of community activity, as opposed to institutional development. The discussion here is not centered on the development of collections and institutions, but on the creation of organizations intended to foster library development. A chronology of the establishment of library entities in Baltimore is appended to this paper.

Except for the almost legendary Bray Library in the vicinity of what would become Baltimore, there appears to have been no such activity until 1773, when Joseph Rathel made a proposal for a circulating library.[51] It was not established then, but one was later, by William Murphy, bookseller; in 1784 he sold the store and library to Hugh Barkley.[52] The next eighteen years saw the establishment of three more library entities: the Library Company of Baltimore in 1795, the Friends Library Association in 1799, and the Baltimore Circulating Library in 1802. From 1802 to 1820 only two more libraries were created in the city: the library of the University of Maryland Medical School in 1813, and Robinson's Circulating Library, in Robinson's Book Store, in 1816. During 1821–1830 five libraries were established; they included two more medical libraries (one of which was the library of the state medical society), an apprentices' library association, and that of the Maryland Institute for the Promotion of the Mechanic Arts,[53] the latter two reflecting the increasing industrialization of the city.

The principal single event in library development in Baltimore up to that time may have been the fire on 7 February 1835, which destroyed the Athenaeum, its libraries, and those of the Maryland Institute.[54] Two of the city's principal libraries were gone; and the third, that of the Library Company of Baltimore, was far from accessible to most of the city's people. No immediate response to the catastrophe was apparent, but in the years 1838–1860 at least fifty-eight library entities were created, organized, or established. They were "popular libraries" in the older sense of the phrase; that is, they were created by diverse organizations of people responding to diverse sets of needs. Rather than following a doctrine of "one big library" for the entire city, they were following one of different libraries for different communities.[55] Fifteen of those were fire company libraries, organized in the neighborhoods where the engine houses were located, and from which they tended to draw the bulk of their members.

The idea of the library associations was not original with the Baltimore firemen; they appear to have been following the example of some of their brethren in Washington.[56] In any case, by the summer of 1839 there were library associations in three fire companies: the Columbian, the Mechanical, and the New Market. During the next thirteen years, twelve other companies followed the example. The fifteen were: Columbian (1838); Mechanical, New Market, and Deptford (1839); Union (1841); Patapsco and Vigilant (1842); First Baltimore, Independent, LaFayette, Liberty, and Washington (1843); Watchman (1845); Howard (1846); and Pioneer (1852).[57]

The motives behind these libraries are not clear. The firemen left relatively scant records of the associations, but the Charter of the Mechanical Company contains a statement of purpose of: ". . . collecting a library of literary and scientific books, and of holding stated meetings for the hearing of lectures and essays, with a view of exciting and fostering among its members a desire for mental cultivation and improvement."[58] Six years later the charter of the Watchman Library Association contained exactly the same statement.[59] In other words, the firemen wanted to improve their opportunities for self-education. There was ample opportunity for it. The volunteer firemen spent a lot of time as do their municipal counterparts: waiting at the firehouse. The volunteers, however, were relatively free to partake of the pleasures of the tap rooms, billiard parlors, and other resorts. On the other hand, the principal public supporters of the fire company libraries were eager to keep the firemen out of the saloons and pool halls, and thus strongly promoted the libraries as incentives to "mental and moral improvement," in the much favored phrase of the day. Francis Bacon's epigram—"reading maketh a full man"—was elaborated into a doctrine that reading would inhibit sinfulness, if not prevent it.[60]

As for the libraries of the associations, relatively little can be said. In 1841 the Deptford Library Association had accumulated about five hundred volumes, gifts from a few residents in its Fells Point neighborhood.[61] "Within a week from its formation," it was reported, the Watchman Library had obtained two hundred volumes; but this report was more than a year after the event, and there was no report of increase from that number.[62] The best records of collection development are from the Mechanical and the Patapsco libraries, and their net effect is to leave one doubtful of the accuracy of contemporary reports about the libraries. A year or so after the Mechanical organized its library association, the librarian reported a diverse collection: 1,130 volumes, all but two of the city's newspapers on free subscriptions, contributions of other newspapers "from all States of the Union," and a "large number of Periodicals and Pamphlets," which increased every week.[63] In August 1848 the collection was reported to be excellent, "of which about two thousand [works] are in good order."[64] The 1858 *Manual of Bibliography* reported the Mechanical Company Library to contain 2,200 volumes, of which 22 were obtained in 1857; 1,800 of them were in English, 100 each in French and German, and 50 each in Greek, Hebrew, Latin, and Spanish.[65] Subsequently the Library was reported to have contained more than 3,000 volumes in 1859.[66] The record of the Patapsco's collection is only slightly more extensive. When it was organized in 1842, the Association held only a "few volumes."[67] About three or four months later the Library was reported to contain "some four hundred well-selected volumes."[68] Seventeen months later it was said to "have swelled into more than 1500 works."[69] In 1848 the number of volumes was reported "near eighteen hundred," of which three or four hundred had been added in the past year.[70] Thirteen months later the number had increased to "about two thousand volumes"; but only three months later (in November 1849) it was said to be 1,200 volumes, "mostly contributions from members."[71] Perhaps the final word about the collections of the fire company library associations should be with reference to the Vigilant Library Association, organized in 1842: In November 1849 the *Sun* reported its members had been "endeavoring to form a library . . . and they have succeeded in collecting together some three hundred volumes of useful and entertaining works."[72] As for the contents of those collections, information is even sketchier than for their numbers. They seem to have been extensive in terms of the range of subjects (for the times, that is); but there is no evidence about the depth of coverage in particular subjects. It is likely their libraries were quite similar to those of other "social library" organizations of the time.[73]

The library associations themselves appear to have been of two kinds: those that were organized separately from the fire companies, and those that were adjuncts to the fire companies. Only two of the library associations appear to have achieved some independence from their parent companies: the Library Association of the Mechanical Fire Company was incorporated by the legislature in 1840, as was the Library Association of the Watchman Fire Company in 1846.[74] Both thus became "bodies corporate and politic," with authority to act independently. Still, persons who wished to join the Mechanical Library Association had to become honorary or special members of the Mechanical Fire Company.[75] It is on record that the Union Library Association had its own constitution and bylaws, and there may have been others; after 1846 literary, charitable, and social organizations were permitted to incorporate without a charter from the legislature.[76]

The question of organizational independence is related closely to questions about membership in the fire company library associations, but information on this point is also limited. In most cases, it appears, the situation was that of the Washington Hose Company Library Association: "The Association embraces the members of the company generally."[77] Membership in the Liberty Fire Company was not necessary for membership in its Library Association, but special circumstances were involved in that case.[78] The most precise and reliable information on fire company library association membership is in the report of George Robinson, librarian of the Mechanical, in June 1840. The Association had 85 members; "many" had joined the Mechanical Fire Company as honorary or special members, in order to join the Library Association.[79] As for the other fire company library associations, they did depend strongly on contributions of books and money from the public, and on friendly press coverage as well, so it is likely there were informal mechanisms for making their libraries accessible to others. The Liberty Library Association, in 1850, began to admit women to use of the library.[80] The Liberty made another significant attempt to extend the usefulness of its library. This one involved the new Apprentices' Library; the first, organized in 1822, was long defunct.[81]

In July 1838 the editor of the *Sun* began to argue for the establishment of a new Apprentices' Library.[82] Early in 1841 the Apprentices' Library Association was organized, and its library was opened in June, in a room at the Patapsco Fire Company.[83] A year later the organization of the Patapsco Library Association apparently compelled the removal of the Apprentices' Library. Exactly what happened does not seem to have been recorded, but there was an attempt to merge the Apprentices' and the Mechanics' Library Associations; it failed, and so did the Mechanics' Library.[84] That may have occurred early in 1843, because by May 1843 continuation of the Apprentices' Library appeared uncertain.[85] Just at this time the Liberty Library Association was starting up; from May to July a merger of the two associations was negotiated, and it was ratified at a joint meeting on 11 August 1843, under the name Liberty-Apprentices' Library Association.[86] As a practical matter the merger was effected in July, when the Apprentices' Library was moved into the Liberty engine house, and opened to apprentices every Friday evening, and the united associations began a subscription drive for money to build a library annex to the engine house.[87] How long the merger continued is uncertain, but by February 1846 the Apprentice's Library Association was again conducting meetings under that name.[88]

The Pioneer Library Association, organized in 1852, was the first fire company library association to be organized in six years; it was also the last one. It appears that by the mid-1840s the enthusiasm for fire company libraries had diminished substantially. There does not appear to be any contemporary record of speculation on the matter, but it seems the unsavory reputations of the fire companies—with only three or four exceptions—did much to diminish perception of them as viable community organizations. Such a reputation undoubtedly took time to become majority opinion in Baltimore, but there can be little question that it was the case by 1858; the relatively quick and easy transition from the volunteer to the municipal fire department—at approximately double the cost to taxpayers—can be explained only partially by the effectiveness of a new fire-fighting technology. In any event, as 1858 ended, so did the era of the "Baltimore Fireman."[89]

Without the base of the fire companies their library associations could not survive long; in themselves they had no effective communal bases, and were in no position to develop them. Their financial conditions were too infirm.[90] During the year leading up to the disbandment of the Baltimore United Fire Department, with extensive press coverage of the subject, there was no discussion of the future of the fire company library associations. Perhaps there was an assumption they would continue. One did, for another fifteen years. The Mechanical Fire Company went out of existence in 1859, but the Library Association remained in existence as a sort of retired gentlemen's club until 15 June 1873, when the remnant of the Association surrendered its charter. The disposition of its library was not recorded.[91] The disposition of two other fire company libraries is known: in February 1859 the Vigilant voted to give its library to the Maryland Penitentiary; and in March 1860 the Columbian presented its library to the East Baltimore YMCA.

"Experiment in neighborhood libraries" was used as a tentative hypothesis for this paper. It did not prove out; "experiment" connotes too strongly the idea of deliberate, organized effort toward a specified objective, and the Baltimore fire company library promoters and their associates and friends just were not that conscious of the "neighborhoodliness" of their libraries. There was some awareness of the communal qualities of the fire companies, and even of their libraries; but it appears that a developing trend toward the institutionalization of urban facilities and services was too attractive and foreclosed the development of alternate modes of organization. As an example, during the time that arguments for a municipal fire department were appearing in the *Baltimore American*, there were equally fervent statements for similar "reform" of the Baltimore Police Department and an end to the so-called "independent police." The doctrines of institutionalism also were entrenched in ideas for the development of Baltimore's public schools. As for libraries, the creationary enthusiasms of the 1840s appeared still strong at the end of the 1850s, but shifting from "local" or "neighborhood" entities toward interest-based organizations, such as the Bar Association Library, a new Maryland Institute for the Promotion of the Mechanic Arts, the Mercantile Library Association, and others. That concept remains vital in Baltimore, as study of the American Library Directory indicates.

The first "modern" American industrial institution, the Baltimore and Ohio Railroad Company, was born there, and others were following. It proved relatively easy to adapt the industrial corporation for use in municipal institutions. For libraries, a model became visible in Boston in 1848. It was in the minds of some Baltimoreans already. A year after the Liberty Library rescued the Apprentices' Library, an official source commented on the merger. While grateful to the Liberty, he also wrote: "It would seem that in no enterprize should the evil of exclusiveness be more palpable than in establishing a public library . . ." and called for a "public institution" to correct the situation.[92] The fire company libraries were not organized on any general principle of exclusiveness, but. . . . Meanwhile, no one appears to have taken seriously the *Sun*'s earlier assertion there should be municipal appropriations to support the fire company library associations.[93] The frost of public disapprobation already was closing on the nettle's flower.

APPENDIX 1
Fire Companies of Baltimore

Name	Date Est.	Membership (1843) Active	Honorary
Baltimore Property Guards and Life Escape Company	1810	NA	NA
Columbian Fire Company	1809	260	14
Commercial Fire Company	1792	NA	NA
Deptford Fire Company	1792	230	30
First Baltimore Hose Company	1810	140	154
Franklin Hose Company	1809	175	34
Friendship Fire Company	1785	130	61
Hercules Fire Company	1843(?)	NA	NA
Howard Fire Company	1835	200	62
Independent Fire Company	1799	350	50
LaFayette Hose Company	1842	248	20
Liberty Fire Company	1794	130	65
Mechanical Fire Company	1763	220	280
Mercantile Fire Company	1787	NA	NA
Monumental Hose Company	1855(?)	NA	NA

Appendix 1 (cont'd)

Name	Date Est.	Membership (1843) Active	Honorary
Mount Vernon Hook and Ladder Company	1853	NA	NA
New Market Fire Company	1805	220	40
Patapsco Fire Company	1822	144	NA
Pioneer Hook and Ladder Company	1852	NA	NA
Union Fire Company	1782	160	30
United Hose and Suction Company	1810	230	63
United States Hose Company	1854	NA	NA
Vigilant Fire Company	1804	342	63
Washington Hose Company	1815	83	60
Watchman Fire Company	1840	320	116
	Totals:	3,582	1,142

APPENDIX 2
A Chronology of Libraries in Baltimore, 1773–1860

1773: Joseph Rathel proposed a circulating library.
1784: Murphy's Circulating Library established.
1795: Library Company of Baltimore organized.
1799: Friends' Library Association organized.
1802: Baltimore Circulating Library established.
1813: Library of the University of Maryland School of Medicine established.
1816: Robinson's Circulating Library established; in existence until 1846.
1821: Webster's Medical Library and Reading Room established.
1822: Apprentices' Library Company organized; defunct by 1829.
1824: Baltimore Athenaeum organized.
1825: Maryland Institute for the Promotion of the Mechanic Arts organized.
1830: Library of the Medical and Chirurgical Faculty of Maryland (the state medical society) in existence.
1835: Athenaeum destroyed by fire; Maryland Institute Library also destroyed.
1838: *Sun* proposal for an Apprentices' Library.
Columbian Fire Co. Library Association organized.
1839: Clinton Lyceum reported organzing library.
Niles Total Abstinence, Beneficial and Library Association of Baltimore Printers organized.
Deptford Fire Co. Library Association organized.
Mechanical Fire Co. Library Association organized.
New Market Fire Co. Library Association organized.
Mercantile Library Association organized.
1840: Library Company of the Baltimore Bar organized.
1841: Young Men's Social Literary Society reported organizing a library.
Franklin Institute and Maryland Lyceum in existence.

Appendix 2 (cont'd)

Apprentices' Library Association organized.
Union Fire Company Library Association organized.
1842: Jefferson Temperance Society Library and Reading Room established.
Mechanics' Library Association organized.
Patapsco Fire Co. Library Association organized.
Vigilant Fire Co. Library Association organized.
Germania Library Association incorporated.
Maryland Institute of Literature, Science and Art incorporated.
1843: Marion Total Abstinence Library Association in existence.
Channing Literary Institute incorporated.
First Baltimore Fire Co. Library Association organized.
Independent Fire Co. Library Association organized.
LaFayette Fire Co. Library Association organized.
Liberty Fire Co. Library Association organized.
Washington Hose Fire Co. Library Association organized.
Merger of Apprentices' and Liberty Fire Co. library associations.
1844: Caledonia Library Association in existence.
Odd Fellows' Library established.
Maryland Historical Society organized.
Library Association of the Young Catholic Friend's Society in existence.
1845: Baltimore Athenaeum reorganized; inc. 1846.
Maryland Farmers' Club organized.
Pioneer Sunday School Library Association organized.
Catholic Library Association of Baltimore in existence.
Irving Circulating Library in existence.
Watchman Fire Company Library Association organized.
1846: Barnum's City Hotel Reading Room established.
Society for Mutual Instruction incorporated.
Light Street Sunday School Library Association organized.
Howard Fire Company Library Association in existence.
1847: Loadstone Library Association organized.
Association for the Encouragement of Literature and the Arts organized.
Maryland Institute for the Promotion of the Mechanic Arts re-established.
Merchants' Exchange Reading Rooms in existence.
St. Peter's Institute Library in existence.
Wesley Chapel Library Parsonage Library Association incorporated.
Philharmonic Society in existence.
1848: Athenaeum Building opened. Tenants: Library Company of Baltimore, Maryland Historical Society, Mercantile Library Association.
Prescott Institute Library established.
Baltimore Female College in existence.
1849: Maryland State Agricultural Society Library established at Farmer's Exchange.

Appendix 2 (cont'd)

Newton Literary Institute Library closed and sold.
Sons of Temperance Library Committee organized, by representatives from various S.O.T. lodges.

1852: Pioneer hook & Ladder Co. Library Association organized.
Loyola College Library established.

1854: Library Company of Baltimore defunct; collection given to Maryland Historical Society.

1856: "An Appeal" (for a free public library) published by Maryland Historical Society.

1857: Peabody Institute created; $500,000 gift by George Peabody.
Charles Street Church Library Association organized.
House of Refuge Library in existence.

1858: Catholic Institute in existence.
St. Stephen's Church Free Library and Reading Room established.
Young Men's East Baltimore Christian Association organized.

Notes

Copies of the original version of this paper, presented at Chapel Hill on 7 March 1985, are available at the Newberry Library, Chicago, the Maryland Historical Society, Baltimore, and the Maryland Fire Museum.

1. In 1849 prefabricated houses, and even a 100-room hotel, were manufactured in Baltimore, for erection in San Francisco (*Balt. Sun*, 18 January 1849: 2; and 10 November 1849:2).

2. The best general study of Baltimore's development is Sherry H. Olson, *Baltimore, The Building of an American City* (Baltimore: Johns Hopkins University Press, 1980).

3. *Map of the City and Suburbs of Baltimore* (Baltimore: 1853), pp. 3–7.

4. Olson, *Baltimore*, p. 140.

5. The image may appear inapt, but such a research program frequently involves reading a month's edition of newspapers in the course of an afternoon.

6. Indeed, in the editorial "Go Forth of the City," the *Sun* advised immigrants to "seek their fortune in the country," and not to stay in "indulgence in illusory ideas of imaginery prosperity" (8 April 1846: 2).

7. See "Annihilation of Space and Time," *Sun*, 8 January 1847: 2.

8. Contemporary newspapers show a strong sense of immediacy in both popular and press responses to events in Europe in 1848, with press reports only two weeks behind events.

9. "New Inventions—Antagonisms," *Sun*, 4 December 1849: 2.

10. "Cholera Confusion," *Sun*, 24 May 1849. 2; and "The Cholera in Baltimore," *Sun*, 1 June 1849: 2.

11. "Juvenile Delinquents" was an index term in the 1841 volume of the Laws of Maryland.

12. "Corner Loungers," *Sun*, 25 August 1838: 2. See also "Prevention—The Youth of Our City," *Sun*, 16 December 1844: 2; and "A Caution to Ladies—Cases of Outrage," *Sun*, 1 June 1849: 4—a letter to the editor.

13. Cf. Olson, *Baltimore*, pp. 118–120.

14. For a contrary view, see the remarks of the House of Delegates Committee on Education, in its 1846 report, quoted in the *Sun*, 4 March 1846: 2, on the agrarian roots of "all the greatest and best men."

15. "Baltimore was more than a city, or even a cultural entity: it was a process as well," Gary L. Browne, *Baltimore in the Nation, 1789-1861* (Chapel Hill: University of North Carolina Press, 1980), p. 216.

16. Olson, *Baltimore*, p. 103. See also the articles about the Mechanical Bakery Co. of Baltimore, in the *American*, 14 May 1858: 1; 15 May: 1, 2; 18 May: 1, 2; and 21 May: 2.

17. "Communism and Individualism," *American*, 4 January 1858: 2. It is noteworthy that the editorial contains no mention of Karl Marx.

18. "Proposed Silk and Fancy Jobbing House," *Sun*, 24 October 1845: 2.

19. "Misgovernment in Cities," *American*, 11 December 1858: 1.

20. The organizer of America's first volunteer fire company was none other than America's first "Renaissance man" and "first librarian," Benjamin Franklin, Donald J. Cannon (ed.), *Heritage of Flames* (Garden City: Doubleday, 1977), p. 91.

21. Olson, *Baltimore*, p. 13.

22. "Statistics of the Baltimore United Fire Department," *Sun*, 26 August 1843: 1.

23. "Fire Engine Houses City Property," *American*, 11 December 1858: 1. The valuations were for real property only, and did not include the values of engines, equipment, uniforms, and so forth.

24. "A Model Establishment," *American*, 29 March 1858: 1.

25. "New Engine House—Patapsco Fire Company," *Sun*, 5 September 1849: 1.

26. Clarence H. Forrest, *Official History of the Fire Department of the City of Baltimore* (Baltimore: Williams and Wilkins Co. Press, 1898), p. 49.

27. Ibid., p. 46.

28. "A Decided Improvement," *Sun*, 7 December 1848: 2.

29. "Contemplated Improvement of the Patapsco Fire Company," *Sun*, 1 February 1849: 2; also 24 February: 2.

30. "LaFayette Fire Company," *Sun*, 27 January 1849: 2.

31. *Sun*, 2 December 1856: 2.

32. Olson, *Baltimore*, p. 14.

33. *Letters of Pliny the Consul* (Edinburgh: J. Ballantyne for W. J. and J. Richardson, 1807), II: 263. Reprinted in the *Albany* (N.Y.) *Argus*, and then in the *Sun*, 17 August 1849: 4.

34. Advertisements by the two companies, Firemen's Insurance Co. and Associated Firemen's Insurance Co., in the *American*, 6 December 1847: 4.

35. Cannon, *Heritage*, p. 352. Lt. Col. William H. Watson, commander of the Baltimore-Washington Battalion, killed in the Battle of Monterrey, was speaker of the House of Delegates, president of the Columbian Fire Co., captain of the Columbian Rifles, and a lawyer, obituary, *Sun*, 21 October 1846: 1.

36. For examples, Gens. James S. Anderson and Samuel S. Mills, of the Mechanical, and Anthony Miltenberger and C. C. Egerton, of the First Baltimore.

37. "Report of the Special Investigating Committee," quoted in Paul C. Ditzel, *Fire Engines, Firefighters* (New York: Crown Publishers, 1976), p. 97.

38. Forrest, *Official History*, pp. 55-56.

39. *Sun*, "A Riot," 1 February: 2; "A Riot and Brutal Murder," 6 February: 1; "Disgraceful Proceedings, Arrests, &c," 12 February: 1; "False Alarm,"

13 February: 1; "False Alarm," 20 February: 1; "Fire and Fire Riot," 20 February: 1.

40. "Disturbances among the Firemen," *American*, 22 September 1847: 3.

41. *American*, 4 April 1858: 2.

42. "Salutary Provisions of the Fire Appropriations Bill," *Sun*, 5 May 1847: 2; "The Fire Riots—Action of the Fire Department," *American*, 27 October 1847: 3; Forrest, *Official History*, pp. 77-78.

43. *Sun*, 17 March 1848: 2.

44. "The Mayor's Message," *Sun*, 16 January 1849: 1.

45. "Hall of the Union Fire Company," *Sun*, 20 April 1849: 2.

46. "Council Proceedings," *Sun*, 16 February 1849: 4.

47. "Arrival of the Steam Fire Engine" and "Trial of the Steam Fire Engine," *American*, 19, 20 February 1858: 1.

48. "Annual Message of the Mayor," *American*, 19 January 1858: 1.

49. "Reorganization of the Fire Department" and "The Fire Department Ordinance," *American*, 18 September 1858: 4; 17 November 1858: 2.

50. *American*, 10, 11 December 1858: 1.

51. John Thomas Scharf, *The Chronicles of Baltimore* (Baltimore: Turnbull Bros., 1874), II: 658. On the Bray Libraries, see C. T. Laugher, *Thomas Bray's Grand Design* (Chicago: ALA, 1973).

52. Scharf, *The Chronicles*, II: 658; Robert I. Vexler, *Baltimore: A Chronological and Documentary History, 1632-1970* (Dobbs Ferry, N.Y.: Oceana Publications, 1975), p. 13, said the store was established by Murphy in 1784.

53. See the appended chronology.

54. *American*, 8 February 1835.

55. The phrase "one big library" was used by George Ticknor, when he proposed a merger of the principal libraries in Boston, in a letter to John Quincy Adams, in 1826, Walter M. Whitehill, *The Boston Public Library* (Cambridge: Harvard University Press, 1956), pp. 2-3.

56. *Sun*, 31 July 1839: 2.

57. One or two other companies may have been involved with libraries, but the record is too vague for certainty.

58. Ch. 240, Laws of Maryland, 1840.

59. Ch. 14, Laws of Maryland, 1846.

60. See, for example, "Improvement of Firemen," *Sun*, 22 August 1843: 2.

61. "Deptford Fire Company Library Association," *Sun*, 15 January 1841: 2.

62. *Sun*, 7 December 1846: 2.

63. "Library Association of the Mechanical Fire Company: Report of the Librarian," *American*, 5 June 1840: 2.

64. "Library Association of the Mechanical . . ." *Sun*, 21 August 1848: 2.

65. W. J. Rhees, *Manual of Bibliography* (New York: W. W. Norton, 1858), p. 84.

66. Scharf, *The Chronicles*, I: 245.

67. C. W. K., "Patapsco Library Association," *Sun*, 20 July 1844: 2.

68. "Patapsco Library Association," *Sun*, 2 March 1843: 2.

69. C. W. K., "Patapsco Library Association," p. 2.

70. "Patapsco Library Association," *Sun*, 25 July 1848: 2.

71. "Patapsco Library Association," *Sun*, 24 August 1849: 2; 24 November 1849: 1.

72. "Vigilant Library Association," *Sun*, 2 November 1849: 1.

73. See, for example, the account of the Mechanical Library Association in the

Sun, 24 August 1848: 2; of the Patapsco by C. W. K., ''Patapsco Library Association,'' p. 2.

74. C. W. K., ''Patapsco Library Association,'' p. 2.

75. See the 1840 report, *American*, 5 June 1840: 2.

76. *Sun*, 20 May 1841: 2; Ch. 323, Laws of Maryland, 1846.

77. *Sun*, 25 March 1843: 2.

78. ''Apprentices' Library Association,'' *Sun*, 19 December 1844: 1.

79. 1840 report, *American*, 5 June 1840: 2.

80. *Sun*, 12 March 1850: 2.

81. Forrest, *Official History*, p. 44.

82. ''Apprentices' Libraries,'' *Sun*, 19 July 1838: 2.

83. ''Apprentices' Library,'' *Sun*, 12 June 1841: 2.

84. ''The Apprentices' Library,'' *Sun*, 19 December 1844: 1.

85. ''Notice of Meeting of the Apprentices' Library Ass'n,'' *Sun*, 4 May 1843: 2.

86. *Sun*, 11 August 1843: 2.

87. ''The Apprentices' Library Association,'' *Sun*, 31 July 1843: 2.

88. *Sun*, 27 February 1846: 2.

89. See the melancholy report of the last Christmas Festival of the Mechanical Fire Co., *Sun*, 27 December 1858: 1.

90. In his euphoric statement about the Patapsco Library, C. W. K. portrayed a flourishing organization, but the last sentence admitted, ''the treasury barely sustains itself,'' ''Patapsco Library Association,'' p. 2.

91. Scharf, *The Chronicles*, I, 245; ''Commendable,'' *Sun*, 25 February 1859: 1; ''The Columbian Fire Company,'' *Sun*, 29 March 1860: 1.

92. ''The Apprentices' Library,'' *Sun*, 19 December 1844: 2.

93. ''Firemen's Library Associations,'' *Sun*, 31 July 1839: 2.

Public Library Development in the United States, 1850–1870: An Empirical Analysis

Robert V. Williams

The ability of the classical "social conditions theory" to explain public library development in the United States during the middle of the nineteenth century is examined. Using data collected by the Census Bureau in 1850, 1860, and 1870 on public, school, church, Sunday school, and college libraries, seven socioeconomic variables are analyzed using correlation and multiple regression techniques. Results indicate that there are both merits and weaknesses to this classical explanation of library development. While the best explanatory variable often differs from one time to the next and from one type of library to another, education and economic ability provide the best overall explanation. Urbanization, industrialization, and literacy are useful additions to the explanation but are generally not as powerful.

Introduction and Problem Statement

The era from about 1850 to 1876 is widely recognized as the critical formative period in the development of the public library in the United States.[1] While less widely acknowledged, this period is probably also very important to the development of a comparatively strong library tradition within the society at large. This tradition bears remarkable fruition in the last quarter of the nineteenth century and the early years of the twentieth century. A considerable array of types of libraries and library associations and a good body of professional knowledge are developed in a short period of time. College and university libraries, school libraries, and specialized libraries have strong roots in this period between 1850 and 1876.

Despite the acknowledged strength of the development of all types of libraries during this period, our understanding of the causes of this development is not good. Even though a good deal of work has been done

Robert V. Williams *is associate professor of library and information science, University of South Carolina.*

on public library development during the nineteenth century, the explanations offered by historians differ considerably. Work on the development of college and university libraries, school libraries, and special libraries, while not nearly as extensive as that for public libraries, also shows a variety of explanations.[2]

This paper is an empirical study of library development in the United States at three specific time points in the middle of the nineteenth century: 1850, 1860, and 1870. The focus of the paper is on public library development, but attention is also given to school, college, Sunday school, and church libraries. The central problem examined here is the extent to which it is possible, using a specific theoretical framework and a limited set of data for each of the three years, to explain library development for the separate types of libraries and library development overall. (Private libraries, that is, those belonging to individuals or families, while certainly a legitimate part of the larger concept of library development, are not examined here.)

Theoretical Framework

The explanations of library development offered by library historians have been reviewed extensively elsewhere and are not repeated here.[3] This study utilizes only one of the approaches discussed previously, the "social conditions theory." In scientific terms this is not really a theory but an argument, or rationale, for the selection of a set of variables considered to be most important to an explanation of library development. The explanation offered is one that has been developed only in the context of public libraries but, in this study, it is also tested for applicability to overall library development and to the development of the several types of libraries. This is being done because no specific theoretical explanations have been advanced for these other types of libraries and because of my interest in examining the larger, or overall, issue of library development.

As presented by library historians, the social conditions theory is a fairly simple one. As noted earlier, it actually lacks the critical elements of theory in that it fails to specify the relative importance of the variables, and, most importantly, *why* these variables affect the establishment and growth of libraries. The central developers of this argument, Shera,[4] Ditzion,[5] Lee,[6] Hassenforder,[7] Jackson,[8] and, to some extent, Johnson and Harris,[9] also show considerable differences in the social conditions variables they choose to list as most important. Depending on the historian consulted, the list contains from about four to over fifty variables.

Careful study of the work of these, and other, historians shows that a few variables receive repeated mention and are stressed as being most important. The following conceptual variables appear to predominate: economic ability, education, urbanization, growth of democracy, industrialization, European examples/influences, spread of mass communication media, a favorable cultural milieu, growth of professions/occupations, and the contribution of religion.

In carrying out the empirical analyses performed in this study, an attempt was made to locate data and develop measures of all of these variables. It was not possible, however, to locate appropriate data on the concepts of European influences, growth of democracy, a favorable cultural milieu, growth of occupations and professions, and the contribution of religion. While the loss of information concerning the effect of the variables on library development may be severe, this is not necessarily the case. Indeed, as was noted earlier, some historians limit themselves to only two or three variables. Quite simply, this is an empirical question but, obviously, not one that is addressed in this study.

Almost without exception, historians view library development as a complex process. Very few, however, attempt to disentangle the factors and say how library development takes place. My *interpretation* of their work leads to the development of a specific theoretical rationale that is tested in this study.

This rationale says that as formal and informal education spreads, it creates a demand (via the process as well as from the educated individuals) for access to increased information resources. These resources will be developed according to the economic ability of the community to pay for them. Recognizing the economic advantages of pooling their funds (through a variety of methods) to provide these resources, the community will do this in a variety of overlapping, but sometimes also exclusive, ways, leading to the development of several types of libraries. Since formal education is also a beneficiary of pooled resources, these educational systems and libraries will begin, spread, and grow most rapidly in urbanized areas. It is also in urban areas that the printed mass communications media develop most rapidly, thus contributing to the education process and forming part of the information resources of the libraries. Industrialization requires greater economic capital and a more concentrated and educated population who will establish and strengthen libraries in their communities.

This rough theoretical rationale is tested in this study. Measures of these concepts are developed and tested on data for the United States for the years 1850, 1860, and 1870. It is hypothesized that there are positive correlations between library development (by type of library and overall) and the measures of these conceptual variables. Further, it is expected that it will be possible to assess the relative importance of each of these variables in an explanation of library development, enabling us to assess the separate components as well as the overall merit of this general theoretical rationale for library development.

Data Collection

The data used in this study were collected by the U.S. Bureau of the Census in the decennial census years of 1850, 1860, and 1870. The data were published in the reports that the Census Bureau made shortly after the years in which the census was taken.[10] The data on libraries appear as part of the Social and Economics Statistics schedules. The data on other variables appear in a variety of additional schedules. The machine-readable files of these data were prepared by the Inter-University Consortium for Political and Social Research (ICPSR) of the University of Michigan from the published reports of the Census Bureau. A codebook identifying the variables and other coded information is available from ICPSR.[11]

The 1850, 1860, and 1870 censuses are the only ones to include data on libraries. Exactly why the Census Bureau decided to include library data is not known, though Peterson speculates that it was caused by the inability of the federal government to respond to earlier international requests for information on libraries.[12] The data were collected in the usual Census Bureau manner, using, in each state, local census enumerators, who were supposed to personally interview the individual from whom the information was obtained. This information was recorded by the census enumerators on (usually) preprinted forms that were collected at the state level and sent to Washington, D.C., for compilation. Census enumerators were responsible for collection of the data at the level of the county or subsections of the county. This results in a manuscript census for each county or part of a county.

At the time of the census, county- (and sometimes subcounty-) level data were available. In 1850 the Census Bureau published library data at the levels of counties and states, but in 1860 and 1870 it published only state-level data. Since the published data were used by ICPSR in preparing the machine-readable file, county-level data on libraries are not available for those years. (County-level data do exist for some states in the form of microfilm copies of the manuscript Social Statistics schedules, which were offered to most states by the National Archives in the 1950s. Information on the existence of these schedules for all of the states has not been pursued in this study.)[13]

The lack of county-level library data for 1860 and 1870 places a severe restriction on the findings of this study. Data at that level are vastly preferable because of the nature of library development as a community-based phenomenon. They are also to be preferred because of the anticipated higher levels of variability in library development at the level of counties than at the level of states.

In addition to the problem of less than ideal data for the years 1860 and 1870, the data on public libraries from 1860 are incorrect and have not been used in this study. In a mixup that even the Census Bureau did not understand, the published data on public libraries from that year were partially mixed in with data on private libraries.[14] It has not been possible to separate these, and the Census Bureau apparently never published a correction.

The issue of data "mixups" naturally brings to question the larger issue of the reliability of the data. In terms of the reliability of the data on libraries, I have examined this using two different approaches. First, an attempt was made to verify the accuracy of the census data by comparing them with the work of other researchers. This is not so simply done because of the differing compilation approaches, definitions, and methods of data presentation used by these other researchers. Nevertheless, a rough comparison of these data with the results presented by McMullen on number of public libraries per ten thousand population,[15] and the total number of public libraries in 1850 and 1870, shows that the results are somewhat comparable. The census data show more public libraries than McMullen in 1850, but, again, comparisons are difficult because McMullen shows public libraries (including social libraries, commercial circulating, and "regular" public) in *existence* in the United States before 1876. The only near comparison that it was possible to make was with McMullen's "in existence before 1876" category for social/public libraries and the 1870 census data on public/circulating libraries. In this case, McMullen shows 4,106 libraries and the census data (see table 1C), 2,315 libraries. Given these discrepancies for both years, it was concluded that the issue of reliability cannot be tested satisfactorily using the published work of other researchers.

To a slight extent the Census Bureau made an assessment of the reliability of the data on libraries after discovering the 1860 mixup on public and private libraries. Writing in 1870, the superintendent of the Census office, Gen. Francis A. Walker, said:

> The statistics of libraries have never been very creditable to the census of the United States. Such improvement as was practicable with the machinery provided for the collection of these statistics, have been effected in the Ninth Census, . . . but no great amount of complacency will be experienced upon a critical examination of the figures. The fact is, the machinery of the census under existing conditions of law, defective as it is in many particulars, is

> less adapted to work out correct results in this matter of the statistics of libraries than in any other use to which it is applied.[16]

This would seem to give the death knell to the reliability of the data on libraries. I have not found this to be the case, however; indeed, careful examination of the entire text of the comments reveals that the superintendent is speaking more about the statistics on private libraries than those for nonprivate libraries.

The second approach to testing reliability of the census data was to determine whether researchers have studied the reliability of any of the nonlibrary variables used in the study. Walsh studied the manufacturing returns for Wisconsin for 1850 and 1860 and found numerous errors in them involving the figuring of product value and wages paid.[17] She also found that errors were made in the compilation process between the manuscript schedules and the published version of the data. Groff, in studying data on literacy for the same period and a different area, however, found the data to be both reliable and valuable in his work.[18] Condran and Crimmons, studying mortality data from 1850 to 1900, found errors but considered the data reliable.[19]

From this work one can only conclude that the census data on libraries probably have errors, but to an unknown extent. Certainly the library data, in terms of complexity of compilation, are not nearly so prone to errors as the more complicated manufacturing schedules. In addition, I compared the published data for South Carolina with the manuscript schedules, and no major errors were located. Nevertheless, it is not possible to estimate a reliability coefficient for the library data at this time. A good deal more work needs to be done.

Measurement Issues and Study Limitations

The theoretical rationale states the central concepts to be dealt with in this study. The measurement of these concepts is not simple. Central to the overall problem investigated here is a satisfactory definition of library development. Complications surrounding this issue have been treated elsewhere and are not repeated here.[20] What is desired is a measure that encompasses the existence of libraries in a geographical area and factors about the strength and usefulness of the library to its intended users. In this study, because of the limitations of data, library development for a specific type of library has been defined as the sum of the number of libraries per ten thousand population (in the state or the county) and volumes per capita in those same libraries (and geographic area). This figure has been calculated for each of the three types of libraries. An overall index of library development, for each census year, has been calculated by summing the separate types of library development indexes into one index. In all cases with the indexes, the potentially contaminating variable, the size of the population of the county or state, has been removed by use of per capita or similar ratios.

In performing the necessary calculations to construct these indexes for each type of library, some assumptions had to be made regarding how the census enumerators defined types of libraries. As far as can be determined from the instructions to census enumerators,[21] no specific instructions were given to them on how to define a type of library. Fortunately, because of the categories available to them, this causes problems only with public libraries. That is, a library in a school, college, Sunday school, or church is easily determined. What appears to have happened then is that the census enumerators (as least in 1850) simply put every other type of nonprivate library into the public library column on their printed forms. This includes identifiable social libraries, private club/society libraries, fee-based circulating libraries, and genuine public libraries that are tax-supported in some way or open to anyone. The exception to this was 1870, when the enumerators had considerable choice in where to place libraries that belonged to the state or federal governments. In this case, public libraries have been defined in this year as those marked "town, city, etc." and "circulating" on the enumerator forms. Hopefully, this provides some consistency across the three census years studied here.

Measuring the explanatory, or independent, variables shares some of the same problems involved in measuring library development. Fortunately, considerably more work has been done in these areas and can be partially relied on for determining the validity of the measures.[22] The seven conceptual explanatory variables mentioned in the theoretical rationale have been defined as given below. In some cases, because of changes in the data-collection procedures in a given census year, it has been necessary to alter slightly the specific definition of a measure from year to year. Insofar as possible, however, efforts were made to maintain consistency across all three census years. It should also be noted that in 1850 and 1860 the white (or, in some cases, the free) population has been used to form per capita figures or proportions, and in 1870 the entire population has been used.

Economic Ability

Desired measure: total dollar value of the production of all goods and services for the state or county for the period.

Actual measures used by year:

1850: value of all farm and manufacturing products per capita (white population).

1860: value of farms, manufacturing products, and capital invested in manufacturing per capita (free population).
1870: value of all farm and manufacturing products per capita.

Education

Desired measure: proportion of the school-aged children attending school.
Actual measures used by year:
1850: proportion of the (white) population (aged 5–19) attending school.
1860: proportion of the (free) population attending school.
1870: proportion of the total population attending school.

Literacy

Desired measure: proportion of the population who can read and write.
Actual measures used by year:
1850: proportion of the (white) population (over 15 years of age) who can read and write.
1860: proportion of the (free) population (all ages) who can read and write.
1870: proportion of the total population (over 10 years of age) who can read and write.

Mass Communications

Desired measure: per capita circulation of newspapers and periodicals.
Actual measures used by year:
1850: no data available.
1860: circulation of all newspapers per capita (white population).
1870: circulation of all newspapers and periodicals per capita (total population).

Urbanization

Desired measure: the extent to which the population is concentrated in one or more areas in the specified geographic area, county or state (note: for state data this is a very poor measure, particularly for the years studied here, because almost all states have extensive rural areas).
Actual measures used by year:
1850: no data available.
1860: inhabitants per square mile in the state (free population).
1870: inhabitants per square mile in the state (total population).

Industrialization

Desired measure: the extent to which the population is employed in industrial or manufacturing establishments.

Actual measures used by year:
1850: proportion of the total (white) population employed in manufacturing.
1860: proportion of the total (free) population employed in manufacturing.
1870: proportion of the total population employed in manufacturing.

Taxation
Desired measure: per capita local and state taxes on individuals and corporations.
Actual measures used by year:
1850: no data available.
1860: total annual local taxes (all types) per capita (free population).
1870: total annual local and state taxes (all types) per capita (total population).

Despite the earlier attention to the validity of the independent and dependent variables, there are, obviously, serious concerns here regarding validity. Optimally, one would like to have a high validity coefficient for each conceptual measure. However, given our limited state of knowledge about all of these concepts, and, particularly, the concept of library development, this is not possible at this time.

Two basic methods of analysis are used in this study. The first, the Pearson product-moment coefficient of correlation, is a measure of the association between two variables and takes on a value from − 1.00 to 1.00. The second, linear, stepwise multiple regression assesses the extent to which a given series of independent variables (here, the socioeconomic variables) explains variation in a dependent variable (the separate and overall indexes of library development). In addition, stepwise regression enables one to assess the amount of variability in the dependent variable that can be explained by each independent variable that has explanatory power. It is thus possible to estimate, using the variables in the theoretical model, the overall explanatory power of the model and the separate contributions that each variable makes to the explanation. It should be noted that no significance-level information has been reported, because in all cases we are dealing with data on the entire population instead of sample data.

Results

Table 1 contains the descriptive statistics of mean, standard deviation, and sum for total number of libraries, number of libraries per ten thousand population, number of volumes, and number of volumes per capita in each of the types of libraries for the three census years. Results are shown for the county-level data for 1850 and for state-level data for 1850, 1860, and 1870. Even a brief examination of these results shows that school and Sunday school/church libraries far outnumber any other type of library. The central implication of this is that the overall (or all-libraries) part of the table consists primarily of information on these two types of libraries. This also must be kept in mind when examining the correlation and regression tables for the overall library development indexes.

The correlation results are, of course, central to the hypotheses stated in the theoretical rationale. However, before examining the correlations between the independent variables and the measures of library development, it is useful to observe the relationships between the various types of libraries. Table 2 shows these results. Interestingly, correlations between the types of library development indexes are weak. This is true generally across all three years, and it makes little difference whether one uses the superior county-level data or state-level data. The exceptions are the relationships between the all-libraries index and the indexes for school/college and Sunday school/church libraries. The strong relationships there, however, are simply an indication that those two types of libraries make up the strongest component of the all-library indexes for the three years.

The 1850 and 1870 state-level data show a weak to moderate relationship between public libraries and Sunday school/church libraries. The 1850 county-level data results, however, give serious challenge to the existence of a real relationship between the development of these two types of libraries.

Table 3 shows the relationships between the several library development indexes and the independent variables for the three years. For 1850 results are shown separately for county-level data and for state-level data; the county-level data, however, should be considered more accurate. It is obvious that, in 1850, education is the single best predictor of overall library development for each of the types of libraries. Literacy is the next best predictor, and industrialization a distant third. For public libraries, education is the single best predictor but a weak one. A similar picture appears with the 1850 state-level data, but the correlations are somewhat stronger in all areas. To some extent this is to be expected, since variations in library development would probably be greater (at least in this period) within states than between states. The strong correlation in the state data between Sunday school/church libraries and industrialization is a curious anomaly.

Table 1A
Descriptive Statistics for Library Variables
1850 (N = 30)

Library Variables	Mean	Standard Deviation	Sum
Number of Public Libraries	40.33	58.90	1,210
Number of School Libraries	402.23	1,969.48	12,067
Number of College Libraries	7.03	6.79	211
Number of Sunday School & Church Libraries	70.60	101.46	2,118
Number of All Libraries	520.20	2,000.00	15,606
Public Libraries per 10,000 Pop.	.78	1.31	23.39
School Libraries per 10,000 Pop.	1.87	6.54	56.08
College Libraries per 10,000 Pop.	.11	.07	3.36
Sunday School & Church Libraries per 10,000 Pop.	1.14	1.18	34.30
All Libraries per 10,000 Pop.	3.90	6.84	117.12
Volumes in Public Libraries	45,997	61,632	1,379,915
Volumes in School Libraries	54,913	252,655	1,647,404
Volumes in College Libraries	30,327	36,818	909,821
Volumes in Sunday School & Church Libraries	20,022	35,818	600,671
Volumes in All Libraries	151,260	331,774	4,537,811
Public Libraries Volumes per Capita	.079	.080	2.34
School Libraries Volumes per Capita	.031	.084	.93
College Libraries Volumes per Capita	.052	.057	1.56
Sunday School & Church Libraries Volumes per Capita	.033	.047	.99
All Libraries Volumes per Capita	.194	.196	5.82

NOTE: Mean and standard deviation are for single state; sum is for all states.

Table 1B
Descriptive Statistics for Library Variables
1860 (N = 35)

Library Variables	Mean	Standard Deviation	Sum
Number of Public Libraries	NA	NA	NA
Number of School Libraries	301.54	1,108.19	10,554
Number of College Libraries	6.26	7.04	219
Number of Sunday School & Church Libraries	192.17	283.99	6,726
Number of All Libraries	499.97*	1,334.04*	17,499*
Public Libraries per 10,000 Pop.	NA	NA	NA
School Libraries per 10,000 Pop.	1.47	3.42	51.57
College Libraries per 10,000 Pop.	.08	.06	2.71
Sunday School & Church Libraries per 10,000 Pop.	2.30	2.08	80.57
All Libraries per 10,000 Pop.	3.85*	4.28*	134.85*
Volumes in Public Libraries	NA	NA	NA
Volumes in School Libraries	50,572	158,464	1,770,038
Volumes in College Libraries	28,290	37,904	990,173
Volumes in Sunday School & Church Libraries	70,822	108,450	2,478,774
Volumes in All Libraries	149,685*	261,092*	5,238,985*
Public Libraries Volumes per Capita	NA	NA	NA
School Libraries Volumes per Capita	.033	.050	1.16
College Libraries Volumes per Capita	.040	.049	1.42
Sunday School & Church Libraries Volumes per Capita	.09	.091	3.16
All Libraries Volumes per Capita	.164*	.153*	5.74*

NA = Not available; see explanation in paper.
*Does not include data on public libraries.

Table 1C
Descriptive Statistics for Library Variables
1870 (N = 38)

Library Variables	Mean	Standard Deviation	Sum
Number of Public Libraries	60.92	105.72	2,315
Number of School Libraries and College Libraries	378.21	1,609.85	14,372
Number of Sunday School & Church Libraries	991.79	1,167.45	37,688
Number of All Libraries	1,466.05	2,442.29	55,710
Public Libraries per 10,000 Pop.	.76	1.05	28.76
School Libraries and College Libraries per 10,000 Pop.	1.41	3.84	53.75
Sunday School & Church Libraries per 10,000 Pop.	9.84	5.46	374.05
All Libraries per 10,000 Pop.	12.40	7.15	471.26
Volumes in Public Libraries	98,017	202,522	3,724,668
Volumes in School Libraries and College Libraries	94,656	203,305	3,596,937
Volumes in Sunday School & Church Libraries	260,888	395,097	9,913,759
Volumes in All Libraries	499,449	771,816	18,979,066
Public Libraries Volumes per Capita	.101	.128	3.83
School and College Libraries Volumes per Capita	.072	.094	2.72
Sunday School & Church Libraries Volumes per Capita	.257	.178	9.76
All Libraries Volumes per Capita	.482	.351	18.31

Table 2
Pearson Product Moment Correlation Coefficients for Relationships between Library Development Indexes

Types of Libraries	Public	School & College	Sunday School & Church
	1850 County Data (N = 1,559)		
Public Libraries			
School & College Libraries	.023		
Sunday School & Church Libraries	.037	.038	
All Libraries	.167	.944	.313
	1850 State Data (N = 30)		
Public Libraries			
School & College Libraries	.014		
Sunday School & Church Libraries	.247	.017	
All Libraries	.250	.956	.240
	1860 State Data (N = 35)		
Public Libraries			
School & College Libraries	NA		
Sunday School & Church Libraries	NA	.166	
All Libraries	NA	.873	.626
	1870 State Data (N = 38)		
Public Libraries			
School & College Libraries	.046		
Sunday School & Church Libraries	.422	.003	
All Libraries	.521	.533	.830

In the results for 1860 a different picture emerges, where urbanization and industrialization are slightly better predictors than education. For school/college libraries and Sunday school/church libraries industrialization is the best single predictor, though followed very closely by education.

The picture becomes even more complicated in 1870 for the individual types of libraries. Again, education is by far the best predictor of overall library development, but different top predictors emerge for public libraries and school/college libraries. For public libraries, economic ability is superior, followed closely by urbanization. For school/college libraries, mass communications is a surprisingly good predictor; no other variables are even close to it.

Even though correlations do a good job of assessing one-to-one relationships and show the single best predictors, they do not enable us to assess a theoretical model of the separate and combined effects of the independent variables on the indexes of library development. The linear stepwise regression results assist in this process.

Table 4 shows the results of the regression analyses using the 1850 county-level data. It is quickly apparent that very little of the total variance in the library development indexes for each type of library and for overall library development can be explained using the variables in the theoretical rationale. The greatest percent of variance explained is the 13.10 percent in overall library development. For the individual types of libraries, the percent of explained variance is very low. Use of the 1850 state-level data shows some improvements in the percentage of explained variance. In terms of the best contributors to an explanation of library development, the variables of education, literacy, and industrialization are fairly consistent throughout both groups of data and across the types of libraries.

A different, and somewhat more complicated, picture emerges in 1860. Here, education plays a secondary role to a variety of variables. Since Sunday school and church libraries make up the strongest group of libraries in this year's data, it is interesting to note that industrialization contributes a high percentage of the explained variance. In all types of libraries, however, education plays a very powerful role in the explanation.

The 1870 results are quite similar to those for 1860. In this case, however, the data include information on public libraries. Here, for the first time, economic ability plays a key role in the explanation; when it is combined with education, the two factors contribute a high percentage of explained variance. Urbanization and industrialization are, however, also important independent contributors. Mass communications continues as a good explanation for school and college libraries, but education is now the best single contributor for Sunday school and church libraries.

Table 3
Pearson Product Moment Correlation Coefficients between the Type of Library Development Indexes and the Independent Variables by Census Year

Independent Variables	Type of Library Development Indexes: Public Libraries	School & College Libraries	Sunday School & Church Libraries	All Libraries
		1850 County Data (N = 1,559)		
Economic Ability	−.010	.051	.011	.049
Education	.188	.266	.185	.332
Literacy	.154	.173	.096	.216
Mass Communication	NA	NA	NA	NA
Urbanization	NA	NA	NA	NA
Industrialization	.082	.138	.117	.176
Taxation	NA	NA	NA	NA
		1850 State Data (N = 30)		
Economic Ability	.136	.211	.697	.350
Education	.461	.246	.524	.413
Literacy	.457	.224	.583	.404
Mass Communication	NA	NA	NA	NA
Urbanization	NA	NA	NA	NA
Industrialization	.315	.231	.885	.436
Taxation	NA	NA	NA	NA

Table 3 (continued)

Independent Variables	Type of Library Development Indexes: Public Libraries	School & College Libraries	Sunday School & Church Libraries	All Libraries
		1860 State Data (N = 35)		
Economic Ability	NA	−.038	.105	.021
Education	NA	.345	.488	.514
Literacy	NA	.275	.450	.440
Mass Communication	NA	.400	.133	.382
Urbanization	NA	.261	.626	.516
Industrialization	NA	.559	.661	.371
Taxation	NA	.011	.043	.030
		1870 State Data (N = 38)		
Economic Ability	.544	.122	.180	.290
Education	.409	.264	.542	.621
Literacy	.477	.257	.467	.571
Mass Communication	.188	.724	.116	.498
Urbanization	.227	.212	.175	.269
Industrialization	.522	.095	.242	.317
Taxation	.446	.208	.271	.388

Table 4
Stepwise Regression of Independent Variables on Library Development Indexes by Year and Type of Library

Independent Variables	Cumulative R^2	R^2 Difference
	1850 County Data (N = 1,559)	
	Public Libraries	
Education	.036	
Literacy	.045	.019
Economic Ability	.046	.001
Industrialization	.047	.001
	School and College Libraries	
Education	.071	
Literacy	.079	.008
Industrialization	.084	.005
	Sunday School and Church Libraries	
Education	.034	
Industrialization	.040	.006
Literacy	.041	.001
Economic Ability	.042	.001
	All Libraries	
Education	.111	
Literacy	.123	.012
Industrialization	.131	.008
	1850 State Data (N = 30)	
	Public Libraries	
Education	.213	
Literacy	.245	.032

Table 4 (continued)

Independent Variables	Cumulative R^2	R^2 Difference
	School and College Libraries	
Education	.061	
Economic Ability	.081	.020
	Sunday School and Church Libraries	
Industrialization	.800	
Economic Ability	.810	.010
Education	.814	.004
	All Libraries	
Industrialization	.190	
Education	.223	.033
	1860 State Data (N = 35)	
	School and College Libraries	
Mass Communications	.160	
Education	.345	.185
Industrialization	.402	.057
Taxation	.448	.046
Literacy	.460	.012
	Sunday School and Church Libraries	
Industrialization	.436	
Education	.667	.231
Economic Ability	.691	.024
Mass Communications	.707	.006
Literacy	.719	.012
Urbanization	.731	.012

Table 4 (continued)

Independent Variables	Cumulative R^2	R^2 Difference
	All Libraries*	
Urbanization	.267	
Education	.437	.270
Mass Communications	.532	.095
Economic Ability	.563	.031
Literacy	.580	.017
Taxation	.588	.008
	1870 State Data (N = 38)	
	Public Libraries	
Economic Ability	.296	
Education	.359	.163
Urbanization	.420	.061
Industrialization	.489	.069
Taxation	.497	.008
	School and College Libraries	
Mass Communications	.524	
Industrialization	.560	.036
Urbanization	.607	.047
Taxation	.613	.006
Education	.623	.010
	Sunday School and Church Libraries	
Education	.294	
Mass Communications	.306	.012
Industrialization	.317	.011
Taxation	.338	.021
Economic Ability	.355	.017

Table 4 (continued)

Independent Variables	Cumulative R^2	R^2 Difference
	All Libraries	
Education	.386	
Mass Communications	.460	.074
Taxation	.468	.008
Industrialization	.484	.016
Economic Ability	.492	.008

*Does not include public libraries.

In the index for overall library development (where Sunday school and church libraries constitute about three-fourths of the index), education is again dominant.

Conclusions and Interpretations

Given these results one is certainly tempted to agree with McMullen's assertion, over ten years ago, that "we do not yet know enough about the reasons why libraries have been founded or why they have remained in existence."[23] If it were an accepted fact, instead of remaining an empirical question, that when using county-level data for 1860 and 1870 the results would be very similar to those for the 1850 county-level analysis, then McMullen's assessment would continue to be a good one. At the moment, however, it is an empirical question and we must go with the best available information.

Therefore, the results presented here tend to confirm two different kinds of conclusions. First, and probably most important, library development is a complex phenomenon. It does vary from type of library to type of library and from one period to another. Second, it appears that there is some merit to the classical explanations about the influence of the traditional socioeconomic factors on library development. Education, literacy, economic ability, industrialization, and urbanization are good contributors to an explanation of library development. Our theoretical rationale, which was derived from the work of the traditional library historians, seems to hold together fairly well, even though it is not a uniform or complete explanation of variability in library development.

For public library development, the explanation over the two different periods is fairly uniform. In 1850 the level of education is the best explanation; in 1870 it is an important supplemental factor to economic ability. These twin factors, education and economic ability, are very much in keeping with the arguments made by several library historians and are fairly well in agreement with the theoretical rationale. What is surprising is that they are strong *independent* contributors to the explanation, an indication that where public libraries are most highly developed (at least in 1870 at the state level), you must have a good economic base *and* a good formal educational system. The fact that urbanization and industrialization also contribute independently of each other and of education and economic ability is an indication that public library development is highest in those states with strong urban and industrialized communities. These independent effects are somewhat surprising and are in contrast to my earlier study of public library development in 1974, where neither education nor economic ability was a sufficient explanation.[24]

When assessing the explanations for overall library development, it is important to keep in mind that Sunday school and church libraries constitute, in 1860 and 1870, the majority of this index. Since this type of library has been of little interest to library historians, it makes this a somewhat less useful measure of overall library development. Despite this problem, the measure is useful because it encompasses all kinds of nonprivate libraries in existence at these times. Again, education proves to be a consistently powerful explanation and, when combined with industrialization and urbanization, it is possible to explain almost half of the variation in total library development.

This basic set of factors continues to be important to the individual explanation for Sunday school/church libraries and school/college libraries. The surprises here are the extent to which mass communication is a good explanation for the development of school/college libraries and industrialization for Sunday school/church libraries. Exactly why this would be different from the explanations for public libraries and overall library development is difficult to determine and not provided for in the theoretical rationale.

In general, it can be said that the theoretical rationale does have merit in that it names variables that have an influence on library development —overall as well as for specific types of libraries. The rationale also states an ordering of these variables as to importance and sequence. The results show fairly well that the stated order of importance also has merit. What has not been tested here is the sequencing, over time, of these influences. To some extent, this may not be necessary because the expectation, based on an analysis of the interrelationships between these variables, is that the ones critical to library development are all occurring at about the same time. Where this is not happening or where one is dominant, library development is apparently being impeded in some way. This assertion, however, as an extension of the theoretical model, needs testing using time series data.

The issue of what is happening over time within a community or state to affect library development is, of course, the heart of the matter, because library development only happens over time. In this regard, the expectation was that the development of one type of library would have strong and positive effects on the development of all others. Based on the results shown in table 2, this is obviously not happening. In fact, the correlations are so low in the 1850 county data that one can safely say that, if you found one well-developed type of library in a community in that year, the probability of finding another well-developed type of library is practically zero. This conclusion does not augur well for the formation of a general theory of library development and implies the need for separate "types of libraries" theories or a "stages of library development"-type theory. These kinds of theories are certainly less desirable than a general one and, more importantly, are in contrast to the findings here that show repeated instances across types of libraries where education, economic ability, industrialization, and urbanization are good predictors of library development.

Obviously, this problem—as well as several others already mentioned—is not going to be answered by this study. Additional research, using county-level (or better) data over time will be needed. It will also be necessary to take a look at geographic differences in various parts of the United States during these periods. This should be particularly interesting because of the well-known socioeconomic differences that existed at these times among the several regions. Alternative measures of the central concepts used in this study (such as library development, education, urbanization, and so forth) also need further examination and validation.

Despite the fact that a good deal of work has been done on the development of libraries in nineteenth century America, a great deal more needs to be done. This study was an attempt to reformulate and empirically test some of the theoretical conceptualizations that arose out of this earlier work. This theoretical rationale has both merit and weaknesses. These weaknesses are in the nature of an incomplete explanation of library development, lack of specification of the sequencing of factors that affect library development, and, most importantly, how these factors affect different types of libraries over time.

Notes

1. See, for example, the comments in Edward G. Holley's *Raking the Historic Coals* (n.p.: Beta Phi Mu, 1968), pp. 3-9.

2. Robert V. Williams, "Theoretical Issues and Constructs Underlying the Study of Library Development," *Libri* 34/1 (Winter 1984): 1-16.

3. Robert V. Williams, "The Public Library as the Dependent Variable: Historically Oriented Theories and Hypotheses of Public Library Development," *Journal of Library History* 16/2 (Spring 1981): 329-341.

4. Jesse H. Shera, *Foundations of the Public Library: The Origins of the Public Library Movement in New England, 1629-1855* (Chicago: University of Chicago Press, 1949), pp. 243-244.

5. Sidney H. Ditzion, *Arsenals of a Democratic Culture: A Social History of the American Public Library Movement in New England and the Middle States, from 1850 to 1900* (Chicago: American Library Association, 1947), p. 190.

6. Robert E. Lee, *Continuing Education for Adults through the American Public Library, 1833-1964* (Chicago: American Library Association, 1966), p. 3.

7. Jean Hassenforder, "Comparative Studies and the Development of Public Libraries," *Unesco Bulletin for Libraries* 22, no. 1 (January-February 1968): 13-14.

8. Sidney L. Jackson, *Libraries and Librarianship in the West: A Brief History* (New York: McGraw-Hill, 1974).

9. Elmer D. Johnson and Michael H. Harris, *History of Libraries in the Western World*, 3rd ed. rev. (Metuchen, N.J.: Scarecrow, 1976), pp. 4-5.

10. *The Seventh Census of the United States: 1850 . . .* (Washington, D.C.: Robert Armstrong, Public Printer, 1853); *Statistics of the United States Census . . . 1860; Mortality and Miscellaneous Schedules . . .* (Washington, D.C.: Government Printing Office, 1866); *The Statistics of the Population of the United States . . .; The Statistics of School Attendance . . . Libraries . . .; Ninth Census, June 1, 1870* (Washington, D.C.: Government Printing Office, 1872).

11. Inter-University Consortium for Political and Social Research, *Codebook for the Historical Census . . .* (Ann Arbor, Mich.: ICPSR, 1963).

12. Kenneth G. Peterson, "Library Statistics and Libraries of the Southeast before 1876," *Southeastern Librarian* 22/2 (Summer 1972): 67-73.

13. For example, the manuscript schedules for 1850, 1860, and 1870 for the state of South Carolina are available on microfilm from the S.C. Dept of Archives and History.

14. "Remarks on the Statistics of Libraries," in *Statistics of the United States, 1870*, pp. 471-473.

15. Haynes McMullen, "More Statistics of Libraries in the Southeast before 1876," *Southeastern Librarian* 27/1 (Spring 1974): 18-28.

16. "Remarks on the Statistics of Libraries," in *Statistics of the United States, 1870*, p. 471.

17. Margaret Walsh, "The Census as an Accurate Source of Information: The Value of Mid-Nineteenth Century Manufacturing Returns," *Historical Methods Newsletter* 3/4 (September 1970): 3-13; "The Value of Mid-Nineteenth Century Manufacturing Returns: The Printed Census and the Manuscript Compilations Compared," *Historical Methods Newsletter* 4/2 (March 1971): 43-51.

18. Harvey J. Groff, "Notes on Methods for Studying Literacy from the Manuscript Census," *Historical Methods Newsletter* 5/1 (December 1971): 11-16.

19. Gretchen A. Condran and Eileen Crimmons, "A Description and Evalu-

ation of Mortality Data in the Federal Census: 1850–1900,'' *Historical Methods* 12/1 (Winter 1979): 1–23.

20. Williams, ''Theoretical Issues and Constructs Underlying the Study of Library Development,'' p. 5.

21. See the introduction in *Seventh Census of the United States: 1850*, pp. xi–xii.

22. Most of this work has been done on current data. See the discussion of a variety of these measures in the following two works: David Lehmann (ed.), *Development Theory* . . . (London: Frank Cass, 1979); Everett M. Rogers (ed.), *Communication and Development: Critical Perspectives* (Beverly Hills: Sage Publications, 1976).

23. McMullen, ''More Statistics of Libraries in the Southeast,'' p. 473.

24. Robert V. Williams, ''Sources of the Variability in Level of Public Library Development in the United States: A Comparative Analysis,'' *Library Research* 2/2 (Spring 1980): 157–176.

American Printers in the East Indies through 1850

Katharine Smith Diehl

My terminus while investigating printing and publishing in the East Indies has been 1850. Few American nationals were identified pre-1800; after that date persons with various interests are mentioned. They represented commerce, the United States government, evangelical Protestantism, printers, linguists, educators, authors, scientists, and journalists. Facing a 9- to 15-month sea voyage and great uncertainty, each was an adventurer. They adapted very quickly to strange circumstances and left some sort of record for us.

From 1492 until 1800 our land had been somewhat beset with wanderers who arrived for various reasons and with more or less intention to remain. Some of us are descendants of those people; we have, somehow, settled down.

There was a reverse migration and, for the purposes at hand, we will consider the movement of Americans to South Asia. Approximately 185 years ago a recent graduate of the medical school in Philadelphia set out with a ship traveling to Java. While a student his specialty field work was a study of regional poisonous plants, especially poison oak and poison ivy. Thomas Horsfield had good reason for being interested in such woody plants for they thrive in Pennsylvania woodlands and fence rows and he was from Bethlehem. Besides, several professors at the college were trying to make an inventory of the area vegetation; his work helped that project.

Dr. Horsfield was in Java (probably Batavia—Jakarta, as we know it) briefly when he suddenly realized the richness of possible investigations and his lack of books and laboratory equipment. He returned to Philadelphia, gathered what he considered essential, and returned to the island. Upon second arrival he began serious investigation of many plants and their known or unknown effects on living beings. One, in

Katharine Smith Diehl *is a printing historian, Seguin, Texas.*

particular, was especially important: the people used it in self-defense. When applied to the tips of arrows, death of the victim—animal or human—was virtually assured. He spent much time on this particular plant, testing its effects on animals (using dogs for many experiments), measuring the time between injection and onset of physical change and/or death spasms. Systematic records were made; then systematic reports followed the study of the records—and these were placed in his own "completed" file.

Horsfield knew of the Bataviaasch Genootschap van Kunsten en Wetenschappen: all important men in the Dutch government were members. He knew they published, but there were many and various travelers in Java and the Dutch Company (usually know as the VOC) was so busy with its own duties that it paid no attention to the wanderers. There were plantings, collections, processing, packaging, and shipping to attend. Besides all this, intra- and inter-island trade for numerous desirable commodities, plus interregional communication with the Company factories elsewhere in the seemingly endless East, had to be managed. Horsfield went unnoticed.

That is he went unnoticed until the briefly resident British set up government at Batavia, 1811–1816. In British tradition, Sir Thomas Raffles became president of Bataviaasch Genootschap, and the Society became known (in English) as Batavian Society of Arts and Sciences. Sir Thomas soon learned of Horsfield; they became acquainted; articles he had written years earlier were accepted for publication. At last some recognition was paid.[1] And, to make a long story end quickly, Raffles's wide interests in Javanese culture, products, and natural life led him to become so impressed by the doctor's field studies—and his ability to report them —that he asked Thomas Horsfield to travel to England and, there, to become head of the East India Company's Museum. The challenge was accepted; so, like many travelers, he made a roundabout voyage to Europe. Included was a visit to the Asiatick Society of Bengal, a Calcutta learned society that continues to be active. Eventually Horsfield assumed the Museum responsibility and remained in that post until his death in 1859 at the age of 86 years; he had been curator for about 40 years.

Some years later another Philadelphian, Dr. Josiah Harlan, arrived at Calcutta as a supercargo. He soon joined the East India Company's Medical Service as a temporary surgeon. This was just the time that the British and the people of Burma were having great misunderstandings—in the early 1820s. Dr. Harlan was involved in the Burmese war; he became ill and returned to Bengal (Calcutta) a sick man. He recovered and remained in the Medical Service several years longer to completely fill the terms of his contract. Apparently posted at Lucknow at Rs. 1,500 per month, he finally left both the Company's service and the region—

proposing to travel to St. Petersburg. By this time he knew Farsi, had assumed the local dress, and certainly crossed Afghanistan. Whether he reached St. Petersburg, I have not learned. Nor have I learned whether he wrote travel accounts for publication.[2]

In the early 1820s several societies interested in agriculture were organized in South Asia. The Agricultural and Horticultural Society of India a Calcutta body, was the first and remained the strongest in both its size and its activities. Quite early it became associated, through correspondence, with various Americans. When they sorted their desiderata, they wrote to Landreth of Philadelphia, a seed firm. Not everything that was shipped by Landreth germinated or matured satisfactorily; however, the interest of each party was quickened. The Society's *Transactions*, its *Journal*, and its other publications (both in English and in Bengali)—through the years to the end of the 1840s—are replete with hopes for new vegetable and horticultural products. Cotton as a commercial crop (a Georgia long staple variety) was desired. Potatoes, garden peas, and other vegetables were introduced in both Bengal and Ceylon (particularly in the Kandyan Hills); there was a Society active on that island. Some flowers became quickly acclimated, and many of us in the warmer parts of the United States realize the great number of woody plants that originated in the sub-Himalayas and elsewhere in Asia. Even our brightly colored houseplant, the begonia, was growing on a bank of a small stream in Assam when I wandered through those lovely woodlands in 1961. And the photinia, which in my own garden may reach 20 feet, I saw in grand maturity at about 75 feet—also in Assam.

Some of this agricultural exchange was the result of the interest that American consuls showed when they reached their Indian offices, both at Calcutta and at Bombay. In each place at least some of the appointees were doctors. There was Edward Ely, M.D., a native of Pennsylvania and our consul at Bombay, who died there on 17 January 1858 at the age of 34 years. Dr. Ely is mentioned as one of 13 Americans (individual or group) whose tombstones have been discovered in the Bombay area. The memorials represent a cross section of travelers, wives, children, husbands (sometimes in a single plot), seamen, and others who died while there.[3] Published in a small Bombay journal, *Indica*, some years ago, this is the only such list of which I know, though the cemetery at Uduvil, near Jaffna in Sri Lanka, is the burial site of quite a number of Americans who had belonged to the mission settled in that part of the island. More about them later.

In the 1840s, Dr. Charles Huffnagle was the American consul in Calcutta. Among my countrymen, I have learned of none so active as he was in the local community. A member of the Asiatic Society of Bengal, he was on the Committee on Papers (they selected articles to be published), and he accepted his share in the Society's activities in whatever manner was appropriate. The same was true of his membership in the Agricultural and Horticultural Society of India, where his responsibility was practical rather than academic. Notice, in retrospect, that these individuals were medical doctors born in our own Northeast where people were most settled and had greatest educational advantages. Philadelphia remained the center of medical education and publishing for many, many more years.

Lindley Murray (1745–1826) was born at a place known as Swatara —now the name of a somewhat large stream emptying into the Susquehanna near Middletown; the village name is lost and the location is unclear. Like Thomas Horsfield, Murray was the child of Quaker parents, and the son of a father who knew exactly what his son was to do in life: be a lawyer. Murray studied law and, indeed, practiced it until 1784 when he retired (about 40 years of age). He went to England. There he began writing and the works of greatest importance were his language books. His *Grammar of the English Language* was standard in both England and the United States for close to 50 years and became almost standard, certainly equally popular, in India in full English and diglot versions.[4] I have found several editions in various language combinations. Most of them, if not full English, are attributed (originally) to the translator and I may have failed to identify some in my own investigations.

There was the Scot, William Robertson (1721–1793), an historian who wrote before the American colonies had rejected British direction. I found it interesting that a full 75 years later some of his writings should have issued from an American press anywhere in the world. His *History of America* (London, 1777), in 2 volumes, was used again and again as the basis for vernacular history texts in the East Indies.[5] Portions were excerpted—the Columbus story being the favorite. I found it in several languages—either as a pamphlet or as an article (possibly continued) in a serial for young people learning both English and history. An 1849 edition of selections from the second volume was prepared in Marathi by a Bombay pundit and printed at the American Mission Press in that city. The fairly large book of 178 pages of text was in Professor A. K. Priolkar's personal library when I collated it. Since his death it is probably among the large collection that he designated for the University of Bombay Library, their Rare Collection.

In addition to individual and United States government influences in the East Indies, there were corporate contributions of a quite different nature. The earliest came as a result of a meeting of the General Association of Massachusetts Proper, held at Bradford on 27 June 1810. The committee that resulted from the June meeting gathered about ten weeks later (5 September 1810) at Farmington, Connecticut, for a very special purpose. Known as the American Board of Commissioners for Foreign Missions, they planned to introduce Adoniram Judson, Jun., Samuel Nott, Jun., Samuel J. Mills, and Samuel Newell. These four were volunteering to represent the Board as missionaries. India was the objective but, because India was under British government, it was decided to send one of them to England to make inquiries concerning possible cooperative or joint Christian missions. Accordingly, it was Judson who was sent. He had some unexpected delays due to international affairs between France and Great Britain, but he did meet officials of the London Missionary Society, which was supplying chaplains where government agreed to have them in India. No cooperative plans could be arranged; Judson returned to New England and the Board decided to proceed independently. By this time the volunteering group had changed a bit. Mills had left; Luther Rice and Gordon Hall had joined. There were five young men, all college graduates with some theological training, and two of them would take some medical courses before departure. Due to travel accommodation delays they had time to spare.

By the time the American Board of Commissioners for Foreign Missions met for the third time (16–17 September 1812) Judson and Newell had married and the two couples had sailed on one vessel; several weeks later Mr. and Mrs. Nott (but recently married), Hall, and Rice sailed. A Mr. Charles Ralston of Philadelphia was actively helpful in securing the travel space for the latter group; he remained interested in the work of the Board until his death in August 1836 and is believed to be the first American layman so involved.

We might call those Americans professional Christians. There were many ordinary Christians living in Calcutta at the time. The Americans, upon arrival, were not the first to receive a greeting of unwelcome. The Serampore Trio—William Carey, Joshua Marshman, and William Ward—had had the same experience some fifteen years earlier: they solved their dilemma by departing British territory and moving into Danish Serampore (about fifteen miles north). When the Americans found themselves in difficulty, the experienced men at Serampore had words of counsel and tried to resolve the troubles. The efforts were futile. Government under Minto was firm: Get out; get out immediately. Stay away from land under the British flag.[6]

They got out—variously and to several destinations. Adoniram Judson and Luther Rice went to Burma; Samuel Newell went to Ceylon, and after a bit less than a year, requested Governor Brownrigg of Ceylon to give a testimonial for his transfer to Bombay, where (following some very serious negotiations) Gordon Hall and Samuel Nott had been permitted to settle. Without going into further details of the migration, the

Bombay American Mission can be considered established from 12 February 1813. Of the men in Bombay, Nott remained until 7 September 1815; Newell died in May 1821; and Hall died in March 1826.

The diaspora had occurred. Instead of five individuals or couples in one community—Bengal/Calcutta—Burma, Ceylon, and Bombay had been visited. The quota of nonchaplain clergy for Ceylon was filled when Newell arrived. But Ceylon was a Crown Colony, thus directly under Home Rule and not under the British Indian government. At each of these locations a press, or presses, was soon at work. The products varied from elementary diglot linguistics, to biblical selections, to job printing of infinite variety. The latter was essential to help pay Mission Station expenses. Now consider the three locations individually.

Both Adoniram Judson and Luther Rice had had religious awakening while on ship or shortly after reaching Serampore. Each was baptized according to the Baptist rite while at Serampore. That cut them from the American Board and placed them with the British Baptists in whose fold the Serampore was situated. Affiliation with their New England sponsors and friends was officially broken but, unlike the other three, this duo was now part of a community experienced in several ways. Principally, they had entered a small informal society that was doing very responsible, unique translating, printing, type-founding, and even paper-making. But Burma was not a politically settled part of the world. For several years Judson could move about, could work on his language investigations, and could begin translating the New Testament (always the first portion to be attempted in a new language). British and Burmese were clashing more and more, and in the early 1820s the situation became violent; Judson was imprisoned and was not always treated gently. The press could not be used, but he did have his dictionary ready to print. Another individual, G. H. Hough, also had a dictionary prepared for the press, smaller than Judson's. Hough was able to get it to the Mission Press at Serampore where it was printed. Judson's had to wait another year. In 1826 *A Dictionary of the Burman Language, compiled from the manuscripts of A. Judson, D.D. and of other missionaries in Burmah*, appeared from the Baptist Mission Press, Calcutta. It was seen through the press by the linguistically competent American Jonathan Wade. Variant languages are many in a riverine/mountainous land such as the Burmese-Malay Peninsula: every valley—even across every river—has its vernacular. Finally, free to be at his translation, Judson completed the New Testament (Moulmein, 1836) and the entire Bible was printed in 1840. This was the third edition for the New Testament and the first edition of the Old Testament; an edition of 5,000 copies of the pair was made.

Less well known than Judson was another American, Nathan Brown, who—with wife and small daughter—was with Judson while learning

Burmese. Printer O. T. Cutter and wife were there too—with Cutter in charge of the American Mission Press. Just after the 1836 biblical printing was completed, an official British committee (chiefly from the Calcutta offices) began search for a tea plant they could propagate, transplant, and harvest profitably. They knew varieties were growing in the hills of what we call Assam, Bhutan, Burma, and the upper reaches of the Brahmaputra River. That was the signal for the Browns, the Cutters, and several others to join the investigators, to introduce printing and Christianity. They actually traveled almost as far as the gorge through which the great Yarlung Zangbo rushes from the north slope of the Snowy Range (as Himalaya is translated) to the south slope, where it is known as the Brahmaputra. First settled at Sadiya (96° E, 28° N) they made it their home for a short time. The press was erected; I found no imprints. However, in a rather short time, the families moved a short distance downstream, to a place then known as Jaipur (no longer named on large atlases and not to be confused with the large Jaipur southwest of Delhi). From that location I found a single language book written by Mrs. O. T. Cutter (using her personal initials, H. B. L. Cutter): *Vocabulary and Phrases, in English and A'sa'mese.* The imprint reads: *Jaipur, printed at the American Baptist Mission Press, 1840.* This 12mo of 252 pages represents a press active in the most remote location I have identified; it remains a very remote part of the world.[7]

On the opposite side of the subcontinent, Bombay became center for Americans' most generally productive publishing operations. I have some difficulty being enthusiastic about their "Christian mission" for they were so intense with printing. Though I made several extended research visits to Bombay, an American "mission" was never identified as a continuing location. They were settled, at least for printing, on Jail Road in the district known as Bhendi-Bazar—a very well-known district some distance from Bombay Harbor. The American Mission Press, Bombay, printed for everybody. Virtually all society publications (non-government) were their products; Bible Society orders (whether British, American, or local), as well as Tract Society 12mos, were printed according to contract. Much government work, and many reports and monographs for local community organizations helped keep them busy. Until the Scots had their lithographic press operating at what is now Wilson College, the American Mission Press did their work. I have found no evidence that they had a lithographic press in Bombay; however, they did have one at their mission located at Ahmadnagar, some distance away from Bombay.

Many, many pages—thousands and thousands of them—came from the American Mission Press, Bombay. Unacknowledged is the actual director of the press and printing establishment, a man named Thomas

Graham. No, he was not an American; no, he was not a Briton; yes, he was a Bengali Christian whom Gordon Hall had found during that brief, not-so-pleasant residence in Calcutta. He was, if the name and childhood residence be any indication, a protégé of the well-known, very able Thomas Graham—close friend of the Serampore Missionaries. On title page after title page Thomas Graham's name appears: always on pages in vernacular languages and type, and on English-language publications intended for local or regional use. His name is not on imprints intended for shipment to the West (either Britain or the United States). I cannot say that it *never* appeared on such title pages, but I certainly do not recall finding it on any text that was intended, primarily, for export. The missionary who had been deputed from our own New England office is named; not T. Graham who really did the work. Of course, you and I can point the finger inwards to the times our library assistants, our student assistants, and our lesser-rank colleagues did some of our groundwork. Even that does not excuse this neglect of Thomas Graham, the boy-turned-man who worked at that printing establishment from the beginning until the late 1850s when it was sold. Historian Henry J. Bruce does give him credit for type-founding and for improvement of the vernacular fonts used in both Marathi and Guzarati work. I read those compliments under the 1882 imprint, but Thomas Graham may not have been around to see them.[8]

In 1812, following Minto's order that Americans get out of the country, Samuel Newell reached Colombo. It was not antagonism that caused difficulty for him to continue residence, but the quota for non-government-appointed, avowedly Christian missionaries was already filled. About a decade later the situation had changed and a group of Americans was permitted to enter. They decided to go to Jaffna to a village they called Batticotta (today, Vaddukoddai). Education was their primary objective; cultural and religious changes would follow.

The Wesleyan Mission Press in Colombo printed several small pieces for the Americans, but the earliest imprint I have found from the Jaffna region is *The First Report of the American Mission Seminary, Jaffna, Ceylon. Nellore: Church Mission Press. 1827*. But eight leaves, it is paged i–ii, 1–14. There are 41 lines in a space of 192 × 135 mm. And the place, Nellore, is another village in Jaffna District where the Church Mission was residing. Obviously, the language of the *Report* is English. It was intended for the American Board in New England, and for the English-speaking community in both Ceylon and India. Local readers would be using Tamil, seminary courses would involve both languages as well as Sanskrit. As events proved, the Americans would become the only missionaries on the island to print in Tamil; government had to use it, but the Wesleyans and the Baptists never did.

In 1829, the first press arrived for the American Mission. Without a printer in the community, it was lent to the Church Mission at nearby Nellore for use until an American professional printer might be found. In 1834 Eastman Strong Minor came; he remained until late 1849. A second press and supplies had arrived earlier.[9]

Individuals representing the American Board received annual cash salaries. By any of our standards the amount was small, but they had few needs requiring money. Theirs was a barter economy and the press, as part of the usual equipment, was supposed to pay some costs. The Board supplied (shipped) fine-to-finest qualities of paper and other essential press supplies. The press may have been the gift of a congregation. Locally-made paper was used for products that probably would have a short life; the fine rag paper was reserved for permanent imprints.

Jaffna may be considered (1) a large village and (2) a district about the size of a county. The American Mission was actually in Jaffna District, and they used the large-city name for geographical identification. By mid-century they had small settlements of one or another kind in several villages, but the village names are always secondary for identification purposes.

Like the sister mission in Bombay, the Jaffna community had close associations with the various Bible and Tract Societies: both were becoming worldwide as well as intermission in their work. For each of these organizations, American Mission Press at Jaffna printed—sometimes by contract with another mission, and at other times, at its own cost for local use. Generally, imported supplies were used.

How many documents did the Jaffna American Press produce? Taking only the General Series of tracts (each bearing a code number for interlingual identification), 86 were issued through 1850 (my terminus). Of these, I found examples of exactly 70 titles, not from a particular edition, but from some edition of the possible 3 to 6 in which it had appeared. Small 12mos, they range from 8 to 80 pages. Number 1 in the series, *The Spiritual Light* (in Tamil), had reached 95,000 copies in 10 editions by 1843. Only 8 pages of 29 lines each, the précis on the title page reads: "Refers to heathen practices and notions, and containing extracts from native writings in refutation of their System. It closes with a poem/hymn of 5 four-line stanzas." I found one example from those 95,000 copies. But of the 70 titles discovered, it was possible to identify most of the individuals primarily responsible for the original texts. The information is not usually in the book.

This press had its type foundry and its very faithful crew of workmen. By using various contemporary sources (government and Mission), I learned that in some years they were actually running a double 8-hour shift in order to meet demands for print.[10] They eventually had four presses and from 50 to 75 men on a single shift; this was split somehow when the double shift was working, when they seem to have added some 15 or 20 more men. Remember that everything was handwork—everything! Stitching, trimming, pasting, all the additional little duties of pasting a bright-colored paper over white paper to present a more attractive 12mo—all motions, every single one, were hand/foot motions.

Recall that for many years infants born into Roman Catholic families were given at least one name commemorating a saint; and in numerous Protestant communities a biblical name was similarly given. In Roman Catholic India, when the village chief became Christian, it meant that the entire village was also Christian. Each individual would be given (as a kind of surname) the name of the visiting priest or bishop who celebrated the rite. In Jaffna the system was different. Any American who made a contribution of twenty dollars (or multiples) was privileged to suggest a name to be given to a newly baptized individual. In *Complete / List / of / Church Members / Connected with the / American Mission Churches, / Jaffna. / May 1839* there are names such as Amy Tompkins, Ebenezer Porter, Susannah Anthony, Timothy Dwight, Martha Washington, Francis S. Key, Cotton Mather, Chauncey Goodrich, and John W. Chickering. In recent years there has been a tendency to recover the original names.

Nowhere in South and Southeast Asia has American influence been so great as in Jaffna District, at the very northern part of Sri Lanka (Ceylon). The first, and continuous, major project was the school (seminary) at Vaddukoddai for youths aged eight to twenty, a 6-year program that seems to have closed with the virtual equivalent of high school standard. Classes were taught in English; the curriculum was general; and there was Bible study and daily chapel. Except for the earliest years of the Portuguese school in Goa (approximately the 1550–1570 period), I have learned of few institutions where every student had his books for every subject. In most schools, the lecture method was normal, and the teacher was lucky to have a real printed book for everything taught. At Vaddukoddai they had sufficient textbooks, among which were Lindley Murray's various English language books (many copies).[11]

Very soon, medical studies were introduced by an American doctor. A girls' school (for prepuberty years) was organized in a neighboring village named Uduvil. Medical studies led to several clinics, but no major hospital; that happened when the Jaffna Mission gradually divided and several went to the mainland. The Women's Medical Hospital at Vellore, its partner and smaller hospital at Chittoor, both in the southern part of the peninsula, gradually developed into a major teaching institution at Vellore and a separate location for the two units. American funds continue to be sent regularly.

Back to Vaddukoddai. In 1841 a twice-monthly diglot paper was started: *Uthayatharaka* or *Morning Star*. Originally an edition of 1,000 copies was printed; half were for sale, and half for later binding and sale as volumes. That paper continues. It serves as the diocesan paper for the Church of Sri Lanka. The Jaffna College chapel serves as diocesan cathedral; it had been built by the Portuguese, remodeled by the Dutch, and again, very slightly, by the British.

In numerous places in British India, individuals or committees were busy preparing dictionaries, and their basis was Johnson's work. The Americans chose Webster's and the director of the Jaffna Press handled two sets of orders for copies of the 2-volume royal octavo first edition. *Morning Star* carries notices of his intentions. Work was begun at Jaffna on a diglot Tamil-English dictionary. Half completed by the original compiler, that portion was printed in Jaffna (pp. 1–128); the work was continued by several individuals who transferred to the American Mission in Madras. P. R. Hunt, printer at the American Mission Press, Madras, printed the balance. So we have a Jaffna imprint for a small section, and a Madras imprint for the balance (pp. 129–830). Individuals involved were Joseph Knight (British) and later the Americans Levi Spaulding and Samuel Hutchings.

Before the first Americans appeared at Calcutta there were contacts between the Serampore Mission and the United States. William Carey, the actual founder of that mission, had made such a great impression on people in the English-speaking world that his name reached New England. In 1807 he was honored by Brown University with the LL.D. degree. In 1811 a similar honor was received by his partner, Joshua Marshman. Both were granted in absentia. The third man of the trio, William Ward, was their press director and many persons believe that he was the best educated (formally) of the three. In 1818 Ward traveled to England and then to New York City, where he remained for three months. During that time, speaking to numerous groups, he made a plea for funds to support the college being organized on their property, Serampore College. By the time he left this country, he had received $10,000 for the single purpose—a college, not a theological school (nor has it ever been a theological school), though biblical studies have been part of the general curriculum until quite recently.[12]

Americans made some interesting impressions here and there and, at certain places in South Asia, or beyond, their influence was very great. I regret their apparent separateness from the local societies—but they were in the minority both nationally and ecclesiastically. They worked hard; they did a lot of local job printing and considerable translating (but not a great deal of really original writing and translating). When it came to church music, they failed. Certainly in the Bombay area they had made the mistake of using local melodies for hymns (usually translations) to be used at worship: not a single one remained in print even thirty or forty years later simply because of the melody's non-Christian association.[13] On the other hand, physicians were usually quite ready to adopt local medicaments that had proved effective; they added what they could from their American learning. These were quickly accepted—save in one respect: women in Asia were cared for medically or during childbirth by women. Even for that critical issue, the Americans found a solution; however, it came some 50 years later than my investigations through organization of the Women's Medical Hospital (mentioned earlier) at Vellore. As Serampore College continues to be a very vital institution, so Jaffna College at Vaddukoddai continues with, perhaps, more emphasis on school than college. The library is now in a new structure, thanks to American gifts. And in that library is the only collection of early imprints that I was able to find—a sample, or office file, collection of products of the local press. Certainly not complete, the joy of finding so many of them under a single roof was greater than I could express then—or now.

Notes

1. *Verhandelingen van het Bataviaasch Genootschap der Kunsten en Wetenschappen* (Batavia, i.e., Jakarta), 7 (1814) contains 12 articles, of which 7 are by Horsfield; and 8 (1816) contains 3 articles by Horsfield and 4 by Sir Thomas Raffles.

2. Victor Jacquemont, *Travels in North India & Kasmir 1829 to 1831*, in H. L. O. Garrett (ed. and tr.), *The Punjab a Hundred Years Ago: as Described by V. Jacquemont (1831) and A. Soltykoff (1842)* (Patiala, New Delhi: Offset Master Printers, 1971), pp. 31-32.

3. Braz A. Fernandes, "American Tombs in Bombay 1794-1868," *Indica* (Bombay) 8/1 (March 1971): 33-39.

4. "Murray, Lindley," in *Encyclopaedia Britannica*, 11th ed., 19: 42a.

5. "Robertson, William," in *Encyclopaedia Britannica*, 11th ed., 23: 406-407.

6. American Board of Commissioners for Foreign Missions, *First Ten Annual Reports . . . with Other Documents* (Boston: Crocker and Brewster, 1834). Years 1810-1820 are reported.

7. Eliza Whitney Ballard Brown, *The Whole World Kin: A Pioneer Experience among Remote Tribes, and Other Labors of Nathan Brown* (Philadelphia: Hubbard Brothers, 1890), pp. 1-192, passim.

8. Henry J. Bruce, *The Literary Works of the American Marathi Mission, 1813-1881. Reprinted from the "Memorial Papers"* (Bombay: Education Society's Press, Byculla, 1882), p. 22.

9. American Ceylon Mission, *Report of the American Ceylon Mission, From Its Commencement in 1816 to the Close of 1846* (Jaffna: American Mission Press, 1846), pp. 73-79.

10. Ibid.

11. American Ceylon Mission Seminary, *The Second Triennial Report* (Nellore: Church Mission Press, 1830), pp. 3, 29-30.

12. John Clark Marshman, *The Life and Times of Carey, Marshman, and Ward, Embracing the History of the Serampore Mission*, 2 vols. (London: Longman, Brown, et al., 1859), 1: 290 for Carey; 1: 465 for Marshman; and 2: 187–222 for Ward.
13. Bruce, *Literary Works*, p. 49.

The several examples used in this paper are from those I discovered during eight and a half years (of the period 1959–1972) of field research in South and Southeast Asia. My focus has been the press, publishers and their products, people involved in the technology. Chiefly, my interest is people, their response to the press, and what they did with it in their tradition. More will be found in my *Printers and Printing in the East Indies to 1850*, in 8 volumes plus a large ninth volume of bibliography, to be published by Aristide D. Caratzas (New Rochelle, N.Y.), beginning with volume I scheduled for Winter 1985–86. Volume II is to follow directly.

German Influences on the Development of Research Libraries in Nineteenth-Century Bombay

Donald Clay Johnson

Between 1859 and 1881 three Germans served as Sanskrit professors in colleges affiliated with Bombay University. In order to teach then-modern linguistic methodologies they required access to Sanskrit manuscripts. The Government of Bombay, and later the Government of India, funded survey and acquisitions trips in western India with the understanding that collected titles must remain in India, although they could be lent to any scholar anywhere in the world. Resulting from this enlightened government support of scholarship is the Bhandarkar Oriental Research Institute Library, a preeminent manuscript research library in western India.

> The Sanskrit language, whatever be its antiquity, is of a wonderful structure; more perfect than the Greek, more copious than the Latin, and more exquisitely refined than either, yet bearing to both of them a stronger affinity, both in the roots of the verbs and in the forms of the grammar, than could possibly have been produced by accident; so strong, indeed, that no philologer could examine them, all three, without believing them to have sprung from some common source, which, perhaps, no longer exists.[1]

These words of Sir William Jones delivered in the third anniversary address of the Asiatic Society of Bengal on 2 February 1786 launched a

Donald Clay Johnson *is head, Reader Services Division, College of William and Mary.*

This paper is based on research conducted at the India Office Library and Records. The author wishes to express his appreciation for the assistance given to him in conducting this study.

tidal wave of scholarship in comparative philology that ultimately led to the formation of both the discipline of linguistics as we know it today and Indic studies, the detailed investigations of the culture and civilization of India. Previously the accepted belief for the diversity of languages in the world derived from the biblical Tower of Babel, and great effort was made to trace all tongues to this origin. Jones in his brilliant observation regarding Sanskrit stumbled upon the heart of the Indo-European family of languages, and over the next century scholars traced the development and evolution of this linguistic tree.

While British scholars were the first Westerners to learn Sanskrit and to introduce it to the West, almost immediately continental scholars, especially German-speaking ones, played key roles in the great linguistic discoveries. For instance, it was Franz Bopp's research that proved Jones's assumption.[2] German universities established chairs for the study of Sanskrit long before British universities did, and by the mid-nineteenth century, German Sanskrit scholars joined a diaspora throughout the world in search of employment. Several of these scholars were hired by the Government of India. Three Germans who played a key role in Bombay Sanskrit scholarship—Martin Haug, Georg Bühler, and Franz Kielhorn—also, by their activities, led to the establishment of the most prominent Sanskrit manuscript library in Bombay Presidency. Their work in Bombay allows one to observe both how well German academic attitudes toward libraries adapted to the Indian setting and how their work assisted or hindered the growth and development of collections in Bombay.

Martin Haug came to India in 1859 as superintendent of Sanskrit studies at Poona College. His appointment, just a year after the assumption of responsibility for India by the British Crown, reflected a determined effort to recruit noted scholars to strengthen Indian academic programs. As such, he was in the enviable position of being able not only to introduce new research and teaching programs, but also to receive government support for related projects. During his first four years at Poona College, Haug successfully introduced his students to then-current European research methodologies for Sanskrit and other classical languages. This work impressed officials in the Bombay Education Department so much that in 1862, when E. I. Howard, director of the department, made an inspection trip through the presidency and learned of various places that had reputed rich holdings of Sanskrit manuscripts, he appended a note to his report indicating the desirability of sending Haug on a trip through Gujarat "in the interest of Zend and Sanskrit philology."[3] The local press supported the suggestion and recommended several additional things Haug could do while on such a linguistic survey.[4] The Government of Bombay approved the project, and Haug made the trip. Had subsequent events not overtaken him, Haug's expedition might never have attracted attention or been remembered. But fate intervened.

Upon his return from Gujarat, Haug submitted a report that discussed his successes and failures in detail. The *Times of India* newspaper, for whatever motivation, published it, without editing, and stirred up a hornets' nest.[5] Two things in particular aroused much ire in an ensuing newspaper war of words. First, Haug accused two prominent Bombay intellectuals, Dr. Bhau Daji and Shastri Pandurang, of sabotaging his work in Surat by telling people there not to show or to sell their manuscripts to him. Second, and far more important for the history of Indian libraries, was his comment that he personally had received several manuscripts as gifts. People wondered whether these titles were going to go into some type of manuscript repository in Bombay or whether Haug intended to keep them for himself. The *Times of India* issues for June and July 1864 contained numerous articles questioning the ultimate disposition of the works. Making the situation particularly ominous was the recently discovered example of Aloys Sprenger, who had assembled a manuscript collection during his career in India and subsequently had sold it for £20,000 in Berlin. People asked if Haug, too, was amassing a collection of manuscripts that would be sold in Europe.

One of the individuals active in the war of words, using the *nom de plume* Bibliophilus, raised questions that forced the government of Bombay to consider the fate of Indian manuscripts. He noted that "these manuscripts, though in the possession of private parties, are, to a certain extent, the property of the race."[6] Hence, they should be kept in India so that "when a race of . . . Sanscrit critical scholars arises in this country they [will not] have to go to Berlin, or Paris, or Copenhagen to consult the genuine manuscripts of their ancestral literature."[7] Bibliophilus thought access to manuscripts should always be provided to those Europeans living in India and copies could always be made for scholars resident abroad. To facilitate access to manuscripts, Bibliophilus indicated he "would gladly see the originals collected and deposited in safe and careful custody under the auspices of Government."[8]

Haug, however, refused to part with the manuscripts, resigned his appointment, and returned to Europe. In 1877 his widow sold the Haug Manuscript Collection to the Königliche Bibliothek of Munich for 17,000 marks. Thus a European library benefited from the gifts Haug received.

Since the last half of the nineteenth century was the age of high imperialism when numerous European museums, archives, and libraries acquired priceless treasures from abroad, one might consider the actions of Haug not so unusual. However, the British defined their administration in India as a trust. As such, the cultural heritage of this trust was to remain in India. The examples of Haug and Sprenger illustrated what could happen if government did not take an interested role in the preservation of culture within India.

The Government of Bombay thus had to face a difficult problem. The need to have access to and copies of Sanskrit manuscripts for research continued. However, to repeat the Haug experience would precipitate numerous difficulties. Would it be better to drop the program at this point, or should government continue to encourage the discovery and distribution of information on Sanskrit manuscripts? The latter course prevailed, and two other Germans played crucial roles in the creation of the Government Sanskrit Collection.

The Government of Bombay asked Franz Kielhorn, Haug's replacement as professor of Sanskrit at Deccan College, to prepare a *catalogue raisonné* of the Sanskrit manuscripts held by government. However, there was no definition of whether these works formed a library, were to become a library, or what was to be done with them.

Also, Haug's infamous search trip did not consume all the funds allotted to it, and before the controversy narrated in the *Times of India* became public, the Government of Bombay had sanctioned a second search trip. The Bombay authorities consequently asked Georg Bühler to make the trip. Bühler, the first professor of Sanskrit at Elphinstone College, Bombay, came to India in 1862 after serving for a year as an assistant to the librarian of the Royal Library at Windsor Castle, and for five months in a similar capacity in the library of the University of Göttingen. Like Haug, Bühler immediately learned how woefully inadequate conditions were in Bombay for the establishment of a Sanskrit studies program comparable to those in European universities. Upon hearing his eloquent expression of concern, a group of Indians in Bombay took up a collection that raised 5,000 rupees to strengthen library holdings of Sanskrit materials.[9] Two years later, in 1864, the Government of Bombay appointed him to a commission charged with producing a digest of Hindu law cases. Most of the materials needed for such a compendium were available only in manuscripts, and Bühler soon became known in various learned circles for his interest in and need for such titles. Many people assisted him, both officially and unofficially. Thus the choice of Bühler to undertake the second search trip was most logical. He made it in 1866, and Elphinstone College's Sanskrit collection grew by 201 manuscripts.

Each of these manuscripts was unique to Bombay city, for Bühler had carefully prepared a union list of works owned by individuals and libraries in Bombay before he made his trip, and he did not duplicate titles on the list in his purchases. He distributed the list to Sanskrit scholars previous to his trip so that those individuals interested in selling works would not offer him titles already in Bombay. Conversely, he collected any lists of holdings of libraries in the presidency, so individuals in Bombay city could learn of unique titles not available in the capital. While on his trip, Bühler tried to hold as many meetings as possible with Sanskrit scholars to publicize his work and government's interest in Sanskrit studies. Bühler's public relations approach and great respect for the traditional methods of Sanskrit scholarship counterbalanced the negative impressions created earlier by Haug. By 1867 work in Bombay Presidency appeared to be well on the way to having government involved in a constructive role in providing the necessary manuscripts to support the Sanskrit programs in its colleges and universities.

As the work in Bombay evolved, another major source of financial support appeared. Thanks to expressions of concern and the presence on the Viceroy's Council of several scholarship-oriented officials, the Government of India passed a law on 3 November 1868 that set aside 25,000 rupees each year for the collection and the preservation of Sanskrit manuscripts.[10] Bombay received annual grants of 3,200 rupees and, with its previous experience in conducting searches, decided both Bühler and Kielhorn deserved support; a bifurcated search program was formed that conducted its first search just a month after the issuance of the central government act.

Although Bühler and Kielhorn undertook identical responsibilities, the realities of manuscript availability within Bombay Presidency meant that their accomplishments were very different. Kielhorn had as his search area the southern or Marathi-speaking portions of the presidency, while Bühler had the northern or Gujarati-speaking areas. Poona in the Marathi area long had been known as a great center of Sanskrit scholarship; unfortunately, only during those years when its famous resident Ramakrishna Gopal Bhandarkar, headed the searches did any significant number of manuscripts come to the government collections from the south. Kielhorn consequently spent most of his time working on bibliographic control of the collected titles, a topic that is discussed below.

Georg Bühler, on the other hand, stumbled upon one of the richest troves of Sanskrit treasures in India, and during his tenure with the searches, he managed to add 2,876 manuscripts to the government collection. When compared to the 362 added by Kielhorn during essentially the same period, one can see the sharp contrast in the acquisitions rates of the two Germans. One reason why Bühler may have been so successful was his transfer in 1868 to the position of educational inspector for the northern portion of Bombay Presidency. The move relocated him to Surat and required constant traveling through the northern areas of the presidency. He soon learned that, in addition to centers of Sanskrit learning previously known, many towns and villages had notable collections that merited consideration under the search program. Upon establishing contact in such places, his rate of acquisitions grew tremendously.

While his new position did not deal directly with Sanskrit research and teaching, Bühler continued his work on the language. He and Kielhorn served as editors of the Bombay Sanskrit Series, one of the notable nineteenth-century compendia for promoting Sanskrit study. His communications with scholarly groups around the world precipitated numerous requests for assistance in gaining access to Sanskrit materials, and Bühler personally escorted a Russian scholar fortunate enough to be sent to India to acquire needed works. All of these activities greatly enhanced the reputation of Bombay as a center for Sanskrit learning and helped to spread the fame of the ever-growing government collection of manuscripts. While Bühler did not take the initiative to convert the collection into a library in the sense that we use the term today, he amassed the essential bulk of materials that eventually would serve as the basis for a library. A summary of his acquisitions activities shows the support government provided to him, the success he enjoyed in his work, and that his work went far beyond the borders of Bombay Presidency.

After an initial flourish of searches generated by the Government of India's 1868 Act, several years passed before Bühler made his most stunning discoveries. In 1872 Major-General Alexander Cunningham, director general of the Archaeological Survey of India, drew government's attention to the comments of James Tod's 1839 book, which mentioned the rich manuscript holdings in the Rajputana princely states of Bikanir and Jesalmir.[11] Government reacted immediately and sent Bühler on a survey that same year to the two states and to Jodhpur, another area known to contain unique titles. Thanks to the personal intervention of the Jesalmir Maharaval, Bühler received access to the library of the Aswal Jains, a collection of extreme rarity. In his report of the trip Bühler recorded finding the oldest extant manuscript in India, dated to 1103 A.D.[12] The Jain community gave him permission to copy any works he wanted. Bühler immediately hired copyists, but after he left Jesalmir all work for him ceased and he never received the titles he had requested.

Another rich library, in Patan, part of the princely state of Baroda, also attracted Bühler's attention and after a great deal of perseverance yielded a breakthrough. In 1873 he visited the city briefly; armed with a letter of introduction from Sir Lewis Pelly, Resident to the Baroda Court, he held meetings with the *Nagarseth* (chief merchant) and the *Panch* (Council of Elders). Some libraries were then opened to him, but not the most famous one, the Hemachandra Bhandar. After Bühler returned to Surat, the guardians of the Hemachandra Bhandar began playing a game of cat and mouse with him. First, they agreed to show him the collection. Bühler rushed to Patan, only to be shown a few dilapidated manuscripts. When he pressed the matter, the keepers showed him 6,000–7,000 works, none of which was of great value. Disappointed, Bühler returned to Surat. Again the keepers changed their minds and, as a measure of good faith, allowed his agent in Patan free access to the library. The agent reported seeing 40 boxes filled with rare works and immediately began to list the holdings of this unique library.[13]

In 1874 the Government of India gave Bühler 11,000 rupees and sent him on a ten-month survey to Kashmir, a princely state far removed from Bombay. The maharajah of Kashmir took a personal interest in Bühler's search and helped whenever possible. Bühler noted the numerous meetings arranged by the maharajah and the use of the royal road as particularly helpful gestures by His Highness.[14] The trip added to the Bombay collection several ancient birchbark manuscripts, works peculiar to Kashmir.

These projects of Bühler point out that survey work and collecting were not confined to British India. Princely states known to have outstanding collections received visits, and whenever possible these treasures were purchased and copied or, at the very least, holdings lists were prepared. Bühler's dedication to promoting Sanskrit scholarship seemed to permeate everything he did. His wide-ranging activities amply appear in his 1873/74 report for the searches, where he said:

> The following steps have been taken in order to make the Government collection known and useful. The report and classified list of purchases made in 1872–73 have been printed and issued. The life of Vikramankadeva has been edited by myself, and will form part of the Bombay Sanskrit series. Articles on the Jesalmir Bhandar and the new manuscripts of the Baialacchi have been published in the *Indian Antiquary*.
>
> Eight of the old palm leaf manuscripts acquired in 1872–73 have been sent to England at the request of the Government of Bombay, and have been exhibited at the Oriental Congress. According to a notice in the *Accademy* [*sic*], they were considered the most valuable among the manuscripts exhibited.
>
> Professor Kielhorn in Puna has received the loan of the Manduki Ajusale and Naradiya Sikshas acquired in Rajputana and in Gujrat.
>
> Dr. S. Goldschmidt in Strassburg has received a copy of Kalidasa's Setubandha, Mr. Griffiths in Benares a copy of Jenedra's commentary on the Kasika, and Mr. Shankar P. Pandit, a number of commentaries of the Kayhuvamsa. Besides, I have been able to procure loans of manuscripts from private libraries to several colleagues in Europe and in India.[15]

The report mentions the loan of manuscripts both within India and to Europe. Lending manuscripts to scholars away from India began in Bombay in 1869, when Professor Theodor Goldstücker of University College, London, borrowed three works. Each year thereafter requests came to Bombay for the loan of titles from the collection, and by the end of the first decade of the searches for Sanskrit manuscripts, 59 works had gone to scholars in the West. The countries and numbers of manuscripts were: Germany (27), Austria (20), Great Britain (9), and Russia (3). The procedure for this intercontinental lending was to send the manuscripts to the India Office Library in London that served as the western distribution center. The India Office Library then shipped them to the various European, and later American, libraries or scholars. If the manuscript went to a library, no indemnity bond was placed on the work. However, if the manuscript went directly to a scholar, a bond had to be placed before the manuscript left London. The program continued until the outbreak of World War I and is, I believe, the earliest example of a sustained and systematic library-to-library intercontinental lending of works. Altogether, between 1869 and 1913, a total of 791 manuscripts went to scholars resident outside India.

In addition to sending manuscripts to Europe via inter-library loan, there were five times when Bühler purchased manuscripts for scholars or libraries in the West. The Government of Bombay allowed these special purchases on the condition that the titles in question were already represented in good copies in the Bombay Collection. The first such request for assistance from Bühler came in 1873 from the Königliche Bibliothek in Berlin.[16] Over the next four years, Bühler bought 485 manuscripts for the Berlin library. In 1874 the Asiatic Society of Bengal asked him if he might help in acquiring manuscripts dealing with the Jains.[17] Bühler secured the necessary government permission, but the Society lost interest in the matter and no works went to Calcutta. A year later, in 1875, Professor E. B. Cowell asked Bühler to purchase manuscripts on the Jaina Agamas for Cambridge University Library. Over the next two years, Bühler sent 30 titles in response to this request.[18] Also in 1875 the Boden Professor of Sanskrit at Oxford, Sir Monier Monier-Williams, asked for some Jain manuscripts.[19] Bühler acquired the needed titles and sent them to Oxford thinking they were for the Bodleian Library. However, Monier-Williams had made a personal request. Subsequently, with the establishment of the Indian Institute at Oxford, Monier-Williams presented the volumes to its library. The last request came in 1878 when the Institut de France asked Bühler if he could obtain a set of the Samhitas of the four Vedas.[20] As a gesture of international scholarly goodwill, the Government of Bombay generously purchased the works and sent them to France as a gift.

During 1880, Bühler's last year in India, the Russian Sanskrit scholar Ivan Pavlovich Minaev (frequently spelled Minayeff) of St. Petersburg visited India in order to acquire manuscripts. Bühler kindly helped him to establish contact with Indian agents, with the proviso that all purchases were duplicates of titles in the Bombay Collection.

One sees in the activities of Bühler a great concern to discover the Sanskrit wealth of western India, for he extended the sphere of his work far beyond the borders of Bombay Presidency. The respect for his activities was so high that he was among the first fifty people to be honored with appointment to the Order of the Indian Empire when it was created in 1878. The acquisitions lists of the new titles added to the Bombay Collection and to selected libraries in India that he produced attracted worldwide attention and numerous requests to gain access to them. By allowing the intercontinental inter-library lending of manuscripts, Bühler solved the problem of allowing scholarly access to unique titles while retaining ownership of them in Bombay. Five times the Government of Bombay agreed that he might purchase manuscripts for others on the condition that the works were already in the Government Collection. Unquestionably, Bühler's great contributions were the acquisition of titles and the public relations to establish the prestige of the Bombay Sanskrit Collection. However, the one area in which he failed was the integration of the numerous acquisitions into a true library. The works were stored under more or less warehouse conditions; there was no building or library that served as the focal point in Bombay, where scholars could come to do extended research in an environment conducive to detailed investigation.

Franz Kielhorn, the last of the Germans involved with the Bombay Sanskrit Collection, did undertake several projects to transform the numerous acquisitions into a library. His contribution was a consistent and persistent attempt to prepare a comprehensive catalog of the ever-growing government collection. This began with his work on the *catalogue raisonné* Haug had begun for the pre-1868 purchases. With the establishment of the searches for Sanskrit manuscripts in 1868, Kielhorn immediately perceived that having copies of the published catalogs of European Sanskrit collections would greatly facilitate both acquisitions and cataloging in India. He requested and received copies of the printed catalogs of the India Office Library, the Royal Asiatic Society, the Bodleian Library, and the Königliche Bibliothek in Berlin.[21] Kielhorn soon assumed the role of maintaining accurate bibliographic description of the discoveries in India. For instance, in 1870 he indicated his inability to identify positively several of the works listed in the *Classified Catalogue of Sanskrit Works in the Saraswati Bhandaram Library of His Highness the Maharaja of Mysore.*[22] Government responded to the criticism by asking that additional information be supplied in cataloging to allow precise identification of works. However, government later informed Kielhorn that it was more important to produce a catalog, even if it contained some errors, rather than to wait an inordinate amount of time in producing an absolutely perfect one.[23]

Each of the search trips of Bühler and Kielhorn resulted in a printed list of the new acquisitions, which the Government of India distributed to scholars and libraries in both India and the West. A printing of the distribution list in 1883 reveals that 103 individuals and 27 Western libraries received these publications, as did 50 Indians and 34 Indian libraries.[24] Unquestionably, the data from these distributed lists formed the basis of knowledge of the Bombay Sanskrit Collection and the initiation of the numerous inter-library loan requests. In the 1870s cataloging as we know it today was in its infancy. Max Müller, in speaking to the 1874 International Congress of Orientalists, described what bibliographic information should be given for Sanskrit manuscripts. He said:

> Several catalogues have been published and there is but one feeling among Sanskrit scholars as to the value of their work. But they also feel that the time has come for doing more. The mere titles of the manuscripts whet our appetite but do not satisfy it. There are of course hundreds of books where the title, the name of the author, the locus and annus, are all we care to know. But of books which are scarce and hitherto not known out of India, we want to know more. We want some information of the subject and its treatment, and if possible of the date of the author and of the writers quoted by him. We want extracts intelligently chosen: in fact, we want something like the excellent catalogue which Dr. Aufrecht has made for the Bodleian Library.[25]

Such detailed catalogs were beyond the capabilities of the government staff, who undertook such work in conjunction with numerous other responsibilities. When Kielhorn retired in 1881, he had produced several lists but had finished only one work that might be called a catalog, namely, his very first charge, the government's pre-1868 collection of manuscripts.

At the time of his departure from India, Kielhorn proposed that the best way to prepare a complete catalog of the Government Sanskrit Collection would be to ship the manuscripts to Europe, where various European authorities on aspects of Sanskrit literature could produce the individual sections. The Government of Bombay accepted the idea of producing a complete catalog of the 3,650 manuscripts, although both Bühler's and Kielhorn's successors protested the move, since funds for its production would be taken from the government grant.[26] Unfortunately, Kielhorn overlooked the willingness or ability of European Sanskrit scholars to complete such a catalog any faster than people in India. At the time the project ceased, only 403 manuscripts had gone to Europe. They went to Georg Bühler, Vienna (30); Richard Garbe, Königsberg (50); Herman Jacobi, Münster (70); Johannes Klatt, Berlin (24); Richard Pischel, Halle (123); and Kielhorn, Göttingen (97). Only in 1914 would a catalog finally appear for the collection, ironically, just as negotiations had begun to transfer the entire collection from public to private ownership.

The twenty-two years from 1859 to 1881 in which the three German Sanskrit scholars played a dominant role in Bombay Sanskrit scholarship at the collegiate level reflect a time when German universities, including their libraries, were viewed throughout the world as the pinnacle of modern scholarship. The transformation of American colleges into the research universities we know today dates from this period and reflects German models. In the American setting there was little the colleges could offer German universities, and the relationship was distinctly one-sided, with Americans imitating the German model. The situation in India was vastly different. German scholarship had long had an interest in India and its culture, particularly the Sanskrit heritage. India possessed the wealth of Sanskrit literature, and to further their studies German scholars needed access to it. The Government of India, however, did not wish to be perceived as depleting India of its cultural wealth. Thanks to the newspaper wars of words, government had to play some role so that individuals such as Haug or Sprenger would not amass collections of manuscripts, pirate them away from India, and then sell them for great profit in Europe. The actions of the Government of India to collect and to preserve Sanskirt manuscripts through annually sponsored survey trips reflect an enlightened approach to the problem and a caring need to take action on those concerns mentioned in the Bombay press by individuals such as Bibliophilus.

The initial development of a manuscript collection in Bombay derives from the need of Haug, Bühler, and Kielhorn to have Sanskrit titles to teach then-modern linguistic methods to their Indian students. Did they also have the goal of developing research libraries in India? With Haug the answer is no. Bühler's great work of amassing a valuable collection that government declared must be kept in India serves as a transition toward having such a library. Although Bühler worked in the Royal Library at Windsor Castle and the University of Gottingen, his actions in India indicate concern primarily to identify unique works of Sanskrit scholarship in India, to publicize their existence, and to assist scholars from around the world in gaining access to such titles. His production of numerous lists, with no cumulation to them or the detail of cataloging so earnestly sought by Max Müller, again reflects the work of a discoverer rather than a library organizer. It is only with Franz Kielhorn that we see a concern for laying the foundations of systematic bibliographic organization for the Sanskrit collection, although he never completed his goal.

Thanks to the efforts of the three Germans, we have today the Bhandarkar Oriental Research Institute Library, a preeminent Sanskrit manuscript collection in what was, in preindependent India, Bombay Presidency. Without the work of Haug, Bühler, and Kielhorn, there would not have been such early and sustained effort to search out and to preserve the Sanskrit wealth of western India and to make it freely available to all scholars. Without the work of the three German scholars, the development of manuscript libraries supporting modern research would have been delayed in Bombay for many years.

Notes

1. Sir William Jones, "Third Anniversary Discourse, Delivered 2 February 1786," *Asiatic Researches* 1: 423–424.
2. Franz Bopp, *Ueber das Conjugationssystem der Sanskritsprache* (Frankfurt am Main: Andrea, 1816).
3. Government of Bombay, Education Department, *Proceedings, 1862–3, No. 1475.*
4. "The Claims of Sanscrit," *Hindu Patriot*, 6 July 1863, in *Times of India*, 18 July 1863, p. 3, col. 6.
5. Martin Haug, "Account of a Tour in Gujarat," *Times of India*, 9–23 June 1864, p. 3, cols. 1–6.
6. Bibliophilus, "Dr. Haug's Manuscripts," *Times of India*, 1 July 1864, p. 2, col. 6.
7. Ibid.
8. Ibid.
9. Government of Bombay, Department of Public Instruction, *Annual Report, 1863–4*, p. 29.
10. Archibald Edward Gough, *Papers Relating to the Collection and Preservation of the Records of Ancient Sanskrit Literature in India*, edited by Order of the Government of India by Archibald Edward Gough (Calcutta: Government Printing Office, 1878), pp. 9–10.
11. James Tod, *Travels in Western India: Embracing a Visit to the Sacred Mounts of the Jains and the Most Celebrated Shrines of Hindu Faith between Rajputana and the Indus, with an Account of the Ancient City of Nehrwalla* (London: W. H. Allen, 1839).
12. Government of India, Home Department, *Public Proceedings, 1875, No. 4810.*
13. Government of Bombay, Director of Public Education, *Annual Report, 1874–75*, pp. 131–132.
14. Georg Bühler, "Extract from Dr. Bühler's Preliminary Report on the Results of the Search for Sanskrit MSS. in Kasmir," *Indian Antiquary* 5 (1876): 27–28.
15. Government of India, Home Department, *Public Proceedings, 1875, No. 4810.*

16. Government of Bombay, Education Department, *Resolution 696, 30 June 1873.*

17. Georg Bühler, "Two Lists of Sanskrit MSS Together with Some Remarks on My Connexion with the Search for Sanskrit" (reprint from *Zeitschrift der Deutschen Morgenländische Gesellschaft* 42 [1888]: 6).

18. Ibid.

19. Ibid.

20. Ibid.

21. Government of Bombay, Education Department, *Resolution 380, 29 July 1869.*

22. Saraswati Bhandaram Library, Mysore, *Classified Catalogue of Sanskrit Works in the Saraswati Bhandaram Library of His Highness the Maharajah of Mysore* (Bangalore: n.p., 1870).

23. Government of India, Home Department, *Public Proceedings No. 3705, 9 August 1870.*

24. Government of India, Home Department, *Public Proceedings, No. 183, 10 February 1883.*

25. Government of Bombay, Education Department, *Proceedings No. 2053, December 1881.*

26. Ibid.

A Circulating Library in the Southwest: J. S. Penn in Austin, Texas

Philip A. Metzger

In spite of the widespread existence of circulating libraries in the nineteenth-century United States, few of them were found west of the Mississippi. One of the exceptions was J. S. Penn's Circulating Library in Austin, Texas, begun in 1872 (not coincidentally, shortly after the arrival of the railroad in Austin) and lasting until about 1880. Penn offered a catalog of about 1,500 titles, mostly fiction, at a rental price suggesting that only the relatively well-off would have been able to afford to borrow books. Not only does Penn's circulating library provide an example of a genre rare in its part of the country, it also provides a glimpse of Austin's reading tastes at the time.

Circulating libraries have been a widespread force in the purveying of books to readers since colonial times, but they differed in one substantial way from other libraries of their time. As a primarily entrepreneurial activity, they operated largely outside the philanthropic or communal motives that led to the creation of mechanics', Sunday-school, YMCA, social, and the many other kinds of public libraries that made their appearance in the United States during the course of its history. The proprietor of a circulating library was—in most cases—a bookstore owner who saw a collection of books to be rented out to anyone able to pay the fee as a way of supplementing income. In short, the proprietor was out to make money, rather than to fill some perceived social need.

In spite of the importance of circulating libraries as a force in the development of library use, little attention, compared to other topics in the history of libraries, seems to have been devoted to them. One happy exception is David Kaser's delightful Beta Phi Mu monograph, *A Book for a Sixpence: The Circulating Library in America,*[1] to which I am heavily indebted for background.

As Kaser suggests, not only is the circulating library an entity worth studying *per se*; it also offers a way to get at one of the most difficult and

Philip A. Metzger *is curator of special collections, Linderman Library, Lehigh University.*

vexing questions in the study of social history; that is, what did the average man or woman (and in the case of reading it appears to have been predominantly women) like to read? Since circulating libraries were largely commercial enterprises, their success depended on stocking books that people would pay, and sometimes pay fairly substantial amounts, to read. For this reason, surviving catalogs of the books offered by individual circulating libraries provide a glimpse into general popular reading tastes probably unmatched by any other source.

The following numbers indicate the general geographical distribution of these libraries during the period covered by Kaser's book, 1762–1890. The leading state was, perhaps not surprisingly, Massachusetts, with 86 circulating libraries. A substantial number of these were, of course, in Boston. Rhode Island followed with 56, possibly due to its position as a popular nineteenth-century resort. Then came Pennsylvania with 48, New York with 47, and Maryland with 21. In the Midwest, Illinois had 18, Indiana 9, and Ohio 21. Closer to Texas, Kaser identified 13 circulating libraries in Louisiana. Many other states east of the Mississippi River can boast of similar numbers.[7]

However, once the great river is crossed, the number of circulating libraries drops drastically; indeed, in many states west of the Mississippi there are none at all recorded. Texas, in fact, barely misses that perfect mark, reporting only one, an antebellum bookstore and circulating library in Houston. Even if a few more existed in Texas that have not yet been detected, the strong imbalance between prevalence in the East and the West will not be changed significantly.

What kept the trans-Mississippi West from the development of these institutions? One paramount factor, at least in the case of Austin, was transportation. Books are extremely heavy objects, and large numbers of them cannot be transported economically over long distances by wagon. Cities without water transportation—that is to say, most of the West—had to wait, it seems clear, for the railroad to pass through before such institutions could develop. Thus I do not think it in the least a coincidence that the circulating library under examination here was begun less than one year after the first railroad line arrived in the capital city of Texas. This is a hypothesis that certainly deserves further examination.

A few words of background on Austin in the 1870s are in order before proceeding further. At the time we are concerned with here, the economic and political life of Texas had only begun to recover from the devastation caused by the Civil War. In fact, at the end of that conflict, civil government in the state had virtually collapsed. By the early 1870s, the state was still in the grip of a highly unpopular, radical Republican government that kept power only through the presence of federal troops. Austin, as the capital, felt these vicissitudes with a special immediacy. Thus the arrival of the first Houston and Texas Central locomotive in December 1871 must have provided quite a boost for the city. This link did not make transportation to and from East Coast book centers completely trouble-free, however. The train connection went through Houston, where the traveler continued the trip by water, either to New Orleans for railroad connections to the East, or else all the way to the Atlantic seaboard by water. Not until 1876 was a direct rail route north through St. Louis constructed.[3]

Economically, Austin was at this time a small frontier settlement set in the middle of cotton-growing and ranching. Besides these, its only other important business was state government, one of the purposes for which it had been established in 1839. Its location on what had only recently been Texas's frontier, 180 miles northwest of Houston and 90 miles north of San Antonio, had kept it relatively isolated from the state's main population centers. With a population in 1870 of about 4,500 people (about 9,000 more in the surrounding county), it was a small city, yet poised for rapid population growth.

Although the city was far from being a center of literary activity or commerce, several bookstores existed in Austin as the 1870s began, the most interesting and enterprising of which was that of J. S. Penn, who had been selling books in some form in Austin for several years before 1870. At first his business was described as a newsstand, but even then he was selling what appear to have been secondhand books of the "cheap literature" variety ("cheap" had none of its less favorable connotations in those days), probably the kind of material many Austinites wanted to read. For example, on one occasion he offered the first volume of the "cheap collected edition" of T. S. Arthur, an extremely popular novelist of the day, perhaps most famous for his temperance tract *Ten Nights in a Bar Room*. This was combined with some other volumes of stories, all for sale at fifty cents per volume.[4]

Perhaps using this kind of experience as a base, in the fall of 1872 Penn opened up his best-documented enterprise, a circulating library.[5] Fortunately, a catalog of this collection has survived.[6] As I have mentioned, many bookdealers in the United States had kept collections that they rented out to patrons on various bases—daily, weekly, monthly, and often yearly. Circulating libraries had developed in colonial America, and had continued their growth into the nineteenth century, but by 1872 this method of circulating books had probably passed its prime. The development of the free public library seems to have been one factor influencing the fate of the circulating library;[7] this movement had, however, developed little strength in Austin at this time, so Penn's circulating library seems to have found a market without much competition.

Although Penn's circulating library was begun in 1872, the only existing catalog of the collection—perhaps the only one ever prepared—dates from about October 1876. It claims to list "two thousand volumes of the most popular works extant." This figure involves what appears to be some puffery, or perhaps just excessive devotion to round numbers. The numerical list of titles runs to 1,750, but with gaps in the numbering there are approximately 1,500 actual titles. It may be that the other 500 "volumes" were duplicates, but that seems doubtful. Still, this a large collection for that place at that time.

The catalog begins with an address "To the Public," in which the usual dignified thoughts about the value of reading are expressed. "No inquiring mind will fail to see," it begins, "the great benefits a community derives from a good Circulating Library." It goes on to say:

> Comparatively few persons are able to purchase all the books they wish to read, and many there are who deem themselves too poor to even purchase books at all, and thus are deprived through life of the great blessings and benefits of a well cultivated mind. Such persons invest their dimes in light, cheap literature, which is to a very large proportion from the pen of third and fourth class authors, and generally considered not worth putting into book form; and while we would not by any means disparage good papers and magazines, yet it is a well known fact that the works of our best writers of both solid and light literature, are scarcely to be found except in book form. And thus, by the advantages of a Circulating Library, so much more of the wheat and much less of the chaff may be obtained, at a small cost to the beneficiary.

After some comments on the cost of buying all the books one might read in a year as compared to the terms of subscription for obtaining those books from the library, the piece concludes with a somewhat veiled appeal.

> A Library of two thousand volumes is not a very small one, and yet we intend making frequent and large additions of new editions as they come out, and also of standard works that have not yet been added. It is true that we could not go on making these additions, should the people of Austin and adjoining country fail to appreciate our enterprise, and not give us their patronage; but we are making no such calculations, for we have too high an appreciation of the community and city of our choice to be fearful.

The last statement, one must say, smacks a bit of whistling in the graveyard.

Certainly for an avid reader the fees charged by Penn amounted to a sizable savings over the cost of buying the books, and yet they were not insubstantial. Penn set his "terms of subscription" as follows:

	3 months	6 months	1 year
1 volume at a time	$2.00	$ 3.75	$ 7.00
2 at a time	3.75	7.00	12.00
3 at a time	5.50	7.00	17.00
4 at a time	7.00	12.00	22.00

In addition, one could rent a book at 5 cents per day, 25 cents per week, or 75 cents per month, in which case a deposit covering the value of the book had to be paid "and no exceptions made." The catalog also listed the retail price of each volume, in case of loss or damage.

It is difficult to determine how many people could have afforded this schedule of rates, especially since barter may still have been an important aspect of the local economy, and ready money may sometimes have been difficult to find. Indeed, the maximum rate, $22.00, would have been a substantial portion of a typical monthly income.

For that reason, I think it is highly useful to attempt to put these figures into some sort of context. In spite of the difficulty of making a comparison of earnings and possible expenditures between one period and another, some suggestions can be made.[8] For example, in terms of earnings, at about this time a schoolteacher in a nearby county was earning $75.00 per month. A further example is that of a particular house repair job that employed a carpenter at $3.00 per day and his helper at $2.00 per day. Interestingly, assuming a six-day work week, the carpenter made about the same monthly income as the teacher if he worked each possible day. A housemaid, on the other hand, made substantially less; in the example I have, she earned only $12.00 per month. Salaries for other kinds of positions might be higher, however. The clerk of the Texas House of Representatives made $240.00 a month; at the same time he was earning $166.00 a month as chief clerk in the office of the superintendent of public instruction.

These salary figures give a sense of what a range of typical Austin citizens might earn, but what do figures such as these mean in terms of ability to afford to rent books from Penn's circulating library? If the maid were inclined to read, for example, she probably would not be able to command the $2.00 in one lump sum that would be necessary to rent one book at a time for three months. Since her daily income works out to about 50 cents, even the 5 cents a day rental fee would be a daunting amount for her. The schoolteacher and the carpenter are much better off, but Penn's fees would still be a significant amount, especially if there were several readers in the family. One suspects, however, that the clerk of the House of Representatives would have had no difficulty with the fees, provided he were not profligate in other areas.

In addition to income, it is also helpful to look at what other uses the Austin citizen of the 1870s might have made of his or her money. At this time, for example, a dining room table and chair set might cost around $28.00, and a suit of men's clothes about the same. These prices seem cheap to us today, but, relatively speaking, they were not particularly so at the time. Other goods were proportionately even more expensive. A Singer sewing machine must be considered a luxury item at $100.00, and a discounted pair of round trip tickets via rail to St. Louis cost $106.00, or nearly one and a half times the monthly income of the school teacher. Of course there were no income taxes, and many of the modern demands on income did not exist. Clearly, however, based on the fees alone, Penn's circulating library customers were probably for the most part middle class and above, although a laborer or maid might rent a book on a daily basis if he or she were an avid reader. However, the average casual reader might well find the expense too great.

After the blast, in the introduction to Penn's catalog, against "third and fourth class" authors and also presumably against the popular dime novel, one may logically be curious as to the quality of the works in the catalog. To use the catalog's own rather imprecise classification system, the authors were primarily of the second class, with the merest sprinkling of those of the first class. In other words, they were, for the most part, "light" reading by the most popular authors of the day. Nonfiction is conspicuous, for the most part, by its absence, representing probably less than 10 percent of the total holdings of the library. One is tempted to substitute "of previous days" for the catalog's statement "of the day," because most of the novels represented were the output of writers who published in the 1840s, 1850s, and 1860s or, if they were still publishing, had had their heyday during that period. They were also, for the most part, by nationality English.

No figures are available to indicate how often a given title circulated, so judgment as to an author's popularity must be based at least in part on the number of his or her titles in the collection. However, since most of these authors were prolific, this basis may not be entirely inaccurate. By these numbers, then, Charles Dickens, with 26 titles to his credit, was the most popular author in Austin, followed rather closely by Sir Walter Scott, with 22 titles. It is certainly not necessary to identify either of these writers. The next in order, however, is not known by most today: G. P. R. James. James was also English, with his primary output and greatest popularity during the 1840s. However, in Austin in 1876, he was represented by 21 novels, although in his lifetime he wrote many more, all light romances, forgettable and forgotten. Alexandre Dumas follows, in translation, with 20 titles, and then Bulwer-Lytton, listed as Lord Lytton, with 15. Interestingly, his good friend and fellow prolific novelist Benjamin Disraeli had only one work in the catalog. A certain Mary Elizabeth Braddon follows, with 12 titles. Only then does the first American appear on the list, James Fenimore Cooper. Another American, probably the most popular American writer of the 1850s, Mrs. E. D. E. N. Southworth, is almost even with Cooper at 10 titles. Other authors could be mentioned, having 5 to 10 works in the catalog —T. S. Arthur, Capt. Marryat, Mayne Reid, Mrs. H. Wood, to name a few—but the overall nature of the list is well represented by the foregoing names.

An examination of Luther Mott's list of "best sellers" for 1865–1874 demonstrates how little interested, if its lack of availability in the circulating library is an indication, the people of Austin were in current fiction.[9] Although Dickens topped the list in popularity, his *Our Mutual Friend* of 1865 does not appear there. One could not borrow *Alice in Wonderland* (1866), or Horatio Alger's first book *Ragged Dick* (1867). About the only available works from this period were Louisa May Alcott's two most popular books, *Little Women* (1868) and *Little Men* (1871). Interestingly, *Uncle Tom's Cabin* is there, along with *A Key to Uncle Tom's Cabin*, also by Stowe. One title foreshadows Texas's future, a work entitled *The Oil Regions of Pennsylvania.* In addition, one or two works were available to German speakers, including a biography of Abraham Lincoln.

Obviously, the development of Penn's circulating library was an important aspect of his business, but his operation of the library must be seen in the context of his other activities. In 1872, when two other Austin book dealers, Nagle and Thompson, formed a partnership under Thompson's roof, it was Penn who bought out Nagle's stock, and apparently moved into Nagle's previous location, where Penn continued to sell "reading matter of every description," including "the best and largest assortment of newspapers, magazines, periodicals, etc. ever kept in Austin."[10]

Perhaps Penn's biggest venture in bookselling, one that makes him unusual, perhaps even unique in Austin book trade annals, is his journey to New York for the Book Fair held in Clinton Hall in July of 1875. This trip also had important implications for the stocking of his circulating library. Penn had made at least one other trip to New York to buy books, the only Austin book dealer on record as having made such a trip. Certainly the result of this trip is found in Penn's claim ("Good news!" began the announcement) a few months later to have already 2,000 volumes in his circulating library.[11]

Penn's departure and return were heralded with some enthusiasm in the *Statesman*, which gave a full acount of his departure.

> Mr. J. S. Penn leaves on Monday for New York to lay in a complete stock of books, stationery, etc. to place in his new store opposite Sampson & Henricks. He says he is determined to keep as choice a stock as to be found in the State, and we believe he will do it. Penn is a live business man and will beyond doubt infuse new life into his line of business at this place. The name of the firm at the new store will be J. S. Penn & Co. The location will be one of the finest in the city, and we are sure a splendid business will be conducted by the new firm.[12]

In 1875, as I have mentioned, the railroad had been completed for several years between Austin and Houston, but the overland connection through St. Louis had not yet reached Austin. So Penn probably had to take a steamer from Houston at least as far as New Orleans, and perhaps the entire distance to New York, which may help to explain the length of his absence from Austin. A few days later, on 14 July, the *Statesman* reported that Penn, of the "extensive book and stationery establishment," had left yesterday for "New York and other eastern cities to purchase a large stock of goods for the fall trade." He had already made room for this stock and would return in a month or six weeks. The longer estimate of the journey's length proved the more accurate, for the *Statesman* on 5 September reported that Penn had just returned and "the large and elegant stock . . . has begun to arrive and in two weeks their stock will be one of the largest and most complete in the state. . . ."

He went, as one of only two booksellers from the entire state of Texas (the other from Dallas), to the first book fair, which was held at Clinton Hall, 19 to 24 July. This book fair was intended to replace the annual, often semiannual, trade sales, which publishers had held in New York for many years. The trade sales allowed out-of-town booksellers to examine the wares of a number of publishers simultaneously, in the days before a well-developed rail network allowed traveling salesmen to visit their customers. But trade sales had a financial liability to publishers for some time. Parcels of books were auctioned off to the highest bidder, and there was always the temptation on the part of publishers to use this method to raise money, especially during hard times, even if they sold batches of books at far less than the normal wholesale price. In the "last" trade sale in the spring of 1875, for example, books fetched only about 30 to 50 percent of retail price, at a time when the normal trade discount was around 20 percent. The result was that wholesalers were undercut when retailers could buy as cheaply as they could; retailers too were harmed when jobbers or "book butchers" suddenly turned up with stocks of popular titles at lower prices than they were compelled to charge. It was an entirely unsatisfactory system, except that an alternative had been found difficult to devise.[13] Certainly it must have been as injurious to the operator of a circulating library as to a bookstore owner.

One attempt, by the publishers' trade group, was the Book Fair that drew Penn to New York. Publishers would not auction their wares, but would instead display samples and take orders. Book buyers were, moreover, required to present an endorsed note for their purchases. By all descriptions, the fair was a complete success. Penn was able to see the output of 97 publishers, big firms and small, from New York, Boston, Philadelphia, and no doubt some of the smaller eastern centers, who were exhibiting 32,694 samples. Harper's alone had 4,000 titles. The samples included both trade and school books; the main reason this fair was being held so soon after the previous trade sale was to afford booksellers an opportunity to stock up on school books before the fall semester began. Books worth more than $300,000 were sold to 94 buyers from 17 states. Unfortunately, Penn's share of this total is not known; perhaps it was in the vicinity of the average purchase of around $3,200.[14]

Penn was not to be tempted by further such book events. Two subsequent fairs, one in the fall of 1875 and one the following spring, proved to be complete failures, the first one having absorbed all the market could bear for a while, and publishers returned to the system of trade sales for a few more years. There is no evidence that any Austin book dealer attended any of the sales, either before or after Penn.[15]

Penn, like other booksellers, carried a wide assortment of other merchandise. No doubt he hoped that his circulating library would draw customers to make purchases. Not only did he feature these items in his store, but in the same busy year of 1875, a month or so before Christmas, he entered several displays in a local fair. He won premiums for the best display of "perfumery," and for the best display of gold pens and pencils. Other displays featured albums in leather and cloth, both imported and domestic, books bound in morocco, ivory, and Russian leather, and "finely bound poetical works." At the same time, Penn was adding to the space in his business by acquiring the room upstairs over the store to contain his wholesale business. He was also offering the staple of booksellers at that season, the sumptuously printed and bound—and largely unread—gift book, the equivalent of the modern "coffee table" book.[16]

Some time before the publication of the 1877–1878 Austin City Directory, probably in 1873 at the time of the *Statesman*'s reference to the "new firm," J. S. Penn took in his brother Robert R. as a partner.[17]

The two of them operated the business for several years, Robert probably managing the store when James went on his trips. In 1879 the firm advertised its entire circulating library for sale "cheap for cash.[18] On 6 November 1879 they dissolved the partnership, and J. S. Penn continued the business alone.[19] Finally, in mid-1880, Penn advertised that he was selling either his Austin store or the one the brothers had operated in San Antonio, as he wanted to consolidate operations.[20] Eventually, no sale took place and the stock was shipped to San Antonio. In August 1880 the store closed, ending Austin's association with J. S. Penn.[21]

J. S. Penn's energetic activities as a bookseller and proprietor of a circulating library mark a significant development in the literary and cultural life of Austin. In this sense, the city lost its isolation from the rest of the country, due both to the arrival of the railroad and to the efforts of one enterprising person to exploit new opportunities. Indeed, Penn was active in a unique and, for Austin, rather short-lived period of the book trade. After the Civil War, railroad lines spread rapidly throughout the country. By the 1880s this form of transportation permitted the rapid development of that class of men well known in song and story, to say nothing of the crude joke: the traveling salesman. No longer was it necessary for a person like Penn to travel many miles to see and buy books to stock his store and library; instead, the information and stock came directly to the bookseller, just as it does today.

Penn's circulating library was successful rather beyond the average. He was in business from 1872 to about 1879 or perhaps a year or two longer. The typical survival length for this type of library was not much beyond five years or so.[22] One suspects that at least some of the success —and it is not known how really profitable the enterprise was—lay in the desire of Austinites to catch up on activities and reading perhaps neglected during the hard days of the Civil War and Reconstruction years. Surely it must have been quite a novelty to have had that many books at one's beck and call all at once. Some of his success must also be due to the growth of the city during that decade. From its 1870 population of about 4,500, it grew to over 11,000 in 1880, the largest percentage increase in a decade ever recorded for the city. Moreover, Penn had little competition during this time. No other circulating library has been identified during this period, and no other bookseller, of which there were only a few, gave evidence of having the same entrepreneurial energy as Penn.

Why did Penn quit the business? The records do not say. The split with his brother may suggest personal problems, and the wish to consolidate all his business in San Antonio may suggest overextension. Kaser suggests that the rise of cheap publications, the same kind that Penn was originally selling, after the Civil War made it possible for potential customers of a circulating library to buy books rather than rent them, at prices roughly equivalent to the cost of renting.[23] Five- and ten-cent books, not of the dime novel genre, but rather closely approximating the kind of literature most prevalent in Penn's circulating library, were becoming widely available during this period. This development was fueled by the mechanization of printing and papermaking, and the concomitant lowering of costs, supported by the lack of a copyright agreement with the prime source of literary supply, England. This may also account for the prevalence of English writers in the inventory and the lack of current American writers. They may simply have been more expensive to stock. Unless further information about Penn is uncovered, the precise answer to these questions probably never will be known.

What did Austinites do for library service after Penn's circulating library closed? This question too has no clear answer. They may have bought the new cheap books, or returned to reading dime novels, or newspapers, or nothing at all. It is possible also that other bookdealers in Austin maintained circulating libraries. Indeed, a faint suggestion in the papers of another, later bookseller hints that this might have been the case. However, a record of these activities no longer seems to exist. For public library service the citizens of Austin had to wait until the twentieth century was a couple of decades old, so Penn's circulating library may be said to mark the first real flowering of library service in the city.

Notes

1. David Kaser. *A Book for a Sixpence: The Circulating Library in America* (Pittsburgh: Beta Phi Mu, 1980).
2. Ibid., pp. 127–172.
3. C. S. Potts, *Railroad Transportation in Texas* (Austin: University of Texas, 1909), p. 40; Mary Starr Barkeley. *History of Travis County and Austin, 1839–1899* (Austin: The author, 1963), p. 274.
4. *Austin Statesman*, 17 March 1872.
5. *Austin Statesman*, 5 September 1872.
6. Located in the Barker Texas History Center, University of Texas at Austin.
7. Kaser, *Book*, p. 92.
8. I offer thanks here to May Schmidt of the Austin Public Library's Austin History Center for searching out these difficult-to-find statistics and cost figures.
9. Frank Luther Mott, *Golden Multitudes; The Story of Best Sellers in the United States* (New York: Macmillan, 1947), pp. 309–310.
10. *Austin Statesman*, 24 October 1872.
11. *Austin Statesman*, 7 November 1873.
12. *Austin Statesman*, 3 August 1873.
13. John Tebbel, *A History of Book Publishing in the United States*, vol. 2: *The Expansion of an Industry* (New York: R. R. Bowker, 1975), pp. 103–108.
14. Tebbel, *Expansion*, pp. 107–108.

15. Ibid., p. 108.
16. *Austin Statesman*, 14 November 1875.
17. Austin City Directory, 1877–1878.
18. *Austin Statesman*, 3 August 1879.
19. *Austin Statesman*, 9 November 1879.
20. *Austin Statesman*, 12 June 1880.
21. *Austin Statesman*, 25 and 27 August 1880.
22. Kaser, *Book*, p. 101.
23. Ibid., p. 103.

The Rental Library in Twentieth-Century America

Philip B. Eppard

Rental libraries flourished in the United States in the 1920s and 1930s, threatening to revolutionize American book buying and reading habits. Libraries were often adjuncts to bookshops, but many operated as independent businesses. The development of chains of libraries enabled a wide variety of retailers to install them. The low rates charged by many of the chains, however, helped keep rental rates too low for adequate profits to be made. The rise of paperbacks and television, coupled with the increased cost of books after World War II, contributed to the demise of the rental business, although rental libraries continue to exist in a few localities.

"When the story of this period of the American booktrade is written," *Publishers' Weekly* editorialized in 1933, "there will have to be much said about the influence of the rental library on book distribution."[1] Rental libraries were all the rage in the 1920s and 1930s, coming seemingly out of nowhere and threatening to transform totally the reading and book-buying habits of the American public. The number of rental outlets in the United States in the 1930s has been estimated to be as high as 50,000, a figure that vastly outdistances the total number of bookstores and public libraries combined. Yet the years after World War II saw a steady decline in the rental business, until today the rental idea persists only in the pay collections in public libraries and in a few devoted and successful purely commercial operations.

The great rental library boom of the twentieth century has received scant attention from historians. It does not seem to have gotten even a footnote in John Tebbel's *A History of Book Publishing in the United States*. The one book on circulating libraries in America, David Kaser's *A Book for a Sixpence*, concentrates almost exclusively on the eighteenth and nine-

Philip B. Eppard *is survey archivist, Harvard College Library.*

The author would like to thank Jean Peters of R. R. Bowker Company and John Baker, editor of Publishers' Weekly, *for granting access to the* Publishers' Weekly *library.*

teenth centuries. It has been neglected by researchers in both library and book-trade history, perhaps in part because it does not belong exclusively to either field. Furthermore, the modern rental library business led a shadowy kind of existence about which very little reliable information was available even to people working in the field. Nelson R. McNaughton, who operated a chain of rental libraries based in Altoona, Pennsylvania, and who later developed the McNaughton system for supplying public libraries with rental collections, offered the following lament in 1949:

> Has it occurred to you that this is one of the very few businesses of fair size for which no general statistics are available anywhere? How many lending libraries are there? Who operates them? How many chains and how many independents? How many detective stories do they buy? How many westerns? How many books in total? What incidence of business failures? What total amount of business do they do annually? Is the field saturated, over-saturated, or under supplied? We have opinions, but we have no facts.[2]

This article is an attempt to rescue the outlines of a bit of lost book history, to characterize the rise and fall of the rental craze of fifty years ago, and to try to evaluate, as *Publishers' Weekly* suggested in 1933, "the influence of the rental library on book distribution."

Rental libraries had existed in the United States since at least 1762, the year William Rind of Annapolis began to lend books to anyone who would pay a yearly subscription fee of twenty-seven shillings. Rind's library was termed a "circulating library," certainly an appropriate term for the eighteenth century, when libraries of this type were virtually the only kind of libraries that circulated books. This term continued to be used, however, well into the twentieth century. With the explosive growth of commercial libraries in the late 1920s, the older term gradually was replaced by the more accurate term "rental library." Many businesses, however, used the term "lending library," which was technically no more accurate than "circulating library," but which did have a more genteel air to it.

Circulating libraries flourished in the early years of the nineteenth century, but their growth began to be stymied by three factors, according to David Kaser. These were the growth of free public libraries that could satisfy the public's appetite for nonfiction; the development of philanthropic libraries, particularly Sunday-school and YMCA libraries; and, most significantly, the explosion of cheap literature, which made buying something to read more affordable than renting.[3] By the end of the nineteenth century, the rental business in the United States was stagnant, if not moribund.

The situation in Great Britain had developed in a considerably different fashion. The circulating libraries dominated the scene there, led by Charles Edward Mudie and his Select Library, established in 1842. Average readers were forced to borrow books because they were generally brought out in the three-volume, or triple-decker, format with a price tag prohibitive for the average pocketbook. The purchasing power of the libraries was strong enough to influence what books were published and in what format. Without a well-developed public library system, the circulating library in Great Britain achieved a much stronger hold on the reading public than it did in the United States. Although fiction was the most popular staple of the libraries, Mudie's, for example, would provide books in any subject category.[4]

At the beginning the the twentieth century, an attempt was made to revive the stagnant rental library business in the United States by the creation of a large-scale operation modeled after Mudie's. An entrepreneur named Seymour Eaton established the Booklovers Library in Philadelphia in 1900; by 1903 it had expanded to fifty cities in the United States with branches in Canada and outposts in London and Paris. Membership in the Booklovers was by invitation only, and the membership rolls were limited. Various forms of membership were available on a subscription basis. Books were delivered, each in its own slipcase. When the rolls of the Booklovers were filled, Eaton established the Tabard Inn Library in 1902. The Tabard Inn offered membership to anyone on payment of an annual fee of $1.50. Lifetime memberships cost only $5.00. Members were entitled to borrow one book at a time and paid an exchange fee of five cents each time they took a new book. In addition to regular libraries, the Tabard Inn installed bookcases in drugstores and other outlets, and members could exchange their books at any outlet in the country. Eaton sold Tabard Inn franchises in a pyramid-like operation. *Publishers' Weekly* looked askance at the whole enterprise from the beginning, but Eaton was able for a while to continue selling stock in his various companies, which expanded to include the Tabard Inn Druggist's Specialty Company and the Tabard Inn Food Company. Eaton's empire collapsed in 1905, ostensibly because of the diversification into other lines. Eaton himself seems to have emerged from the debacle unscathed. He moved on to the insurance business, leaving behind a vast reading public whose appetite had been whetted for borrowing current fiction at bargain basement rates.[5]

The Booklovers and Tabard Inn libraries offered a model for what became a very important ingredient in the later success of rental libraries —the chain system, in which one central office serviced many small libraries. Significantly, it was one of Eaton's lieutenants, Arthur R. Womrath, who developed perhaps the most important chain of libraries.

Womrath was a Philadelphia native and a graduate of Lehigh University, who gave up engineering to establish a circulating library in Pottsville, Pennsylvania, in 1896. Eaton recruited him for the Booklovers in 1900, but Womrath didn't like the way Eaton did business and pulled out in 1902. He went to New York City and set up a rental library of his own, charging fees of twenty-five cents a week and up. By 1930 Womrath had 72 branches in 14 cities. In 1929 alone, 15 new branches were opened. In addition to the Womrath bookshops and libraries, in 1930 the company serviced over 1,500 additional outlets in drugstores, gift shops, and small bookstores. With this many outlets and a total staff of nearly 400, Womrath was clearly a potent force in the distribution of books. Part of the chain's success could be attributed to the close control exerted by the central office. Library operators were instructed to examine their stock regularly, and lists from the home office gave them guidance on what titles to pull, either for sale or for transfer to another unit where the demand was greater. This control relieved the individual library operator of the most delicate decisions in the rental process: when to pull a book, when to add more copies, or what new titles to add. Womrath libraries set high standards for the field, and their success was surely an encouragement for others to enter the rental business.[6]

While Womrath's operated principally in the New York to Washington corridor, the entry of the American News Company into the rental library market late in 1924 was an important factor in developing large numbers of outlets across the continent. As the principal supplier of magazines to dealers in railroad stations, newsstands, drugstores, and stationery stores, American News, through its local affiliates, was in a unique position to exploit markets with limited access to bookstores or libraries. Its monthly magazine, the *American News Trade Journal*, had been campaigning for several years for newsdealers to expand their offerings to include books. The November 1924 issue announced the launching of the Readmore Lending Library program. For a minimum investment of $50.00, a dealer would receive a bookrack, a selection of books, and the necessary supplies and guidelines to set up a rental library. Subsequent accounts of the program's successes were colored by the fact that they were designed to induce other dealers to establish libraries. Even taking these accounts with a grain of salt, however, one senses that the program struck a responsive chord. After one year it was announced that over 1,500 dealers had installed libraries. Community size seemed to be no obstacle. "One dealer in a town of such small population that you had to look twice in the postal guide for the figures is now averaging over fifty loanings a day at an average of three cents per day rental per book."[7] Besides regular outlets for magazines and books, "Readmores" were installed in drugstores, department stores, barber shops, sporting goods stores, variety stores, flower shops, and candy shops. Headlines in the *Journal* confidently boasted of the success of the Readmore program. In all of its book operations, American News stressed that knowledge of books was not necessary to sell or rent them. Concerning the Readmore Libraries, the *Journal* proudly asserted that many of the dealers who installed them "didn't know Zane Grey from William Shakespeare."[8] Here was true democratization of literature.

Chains of rental libraries of varying size and quality proliferated in the 1920s and 1930s. The extensive chain operations make it very difficult to estimate the number of rental libraries in operation. The principal source for statistics on the booktrade is the *American Booktrade Directory*, which lists booksellers across the country. An examination of its listings of specialties for each business can be made to determine rental outlets. This figure is not a true reflection of the number of places renting books, however, since it excludes the numerous outlets of the chain libraries. Only bookstores with libraries and independent rental libraries are included. The 1935 *Directory*, for example, records 2,066 firms that rented books.[9] This figure gains some additional meaning when compared to the same year's figure for the total number of bookstores—5,949. In 1935 Frederic G. Melcher, editor of *Publishers' Weekly*, in consultation with the American News Company and Baker and Taylor, a principal supplier of books to rental libraries, estimated that there were between forty and fifty thousand rental libraries in operation "including deposit stations" and that independent libraries were probably a quarter of that total.[10] Clearly it was easier in the 1930s to find a place to rent a book than it was to find a place to buy one.

Some generalizations about the rise and fall of rental libraries can be made from an analysis of libraries in Boston listed in the classified business listings of the *Boston City Directory*. Like the *American Booktrade Directory*, the *City Directory* has its problems as a statistical source, the principal one being that it seems to have been restricted to businesses for which the renting of books was the primary purpose. Department stores or bookshops with rental departments were for the most part omitted. There is a surprisingly low amount of overlap between the listings in the *City Directory* and the *American Booktrade Directory*. Of the twenty-eight firms shown as having rental businesses in the *American Booktrade Directory* for 1935, only ten appear in the *City Directory* under the heading "Libraries—Circulating." Conversely, the *City Directory* lists twenty-seven businesses that are not listed as rental outlets in the *American Booktrade Directory*.

According to the *City Directory*, there were ten circulating libraries in operation in Boston in 1900, and this figure held more or less steady until the mid-1920s. In 1921 it dropped to seven, but climbed slowly to twelve in 1925. Then real growth began. In 1926 there were fifteen, and in 1927 there were nineteen. In 1928 the figure shot up to twenty-eight, and it reached thirty-two by 1930. It peaked at forty for the years 1932–1933, then gradually dropped back to thirty-one in 1936 and to twenty-eight in 1940. One striking aspect of this analysis is the percentage of turnover in businesses, a feature of the rental trade that was characteristic of the nineteenth century as well.[11] Anywhere from four to fourteen of the new listings for each year of the 1930s represented new entrants in the field. Of the thirty-two rental operations listed in 1930, only four were still listed in 1940. The total number of businesses listed from 1930 to 1940 was 107, and approximately one-third of them were listed for only one year.

By the end of World War II, the number of rental libraries listed in the *Boston City Directory* was cut in half to fourteen, and the figure continued to drop annually until 1954 when there were just three listings. The last survivor, Catherine M. Clare, who operated a library and card shop in the downtown financial district, was listed through 1965. The 1965–1966 edition of the *American Booktrade Directory* recorded six rental outlets in Boston, all housed in bookshops or department stores. Even when the inadequacy of these statistical sources is granted, the shape of the declining curve cannot be disputed.

One additional way to gauge the curve of rental library activity is to examine the space given the subject in *Publishers' Weekly* and in the *Retail Bookseller*, Baker and Taylor's journal for the booktrade. In *Publishers' Weekly*, the greatest concentration of articles and news items occurred from 1929 to 1936. In 1934 R. R. Bowker gave its imprimatur to the rental movement by publishing Groff Conklin's book, *How to Run a Rental Library*. After 1940, however, very little attention was given to rental libraries in *Publishers' Weekly*. The only significant piece to appear subsequently was Conklin's elegiac "Rental Libraries: Problems and Prospects" in 1954. The *Retail Bookseller*, as an organ interested primarily in book distribution, devoted a little more attention to rental libraries after World War II, but the tone was often the defensive one of a besieged industry. A visible measure of the decline in rental libraries can also be seen by comparing the 1934 edition of Groff Conklin's *How to Run a Rental Library* with the "new and revised edition" published by Bowker in 1947. The former is a small but attractive clothbound book of 136 pages. The latter is a pamphlet of 94 pages. In 1934 Conklin wrote of independent libraries as viable businesses, but in 1947 he advised against expecting the receipts from a library alone to provide a livelihood, saying, "Rather, consider your library a valuable adjunct to some other allied type of retail business."[12]

Much of the discussion of rental libraries in *Publishers' Weekly* and the

Retail Bookseller centered on the question of rates. Since rates are obviously crucial to the success of the rental business, some attention must be given to what happened to rental rates during these years. In the early years of the century, Arthur Womrath made his rental business a success by charging twenty-five cents a week. In a 1933 survey of Manhattan libraries, Groff Conklin reported that that rate was disappearing quickly. He found a variety of rates as low as three cents a day with a six-cent minimum for novels. A rate of fifteen cents for three days was the most common rate in the early thirties. Nonfiction, which usually had a higher retail price as well as a smaller appeal, went at a higher rate. Conklin recommended 10 percent of the retail price for nonfiction, charged on a weekly basis. Experts in the field felt that the twenty-five-cent rate was necessary to run a rental business profitably. A $2.00 novel whose cost to the library was $1.34, for example, would have to be rented nine times at the fifteen-cent rate in order to cover its initial cost, to say nothing of overhead. If it were rented continuously, those nine rentals would cover twenty-seven days, or four weeks. Given the short life span of much new fiction, it is easy to see how difficult making a profit out of the rental business could be.

The expansion of the business and the growth of chain outlets forced rates even lower, however. In 1937, three years after Conklin's book was published advocating the fifteen-cent rate, a *Publishers' Weekly* survey found that the predominant rate for fiction was now three cents a day, although there were a variety of minimum charges employed to soften the impact of that cut-rate price. If the complaints of bookshop and rental library operators are to be believed, the rental shelves in the corner drug or candy store supplied by a chain were operated primarily as loss leaders that served to get customers into the stores to make other purchases. Bookstore operators often claimed to have added libraries reluctantly because their customers demanded the service. They then felt the pressure to compete with the corner drugstore in setting rates. As the paperback rack replaced the rental rack in the corner drugstore in the 1940s, bookstore owners were probably quite willing to scuttle their libraries now that the local competition was gone.

Pleas in the *Retail Bookseller* for higher rates or for some uniform system of rates could have little impact because of the variegated and diffuse nature of the business. Pegging the rental rate to the retail price of the book was one way to meet the challenge of rising book prices. In 1954 an average rate for a book costing $3.50 was twenty cents for three days and five cents per day after that. This rate, however, was still lower than many rates twenty-five years earlier when books were cheaper. Today a rental collection operated by the Womrath chain in Manhattan charges $1.50 for three days and fifty cents a day thereafter. Anderson's

Book Shop in Larchmont, New York, which has continued to operate a library successfully, charges on a sliding scale based on the retail price of the book. Books costing up to $14.49 rent at $1.75 for the first three days and ten cents a day thereafter. Up to $18.99 the price is $2.00 for the first three days and ten cents a day thereafter. For books costing over $19.00, the charge is $2.50 for the first three days and ten cents a day thereafter. The initial charge, therefore, is over 10 percent of the retail price compared to the 1954 example cited, where the basic charge was roughly 6 percent of the retail price. Those businesses that have survived have obviously been forced to put the renting of books on a sounder financial basis.

Turning to a consideration of the impact the libraries had on reading, we must first consider what kind of books they offered. Fiction, of course, predominated. This had been the case since the middle of the nineteenth century, as Kaser had demonstrated in an analysis of the printed catalogues of nineteenth-century circulating libraries. The predominance of fiction was even incorporated into some of the libraries' names. Publix Fiction Circulating Libraries was a chain in New York City, for example, and Fiction Lover's Library was a chain in Washington, D.C. In most of the first-class libraries, however, some nonfiction found a place. Part of the problem with nonfiction, however, was that the public taste for it was not as predictable as for fiction, and therefore there was less assurance that any given title could turn a profit, which was, of course, the name of the game. In the 1934 edition of Groff Conklin's *How to Run a Rental Library*, it was assumed that nonfiction would be a part of a quality library. In a declining market, however, nonfiction was too much of a luxury. The revised edition of 1947 cautioned, "Go very easy on the non-fiction. Even if it is a best-seller, do not buy it unless you have two or three requests for it. Non-fiction is only too often a money-loser for the library."[13] This would surely have been the advice of the library operator who wrote in a letter to the editor of the *Saturday Review of Literature* of her attempts to run a "quality" library including a healthy selection of nonfiction. After six months, no reader had asked for nonfiction. "They all say 'I want a *new* book.' And regardless of what it is, just so it is new, light, *and* fiction they take it."[14]

The quality of the fiction carried by rental libraries was often alluded to in the trade magazines. To a great extent the libraries were associated with light fiction and sometimes even fiction of dubious moral quality. I came on one or two references to the practice of keeping a special selection of books under the counter for particular customers. In the main though, it was dubious literary quality, not dubious moral quality, that made many rental operations suspect. Light romances of the Grace Livingston Hill or Kathleen Norris type, westerns by Zane Grey and Max

Brand, and a heavy dose of mysteries formed a large percentage of the stock of the libraries. Usually it was the outlets of the cheaper chain operations that often stocked cheap reprints, what were termed "popular copyright fiction," as well as remainders and sometimes even the older discards from the better-quality libraries.

Some hard evidence concerning the stock of the libraries comes from Nelson R. McNaughton, who analyzed in the *Retail Bookseller* how his chain business had changed during the ten years from 1939 through 1948. In 1939 he was spending 18.1 percent of his new books budget for detective stories, 7.6 percent for westerns, and 74.3 percent for other fiction and nonfiction. In 1948 the figure for detective fiction was 19 percent, although it had been as high as 29.6 percent in 1943. Westerns had plummeted to a scant 0.4 percent share of the budget. Beginning with the year 1944, McNaughton kept separate figures for light romances, on one hand, and for serious fiction and nonfiction, on the other. The combined figure for these two areas for 1948 was 80.6 percent, compared to 74.3 percent in 1939 and a low of 67.4 percent in 1943. The breakdown of this category into light romances and serious fiction and nonfiction, however, shows a marked decline in light romances from 23.5 percent in 1944 to 9.6 percent in 1948 and a corresponding rise in serious fiction and nonfiction from 51.7 percent to 71 percent. McNaughton argued that his experience proved that the quality of the taste of rental library patrons was now equal to that of book buyers. He recalled his own library in Altoona in the 1920s. "We had on our shelves about 15% detectve stories, 15% westerns, 35% light fiction, and about 30% more serious fiction and non-fiction. It was no uncommon thing for us to put in the library fifty copies of a Grace Livingston Hill title, twenty of Ethel Dell, and up to thirty or so of Zane Grey. Practically anything would pay its cost and overhead, and practically anything did just that."[15] The reasons for this shift in taste, McNaughton felt, were that "really literate people have discovered that the lending library offers the best and least expensive entertainment value for their money" and that "literary taste, by and large, is improving."

One means to gauge how rental tastes may have differed from buying tastes is to compare the monthly list of "Best Renters" published in Baker and Taylor's *Retail Bookseller* with their list of "Best Sellers." Analysis of the lists for 1935 would seem to suggest that, at least by then, rental tastes had become more sophisticated than book-buying tastes. John O'Hara's *Appointment in Samarra*, published in August 1934, was listed among the top ten best renters for the first five months of 1935 without showing at all on the best sellers list for that time. Thomas Wolfe's *Of Time and the River* stayed on the best renter list for five months, but only showed up one time on the *Retail Bookseller*'s monthly best sellers list. Clearly, books that were perceived to be slightly risqué did better in the rental market than in the sales market. *Appointment in Samarra* is a case in point, as is O'Hara's second novel, *BUtterfield 8*, which was promoted in advance as being even more forthright than his first. It appeared in seventh place on the *Retail Bookseller*'s best renter list in December 1935. The same month it first appeared on the best seller list in the tenth position. The fact that it shot so quickly onto the best renter list is unusual, because for most books there was a lag of a month between appearance on the best seller list and appearance on the best renter list. Good sales tended to turn titles into good rental property. Another notable feature of the best renter list is the length of time that the most popular titles remained on it. A popular book such as Lloyd C. Douglas's *Green Light* continued to appear on the best renter list for several months after dropping off the best seller list. The staying power of these popular books must have been a real blessing to library operators with twenty or thirty copies of a popular title.

What effect did all of this rental activity have on the publishing of books? Like other questions about the rental industry, this one is difficult to answer because of a paucity of hard evidence. That the libraries had an important role in book sales is undeniable. O. H. Cheney's *Economic Survey of the Book Industry 1930–1931* concluded that rental libraries had increased the sale of certain popular titles. "In some cases as much as 50 to 75 percent of the total sale of a title may be, ultimately, to rental libraries."[16] A survey in 1932 by the *Retail Bookseller* of bookshops with rental libraries indicated that 60 to 70 percent of their purchases were copies intended for resale, meaning that 30 to 40 percent were destined for libraries.[17] When one considers the large purchases made by the library chains and the independent libraries, however, it is possible that the percentage of books destined for the rental market was higher. For certain types of books this was surely true. According to one source in the late 1940s, more than 70 percent of new mysteries were bought by rental libraries.[18] Despite these impressive sounding statistics, American rental library operators were such a diverse and disorganized lot that they could not bring their collective weight to bear on publishers, certainly not in the way Mudie was able to do with British publishers in the nineteenth century. There was no clear voice demanding certain kinds of books from publishers and authors that was substantially different from that of the general book-buying public. Publishers and authors voiced concern about the lost revenues and royalties when a single copy of a book was rented twenty-five times, but presumably the guaranteed sale to the rental market of a substantial percentage of the copies printed was a definite asset to both publishers and authors, particularly during the Depression years.

The two most visible reasons for the decline of rental libraries are television and the paperback book. These were the top two reasons cited in a survey of bookstores conducted by Groff Conklin in 1954. He dated the steep decline in the business to 1950–1951 "when television began claiming more and more leisure hours."[19] The third most cited reason was the high cost of books, a feature that Nelson R. McNaughton had called attention to in 1949. He showed that the percentage of his book budget that was spent on books with a retail price of $2.00 had declined from 52.7 percent in 1941 to 8.8 percent in 1948. In 1941 books costing $3.00 or more claimed only 6.2 percent of the budget, whereas in 1948 they took 67.5 percent.[20] Price was probably a factor in Conklin's examples of how purchases by chains had altered from 1948 to 1953:

> In 1948 the six chains answering this question bought a total of 1,364 copies of that year's Van Wyck Mason title, which listed at $3. In 1953 the same chains bought 478 copies of his best seller for that year at $3.75. This is a decrease of nearly two-thirds in number of copies bought. The picture was not *quite* as gloomy for the James Hilton best sellers in the respective years: 1,884 copies in 1948 at $2.75, and 827 in 1953, at $3.75. This is a decrease of about 56 percent.[21]

The problem for the chains was that they had no other source of income beyond that which they took in from renting books. Bookstores at least derived some higher return from higher book prices, but a chain operator was caught in a price squeeze because rental rates did not rise as sharply as book prices. Furthermore, the chains had to split their gross with the store housing the library. One experiment to deal with the price squeeze was the development of special rental library editions by several different publishers. Conklin lists nine titles that had special printings of a few thousand copies each especially for the rental market. The chains received a lower price; the publisher had a guaranteed order with no returns; and since the chains organized distribution among themselves, shipping was simplified for the publishers. Probably the biggest reason why such schemes did not work to save the chains was that it would not have been in the publishers' interest to produce low-priced editions of those best sellers that would have drawn the largest orders and meant the biggest savings for the chains. The demand for these books would ensure a good sale to the libraries at their regular price.

The other reasons for decline cited in Conklin's survey were book clubs, competition from public libraries, the poor quality of new books, and poor service from rental chains. Of these, the role of public library competition was probably the most significant. As the public libraries undercut the circulating libraries' role as a supplier of nonfiction in the nineteenth century, the growth of public library budgets after World War II and the shedding of old prejudices against popular fiction made public libraries stiff competitors of the commercial libraries in supplying fiction to the public.

Insofar as booksellers did add libraries to their stores reluctantly to meet a perceived demand or neighborhood competition, the resulting libraries could hardly be successful. A personal commitment to the business was essential for the individually run library. Library operators needed to know their customers personally and attend to their wants accordingly. It required the same kind of attention an old-fashioned personal bookshop would give its customers, except that it was even more demanding because regular patrons would be renting books far more often than book buyers would be buying them. Add to this the difficulty in a highly mobile society of maintaining such a core of regular customers and the precarious financial yield of the enterprise with its tedious record-keeping, and it is easier to understand why rental libraries continued to disappear in the 1950s and 1960s.

Yet the rental movement had surprising strength for a couple of decades, for which several reasons can be advanced. There was the continued reluctance of public libraries to stock fiction. *Publishers' Weekly* noted that the libraries were in part compensating for the decline of fiction in magazines.[22] Probably the faddishness of the rental library was part of its appeal as well as part of its undoing. Above all, it seems, the impact of the Depression must be considered. The greatest growth in the movement coincided with the worst years of the Depression. Reading a rented book was not as cheap a form of entertainment as listening to the radio, but it was certainly far cheaper than buying a book. It was probably not just coincidental that the *New York Times* featured an article headlined "Rental Libraries Enjoying Comeback" in 1982, at the height of the recent recession. The result of the rental boom of fifty years ago was not to turn us into a nation of book borrowers instead of book buyers, as many publishers and authors apparently feared. It did serve to put millions of books into circulation and to foster the habit of reading in countless numbers of people. For a few years the mass reading public, which had thrived on the cheap books of the nineteenth-century days before the international copyright, could read cheaply again by renting. Then the more convenient paperback altered reading habits once more. The rental library as a service of local bookshops continues to hang on in certain localities, but its brief moment of glory is past.

Notes

1. "The Rental Library," *Publishers' Weekly* 123 (22 April 1933): 1338.
2. Nelson R. McNaughton, "S'Matter?" *Retail Bookseller* 52 (April 1949): 34.
3. David Kaser, *A Book for a Sixpence: The Circulating Library in America* (Pittsburgh: Beta Phi Mu, 1980), pp. 86–94, 103–104.
4. For information on Mudie's, see Guinevere L. Griest, *Mudie's Circulating Library and the Victorian Novel* (Bloomington: Indiana University Press, 1970).
5. For information on Seymour Eaton and his enterprises, see Dal Hitchcock, "The Booklover's Library," *Publishers' Weekly* 116 (6 July 1929): 44–47; and Grace Ashley, "A Visit to the Booklover's," *Public Libraries* 10 (January 1905): 8–10.
6. For information on Arthur R. Womrath, see "The Famous Womrath Libraries," *Publishers' Weekly* 117 (15 March 1930): 1543–1546; and Wallis P. Howe, Jr., "Arthur Womrath Circulates," *Publishers' Weekly* 123 (4 March 1933): 843–844.
7. "One Year with the Readmore," *American News Trade Journal* 8 (January 1926): 21.
8. Ibid.
9. These cumulations have been taken from Louis R. Wilson, *The Geography of Reading: A Study of the Distribution and Status of Libraries in the United States* (Chicago: American Library Association and the University of Chicago Press, 1938), pp. 210, 201.
10. Telegram, Frederic G. Melcher to Edward A. Weeks, 22 March 1935, *Publishers' Weekly* library, R. R. Bowker Co., New York.
11. See Kaser's findings for the nineteenth century in *A Book for a Sixpence*, pp. 101–102.
12. Groff Conklin, *How to Run a Rental Library*, new and rev. ed. (New York: R. R. Bowker, 1947), p. 5.
13. Ibid., p. 29.
14. A Circulating Librarian, "Catch Your Reader," *Saturday Review of Literature* 11 (30 March 1935): 580.
15. McNaughton, "S'Matter?" (April 1949), p. 32.
16. O. H. Cheney, *Economic Survey of the Book Industry 1930–1931* (New York: National Association of Book Publishers, 1931), p. 255.
17. "Sales vs. Rentals," *Retail Bookseller* 35 (1 June 1932): 19–21.
18. McNaughton, "S'Matter?" *Retail Bookseller* 52 (March 1949): 32.
19. Groff Conklin, "Rental Libraries: Problems and Prospects—Part I," *Publishers' Weekly* 165 (24 April 1954): 1818.
20. McNaughton, "S'Matter?" (March 1949): 33.
21. Groff Conklin, "Rental Libraries: Problems and Prospects—Part 2," *Publishers' Weekly* 165 (1 May 1954): 1893.
22. "The Rental Library," *Publishers' Weekly* 123 (22 April 1933): 1339.

Mosques as Libraries in Islamic Civilization, 700–1400 A.D.

Hedi BenAicha

"Read in the name of thy Lord and cherished Who created, created man out of a mere clot of congealed blood: Read! and thy Lord is most bountiful, He who taught the use of the pen, taught man that which he knew not . . ." (Sura XCVI, Qur'an).

This excerpt provides the Qur'an's basic justification for the rise of literacy; it was a clear indication to the Arabs to make a break with their mnemonic traditions and move toward a new literary era.

With the establishment of Islam as the cultural and political foundation of the Arab world, mosques flourished beyond being mere places of worship. Used as schools and informal gathering places for the exchange of ideas and impromptu poetry readings, mosques were a natural choice for establishing the first libraries in the Arab world. How these libraries developed, and their role in nurturing the germ of the European Renaissance, is the focus of this paper.

The Qur'an: From "It is said . . ." to "It is written . . ."

The words *Iqra* (read) and *Kitab* (book) occur frequently in the Qur'an. Reading and respect for books was strongly encouraged by the Qur'an, which served as the principal force behind the development and maturity of intellectualism in the Arab world. With the birth of Islam, the Arab peninsula emerged from obscurity to enter a new stage of creativity and cultural ferment that far surpassed two great civilizations, Persia (Sassanids) and Byzantium.

Before the dawn of Islam, no real education system existed for the Arabs. There was no significant written literary tradition. Rather, they relied heavily on memorization, preserving most of their legends, poetry, and (especially) genealogies through an oral tradition passed from

Hedi BenAicha *is a member of the American-Arab Anti-Discrimination Committee, Washington, D.C.*

generation to generation. Young Arabs learned from their parents not only how to tend camels and other livestock, how to care for tents or how to conduct oneself honorably in battle, but also how to speak with authority, drama, and inflection—an art known as *balagha* or rhetoric. This oral tradition did not disappear abruptly with the development of written literature, but rather dovetailed with and continued to thrive throughout the early Islamic years.

Through the discipline and rigor of *balagha* and the Arab oral tradition, Muslims were able to preserve the Qur'an until it was formally written down. The Huffadh were among the faithful and closest companions of Muhammed who were charged with memorizing the Qur'an.[1] These Huffadh not only taught and transmitted the teachings of the Qur'an from memory, but were instrumental in having it recorded. When a large number of Huffadh died in early Islamic battles for the conquest of Iraq and Syria, Muhammed's successor, Abu Bakr al-Siddiq (d. 634 A.D.), directed those Huffadh remaining to collect the complete text of the Qur'an into one comprehensive manuscript. Thus the oral tradition of the first Muslims paved the way for the development of literature in Islam.

The third caliph, Uthman Ibn Affan (d. 656 A.D.), ordered the duplication of a few copies of the manuscript to be sent to each of the new conquered provinces. These copies were made under the caliph's own supervision and in consultation with those Huffadh who were still living. In turn, it was from these approved copies that dispersed Muslim communities prepared their own multiple copies, resulting in a second wave of duplication of the original text.[2]

The compilation of the Qur'an and production of multiple copies not only served to propagate the faith, but, especially, it provided a model for the standardization of the Arabic language. As history tells us,[3] there were many other dialects spoken besides that of Muhammed and his tribe, the Quraish of Mecca. Writing the Qur'an in a Quraishi dialect established it *de facto* as the official dialect of Arabic, and the language of Islam, both spoken and written. This standardization was elaborated and improved as the writers developed and created new scripts.[4]

For early Arabs the Qur'an itself represented a real intellectual, social, legal, and historical revolution. It was with the Qur'an and for the Qur'an that Muslims built their system of worship and education. There are Islamic sayings that "man should seek knowledge from birth to death"; and that "knowledge and fire are the only two things that grow by being spread." Islamic proverbs such as these unleashed an incomparable eagerness among Muslims for learning, teaching, and discovery.

This deep intellectual thirst was not limited to a learned elite of scholars, but included military and political leaders. Caliphs themselves often set the pace for expanded literary and scientific achievement. Amidst this ferment the Qur'an was taught in the mosques and regarded as the foundation of all knowledge and learning, both religious and secular (although the distinction between the two would have been meaningless to an early Muslim).

The Mosque: Place of Prayer, Government, and Learning

The mosque was the first institution Muhammed ordered built when he moved to Khaybar or al-Madinah. Primarily a place of worship, the mosque also served as classroom, where Muhammed expounded on Qur'anic passages; and as courtroom, where legal squabbles and moral questions were settled in light of Islamic teaching. As Arab-Muslim communities grew too large for one mosque, new ones would be constructed nearby, allowing the mosques to assume different roles within one community. This division of responsibility resulted in a hierarchy of importance among mosques in the same city, town, or village. Always it was the largest mosque that housed the largest, most complete library.

With Islamic expansion, mosques in non-Arab, originally non-Muslim provinces of the empire played a crucial role in the Islamization of each conquered nation. At the mosque, newly converted Muslims first learned Arabic in order to master the words and the teaching of the Qur'an. Often, a by-product of Islamization was Arabization. This served to cement the non-Arabs' identification with their conquerors. In an Arab-Muslim empire becoming increasingly pluralistic, the mosque served as a symbolic, yet very real, site for religious and cultural unity among Muslims of all nations.

Teachers, like missionaries, would staff the mosques in new territories and begin their task of exhorting the population to embrace Islam. But that was not all they did. Taking their cue from the Qur'an itself, these teachers set out imbuing new Muslims with the same zeal for learning that consumed them. The means for this Arab-Islamization was the written word: books. Thus it was only logical that manuscript collections and formal libraries would be housed in mosques.

Mosques as Libraries: Translation, Preservation, and Creation of Literature

The greater, more prestigious libraries of Muslim communities often were founded by learned individuals through the philanthropy of scholars, aristocrats, governors, and caliphs. Under this patronage, many mosques flourished and developed enviable libraries accessible to scholars from all over the Islamic world.

One such scholar was al-Waqidi, who bequeathed his private collection to a mosque. "After his death al-Waqidi left behind six-hundred cases of books, each case a load for two men. He had two young male slaves who wrote for him night and day. He also collected some books costing two thousand gold coins."[5]

The Bayt al-Hikmah (House of Wisdom) was another renowned collection established in Baghdad by the Abbasid caliph, Al-Ma'mun (813 A.D.). In addition to its function as a mosque for scholars and employees there, the Bayt al-Hikmah possessed a collection of Greek manuscripts that were translated into Arabic by the most competent scholars of the Islamic empire. Bayt al-Hikmah was ransacked by the Mongols in 1258 A.D.,[6] its rich holdings washed away in a river of ink in the Tigris and Euphrates.

In 988 A.D. a member of the Fatimid dynasty in Egypt donated funds to encourage higher learning at Cairo's Al-Azhar Mosque, where astronomy and other sciences were taught in addition to the Qur'anic literature.[7]

As Islamic libraries collected more and more documents and manuscripts, rooms and shelves were designed and constructed to house the burgeoning collections. The scheme for shelving books varied from library to library, with the exception of the location of the Qur'an, which was always placed on the highest shelf, a practice that is still observed today in the mosques. Duplicate copies of the Qur'an were available for daily use; and any passages too worn to be legible were verified from the original.[8] All manuscripts and books were classified and catalogued. One of the earliest known library catalogues, a bibliography really, is Al-Fihrist, written by al-Nadim (987 A.D.) using the dominant method of cataloguing of his time.[9] It ranges from Qur'anic studies and exegeses to literature, philosophy, and the sciences.

As political and military superiority shifted from one region to another, mosques of capital cities underwent corresponding surges and declines in reputation and influence. After the conquest of North Africa in 674 A.D., the army general Uqba Ibn Nafi ordered the building of a mosque in a rural area in what is modern-day Tunisia. The city that eventually grew up around the Qayrawan mosque was and still is considered among the oldest and most authentic Arab-Muslim cities in all North Africa. It was founded two centuries before Fez in Morocco and three centuries before Cairo in Egypt. As part of the Arab settlement in North Africa, Qur'an readers and Muslim scholars from the Arab east were brought to Qayrawan for the Islamization of the indigenous inhabitants. In this process, much of the population was also Arabized. Copyists were imported to prepare manuscripts of the Qur'an for the new converts.

As successive dynasties ruled North Africa from Qayrawan, the mosque was enlarged to accommodate the growing number of worshipers who were attracted by the wealth and renown of the politico-religious center. New space was also provided for the libraries' increasing collection of manuscripts. The concentration of religious scholarship and political power within its walls enabled Qayrawan to exercise enormous influence on the literary flowering of Muslim North Africa. With the expansion of Islam further west into Morocco, an elite of Qayrawani scholars established themselves in Fez to teach in its mosque, which still bears the name of Qarawiyyin, signifying its role as a satellite mosque of Qayrawan.

In the establishment of Qayrawan mosque, as in mosques in Damascus, Cairo, Baghdad, and elsewhere, two phases of activity characterized its growth. First, there was a period of intense translation of foreign-language manuscripts into Arabic. Second, there was an era of creative literary outpouring and scientific discovery. Many of Qayrawan's manuscripts have been partially preserved in the National Library of Tunisia, in Tunis.

The eventual decline and deterioration of Qayrawan came about after its conquest by the Fatimid dynasty in 909 A.D. The Fatimid, who derived their name from Fatimah, the daughter of Muhammed, were a shi^{c}a Islamic sect known as Isma^{c}ilia.[10] Originally from Salamiya in Syria, the Fatimid unsuccessfully tried to depose the ruling Abbasid caliph of Baghdad. Fleeing west, the Fatimid decided to try their military strength against Qayrawan in North Africa, which was a distant province of the then-declining Abbasid empire. For the Fatimid, the conquest of Qayrawan was only a stepping stone to regaining a foothold in the east. Using the city as a place to regroup and refill their coffers in order to finance another offensive, the Fatimid moved the provincial capital of North Africa to Mahdiya on the east coast of Tunisia in 912 A.D.[11] From there the Fatimid caliph Al-Mu^{c}izz successfully led his forces back into Egypt.[12] An important means by which the Fatimid established themselves in Egypt was the building of the Al-Azhar Mosque in 970 A.D. The Fatimid presence in Egypt differed fundamentally from their stay in Tunisia. For while the Fatimid left no cultural legacy in Qayrawan, and in fact actually stripped it of its political and intellectual preeminence, they settled more permanently in Egypt and nurtured the prestige and influence of Al-Azhar Mosque. In an effort to overshadow the Abbasid in Baghdad, the Fatimid lavished much attention on Al-Azhar, making it a showpiece and the focus of rivalry between the two rival dynasties. Moreover, the Fatimid used the mosque as the center point of their Isma^cili ideology.[13] In Al-Azhar, as in other mosques, religious, political, judicial, and educational affairs were all managed simultaneously. Bayard Dodge has described learning of this great mosque, where "archives were stored in the inner part of the building, while classes were held in the sanctuary and courtyard."[14]

Mosque Libraries in Christendom

The Arab-Muslim push into Sicily and Spain from North Africa was characterized by the same cultural transplantation and growth witnessed in Tunisia and Morocco. The Arabs did not dismantle Christian institutions already in place; they did, however, establish mosques and libraries that coexisted with Christian churches. In Spain, Muslims and Christians peacefully practiced their religion and supported their respective scholarly pursuits side by side. Christians and Muslims intermarried, too, as demonstrated by the marriage of Abd al-^cAziz Ibn Nsayr to princess Egilona in 718 A.D.[15]

The creative wealth of Islamic literature and scholarship coupled with its cultural and religious tolerance earned Muslims such a good reputation among Christian Spaniards that many identified themselves with the Arabs. Alvaro, a Christian of Cordova in the ninth century, remarked with regret:

> Many of my co-religionists read the poetry and tales of the Arabs, study the writing of Muhammadan theologians and philosophers, not in order to refute them, but to learn how to express themselves in Arabic with greater correctness and elegance. Where can one find today a layman who reads the Latin commentaries of the Holy scripture? All the young Christians noted for their gifts know only the language and literature of the Arabs, read and study with zeal Arabic books, building up great libraries of them at enormous cost and loudly proclaiming everywhere that this literature is worthy of admiration. Among thousands of us there is hardly one who can write a passable Latin letter to a friend, but innumerable are those who can compose poetry in that language with greater art than the Arabs themselves.[16]

Lament though it was, Alvaro's observation underscored the profound effects of the cultural grafting of Islamic thought in Christian Spain, a process that mosque libraries not only facilitated, but induced. The use of Arabic was so widespread that a priest named Vicencius translated the Bible into Arabic.[17]

The Arab-Muslim rulers in Spain spurred this cultural advancement by diligently patronizing their mosque libraries, so as to rival the intellectual accomplishment of the Abbasid Muslims in the East.[18] Once again the mosques and their libraries, and ultimately the scholars and students using them, reaped the greatest benefits of dynastic rivalry within the Islamic world.

Given the dramatic explosion of ideas and information to come out of Spain, it was natural for these institutions to gain a reputation beyond the Iberic peninsula. Two of the few Europeans outside Spain to learn Arabic were Robert Retenensis and Hermano Delmarta. Sent by Petrus Venerabilis, the chief abbot of Cluny monastery, these scholars stayed in Spain to study astronomy and mathematics. They also translated the Qur'an into Latin in 1143 A.D. and wrote two books on Islamic doctrine and culture, *Doctrina Machumat et Nutrituraeus* and *Mendosa et Ridiculosa Saracenorum*.[19]

The eleventh century marked the awakening of Christian European nations to retrieve territories lost to the Arabs. In 1085 A.D. Toledo was once again under Christian control, though its Arab character and cultural greatness remained unweakened. Christian kings, such as Alphonso VII, astutely avoided interfering with the creative momentum by encouraging Christians, Jews, and Arabs to continue their endeavors in their respective institutions. Thus it was in Toledo that the translation of books from Arabic reached its apex. Dictionaries were written to help translators in this seemingly endless task. Johanne Fück mentions the *Glossarium Latino-Arabirum*,[20] one of a number of dictionaries that permitted the translation of the work of Arab scholars such as Averroës and opened the way for Christian research citing sources from farflung Byzantium.

The tradition of learning continued, even though there was a substantial decline in the role and importance of the mosque beginning in the fourteenth century. However, the existence of secular institutions such as colleges carried on the tradition of maintaining manuscripts and, after the invention of the printing press, books. Thus today the important libraries in the Arab world are no longer associated with mosques, but instead are attached to the European-style secular universities and institutions.

Notes

1. *Huffadh*, plr. *hafidh*, the one who memorizes; it can also be taken to mean a guardian or keeper (e.g., *hafidh maktaba*, keeper or director of a library).

2. Nasser al-Naqshabandi, "Early Islamic Manuscripts of the Quran," *Islamic Review* 1/18 (January 1958): 46–47.

3. Bernard Lewis, *The Arabs in History*, rev. ed. (New York: Harper Colophon Books, 1966), p. 9.

4. Abu al-Faraj Muhammed Ibn Ishaq Nadim (Ibn al-Nadim), *Kitab al-Fihrist*, ed. Gustav Flugel (Leipzig: Vogel, 1871) pp. 7–8.
5. Ibid., p. 98.
6. F. Krenkow, "Kitab Khana," in *Encyclopedia of Islam* (Leiden: Brill, 1925–1928), vol. 2, part 2, p. 1045.
7. Muhammed Kamil Husayn, *Diwan al-mu'ayyad fi al-din* (Cairo: Dar al-kitab al-Misri, 1949), p. 57 *n*2.
8. Nadim, *Kitab al-Fihrist*, p. 1046.
9. S. Vilayat Hussain, "Organization and Administration of Muslim Libraries (from 786 to 1492 A.D.)," *Pakistan Library Association Journal* 1/1 (July 1966): 8–11.
10. Henri Laoust, *Les schismes dans l'Islam* (Paris: Payot, 1966), p. 140; Bayard Dodge, *Al-Azhar: A Millennium of Muslim Learning* (Washington, D.C.: Middle East Institute, 1974), pp. 1–2. See also Bernard Lewis, *The Origins of Ismailism* (New York: W. Heffer and Sons Ltd., 1940), and "The Route to India," in *La Revue de la Faculté des Sciences Economiques d'Istanbul* (1953).
11. Abdallah Laroui, *L'Histoire du Maghreb: Un essai de synthèse* (Paris: Maspero, 1975), I: 120.
12. al-Maqrizi, *Al-Mawa^{c}iz Wal I^{c}tibar Fi Dhikr Al-Khitat wal Athar* (Cairo: Institut Français d'Archéologie Orientale, 1911–1927), part II, p. 180; part IV, pp. 49–55.
13. Dodge, *Al-Azhar*, see chapter "Al-Azhar and the Fatimid Caliphate."
14. Ibid., p. 4.
15. Abu Muhammed Abd Allah al-Marrakushi Ibn Adhari, *Al-Bayan al-Mughrib*, ed. G. S. Collin et Lévi-provençal (Paris: Dozy, 1948–1951), part VI, p. 30.
16. Lewis, *The Arabs in History*, p. 123.
17. Francisco Javier Simonet, *Historia de los Mozárabes de España* (Amsterdam: Oriental Press, 1903), p. 720.
18. Lewis, *The Arabs in History*, p. 124.
19. Johanne Fück, *Die Arabischen Studien in Europa* (Leipzig: O. Harrassowitz, 1944), pp. 89–90.
20. Ibid., p. 94.

References

Ahwani, Ahmad Fuʾad. *Al-Tarbiyah fi al-Islam* (Cairo: Dar Ihya al-Kutub al-Arabiyah, 1955).

al-Baladhuri, Ahmad. *The Origins of the Islamic State*, trans. Philip K. Hitti (New York: Columbia University Press, 1916).

Bukhari. *Kitab al-Jami^{c} al-Sahih*, ed. M. L. Krehl (Leiden: Brill, 1862).

Fadl (Mirza abul Fazl). *Sayings of the Prophet Muhammad* (Allahabad: Reform Society, 1924).

Ibn-Jubayr, Abu al-Husayn Muhammad. *The Travels of Ibn Jubayr*, trans. R. J. C. Broadhurst (London: Jonathan Cape, 1952).

Pedersen, Johannes. *The Arabic Book*, trans. Geoffrey French (Princeton: Princeton University Press, 1984).

The Richtungstreit: The Philosophy of Public Librarianship in Germany before 1933

Margaret F. Stieg

The Richtungstreit is the name given to the disagreement that dominated German public librarianship from approximately 1910 to 1933. At its center was the fundamental question, what is the purpose of the public library? The Alte Richtung, led by Erwin Ackerknecht and including Eugen Sulz and Paul Ladewig, and the Neue Richtung, synonymous with Walter Hofmann, approached this question from different perspectives. Argument focused on such issues as the goals of education, the scope of the book collection, the definition of a "good" book, the role of readers' advising, and whom the library should serve.

Modern public library service began in Germany with the Bücherhallenbewegung (Reading Room Movement) of the 1890s, although the concept of a public library can be traced back to the late eighteenth century. The Bücherhallenbewegung was the German counterpart of the somewhat earlier public library movement in the United States; indeed, its leaders looked to the American movement for inspiration. Like the American public library movement, the Bücherhallenbewegung can take credit both for establishing many public libraries and for creating the rudiments of a theory.

Within fifteen years of its beginnings, the Bücherhallenbewegung was in outward disarray. The discrepancy between its ideals and actual practices in the new libraries stimulated criticism that rapidly grew into a full-fledged debate over theory and practice. This debate addressed all aspects of librarianship: the creation of knowledge, its collection, organization, dissemination, and use.[1] The movement split into two warring camps, the Alte Richtung (Old Direction) and the Neue Richtung (New Direction), both claiming to represent the true faith. From these two groups the controversy itself derived a name, the Richtungstreit (dispute over direction). Both a sign of professional maturity and a source of

Margaret F. Stieg *is associate professor of library service, University of Alabama.*

weakness, the conflict dominated German public librarianship and became more bitter and more debilitating with the passage of time.

A sharply critical review in 1912 of Paul Ladewig's book *Politik der Bücherei* by Walter Hofmann, then librarian of Dresden-Plauen, opened the Richtungstreit. Hofmann had already written several revisionist articles, but his review and the response it provoked—an open letter to him signed by sixteen leading German public librarians taking issue with his presentation of certain facts—formalized the division between the two groups. In the ensuing years a new attack, usually by Hofmann, and yet another sharp response would periodically renew the conflict. There are some indications in the late 1920s of attempts to reduce friction and of tentative efforts by younger librarians to find some common ground, but it was left to the Nazis to end the Richtungstreit. The redirection of public librarianship to serve Nazi goals and the assertion of a Nazi philosophy for the profession rendered the Richtungstreit irrelevant, although lingering personal animosities occasionally surfaced during the Nazi period.

The leading figures of the Alte Richtung were Erwin Ackerknecht, librarian of the Stettin Public Library, Eugen Sulz, librarian of Essen, and Paul Ladewig, who had created the Krupp library in Essen and written *Politik der Bücherei*. Because Constantin Nörrenberg, one of the founders of the Bücherhallenbewegung, signed the open letter of 1913, he too can be identified with it to some extent. The Neue Richtung was practically synonymous with Walter Hofmann, librarian first of Dresden-Plauen and then of Leipzig, who was unusual in coming from a working-class background. Others accepted and propagated his ideas, but the prolific and creative Hofmann so clearly dominated that it is impossible to conceive of a Neue Richtung without him.

They came from different philosophical traditions. The men of the Alte Richtung looked to England and the United States for models of public librarianship; their thinking reflects pragmatic, unsystematized Anglo-American ideas and values. Hofmann, on the other hand, was clearly a German idealist and strongly influenced by German Romanticism.

Over the years the two groups found many points over which to differ, but most had a single basis: an irreconcilable disagreement over the purpose of the public library, an issue that is necessarily central to any theory or philosophy of public librarianship. This conflict derived from divergent definitions of culture and education, and even more fundamentally, from differing views of human nature. It expressed itself largely in the areas of book selection and the nature of readers' advising.

The Bücherhallenbewegung had to some extent defined the purpose of a public library. In an 1895 lecture that served as the movement's intellectual manifesto, Constantin Nörrenberg unequivocally asserted that the primary task of the public library was educational. The library was an extension of the public school. In minimizing economic inequalities, it had an essential social role to perform, and in keeping the citizenry informed, an essential political one.

More specific statements amplified Nörrenberg's statement of purpose. The library should be free, open to all classes, and should maintain hours that make it readily accessible. It should maintain a well-equipped reading room (or book hall, hence the movement's name). Its collections should contain material at varying educational levels on topics of interest to the community. Different political views should be represented. It should be staffed by professionally trained librarians and be supported by public funds. Above all, it should offer professional service: a library was more than just a collection of books.[2]

This vision of the role of the public library was shaped in the social and economic conditions of late-nineteenth-century Germany, the outstanding features of which were rapid industrialization and urbanization. It could not ignore that libraries in Germany were not yet viewed as a public responsibility. Most public libraries were public in the sense that they sought to reach all sectors of the community rather than in the sense of being supported by taxation. This ideal also reflected the close connections of public librarianship with the adult education movement. It left much unstated, and its interpretation would be a fruitful source of controversy in the ensuing decades.

Because Nörrenberg's ideas were the starting point for both Alte and Neue Richtung, at a very general level the two groups agreed that the primary purpose of the public library was educational. Their agreement did not, however, extend far, since the two groups defined education differently and even used different words for it. Hofmann always used *Bildung* (the result, education), while the men of the Alte Richtung preferred to use *Erziehung* (the process, education) whenever possible. *Bildung* especially has connotations of some significance; the word can also be translated as culture or refinement.

Central to the Alte Richtung's view was the conviction that the goal of education is to enable an individual to achieve full humanity. People must become rational and goal-oriented. Education could help an individual to do that and could fruitfully enlarge experience. It was not a passive object to be given or acquired; only when a reader responded to a book with active, or at least awakening, mental activity could reading be called education. Ultimately, education (*Bildung*) was a harmonious intellectual-spiritual relationship.[3]

On the surface, many of Hofmann's ideas sound similar. Early in his career he declared that education should concern itself with people. It should develop a concern for books, a true humanism; for example, the most important aspect of worker education was not intellectual, but the strengthening of the soul. His statement that education is at once a form, an inner attitude, an inner movement of the individual, and consequently something that belongs to the innermost life of the individual, is not far from Ackerknecht's view of it as a harmonious intellectual-spiritual relationship. But by insisting that education takes place only when the librarian acts as middleman, Hofmann makes it clear that there is a profound conflict. Instead of education being a process of self-realization, it is a product, and one, moreover, with little room for variation.[4]

These differences over the methods and purposes of education were rooted in their respective views of humanity. Hofmann may have made personalized advising the hallmark of his school of librarianship, but he was essentially a collectivist, thinking in terms of The Public or The Bourgeois Housewife, however often he denied it.[5] For Hofmann and the Neue Richtung, "individualism" and "liberalism" were dirty words. The Alte Richtung, in direct contrast, prided itself on its concern for the individual and its liberal principles. They spoke of basing their ideas upon psycho-sociological theories, but ultimately their view of human nature was Kantian. They valued human personality as an end in itself and tried to adhere to the categorical imperative.[6]

The implications of the divergent views of human nature were very apparent when the political role of the library was discussed. Both Alte and Neue Richtung agreed that the library had a political role; both agreed that that role was to strengthen national unity.[7] But they differed sharply over a definition of the nation, because the concept of *Volk* was integral to Hofmann's thinking, while it was totally absent in that of the Alte Richtung.[8]

Völkisch ideology was peculiarly German and traced its origins to Fichte and Herder. It was at once political and cultural: it affirmed that the German antiliberal, antienlightened political tradition was superior and that German culture was unique (and superior) and must be protected from alien influence. The nineteenth century added overtones of racial purity and a siege mentality. *Völkisch* ideas could blend with party views across almost the entire political spectrum. Walter Hofmann was not uncommon in combining them with socialism.[9]

Hofmann exhibits many characteristics typical of those influenced by this movement; his constant iteration of the word *Volk* is only the most obvious. His ideal was the social and spiritual unity expressed by the term "*Volk* community" (*Volksgemeinschaft*), a phrase that also implied the disappearance of class barriers. He interpreted adult education as an attempt to revive the roots of Germanness.[10] He indulged in the cloudy philosophizing typical of *völkisch* thinkers: for example, "Adult education is the forming of the *Volk* to *Volk*ness."[11]

Closely related to Hofmann's *völkisch* ideas was his view of culture. For him culture was a coherent, knowable entity, a creation at which to marvel. It was, above all, German, shaped by historical experience. Hofmann defined culture in the following paragraph:

> Culture is the form of the common life of men that is given when men—a group, a circle, a *Volk*—have been united by something that stands outside and over the individual, which soars ahead of the group, of the *Volk*, a belief as religious ages called it, an ideal as it was designated in the German classical period, the illusion, as Gustav Landauer, tired of the old clichés, described it. Culture is there where ordinary men educate themselves about a belief, about an ideal, about an illusion, and where then from this life of ordinary men the high symbols of ordinary, brotherly life arise, the cultural acts, customs, which animated, limited by the ethos of the time and forms of work and arts that grew out of cult, custom, and inspired work.[12]

It was the library's task at once to create this national culture and to protect it, to serve as the memory of the nation.[13]

The Alte Richtung might agree that the German language and culture were to be treasured and protected, a concern that all educated Germans shared, but Sulz's statement that "[libraries] fulfill their purpose best when they satisfy as far as possible cultural need in all forms in which it appears" shows how far apart they were.[14] For Homann culture had only one form. The implications of this disparity were apparent whenever the two groups applied their principles, as, for example, in book selection.

The question of whom the library should serve is another aspect of purpose in which ostensible agreement between Alte and Neue Richtung concealed fundamental disagreement. To this question both groups unhesitatingly responded "all"; both were convinced that it was important to reach the working class and prevent the library from becoming the preserve of the bourgeoisie.[15] But their respective interpretations of "all" are so unlike that this agreement means little. Hofmann held that the public library was to serve the entire nation, a statement with *völkisch* overtones.[16] He then qualified this position by arguing that the library should concentrate its efforts on those who were receptive. Just as not everyone could appreciate music, so there were those who could not appreciate books. Was it not better for the librarian to spend his resources helping those who could be helped?[17] Hofmann's attitude is similar to Nörrenberg's, who qualified "all" in his statement "Its [the public library's] proper task is to spread the healthy education of heart and mind among those who need and seek it."[18]

Ladewig's position, and that of the Alte Richtung, was that the library as a publicly supported institution must admit all.[19] They rejected the idea of serving only the receptive reader as unacceptably elitist, since public means contributed to the support of the library.[20]

The thinking of the two groups on this issue was suffused by an awareness of class. There appears, in fact, to be an unstated assumption that the public library was for the lower classes, although Nörrenberg had clearly rejected the view that the public library was a charitable institution.[21] Often the idea of class was explicitly present. Walter Hofmann spoke frequently in terms of class, whether to deny that he equated educability with class or, somewhat contradictorily, to argue that education is tied to class.[22] The Alte Richtung repeated on a number of occasions that its goal was to serve all classes.[23]

When the two groups began to translate ideas into the realities of library service, further differences appeared. The areas of greatest controversy were those of book selection, the advising of readers, and circulation policies. Neither Alte nor Neue Richtung seems to have had much interest in questions of administration and management, and on professional issues such as the qualifications of a librarian, they held substantially the same opinions.

The problem of book selection or, in broader terms, the nature of the collection unquestionably attracted the most attention. It was an issue that focused all their theories; and many of their theories were developed under its stimulus. Discussion of book selection involved such questions as: who was the public library to serve? what was a "good" book? what was educational?

The differences between Alte and Neue Richtung in this area began at the most basic level: what kinds of materials should the library include? The Neue Richtung took a conservative view. Hofmann believed that the public library should confine itself to the traditional media, that is, to books and periodicals. His position was a direct consequence of his views on culture; writing is the most important element in preserving the nation's culture, and the public library is supposed to serve as the collective cultural memory for the nation. To that he added a more practical argument: the book is the best means of education.[24]

Both because they defined culture less restrictively and because they wished to reach a broader clientele, adherents of the Alte Richtung were interested in media other than the book. Although there is no question that they considered the book the primary form, it is equally unquestionable that they considered it necessary to look beyond the book. For the public library to serve all, as they held it was duty-bound to do, it would have to use other media for those who were unreceptive to the written word. Ackerknecht, for example, early interested himself in the potential of movies.[25] The Alte Richtung also integrated nonbook activities into its library activity in a number of ways. Ackerknecht's ideal library included an auditorium for lectures and a piano in its music library.[26]

The two groups did agree that the public library should hold "good" books, a legacy of their common origin in the Bücherhallenbewegung. The Bücherhallenbewegung had asserted the importance of goodness in defining the difference between the public library's and the lending library's task.[27] Neither Alte nor Neue Richtung ever actually tried to define "good," tending to treat good and bad as self-evident. In fact, their concepts must have been very similar, with vague generalizations such as elevating ideas, good writing, and sensible plots prominent. Unlike their American counterparts, German librarians did not dislike all fiction by definition. They regarded novels and other imaginative literature as an important part of their cultural heritage.

Where they disagreed was over whether the library should hold *only* good books. In practice the question became: is it appropriate for the public library to provide entertaining books? As usual, Hofmann's position was one of lofty, uncompromising principle. The library had to make a choice between entertainment, which led nowhere, and education. Only the authentic and legitimate, the educational, belonged in the library. If the library's money was spent on entertainment, nothing would be left over for its proper task. His views on culture made him even more adamant. Perhaps there is something of the parvenu in his insistence that culture was to be defined by academics, but whatever the antecedent, for Hofmann only the highest of high culture was acceptable.[28]

To provide guidelines for implementing his views, Hofmann devoted considerable effort to developing criteria for book selection, which included a discussion of formal value, value with regard to content, and value for the enhancement of experience. He also delivered himself of a number of more straightforward pronouncements; for example, although different people found different things educational, modernist works could not by definition educate since they were individualistic.[29] For him, the issue was a moral one. Providing entertainment was the equivalent of bread and circuses and would undermine the health of the *Volk* along with beer and movies.[30]

The more pragmatic Alte Richtung did not regard goodness as absolute and immutable, but culture-determined, and changing over time. They took the down-to-earth position that if the masses did not find what they wanted in the public library, they would not use the library.

They very noticeably refrained from defining goodness, and the only principle of book selection they established was that the reader should be studied. They preferred to see the public library as a place for enjoyment rather than, as Ladewig put it, a police institution.[31]

Another specific point of book selection over which they differed was the relative importance of German materials. Hofmann's perception of the public library as the memory of the nation and his emphasis on its role in shaping the *Volk* dictated emphasis on literature written by Germans. The Alte Richtung, although hardly unpatriotic, was interested in expanding readers' perspectives and considered it important to include books that would make them aware of the viewpoints of other nationalities.[32]

It is the issue of *Schundliteratur* (trashy books), however, that more than any other is the touchstone for differentiating between Alte and Neue Richtung in the area of book selection. Very simply, the issue was, did trash belong in the public library? The Neue Richtung's answer was no; the Alte Richtung's, yes.

The two groups agreed that *Schundliteratur* meant books without literary value; they disagreed over its dangers. Paul Ladewig described it as

> literature that apparently is read for relaxation, but in reality agitates the tired nerves of modern men (for the most part poor) through grossly exciting plots to complete exhaustion. A clear means of differentiating between *Schundliteratur* and exciting, but valuable, books, lies in the fact that the good book in its most rousing moments compels thoughtfulness and consideration while the *Schund* novel would make reflection over its contents impossible, yes, even grotesque. The *Schund* book can be summarized with a word: the search for thoughtlessness.[33]

Although *Schundliteratur* was not something the members of the Alte Richtung could endorse, they could accept it. For practical reasons, they were willing to include it in their collections.

There were several elements in the Alte Richtung's defense of *Schund*. They argued that there were distinctions to be made; there was true *Schund*, but much of what Hofmann dismissed as *Schund* was really kitsch, uninspiring but hardly dangerous. In any case, they believed that *Schund* was nothing new and did not harm the adult reader who had already formed values.[34]

Their attitude toward *Schund* also had a positive side. Fundamentally, the Alte Richtung believed that it was better to read than not to read, and that one could hope that a reader of *Schund* would move on from there to something better. They were satisfied if a reader at least recognized that something better did exist. Ackerknecht quoted several important German authors to this effect and aligned himself firmly with Schiller.

> Until our better authors disregard the tricks of bad writing and make use of good or until our public becomes cultivated enough to prefer the true, the beautiful, and good without strange supplements, it is a gain if an entertaining book achieves its purpose without harmful consequences that one must admit corrupt much of this category of writing. At least it drives out, as long as it is read, worse, and contains somewhere a reality for the mind, sows the seed of more useful knowledge, serves in addition to direct the consideration of the reader to more useful purposes, so that the category to which it belongs cannot be dismissed.[35]

Unlike the Alte Richtung, which tended to see *Schundliteratur* as the worst along a continuum, for Hofmann there were no gradations. A work either had or did not have aesthetic value. Hofmann reacted to *Schund* emotionally, seeing it as an influence corrupting a pure and noble *Volk*. He equated it with liquor: people were seeking oblivion from the pressures of mechanization in alcohol and trashy literature. The classes that supplied trash were particularly to be blamed; it was more shameful to provide *Schund* than to read it. *Schund* was a part of a larger cultural question and a symptom of a general societal malaise that called for total reform.[36]

The author Karl May became a symbol of *Schundliteratur*. May was a prolific adventure writer who single-handedly could claim credit for introducing the Germans to the American West and its cowboys and Indians. His novels featured settings as diverse as East Prussia during the great period of the Teutonic knights, the battlefield of Waterloo, and the late-nineteenth-century American Far West. His works were phenomenally popular and have retained their appeal to this day. Hofmann objected to the library holding May; someone reading May wouldn't be reading Goethe or Schiller. The Alte Richtung was unwilling to abandon the May reader who had paid the fees and taxes that supported the library. They also found some redeeming virtues in May. Such literature was admittedly fantasy, but fantasy was a psychological necessity. May presented much useful ethnographic information, created characters who embodied the primitive virtues, and did it all without a surfeit of blood and violence. In any case, what were the alternatives?[37]

Circulation information about Leipzig and some of Hofmann's own statements indicate that Hofmann's practices were probably much more similar to those of the Alte Richtung than his theory suggests. May and his ilk were what readers sought at the public library, and Hofmann appears to have included at least some entertaining and "trashy" works in his collections. He combined this reluctant accommodation to reality, however, with the precept that it was the task of the public library, indeed, its central responsibility, to redirect the reader from such trash to works that he, Hofmann, considered culture. Only such works could educate, and education was the role of the public library. Only then was the librarian functioning as an educator.[38]

Hofmann would accomplish his purpose by providing individualized readers' advisory services. He developed an elaborate theory of circulation, the central idea of which was that the reader and the book collection were two systems, each of which had its correlative in the other. The librarian served as the contact point between the two. The lending process he then divided into *Bestimmungsakt* (act of making a decision, an inner, intellectual act), and *Executivakt* (delivery act, a physical, mechanical action). These he in turn further subdivided, the *Bestimmungsakt* into *Feststellungsakt* and *Einschränkungsakt* (identification act and limitation act), and the *Executivakt* into *Notierungsakt* and *Erledigungsakt* (notification act and fulfillment act).[39]

Hofmann was adamant in his opposition to open stacks and mechanical aids, such as the Indicator, a display board that showed whether a book was in the library or in circulation. He even disliked catalogs that informed the user if the library held a book. All such devices cut down on personal contact between reader and librarian and enabled the reader to evade education. Instead, Hofmann advocated the creation of an elaborate series of forms and registers, designed to assist librarians in giving advice and inform them about the holdings of the library, the content of a book, what an individual had read, what books were out, what books a reader had out, and more. This proliferation of records was an aspect of Hofmann's thinking particularly distasteful to the Alte Richtung. Ladewig commented astringently that you shouldn't spend more time on a thing than it was worth and that too often the public saw the forms associated with borrowing as the *raison d'être* of the public library.[40]

The Alte Richtung's position on readers' advisory work reflected its lesser emphasis on the educational purpose of the public library and its greater concern to serve all readers. Its adherents' objections to Hofmann's ideas fall into three principal groupings. They felt that because the schools were already providing the kind of schoolmasterly guidance Hofmann advocated, it was unnecessary for the public library to duplicate it. They considered his methods entirely too rigid, taking a less structured, less formalized approach. And they preferred to concentrate their efforts on the vast majority of readers rather than on the exceptional one who was genuinely trying to become educated in the public library.[41]

To reinforce the guidance given to readers, Hofmann also established fees structured to deter them from inappropriate use of the library. He was much concerned with the problem of voracious reading (*Vielleserei*) and wished to restrict it as much as possible. This seems an odd thing for a librarian to find objectionable, but Hofmann believed that a reader who was reading a lot must be reading entertaining books. To discourage this, he advocated that a reader be limited to four nonfiction and two fiction books each month. If a reader wished more, he or she would be charged. Hofmann was pleased at the response when he implemented such a plan; when circulation figures dropped but the number of readers rose, he interpreted the change as an improvement in the quality of reading. The Alte Richtung did not like charges of any kind and found such a charge especially offensive because it discriminated against the reader who was disadvantaged to begin with. They argued, moreover, that external constraints do not change taste.[42]

His emphasis on educational reading and the advisory process determined Hofmann's attitude toward the seemingly innocuous matter of library statistics. German librarians habitually kept detailed statistics and only superficially considered their meaning. Hofmann criticized this practice repeatedly. His basic premise was that high circulation figures did not mean that a library had achieved its goals. Although the Alte Richtung agreed with him on this point—Ladewig used almost the same words as Hofmann to state that high circulation figures showed nothing of results—Hofmann continually reproached them for an emphasis on statistics.[43]

Hofmann carried his arguments further. He not only regarded high circulation figures as meaningless, but held them to be evidence of bad librarianship. If a librarian was concentrating on statistics, it showed that he was unwilling to do appropriate advising of readers. Advising would reduce the absolute number of loans by making it unnecessary for a reader to take home a book to see if it *might* interest him and, by its mere presence, would discourage the less serious reader, who in Hofmann's terms did not belong in the public library. Cheap work was poor work and to Hofmann, a high circulation was *prima facie* poor work.[44]

By 1933 German public librarianship had developed not one, but two philosophies. Expressions of radically different philosophical traditions, the two systems offered alternative views on almost all aspects of librarianship.

Their disparate conceptions of human nature and of the rights of individuals produced sharply contrasting attitudes toward library users. Where the Neue Richtung would impose a librarian-defined culture on users, the Alte Richtung believed that what the user wanted deserved consideration. In the divergence are apparent two of the Neue Richtung's dominant themes, its elitism and its authoritarianism, as well as the Alte Richtung's more relaxed, less rigid approach. These attitudes toward library use determined the groups' respective positions on both readers' advising and collection development.

Their thinking on education illustrates another important contrast, the more collectivist-minded Neue Richtung vs. the more individualistic Alte Richtung. Education has a twofold thrust: it serves the purposes of a society by socializing children and preparing them to function in the economy, and it benefits the individual by enabling him or her to lead a richer, fuller life. Both Alte and Neue Richtung recognized the dual nature of education,[45] but they emphasized different sides. Hofmann regarded the public library and more specifically the librarian as instruments to assist in molding the fragmented society into a *Volk*. The Alte Richtung considered the library and its resources as offering the individual an opportunity for self-realization.

Widening the distance between the two groups was their whole approach to a "philosophy" of German public librarianship. Hofmann was a systematic thinker, to whom the development of comprehensive theories came naturally. Early in his career he argued the need for a new theory of public librarianship,[46] and he single-handedly filled volumes to create one. The Alte Richtung did not have the same affinity for theorizing. Ackerknecht, for example, commented rather acidly that, in contrast to Hofmann, *his* duties as librarian did not allow him the time to pursue "theoretical superficialities and sophistical distortions."[47] The Alte Richtung's views, therefore, were more often a response to Hofmann's rather than a spontaneous exposition, its subject necessarily determined by Hofmann's interests rather than its own.

Disagreement over the role of theory extended beyond the bounds of librarianship. While the Alte Richtung confined its discussions to librarianship's immediate concerns, Hofmann saw these same concerns in a wider context. For him, the public library was one unit in society, its role integrated with that of other units.[48] Like other contemporary German writers influenced by Romanticism and idealism, he deplored the modern world. He wrote, for example, of the workers' losses: of their satisfaction in their work, of their understanding of nature's language, of their connection with the spiritual world.[49] He wrote of atomization and of anomie. Workers naturally suffered the most and, if education did not strengthen their souls, the anarchism of despair would destroy Germany and German culture.[50] The Alte Richtung displays none of this nostalgia for a healthier, happier past.

The relative ease of the two groups with theorizing is symptomatic of their very different styles, and in many ways the Richtungstreit is as much a conflict over style as substance. An American reader immersed in the literature of the Richtungstreit comes away with the overall impression of a precise, disciplined, and very German Neue Richtung and a relaxed, pragmatic, nonauthoritarian Alte Richtung, open to outside influences. The participants themselves recognized their stylistic incompatibility. Eugen Sulz delivered a stinging rebuke to Hofmann in his essay "Fortschritt und Reaktion": "One of the inherited failings from which the German soul suffers is the will to be a schoolmaster, to prefer compulsion to other intellectual persuasion."[51]

Stylistic differences are the outgrowth of personality differences, and it is obvious that personality played an important role in exacerbating the Richtungstreit. Hofmann was perpetually combative, something of an intriguer, and as an individual without formal educational credentials, seemingly uncomfortable in an environment where library leaders commonly held a doctorate. One writer on the Richtungstreit argues that he isolated himself.[52] The idiosyncrasies of the various members of the Alte Richtung are less clear-cut, but collectively they appear far more tolerant, flexible, and influenced by their experience.

The trauma of the Nazi period, far-reaching postwar changes, and the death of the individuals most immediately involved have relegated the Richtungstreit firmly to the past. It remains, however, more than an incestuous quarrel over trivialities or a minor historical curiosity. It gave serious consideration to a number of important theoretical and practical issues and to others relating to the identity of the profession. By making concerns explicit, it gave shape and direction to public librarianship. But it also had serious negative consequences. The mere existence of two competing and irreconcilable groups weakened public librarians in dealing with the political authorities who controlled the resources essential for growth and development. The failure to consider the ethical implications of ideas and practices left the profession without intellectual resources when confronted with the Nazi challenge. One can understand the German librarian who declared that the most positive accomplishment of the Nazis in the area of public librarianship was their abrupt and unceremonious termination of the Richtungstreit.

Notes

1. Rudolf Joerden, "Die Volksbücherei," in *Handbuch der Pädagogik*, ed. Hermann Nohl and Ludwig Pallat (Langensalza: Verlag Julius Beltz, 1928), 4: 412.

2. Constantin Nörrenberg, *Die Volksbibliothek: Ihre Aufgabe und ihre Reform* (Berlin, 1895); Wilhelm Schuster, "Historische und andere Irrtümer in der Kritik der Volksbildungbewegung," *Bücherei und Bildungspflege* 7 (1927): 375–376.

3. Erwin Ackerknecht, "Buch und Bildung (1924)," in his *Büchereifragen* (Berlin: Weidmannsche Buchhandlung, 1926), pp. 10–12; E. Ackerknecht, "Jugendlektüre und deutsche Bildungsideale," in *Büchereifragen: Aufsätze zur Bildungsaufgabe*

und Organisastion der modernen Bücherei, ed. E. Ackerknecht and G. Fritz (Berlin, 1914), p. 58; E. Sulz, "Fortschritt und Reaktion," in *Büchereifragen* (1914), p. 15; Erwin Ackerknecht, "Deutsche Bildungspflege in Oberschlesien," in *Oberschlesien: Ein Land deutscher Kultur* (Gleiwitz: Heimatverlag Oberschlesien, 1921), p. 60.

4. Walter Hofmann, "Bildung und Ausbildung des Volksbibliothekars," *Volksbildungsarchiv* 2 (1911): 408; Walter Hofmann, "Um Buch und Volk," in his *Buch und Volk: Gesammelte Aufsätze und Reden zur Buchpolitik und Volksbüchereifrage* (Köln: Verlag der Löwe, 1951; originally published 1916), p. 33; Walter Hofmann, "Grenzen der Volksbildungsarbeit," in his *Buch und Volk* (originally published 1920), pp. 77–78; Walter Hofmann, *Die Praxis der Volksbücherei* (Leipzig: Quelle und Meyer, 1926), p. 24.

5. Walter Hofmann, "Die kleine Ausleihschule," in his *Buch und Volk* (originally published 1915), p. 411.

6. Eugen Sulz, "Die Neue Richtung: Eine prinzipielle Auseinandersetzung," in *Politik der Bücherei: Paul Ladewig und die jungere Bücherhallenbewegung*, ed. Wolfgang Thauer (Wiesbaden: Otto Harrassowitz, 1975; originally published 1913), p. 88; Erwin Ackerknecht, "Bibliothekarische Berufsinnung (1925)," in his *Büchereifragen* (1926), p. 72.

7. Walter Hofmann, "Das Gedächtnis der Nation," in his *Buch und Volk* (originally published 1932), p. 72; Ackerknecht, "Bibliothekarische Berufsinnung," p. 74.

8. *Volk* is one of those untranslatable words that is variously rendered in English as people, nation, and race, and is at once all and none of them.

9. Karl Dietrich Bracher, *The German Dictatorship: The Origins, Structure, and Consequences of National Socialism*, trans. Jean Steinberg (n.p.: Penguin, 1978), pp. 38–44.

10. Hofmann quotes Robert Erdberg in *Vergangenheit, Gegenwart und Zukunft der volkstümlichen Bücherei* (Leipzig: Quelle und Meyer, 1928), p. 20.

11. This sounds even worse in German: "Volksbildung ist Formung des Volkes zur Volkheit," ibid., p. 94.

12. Hofmann, "Grenzen der Volksbildungsarbeit," p. 78.

13. Walter Hofmann, "Detsche Volksbildung," in Thauer, *Politik der Bücherei* (originally published 1918), pp. 132–133; Hofmann, "Das Gedächtnis der Nation."

14. Ackerknecht, "Deutsche Bildungspflege in Oberschlesien," p. 61; Sulz, "Die Neue Richtung," p. 87.

15. Walter Hofmann, "Das Buch, die Bücherei, das Volk und die Jugend," *Volksbildungsarchiv* 5 (1917): 100–116; Sulz, "Fortschritt und Reaktion," p. 22.

16. Walter Hofmann, "Die gesellschaftliche Funktion der öffentlichen Bücherei," in his *Buch und Volk* (originally published 1925), p. 37.

17. Walter Hofmann, "Die Organisation des Ausleihdienstes in der modernen Bildungsbibliothek: III. Die Organisation, Zweiter Teil," *Volksbildungsarchiv* 3 (1913): 373; Hofmann, "Um Buch und Volk," p. 29.

18. Nörrenberg, *Die Volksbibliothek*, p. 7.

19. Paul Ladewig, "Zur Systematik der Ausleihe," in Ackerknecht and Fritz, *Büchereifragen* (1914), p. 80; G. Fritz, "Organisationsformen der modernen Bücherei," in ibid., p. 30.

20. "Offener Brief an Herrn Walter Hofmann," in Thauer, *Politik der Bücherei* (originally published 1913), p. 65; Erwin Ackerknecht, "Was Herrn Hofmann und mich beruflich unterscheidet," *Blätter für Volksbibliotheken und Lesehallen* 20 (1919): 92–94.

21. Nörrenberg, *Die Volksbibliothek*, pp. 6–7.

22. Hofmann, "Um Buch und Volk," pp. 26–29; "Grenzen der Volksbildungsarbeit," p. 83.

23. For example, Erwin Ackerknecht, Gottlieb Fritz, and Wilhelm Schuster, "Erklärung," *Bücherei und Bildungspflege* 7 (1927): 143.

24. Walter Hofmann, *Der Weg zum Schrifttum* (Berlin: Verlag der Arbeitsgemeinschaft, 1926), pp. 17, 20; Hofmann, "Das Gedächtnis der Nation."

25. Erwin Ackerknecht, *Das Lichtspiel im Dienste der Bildungspflege: Handbuch der Lichtspielreformer* (Berlin: Weidmannsche Buchhandlung, 1918).

26. Erwin Ackerknecht, "Besuch in einer Volksbibliothek (1921)," in his *Büchereifragen* (1926), pp. 23–24.

27. "Offener Brief an Herrn Walter Hofmann," pp. 64–65; Walter Hofmann, "Erwiderung auf den an ihn gerichteten offenen Brief," in Thauer, *Politik der Bücherei* (originally published 1913), p. 69; Schuster, "Historische und andere Irrtümer," p. 375.

28. Walter Hofmann, "Zur Reform des Volksbildungswesens," *Blätter für die gesamten Sozialwissenschaften* 4 (1908): 149; Hermann Herrigel, "Die Problematik der Volksbibliothek," in Thauer, *Politik der Bücherei* (originally published 1915), p. 128; Hofmann, *Der Weg zum Schrifttum*, p. 20; Hofmann, "Um Buch und Volk," p. 25; Hofmann, *Der Weg zum Schrifttum*, pp. 20–24; Walter Hofmann, "Die Erlebensnähe: Grundsätze für die Auswahl der Bildungsmittel," in his *Buch und Volk*, p. 162.

29. Hofmann, "Die Erlebensnähe," pp. 164–165.

30. Hofmann, "Um Buch und Volk," p. 23.

31. Paul Ladewig, "Politik der Bücherei," in Thauer, *Politik der Bücherei*, p. 46.

32. Hofmann, "Die gesellschaftliche Funktion," p. 37; Hofmann, "Das Gedächtnis der Nation"; Erwin Ackerknecht, "Leitsätze: Bedeutung und Aufgabe der Volksbücherei (1919)," in his *Büchereifragen* (1926), p. 175.

33. Ladewig, "Politik der Bücherei," p. 40.

34. Sulz, "Fortschritt und Reaktion," p. 7; Erwin Ackerknecht, "Zur Psychologie der Schundliteratur (1919)," in his *Büchereifragen* (1926), p. 143; Ackerknecht, "Jugendlektüre und deutsche Bildungsideale," p. 63.

35. Sulz, "Die Neue Richtung," pp. 90–91; Ackerknecht, "Zur Psychologie der Schundliteratur (1919)," p. 150.

36. Walter Hofmann, "Bücher des Lebens," in his *Buch und Volk* (originally published 1922), p. 178; Hofmann, *Der Weg zum Schrifttum*, p. 20; Hofmann, "Um Buch und Volk," p. 18; Walter Hofmann, "In Sachen Scherls," in Thauer, *Politik der Bücherei*, p. 72; *Vergangenheit, Gegenwart und Zukunft*, p. 49; Walter Hofmann, "Buchpolitik," in his *Buch und Volk* (originally published 1929), pp. 11–12.

37. Hofmann, "Um Buch und Volk," p. 21; Ladewig, "Politik der Bücherei," p. 42; Sulz, "Fortschritt und Reaktion," pp. 11–12; Sulz, "Die Neue Richtung," pp. 88–92.

38. Hofmann, *Die Praxis der Volksbücherei*, p. 15; *Vergangenheit, Gegenwart und Zukunft*, p. 35; Hofmann, "Die Organisation des Ausleihdienstes, III," p. 42.

39. Hofmann, *Der Weg zum Schrifttum*, p. 27; Hofmann, "Die Organisation des Ausleihdienstes, III," *Volksbildungsarchiv* 2 (1911): 38–44.

40. Hofmann, "Die Organisation des Ausleihdienstes, III," *Volksbildungsarchiv* 2 (1911): 51, 74, 77, 94–132; Paul Ladewig, "Zur Systematik der Ausleihe," in Ackerknecht and Fritz, *Büchereifragen* (1914), pp. 71–74.

41. Sulz, "Fortschritt und Reaktion," pp. 16–18; Ladewig, "Zur Systematik der Ausleihe," p. 71.

42. Walter Hofmann, "Das bedingte Lesegeld," in Thauer, *Politik der Bücherei* (originally published 1910), pp. 83–85; Sulz, "Fortschritt und Reaktion," p. 10; Sulz, "Die Neue Richtung," p. 95; Gottlieb Fritz and Otto Plate, *Volksbüchereien* (Berlin and Leipzig: Walter de Gruyter, 1924), p. 97.

43. Hofmann, "Um Buch und Volk," p. 32; Walter Hofmann, "Politik der Bücherei," in Thauer, *Politik der Bücherei* (originally published 1912), p. 60; Ladewig, "Politik der Bücherei," p. 51.

44. Hofmann, "Zur Reform des Bibliothekswesen," p. 164; Hofmann, "Politik der Bücherei," p. 60.

45. For example, Joerden, "Die Volksbücherei," p. 411; Hofmann, "Grenzen der Volksbildungsarbeit," p. 86.

46. Hofmann, "Die Organisation des Ausleihdienstes in der modernen Bildungsbibliothek: III. Die Organisation, Zweiter Teil," p. 374.

47. Ackerknecht, "Was Herrn Hofmann und mich beruflich unterscheidet."

48. For example, he argued that the lack of adequate housing did not justify allowing the poor to use reading rooms to keep warm; it should instead encourage housing reform (*Der Weg zum Schrifttum*, p. 48).

49. Hofmann, "Um Buch und Volk," p. 19.

50. Walter Hofmann, "Menschenbildung, Volksbildung, Arbeiterbildung in der volkstümlichen Bücherei," in his *Buch und Volk* (originally published 1925), pp. 98–101.

51. Sulz, "Fortschritt und Reaktion," p. 2.

52. Tibor Süle, *Bücherei und Ideologie: Politische Aspekte im Richtungstreit deutscher Volksbibliothekare 1910–1930*, Arbeite aus dem Bibliothekar-Lehrinstitut des Landes Nordrhein-Westfalen, Heft 42 (Köln: Greven, 1972), p. 21.

The Working Library of Samuel Taylor Coleridge

Ralph J. Coffman, Jr.

The reconstruction of Coleridge's working library sheds light on the tension between the democratization of the printed word and the persistence of the elitist constraints on access to information in early-nineteenth-century England. The liberating climate of publishing, akin to the Wesleyan climate of the English Broad Church, was embodied in Coleridge's career as a preacher and as a publicist. However, there persisted the vestiges of an authoritarianism in which the institutions of religion and knowledge were protected from easy public access. Ironically, the democratizing forces of religion and the printed medium facilitated a renewed importance of private religion and the personal library. Coleridge's uniquely documented reading history allows us to examine this clash of reason and authority in the career of one who was on the periphery of the clerical and professional orders and who successfully penetrated their elitist, authoritarian institutions.

The importance of libraries and their usage for the social and intellectual underpinnings of English Romanticism has not been fully appreciated. Circles of individuals, such as the ones that encompassed Coleridge throughout his life, were nurtured by a diversity of libraries, which exemplify the tension in early-nineteenth-century English society between the "revolutionary social concept," that of "the democracy of print," and the persistence of an elitist attitude to information access.[1]

Coleridge relates an anecdote illustrative of the democracy of print in the *Biographia Literaria*. In 1796 he had just completed a series of successful lectures in Bristol against war with France. He "set off," he recounts, dressed in a blue and white waistcoat "on a tour to the North," from Bristol to Sheffield, on the commercial task of soliciting subscriptions to his periodical, the *Watchman*, and on the inspired errand of preaching in Unitarian chapels on its theme, "knowledge is power." His first potential customer-convert, "a rigid Calvinist of severe countenance, a

Ralph J. Coffman, Jr. *is the director of the Burns Library, Boston College.*

tallow chandler by trade,'' was, for half an hour, harangued, promised, prophesied, and warned of the impending millennium:

> When in the solemn hour of jubilee
> The massive gates of paradise are thrown wide open.[2]

Thereupon the wide-eyed and somewhat terrified chandler burst in:

> And what Sir! (he said after a short pause) might the cost be? *Only* FOUR PENCE (O! how I felt the anti-climax, the abysmal bathos of that *four pence*!) *Only four pence, Sir, each number, to be published on every eighth day*. That comes to a deal of money at the end of the year. And how much did you say there was to be for the money? *Thirty-two pages, Sir! large octavo, closely printed.* Thirty and two pages? Bless me, why except what I does in a family way on the sabbath, that's more than I ever reads, Sir! all the year round. I am as great a one, as any man in Brummagem, Sir! for liberty and truth and all them sort of things, but as to this (no offence, I hope Sir!) I must beg to be excused.[3]

The new democratizing spirit of the printed word would soon seep into the chandler's veins, while the Coleridge circle espoused its cause both as authors who wrote, as Carlyle quipped, ''not for rich men alone but for all men,'' and as readers, who advocated in an almost evangelical tone the right-to-read credo, much like the later Chartists would.[4] However, it is crucial to remember that, coexistent with this liberating impulse was the enduring fact that free access to information and books was still not regarded as a right, as, indeed, Coleridge's ingenuity in securing the books he needed for his work indicates.

This essay explores Coleridge's use of a variety of different types of libraries, the social and intellectual circles they served, and the formation of his own working library. The saga begins with his first exposure to libraries in London in the 1780s, followed by his studies at the University of Göttingen in 1798 and 1799, his use of libraries in the Lake Country and the north of England in 1800–1801, and the libraries he encountered during his Malta sojourn from 1804 to 1806, ending with an appreciation of Dr. James Gillman's personal library at Highgate, which he used during the last eighteen years of his life. The waves that encircled Coleridge on his life voyage to realms even beyond Xanadu bore on their crests ever-wandering missive books that, like so many bottles in the flotsam of sea foam, conjure a phantom ship from whence they were launched on their eternal errand.

Coleridge's Working Libraries in London

In Coleridge's day, London abounded with a Pandora's box of libraries—public, private, and commercial. John Bagford, the antiquarian, published the first list of them in the 1808 *Monthly Miscellany*, and William Oldys (d. 1762) expanded this list by adding book collectors, booksellers, and published catalogues.[5] By 1819 the variety and number of London libraries were so complex that a guide to them was compiled by William Clarke, listing all the principal libraries—foreign, public, private, and personal. Clarke's list is most noteworthy for its inclusion of notices of selected sale catalogues, since the personal collector (such as Robert Southey, who owned an extensive Spanish manuscript collection) still retained a distinctive social role as a steward of knowledge otherwise unavailable.[6]

Coleridge's contact with London libraries spanned five decades. The first two decades encompassed his school libraries at Christ's Hospital, commercial libraries, London Hospital, and coffeehouses. To this list were added at least three more in the 1820s—Sion College, Dr. Williams's, and the British Museum.

In July 1782 Coleridge, nicknamed "Coly," was enrolled in Christ's Hospital lower grammar school in Hertford, run by a lenient master, Matthew Field. In September he was transferred to the upper school on Newgate Street, London, run by James Boyer (1736–1814), a classicist and sometime poet, who stuffed his students with a *pot-pourri* of Theocritus, Catullus, Homer, Virgil, Pindar, Iamblichus, Plotinus, and even Jacob Boehme, the Silesian mystic, whose *Aurora*, translated by John Sparrow, resonated with the school's Wesleyan pietism.[7]

Near the upper grammar school on Newgate Street was the mathematical school run by William Wales (1734–1798), Captain James Cook's accomplished co-navigator. Wales was in charge of an intriguing library devoted to navigation, seamanship, meteorology, and geography, with an extensive collection of travel accounts by Carteret, Crantz, Forster, Wallis, and Purchas. This was the library where Coly may have first come into contact with the esoteric imagery he incorporated into "Kubla Khan" and "The Rime of the Ancient Mariner."[8]

While Coly was at Newgate Street, his brother Luke (1765–1790) was enrolled at London Hospital, Mile End, as a surgical intern. Luke was in its first graduating class, and although its library was not formally constituted, it did have a rudimentary assortment of standard medical texts to which Coly had access, including works by Harvey, Galen, Bartholin, and Blanchard. *The Edinburgh Dispensatory* was a standard reference work in the wards, as was James Burgh's *Art of Speaking*, recommended to him by Luke for improving his professional manner as an orderly.[9]

History, romance, and poetry, Coly's other early interests, were nurtured by the fortuitous gift of a ticket to a commercial subscription library. One afternoon, so goes the story, after classes on Newgate Street, Coly was churning up and down the Strand with arms outstretched emulating Leander swimming the Hellespont. He crashed into a pedestrian who thought him a pickpocket at first, but so ingenuous was his explanation that he was presented with a ticket to "a great Circulating Library" at 39 King Street, owned by John Boosey, Sr. (1740–1820), an importer and bookseller, whose son Thomas later would procure German books for Coleridge.[10]

The commercial subscription or rental library had developed in the late eighteenth century as an extension of the common bookseller's practice of loaning surplus stock free of charge. Some, like John Murray on Fleet Street and J. H. Bohte on York Street, continued this practice into the nineteenth century for valued customers like Coleridge. The demise in 1774 of the perpetual copyright act assisted in reducing the price of popular editions of standard titles. However, new works in the sciences and foreign languages remained expensive and made their lending by commercial libraries attractive. By 1790 over one thousand commercial libraries had been established to meet this demand in England.

It was rare for a commercial library to issue a rental catalogue; while there is no indication that Boosey ever did, his chief competitor, Bell and Cathorne, did publish a list of their rental stock.

Table 1
Bell and Cathorne's City Circulating Library, 1778

Subject Categories	Percent of titles
1. History, Lives, Antiquity	46
2. Romances, Comic Literature, Fables	19
3. Poetry and Plays	15
4. Physics, Surgery, Science	9
5. Voyages and Travels	6
6. Divinity, Church History, Theology	5

Emphasizing the humanities rather than the sciences, this professional circulating library was distinguished from popular circulating libraries by its stock of multiple-volume sets and its lack of cheap editions. Its collections were especially strong in history, lives and antiquities, science, and theology. When Coly claimed he had read the entire stock (minus the French titles, a language he did not read), it would have taken him three years at the rate of twelve volumes a week. By 1788 it was conceivable that he had completed his task, at least in part, the same year he reported that he was "sporting infidel" by having read Junius's *Letters*, Voltaire's *Dictionary*, and Trenchard and Gordon's *Cato's Letters.*[11]

Commercial ventures to purvey current news of poetry, politics, and Parliament often took strange forms, such as the disguised libraries of the London coffeehouses. Coleridge had frequented them ever since he had gone to live with his uncle John Bowdon on Threadneedle Street in October 1781, shortly after his father's death. Cornhill coffeehouses touted cheap editions of favorite authors, which they frequently rented at a penny a day, and popular periodicals, such as the *Spectator*, which enjoyed an estimated readership of twenty times its issue run of three or four thousand because of its availability in the coffeehouses.[12] In August 1793 Coleridge, now *alias* Silas Tomkyn Comberbach, and Robert Southey spent their evenings at the Salutation and Cat coffeehouse with would-be fellow utopians George Dyer (1755–1841) and Robert Lovell (1770–1796), amidst aromas of Turkish tobaccos, heady ale, and opium. Here was expounded Unitarian Joseph Priestley's Pantisocratic scheme for the youth to leave England and settle the banks of the Susquehanna River in Pennsylvania, together with William Bartram's alluring accounts of life there. The call seemed welcome after hearing Pitt's and Burke's alarming reports on the aftermath of the French Revolution, while the latest poetry of William Lisle Bowles, Conyers Middleton, and William Gilbert provided welcome diversions—all of these books were supplied by the Salutation and Cat's proprietor.[13]

As Coleridge's interests became more erudite, he resorted to libraries that had subject specialties. When he was in London in the fall of 1801 as a correspondent for the *Morning Post*, he was working on "a curious metaphysical work" for which he resorted to the "old libraries" of the city, one of which was the London Library.

The London Library had been founded in 1785 as a private subscription society located on Jermyn Street. Such libraries had developed to meet the demands of a clientele who required, as its prospectus indicated, "works so costly and expensive, as to be beyond the reach of most private fortunes."[14] It had an outstanding reference collection that concentrated on continental editions of scientific and philosophical works in the original languages. Its periodical collection included complete runs of contemporary publications such as the *Adventurer*, the *Connoisseur*, the *Critical Review*, the *Guardian*, *Maty's*, the *Mirror*, the *Monthly Review*, the *Observer*, the *Spectator*, and the *World*. A tabulation of its holdings allows one to compare its emphasis on science and philosophy to Bell and Cathorne's emphasis on history, classics, and romances.

Table 2
The London Library, 1785

Subject Categories	Percent of Titles
1. Anatomy, Botany, Chemistry, Math, Natural History and Philosophy, Physics	33
2. Religion, Morality, Metaphysics	15
3. History, Antiquities, Biography, Heraldry	13
4. Law, Politics, War, Trade, Commerce	11
5. Polite Literature, Education, Language, Grammar, Rhetoric, Criticism, Logic, Polite Arts	9
6. Astronomy, Geography, Voyages, Travels	8
7. Miscellanies	6
8. Poetry, Plays, Novels, Romances	5

Coleridge's choice of the London Library and other commercial subscription societies during the 1800–1801 period was apposite to his study of philosophy, science, medicine, and religion. Unlike Bell and Cathorne's Library, for instance, which had 4 percent of its stock in religion and 9 percent in physics, surgery, and science, the London Library had 15 percent in the former and 33 percent in the latter. Commercial libraries prided themselves on the emphasis of their collections, catering to widely differing readerships.

In 1811 Coleridge was in London again, having just returned from a two-year Lake Country sojourn with Southey and Wordsworth. At this time he was preparing a series of Shakespearean lectures and needed some anecdotal material to spice up his talks. Again he visited the London Library, which had been consolidated since 1806 with the Westminster Library, noted for its fine collection of sixteenth- and seventeenth-century editions. Coleridge selected John Selden's *Table Talk*, in which there was a mine of curious stories. Instead of recording his use of Selden's book, in his notebook "M", he annotated the margins of the book, as was his notorious habit. We know of his use of the London Library at this time only because its books were auctioned in 1821 after it had become insolvent, and one of Coleridge's friends, the Reverend Henry Francis Cary, bought the book and found the unmistakable notes in its margins.

In 1811 Coleridge was also using Rolandi's foreign-language subscription library on 20 Berners and Oxford Streets. Once again, the only record of his use of it is in the identification of marginalia. In 1860 Sir Matthew Digby Wyatt (1820–1877), secretary emeritus of the Royal

Institute of Architects, recorded how he strolled from his lodgings at 54 Guildford Street to Rolandi's, where he borrowed volume two of Wieland's *Comische Erzählungen*. When he brought the book home, he recalled, "I found some MS. notes written on the flyleaves at the commencement and end of the volume. They were signed with the initials 'S.T.C.,' and even had they not been so signed, and in Coleridge's unmistakeable handwriting, the vigour of the thought and language which characterized them could leave but little doubt as to the author, by whose masterly pen they had been written."[15] Sixty-four years later, Professor Leonard Mackall found volume one still with Rolandi's faded yellow label in a London bookstall. Rolandi's, we may surmise, provided Coleridge with German texts otherwise unavailable to him in London.

When Coleridge began his work on *The Aids to Reflection* in 1823, he resorted to Dr. Williams's Library and the Library of Sion College for materials on Robert Leighton (1611–1684), the Archbishop of Glasgow, whose theology was ostensibly the inspiration of the project.

Dr. Williams's Library, in Gordon Square, proved a rich resource for this work, and its librarian, the Reverend J. Coates, was sympathetic to Coleridge's endeavor. Dr. Williams's Library was established by the Presbyterian minister Dr. Daniel Williams and incorporated the libraries of Dr. William Bates and Dr. William Harris. In 1823, through its collections, Coleridge was able to gain access to tracts and pamphlets of the Civil War period, letters and treatises of the Reverend Richard Baxter, and several manuscripts concerning English church history, all of which pertained to the theme of *The Aids to Reflection*.

One work, however, *The History of the Church and State of Scotland* (1677) by John Spottiswoode, was not in Dr. Williams's Library, and Coleridge resorted to the Library of Sion College on Victoria Embankment. The Library dates to 1635, five years after the College was founded. As in Dr. Williams's Library, its collections are especially rich in Puritan literature and theology with 357 volumes of pamphlets and sermons gathered by Edmund Gibson, the eighteenth-century Bishop of London. Its collections were open to members of the College or those with recommendations from a beneficed clergyman, such as the Reverend Joseph Hughes, secretary of the British and Foreign Bible Society, who had helped Coleridge acquire books before.

Coleridge always displayed ingenuity for tracing books in out-of-the-way libraries, sometimes requiring abstruse bibliographic knowledge. The work by Spottiswoode, in fact, occurred as part two of a volume by Gilbert Burnet; its existence required a knowledge of the contents of Burnet's book. By 9 September 1823 he had gathered and "arranged" his sources, including the Spottiswoode account, for his life of Leighton.[16]

It is a pity that the British Museum was never a primary resource for

Coleridge. Admission to the reading room required an introduction from a peer or other eminent person, and this Coleridge lacked. Instead, after 1827 he relied on *bona fide* readers, Dr. Joseph Henry Green and the Reverend Henry Francis Cary. The difficult accessibility of English libraries and particularly the British Museum to the common person was deplorable; the *Westminster Review* pleaded in 1827, "We cannot believe that any nation under the canopy of heaven can equal, much less surpass us, in locking us out of libraries; we are unrivalled in all exclusions."[17] While this is an exaggeration, it does indicate the rampant anxiety many felt for being excluded from the world of information, a secular impulse that parallels the evangelical impulse of the pious in the previous century.

Coleridge's Working Libraries in Bristol

In 1795, when Coleridge was lecturing in Bristol, a number of Romantics had gathered there, including John Matthew Gutch, Thomas Beddoes, William Wordsworth, Robert Southey, John Pinney, George Dyer, and Robert Lovell. Collectively, their interests in German philosophy and poetry, and a sympathy for the French Revolution, inspired *The Annual Anthology*.

These Romantics had a social circle that revolved around the two major literary institutions in Bristol, the Library Society and the Education Society. Both were examples of private subscription institutions that had been founded by professionals and merchants in three regions extending from Liverpool to Warrington, from Carlisle to Halifax, and from Macclesfield to Sheffield. Indeed, Coleridge was aware of their proliferation when he wrote in 1795 that these "book-societies" had been "established in almost every town and city of the kingdom," spreading news and ideas.[18]

The Bristol Library Society was a venerable institution that was founded in 1613 by Robert Redwoode in his private "lodge adjoyinge to the town Wall," but it was moved the next year to its own quarters on King Street, with book donations from Toby Matthews, the Archbishop of York, a collection strong in pre-Civil War English titles. With the rise of the popular circulating library, the town corporation alienated itself from the Society in 1772, since there was no longer adequate municipal support for its antiquarian collections. The following year, its jurisdiction fell to a private club of 132, with an entrance fee of one guinea and a yearly subscription fee of the same amount.[19] These fees restricted its membership to the middle classes. Between 1774 and 1798 its membership increased only by 30 percent, and while it allowed women to join, only five had done so by 1798. It was, therefore, an exclusive club with a fairly static clientele.

The Bristol Library Society's circulation "Registers" cover the period from 1773 to 1857 and make it possible for us to study the reading habits of the Coleridge circle in Bristol.[20] They were deposited in 1857 in the upper story of the Library, where they remained forgotten for thirty-two years, until a distant descendant of Archbishop Matthews, E. R. Norris Matthews, discovered the dusty volumes with Coleridge's and Southey's names listed as borrowers.[21] Matthews reported his findings to the *Bristol Times and Mirror*, which attracted James Baker to the scene, and he published a more complete account.[22]

The Bristol Library Society's collections expanded nearly tenfold between 1774 and 1798, and the relative ranking of its subject holdings, realigned to Bell and Cathorne's, indicates that they were both generally comparable.[23]

Table 3
The Bristol Library Society, 1773–1784

Subject Categories	Percent Titles	Percent of Circulation
1. History, Antiquities, Geography	31	45
2. Belles Lettres	26	25
3. Theology, Church History	9	5
4. Natural History, Chemistry	8	6
5. Philosophy	7	6
6. Jurisprudence	6	3
7. Miscellanies	5	7
8. Mathematics	5	2
9. Medicine, Anatomy	3	1

Furthermore, the collection's strengths correlated with the respective circulation figures for each category, indicating that the Reverend Thomas Johnes's process of selecting books acutely reflected the tastes of his readers. Coleridge, however, appears not to have made use of the Reverend Johnes's expertise during his two periods in Bristol from 1794 to 1798 and from 1814 to 1816. Rather, he had contact only with the sublibrarian, George Symmes Catcott, who repetitiously requested him to return overdue books that had been borrowed on his behalf by Robert Southey.[24]

A host of Bristol friends procured volumes from the Society for Coleridge. Robert Lovell (1770–1796), the fellow Pantisocrat, loaned Coleridge his copy of Mary Wollstonecroft's *Vindication of the Rights of Women* and Gibbon's *History.* In 1794 John Pinney procured the Society's copy of Bruce's *Travels* for Coleridge when he was drafting "Religious Musings." Pinney's father owned Racedown Lodge, where Coleridge first met Wordsworth in 1795. In addition, Wordsworth was residing at Racedown and had a portion of his library and may have loaned Coleridge some of his own books. Subsequently, Joseph Cottle (1770–1853), a Bristol bookseller and publisher and a Society member, loaned books to Coleridge when he was writing the *Watchman* in the spring of 1796.[25] Finally, the minister of Lewin's Mead Chapel, John Prior Estlin (1747–1817), borrowed Stewart's *Political Economy* for Coleridge from the Library Society when Coleridge was still writing his essays a year later.[26]

The other private subscription institution in Bristol was the Education Society, which had an extensive collection comparable to the Library Society. When Coleridge was in Bristol prior to going to Highgate, he again used these libraries. Our information is conjectural, but he probably resorted first to the Library Society for a copy of Harte's *Life of Gustavus Adolphus.* Failing to locate it there, he resorted to his friend John Matthew Gutch, a member of the Education Society, to help him procure a copy from its holdings. In addition, the Cathedral Church housed one of the most extensive ecclesiastical collections in England, with holdings approaching 7,000 volumes, which admirably supplemented Archbishop Matthew's collection in the Library Society. Unfortunately, 90 percent of the Cathedral Library's collections and all of its circulation registers were destroyed in the 1831 riots, so that its use by the Coleridge circle remains conjectural.[27]

The circle of Bristolian Romantics who fostered Coleridge's reading illustrates how various library resources supplemented each other in a competitive environment of providing books for the city's readers.

Coleridge's Working Libraries in Germany

Wordsworth, his sister, Coleridge, and John Chester of Nether Stowey set sail from Yarmouth on 18 September 1798, bound for Hamburg, an odyssey interpolated into the *Biographia Literaria* as "Satyrane's Letters." At Hamburg they met Klopstock, the patriarch of German poetry. The Wordsworths settled at Goslar for a particularly grisly winter. Coleridge walked to the half-timbered town of Göttingen, where he attended classes in the various professors' homes since there were no lecture halls at Göttingen University.

It was between October 1798 and August 1799 that Coleridge made use of the Göttingen University Library; examinations of its circulation records indicate that Coleridge read only literary history, Swabian poetry,[28] or English titles charged out to his friend Clement Carlyon.[29]

However, at Göttingen it was customary for students to purchase the works of individual faculty, past and present, for their personal libraries or to borrow them from professors' private libraries. Through an examination of books that Coleridge either acquired for his own library or cited in his letters and notebooks, we can reconstruct a large body of material written by Göttingen faculty that he studied during this period but did not borrow from the University Library. In theology, for instance, he knew of Gottlieb Jacob Planck (theology chair, 1784–1833), and he read the works of Planck's predecessor, Johann Lorenz Mosheim (professor of theology and church history, 1694–1755). Similarly, he knew of the lectures of constitutional law privat-docent Friedrich Christoph Willich (1745–1827), and he studied the works of his predecessor Johann Heinrich von Selchow (law chair, 1762–1782). Impressed by the lectures of Johann Friedrich Blumenbach (professor of medicine, 1776–1835), he read the works of his predecessor, Albrecht von Haller (professor of anatomy, surgery, and botany, 1736–1753). Coleridge studied the works of various members of the philosophy faculty, including Johann Georg Heinrich Feder (professor of philosophy, 1768–1798), Georg Christian Lichtenberg (professor of philosophy, 1775–1799), Christoph Meiners (professor of cultural history, 1775–1810), Johann David Michaelis (privat-docent of philosophy and Oriental languages, d. 1791), and Michaelis's successor, Gottfried Eichorn (professor of Oriental languages and biblical exegesis, 1788–1827), from volumes purchased later. This considerable list of Göttingen scholars' works ranging from medicine to biblical exegesis[30] broadens our view of Coleridge's intellectual development and cautions one to document the reading habits of an individual through as many sources as possible, such as notebooks and private correspondence, and not to attribute sole evidence to one source, such as circulation records.

Coleridge's Working Libraries in the North

In April 1800 Coleridge moved from the Wordsworths house at Town End, Cumbria, to Greta Hall, Keswick, a house magnificent for its views of the hills high above the river.[31] Coleridge had brought many books with him, such as works of Bruno, Descartes, Hobbes, Newton, Locke, Wolff, and Kant,[32] but his continuing study of the seventeenth century philosophers led him to look beyond Keswick.

Coleridge decided that cathedral libraries were another good source for his needs, so he contacted a friend, James Losh (1763–1833), of the diocese of Carlisle, to procure books from its library.[33] Losh had been an enthusiastic supporter of the *Watchman*, as he was a member of the Friends of the People and the translator of Benjamin Constant's *De la force de la gouvernement.*[34] Through Losh's intercession, Coleridge was able to "carry off a record number of volumes at one time" from the library, "no less than fourteen."[35]

In September 1801 Coleridge was engaged in an examination of various medieval scholastics. This time he turned to another cathedral library, that of Durham, which had a seventeenth-century catalogue and subject index prepared by its librarian, Elias Smith (1633–1676).[36] Coleridge made application to James Deason, the minor canon (1773–1810), and was granted access to its collections. On 25 July 1801 he borrowed volumes of Aquinas, Suarez, and Casaubon.[37] Two months later he borrowed George Campbell's *Lectures on Ecclesiastical History*, which he supplemented with information in his own copy of Cave's *Scriptorum Ecclesiasticum.*[38] It is impossible to verify how many other volumes were borrowed from Durham, but many of the works of the schoolmen studied in the winter of 1801–1802 could have been found.

By 1803, however, Coleridge needed works that Carlisle and Durham Cathedral libraries did not have, so he resorted to a Puritan charity school, Sandys Hospital, in Kendal. Thomas Sandys had founded the school in 1659 for local widows and orphans. The library he donated to it contained Puritan works on the early church fathers, church history, sermons, medieval philosophy, history, and cosmography.[39] Unlike Durham Cathedral Library, these must have been known to Coleridge firsthand, since he asked for a 1505 edition of Duns Scotus. After this one recorded borrowing, however, the library was never mentioned again.

When Coleridge returned to Greta Hall in 1808, he found Southey perambulating with the regularity of Kant and working with the imperturbability of Baxter. Southey had moved his entire library from London to Greta Hall, and "with great ingenuity" he had made all of the long narrow passages hold bookcases from top to bottom.[40] Southey was a voracious reader, being able to glance at a page and note on a slip of paper what might be of future use to him.[41] These loose notes, Southey's equivalent of Coleridge's notebooks, became his *Commonplace Book*, and were posthumously edited by his son-in-law, the Reverend John Warter. Coleridge used many of Southey's books at Greta Hall, but he also supplemented his reading with copies from Bull's Proprietary Library at Bath (Southey's "Bodleian"!) and the Keswick Book Club.[42]

Coleridge left Southey in 1808 to live with the Wordsworths, and Mrs. Coleridge and daughter Sara shared the responsibility for transporting his books from Keswick to Allan Bank. Wordsworth was very unlike Southey and Coleridge in his appreciation of books, confessing,

"And as to buying books, I can affirm that on *new* books I have not spent five shillings for the last 5 years."[43] His somewhat apocryphal mistreatment of books was notorious. It was Southey who quipped that in a library Wordsworth was like "a bear" in "a tulip garden," and De Quincey caricatured Wordsworth, armed with a greasy knife, subtly but effectively buttering an edition of Burke at high tea. At best, Wordsworth was indifferent to books, but he did appreciate Coleridge's library, which was enclosed at Allan Bank in 1810 and which William brought with him to Rydal Mount in 1812.[44] There are five sources that enable one to trace the Wordsworth-Coleridge Library. The first is an 1823 catalogue produced when Coleridge was writing *Aids to Reflection*. The second is an 1829 inventory of Coleridge's books therein. The third is a Rydal Mount circulation register. The fourth is a Rydal Mount shelf-list, produced after Wordsworth's death in 1850 by John Hudson of Ambleside, that gives an indication of the size of individual volumes and helps us identify otherwise dubious editions. The fifth source is the 1859 Wordsworth sale *Catalogue*. Between the 1850 shelf-list and the 1859 sale *Catalogue* of Wordsworth's library, most of the Coleridge association titles and about 20 percent of Wordsworth's own library disappeared.

The 1859 sale of Wordsworth's library enables one to identify admirers of Coleridge and Wordsworth by the books that they purchased and thereby documents a further extension of the Coleridge-Wordsworth circle. Only two copies of the catalogue were annotated, one at the Bodleian containing only a dozen prices, and a second inscribed "A. W. D." owned by the proprietor of the Commercial (now Queen's) Hotel, Ambleside, John Brown. In November 1925 Gordon G. Wordsworth transcribed A. W. D.'s annotations into his copy, which is now in Dove Cottage.[45] From these sources we now know that there were not more than fifty prople at the sale each day. Local residents included the Reverends Graves of Ambleside and Tatham of Rydale, Lady Ainsworth, James Mason Hoppin, the Viscount of St. Asaph, William Wordsworth, Jr., and W. D. Heelis of Hawkshead.[46] From farther afield came F. Merewether,[47] John Peace of Bristol,[48] Mrs. Clayton,[49] Isaac H. Storey, and the Reverend J. J. Taylor. Five bookdealers were present, including Waller and Son from Fleet Street,[50] Bentinck, Saul and Company, Thomas Kerslake of Bristol, George Dawson of London, and George Clayton of Derby. Only Bentinck's *Catalogue* of items purchased has been recorded as having been published, but not one copy has been located. From this point the Coleridge-Wordsworth books were widely dispersed; through the assemblage of those present at the sale, we can view their subsequent provenances as an aspect of the transmission of ideas.

Coleridge's Working Libraries in Malta

On 9 April 1804 Coleridge embarked for Malta as undersecretary to Sir Alexander Ball. He took with him mementos of his stay in the Lake Country: a box of pens from Charles Lamb, a seal with his initials from Sara Hutchinson, and an escritoire containing an Italian grammar from Lady Beaumont. He also packed some of his more valued books.[51]

After an uneventful voyage Coleridge disembarked the *Speedwell* at Valetta, where he contacted John Stoddart at the Casa di San Poix and was introduced to Sir Alexander Ball. His first assignment as undersecretary was to finish Ball's summary of the American Consul's report on Great Britain's diplomatic crisis with the Algerian government.[52] Ball introduced Coleridge to Vittorio Barzoni, and Coleridge procured copies of *Il Cartaginese* and *Rivoluzioni della Republica Veneta* from their illustrious author.

Ball had a large personal library that was especially strong in the recent history and diplomacy of the island and of Italy, and Coleridge read widely in it, covering works by Henry Dundas, First Viscount Melville, Lord Minto, Granville Penn, Charles William Pasley, and Ball himself.

He also became interested in the religious life and the liturgy of the Malta Cathedral Church, with which Ball had worked out an accommodation policy. Coleridge procured two orders of worship and a liturgy in order to become more familiar with its service.[53]

As undersecretary, Coleridge had access to the Royal Library on the Strada Reale, noted for its rare works on philosophy and history in Latin, Italian, and French. There he discovered Giordano Bruno's *De Progressu* in the 1587 edition by Zachariah Craton.[54] Coleridge wanted to borrow this rare work from the Library, but because it was against its policy to loan rare books, and because Coleridge did not succeed in finding a voucher such as Henry Phipps, the First Lord of the Admiralty, the books in the Royal Malta Library were available to him only in the reading room during the day. There he read sixteenth-century theology and books on casuistry such as Antonio Deana's *Resolutiones Morales.*[55] For cheap editions of classical works Coleridge frequented the Piazza Tesorerice, where he procured several works over the next two years.[56]

By the end of the summer of 1805 Coleridge was given the project of applying a theory of colonization to the contemporary Egyptian situation; this became his *Observations on Egypt*. He relied heavily on sources in Ball's library, such as Sir Mark Wood's *Remarks* on the history of East Indian colonies, Lord Brougham's *Colonial Policy*, Ball's *Observations on the Importance of Malta*, and his *Plan for the Defense of Alexandria.*[57] Then Ball sent Coleridge to Sicily to confer with Sir Francis Leckie on the project.[58]

Coleridge presented Leckie with a copy of Barzoni's *Revoluzioni* and found his host friendly and his private library accommodating.[59] There Coleridge made good use of Byron's *Tour through Sicily and Malta* and Swinburne's *Travels through the Two Sicilies* for background information on local life and customs. He also read with interest Metastasio's *Letteri* and Abbe Fortis's *Viaggio in Dalmazia* with its curious accounts of Morlack songs.[60] On departing, Coleridge was given a beautiful edition of Arrian's *De Venatione*, and he returned the compliment with a copy of Richard Price's *Observations*.[61]

In November 1805 Coleridge was back in Malta, with his diplomatic mission nearing completion. As a result, he began to study philosophy and religion again, notably Kant's critical philosophy, its critics and predecessors. He resorted to Christian von Wolff's works on natural theology and Rehberg's *Verhaltness der Metaphysik zu der Religion*, which provided him with additional thoughts on Kant's *Religion innerhalb der grossen blossen Vernunft*.[62] Furthermore, he delved into gnostic Christian thought and its sources, namely Plotinus, the middle Platonists, Pseudo-Dionysius, Paracelsus, Bruno, and Sir Thomas Browne.[63] He wrestled with Hume's scepticism and finally found what he deemed to be a philosophical standpoint compatible with his own in Fichte's subjective transcendentalism.[64] An old issue of the evangelical *Christian Observer* (perhaps borrowed from Ball or Leckie) gave him cause to reflect on his struggles with Unitarianism and gnostic Christianity.[65] Indeed, Crashaw's hymn to St. Theresa in his copy of Anderson's *British Poets* seemed to affirm his maturing religious orthodoxy:

> Angels thy old Friends there shall greet thee
> Glad at thy own Home now to meet thee.[66]

On 20 November 1805 Coleridge embarked at Naples for his return to England. It had been an interesting trip, one filled with local color and religious significance. He reflected on Italian customs in an account by John Moore borrowed from Leckie's library, and when he visited Virgil's tomb at Posillipo, he was more intrigued with a girl's story of her father confessor than he was with the Latin poet.[67] At Herculaneum, Coleridge did manage to procure from John Hayter (1756–1818) at the Museum of Portici a list of papyri excavated from the ruins, but he left no record of having used the Museum's library.[68]

The tragedy of the trip occurred on 23 June 1805, when he lost a trunk containing "some 40 volumes" including his own manuscripts.[69] When he arrived at Halstow on 17 August 1805, in spite of the loss of the books and his marital separation, the trip had been a success and crucial to his own religious and philosophical development. Without the libraries he had encountered on the way, it would have been much less of a watershed in his life.

Coleridge's Working Library in Highgate

In April 1816 Coleridge went to live with James Gillman (1782–1839), a surgeon, and his family at their home in the London suburb of Highgate, first at Moreton House, then, from December 1823, at No. 4, The Grove. Gillman took an active interest in Coleridge's health and his work. He wrote volume one of a projected two-volume biography of the poet, superintended Pickering's 1828 Aldine edition of *The Poems*, and, with his wife Anne, regularly transcribed notes from Coleridge's books into his own.

Gillman's library has not been studied hitherto as a resource that Coleridge used on a daily basis. After Coleridge's death in 1834, some Gillman-Coleridge association items were removed. One was *The Works* of Archbishop Leighton, which had been the main inspiration for *The Aids to Reflection*, and its provenance illustrates the circuitous route of literary transmission. Professor W. B. Elwyn of Queen's College, Oxford, managed to acquire the volume, which he then sent to his kinsman Alfred Elwyn (1804–1884), the Harvard founder of the Pennsylvania Agricultural Society, a man who had studied medicine in Germany. In 1838 Alfred Elwyn communicated Coleridge's marginalia in his copy of Leighton to Charles Lamb's executor, Edward Moxon, and they were included in Henry Nelson Coleridge's 1839 edition of the *Literary Remains*.

Apart from any Gillman-Coleridge volumes that vanished after Coleridge's death, Gillman's library remained intact until it was auctioned by Henry Southgate in 1843. The largest portion was incorporated into 773 lots to be sold, while a small portion of under 50 volumes was retained by the family.

The dispersion of the Gillman library offers some complex provenance histories. William Pickering (1796–1854), who had published the *Literary Remains* in 1839, was desirous to expand the notes he had already promulgated, and purchased twenty-one titles. However, when Pickering's own library was auctioned in 1854, the Gillman-Coleridge association volumes were not noted except for a 1796 edition of Horace; many were lost subsequently.[70] William Henry Miller (1789–1848), the Newcastle-under-Lyne collector, purchased one of the few United States editions, Upham's *Lectures on Witchcraft.* John Bohn (1806–1898), the son of the prominent bookseller in Soho, acquired several volumes, including Bishop Berkeley's 1744 *Siris.*[71] Also present at the sale were old Coleridge friends and admirers, such as Thomas Allsop, James Tregaskis,

W. S. Jackson, John Taylor Brown, Dr. Wright, and Messrs. Baldock and Steward.

The portion of Gillman's library retained by the family included ten volumes that had annotations published in the *Literary Remains* later purchased by Thomas James Wise. Gillman's granddaughter, Lucy E. Watson, wrote a 1925 account of her life at Highgate, making reference to additional Gillman-Coleridge volumes that were auctioned in 1929 after her death.

The Gillman-Coleridge library was well rounded, with distribution of subjects ranging from religion, theology, and philosophy,[72] to medicine and jurisprudence,[73] to world literature,[74] and history.[75] About a third were pre-1800 titles, with the majority printed in the nineteenth century.

After Coleridge's death in July 1834, Coleridge's own volumes that were not associated with Gillman's library were retained by his estate and purchased by his literary executor, Joseph Henry Green (1791–1863), a surgeon of Lincoln's Inn Fields, and honorary lecturer on anatomy at St. Thomas's Hospital, London. Green used Coleridge's Highgate books for thirty years, with the intention of completing Coleridge's philosophy.[76]

Coleridge had first met Green at a dinner party at Lincoln's Inn Fields on 13 June 1817, at which Henry Crabb Robinson, the Germanophile, and Ludwig Tieck (1773–1853), the German poet, were also present. After reciprocating the dinner at Highgate on the twenty-fourth, Green, stimulated by Tieck's account of the Berlin philosophy professor Carl Wilhelm Solger (1780–1819), hurriedly departed for the continent to hear the latest improvements on Fichte and Schelling. After returning, Green met with Coleridge every Sunday from the spring of 1818 until Coleridge's death.[77] The nature of their collaboration need not concern us here, except that, apart from acting as an editor and colleague, Green wrote four essays and a major work under Coleridge's influence,[78] and Coleridge continued work on the "Estecean" philosophy, sometimes referring to it as the "Jahagean";[79] Coleridge and Green thus mutually supported and stimulated each other.

When Green died on 13 December 1863 at The Mount, Hadley, it was predetermined that he was to be buried in Highgate near Coleridge. The prestigious *Medical Times* and the *Lancet* lauded Green's medical accomplishments and his publications. Yet Green had spent the last thirty years of his life working with Coleridge's manuscripts and his library. It was not until July 1880 that 239 Green-Coleridge association books were auctioned at Sotheby's.

About a quarter of these went directly to the British Museum, and the remaining portion went to a variety of collectors, some of whom can be considered part of the Coleridge circle. For instance, John Wilson, the antiquarian, purchased fifty-eight titles, and bookdealer Edward

William Stibbs secured some seventy-two.[80] Dr. Edward Riggall of 141 Queen's Road, Bayswater, purchased three, one of which has disappeared,[81] while the Lancashire novelist William Bury Westall (1834–1903) purchased nine, eight of which have vanished.[82] The eminent bookman Bernard Quaritch selected three titles,[83] while the Broad Church leader and founder of the Working Men's College, Frederick Denison Maurice (1805–1872), selected German authors.[84] Bibliographer Joseph Sabin (1821–1881) acquired three titles,[85] and William Pickering, Jr., the son of the London publisher, acquired two.[86]

These individuals represent a further extension of the Coleridge circle—those who, in the generation after his death, would carry on interest in his life and thought. Today some of these Coleridgeans can be identified only by the association volumes that link their names to his. Such networks of affiliates attest to an important yet infrequently studied reticulation of ideas and associations transmitted and embodied in a library circle that served as an important social and intellectual vehicle of ideas in a past age.

Summary

The reconstruction of Samuel Taylor Coleridge's working libraries from his London and Bristol periods, to his sojourns in the north and his trip to Malta, to his final eighteen-year period at Highgate, provides us with a consummate vantage point to view the struggle for democratizing the printed word. Technologically, new printing methods were being developed to enable the production of cheap editions of standard authors, a situation made legally possible by the demise of the perpetual copyright law. The print medium became the focal point for a number of different social expressions, such as the coffeehouse, commercially run subscription libraries, private clubs, and circles of friends.

The new milieu of burgeoning information exchange that enabled the printed word to be liberated coexisted with older exclusivist institutions, where authoritarian access to knowledge persisted. It was a tension-filled environment, with the gates of knowledge open to some and closed to others. Coleridge's own information needs spanned the gamut; he resorted to the coffeehouse, the professional circulating library, the cathedral library, and libraries of charity schools and colleges. The so-called public library, the British Museum, was closed to him except through friends with proper introductions from eminent people. The private library society was also inaccessible, except through friends, because of the expense of membership.

By tracing in detail Coleridge's use of libraries, one can begin to appreciate how the democratization of the word was a phenomenon born of many factors: the demise of perpetual copyright, the mass publication of cheap editions, the proliferation of commercial libraries, and the popular dissemination of pamphlets and periodicals. Alongside this liberating spirit akin to the emergence of evangelical religion, there persisted, however, the vestiges of an older world in which the printed word had been guarded from the people, in which reading was still a privilege and not a right. Coleridge stood astride these two eras, as did many of those in his circle. Yet he fared the worse for it. Because he was neither a university graduate nor a cleric, his lack of credentials excluded him from the ranks of library membership, a privilege his peers enjoyed. Furthermore, he was constantly plagued by financial problems and this prevented his membership in the clubs and societies apposite to his needs. In these instances he relied heavily on friends.

Indeed, friends played an important informational role throughout his life. It was through friends that Coleridge gained access to an otherwise closed world. Friends shared their special books with him, and he with them. Before the public library in England assumed its egalitarian posture, personal libraries and the circles that formed around them continued to play important roles in the social and intellectual fabric of the nation. The forces at work to make the printed medium more public conversely contributed to a renewed importance of the personal library circle.

Through the reconstruction of Samuel Taylor Coleridge's working libraries, one is able to reconstruct from the provenance history of particular books the library circles that intersected in common social and informational needs and that nurtured and promulgated commonly held ideas. Coleridge's uniquely documented struggle with reason and authority allows one to examine with rare thoroughness the informational problems of a reader who was on the fringes of the clerical and professional orders in the early nineteenth century.

Notes

(Note: when specific titles to works Coleridge used are cited in this paper, the reader is referred to my forthcoming *Samuel Taylor Coleridge's Library: A Reconstruction* [Boston: G. K. Hall, to be published in 1986] for the relevant documentation.)

1. Richard D. Altick, *The English Common Reader* (Chicago: University of Chicago Press, 1957), p. 1.

2. Coleridge, "Religious Musings," ll. 345–316.

3. Coleridge, *Biographia Literaria*, ed. J. Engell and W. Jackson Bate, 2 vols. (Princeton: Princeton University Press, 1983), I: 180–182 (hereafter cited as *BL*).

4. *New Letters of Thomas Carlyle*, ed. and annotated Alexander Carlyle (London: John Lane, 1904), I: 212.

5. William Oldys, *London Libraries*, printed in James Yeowell, *Memoir of William Oldys* (London: privately printed, 1862), pp. 58–109.

6. William Clarke, *Repertorium Bibliographicum*, 2 vols. (London, 1819).

7. Leapidge Smith, "Reminiscences of an Octogenarian," *Leisure Hours* 9 (1860): 633–634. Smith was Coly's valet.

8. Bernard Smith, "Coleridge's 'Ancient Mariner' and Cook's Second Voyage," *Journal of the Warburg and Courtald Institute* 19 (1956): 117–154.

9. Matthew Audley, *An Account of . . . London Hospital*, in *A Sermon Preached . . . April 27, 1775* (London: H. S. Woodfall, 1775), second pagination, pp. 1–28. Coleridge, *Notebooks*, ed. Kathleen Coburn, 3 vols. (Princeton: Princeton University Press, 1957–1973), entries 2227, 2420 (hereafter cited as *N*); Coleridge, *Collected Letters*, ed. Earl Leslie Griggs, 6 vols. (Oxford: Oxford University Press, 1956–1971), no. 1 (4 February 1785) (hereafter cited as *CL*).

10. James Gillman, *Life of Coleridge*, 2 vols. projected, only vol. 1 printed (London: W. Pickering, 1838), pp. 17, 20; John Beer, "Coleridge's 'Great Circulating Library,'" *Notes and Queries*, new series 3 (June 1956): 264. An inventory of all commercial libraries in the 1780s indicates Bell and Cathorne's as the only other possibility, but their location was never on King Street. Thomas Boosey imported German books for Coleridge later. C. F. Schreiber, "Coleridge to Boosey, Boosey to Coleridge," *Yale University Library Gazette* 22 (1930): 6–10.

11. *BL*, I: 48.

12. Donald F. Bond, "The First Printing of the *Spectator*," *Modern Philology* 47 (1950): 166–167.

13. Gillman, *Life*, p. 69.

14. London Library, *Catalogue* (London, 1785).

15. Matthew D. Wyatt, *Athenaeum* 1691 (24 March 1860): 409.

16. *CL*, V: 300.

17. Anon., "Public Libraries," *Westminster Review* 8 (1827): 106.

18. See Frederick Erastus Pierce, *The Eddy around Bristol: Currents and Eddies in the English Romantic Generation* (New Haven: Yale University Press, 1918); Carl A. Weber, *Bristols Bedeutung für die englische Romantik and die deutsch-englischen Beziehungen* (Halle: M. Niemayer, 1935).

19. Charles Tovey, *History of the Bristol City Library: Its Founders and Benefactors* (Bristol, 1853); Edward Robert Norris Mathews, *Early Printed Books and Manuscripts in the City Reference Library, Bristol* (Bristol: printed for the Libraries Committee by W. Crofton Hemmons, 1899), pp. vii–viii; Ronald A. Marchant, *The Church under the Law: Justice, Administration and Discipline in the Diocese of York, 1560–1640* (London: Cambridge University Press, 1969), p. 132.

20. Paul Kaufman, *Borrowings from the Bristol Library 1773–1784: A Unique Record of Reading Vogues* (Charlottesville: Bibliographical Society of the University of Virginia, 1960), p. 8.

21. E. R. Norris Mathews, "Southey and Coleridge in Bristol: Reminiscences of the Old Bristol Library, King Street," *Bristol Times and Mirror* 7600 (11 April 1889): 3.

22. James Baker, "Books Read by Coleridge and Southey," *Chamber's Edinburgh Journal* 7 (1 February 1890): 75–76.

23. *A Catalogue of the Books Belonging to the Bristol Library Society: To Which Are Prefixed the Rules of the Institution and a List of the Subscribers* (Bristol, 1798): *A Catalogue of Books in the Bristol Reference Library* (Bristol: Bristol Public Library, 1954–1958), 3 vols.

24. See Helene Richter, "Thomas Chatterton," *Wiener Beiträge zür Englischen Philologie* 12 (1900): 57–60. The correspondence is at Houghton Library, Harvard.

25. Among the titles Cottle procured for him were George Chalmers's *An Estimate of the Comparative Strength of Great Britain during the Present and Four Preceding Reigns*, which Coleridge used as propaganda against a war with France, David Crantz's *History of Greenland*, and Broughton's *Dictionary*.

26. *N*, entries 308–309.

27. *A Catalogue of the Bristol Education Society* (Bristol: Bristol Education Society, 1795); Beriah Botfield, *Notes on the Cathedral Libraries of England* (London: Charles Whittingham, 1849).

28. Henri Nidecker, "Notes Marginales de S.T. Coleridge," *Revue de Littérature Comparée* 7 (1927): 133.

29. Alice D. Snyder, "Books Borrowed by Coleridge from the Library of the University of Göttingen," *Modern Philology* 28 (1928): 377–380.

30. Full biographical references can be found in Wilhelm Ebel, *Catalogus Professorum Göttingenesium, 1734–1962* (Göttingen: Vandenhoeck and Ruprecht, 1962).

31. *CL*, no. 1631.

32. See *N*, entries 369–928.

33. The other potential candidates were the cathedral libraries of Canterbury, Durham, Gloucester, Winchester, York, Exeter, St. Paul's Lichfield. See Paul Kaufman, *Libraries and Their Users* (London: Library Association, 1969), pp. 77, 89*n*.

34. Paul Kaufman, "Wordsworth's Candid and Enlightened Friend," *Notes and Queries*, new series 9 (1962): 403–408.

35. Kaufman, *Libraries*, p. 83.

36. Huntington Library, San Marino, California, ms. B, IV, 47.

37. See *N*, entry 988.

38. *CL*, no. 528.

39. Edwin Seton Sandys, *History of the Sandys of Cumberland* (n.p.:Barrow, 1930).

40. Charles Cuthbert Southey, *The Life and Correspondence of the Late Robert Southey*, 6 vols. (London: Longmans, 1849–1850) VI: 15–16.

41. C. C. Southey, *Life*, II: 17–18. The four volumes of Southey's *Commonplace Book* entries were published between 1848 and 1851 by J. W. Warter from the original slips of paper in his notebooks.

42. W. Haller, *The Early Life of R. Southey* (New York: Columbia University Press, 1917), p. 25; *N*, entry 3822.

43. William and Dorothy Wordsworth, *The Letters: The Middle Years*, 2nd ed., E. de Selincourt, 2 vols. (Oxford: Oxford University Press, 1970), II: 524.

44. *A Catalogue of the Books and Manuscripts of Harry Elkins Widener*, ed. A. S. W. Rosenbach (Philadelphia: privately printed, 1918). The 1829 *Catalogue* and the 1824 *Library Book* have been analyzed by Chester L. Shaver and Alice C. Shaver in *Wordsworth's Library. A Catalogue* (New York: Garland Publishing, 1979) and have become, therefore, part of the public record.

45. See Roy Park, "William Wordsworth," in *Sale Catalogues of Libraries of Eminent Persons*, vol. 9: *Poets and Men of Letters* (London: Mansell with Sotheby, Parke-Bernet Publications, 1974), p. 4.

46. Ibid., verso title page and passim, Dove Cottage copy.

47. *The Cornell Wordsworth Collection: A Catalogue*, comp. G. H. Healey (Ithaca: Cornell University Press, 1957), no. 2272.

48. Ibid., no. 2266.

49. Ibid., no. 2262.

50. *The Correspondence of Henry Crabb Robinson with the Wordsworth Circle*, ed. E. J. Morley, 2 vols. (Oxford: Clarendon Press, 1927), II: 834.

51. *CL*, II: 1139; *N*, entries 2223, 2438, 2442, 2132. Marcus Aurelius's *Medi-*

tations, Anderson's *British Poets*, Erasmus Darwin's *Botanic Garden*, Kant's *Critique of Judgment*, Condillac's *Logic*, Aleman's *Roque*, Browne's *Religio*, Harrington's *Oceana*, Bishop Latimer's *Sermons*, Hutchinson's *Cumberland*, Pascal's *Provinciales*, and German poetry by Schiller, Voss, Stolberg.

52. Victoria University Library, Toronto, ms. F. 14. 2 (hereafter cited as VUL).

53. *N*, entry 2101.

54. *N*, entry 3825.

55. *N*, entry 3435.

56. *N*, entries 2590, 2625, 2670; *CL*, III: 58; *N*, entry 2433. Franciosini's *Dictionary*, Guarini's *Pastor Fido*, Machiavelli's *Istorie*, old issues of the *Christian Observer*, *Baldwin's Weekly Journal*, and Marion's *Sonnets*.

57. *CL*, II: 1178.

58. British Museum add. ms. 34932 (hereafter cited as BM); Coleridge, *Essays on His Own Times*, 3 vols. (Princeton: Princeton University Press, 1983), II: 200ff.

59. BM add. ms. 3544, f. 263.

60. *N*, entries 2222, 2224.

61. *N*, entries 2236, 2230.

62. *N*, entry 2219.

63. *N*, entries 2447, 2326, 2269, 2329, 2375.

64. *N*, entries 2370, 2382.

65. *N*, entry 2446.

66. *N*, entries 3102–3103.

67. *N*, entries 2721, 2731.

68. *N*, entry 2728.

69. Reconstruction of these lost items is sketchy.

70. *CL*, II: 1186; III: 42. A series of seventeenth-century tracts including William Lilly's rare *Newes from Tvrkie*, Geree's *Character of an Old English Puritane*, and others by Hall and Dymock dropped from sight completely. An 1807 Rabelais went to Dr. Joseph Henry Green, and Hales's *American System* went to one William S. Perry and finally to Harvard. Fielding's *Joseph Andrews* and Southey's *Omniana* went to the British Museum.

71. Bohn's acquisitions included two editions of Bishop Burnet's *History*, Byron's 1815 *Works*, and Prior's *Narrative*.

72. Including works by Bentham, Berkeley, Donne, Fénelon, Fuller, Heylyn, Hooker, Henry More, and Swedenborg.

73. Including works by Boerhaave, Seip, Soame, and Haslam.

74. Including works by Cervantes, Fielding, Shakespeare, Milton, Byron, Pepys, Jonson, Horace, Burton, and Beaumont and Fletcher.

75. Including works by Laing, Fitzgibbon, and Commines.

76. The charge to Green is found in Coleridge's will, BM add. ms. 40057.

77. See H. J. Jackson, "Coleridge's Collaborator: Joseph Henry Green," *Studies in Romanticism* 21/2 (Summer 1982): 161–179.

78. Namely, *An Address Delivered . . . at King's College, London* (1832), *Suggestions Respecting the Intended Plan of Medical Reform* (1834), *Vital Dynamics* (1840), *Mental Dynamics* (1847), and the posthumous *Spiritual Philosophy* (2 vols., 1865).

79. Including the following mss.: BM ms. Egerton 2800, fols. 100ff.; BM ms. Egerton 2801, fols. 107ff.; BM add. ms. 34225, fols. 140ff.

80. Thirty-nine were procured by Scribner and Welford, who had sold Lamb's library. Three of the Wilson titles are in the United States at the Huntington,

the Beinecke, and Johns Hopkins. The located Stibbs titles are now at Harvard, University of Vermont, New York Public Library, Columbia, Princeton, Huntington, University of Pennsylvania, Library of Congress, and the College of St. Mary of the Woods.

81. Including Fleury's *Ecclesiastical History*, Southey's *History of Brazil*, and Paullini's *Disquisitio*. The first went to Harvard and the second to the British Museum.

82. Including a 1670 Erasmus, a 1689 Beughem, an 1801 Hauterive, a 1798 Mueller, a 1798 Bruns, a 1783 Michaelis, a 1742 Quevedo, a 1796 Manu, and Sotheby's 1807 *Saul*. All have been lost from view except the Beughem, which was deposited by the Coleridge family at Victoria University.

83. Including Gilbert's 1633 *Tractatus*, Paracelsus's *Opera*, and Young's *Course of Lectures*.

84. Including Ruedigger's 1704 *Vitae*, Tieck's *Phantasus*, Varen's 1672 *Geographia*, and Wilken's commentary on Kant.

85. Including James's 1829 *Adra*, Voltaire's 1749 *Treatise*, and Sir Francis Wrangham's *Scraps*.

86. Tennyson's 1830 *Poems* and Hyman Hurwitz's 1820 *Hebrew Dirge*.

Private Libraries of American Authors: Dispersal, Custody, and Description

Alan Gribben

The personal libraries of eminent American authors, though indispensable resources for research, have sometimes undergone hazardous stewardships. The families of nineteenth-century authors often sold the book collections, scattering their volumes and resulting in numerous losses. But scholars have employed surviving documents—including correspondence, bookstore receipts, and public library lending records, together with literary allusions in the authors' works—to reconstruct the reading of Melville, Twain, and others. Fortunately, many families and literary executors were conscientious and maintained the library collections. Authors' working libraries are gradually being recognized as significant components of scholarship in literary and cultural history as well as biographical studies. However, librarians and professors face a continuing challenge in educating families and estates about the scholarly value and proper care of books as artifacts and the advantages of making them available for scholarly purposes in a well-maintained academic environment. English professors and research librarians need to collaborate in protecting and describing the private libraries of American authors.

Even before the current concern with environmental issues developed, university botany classes were routinely instructed about the "ecosystem," an interdependent linking of plant and animal life in a given region. And it has long been known that where this carefully balanced, self-perpetuated system is disrupted by lumber operations or by great natural disasters such as forest fires, or where a prairie land becomes suitable for forestation, the climax ecosystem of oak and hickory forests, for instance, does not immediately appear; rather there is an ecological succession of increasingly diverse and complex phases leading toward ecological maturity, with grasses, shrubs, pine trees, and various intervening young ecosystems necessary before the area establishes itself as the mature hardwood forest for which the soil and climate may ultimately have destined it.

Alan Gribben *is associate professor of English, University of Texas at Austin.*

However remote this botanical order may seem from the world of books, there often appear to be analogous natural laws at work in the field of literary study, where it is possible to observe an inexorable progression in the research conducted on any author who attracts scholarly attention. Within the ecosystem of a newly fertile subject, the biography is usually the first green growth to appear; then a bibliography grows up within its shade; several boldly broad critical surveys follow; and soon, if the quality of the literary canon is sufficient, a grove of increasingly specialized studies takes root, affording protective habitats for modish critical approaches. Competing biographies and new editions of the works eventually flourish among the dense woodland vegetation of the climax stage.

Somewhere in the evolution of this delicate ecosystem of academic books, a study of the author's knowledge of others' writings—an examination of his or her library and reading—manages to thrust itself through the foliage of this timber into the sunlight, and it is the often-unnoticed arrival of this seed-bearing plant that I would like to examine. I concentrate on the American species of this flora, and since the listing of and commentary on an author's working library is essentially a twentieth-century component of literary research, the United States already rivals the United Kingdom in the attention paid to the contents of its writers' library shelves. Anyone who gives the matter a few minutes' thought can probably guess accurately the names of some of the earliest American recipients of studies of their libraries. It was our colonial and patriotic figures—those connected with the national destiny who left behind historical, philosophical, or political reputations—whose personal libraries gained the promptest attention. One can understand how colonial writers would appeal to the early-twentieth-century literary historians, and how foundations and associations dedicated to the collection and dissemination of information about colonial and Revolutionary War heroes would encourage the study of their personal collections of library books. William Byrd's library was written about in 1901;[1] the Mathers' in 1910;[2] John Winthrop's library received treatment in scholarly articles in 1928 and 1937;[3] John Woolman's in 1942;[4] Benjamin Franklin's personal book collection produced six scholarly articles that commenced in 1884 and culminated in Edwin Wolf II's essay, "The Reconstruction of Benjamin Franklin's Library: An Unorthodox Jigsaw Puzzle," in 1962;[5] and the contents of Thomas Jefferson's library have elicited three books and several articles.[6]

But those with purely literary careers have eventually won such studies, too, for the listing and analysis of someone's library is one of the surest approaches to that person's intellectual life, aesthetic tastes, and artistic development. Yet the personal libraries of eminent American authors, though indispensable resources for literary and historical research, have sometimes undergone hazardous stewardships. The families of nineteenth-century authors often sold the book collections soon after the deaths of the owners, scattering volumes in many directions and resulting in numerous losses. This was the case with Herman Melville, Mark Twain, and Stephen Crane, for example. Scholars have tried to arrest destructive erosions resulting from the careless mistakes of disinterested relatives (and nodding bookstore clerks) by employing other surviving documents, including library inventories, correspondence, bookstore receipts, and public library lending records, together with literary allusions in the authors' works, to reconstruct the reading of Thoreau, Melville, Hawthorne, Twain, Crane, and others. Fortunately, some families and literary executors were conscientious, maintaining the library collections of Ralph Waldo Emerson, William Dean Howells, and Ernest Hemingway, to name a few, as monuments to the writers' achievements.

Still, the treatment accorded the private libraries of prominent American authors following their deaths is revealing in what it teaches about the continuing challenge that librarians and university professors face in educating families and estates about the scholarly value and proper care of books as artifacts and the advantages of making these assets available for scholarly purposes in a well-maintained academic environment. Depredations are likely to continue until authors' private libraries become recognized outside academic communities as a significant tool of scholarship in literary history and criticism and in intellectual and cultural history, aside from their essentialness to biography.

Occasionally the inquiring scholar is fortunate enough to find an author's library that has been preserved as a unit. Walter Harding wrote in 1967 that he "was astounded . . . to discover that no catalogue of Emerson's library had ever been published despite the fact that, unlike Thoreau's, Emerson's library is still almost intact. It is in the Concord Antiquarian Society in Concord, Massachusetts, just across the street from Emerson's home."[7] Usually the literary researcher is not so fortunate as Professor Harding. The book collection of the author has incurred at least one major removal; there have been problems of storage, of division among heirs, of capricious sales and gifts by literary executors and relatives, of dispersal by public sale to private collectors—not to mention the difficulty in locating those volumes that have been donated to or purchased by public and academic libraries. In researching another book, *Thoreau's Library* (1957), Walter Harding was obliged to preface the catalog with a warning that "unfortunately Thoreau's library has been spread to the four corners of the earth (or, at least of this country) for ninety years, so no completely accurate checklist is possible."[8] On the other hand, Harding was relieved to discover that "Thoreau himself kept a catalog of his books," preserved in the Huntington Library in San Marino, California. But many of them will never be seen again. The Concord Free Public Library did not initially realize the special value of the volumes from the library of Sophia Thoreau's brother that she donated in 1873, and the books were in general circulation for many years until they were rescued in the mid-twentieth century. Thoreau's copy of the Bhagavad-Gita was stolen from the Concord Antiquarian Society in 1941.

Sometimes even the presence of a surviving spouse fails to secure for literary history the best possible record for compiling this reference tool. James E. Kibler's informative article, "The Library of Stephen and Cora Crane" (1971), concedes that "the Crane library must be a Platonic concept because the Cranes moved about so frequently."[9] There was an even more serious difficulty: after Stephen Crane died, his wife moved back to Florida and resumed her occupation as madam of a brothel; following her death, her belongings were auctioned on the steps of the Jacksonville courthouse in 1911—the inventory of this sale mentions a lot of 176 books, now assumed to have been Stephen Crane's. Happily, the Butler Library of Columbia University possesses two helpful manuscripts—attempts by the Cranes to make a formal catalog of the books they owned at Brede Place, their Sussex residence from February 1899 to June 1900. The Cranes' library included standard authors, which suggests that we should no longer consider Crane to have been "ignorant of literary tradition. Far from being an untutored genius or the man Howells imagined as having sprung into life fully armed, Crane evidently was an avid reader." Among the books inscribed by Stephen or Cora Crane are volumes written by Harold Frederic, Thomas Hardy, and Rudyard Kipling.

One example of the ingenuity necessary in the scholar seeking proof of an author's reading patterns is represented by Marion L. Kesselring's transcription of titles that Nathaniel Hawthorne and his family borrowed from the Salem Athenaeum, as recorded in its charge-books between 1828 and 1850.[10] These astounding resources, "tall, narrow volumes, kept by the librarian," provide "direct evidence of what an eminent American author was reading day by day." (One doubts whether such permanent records of library borrowings will survive from our contemporary computer-assisted libraries.) Kesselring, a Brown University librarian, transcribed the abbreviated and dated entries of the Athenaeum charge-book and then identified the books mentioned. Few other researchers have enjoyed the thrill of unearthing a comparable treasure of literary and biographical facts.

I myself serendipitously joined this privileged elite in 1977 when two elderly volunteers I had recruited to assist my search for clues to Mark Twain's library and reading discovered the long-lost original accession record of the small community library in Redding, Connecticut, to which Twain donated many hundreds of his library books between 1908 and 1910. In the 152 ruled pages of this notebook, a librarian had neatly inscribed the authors, titles, publishers, pages, number of illustrations, bindings, prices, dates of publications, and—providentially—*donors* of 2,315 books given to the Mark Twain Library. Of these, 1,751 were explicitly identified as the donations of Samuel L. Clemens or his daughter. Here at last we could learn the titles and dates of novels by Walter Scott, Charles Dickens, Jane Austen, and other books strangely absent from his library when he died in 1910.[11] At moments like those I knew firsthand the pleasures of historical sleuthing celebrated in Richard D. Altick's *The Scholar Adventurers* (1950). In another instance, I salvaged forty books containing Twain's marginalia that had been accidentally placed in paper sacks and boxes among miscellaneous donations to a religious charity's bargain store. The Wisconsin owner of these volumes, seriously ill and in the process of moving her household, had absentmindedly instructed her maid to discard the volumes on those bookshelves, and I arrived at her doorway on my research trip in 1970 only minutes before the truck was scheduled to pick up the books. Imagine my gratification at saving these books from almost certain loss, since none of the future purchasers was likely to have recognized Twain's handwriting.

Most of my research was far more mundane, of course, but ultimately I located nearly 700 books from Twain's personal library that still survive and was able—from Twain's journals, letters, published and unpublished writings, auction and booksellers' catalogs, newspaper magazines, records of his household expenditures, family correspondence, memoirs of his associates, and scholarly books and articles that demonstrate literary influences in his writings—to publish a two-volume annotated catalog with almost 5,000 entries tracing the books, stories, essays, poems, plays, operas, songs, newspapers, and magazines with which Twain was familiar.[12] As with so many other authors' library collections, Twain's had been routinely dispersed after his death—principally by two auctions in 1911 and 1951. The little community library to which he and his daughter donated a large proportion of his collection had treated them—in the manner of Thoreau's books in Concord—as ordinary accessions, and left them on the circulating shelves until 1959. Only 240 survived the decimations of circulation, loss, and sale (in 1952 a well-meaning librarian disposed of seldom-consulted books to obtain more shelf space). So few of Mark Twain's library books are still in existence, and so popular are his novels, that Twain association copies regularly sell for $600 to $1,000 at book auctions and rare book stores these days, and exceptionally important and annotated volumes can bring prices as high as $3,500 or more. Indeed, the most unexpected conclusion emerging from my research is that the meticulous cataloging of a well-known author's library triples or quadruples the price of any volumes that subsequently enter the rare book market, by bestowing a certified pedigree on the majority of extant titles.

This inflation of prices for association copies is the literary scholars' great boon as well as hindrance. It stimulates the discovery and prompt sale of private libraries, but the staggering prices of volumes linked with literary masterpieces forestall most research libraries from bidding on many items; such books are typically purchased by private collectors or investors, who often recede with them from view for long periods. But at least the scholar can find proof in the rare book catalogs of the existence of specific books.

Equally distracting is the proliferation of forgeries on the current book market. I recently was asked my opinion about a costly ten-volume set of Plutarch supposedly signed by Mark Twain; a deftly executed forgery of his autograph in the first volume could have been persuasive, but I know that Twain almost invariably signed his name as "Samuel L. Clemens" or "S. L. Clemens" in his library books. A handwriting expert subsequently corroborated my doubts about the false autograph. These forgeries abound for all major authors nowadays, and a library or individual must consequently use great caution in making acquisitions or inventorying collections. It is more common to find the forger adding a spurious signature to expensive volumes or sets of volumes, but one sometimes finds autographs forged in relatively common books contemporary to the author. Here is where the specialist on the author's library can be of invaluable assistance, lining up the suspected forgery against numerous other examples drawn from the author's library collection; comparing the writing instruments; considering the likelihood of that particular book or edition's having belonged to the author's collection; and factoring in other telltale details (or the lack of them) that can corroborate or dispute authenticity. Twain, for instance, never employed a bookplate after his teens, favored front free endpapers over title pages for his signature, and predominantly used pencil in the 1870s, three shades of ink in the 1880s and 1890s, and usually black ink after 1900.

Considering the similarity of goals for all studies of authors' libraries, it might seem odd to note the diversity of their approaches and methods. The reason is simple but it merits underscoring: the contents of each man's or woman's library have been treated differently by its original owner as well as by the writer's family or friends, and thus the record of every writer's reading must inevitably be established from varying sources. Although common problems exist for researchers, the answers to them are wondrously multiple. The tasks of listing and discussing an author's acquaintance with books are as challenging and infinitely capable of variations as the responsibilities for editing literary works, whose texts may exist in every conceivable state of preparation, from manuscript to galley proof, page proof, first edition, or revised edition. A scholar reconstructing a library must constantly make decisions about which process would give the user the fullest and most accurate report of the author's ownership of, access to, and interest in a piece of reading matter. It is a complicated and absorbing intellectual activity.

To illustrate with the case of Herman Melville, Merton M. Sealts, Jr.'s *Melville's Reading: A Check-List of Books Owned and Borrowed* (1966) charts Melville's access to thousands of volumes he might have consulted, first in the Young Men's Association of Albany, then in the library of the Lansingburgh Academy, the New York Society Library, the Pittsfield Library Association, and additionally (through his father-in-law, Chief Justice Lemuel Shaw) the Boston Athenaeum.[13] Sealts relied on ledgers for the Library of the Boston Athenaeum and the New York Society Library, statements of Melville's accounts with book firms, entries in Melville's journals, and many other sources. But problems related to the actual volumes once in Melville's personal library were hard to resolve. His widow initially tried to retain all of his books, but when she moved to smaller quarters in 1892, she disposed of a large portion of them as gifts to relatives and friends and by sale to bookshops. It is believed that Mrs. Melville sold at least 500 volumes—possibly more—to the New York City firm of John Anderson, Jr. Another bookseller, A. F. Farnell of Brooklyn, took a "cartload" to his shop, outbidding (at $120) another dealer who offered only $100; Farnell regarded the "theological" works in the collection as a dead loss and scrapped them for waste paper. Mrs. Melville also sold additional books to Francis Harper, whose records concerning the purchase were destroyed in a fire. She may have had dealings with other bookshops as well. Sealts tenaciously followed up many leads, even investigating the subsequent dispositions of the book collections of buyers who patronized these bookstores and supposedly acquired pieces of Melville's library, but too often his pursuit ended as it did with the library of James A. H. Bell, whose collection of 10,425 volumes, including association volumes bearing Melville's signature or notes, was presented in 1896 to the Brooklyn Public Library without any separate designation of the Melville books. (A similar fate befell "a couple of bushels" of books that Mark Twain donated from his personal library to a lending library in Riverdale-on-the-Hudson in 1903; eventually these joined the millions of volumes in the New York Public Library system, and are presumably lost forever.) He was able to locate 229 of 257 titles that apparently survive, to establish Melville's ownership of a total of 390 titles, and, by including the titles Melville demonstrably borrowed, to prepare a checklist of nearly 600 titles.[14]

James D. Brasch and Joseph Sigman, compilers of *Hemingway's Library: A Composite Record* (1981),[15] restricted their inquiry to "books that Hemingway is known to have owned. We have not attempted to identify the other books that Hemingway may have read or known about, but only those books which can be proved to have been in his possession." Even so, what an enormous task was theirs! *Hemingway's Library* contains 7,368 entries, each one keyed to one of eight locations or prior lists. In 1953 Hemingway would write to Bernard Berenson that he customarily read three or four books at once, and that over the course of a year he might average a book and a half a day (p. xix). This is one of the conclusions that arises repeatedly from these studies of the library and reading of supposedly untutored-genius writers like Twain, Crane, and Hemingway: in spite of appearances they sometimes gave to the contrary, they were voracious, wide-ranging, habitual readers who mastered many of the classics and knew contemporary books as well. Professors Brasch and Sigman reproduce several lists he periodically made of his favorite works, which generally included *War and Peace*, *Dubliners*, *Huckleberry Finn*, Stephen Crane's short stories, and several of James's novels.

By coincidence, in the same year that *Hemingway's Library* appeared —1981—Michael S. Reynolds brought out *Hemingway's Reading 1910–1940: An Inventory*.[16] Reynolds also ignored literary allusions, instead inventorying "those books, periodicals, and newspapers that Hemingway owned or borrowed between 1910 and 1940." Although Reynolds's 2,304 entries are less than a third as long as the record that Brasch and Sigman compiled, they augment the other study nicely. One of the most fascinating inclusions in Reynolds's study is the course descriptions and assigned textbooks from Oak Park High School while Hemingway was enrolled there; Professor Reynolds also prints Hemingway's high school transcript of courses and the Oak Park High School Library acquisition records.

Henry James's library was not as carefully preserved as Hemingway's, but recently Leon Edel and Adeline R. Tintner reconstructed that collection of some two thousand books as a special feature article for the *Henry James Review*.[17] In an introduction, Edel recounts a visit he made to Lamb House, the novelist's residence in Rye, Sussex, in 1937. "The basic library remained there after his death in 1916 with most of his furniture and pictures." There was, Edel recalled, "some part of it in every room of Lamb House" (p. 158). When the Nazis bombarded

Britain in 1940, Lamb House was damaged, and the James library was moved by bookdealer Gilbert H. Fabes to a safe place. Dorothea James, widow of James's nephew, casually mentioned to Edel afterwards that she had sold these books to Fabes for £200. "I must have coughed, or moved nervously, for she said, 'Mr. Edel, did I do anything wrong?' 'Those are very valuable books,' I said. . . . I didn't tell her that any of the American libraries—the Houghton, Yale, the Library of Congress—would have paid her handsomely (including the costs of shipping) to obtain volumes signed by James or his contemporaries and especially books he had marked and annotated." Edel was stunned. "As she went to another room, I thought of her insouciant attitude toward material scholars valued. . . . Dorothea James was a wealthy society woman; she worked generously in many charities; but she was not a bookish woman, and seemed a bit lost in this bibliophile world."

At least Leon Edel was there to inquire repeatedly about the dispersal of Henry James's library. The collections of more recent authors have sometimes fared worse. J. M. Edelstein opens his exemplary essay about the private library of the poet Wallace Stevens with a series of sad admissions.[18] "The reconstruction of Wallace Stevens's library, if it is ever to be undertaken," Edelstein writes, "will not be easy; it may even be impossible. Too much is missing" (p. 55). This situation prevails despite the fact that "it can be said with some certainty that most of the books Stevens acquired during his lifetime, particularly in his middle and late years, were together at the time of his death" in 1955 (pp. 55-56). Edelstein adds wistfully: "When, but rarely, a book which had been in Stevens's library does surface in the market, it happens because, not long before her death in 1963, the poet's widow called in a bookseller who carried off shelf after shelf of books from the house in Hartford. The problem for the student of Stevens and anyone interested in his books and reading is . . . that the bookseller who bought them simply added them to his general stock" (p. 56). Kenneth A. Lohf, librarian at Butler Library of Columbia University, repeated nearly the same laments, though for different reasons, about the books owned by the poet Hart Crane.[19] The problem was that "Crane seldom remained in one place for longer than a few months. . . . At all of these locations, he read books that were purchased or borrowed, and most often these books were simply left behind when he moved on" (p. 285).

There are other studies of private libraries that deserve mention. The tireless Kenneth Walter Cameron produced studies of Henry Wadsworth Longfellow's library reading according to charging records, and also documented American Transcendentalists' reading patterns as recorded by charging lists.[20] M. E. Baym's "The Catalogue of Henry Adams' Library" made accessible an essential document.[21] Researchers have identified the final contents of the libraries of Hamlin Garland, Frank Norris, Sherwood Anderson, and William Faulkner.[22] Robert J. DeMott has compiled more than 900 entries relating to books that John Steinbeck owned or borrowed, attaching explanatory notes concerning indications of influence and tastes.[23] Very recently a welcome study by Arthur F. Kinney, *Flannery O'Connor's Library: Resources of Being*, has been published by the University of Georgia Press.[24]

In view of this abundance of books and articles concerning American authors' private libraries, do there yet remain promising, unclaimed topics for other scholars to investigate? I hardly know where to begin, the possibilities are so ubiquitous and so beckoning. To take the research library on my own campus (the University of Texas at Austin), the Harry Ransom Humanities Research Center, as a convenient and well-stocked example, the personal libraries of at least half a dozen American writers await scholarly cataloging and analysis a hundred yards from my academic office. Anne Sexton,[25] Louis Zukofsky, Robinson Jeffers, Charles Henri Ford, Ellery Queen, and Ezra Pound are among the authors whose libraries are partially or completely gathered there. Only the Pound materials have received substantial attention.[26]

Other research collections afford similar opportunities. The Department of Rare Books and Special Collections in the McFarlin Library at the University of Tulsa, for instance, has obtained the 10,000-volume library of Edmund Wilson, one of the most influential men of letters in the twentieth century. These holdings include the self-published first edition of Anaïs Nin's *Under a Glass Bell*, handprinted by the author herself, that Wilson reviewed favorably in the *New Yorker* in 1944, launching her career. Vassar College has acquired Elizabeth Bishop's books and papers.[27] The Beinecke Library of Yale University possesses the private libraries of Gertrude Stein, H. D., Josephine Herbst, and Eugene O'Neill. In 1983 Maggs Brothers of London offered for sale the massive library of Henry James's friend and fellow novelist Edith Wharton.[28] A decade ago Anthony Rota supplied the first glimpse of F. Scott Fitzgerald's library.[29] More recently David J. Nordloh briefly sketched the contents of William Dean Howells's private library in the W. D. Howells Memorial at Kittery Point, Maine;[30] Howells's heirs recently presented the house, which Howells bought in 1902 and spent summers in until 1911, to Harvard University.

These and many recently accessible libraries merit reliable checklists. But there exist a few difficulties in arranging the next step and its natural extensions—annotated descriptive catalog, interpretative essays that analyze findings presented in the catalog, and book devoted specifically to the author's library and reading. In the first place, descriptive catalogs of authors' libraries call for cross-disciplinary skills. A professional librarian who has the bibliographic training to construct such a project can feel somewhat uncomfortable about asserting the literary knowledge and critical judgments necessary for the fullest treatment of the library books and their annotations. An English professor, on the other hand, might be completely familiar with the social and literary relationships and artistic accomplishments of Emerson and Thoreau, Twain and Howells, Wharton and James, but possibly has misgivings about proper cataloging techniques, or—even more likely—might be concerned about the prospects for recognition and reward within the profession for this sort of research. The study of an author's library and reading is a borderline area between literary studies and library sciences, and in the field of English the slighting of such labors is endemic. One evidence of this is the dishearteningly large proportion of library reconstructions routinely relegated to the "Other Books Received" columns in leading journals devoted to American literary scholarship. For many journal editors, recruitment and promotion committees, and English Department chairs and professors, this research smacks of pedantry and the supposedly outmoded methodology of the "source-study."[31] Thus the "private library" book often languishes in a bleak interdisciplinary borderland without receiving thoughtful, detailed reviews except in a handful of specialized journals such as *Literary Research Newsletter* and *Analytical and Enumerative Bibliography*. Whereas nearly anyone on an English faculty might wish to *consult* the findings assembled in these books, few are willing to concede that the intellectual effort of creating this research tool is as impressive or imaginative as, say, that expended by colleagues endeavoring to master the subtleties of recent literary critical theory. In this connection, Jack L. Capps's useful study, *Emily Dickinson's Reading* (1966), illustrates one way that a resourceful scholar can attempt to counter these prejudices.[32] Three-quarters of his book is given over to a cogent discussion of the impact that the reading materials accessible to Dickinson seemingly had on her thought and poetry; almost incidentally, as it were, he provides at the rear of the volume an annotated checklist of Dickinson's reading.

Still, there is little need to be anxious about the future of these studies of private libraries of American authors. Certain scholars will always be drawn to this line of investigation, recognizing it as a tribute that is one sign of an author's arrival at full literary stature. Several major scholarly publishing houses like Garland and G. K. Hall are encouraging the cataloging of private libraries. Already, too, the computer is making feasible the types of indexes and cross-files that previously would have seemed extravagant. The time is not too distant when the student can conveniently learn which American authors were familiar by a given date with the writings of Melville, Thoreau, and Whitman or Marx,

Freud, and Jung. Soon it will grow even easier to determine how an author acquired a particular book—by bookstore, library, or gift—and whether evidence indicates that the author actually read or marked its pages.

Perhaps fairer academic rewards for this work will be more uniformly forthcoming for scholars. It occurs to me that professional librarians should often team up with literary scholars for joint efforts on these projects—the resulting studies would be less eccentric in catalog form, would offer fuller cross-indexes and bibliographies, and yet could link the association volumes to the authors' writings. This area of literary scholarship proffers a potential opportunity for the marriage of two related but sometimes artificially separated disciplines. Community librarians need to be less hesitant about seeking the advice of professors and librarians at research institutions regarding proper conservation measures for important private libraries that come into their custody. We may also see within our lifetimes a shift in public attitudes, so that these reading records are perceived as irreplaceable artifacts of a cultural period as well as signposts that have guided someone's intellectual and artistic journeys. It could be that authors will eventually make premeditated arrangements to donate their working libraries to institutions that can preserve them carefully, or that they will at least stipulate that their families or literary executors must sell the book collections intact rather than piecemeal. New printing procedures may allow the facsimile reproduction of complete marginal notes in instances where they are extremely important, along with accompanying parallel passages from the text the author annotated. For those private libraries that survive into the next century, the odds are very favorable for their rescue, description, and analysis in ways more sophisticated and efficient than we are yet accustomed to. The technology and determination that enable us to penetrate outer space will most likely also give us better means to explore the intellectual lives of our cherished authors. Word-processors, as well as other apparatuses now beyond our ken, will ultimately supplement the researcher's notecards and file boxes, but an unquenchable curiosity about the creators and backgrounds of great literary manuscripts will continually bring forth dauntless scholars in each generation.

Notes

1. "A Catalogue of Books in the Library at Westover," in John Spencer Basset (ed.), *The Writings of "Colonel William Byrd"* (New York: Doubleday, Page, 1901), pp. 413–433.

2. J. H. Tuttle, "The Libraries of the Mathers," *Proceedings of the American Antiquarian Society* 20 (1910): 312–350.

3. C. A. Browne, "John Winthrop's Library," *Isis* 11 (1928): 328–341;

H. Greenberg, "The Authenticity of the Library of John Winthrop the Younger," *American Literature* 8 (1937): 448–452.

4. F. B. Tolles, "John Woolman's List of 'Books Lent,'" *Bulletin of Friends' Historical Association* 31 (1942): 72–83.

5. M. Blake, "Books Taken from Dr. Franklin's Library by Major Andre," *Pennsylvania Magazine of History and Biography* 8 (1884): 430; G. S. Eddy, "Dr. Benjamin Franklin's Library," *Proceedings of the American Antiquarian Society* 34 (1924): 206–226; J. B. Shipley, "Franklin Attends a Book Auction," *Pennsylvania Magazine of History and Biography* 80 (1956): 37–45; Margaret Korty, "Franklin's World of Books," *Journal of Library History* 2 (1967): 271–328; E. Wolf, "A Key to Identification of Franklin's Books," *Manuscripts* 8 (1956): 211–214; Edwin Wolf, II, "The Reconstruction of Benjamin Franklin's Library: An Unorthodox Jigsaw Puzzle," *Proceedings of the Bibliographical Society of America* 46 (1962): 1–16.

6. L. B. Wright, "Jefferson and the Classics," *Proceedings of the American Philosophical Society* 87 (1943): 223–233; E. Millicent Sowerby (comp.), *Catalogue of the Library of Thomas Jefferson*, 5 vols. (Washington, D.C.: Library of Congress, 1952–1959); M. Sowerby, "Thomas Jefferson and His Library," *Proceedings of the Bibliographical Society of America* 50 (1956): 213–228; W. B. O'Neal, *Jefferson's Fine Arts Library: His Selections for the University of Virginia* (Charlottesville: University Press of Virginia. 1976)—based on an earlier, briefer version published in 1956; C. B. Sanford, *Thomas Jefferson and His Library: A Study of His Literary Interest and of the Religious Attitudes Revealed by Religious Titles in His Library* (Hamden, Conn.: Shoe String Press, 1977); A. D. Ladenson, "'I Cannot Live Without Books': Thomas Jefferson, Bibliophile," *Wilson Library Bulletin* 52 (April 1978): 624–631.

7. Walter Harding (comp.), *Emerson's Library* (Charlottesville: University Press of Virginia for the Bibliographical Society of the University of Virginia, 1967). See, as well, Kenneth Walter Cameron, *The Transcendentalists and Minerva* (Hartford, Conn.: Transcendental Books, 1958), 3: 855–862. Cameron also produced *Ralph Waldo Emerson's Reading: A Guide for Source-hunters and Scholars* (Raleigh, N.C.: Thistle Press, 1941) and *Ralph Waldo Emerson's Reading: A Corrected Edition* (Hartford, Conn.: Transcendental Books, 1962)—a reproduction of the 1941 edition, with additional matter.

8. Walter Harding, *Thoreau's Library* (Charlottesville: University of Virginia, 1957)—published jointly by the Thoreau Society and the Bibliographical Society of the University of Virginia. Harding provides additional facts in "A New Checklist of the Books in Henry David Thoreau's Library," in *Studies in the American Renaissance, 1983*, ed. Joel Myerson (Charlottesville: University Press of Virginia, 1983), pp. 151–186. See also *Thoreau's Fact Book in the Harry Elkins Widener Collection in the Harvard College Library: Annotated*, ed. Kenneth Walter Cameron, 2 vols. (Hartford, Conn.: Transcendental Books, 1966). Also *Thoreau's Literary Notebook in the Library of Congress: Facsimile Text* (Hartford, Conn.: Transcendental Books, 1964); *Young Thoreau and the Classics: A Review* (Hartford, Conn.: Transcendental Books, 1975); *Thoreau Discovers Emerson: A College Reading Record* (New York: New York Public Library, 1953).

9. James E. Kibler, Jr., "The Library of Stephen and Cora Crane," *Proof: The Yearbook of American Bibliographical and Textual Studies* 1 (1971): 199–246.

10. Marion L. Kesselring, *Hawthorne's Reading 1828–1850: A Transcription and Identification of Titles Recorded in the Charge-Books of the Salem Athenaeum* (New York: New York Public Library, 1949).

11. I have described this moment and other surprising finds in "Reconstruct-

ing Mark Twain's Library,'' *A B Bookman's Weekly* 66 (11 August 1980): 755–773; reprinted in *A B Bookman's Yearbook, Part I* (1980), ed. Jacob Chernofsky (Clifton, N.J.: A B Bookman's Weekly, 1982), pp. 3–11.

12. Alan Gribben, *Mark Twain's Library: A Reconstruction*, 2 vols. (Boston: G. K. Hall, 1980). See also ''The Formation of Samuel L. Clemens' Library,'' *Studies in American Humor* 2 (January 1976): 171–182; ''The Dispersal of Samuel L. Clemens' Library Books,'' *Resources for American Literary Study* 5 (Autumn 1975): 147–165; and '' 'Good Books & a Sleepy Conscience': Mark Twain's Reading Habits,'' *American Literary Realism* 9 (Autumn 1976): 294–306.

13. Merton M. Sealts, Jr., *Melville's Reading: A Checklist of Books Owned and Borrowed* (Madison: University of Wisconsin Press, 1966), pp. 9–20.

14. Sealts provides these updated figures in a recent reprinting of part 1 of *Melville's Reading* included in *Pursuing Melville 1940–1980: Chapters and Essays by Merton M. Sealts* (Madison: University of Wisconsin Press, 1982), pp. 31–57. The revised figures appear on page 33.

15. James D. Brasch and Joseph Sigman, *Hemingway's Library: A Composite Record* (New York: Garland Publishing, 1981). They previewed this book by interpreting Hemingway's collection of poetry in ''Hemingway's Library: Some Volumes of Poetry,'' *College Literature* 7 (Fall 1980): 282–290.

16. Michael S. Reynolds, *Hemingway's Reading 1910–1940: An Inventory* (Princeton: Princeton University Press, 1981).

17. Leon Edel and Adeline R. Tintner, ''The Library of Henry James, from Inventory, Catalogues, and Library Lists,'' *Henry James Review* 4 (Spring 1983): 158–190.

18. J. M. Edelstein, ''The Poet as Reader: Wallace Stevens and His Books,'' *Book Collector* 23 (Spring 1974): 53–68.

19. Kenneth A. Lohf, ''The Library of Hart Crane,'' *Proof: The Yearbook of American Bibliographical and Textual Studies* 3 (1973): 283–333.

20. Kenneth Walter Cameron, *Longfellow's Reading in Libraries: The Charging Records of a Learned Poet Interpreted* (Hartford, Conn.: Transcendental Books, 1973). Also *Transcendental Reading Patterns: Library Charging Lists for the Alcotts, James Freeman Clarke, Frederic Henry Hedge, Theodore Parker, George Ripley, Samuel Ripley of Waltham, Jones Very, and Charles Stearns Wheeler* (Hartford, Conn.: Transcendental Books, 1970).

21. M. E. Baym, ''The 1858 Catalogue of Henry Adams' Library,'' *Colophon* 3 (1938): 483–489.

22. Lars Ahnebrink, ''Books of Hamlin Garland in the University of Southern California Library,'' in Appendix A of *The Beginnings of Naturalism in American Fiction*, in Essays and Studies on American Language and Literature, ed. S. B. Liljegren, No. 9 (New York: Russell and Russell, 1961), pp. 415–437; Lars Ahnebrink, ''Books of Frank Norris in the Possession of His Widow, Mrs. Jeanette (Charles N.) Black,'' in Appendix F of *Beginnings of Naturalism*, pp. 460–462; Hilbert H. Campbell and Charles E. Modlin, ''A Catalog of Sherwood Anderson's Library,'' in *Sherwood Anderson: Centennial Studies* (Troy, N.Y.: Whitston Publishing Co., 1976), pp. 83–144; Joseph Blotner, *William Faulkner's Library—A Catalogue* (Charlottesville: University Press of Virginia, 1961).

23. Robert J. DeMott, *Steinbeck's Reading: A Catalogue of Books Owned and Borrowed* (New York: Garland Publishing, 1984).

24. Arthur F. Kinney, *Flannery O'Connor's Library: Resources of Being* (Athens: University of Georgia Press, 1985).

25. See "Anne Sexton Archives Acquired by Humanities Research Center," *A B Bookman's Weekly* 68 (3 August 1981): 627.

26. Michael J. King, "An A B C of E. P.'s Library," *Library Chronicle*, new series 17 (1981): 30–45. A librarian in the Humanities Research Center, Willard Goodwin II, has in progress an elaborate descriptive catalog of the Pound library.

27. "Vassar Acquires Papers of Elizabeth Bishop," *Wilson Library Bulletin* 56 (Fall 1982): 410.

28. "The Library of Edith Wharton," sale catalogue of Maggs Brothers, London (1983); copy consulted in the Harry Ransom Research Center, University of Texas at Austin.

29. Anthony Rota, "F. Scott Fitzgerald Appraises His Library," in *Pages: The World of Books, Writers, and Writing, 1* (Detroit: Gale Research, 1976), pp. 83–89.

30. David J. Nordloh, "W. D. Howells at Kittery Point," *Harvard Library Bulletin* 28 (October 1980): 431–437.

31. I should note that my *Mark Twain's Library* has been unusually fortunate in most of these respects, encountering exceptional broadmindedness among book review editors, department committees and officers, and university administrators.

32. Jack Capps, *Emily Dickinson's Reading, 1836–1886* (Cambridge: Harvard University Press, 1966).

Americans in France: Cross-Cultural Exchange and the Diffusion of Innovations

Mary Niles Maack

The impact of American librarianship on the dramatic changes in the philosophy and practice of public librarianship in France from 1900 to 1950 is analyzed in terms of specific stages identified in the theory of the diffusion of innovations. The five main steps in this process are conceptualized as: (1) knowledge, (2) persuasion, (3) decision, (4) implementation, and (5) confirmation. Due to limitations of space, this paper concentrates on the diffusion of the most far-reaching innovation—open access public libraries—as it was communicated through specific channels (professional literature, the general press, library association forums) over a fifty-year time span to the members of one specific social system—the professional library community.

The earliest study identified as a predecessor of modern diffusion research was a work published in 1903 by Gabriel Tarde, a French judge who was one of the forefathers of sociology and social psychology. In this pioneering work, Tarde discussed the spread of new ideas and processes, formulating certain generalizations that he described as the "laws of imitation."[1] During the 1920s a few sociologists and anthropologists also began to study diffusion, but it was not until the 1940s that a significant number of empirical studies were produced in disciplines such as rural sociology and education. In 1962, when Everett Rogers published the first comprehensive survey of this emerging field, 405 publications could be identified. The second edition of Rogers's work, which appeared nine years later, listed 1,500 studies, and of these 1,200 were empirical research reports. By the time Rogers completed the third edition of his cross-cultural survey of the field in 1983, the number of diffusion publications had doubled reaching a total of 3,085 titles.[2]

In his most recent analysis of trends in diffusion research in various disciplines, Rogers observed that the largest number of studies fall in the field of rural sociology (791 publications), followed by communications

Mary Niles Maack *is associate professor of librarianship, University of Minnesota.*

(372), education (336), marketing (304), and general sociology (282). A significant number of contributions have also been made by medical sociologists, anthropologists, geographers, economists, political scientists, psychologists, and scholars in various applied fields like public health, industrial engineering, statistics, and agricultural economics. No historical studies have been identified by Rogers, although certain theoretical articles do discuss the spread of innovations in the past, such as controlling scurvy in the British navy.[3] At this point, when a significant body of empirical data from many fields has led to the formulation of a series of generalizations and hypotheses, it seems particularly relevant that these theories be tested against experience in the past to discover whether they are valid over a more extended period of time. Because the introduction and spread of new practices in librarianship, such as the use of relative classification systems and open stacks, is fairly well documented, library history can both contribute to and benefit from the body of knowledge designated as "diffusion research."

It is the goal of this paper briefly to describe the role of American influence in the diffusion of certain innovations that transformed French public library service between 1900 and 1950. The changes in question were complex, representing all three elements identified in the standard definition that describes an innovation as "an *idea*, *practice* or *object* that is perceived as new by an individual or other unit of adoption."[4] The *ideas* centered on a new philosophy of free, publicly supported libraries administered by trained librarians, who carefully selected a broad range of books and made them accessible to the entire community—including children. The goal was to offer the public materials for their education, amusement, and information. At the turn of this century such ideas were not widely accepted in France, where the best municipal libraries, with rich collections of rare books, catered to scholars. Some circulating libraries known as *bibliothèques populaires* existed. However, these meager collections, made up mostly of novels, were frequently relegated to "the darkest dingiest room of the city hall or the village school, entrusted . . . to a local caretaker who knows neither their contents or use."[5] The new *practices* influenced by American librarianship included special training for librarians, creation of author/title card catalogues, and the use of the Dewey Decimal Classification, as well as the introduction of reference service, children's work, and programs for adults and children. Although little American library equipment was exported to France, the *physical organization* of the library (open stacks, comfortable furnishings, an inviting children's section), as well as the provision of a separate library building, was very much influenced by what was observed in the United States and by what was used in the American model libraries set up in France. The introduction of bookmobiles also illustrates the influence of

American librarianship on the development of new library equipment in France.

The American Role in the Innovation Diffusion Process

The impact of America on the dramatic changes in the philosophy and practice of public librarianship in France and on the professionalization of the field can best be analyzed in terms of specific stages identified in the theory of the diffusion of innovations. The five main steps in this process are conceptualized as: (1) knowledge, (2) persuasion, (3) decision, (4) implementation, and (5) confirmation.[6] From 1900 to 1950 this process can be observed as it operated upon three separate but interrelated innovations—open access public libraries, children's work, and bookmobiles.

Due to limitations of space, this paper concentrates on the diffusion of the most far-reaching innovation—open access public libraries—as it was communicated through specific channels (professional literature, the general press, library association forums) over a fifty-year time span to the members of one specific social system—the professional library community. The first stage of this process, knowledge of the innovation, undoubtedly began during the last quarter of the nineteenth century. However, since the first French journal of librarianship, the *Revue des Bibliothèques*, did not begin publication until 1891, there was no single or significant channel for professional communication prior to the last decade of the century. French librarians met with their British colleagues in Paris in 1892 when the Library Association held its first meeting on the continent. At this conference there was much discussion of public library service in Britain, but in France there was no regular forum to continue debate on these ideas until the Association des Bibliothécaires Français (ABF) was founded in 1906. Meanwhile, new interest had been generated in public librarianship through the American model library exhibit at the Paris exposition of 1900.

Knowledge of the Innovation

In 1900 when the American Library Association designated the New York State Library to prepare an exhibit for the Universal Exposition of Paris, American librarians quickly seized the opportunity to display their growing literature, new techniques, and modern appliances. However, for Melvil Dewey, who directed fifty of his staff in the preparation of the ALA exhibit, the real goal was not to display material achievements but to "represent at Paris this spirit of hearty cooperation among American librarians."[7] Because the organizers wished to emphasize the professionalization of library work, they stressed "the importance of having an experienced and enthusiastic librarian to infuse life into the whole and represent what is best in the profession . . ."[8] One of Dewey's most distinguished protégées, Mary Wright Plummer (then head of both the Pratt Institute Free Library and the Library School), agreed to serve at the exhibit.

The optimism of Dewey, Plummer, and other ALA organizers was rewarded by the presentation of a Grand Prize—one of nine given to the United States. Even before receiving the highest honor awarded by the international jury of the Exposition, the ALA exhibit had attracted the attention of distinguished continental librarians and bibliographers. Among these were Paul Otlet and Henri LaFontaine, co-founders of the Office of International Bibliography (OIB) in Brussels. Both visited the exhibit frequently, and LaFontaine even suggested that a permanent display on American public library work at the OIB would be "a revelation" to Europeans and could serve as "an entering wedge marking the beginning of a new era in European libraries."[9] Although LaFontaine's "library museum" was never created, European interest in American library development had been awakened. Even in France, where there was a great reluctance to accept new techniques used overseas, American librarianship began to be discussed.

In addition to her work at the ALA exhibit, Mary Wright Plummer was also designated by the Association to represent the United States at the Congrès International des Bibliothèques, held at the Sorbonne in 1900 in conjunction with the Paris Exposition. Plummer's previous trips to Europe had made her aware of long-standing prejudices, so she carefully tailored her paper on school and public library cooperation to underline the democratic values that made American librarians "as much concerned with the pedagogical and social aspect of [library] work as with its technique."[10] Mary Wright Plummer received a sympathetic hearing in France, and during the next two years she was invited to contribute a news column on American libraries to France's only journal of librarianship, the scholarly *Revue des Bibliothèques*. Plummer gave enthusiastic accounts of two ALA conferences and discussed a wide range of topics, such as the new program for issuing printed cards at the Library of Congress, children's work, library publications, training programs, and the development of state library agencies.

Although there was little immediate concern for most of these issues in France in 1902, attitudes were slowly changing. By 1913, when the ABF leader, Charles Sustrac, made a trip to the United States, his goal was "to see if the marvels that are recounted about libraries in America are accurate."[11] An ardent advocate of public library reform, Sustrac's curiosity had been piqued by a number of books, articles, and lectures on American libraries written by French educators and librarians.

Among contemporary French publications on libraries were three comparative surveys, each of which gave a prominent place to American public libraries. The first such work to appear was a slim volume by Maurice Pellison on popular libraries in France and abroad. Pellison, a distinguished French educator, was especially concerned with the role that libraries could play in adult education. Of the sixteen countries he surveyed, Pellison felt that the Americans had made the most rapid and "surprising" progress, in both the number and importance of their public libraries. In fact, in the first paragraph of his study, he unequivocally stated that the administration and organization of American public libraries gave them "a democratic character which is shown nowhere else to the same degree."[12]

Two years after Pellison's favorable account appeared, Eugène Morel from the Bibliothèque Nationale issued his famous and highly polemical work entitled *Bibliothèques*.[13] This two-volume comparative "essay" dealt with all aspects of library development in France, Great Britain, and the United States. Despite the caustic style of the work, it was unquestionably well documented with numerous tables, statistics, budgets, and extracts from annual reports.

The biting tone of Morel's 1908 work ensured that its content could not be ignored. The most virulent critique was offered by Emile Chatelain, librarian of the Sorbonne, who implied that Morel's "brilliant imagination" as a novelist led him "to prefer chimeras to reality" and to champion reforms that were "pure utopias."[14] In another review, Victor Chapot, librarian at the Sainte-Geneviève, described Morel's work as "passionate highly colored . . . brutal and shocking . . . [with] both the solicitude of an accurate survey and the bad taste of a journalist bemired in exaggeration and paradox."[15] Chapot also observed that class distinctions were more rigid in France than in the United States or Great Britain. He remarked: "In public libraries people of every condition rub shoulders without embarrassment. I can scarcely see such a regime implanted in France for a long time to come."[16]

Other library leaders were much more sympathetic to Morel's views, and he soon attracted a group of colleagues, educators, and writers who were eager to promote the kind of public library service he advocated. At the urging of these supporters and enthusiasts, Morel soon began to condense and re-edit his work, eliminating his discussion of academic and research libraries. The result of these efforts was *La librairie publique*, later described as the first book in France to be devoted entirely to public libraries. In his choice of title for this pioneering work, Morel intentionally avoided the word *bibliothèque* with its scholarly connotations and attempted to repatriate the word *librairie*, which had been adopted by the English.[17]

In a favorable review of this work, Charles Sustrac observed that Morel continued his crusade for "the modern library," and although he had "eased the polemic, corrected and updated the statistics and softened the expression of his indignation . . . the principal of the work . . . [remained] an apostolate for the public library such as it exists in the United States . . ."[18] In his chapter on the United States, Morel's leitmotif was the theme that the public library movement stemmed "from the fundamental character of a new people, that which perhaps most clearly differentiates them from the Old World; the era of libraries [has succeeded] the era of cathedrals." Although Morel also discussed many British libraries, which he knew firsthand, he did not hesitate to affirm that " 'la librairie publique' was an American invention!" Caught up by the missionary fervor of his American colleagues, Morel painted an idealistic portrait of American libraries—"free, absolutely free, open all day; every day and evening . . . not waiting for the public to come, going out to [the public] . . . they are for the grown man what the school is for the child."[19]

In order to extend the public library movement to France, Morel felt that propaganda was essential. He therefore organized a series of conferences aimed at the general public as well as librarians, booksellers, scholars, and bibliophiles. This lecture series, held at the Ecole des Hautes Etudes Sociales each year from 1910 to 1914, was co-sponsored by the French library association and by the publishers' society. Much to Morel's satisfaction, the conferences also attracted the interest of certain municipalities, and in 1911 he received an invitation to recatalogue the municipal library of Levallois-Perret. This working-class industrial community on the northern outskirts of Paris offered Morel the first opportunity to introduce France to the Dewey Decimal Classification, which had been "rejected without being known."[20] Morel's classified catalogue was published in 1913; six months after it appeared, both consultation of books and circulation figures had doubled, while the loan of nonfiction works rose from 3 percent to 40 percent of all books borrowed.[21] This change, which was all the more impressive considering that the public *did not have open access to the shelves*, further convinced Morel that American library methods could be adapted successfully in France.

Buoyed up by this practical experience and eager to continue the successful lecture series at the Ecole des Hautes Etudes Sociales, Morel and his supporters were in the midst of an active campaign for public libraries when war was declared against Germany in 1914. Wartime conditions and the rapid mobilization of scores of librarians brought discussions of library reform to an abrupt halt. Nonetheless, the seed had been sown that was to lie dormant during four years of agonizing fighting.

Persuasion and Decision

From 1900 to 1914 the knowledge of public library development abroad was spread through discussion at ABF meetings, and by library periodicals and books as well as occasional articles in the general press. This period also marked the second stage in the innovation-decision process, when *persuasion* occurred as individuals formed "a favorable or unfavorable attitude toward the innovation."[22] While some influential librarians openly rejected such libraries as being inappropriate to France, others were sympathetic to library reform but felt that long-standing problems, such as "the lack of money and indifference of the public," would make it impossible to modernize French municipal libraries.[23] Still others, like Ernest Coyecque, inspector general of the municipal libraries of Paris, had begun a long, difficult struggle against the bureaucracy to obtain proper funding for libraries.

Morel's election as ABF president in 1918 may have marked a softening of old antagonisms within the field, as well as demonstrating the profession's renewed concern for the development of public libraries. Certainly a small but vocal group of his colleagues had been persuaded that France should have free, open-access public libraries. Their goals were also quite consistent with those of other social reformers, such as the Catholic movement (known as Equipes Sociales), that sought to democratize access to educational and cultural resources by organizing free classes and discussion groups for workers.

Despite the growing interest in new kinds of public libraries among leaders within the profession and the broader community, and despite the success of a limited application of American library organization in Levallois-Perret, the prospects for further implementation of these principles seemed unlikely in 1919, when one noted educator, Professor Marie Hollebecque, commented:

> Like our American friends we believe in the educational value of books. . . . [However] with us any new enterprise should be preceded by a movement of public opinion. . . . To succeed then, it becomes necessary to establish a library modeled after the American public library . . . but France in her present impoverished condition could not . . . find adequate financial support . . . to maintain an institution of this importance.[24]

Implementation and Confirmation

The first American model library that was financed by a philanthropic group, the Comité Américaine pour des Régions Devastées (CARD), was undoubtedly much more modest than that envisioned by Professor Hollebecque. Nonetheless, André Tardieu, a French statesman who served as honorary president of CARD, remarked that this small library run along American lines "gave the devastated regions the first public library France had ever had. Open all the time, well furnished, well heated, well lighted, with card indexes, dictionaries, works of reference and agricultural works, it was always full."[25] While this unpretentious library, housed in wooden barracks, bore little resemblance to the photographs of solid Carnegie buildings displayed at the Paris Exposition of 1900, it did reflect the spirit of American librarianship so frequently praised by Morel and other public library pioneers.

Soon three other small libraries were created by CARD in response to local demand for literature in the most devastated region of France where "the few books that had been saved from destruction . . . had been passed from peasant to peasant."[26] As a war relief agency, CARD naturally gave first priority to food, clothing, medicines, and agricultural supplies; nonetheless, the need to create social services and libraries was recognized early by the chairperson of CARD's executive committee, the heiress Ann Morgan. Thus, in June 1920, library work became an integral element in CARD's five-part program that also included public health, social service, construction, and agricultural syndicates.

The director of the new Library Department was CARD's assistant treasurer, Jessie Carson, a woman who had begun war relief work in 1917 as a member of the National League for Women's Services. Carson was also an experienced professional librarian. A 1902 graduate of the Carnegie Library School in Pittsburgh, she had worked as a children's librarian in Pittsburgh and in Tacoma, Washington, before becoming assistant to Anne Carroll Moore in the children's department at New York Public Library (NYPL) in 1914. To aid her in her work in France, Carson recruited several colleagues from NYPL whom she chose because they spoke French fluently and "because they were here during the war and know the conditions very thoroughly in the devastated regions where they are to work."[27]

The devastation Carson spoke of had deeply scarred 20,000 square miles in Aisne, a department in northeastern France that had been twice occupied by the Germans during the war. André Tardieu, who served as one of Clemenceau's aides, vividly described the territory that France repossessed in 1918:

> . . . it was pitted with shell holes and seared with trenches; . . . entangled with millions of miles of barbed wire; covered with fifty million cubic miles of debris. . . . There were no roads . . .; there were no railroads . . .; there were no factories . . .; villages had been destroyed by the war; in one third of them the destruction was total . . .[28]

While the enormity of reconstruction in such a setting challenged CARD volunteers, the stoicism and courage of French peasants returning to their shattered villages touched them deeply. Carson later recalled: "It is hard to express what it meant to find ourselves in the center of destruction on all sides. . . . What wonderful response we had. What graciously expressed appreciation. Our heads might well have been turned if it had not been for the desperate sadness which hemmed us in on all sides, and which gave us poise."[29] It was in Aisne among makeshift dwellings that new social agencies came to life, born out of CARD's response to local needs.

In a tribute to Jessie Carson, Ernest Coyecque, inspector of Parisian municipal libraries, avowed that if the population of Aisne had demanded books of the French authorities, such a request would have provoked "a smile of pity, a conceited skepticism and the habitual exclamation 'Ah, vraiment, we have better things to do!' " Or, at best, donations of old books would have been solicited and then relegated to quarters unusable for any other purpose. Coyecque continued: "This shadow of a library would have been placed in the charge of a shadow of a librarian —bad humored and infirm. . . . [However,] with the Americans it was the opposite. The creation of libraries was decided upon immediately; . . . the section . . . for libraries was confided to a real librarian knowing her trade . . . to the librarian who appeared the best suited to the unique and formidable task to be completed."[30]

During her first nine months as director of the new Library Department, Carson supervised the selection and cataloguing of 6,000 books and oversaw the creation of small libraries in four of the war-damaged villages. The first users of these new libraries were surprised to find small tables and chairs for children as well as comfortable reading facilities for adults. Carson recalled the opening days when adults hastily selected their books and left. By 1921 she described the library as full of children whose talk and laughter did not "annoy in the least the blacksmith, the veterinary, or the lord of the Chateau . . . carefully reading the political news on the other side of the room."[31] A decade earlier, a scene such as this had been described as impossible in France by conservative librarians like Victor Chapot. While the war did not end class distinctions, attitudes had changed, and the ideal of extending culture to the masses was already being expressed by Catholic intellectuals and other social reformers.

Carson herself attributed the success of the CARD libraries not to American techniques or innovations, but to the enthusiastic cooperation of the community. In 1921 she confidently described these libraries as an expression of the French people themselves:

> They asked for them; they insisted upon having them. They were even willing, as expressed by the school teacher at Cessières, to do with less of the actual physical necessities to have "food for their minds."
>
> With so many homes, schools and churches to be repaired and refurnished—with the lack of workmen and the slowness of transportation—the only way the libraries have developed is because everybody has been keen to help.[32]

Carson went on to describe the creation of CARD's fifth and largest library at Soissons, which involved the cooperation of many individuals, from the mayor, who gave ground on the central square; to the Chief of Construction of the Liberated Regions, who put up the barrack in record time; and the Lord of the Chateau at Vic, a literary man who helped with book selection. Carson was also in contact with certain French library leaders in Paris and she saw to it that Eugène Morel and Ernest Coyecque were invited to participate in the opening ceremonies, held on Easter day in 1921.

Coyecque later recalled that both he and Morel "were filled with admiration" (*émerveilles*) for the work in Aisne.[33] In a short speech Morel described his efforts to promote public libraries and declared: "In the future when I am asked what I mean by a modern, popular library such as I have preached and written about for decades, I shall advise a visit to this library at Soissons."[34] However, after the inauguration ceremonies ended, both Morel and Coyecque responded spontaneously: "If only Soissons were Paris!"[35]

The dynamic Jessie Carson was not one to let such an opportunity slip by, and within a few days she informed her French colleagues that CARD was willing to offer the capital a similar library. CARD also agreed to train personnel for the Paris library and to finance its operation for one year. As inspector of the Paris municipal library system, Coyecque was able to secure French support and acquire an empty lot on the rue Fessart in Bellevue, one of the poorer sections of Paris. From then on, the process was long and drawn out. During the eighteen months of negotiations and effort, "nothing was finished on time—every step was won with a struggle . . .''[36] For Jessie Carson, who had taken only ten months to establish five center libraries and forty-five traveling libraries in Aisne, the experience in Paris showed that "it is always much easier to introduce a completely new idea than to change or adapt an old one."[37] Despite frustrations and setbacks, Carson was not easily discouraged. Her boundless enthusiasm for libraries proved equal to facing both the ruins of Aisne and the complex, unwieldy bureaucracy of Paris. The creation of the rue Fessart library marked the culmination of Carson's efforts in the field. From 1919 to 1924 she and her American colleagues had participated at a crucial stage in the innovation-decision process, acting as *change agents* who implemented new ideas and practices already publicized and advocated by pioneers such as Morel.

One of the key factors leading to the adoption or rejection of an innovation is its *triability*. Prior to World War I, the inertia of long-entrenched bureaucratic procedures and vested interests made it difficult to obtain the funding and support needed to create a genuine model library. In Aisne this cycle had been broken, making it possible for new agencies to be created in the barren waste left by the war. While the destruction of normal forms of communal activity, entertainment, and cultural life led the population to ask for books, *it can not be inferred that they asked for public libraries*. In fact, most adults were so unaware of this kind of library that they initially checked out their books and left quickly, without using the reading room or other facilities. However, once they understood the service available to them, they readily accepted the public library as *an innovation that filled a need not previously perceived*.

The initial success of these small model libraries defied even their most severe critics. It soon became difficult to contend that free public libraries, organized along American lines, were inappropriate to France and would be rejected by the public. According to Tardieu's account, the CARD libraries *confirmed* the hopes of the most outspoken library reformers:

> The success was so unprecedented that from all sides specialists came to follow the experiment. . . . The new Soissons library with its 6,000 new books . . . with its 4,000 readers out of less than 15,000 inhabitants, aroused emulation. . . . Paris itself turned to the American committee. . . . Within a year the Bellevue library rejuvenated, well lighted and heated, had a circulation of 700 volumes a day as against a former maximum of 90.[38]

The Paris Library School and the Diffusion of Public Libraries

Not content to assume that the popular response to these libraries would guarantee their continuation, CARD leaders immediately sought support for their work among those whose opinions could influence the broader public as well as governmental authorities. One of these individuals was André Chevrillon (a distinguished author and member of the Académie Française), whom Jessie Carson and Ernest Coyecque personally recruited to the library cause. Chevrillon had expressed a passing admiration for American public libraries during a visit to the United States, but he did not at first see what connection he could possibly have with public libraries in France. However, after a two-hour interview with Coyecque and Carson, he diligently read through an armful of reports and books that helped convince him to chair the Comité Française de la Bibliothèque Moderne. This committee, founded in June 1922, also included another member of the Académie Française, five members of the Chamber of Deputies, and one member of the Paris City Council in addition to a number of modernist library leaders such as Morel.[39] Initially created to ensure the continuation of CARD's library work in Aisne and Paris, this distinguished French Committee also played a role in the general reform of the Parisian library system, and later became involved with CARD's efforts to provide American-style training for young French librarians.

Although Carson had obtained support from the French Committee and from the Carnegie Endowment for International Peace to provide scholarships for six French women to study in American library schools, she was convinced that the innovations introduced by CARD would not be spread unless modern library training was available *in France*. Others agree, and once again cooperation was solicited on both sides of the Atlantic. CARD provided $2,500 for a two-month demonstration library course to be held in Paris; ALA offered the services of its assistant secretary, Sarah Bogle, who designed the curriculum; and representatives from the Bibliothèque Nationale, the Parisian municipal libraries, and the French national office for university exchange presented lectures. In the end, the success of this training program, known as the Paris Library School, proved to be CARD's most lasting legacy, and one that was perceived as having a significant impact on the transformation of public librarianship.

During the school's brief six-year history (1923 to 1929), over 100 French students received certificates or diplomas. Although many of these graduates left the field, a small core of alumni became very instrumental in promoting a new image of librarianship in France.

Founded in 1923 at the end of the first summer session, the alumni association grew rapidly as a result of the close ties that were forged between students and faculty. Gabriel Henriot, a former president of the ABF who served as *professeur-directeur de cours* in 1925, commented on the "close collaboration between the American instructors and their French colleagues [which has] enlarged the horizon of each. . . . Professors and students at the end of the year constitute a *veritable family* whose members are animated by the same zeal for a cause equally dear to all."[40] By 1926 the association counted 106 active and 28 honorary members of several different nationalities. That year Mary Parsons, resident director of the school, noted that alumni "have employed younger graduates, have notified the School about positions to be filled, have recruited some of the best students in recent classes and have returned often . . . as visiting lecturers." She also noted that many came "to talk informally with the faculty about their work."[41]

Even after the school closed its doors, a few graduates continued to correspond with former faculty such as Sarah Bogle and Margaret Mann, who were kept informed of new library developments in France and of efforts to revive the school. Throughout 1929 the association continued to receive small gifts from alumni, and in 1930 a final attempt was made to interest European library leaders in the prospect of an international school. Yvonne Oddon, who was elected president that year, also continued to explore possible ties with a French institution, such as the Sorbonne.

Although Oddon and her colleagues were eventually forced to abandon this idea, they remained optimistic about the potential role of the school. In her final letter to Bogle, written in December 1931, Oddon declared: "In spite of the fact that I know our French conditions rather well, I am still surprised to find that the school's influence is somehow felt more strongly now. It reminds me of the light we get from the long extinct stars."[42] Yvonne Oddon and a small group of other alumnae managed to keep this faint light alive, convinced that "each one has to work and keep fighting in order to maintain and develop our influence."[43]

Oddon was quite aware of opposition to the school by certain conservative librarians who ridiculed it as the "Ecole des Chartes of the Far West," where some of their distinguished colleagues were "constrained . . . to cook up digestible training in popular librarianship . . ."[44] Nonetheless, she sought to win over "the elder librarians" and to influence Julien Cain, the new *administrateur-général* of the Bibliothèque Nationale, who was involved in drafting library legislation for France. Despite the fact that she spent most of her career organizing a scholarly ethnographic library at the Musée de l'Homme, Oddon remained in close touch with colleagues involved in the public library movement. Her influence on Julien Cain and her role in preparing the French library exhibit for the International Exposition of 1937 marked the first stages of her rise to national prominence.

Meanwhile, Oddon and a number of other activist colleagues became involved in the creation of the Association pour le Développement de la Lecture Publique (ADLP), a group made up of Paris Library School alumni, other progressive librarians, and a few officials, intellectuals, publishers, educators, and writers. Although many of the librarians who belonged to ADLP remained ABF members, they felt that a more militant group was needed to publicize and promote library service. When ABF failed to submit innovative library projects to the new undersecretary of leisure created by the Popular Front government, these librarians rallied to form a more dynamic association.[45]

Founded in July 1936, ADLP generated a great deal of publicity for libraries, held public conferences, sponsored book festivities, cooperated with union organizers, and maintained close contact with publishers, writers, and government officials. By 1938 the new association had also secured funding from the Ministry of National Education and from the Sous-Secrétariat des Loisirs for a bookmobile project in the Marne.[46] At the same time ADLP was working with several private groups to create a more modest book box service in the western suburbs of Paris (Poissy and Argenteuil). Coordination of these efforts fell to the general secretary, Georgette de Grolier, a Paris Library School alumna whose effectiveness was warmly acknowledged at ADLP's first public conference in 1937.

Mme. de Grolier, librarian at Boulogne-Billencourt, was best known at this time for her innovative periodical, the *Revue du Livre*. Begun in 1933, the *Revue* was the first French periodical to concentrate entirely on modern developments in bibliography, library service, and documentation. The *Revue* was at first an independent publication under the editorship of Mme. de Grolier and her husband. The following year it became the official organ of the Paris Library School alumni association and of the Bureau Bibliographique de France—the French affiliate of the Institut International de Bibliographie in Brussels. Due to lack of adequate funding and permanent staff, the journal appeared irregularly until December 1937, when it received a government subsidy and became the official organ of ADLP. In addition to regular editorials and reviews of professional books, Mme. de Grolier authored numerous articles on a wide range of topics—from subject cataloguing and reader services to library facilities in a Methodist social center. Georgette de Grolier firmly believed that "libraries . . . should become an active element in the intellectual and social life of the country," and in a 1936 editorial she stated that the goal of the *Revue* was to encourage efforts "*to adapt technical progress achieved abroad to French libraries.*"[47]

Innovators and Opinion Leaders

During the 1930s Georgette de Grolier, Yvonne Oddon, and a dozen other American-trained librarians served as innovators—adapting new practices in their own libraries and influencing other progressive librarians to experiment with these techniques. However, since most of the Paris Library School alumni were not employed in the major municipal libraries (known as *bibliothèques classées*), their status was somewhat marginal in the French library hierarchy. Quite sensitive to this, and to the fact that certain ''elder librarians'' strongly disapproved of foreign practices such as open stacks, these modernists were at times quite careful not to overemphasize the influence of the American model.

Yvonne Oddon, who had also worked for a year in the United States, was even reluctant to be identified as co-author of a manual on librarianship (*Le petit guide du bibliothécare*), which she wrote in collaboration with Charles Henri Bach, who had only studied at the American library school during one summer session. Much later Oddon recalled:

> I did not sign the 1930 edition with Mr. Bach in order not to compromise the success of the book. it would have been considered by a certain category of (prominent) French librarians as mere propaganda for new revolutionary methods they did not approve of (among which this unbelievably wild Dewey classification . . .) I had just come back from U.S.A. and was adopting the not less criticized L.C. classification for the Musée de l'Homme.
>
> Time and experience, and the passing out of old librarians gradually modified professional opinion about American techniques so that in 1941 the French library association itself was favorable to a second edition. In 1948 I was able to sign my contribution to a 3rd edition with my title of assistant secretary to the French library association and with the approval of the Government Bureau of libraries.[48]

The gradual acceptance of the innovations presented in the manual by Bach and Oddon was, to a large degree, the result of the enthusiastic, persistent, but discreet efforts of American trained librarians who understood how to effectively exercise *opinion leadership* as it has been defined by innovation-diffusion scholars:

> Opinion leadership is the degree to which an individual is able to influence other individuals' attitudes or overt behavior informally in a desired way with relative frequency. It is a type of *informal leadership rather than a function of the individual's formal position or status in the system*. Opinion leadership is earned and maintained by the individual's technical competence, social accessibility, and conformity to the systems norms. . . .

> In general when opinion leaders are compared with their followers, we find that they (1) are more exposed to all forms of external communication, (2) are more cosmopolite, (3) have somewhat higher social status and (4) are more innovative (although the exact degree of innovativeness depends, in part, on the system's norms).[49]

The articles written by the Paris Library School alumnae clearly show that they were very aware of developments on the continent as well as in the United States, that they were quite cosmopolitan and were generally much more innovative than most of their colleagues. However, their social status within the professional library community would not have been considered high during a period when librarians with the greatest prestige and authority directed large research libraries where scholarship rather than public service was emphasized. Quite aware that the public library movement needed support of individuals with established rank, the younger American-trained professionals sought support from prominent librarians such as Julien Cain, *administrateur-général* of the Bibliothèque Nationale, Charles Schmidt, inspector-general of libraries, and Henri Lemaître, editor of the *Revue des Bibliothèques*. They also recruited a few progressive young librarians who directed important municipal libraries, such as Henri Vendel at Chalons-sur-Marne and Georges Collon at Tours. These individuals, along with the earlier public library pioneers (including Morel, Coyecque, Henriot, and Sustrac), helped overcome the apathy or opposition of more conservative colleagues.

The other factor that promoted the diffusion of American influence was the continuing success of the original model libraries in Soissons and Paris—including a model children's library, L'Heure Joyeuse, which had been set up in 1924 with the aid of another American philanthropic group, the Book Committee on Children's Libraries. The French library historian Noë Richter has observed that this latter library served as an important vehicle for the diffusion of American public library philosophy and practice:

> It is difficult to measure the influence of the institutions created by the Americans on French libraries. . . . However, there is no doubt that it is L'Heure Joyeuse that had the most profound effect in professional circles where it contributed, discreetly and efficaciously, to the diffusion of modern ideas. *New, unique, and because of this fact, marginal, its activities were not of the kind to disturb the "traditionalists."* Its librarians, Marguerite Gruny and Mathilde Leriche, thus escaped the reprobation addressed to those librarians who were looked down upon for concerning themselves with libraries for everyone . . .[50]

The impact of L'Heure Joyeuse was also due to the fact that the obvious success achieved at this model library for children could not be contradicted by even the most skeptical *conservateurs*, who had to admit that the innovations they had rejected for their scholarly collections could, indeed, be effectively applied in public libraries. The fact that children soon learned to use the card catalogue and the Dewey Decimal Classification (and even helped maintain order on the shelves) made it difficult to contend that "modern" principles of library organization could not be used by the general public. It was perhaps this that Eugène Morel meant in 1924, when he eloquently declared: "The children's library precedes and provides the blueprint for the library for everyone that France is eagerly awaiting, that France will surely have. Children, we will follow you."[51]

Conclusions

A preliminary review of the diffusion of those innovations in librarianship first implemented in model libraries set up by Americans in France in the 1920s demonstrates that the general model developed by innovation-diffusion researchers can be effectively used to identify significant stages in this historical process. Such an approach also facilitates the identification of several key factors that influenced the introduction and spread of a new model of public librarianship:

(1) Knowledge of the innovation had been spread through discussion and publication prior to the creation of the first model library.
(2) Although Americans were the first to fully *implement* these innovations, they were sensitive to French needs and emphasized the French role in *adapting* the innovation.
(3) CARD correctly perceived the need to train French professionals to continue the work of the model libraries.
(4) American-trained individuals served as *opinion leaders*, forming a nucleus of modernists who actively promoted public libraries as well as implemented new practices.
(5) The Paris Library School alumnae effectively gained the support of more prominent library leaders whose opinions were widely respected, and who occupied key positions in the French library *network*.
(6) Broader support was also sought among writers, educators, publishers, and statesmen who served on the French committee and in ADLP.

The most significant departure from the diffusion-innovation model described by Rogers concerns the issue of high status among opinion leaders; in a sense this problem was overcome through the development of effective networks as described above.

Notes

1. Gabriel Tarde, *The Laws of Imitation* (New York: Holt, 1903).

2. Everett M. Rogers, *Diffusion of Innovations*, 3rd ed. (New York: Free Press, 1983), pp. xv and 52–53.

3. Fredeick Mosteller, "Innovation and Evaluation," *Science* 211 (February 1981): 881-886.

4. Rogers, *Diffusion of Innovations*, p. 11.

5. André Tardieu, *France and America, Some Experiences in Cooperation* (Cambridge, Mass.: Riverside Press, 1927), p. 202.

6. Rogers, *Diffusion of Innovations*, p. 20.

7. Florence Woodworth, "A.L.A. Exhibit at the Paris Exposition of 1900," *Library Journal* 25 (March 1900): 116.

8. Ibid.

9. Quoted in J. L. Harrison, "A.L.A. Exhibit at the Paris Exposition," *Library Journal* 25 (July 1900): 331.

10. Mary Wright Plummer, "International Congress of Librarians, Paris, August 20–23, 1900," *Library Journal* 25 (September 1900): 582.

11. Charles Sustrac, "Impression d'Amérique," *Bulletin de l'ABF* 6 (November–December 1913): 89.

12. Maurice Pellison, *Les bibliothèques populaires à l'étranger et en France* (Paris: Imprimerie Nationale, 1906), p. 1.

13. Eugène Morel, *Bibliothèques: Essai sur le développement des bibliothèques publiques . . .* (Paris: Mercure de France, 1908–1909). This volume "essay" contained 865 pages.

14. Emile Chatelain, "Bibliographie" (book review of *Bibliothèques*), *Revue des bibliothèques* 19 (1909): 188.

15. Victor Chapot, "L'Organisation des bibliothèques," *Revue de Synthèse Historique* 19 (1909): 139.

16. Ibid., p. 139.

17. Eugène Morel, *La librairie publique* (Paris: Armand Colin, 1910), pp. 8–9. Because *librairie* was already used in French to mean bookstore, the phrase *librairie publique* was seldom used by library reformers other than Morel.

18. Charles Sustrac, "La librairie publique par E. Morel," *Bulletin de l'A.B.F.* 5 (1911): 32.

19. All the preceding citations are drawn from Morel, *La librairie publique*, pp. 99, 101, 73, and 104.

20. Eugène Morel, "Préface," in *Catalogue de la Bibliothèque de Levallois-Perret 1925* (Paris: L'Emancipatrice, 1925), p. 8.

21. Ibid., p. 9.

22. Rogers, *Diffusion of Innovations*, p. 169.

23. Charles Mortet, "A propos du livre de M. Morel sur les bibliothèques," *Bulletin de l'A.B.F.* 4 (1910): 15–16.

24. Professor Marie Hollebecque, quoted in "The Public Library Situation in France," *Public Libraries* 24 (June 1919): 204.

25. Tardieu, *France and America*, p. 207.

26. Jessie Carson, ''Library Report,'' in A. M. Dike, *Special Report of the Commissioner, American Committee for Devastated France, for Nine Months from April 1, 1920–January 1, 1921* (Paris: CARD, 1921), p. 34.

27. Annie Caroll Moore, ''Children's Libraries in France,'' *Library Journal* 45 (15 October 1920): 832.

28. Tardieu, *France and America*, p. 182.

29. Jessie Carson, ''The Library Work of the American Committee,'' paper presented at the New York Library Conference, 13 December 1922, pp. 1, 3.

30. Ernest Coyecque, ''L'Oeuvre française d'une bibliothécaire américaine Miss Carson,'' *Revue des Bibliothèques* 34 (1924): 260.

31. Carson, ''Library Report'' (1920–1921), p. 37.

32. Ibid., p. 38.

33. Coyecque, ''L'Oeuvre française,'' p. 261.

34. Quoted in ''Americans Donate Soissons Library,'' *New York Herald*, 27 March 1921.

35. Quoted by Marguerite Gruny, ''Un pionnier des bibliothèques, Ernest Coyecque: 15 août 1864–15 janvier 1954,'' *Bulletin de l'A.B.F.*, n.s. no. 13 (March 1954): 11.

36. Carson, ''The Library Work of the American Committee,'' p. 11.

37. Jessie Carson, ''Library Work,'' in American Committee for Devastated France, *Description of the Work in France, April 1, 1923* (Paris: CARD, 1923), p. 18.

38. Tardieu, *France and America*, p. 207.

39. ''Comité Français de la Bibliothèque Moderne,'' A Complete List of Members in Sarah Bogle's Correspondence File for 1923. Urbana, Ill., ALA Archives, Paris Library School File, Box 1 (henceforth abbreviated as AALA).

40. Letter, Gabriel Henriot to Carl H. Milam, 25 mai 1925, AALA, Paris Library School File, Box 3.

41. Mary P. Parsons, ''Report of the Library School, June 1, 1925, to May 31, 1926,'' AALA, Paris Library School File, Box 3.

42. Letter, Yvonne Oddon to Sarah Bogle, 17 December 1931, AALA, Paris Library School File, Box 4.

43. Letter, Yvonne Oddon to Sarah Bogle, 14 August 1930, AALA, Paris Library School File, Box 4.

44. Hurepoix, ''Un beau métier que l'on n'apprend plus,'' *Revue des Bibliothèques* 40 (1930): 123.

45. Interview with Marguerite Gruny, Paris, 26 September 1980

46. ''L'Association pour le Développement de la Lecture Publique de juillet 1937 a janvier 1938,'' *Revue du Livre et des Bibliothèques* n.s. (March 1938): 60–61

47. Georgette de Grolier, ''Editorial,'' *Revue du Livre et des Bibliothèques* 3 (January–March 1936): 1.

48. Yvonne Oddon to Mrs. Potter, Paris, 17 November 1949, Paris, Library of the Institut Catholique, Fonds Yvonne Oddon.

49. Rogers, *Diffusion of Innovations*, pp. 27–28.

50. Noë Richter, *Bibliothèques et éducation permanente, de la lecture populaire à la lecture publique* (Le Mans: Bibliothèque de l'Université du Maine, 1981), p. 82 (emphasis mine).

51. Quoted by Henri Lemaître, ''La bibliothèque enfantine de la rue Boutebrie,'' *Revue des Bibliothèques* 35 (1925): 37.

The New Censorship: Censorship by Translation in the Soviet Union

Marianna Tax Choldin

This paper discusses the results of a comparison of the 1978 Soviet translation of Studs Terkel's book *Working*, entitled *Rabota*, with the original. The Soviet practice of prohibiting importation of foreign originals and employing a combination of translating, editing, and rewriting techniques to produce "custom-made" versions of foreign works for domestic readers is contrasted with imperial Russian practices. Examining material included in and excluded from the translation, this study concludes that *Rabota* is not simply an abridged translation of *Working*; it is a censored version of the book, in the Russian and Soviet traditions.

When I was fourteen years old I was taken to task quite severely by a visiting Soviet anthropologist—a colleague of my father's—for reading a translated and abridged version of *War and Peace*. He grudgingly forgave me the translation, but took a hard line regarding the abridgment: "How can you know what some stupid editor might have cut out?" he demanded. "Tolstoy knew what he was doing when he wrote every word of that book. You should throw away that wretched abridged version immediately," he said, glowering at me, "learn Russian, and read the *entire original*!" Obviously the professor got to me at the right time; in my adolescent fervor I vowed that I would follow his advice, and I did!

During the past few months, while comparing the 1978 Soviet translation of Studs Terkel's book *Working*, entitled *Rabota*,[1] with the original, I have thought often about that Soviet anthropologist (now deceased) and the sad irony of his advice to me. For while I am free (although perhaps ill-advised!) to read *War and Peace* in any one of several abridged or complete English translations as well as in Russian, the ordinary Soviet citizen is likely to have access *only* to the drastically abridged official

Marianna Tax Choldin *is head, Slavic and East European Library, and research director, Russian and East European Center, University of Illinois at Urbana-Champaign.* *An earlier draft of this paper was presented orally at the sixteenth annual convention of the American Association for the Advancement of Slavic Studies, New York, 1–4 November 1984.*

translation *Rabota*, a small and pallid fragment of the rich, varied, and colorful original. But before discussing the Soviet treatment of *Working*, let me backtrack briefly to imperial Russia, where I believe the roots of this treatment lie.

In an earlier study I described the roots of Russia's nineteenth-century censorship operation,[2] particularly the ways in which the imperial government attempted to protect Russians from insidious Western influences, and examined the themes that caused official concern. These themes can be grouped into four main categories, each with numerous variations: disrespect toward Russian royalty, opposition to the existing social order, the portrayal of Russians as non-European barbarians, and ideas offensive to religion and morality. That study described the four general categories into which foreign publications were grouped in imperial Russia: (1) those permitted by the censorship authorities to circulate freely; (2) those banned absolutely; (3) those under a ban "for the public," accessible only to individuals who applied at the Foreign Censorship Committee offices and were approved by the authorities; and (4) those permitted for circulation only after the excision (by blacking or pasting over, or by cutting out) of specified words, lines, or pages.

Subsequent research on the treatment of foreign publications in the Soviet Union—in connection with my first study of Soviet translations of Western works,[3] discussed below—has led me to conclude that there appear to be four categories of foreign publications in the Soviet Union today analogous to those of tsarist Russia. (As I pointed out in that study, I say "appear to be" rather than "are," because even the existence of censorship is no longer officially acknowledged in any published Soviet source—in striking contrast to tsarist Russia—so the researcher must rely heavily on material of an inferential nature.)

As I have come to see the analogy, the Soviet category of foreign publications permitted to circulate freely includes writings with a socialist orientation as well as some science, technology, and art titles. The category of works banned absolutely is difficult to describe in any precise way, since we do not have access to official Soviet lists of banned titles, as we do for much of the tsarist period. It is safe to assume, however, that some kind of list almost certainly does exist; in any case, there is no doubt that many foreign publications are not permitted to circulate in the Soviet Union, and we would be justified in considering these works to be "banned absolutely."

The ban "for the public" of tsarist times has its equivalent in the Soviet system of restricted "special" collections and reading rooms in libraries and institutes to which only authorized individuals are admitted. (It is from such a source that my anthropologist might have been able to obtain a copy of the original *Working*.)

The Soviet counterpart of the fourth category in the imperial system, including publications permitted only with excisions, would appear to be the group of works selected for translation. It was this category that I found to be especially valuable for understanding censorship in the tsarist period because it revealed very clearly and directly the themes of concern to the imperial censorship. This category may be equally valuable for understanding at least some aspects of Soviet concern regarding foreign publications.

That study focused on *The Arrogance of Power* by Senator J. William Fulbright (1966, Soviet translation 1967).[4] Three other works were included to broaden the picture: *The Evolution of Diplomatic Method* by Sir Harold Nicolson (1954, Soviet translation 1962);[5] *I Speak of Freedom* by Kwame Nkrumah, president of Ghana (1961, Soviet translation 1962);[6] and *India's Foreign Policy: Selected Speeches, September 1946–April 1961*, by Jawaharlal Nehru, prime minister of India (1961, Soviet translation 1965).[7]

My comparisons of a number of translations with the originals certainly convinced me that qualitative differences do exist. These changes constitute what we might call an "active" censorship rather than the "reactive" type characteristic of tsarist times, and they seem to be aimed primarily at altering the images presented of the Soviet Union and communism and those of the United States and the West, with the result that the Soviet Union is made to appear in a more positive light and the West looks worse.

On the basis of my study of translations of relatively recent works, I concluded that the themes of concern to the imperial and Soviet governments are, at least in a general sense, comparable: they are still concerned about treatment by foreign authors of their leadership, their form of government, and the image of their country. But the significant and interesting difference lies not so much in the themes as in the techniques employed. Translation Soviet-style is infinitely more effective than "applying the caviar," as tsarist censors used to describe the inking out of offending passages, because the ink, as well as what it covers, is now invisible. Before the Revolution there was no system for replacing unwanted passages with something more desirable; the caviar-covered work was clumsy and unconvincing; and the authorities were unable to prevent illegal copies of many foreign works from entering the empire and circulating quite freely. The Soviets changed all that: by prohibiting the importation of foreign originals and employing a combination of translating, editing, and rewriting techniques, they could produce "custom-made" versions of foreign works for domestic readers, very few of whom would have access to the original.

Translations published in the sixties were not subject to copyright, and consequently Soviet editions from this period were not required to include any reference to changes made. After May 1973, when the Soviet Union acceded to the Universal Copyright Convention, a translation that had been altered in any way was required by law to contain a statement like the one found on the verso of the title page of *Rabota*, "Pechataetsia s sokrashcheniiami" (printed with abridgments). However, this kind of general statement hardly tells the whole story, and the Soviet reader, without access to the original, is in no position to assess the kinds of changes that have been made, or the extent of those changes. There is also ample evidence that the legalities are not always observed.[8]

I was unable to learn from Studs Terkel the terms of his agreement with Progress Publishers and with VAAP (the Soviet copyright agency), so I do not know whether he approved the selection of interviews to be included in the Soviet edition.[9] In any case, there is no doubt that the deletion from the translation of 97 of the 133 original interviews is the single most striking and significant feature emerging from the comparison of the two books. Webster defines abridgment as "A reduced form of a work, retaining the general sense and unity of the original." *Rabota* fits the first part of the definition—it is certainly a reduced form of *Working*—but not the second part: I maintain that the general sense and unity of the original has been destroyed. It is difficult to recognize *Working* in *Rabota*: Nearly three-quarters of the interviews are gone, and the ones chosen for inclusion tell only parts of the story. Terkel's introduction is omitted, as are his acknowledgments, his numerous epigraphs, his three prefaces, and his arrangement of the interviews into books with well-chosen titles and subtitles. These are visible, "structural" differences (visible, that is, to those of us with access to both versions!); to them must be added a variety of textual differences, some rather troubling.

Let us begin by comparing introductions. In his, Terkel writes that *Working* (subtitled *People Talk about What They Do All Day and How They Feel about What They Do*), is about "violence—to the spirit as well as to the body," about "a search . . . for daily meaning as well as daily bread, for recognition as well as cash, for astonishment rather than torpor; in short, for a sort of life rather than a Monday through Friday sort of dying." He acknowledges "the happy few who find a savor in their daily job," mentioning four interviews (all excluded from *Rabota*), but observes that "for the many there is a hardly concealed discontent. The blue-collar blues is no more bitterly sung than the white-collar moan." He notes that "The most profound complaint, aside from non-recognition and the nature of the job, is 'being spied on,'" and points out that "The indignation of those being watched is no longer offered in muted tones," a change from the thirties, when "Those rebels who found flaws in our society were few in number." Nor is age necessarily a factor; he interviewed rebellious old people and complacent young ones. Terkel concludes that "No matter how bewildering the times, no matter how dissembling the official language, those we call ordinary are aware of a sense of personal worth—or more often a lack of it—in the work they do."[10]

In *Rabota* the author's own introduction is replaced by one written by B. Gilenson entitled "Trudy i dni sovremennoi Ameriki" (the works and days of contemporary America; Gilenson's title would appear to be taken from Lewis Mumford's review of *Working*, part of which is reproduced on the back cover of the original hard-cover edition, and which Gilenson quotes at the close of his essay). But another Soviet introduction should be mentioned first, this one written by S. Kondrashov, a well-known Soviet correspondent who spent some years in the States. His piece, prefacing thirteen translated interviews from *Working*, was published two years before *Rabota* in the widely read journal *Inostrannaia literatura* (Foreign Literature), where foreign works are often introduced to the Soviet public before being published in book form.[11] (All thirteen interviews were subsequently incorporated into *Rabota*.)

The main points of Kondrashov's essay—entitled "Priamoi golos massy" (the direct voice of the masses)—are echoed later by Gilenson. Kondrashov writes: "Judging by the fruits of his labor the American worker is equal to a titan. But when this aggregate titan is disassembled in Terkel's book into its component parts, we see dissatisfied, exhausted, joyless people." Discussing blue-collar and white-collar workers, he says "they swim in the same pond of labor, which they consider forced labor, they are brothers and sisters, alas, in unhappiness." All "recognize themselves as objects of capitalist exploitation, . . . complain about the oppressive automation of work. . . . speak of employers, bosses, corporations as the enemies."[12]

In his introduction Gilenson places Terkel in the tradition of John Reed and Theodore Dreiser, who let the voices of common people be heard, and compares him with Walt Whitman, who celebrated work in American life; he states that Terkel's heroes represent "virtually all the main professions found throughout American society." It should be noted here that in his own introduction Terkel explains that he deliberately omitted some categories—the clergy (with one exception); doctors (although he did include a dentist); politicians, writers, and journalists (with the exception of one movie reviewer)—because in his view "their articulateness and expertise offered them other forums."[13] As we shall see when we look at the selection of interviews, neither the priest nor the dentist was included in *Rabota*, nor were numerous other professional people interviewed in *Working*. (The movie reviewer, Pauline

Kael, *was* included, for reasons that I think make good sense from the Soviet point of view; in this interview Kael is critical of the movie industry's treatment of its workers and of its neglect of topics such as strikes.)

Like Kondrashov, Gilenson stresses the exploitation, alienation, and dehumanization of American working people, who, he notes, worry about the quality of their lives, not only about making money. Millions are unemployed, and those fortunate enough to have jobs suffer terrible indignities: "Wherever a person works in America, he is constantly under someone's vigilant surveillance," he claims, and he goes on to state that "Terkel's book proves unequivocally that man in the society calling itself 'free' is in reality not free; uncertainty and the fear of losing one's job shape people's behavior and appearance, standardize them to the utmost." Gilenson finds the portraits created in *Working* "truthful and 'unretouched'; they make a deep impression." Terkel's book, he says, is "very American in coloration, details, characters,"[11] and I expect most of us would agree with him. But do the interviews included in *Rabota* portray that same America?

To answer that question I decided to examine not only those 36 interviews selected for inclusion in *Rabota*, but also the 97 interviews not included, and to compare the two groups. Then, with the help of several native speakers of Russian, I looked closely at several of the 36 translated interviews to learn what kinds of changes—if any—had been made. Some results of these investigations are discussed below. (Unfortunately, space does not permit reproduction of the contents pages of *Working*, showing Terkel's arrangement of the 133 interviews, but the 36 interviews selected for *Rabota* are listed in the appendix, with an asterisk marking the 13 that appeared first in *Inostrannaia literatura*.)

I must add that in the three studies of this type that I have undertaken, I experienced a sort of Dr. Jekyll/Mr. Hyde transformation, from scholar to censor, as I became immersed in the material. Once the researcher develops a "feel" for the themes of concern and the techniques used, it is frighteningly easy to do what needs to be done, and frequently I have caught myself shaking my head over a passage or an entire interview and muttering that, of course, it was unacceptable. I was also thoroughly puzzled in some cases, and found myself unable to decide whether something was acceptable or not; I imagine that Soviets involved in this work find themselves in the same situation from time to time! I did find that when I looked at the interviews from what I imagined to be the Soviet point of view, I found several that had been excluded from *Rabota* that I thought might well have been included; perhaps these were considered "duplicates," obvious cuts for an abridged edition. In the majority of cases, however, I believed I could see clear reasons for the choices made.

I cannot know, of course, how the selection of interviews was actually made, or by whom (the translator? the editor? the publisher? someone else?); nor can I do more than suggest explanations for certain discrepancies between translation and original. But some patterns and trends do emerge, and some educated guesses are certainly in order. Let us turn now to the first parts of *Working* and see how they compare with *Rabota*.

Prefaces

As I have mentioned, none of the material in Terkel's three prefaces was included in *Rabota*. Steelworker Mike LeFevre (in preface 1) has some unkind things to say about communism: ''Why is it that the communists always say they're for the workingman, and as soon as they set up a country, you got guys singing to tractors? They're singing about how they love the factory. That's where I couldn't buy communism. It's the intellectuals' utopia, not mine. I cannot picture myself singing to a tractor, I just can't. (Laughs.) Or singing to steel. (Singsongs.) Oh whoop-dee-doo, I'm at the bonderizer, oh how I love this heavy steel. No thanks. Never happen.''[15]

Two of the three young newsboys in preface II like delivering papers and earning money. The third, fourteen-year-old Terry Pickens, does not, and Soviet readers miss the chance to read his vehement rejection of an American myth: ''I don't see where people get all this bull about the kid who's gonna be President and being a newsboy made a President out of him. It taught him how to handle his money and this bull. You know what it did? It taught him how to hate the people in his route. And the printers. And dogs.''[16]

Stonemason Carl Bates (preface III) is one of several Americans interviewed who derive genuine and lasting satisfaction from their work: ''Stone's my life. I daydream all the time, most times it's on stone. . . . I can't imagine a job where you go home and maybe go by a year later and you don't know what you've done. My work, I can see what I did the first day I started.''[17] A few positive comments similar to this one found their way into *Rabota*, but many more were excluded.

Book 1

Of six interviews, only one was included in *Rabota*: Roberto Acuna, farm worker and organizer for the United Farm Workers of America. Acuna describes a terrible, shameful side of American life, and I expect many people reading this interview feel horror and guilt, as I do: ''If people could see—in the winter, ice on the fields. We'd be on our knees all day long. We'd build fires and warm up real fast and go back onto the ice. We'd be picking watermelons in 105 degrees all day long. When people have melons or cucumber or carrots or lettuce, they don't know how they got on their table and the consequences to the people who picked it. If I had enough money, I would take busloads of people out to the fields and into the labor camps. Then they'd know how that fine salad got on their table.''[18]

But different, equally valid feelings, such as pride in one's work, are expressed in other interviews in this book that were excluded from *Rabota*. Pierce Walker, a small farmer, observes: ''When you get a good crop, that's more or less your reward. If you weren't proud of your work, you wouldn't have no place on the farm. 'Cause you don't work by the hour. And you put in a lot of hours, I tell ya. You wouldn't stay out here till dark and after if you were punchin' a clock. If you didn't like your work and have pride in it, you wouldn't do that.''[19] And Hub Dillard, a heavy equipment operator, has similar feelings: ''There's a certain amount of pride—I don't care how little you did. You drive down the road and you say, 'I worked on this road.' If there's a bridge, you say, 'I worked on this bridge.' Or you drive by a building and you say, 'I worked on this building.' Maybe it don't mean anything to anybody else, but there's a certain pride knowing you did your bit.''[20]

Book 2

Chosen for inclusion in *Rabota* from the first section of this book, ''Communications,'' was Heather Lamb, a telephone operator who commented on the telephone company's exploitation of poor people, the intense pressure of her job, and the constant surveillance of employees by ''Ma Bell'' supervisors. Frances Swenson, however, a switchboard operator at a large motel who was not included in *Rabota*, has a similar job but different feelings about it: ''Anybody that has done switchboard likes switchboard. It's not lonesome. You're talking to people. You ask another switchboard operator, they like it.''[21] Clearly neither woman is right or wrong; this is a difference of opinion, and exposure to both views helps the reader to visualize that kind of work.

Four of the five interviews with women in the second section, ''A Pecking Order,'' are included in *Rabota*. Three of those four—the airline stewardess, the airline reservationist, and the model—are dissatisfied with their work: they feel exploited both by their employers and by men; they are overworked, bored, resentful. Says Beryl Simpson, ''My job as a reservationist was very routine, computerized. I hated it with a passion. . . . They monitored you and listened to your conversations. If you were a minute late for work, it went into your file.''[22] ''You feel like you're someone's clothes hanger,'' observes model Jill Torrance; and stewardess Terry Mason complains, "It's always: the passenger is right. When a passenger says something mean, we're supposed to smile and say, I understand. . . . Even when they pinch us or say dirty things, we're supposed to smile at them."[23] The fourth woman included in *Rabota*, executive secretary Anne Bogan, enjoys her job because "I feel like I'm sharing somewhat of the business life of the men. . . . I think if I've been at all successful with men, it's because I'm a good listener and interested in their world."[24]

Kondrashov's and Gilenson's introductions make clear why three of these four interviews were included in *Rabota*: Mason and Torrance are among those cited by Kondrashov as "examples of capitalist exploitation"; and Gilenson describes Bogan as representative of that group of American workers who show the effects of what he calls "Babbitt ideology"—those who are integrated into, and advocates of, the very system that exploits them.[25]

But the most articulate woman in the group, and the one whose job is often considered the most exploited in any society, is not portrayed in *Rabota*: Roberta Victor, prostitute since the age of fifteen, highly intelligent and extremely cynical, who describes her work in detail and observes that

> What I did was no different from what ninety-nine percent of American women are taught to do. . . . You become your job. I became what I did. I became a hustler. I became cold, I became hard, I became turned off, I became numb. . . . I don't think it's terribly different from somebody who works on the assembly line forty hours a week and comes home cut off, numb, dehumanized. . . . In the outside society, if I tried to be me, I wasn't in control of anything. As a bright, assertive woman, I had no power. As a cold, manipulative hustler, I had a lot. . . . Most women are taught to *become* what they act. All I did was act out the reality of American womanhood.[26]

It would be interesting to know whether it was simply Soviet prudery that kept this interview out of the journal and the book, or whether Roberta Victor's comments were considered inappropriate for other reasons.

Section 3 of book 2 of *Working* contains one interview (excluded from *Rabota*) with writer/producer Barbara Herrick, a successful single woman of whom Terkel writes: "According to Department of Labor statistics, she is in the upper one percent bracket of working women."[27] The two included interviews from the next, or fourth, section, "The Commercial," are with black telephone solicitor Enid du Bois, who finds her job distasteful because it makes her exploit poor people; and with actor Rip Torn, who sees American society using actors "to sell products primarily. . . . Who's running things now? The salesman . . . To the American public, an actor is unsuccessful unless he makes money."[28] The other interview with an actor would have shown another view. Arny Freeman finds some satisfaction in making commercials: "I have in recent years found my work somewhat meaningful. So many people have stopped me on the street and said, 'I can't tell you how much I enjoy what you've done.' If, for a moment or two, he can turn on his TV set and see you in a show or a commercial and it makes him a little happier—I think that's important . . . I love to find the qualities in a person, in a character, that are alive and human—even in a commercial."[29]

Book 3

In the first section, "Cleaning Up," Terkel gives us interviews with two members of a Chicago sanitation truck team: Nick Salerno, the driver, and Roy Schmidt, garbage man. Schmidt, included in *Rabota*, is not particularly negative about his work—"I don't look down on my job in any way. I couldn't say I despise myself for doing it"—but his partner Salerno, excluded from *Rabota*, is certainly more positive: "I have nothing to be ashamed of. . . . We make a pretty good salary. I feel I earn my money. I can go any place I want."[30]

Terkel also gives us Maggie Holmes, domestic, and Louis Hayward, washroom attendant, both black. We respond to the force of Maggie Holmes's anger much as we responded to the farm worker Roberto Acuna: "This Nixon was sayin' he don't see nothin' wrong with people doin' scrubbin'. For generations that's all we done. He should know we wants to be doctors and lawyers like him. I don't want my kids to come up and do domestic work. It's degrading." I can see why the Soviets included the fiery Holmes rather than the gentler Hayward, a former Pullman porter working out his last years in a men's room at the Palmer House. "'Most people like to say how rich and rewarding their jobs are. I can't say that.' (As he laughs softly, he walks off toward the washroom.)"[31] I can see, too, why Lincoln James, who works in a rendering and glue factory, and Eric Hoellen, janitor, were excluded. James says "I like what I'm doing. . . . I look forward to going to work. I'd be lost if I wasn't working"; Hoellen observes that "For no college education you can't get a better job as far as paying is concerned. It's interesting. . . . I make a pretty good buck. . . . I'm proud of my job."[32]

Of the two interviews with policemen in the second section, "Watching," the Soviets chose Renault Robinson—founder of the Afro-American Patrolmen's League, black, angry, and disillusioned—rather than Vincent Maher, white, who says his is "one of the most gratifying jobs in the world."[33] Industrial investigator Anthony Ruggiero illustrates the surveillance mentality stressed in the Soviet introductions, and film critic Pauline Kael points out that work is glamorized in the movies: "It's going to have to be a very tough muckraking film maker to show us how industry discards people. . . . We now have conglomerate ownership of the movie industry. Are they going to show us how these industries really dehumanize their workers? It's a long time since we've had a movie about a strike, isn't it?"[34]

The pattern established in these first books is maintained throughout. The Americans portrayed in *Rabota* tend to be people (often highly politicized) who fight and criticize "the system," including Hispanics and blacks as well as some whites who fit that description; people who are racially prejudiced and those who are victims of prejudice; "little people" who feel they are no more than cogs in the big capitalist machine, faceless, with no identity or power; people whose immoral jobs exploit or demean others; people who chafe against the cruelties, callousness, corruption, and commercialism of our business world; people at the bottom of the social ladder; people with low self-esteem who feel marginal, unhappy with their status in life, ashamed of and dissatisfied with their work, resentful, rootless, and alienated. A few of these interviews reflect positive sentiments about life or work, but the great majority—by my count more than three-quarters of the 36 included in *Rabota*—range from neutral to strongly negative.

The Americans excluded from *Rabota*, on the other hand, tend to be people who find satisfaction and pride in their jobs—blacks, whites, and Hispanics from all levels of society; professionals with high-paying and high-prestige jobs; retired people, housewives, and those with the means to be idle; avowed capitalists and successful self-made businessmen and businesswomen who love competition and pressure and the sense of power derived from their work; people who work through established channels to fight prejudice and improve life for others less fortunate. Of the 97 excluded interviews I noted perhaps 68—more than two-thirds—that reflected at least some positive views, often stated quite emphatically.

These are only general patterns, and I must emphasize again that there are certainly exceptions: supermarket checker Babe Secoli, waitress Delores Dante, baby nurse Ruth Lindstrom, gravedigger Elmer Ruiz (all included in *Rabota*) find some satisfaction and dignity in their jobs, while press agent Eddie Jaffe, auditor Fred Roman, stockbroker Ray Wax, and government employees Steve Carmichael, Lilith Reynolds, and Diane Wilson (all excluded from *Rabota*) are unhappy or frustrated in theirs. But the pattern is no less valid because of these exceptions.

Turning now to questions of translation, my comparison of the texts of interviews included in *Rabota* with the originals revealed five kinds of changes:

1. *Simple errors*. There is little to be said about this category, which undoubtedly can be found in most, if not all, translations and may just be due to poor proofreading, as was probably the case in this example: Roberto Acuna says "Illness in the fields is 120 percent higher than the average rate for industry"; somewhere along the line the zero was dropped, and "120 percent" becomes "12 percent" in the translation.[35] Stewardess Terry Mason says "I was in uniform," in the original, but "I was in plain clothes" in the translation,[36] and again I would consider this to be a straightforward error on the part of the translator.

2. *Omission of words or phrases unfamiliar to Soviet audiences*. I assume this is the reason for the omission of "Muzak" from the translation of the interview with supermarket box boy Brett Hauser.[37] (Another technique sometimes used in Soviet translations—and in *Rabota* in cases such as this is the addition of an explanatory note. Terkel also has several of these notes of his own in *Working*, and they are reproduced faithfully, for the most part, in *Rabota*.) A second example of this type of change: "Golden Rule" is omitted from a poem quoted by schoolteacher Rose Hoffman,[38] presumably because Soviet readers would not be familiar with the reference.

3. *Use of more negative or stronger language*. Speaking of a poor customer, telephone solicitor Enid du Bois uses the words "taking his money"; in the translation the phrase is "swindle him out of his last penny."[39] Black policeman Renault Robinson says, "Whites control the vice and gambling in this city," translated as "all the vice and gambling houses belong to the whites."[40]

4. *Omission of language unacceptable for Soviet readers*. Soviet prudery is probably behind the translation of "vaginal sprays" as "aerosols" in the interview with Walter Lundquist, industrial designer (Mr. Lundquist is extremely explicit, the translation very vague!) [41] And the prohibition against any mention of George Orwell's *1984* is certainly behind the translation of a remark by Ernest Bradshaw, head of the audit department in a bank, about "Big Brother watching you" as "a real system of shadowing."[42]

5. *Substitution of Marxist or special Soviet terminology*. Bill Talcott, organizer, refers to "middle-class people in Lexington"; "middle-class" is translated as "bourgeois public, the so-called middle class."[43] Copy boy Charlie Blossom talks about young women who are "attractive by white, bourgeois standards," rendered as "Anglo-Saxon bourgeois standards," a uniquely Soviet definition of "white"![44]

A word about style: the 36 interviews in *Rabota* were translated by 10 different people, and I wondered whether the style would be very uneven, or whether an editor had smoothed out any differences. The latter proved to be the case; indeed, the native speakers with whom I consulted confirmed that the Russian was not only uniform throughout, but was a Soviet bureaucratic style familiar to them all. This is certainly a far cry from the rich variety of English recorded by Terkel!

Abridgments and translations are not, of course, uniquely Soviet problems. Publishers in the West tell me that they or their authors are often unhappy with the quality of translations—abridged or not—produced in other Western countries. But it seems to me that Western publishers and authors need to be aware of that fundamental difference between these countries and the Soviet Union that I mentioned at the beginning of this paper: someone in France or Germany who wishes to read a translated work in the original can find it in a library or bookstore, or order it from abroad; these options are simply not available to most Soviet readers.

A censor, according to one of Webster's definitions, is "an officer or official charged with scrutinizing communications to intercept, suppress, or delete material harmful to his country's or organization's interests."[45] I am suggesting that *Rabota* is not simply an abridged translation of *Working*; it is a censored version of the book, complete with excisions in the Russian tradition, and a little rewriting in the Soviet continuation of that tradition.

Terkel's book is so compelling because he presents us with such a wide variety of people who respond to work in so many, often surprising, ways. There is unhappiness, frustration, boredom, anger, degradation—but there is dignity, pride, humor, satisfaction, too, and in surprising and wonderful combinations. Because of the sameness of the translation, but especially because of the nature of the abridgment, *Rabota* lacks those qualities that make *Working* an extraordinary book. *Rabota*, published in an edition of 50,000 and priced at 45 kopeks, was obviously intended to reach a wide Soviet audience. The introduction spells out the message clearly, and the book delivers it. What a pity that *Rabota* bears so little resemblance to *Working*!

Notes

1. *Rabota: Liudi rasskazyvaiut o svoei kazhdodnevnoi rabote i o tom, kak oni k etoi rabote otnosiatsia* (Moskva: Progress, 1978). I used the paperback edition of *Working* (New York: Avon Books); the original publisher is Pantheon Books (copyright 1972, 1974).

2. Marianna Tax Choldin, *A Fence around the Empire: Russian Censorship of Western Ideas under the Tsars* (Durham: Duke University Press, 1985).

3. Marianna Tax Choldin, "Censorship via Translation: Soviet Treatment of

Western Political Writing'' (presented at a conference at the Kennan Institute for Advanced Russian Studies, 2-3 May 1983; to be published in the proceedings).

4. J. William Fulbright, *The Arrogance of Power* (New York: Random House, 1966): Soviet translation: *Samonadeiannost' sily* (Moskva: Mezhdunarodnye otnosheniia, 1967).

5. Harold Nicolson, *The Evolution of Diplomatic Method* (New York: Macmillan, 1954); Soviet translation: *Diplomaticheskoe iskusstvo* (Moskva: Institut Mezhdunarodnykh otnoshenii, 1962).

6. Kwame Nkrumah, *I Speak of Freedom: A Statement of African Ideology* (London: Heinemann, 1961); Soviet translation: *Ia govoriu o svobode: Izlozhenie afrikanskoi ideologii* (Moskva: Inostrannaia literatura, 1962).

7. Jawaharlal Nehru, *India's Foreign Policy: Selected Speeches, September 1946–April 1961* (Delhi: Publications Division, Ministry of Information and Broadcasting, Government of India, 1961); Soviet translation: *Vneshniaia politika Indii: Izbrannye rechi i vystupleniia 1946–64* (Moskva: Progress, 1965).

8. Henry Glade, ''Aspects of Soviet Censorship of West German Belles Lettres, 1974–1980: An Overview,'' *Germano-Slavica* 4 (1983): 151–157.

9. I should mention that I spoke with Terkel about my study, and although at first he seemed interested and willing to send me the information I asked for, he never followed through.

10. Introduction to *Working*, quotations from pp. xiii, xiv, xxvii, xxix, xxx.

11. *Inostrannaia literatura* 1976, no. 1: 224–255. Selections from *Division Street: America*, an earlier book by Terkel, were included in numbers 8 and 9 of 1969.

12. Kondrashov introduction, p. 225, 227. Incidentally, Kondrashov accurately describes *Working* as a thick volume of almost 600 pages and more than 130 interviews (p. 225). In his introduction to the book, Gilenson refers more vaguely to ''desiatki'' (tens—probably best translated in this context as dozens) of interviews and pages (pp. 8, 10). A Soviet reader who remembered Kondrashov's essay and hoped to find 130 interviews in the book must have been sorely disappointed to find only 36!

13. *Rabota*, pp. 8–10; *Working*, xxvi.

14. *Rabota*, pp. 12, 14.

15. *Working*, pp. 5–6.

16. Ibid., p. 16.

17. Ibid., pp. 20, 22.

18. Ibid., p. 38.

19. Ibid., p. 29

20. Ibid., p. 54.

21. Ibid., p. 64.

22. Ibid., pp. 82, 83.

23. Ibid., pp. 88, 78

24. Ibid., p. 91.

25. *Inostrannaia literatura*, p. 227; *Rabota*, pp. 13–14

26. *Working*, pp. 102–103.

27. Ibid., p. 104.

28. Ibid., pp. 124, 126.

29. Ibid., p. 123.

30. Ibid., pp. 152–153, 149.

31. Ibid., pp. 166, 158.

32. Ibid., pp. 161, 169, 173, 178.

33. Ibid., p. 183.
34. Ibid., p. 218.
35. *Working*, p. 36; *Rabota*, p. 21.
36. *Working*, p. 74; *Rabota*, p. 32.
37. *Working*, p. 371; *Rabota*, p. 142.
38. *Working*, pp. 632–633; *Rabota*, p. 207.
39. *Working*, p. 142; *Rabota*, p. 61.
40. *Working*, p. 193; *Rabota*, p. 75.
41. *Working*, p. 680; *Rabota*, p. 223.
42. *Working*, p. 524; *Rabota*, p. 185.
43. *Working*, p. 466; *Rabota*, p. 172.
44. *Working*, p. 575; *Rabota*, p. 191.
45. *Webster's Third New International Dictionary of the English Language* (1961), s.v. "censor."

Appendix

Interviews included in *Rabota*

(*denotes interview previously published in *Inostrannaia literatura*)

1. *Roberto Acuna, farm worker
2. *Heather Lamb, telephone operator
3. Terry Mason, airline stewardess
4. Beryl Simpson, airline reservationist
5. Jill Torrance, model
6. Anne Bogan, executive secretary
7. *Rip Torn, actor
8. *Enid du Bois, telephone solicitor
9. *Roy Schmidt, garbage man
10. *Maggie Holmes, domestic
11. Renault Robinson, policeman
12. Anthony Ruggiero, industrial investigator
13. Pauline Kael, film critic
14. *Phil Stallings, spot-welder
15. Jim Grayson, spot-welder
16. Gary Bryner, president, Lordstown Local, UAW
17. *Jean Stanley, cosmetics saleswoman
18. Doc Pritchard, hotel clerk
19. Hots Michaels, bar pianist
20. *Tim Devlin, janitor; ex-salesman
21. *Brett Hauser, supermarket box boy
22. *Babe Secoli, supermarket checker
23. Dolores Dante, waitress
24. *Nino Guidici, pharmacist
25. Bill Talcott [organizer]
26. Eric Nesterenko, hockey player
27. *Ernest Bradshaw, audit department head, bank
28. Charlie Blossom, copy boy
29. Ruth Lindstrom, baby nurse
30. Rose Hoffman, public school teacher
31. Elmer Ruiz, gravedigger

32. Nora Watson, editor
33. Walter Lundquist, industrial designer
34. Rebecca Sweeney, nun to naprapath
35. Philip da Vinci, lawyer
36. Steve Dubi, steelworker

"Good Books are a very great mercy to the world": Persecution, Private Libraries, and the Printed Word in the Early Development of the Dissenting Academies, 1663–1730

David L. Ferch

Early Dissenting academies showed no uniformity in providing students with books. No institutional library existed among the fifty earliest academies (1663–1730). State and local persecution was the principal reason for the slow development of institutional libraries. Instability of purpose also hindered their growth, since many Puritans believed university education would soon reopen to them. Despite these problems, selected academies were successful in meeting their objectives without institutional book collections. The most successful were located in cities with accessible public or chapel libraries. But the most important source of books for academy use was the private libraries of the Puritan divines.

"Good Books," wrote Richard Baxter in 1673, "are a very great mercy to the world."[1] Writing a decade after the Great Ejection, the bookish Reverend Baxter succinctly summarized the importance of the printed word to the harassed Nonconformist of the later seventeenth century. The desire to acquire "Good Books" was a central force in the lives of many of the Puritan leaders. Oliver Heywood (d. 1702), considered the "most active evangelistic itinerant in the north,"[2] compiled a lengthy list of what "god had wonderfully provided" during his twenty-two years of ejection—the second entry was: "for buying books."[3] After losing half of his sizable library in the great London fire of 1666, Thomas Goodwin (d. 1680) remarked that "God had struck him in a very sensible part, and acknowledged it as a rebuke of Providence, for having loved his library too much."[4] Indeed, so important were books to the Puritan divines that Baxter could respond in all earnest to the question, "What Books Especially of Theologie should one choose, who for want of money or time, can read but few?" by suggesting not only the Bible, a concordance, a commentary, several books on grace, justification, free will, and duty, and seven catechisms, but also the writings of sixty-five "Affectionate Practical English Writers."[5]

David L. Ferch *is assistant professor of history, Mount Mercy College, Cedar Rapids, Iowa.*

Yet the early Dissenting academies, charged with maintaining the supply of educated Nonconformists, showed no uniformity in providing their students with the books and libraries necessary to achieve Baxter's standard. In fact, their failure to maintain adequate libraries was surprisingly common. Daniel Defoe, himself an alumnus of Newington Green academy (1667?–1706), regarded the lack of access to good libraries as the major disadvantage of students educated at Dissenting institutions.[6] Another former academy pupil stated the case against the academies more bluntly: they provided "all the Dangers and Vices of the Universities, without the Advantages."[7] The Presbyterian historian Herbert McLachlan gave credit to Samuel Cradock (d. 1706) for teaching logic, natural philosophy, and metaphysics at his Wickambrook academy (1678–1696),[8] but failed to mention that Cradock's pupils were required to copy his lectures for lack of books on these subjects.[9] McLachlan did note, however, the widespread forced migration of Nonconformist students from one academy to another in order to "extend their acquaintance with the printed word."[10] Even Samuel Palmer, the great defender of the academies during the hostile reign of Queen Anne, acknowledged the inferiority of academy libraries when compared to those of Oxford and Cambridge: "If their laboratories, gardens and noble libraries are to be brought into the balance, I know no Dissenter that is fool enough to deny their superiority."[11]

Of more importance than a comparison to the university libraries is the fact that it was not until 1730 that an academy library, based on student fees and augmented on a yearly basis, was established.[12] That is, no *institutional* library attached to an academy existed during the first sixty-seven years of Nonconformist higher education—a period that saw the establishment of approximately fifty academies. Moreover, the first Nonconformist endowed library, that of Dr. Daniel Williams in London, opened its doors to Dissenting scholars and students only the year before (1729).[13]

The focus of this paper is the period prior to the establishment of this first institutional library at Philip Doddridge's Northampton academy, that is, the period 1663 to 1730. Its purpose is twofold: to identify and analyze the reasons for the slow evolution of institutional libraries in the academies, and to discuss the alternatives to institutional libraries employed by the academies' tutors and students in their efforts to obtain printed material necessary to the educational objectives of Nonconformity. The paper makes a contribution to the study of Nonconformist education, since the principal historians of the Dissenting academies—Irene Parker (1914), Herbert McLachlan (1931), J. W. Ashley Smith (1954)—largely have skimmed over these uncertain early years to focus on the better-documented, stable years of the mid- and latter eighteenth century.[14]

The major factor hindering the establishment of even the most modest Dissenting academy library was persecution by Anglican authorities. Especially during the period prior to the Glorious Revolution, Anglican-inspired tirades against the academies were frequent. Reverend Robert South, for example, in a 1685 sermon, admonished his audience "to employ the most of this your power . . . to suppress utterly and extinguish, those private . . . academies of grammar and philosophy set up and taught secretly by Fanatics here and there all the kingdom over."[15] Such zealous persecution forced many academies to take on a transitory character, which in turn influenced their generally small size and simple organizational structure. Persecution required Richard Frankland (d. 1698) to move his famous academy, founded at Rathmell in 1670, six times during its eighteen-year history, while the lesser known Isington academy (1672–1680) of Thomas Doolittle was required to migrate five times in its eight-year history.[16]

The continuous pressure applied to the early academies by local and state authorities made it impossible for academies to develop in a stabilized environment necessary for the establishment of institutional libraries. The period 1663–1688 was characterized by an especially high mortality rate for Dissenting academies. This situation was eased only partially by the Glorious Revolution; for despite the influence of a Protestant, though Anglican, throne, persecution at the local level continued. John Moore (d. 1717), for example, was arrested during this period of limited state persecution on a warrant issued by the mayor of Bridgwater for keeping an academy in that city.[17]

With King William's death, the church party's demand for the suppression of the academies returned to the level of the pre-Revolution era. Beginning with Henry Sacheverell's June 1702 sermon before the Oxford judges at assize, the Nonconformist institutions came under severe attack. In this sermon, Sacheverell called for the suppression of these "foundations of lewdness" as a subversive danger to church and state, and he was critical especially of their supposed role in maintaining "all descriptions of heterodox, lewd, and atheistical books."[18] The controversy grew with the Samuel Wesley–Samuel Palmer debates of 1703–1707, and Sacheverell's trial over his *False Brethren* sermon of 1709, culminating in the passing of the Schism Bill, which would have suppressed the academies entirely. The death of Queen Anne on the morning of the Bill's planned enactment prevented the measure from coming into force, but not before Anglican leaders again suppressed John Moore's academy at Bridgwater.[19]

Even with the prospect of a more sympathetic Hanoverian on the throne, local persecution continued during the early years of the Georgian reign. Instability, generated by acts of violence as well as the more common forms of persecution through legal action, continued to be the prime hindrance to the development of institutional academy libraries. At least one library used by an academy, that of Shrewsbury (1680–1715), was destroyed in July of 1715 when anti-Hanoverian rioters burned down the Dissenters' meeting-house, which contained a collection of books used by the academy students.[20] Legal actions, however, were the most often used forms of suppression and harassment, and these continued well into the eighteenth century. In fact, it was not until the early 1730s that legal persecutions ceased, when George II personally intervened on behalf of Philip Doddridge to prevent legal proceedings being carried out against the tutor under the Five Mile Act. It was only after this action that the Dissenters began to establish and endow more permanent educational facilities.[21]

One form of persecution was especially noxious to Nonconformist intellectuals and adversely affected the development of private libraries among Dissenting tutors. This was the confiscation of a Dissenter's books upon being convicted of preaching or teaching without an ecclesiastical license under the Act of Uniformity. For Richard Baxter, as well as countless others of his character, his Anglican persecutors had found an especially appropriate cruelty in depriving him of his books in an effort to keep him from preaching.[22] Oliver Heywood kept a list of books under the heading: "THESE TAKEN FROM ME FOR PREACHING THE GOSPEL."[23] Robert Traill (or Trail) (d. 1716), who tutored students in London, was required to conceal himself and his family for some time after copies of a book "which the privy council had ordered to be publicly burnt" were confiscated from his library.[24] Such harassment may have kept some academy tutors from acquiring too large a collection. Indeed, Thomas Hill (d. 1719/1720), for instance, successfully defended himself in 1712 against a charge of unlicensed school-keeping by the very lack of a library. His defense was that he merely gave lodging to young men and occasionally advised them on what books to read and answered questions they might ask.[25]

To instability caused by persecution must be added instability of purpose; for several tutors during the first decades after ejection believed academy education was only a temporary substitute for university education. Among these was the influential Charles Morton (d. 1698), who believed the lesser halls of the universities would open soon to Dissenters. Similarly, Theophilus Gale (d. 1678/1679), one of the few wealthy tutors, left part of his estate to be used for the academy education of young men under the provision that each recipient must first register his name at one of the university colleges so that the stipend could be applied to Oxford or Cambridge as soon as Dissenters were allowed to take degrees.[26] Furthermore, in anticipation of the day when Nonconformist students would have access to the university libraries, Gale willed his large library, with the exception of his philosophical books, to America's needy Harvard College.[27] Like Morton and Gale, many of the tutors of the seventeenth century were educated at Oxford or Cambridge, and the desire to see a return to university education probably slowed the development of a Nonconformist demand for permanent, separate educational facilities until these early tutors were replaced by tutors educated in the academies themselves.

Before turning to a discussion of the alternatives employed by tutors and students to satisfy their need for printed material, a final factor should be added to the reasons noted previously for the slow emergence of institutional academy libraries. It has been estimated that during the last decade of the seventeenth century fully one-third of the Dissenting ministry were too poor to provide themselves with even the most basic books considered by the various denominations to be essential in adequately fulfilling the duties of a pastorate.[28] As a profession, the Dissenting ministry was supported better than Dissenting education, though in reality a tutor was most often the head of a congregation first, adding an academy as a means of increasing his income.[29] Hence, it may be argued that the problem of low income among the ministry was at least as acute among the segment that supplied Nonconformists with their educators. The prospect of maintaining a small private collection of books, let alone of building a library for the use of students, was, therefore, clearly beyond the means of many academy tutors.

Despite the numerous adversities associated with the development and maintenance of a collection of books, a few Dissenting tutors were able to acquire private libraries of several hundred volumes that were used by their pupils. The large library of Theophilus Gale has been mentioned already. A collection that rivaled Gale's belonged to John Woodhouse (d. 1700). Woodhouse obtained a considerable fortune by marrying into the opulent Hubbert family, thus enabling him to assemble rapidly an outstanding library and later to put it at the disposal of his Sheriffhales academy (1676–1697) students.[30] Besides a strong collection in the various branches of theology and philosophy, Woodhouse's library included works in the fields of mathematics, logic, history, geography, law, and anatomy. In the area of theology, Woodhouse's collection followed the common Puritan path from Calvin to Baxter and William Bates (d. 1699), but also included such diverse works as Daniel Williams's *Gospel Truth* (1692) and Bishop Wilkins's *Principles and Duties of Natural Religion* (1678). In secular fields, his library included the works of Euclid, Descartes, Heereboord, and Coke, among others, as well as a number of ground-breaking studies, including Thomas Gibson's *Anatomy of Human Bodies* (1682), Lawrence Eachard's *Compendium of Geography* (1691), and

Samuel Puffendorf's *Introduction to History*.[31] A later example of an outstanding collection is the library of John Moore (d. 1730?), not to be confused with the much persecuted John Moore of Bridgwater mentioned previously. Between 1705 and 1721 Moore recorded in his diary the systematic acquisition of works in theology, philosophy, and history, as well as of an outstanding multilanguage collection on medicine and surgery, in preparation of the opening of his Tiverton academy (1721–1729).[32]

Often a tutor would build a library that reflected an especially strong interest in a particular field. James Forbes (d. 1712), for example, had an excellent theological library and, therefore, restricted his Gloucester academy (1696–1712?) exclusively to ministerial studies.[33] Although Samuel Jones (d. 1719) opened his Tewkesbury academy (1708?–1724) to both ministerial and nonministerial students alike, he gained his reputation as an educator in the fields of Hebrew and Jewish antiquities. Of these fields, Jones's most eminent student, Thomas Secker, wrote in 1711: "We have scarce been upon any thing yet but Mr Jones has had those writers which are most valued on that head, to which he always refers us. . . . [His] library . . . is composed for the most part of foreign books, which seem to be very well chosen. . . ."[34]

Compared with those few tutors who could offer their students access to personal libraries of some substance, the number of tutors with meager collections seems to have been rather large. However, it also appears that this lack of libraries kept few tutors from running academies, and several of these academies were actually quite successful institutions.

One of the chief means of acquiring the necessary books to run an academy was with the support of various funds established by the Nonconformist leadership. These funds, which sprang up only after the Toleration Act of 1689, assisted ministry students in purchasing books and occasionally granted monies to assist tutors in the acquisition of books as well. Between 1689 and 1693 the joint Presbyterian-Independent effort, known as the Common Fund of the United Brethren, supported 100 academy students in England, while aiding smaller numbers in the academies at Edinburgh, Glasgow, and Utrecht.[35]

Support of the education of ministerial students also was carried on at the local level. The Exeter Assembly, for example, assisted pupils at Joseph Hallett's academy (1690?–1722).[36] When the Baptist leaders of Bristol saw the advantages of having a theological seminary in their city—Bristol Baptist academy, established in 1690—they quickly provided funds for the creation of a library, which soon contained "almost every production of importance upon subjects in theology."[37] Though this library remained separate from the academy, its quasi-institutional nature may have been a factor in the continuation of the academy through successive tutors, until it emerged into Bristol Baptist College in the early nineteenth century.

When available, other types of libraries and book collections were used by tutors and students who could not provide their own materials. This was the case with the academy run by John Moore and his son at Bridgwater (1688–1747, intermittently). Although Moore was harassed into closing his academy on several occasions, he was able to reopen it each time on quick notice due to the fact that his academy relied on the congregation's chapel library.[38] Similarly, John Chorlton (d. 1705) found the lack of a library no hindrance in beginning his career as a tutor; for Chorlton wisely founded his academy in Manchester (1699–1713) in order to take advantage of the Chetham Public Library. The result was a highly successful academy. A student of Chorlton's academy recalled the general procedure: "He [Chorlton] read Lectures to us in the forenoon in Philosophy and Divinity and in the afternoon [we] read in ye Publick Library."[39]

But before the Act of Toleration, and throughout the early period of academy education, it was the private library of the Puritan divine that often supplied the necessary books for Nonconformist tutors and pupils. The relationship between private library and Dissenting academy may be illustrated by noting the relationship between Oliver Heywood's private library and Richard Frankland's academy. Frankland's Rathmell academy is the most famous of the first-generation academies, having educated some 300 students, "among them being the majority of the Nonconformist ministers of the North."[40] Yet almost nothing is known about the use of books at this academy. Ashley Smith has published a scant list of thirty-four titles mentioned in the papers of a Frankland student as works read at the academy.[41] However, more information regarding the books and authors influencing Frankland's students may be obtained by consulting the holdings in Heywood's library. Heywood's two sons, John and Eliezer, attended Rathmell, and, throughout Frankland's career as tutor, Heywood remained a close friend. On many occasions Heywood would visit the academy for a day or two and "discourse" with the students. More importantly, he would bring books on loan from his library for use at the academy.[42] He also was in the habit of setting aside copies of his own newly published writings for Frankland. In this way, Frankland, like many other tutors, was able to acquire such works as *Life in God's Favour* (1679), *Father Angier's Life* (1684), and *Heavenly Concourse* (1697) for his academy at no cost.[43]

A partial impression of what was available to the Rathmell students may be gathered from an early catalog of Heywood's library, recorded a few years before Frankland opened his academy.[44] Reflecting both the interest of a Puritan leader and the ultimate vocation of most of Frankland's pupils, the strength of Heywood's library was in the area of seventeenth-century religious controversy. As could be expected, Richard Baxter's writings dominated with nineteen titles, followed by twelve works authored by Joseph Hall (d. 1656), the onetime bishop of Norwich, whose writing had been suppressed by the Stuarts during the pre-Civil War period.[45] Several of the more famous academy tutors also were represented, including Thomas Goodwin, James Forbes, Samuel Cradock, Thomas Doolittle, and Theophilus Gale. Among older theological writers, the library contained the works of Ambrose, Bede, Aquinas, Luther, Erasmus, and Calvin. The importance of scriptural study to the Puritan was manifest in the collection's two Latin Bibles, two Greek Testaments, two concordances, four Hebrew grammars, and a half-dozen lexicons. In the area of the classics, however, Heywood's library was less complete, containing only the works of Aristotle and Seneca and the orations of Demosthenes. Other titles available to the Rathmell students through Heywood's library included numerous "histories" and "lives," works on physics, logic, and "human learning," and a few books on popery and witchcraft.

Heywood not only lent books from his library to Frankland and the Rathmell students, but he seems to have opened it up to so many that it could be regarded as a sort of "lending" library. At any one time, twenty to thirty titles would be in circulation.[46] Indeed, the circulation of books among Dissenters was an important means of spreading the printed word to those unable to purchase reading material. As a student at Kibworth academy (1715–1723), Doddridge expressed a desire for a better library.[47] The circulation of books from the libraries of wealthy Dissenters helped fill his reading requirements. Recounting his reading activities to a friend, Doddridge wrote: "The New Testament I read in the Original without any commentator; but more of my time is spent in the Old, for I would willingly finish Patrick's Commentary before it is taken from Kibworth, which will be in a few months."[48] The reading needs of his Gloucester community prompted academy tutor James Forbes to transform his outstanding theological library into a circulating library. By his will, Forbes established a trust:

> to permit the Dissenting Protestant Ministers wh[o] sh[oul]d succeed the said James Forbes and live in the said city to use [his library] and at their discretion to lend one book at a time to any of the Protestant Ministers in the County of Gloucester or to any of the Protestant Dissenting Congregation in the said city so as they return it within a month.[49]

It was in London, however, that the circulation of books from the private libraries of Puritan divines was most prevalent. In the early years of Nonconformist education, the need for cooperation had been greatly increased by the London fire of 1666, which not only destroyed "most of the libraries of ministers, conformable and nonconformable, in the city," but also "the libraries of many Nonconformists of the country, which had been lately brought up to the city."[50] Within a few years, some of the great private libraries of the Dissenters were rebuilt. The library of Thomas Goodwin, partially destroyed by the fire, was still the most impressive tutor's library in London.[51] But for every tutor in London with a library of even modest holdings, there were scores with virtually no books at all. These "bookless" tutors relied on the generosity of Puritan divines such as Lazarus Seaman and Thomas Jacomb. Seaman (d. 1685) and Jacomb (d. 1687) had each collected a valuable library that was used by ministers, tutors, and students.[52]

Through a variety of means, then, the tutors and students of the early Dissenting academies were able to acquire the books necessary to the maintenance of Nonconformist education during the years of persecution and institutional instability following the Great Ejection. Although the early academies lacked institutional libraries and were subjected to much state and local harassment, Dissenting tutors and students were able to overcome these adversities on most occasions through access to chapel, public, and private libraries. Indeed, the readiness with which the Puritan divines opened their private libraries for use by the academies stands as a key factor not only in the mere survival of Dissenting education, but in the actual expansion of the Nonconformist intellectual tradition at a time when university education was denied to future generations of Dissenters. As a consequence, and although in short supply and poorly distributed among Dissenting educators, books and libraries were accessible to most segments within Nonconformist education.

Notes

1. Quoted in Gerald R. Cragg, *Puritanism in the Period of the Great Persecution, 1660–1688* (Cambridge: Cambridge University Press, 1957), p. 148.
2. A. G. Matthews, *Calamy Revised: Being a Revision of Edmund Calamy's Account of the Ministers and Others Ejected and Silenced, 1660–2* (Oxford: Clarendon Press, 1934), p. 259.
3. Oliver Heywood, *The Rev. Oliver Heywood, B.A. 1630–1702: His Autobiography, Diaries, Anecdote and Event Books; Illustrating the General and Family History of Yorkshire and Lancashire*, ed. J. Horsfall Turner (Leeds: A. B. Bayer, 1881–1885), III: 219.
4. Walter Wilson, *The History and Antiquities of Dissenting Churches and Meeting Houses, in London, Westminster and Southwark: Including the Lives of Their Ministers,*

From the Rise of Nonconformity to the Present Time (London: Printed for the author, 1808–1814), I: 219.

5. Geoffrey F. Nuttall, "Richard Baxter and Philip Doddridge: A Study in a Tradition," Fifth Lecture, Friends of Dr. Williams's Library (London, 1951), p. 14.

6. Henry Morley (ed.), *The Earlier Life and the Chief Earlier Works of Daniel Defoe* (London: G. Routledge, 1889), p. 16.

7. Quoted in J. W. Ashley Smith, *The Birth of Modern Education: The Contribution of the Dissenting Academies 1660–1800* (London: Independent, 1954), p. 30. See also Matthews, *Calamy Revised*, p. 125.

8. Herbert McLachlan, *English Education under the Test Acts: Being the History of the Nonconformist Academies* (Manchester: Manchester University Press, 1931), p. 15.

9. Joshua Toulmin, *An Historical View of the State of the Protestant Dissenters in England, and of the Progress of Free Enquiry and Religious Liberty, from the Revolution to the Accession of Queen Anne* (London: Longman, Hurst, Rees, Orme, and Browne, 1814), p. 240. See also Matthews, *Calamy Revised*, p. 141.

10. McLachlan, *English Education under the Test Acts*, p. 43.

11. Quoted in ibid., p. 42.

12. This library was established at the Northampton academy (1729–1751) of Philip Doddridge, ibid., p. 43; A. Victor Murray, "Doddridge and Education," *Philip Doddridge, 1702–51: His Contribution to English Religion*, ed. Geoffrey F. Nuttall (London: Independent Press, 1951), pp. 103–104; Irene Parker, *Dissenting Academies in England: Their Rise and Progress and Their Place among the Educational Systems of the Country* (Cambridge: Cambridge University Press, 1914), p. 151.

13. Thomas Kelly, *Public Libraries in Great Britain before 1850*, pamphlet no. 26 (London: Library Association, 1966), p. 19.

14. Parker, *Dissenting Academies in England*; McLachlan, *English Education under the Test Acts*; Ashley Smith, *Birth of Modern Education.*

15. Quoted in John T. Wilkinson, *1662 and After: Three Centuries of English Nonconformity* (London: Epworth Press, 1962), p. 105.

16. Ibid., pp. 104–105.

17. Jerom Murch, *A History of the Presbyterian and General Baptist Churches in the West of England: With Memoirs of Some of Their Pastors* (London: Hunter, 1835), p. 178.

18. Quoted in Herbert S. Skeats and Charles S. Miall, *History of the Free Churches of England, 1688–1891* (London: Alexander and Shepheard, 1891), p. 161.

19. McLachlan, *English Education under the Test Acts*, p. 7. For persecution under Anne, see R. W. Dale, *History of English Congregationalism*, ed. A. W. W. Dale (London: Hodder and Stoughton, 1907), pp. 503–504; Wilkinson, *1662 and After*, pp. 105–107.

20. Hugh Owen, *Some Account of the Ancient and Present State of Shrewsbury* (Shrewsbury: P. Sandford, 1808), p. 317.

21. Nicholas Hans, "The Puritan Tradition in Education," *Year Book of Education* (London: Evans Bros., 1938), p. 823.

22. Geoffrey F. Nuttall, "A Transcript of Richard Baxter's Library Catalogue: A Bibliographical Note," *Journal of Ecclesiastical History* 2/2 (1951): 207–208; Richard Baxter, *The Autobiography of Richard Baxter*, ed. N. H. Keeble (London: J. M. Dent and Sons, 1931), pp. 232, 235, 251, 254.

23. Heywood, *Autobiography*, II: 128.

24. Wilson, *History and Antiquities of Dissenting Churches*, I: 236.
25. Ashley Smith, *Birth of Modern Education*, p. 81.
26. Ibid., p. 10; Matthews, *Calamy Revised*, p. 216.
27. Matthews, *Calamy Revised*, p. 216. Charles E. Whiting, *Studies in English Puritanism from the Restoration to the Revolution, 1660–1688* (London: Society for Promoting Christian Knowledge, 1931), p. 456.
28. Thomas Kelly, *A History of Adult Education in Great Britain*, 2nd ed. (Liverpool: Liverpool University Press, 1970), p. 45.
29. Murray, "Doddridge and Education," pp. 108–109.
30. Matthews, *Calamy Revised*, p. 544; Wilson, *History and Antiquities of Dissenting Churches*, I: 371–372.
31. McLachlan, *English Education under the Test Acts*, pp. 46–47; Toulmin, *Historical View of the State of the Protestant Dissenters*, pp. 227–228. Woodhouse's academy was not typical of the period. While most tutors conducted courses for no more than a half-dozen students, Woodhouse enrolled between thirty and fifty students at a time, maintained three assistant tutors, and housed them all in his Shropshire mansion (see McLachlan, pp. 24, 45, 48–49).
32. McLachlan, *English Education under the Test Acts*, p. 14.
33. Matthews, *Calamy Revised*, p. 205.
34. Thomas Secker to Isaac Watts, 18 November 1711; Thomas Gibbons, *Memoirs of Isaac Watts* (London: James Buckland, 1780), pp. 350–351. Ashley Smith has noted that Jones studied in Leyden and that his library probably was collected on the basis of his Dutch educational experience, Ashley Smith, *Birth of Modern Education*, pp. 84–85.
35. Hans, "Puritan Tradition in Education," p. 822. The two denominations separated in 1693, with each establishing a fund.
36. Allan Brockett, *Non-conformity in Exeter, 1650–1875* (Manchester: Manchester University Press, 1962), pp. 66–67.
37. John Evans, *The History of Bristol, Civil and Ecclesiastical: Including Biographical Notices of Eminent and Distinguished Natives* (Bristol: W. Sheppard, 1816), I: 336.
38. Murch, *History of the Presbyterian and General Baptist Churches*, pp. 177–178, 184.
39. Quoted in Ashley Smith, *Birth of Modern Education*, pp. 105–106.
40. Matthews, *Calamy Revised*, p. 212.
41. Ashley Smith, *Birth of Modern Education*, pp. 269–270.
42. Heywood, *Autobiography*, II: 97, 100, 184, 189.
43. Ibid., pp. 211–212, 215–216.
44. Ibid., pp. 124–128. Heywood's inventory, entitled "A Catalogue of My Bookes," consists of 258 randomly entered titles with prices.
45. On Hall, see Christopher Hill, *The Century of Revolution, 1603–1714* (Edinburgh: T. Nelson, 1961), p. 98.
46. Heywood, *Autobiography*, III: 65, editor's note.
47. Ashley Smith, *Birth of Modern Education*, p. 132.
48. Quoted in John Waddington, *Congregational History, 1700–1800: In Relation to Contemporaneous Events, Education, the Eclipse of Faith, Revivals, and Christian Missions* (London: Longmans, Green and Co., 1876), p. 275.
49. Quoted in Matthews, *Calamy Revised*, p. 205.
50. Baxter, *Autobiography*, pp. 198–199. The existence of the "country" libraries in London at the time of the fire may be explained by Baxter's earlier remark that "when the plague grew hot most of the conformable ministers

fled,'' and the spiritual needs of the citizenry were met by an influx of Dissenting ministers (see ibid., p. 196).

51. Wilson, *History and Antiquities of Dissenting Churches*, I: 218–219.

52. Ibid., III: 12, 19.

Sheldon's Serial Sermons

Jonathan A. Lindsey

Charles M. Sheldon produced thirty volumes of sermons while he was pastor of Central Congregational Church, Topeka, Kansas. Fourteen were produced between 1891 and 1900 and reflect the social and theological mores of that decade. Sheldon's sermons provide insights into evangelical piety, social responsibility, personal responsibility, and other questions. These sermons are unique because he chose the story format. Each of the books is a complete novel or novella, read to his congregation on successive Sunday nights. The best known, *In His Steps* (1896), is still in print with at least thirteen editions. This paper places the volumes produced between 1891 and 1900 into a personal and social context, reflects the primary content of each, and raises questions of relevance.

Charles M. Sheldon was a prominent Congregational minister in the late nineteenth and early twentieth centuries who used a unique approach in homiletics: the serial sermon. That approach was preserved in thirty volumes of sermons. If you recognize Sheldon by name, it is probably on the basis of your acquaintance with one volume, *In His Steps, Or What Would Jesus Do?* I have chosen for this paper to examine Sheldon's sermon production during the decade 1891–1900, looking at a biographical and cultural context, reviewing in broad strokes the issues and content addressed in the sermons, considering publication experiences, and raising some questions of relevance. First, the biographical context.

Who Was Charles M. Sheldon?

Sheldon was born 26 February 1857 in Wallsville, New York, son and grandson of Congregational ministers. His boyhood was spent in several locations in New York, Rhode Island, Missouri, Michigan, and South Dakota. He was educated at Phillips Academy, Brown Univer-

Jonathan A. Lindsey *is coordinator of library affairs, Baylor University.*

sity, and Andover Theological Seminary. Following graduation in 1886 from Andover, he spent a summer in England and then began his ministry in Waterbury, Vermont, as pastor of the Congregational Church. He was called to the Central Congregational Church, Topeka, 1888, and began his tenure there in 1889. Sheldon married Merriam Ward, whom he met in his first parish, in 1891, and they had one son, Stewart. He served the Central Congregational Church until 1912, when he became minister at large, and served again as its pastor from 1915 to 1919. He spent 1920–1924 as editor of the *Christian Herald*, returned to Topeka, and remained there until his death on 24 February 1946. In addition to his pastoral work he was active in prohibition causes. He attended four international conferences on prohibition between 1900 and 1918, in Great Britain, Australia, and New Zealand.

Sheldon's autobiography is a primary source for information about his activity.[1] Readers today will not find it to be a gripping narrative, but it does provide a source for seeing some of his activity from his perspective. Out of the autobiography comes a picture of a man who was devoted to a single profession: the parish ministry.

Topeka, Kansas, Early 1890s

Another way to place Sheldon into an historical and cultural context is from a knowledge of the locale in which he functioned. To gain a glimpse into this approach, the *Topeka Daily Capital*, one of four dailies, provided some data, supported by census data from 1890 and 1900.[2]

Commerce, industry, agriculture, and education are all part of the picture that emerges from a review of the *Topeka Daily Capital*. It appeared to be a growing city, not following reported depression in other parts of the United States. The newspaper reflected awareness of national and some international events, but it was primarily regional in its orientation. All of these factors, however, form a sense of the cultural milieu in which Sheldon functioned. The single issue of prohibition occurred frequently. By popular referendum Kansas declared itself an antisaloon state in 1880, but the enforcement of that decision was a continuing problem, referred to regularly in the content of Sheldon's sermons.

On 1 January 1890 the *Capital* reported the claim that Topeka was the milling center for the West, and that the $2,000,000 produced by the mills in 1889 was the best year yet. Exports to Liverpool were noted. The seven banks in Topeka reported $2,061,000 in capital stock, with a $459,014 surplus, and loans and discounts of $3,157,137. The population of Topeka in 1877 was 8,494; in 1889 it was 38,000. Two thousand new buildings at a cost of $2,000,000 were built in 1889, even though the rest of the United States experienced a depression.

The *Capital* reported that Washburn College had an enrollment of 250 students, and that three parochial schools—Sisters of Bethany (girls only), Catholic School, and German School—enrolled more than 800 students. In addition, two unnamed business schools were listed, and the Methodist Church had purchased 1,000 acres for the University of Topeka.

In 1880 Topeka recorded 390 marriages; in 1889, 481 marriages. The library report indicated that 900 books were added to the collection, 783 cards were issued, 47 of which were on the basis of a $3.00–$5.00 deposit, and circulation for the year was 46,810, plus 1,617 recorded in-house uses.[3]

The 1 June 1890 *Capital* carried a half-page advertisement for the Twelfth Annual Chatauqua Assembly, at which R. H. Conwell and J. C. Price would be featured speakers.[4] The Prohibition Convention was scheduled for 12 July 1890.[5] The 17 July issue carried this headline series:

> The People Speak
> They declare against the Supreme Court's Whiskey decision
> The largest delegate convention ever assembled in the state
> The people determined that the saloon shall not be reinstated
> Rum in original packages or any other form cannot come into Kansas[6]

In 1891 the newspaper raised the issue of child labor. One-third of the 76 counties of Kansas reported that the school attendance law was inadequate. Fifty-six of the counties favored an age minimum of fifteen years for work in the mines, factories, and other workshop industry; 70 of the 76 counties favored compulsory education.[7] On 9 January 1891 the newspaper reported favorably on the Vermillion, South Dakota, post office decision not to distribute *Plain Folk* because it contained an advertisement for a music box raffle.[8] And the 5 March 1891 issue defended women who attend medical school.[9]

The churches of Topeka were encouraged by the editor of the *Topeka Daily Capital* to provide weekly notices for the newspaper. In the 5 April 1891 issue, as part of other narrative about church activities, is the statement: "Rev. C. M. Sheldon will speak tonight on 'The Newspaper as a Field for Young Men.'"[10] There is no listing of the Central Congregational Church among the churches until 5 May 1891.[11] On 5 April, however, the list included nine Methodist churches, two Baptist, two Presbyterian, and one each Lutheran, Spiritual Unitarian, German Lutheran, Spiritualist Society, New Jerusalem, Cumberland Presbyterian, and Congregational. The Episcopal church had no listing that week, but it did appear regularly in the other issues of the newspaper. Reviews of the *Topeka Daily Capital* included little local religious news other than the weekly notices.

Published Sermons

The publication of sermons is a phenomenon in American Protestantism. It was popular in the nineteenth century, and has continued into the twentieth. The best-known preachers in America have allowed their sermons to be published, and they have experienced varying success. Certain publishing houses have specialized in sermon publication, such as Fleming H. Revell and Eerdmans, as well as Moody. Mainline publishers like Harper and Row have also provided some outlet for sermon publication. Today Word, Inc., Waco, Texas, is a primary publisher of sermons in the evangelical tradition.

During his active ministry Sheldon produced thirty volumes of sermons. But Sheldon's corpus was different from the traditional form of published homiletics. "I found that sermonic preparation reached a limited number of hearers, and the printed page many more."[12] He said further:

> I found also a real mental relief to turn from the sermonic and homiletic style of sermon preparation to the story form. I also think it lies within the reach of any man whose business in life is expressing thought in speech to learn to do the same thing for print, and thus enlarge his parish and remove the feeling of limitation of one's audience as confined to the members that he faces from the pulpit.
>
> But there is another reason for the use of writing apart from the relief from the didactic or sermonic style, and that is the enlarged range of subjects that can be treated in a story form as compared with the sermon form. It is true that the love chapter of life can be told in a sermon and preached from a pulpit, but not with the freedom possible in a story, or by the use of fiction to illustrate the theme. The sermon, in the nature of its composition, is restricted to the conduct of the human in his relation to God and his neighbor. The evolution of this theme may take the preacher very far afield, but it is necessarily limited in the use of incident and adventure. The story form allows of more latitude and the listener expects more detail than would be allowed to a sermon without the criticism that the matter is being "lugged" in to fit the text. Whether I am right in this philosophy of the story for teaching certain vital

> things like love and the social side of life, it has at any rate been a great relief to my mental needs to turn from the sermon to the story form of teaching.[13]

Sheldon wrote his first book, *Richard Bruce*, in 1891, in order to say some particular things to young people. The personal pleasure that the story format provided Sheldon was a strong reason for its perpetuation in his ministry.[14] Sheldon's attitude toward writing was probably in a continual tension with the other demands that he experienced as his church grew from less than 100 members in its first year to 1,000 in the 1920s. One of the constants in that growth was the serial sermon.

The American Catalog, 1890–95 listed four publications by Sheldon, each selling from $0.90 to $1.50.[15] In 1903 *The United States Catalog, Books in Print, 1902* listed nineteen publications, the most expensive of which sold for $1.50. Many paperback titles were $0.25, $0.50, or $0.75. Nineteen editions of *In His Steps* were reported, with the next highest number of editions being *Robert Hardy* with seven.[16] By 1912 his list of available titles was twenty-one, with *In His Steps* showing twelve available editions and *Robert Hardy* showing five.[17] The *National Union Catalog Pre-1956 Imprints* provides a record for thirty-three English editions of *In His Steps*, ten for *Robert Hardy's Seven Days*, and seven for the *Crucifixion of Philip Strong*.[18]

Sheldon's Serial Sermons

For the purpose of this paper I have limited an evaluation of Sheldon's serial sermons to the fourteen series produced between 1891 and 1900. Two reasons exist for this limitation: (1) the decade of the 1890s provides a block of productivity that is extended into the second decade of Sheldon's work, with little or no change in emphasis; (2) access to almost all materials has been via interlibrary loan. The fourteen titles produced between 1891 and 1900 were all available, while thirteen titles of the post-1900 works could not be located for review for this paper.

When Sheldon arrived in Topeka, his task was to build a church. In the early days of his ministry the congregation met above a meat market, with fewer than a hundred members in its first year. Sheldon set out to recruit a larger congregation. He organized a Christian Endeavor Society, which in a short time was composed of 150 young adults and college students. Later, the church was located on the edge of the residential district in Topeka, and the area around the church was said to have been sparsely populated. Sheldon was discouraged because of low attendance at the Sunday evening service. He decided to try the approach of writing a story in parts, reading a part each week. Before he completed the first series, Sheldon's Sunday evening worship services were filled to capacity, with the Christian Endeavor Society attending en bloc.[19] The approach was novel, the response mutually satisfying. In 1891 *Richard Bruce or The Life That Now Is* began a phenomenon among sermons. Sheldon's first series has four principal characters: Richard Bruce, a young writer; Tom Howard, Bruce's college friend, a reporter; John King, a minister; and Adam Tower, a labor organizer.

Sheldon based the plot on the relationship between Richard and Tom. Richard writes for the artistic needs met through writing; Tom is a reporter for one of the newspapers. One of the moral dilemmas faced by Richard is whether he should write for a sensational publication. He takes a story to the editor and it is published, but he returns the check. Richard is the confessing Christian in the story. Tom is not. Sheldon pictures them in a Jonathan/David type of friendship. This is acted out through the loss of Richard's first major manuscript in a rooming house fire; Tom is stabbed through the hand by a roughneck in a tenement night school operated by John King; Richard takes Tom's job, but then loses it because he refuses to work on Sunday. When Tom can return to his reporter's job, he subsequently loses it because he, too, refuses Sunday assignments.

This novel introduces a number of themes that Sheldon addressed for the rest of his life. Through the situation of the novel, Sheldon described the tenements of an 1890s mill town in the Midwest; the gulf between the affluent and the poverty-stricken; the social evils of the day, particularly alcohol and tobacco; the proper role of the church in society; and the impact a single individual could have if responsive and faithful to an encounter with Jesus Christ. This last item is illustrated by Sheldon through the person of Adam Tower, a union leader, and the effect of a revival on stalemated union negotiations. Tower loses his power over the workers because of an amicable settlement. He is infuriated with John King, whom he perceives as the agent of his loss of influence. In a private meeting between the two men in King's home, King confronts Tower with his ego and his loss of leadership, but respects his religious skepticism.

Sheldon's first serialized sermons combined the story motif with a realistic setting. He spoke about conditions faced by all sorts of people and systematically set out to learn about their daily lives. He spent several weeks dressed in workmen's clothes, making the rounds trying to find a job, and never gained employment. Nor was his masquerade discovered until he revealed it. Through various means Sheldon made it his business to know at firsthand how people lived and the problems they faced. These insights were translated into his stories. Sheldon's first story focused primarily on the needs of the working classes; his second focused on the needs of the affluent. These two poles are reflected in each story series that he produced.

Since *Richard Bruce* was successful in 1891, Sheldon's second sermon series took place in the spring of 1892. There is one chapter that is only half-a-page long. Church was canceled that night because of an unusually bad rainstorm![20] *Robert Hardy's Seven Days* addresses personal selfishness, Sunday labor, labor/management relations in the railroad industry, alcohol and gambling, personal suffering, and personal salvation. This story has a Job-like theme, never referred to specifically, but, in a biblically literate culture, the parallel could be noted. The difference, however, is that while Job was righteous and faithful in the face of intense personal suffering, Robert Hardy never approaches the true level of Job's righteousness. He is a characterization of the official Christian frightened by a confrontation with his own death. One of Hardy's final acts, a profuse apology to the 800 + men employed in the railyard, articulated the impact of Christian experience on an individual. The story ends with Robert Hardy surrounded by his family, kneeling in prayer, the clock having struck midnight of the seventh day. "He continued kneeling there, nearer God than he had ever been in all his life before. Thus Robert Hardy's seven days came to an end."[21]

The Twentieth Door, read during the winter of 1892–1893, is an autobiographical treatment of college life. The descriptions of academic life are Sheldon's acknowledged reconstructions of events he experienced at Phillips Academy, where he spent "five of the happiest years" of his life.[22] *The Crucifixion of Philip Strong* (1893) is the story of a young clergyman who faces issues such as right/wrong uses of property, evils of the saloon, Sabbath observance, relation of church to tenements, need for a simple lifestyle, integrated church membership, and proper uses of wealth. In this series Sheldon raised for the first time the question: "Would Jesus Christ, if he were the pastor of the Calvary Church in Milton today, speak of this matter next Sunday, and speak regardless of all consequences?"[23]

John King's Question Class (1894) continues the story of Richard Bruce and Tom Howard, and ends with each of them married. The dramatic element in the series revolves around Victoria Stanwood, a talented violinist; her twin brother Victor, equally talented, but dissipated, which leads to his eventual self-destruction; and Victoria's romance with Richard Bruce. The questions provide a snapshot of Victorian middle-class morality and piety in evangelical circles. They treat smoking, dancing, selfishness, existence of a personal devil, lynch laws, and eighty-five other subjects in a random fashion. Young people in the church handed questions to Sheldon each Sunday evening, and he answered them in the following Sunday's serial sermon.

His Brother's Keeper (1895) was based on the miners' strike of the summer of 1895. It is a story of intense experiences centered around the questions of who suffers most in a labor dispute, stewardship of money, and responsible commitments to friends; and portrays a protagonist in the character of Dr. Saxon, the nonbeliever but the true servant. Unique in this volume are lyrics to five Salvation Army songs. This series stands out among all the others for the development of writing skill, characterization, and being less "preachy." *In His Steps, or What Would Jesus Do?* (1896) is the volume for which Sheldon is best known, and through which his literary fame continues to be promulgated. In it he returned to more familiar themes of the power of personal salvation on the life and actions of an individual. Each of the primary characters agrees to act for one year on the basis of a personal response to the question, "What would Jesus do?" The Christian newspaper first mentioned in *Richard Bruce* takes a prominent role. The evil of the saloon is prominent, alongside responsibility for the poor. In *Malcolm Kirk: A Tale of Moral Heroism in Overcoming the World* (1897), Sheldon set out a portrait of the ideal minister, whose life is devoted to one parish and who subverts personal ambition. Besides the evils of alcohol, one social problem treated in this series is the plight of young working girls, both those seeking a profession and those whose work is domestic.

Several short works fill out the corpus near the end of the decade. *Lend a Hand* (1897) speaks to responsible use of one's possessions as Judge Brewster's grief for his son is worked out by loaning his personal library to a couple of young people who are taking a Chautauqua course. *The Redemption of Freetown* presents action resulting in the building of a settlement house, the *sine qua non* of the institutional church in the 1890s. In *The Miracle at Markham*, Sheldon addressed the question of denominationalism and ecumenicity through an examination of the need for cooperation among the churches of a mythical Markham. The list of churches in Markham nearly paralleled the list in the *Topeka Daily Capital* in the early 1890s. The focus for the churches' common action is temperance.

One of the Two (1899) is a different piece, because it portrays a contest between Good and Evil for the soul of a newborn. The strong sense of personal responsibility, however, which permeates all of Sheldon's work, is reflected in the conclusion. "For the eternal struggle between Love and Hate goes on as the earth rolls around the sun, and whether one or the other wins at last may depend upon my conduct, upon my influence, upon my character; for I myself am either the Angel of Love or the Demon of Hate to some new-born soul of humanity. I am one of the two."[24]

For Christ and the Church (1899) also is different from previous series, because it does not contain alcohol or institutional church issues. The sermons are an examination of the commitment of church members to activities of the church or the pledge of Endeavor Society members to support midweek prayer services. The literary device is an interview with the devil.

The final volume of the decade, *Edward Blake: College Student* (1900), was written with "special reference to the students of Washburn College, Topeka, who make up the majority of young people in my church."[25] Edward Blake is not a professing Christian; yet he is the product of a soundly Christian environment. Blake deals with dashed hopes, college finances, his own integrity, self-conceit, alcohol and gambling as well as card-playing, the Spanish American War, and the abuse of power by a college trustee. Blake suffers immense guilt over his fascination for the theater, where he "lost his sense of personal purity."[26] Even sex was treated with an assertion that "The life of students at Hope College was remarkably free from any foolish, sentimental or harmful love-making."[27] But Blake comes through as the quintessential good person.

This review of fourteen of Sheldon's corpus fails to capture the real flavor of his literary product. Generally his writing was free from strain. He appears to have the knack of the storyteller. Also, the stories are generally free of Biblical references, except in a volume that has one of the characters preaching. There is enough detail to allow the reader to picture the event in the description of a town, a tenement, or the fire among the mines in *His Brother's Keeper*. Sheldon generally knew the value of sustained suspense and worked at that feature to include a sense of completeness in each episode, yet provide the appropriate links to tie the episodes together. There are many autobiographical sources for the novels. Those dealing with education call directly on Sheldon's experiences at Phillips, Brown, and Andover. Those dealing with the ideal minister reflect his strong commitment to the parish, but also the pulls of other professional opportunities. His fascination with the idea of a Christian newspaper was finally acted out in March 1900, when for one week Sheldon assumed editorial direction of the *Topeka Daily Capital*, and circulation rose to 367,000 with production in several cities.

Publication of the Sermons

Sheldon's serial sermons were written first for Sunday night services as a means of instructing without formal preaching. Some were distributed serially through the *Advance* (Chicago) and through publications of the Congregational Sunday School and Publishing Society. As monographs, the works were distributed by a variety of publishers: David C. Cook, Fleming H. Revell, Advance Publishing, Frederick L. Chapman, United Society of Christian Endeavor, and Congregational Sunday School and Publishing Society. The editions were inexpensive and meant for a mass market, as can be seen from a scan of the lists in *The United States Catalog, 1902*.

In His Steps was serialized in the *Advance*, but only the first unit was sent to the copyright office. This constituted a faulty copyright, so that when the serialization was complete, publishers reset the book and put out their own editions, without regard for the author.

Sheldon's autobiography commented at length on the publishing history of *In His Steps.*[28] There appears to be no rancor from the irony that publishers of religious materials used a technicality to deprive him of a royalty for his best-known work. In 1925 Sheldon reported that three publishers rejected *In His Steps* when the serialization in the *Advance*, for which he was paid $75.00, was complete. The *Advance* did agree to publish some $0.10 paper copies, and that copy was the base for sixteen publishers to issue the book in the second half of 1897. In 1925 Sheldon calculated that 8,000,000 copies had been sold! My copy, copyrighted by Pyramid in 1960, and in a sixth printing in 1969, carries the legend on the cover "The most widely read religious novel of all time. Over 8,000,000 copies sold!"[29]

Frank Luther Mott in *Golden Multitudes* says that *His Brother's Keeper* was the first of the serialized sermons of Sheldon.[30] This work was his sixth. Mott may have meant that *His Brother's Keeper* was the first to be published serially, but that is questionable, since the Congregational Sunday School and Publishing Society copyrighted *Richard Bruce* in 1892, and three publishers offered five editions with prices ranging from $0.25 to $0.75 in 1902. Today only *In His Steps* is available, except from the secondhand market.

An OCLC search for copies of Sheldon's work reveals no central location. Many are collected at Washburn University, Topeka, but I obtained one copy from University of Texas/Arlington, and one from Drew University. Few public libraries show a holding of a Sheldon work. Primarily they are in scattered colleges and universities, historical societies, and an occasional copy in a theological library.

By 1912 public interest in the Sheldon corpus was apparently low. He continued writing throughout his lifetime, but the impact of his serialized sermons reached its mark in the flood of the market with *In His Steps.* The popularity of that publication, however, eclipsed the others. Today's public is unaware of the larger corpus of which this title was a single manifestation.

The Significance of Sheldon Today

Why is the work of Charles M. Sheldon of any concern nearly 100 years after he began his approach of the serial sermon? This question is not easy to answer, but is certainly worth consideration. One of the most obvious reasons for considering Sheldon's sermons is the record of late-nineteenth-century culture and piety they represent. The 1890s are a fascinating decade filled with contrasts. Until the end of World War II, American culture was heavily influenced by the impact of that single decade. The energetic struggle of developing industry and the inevitable contrasts of economic extremes are preserved within the novels. The Kansas struggle to maintain a strong line on prohibition permeates the novels, and the political realities in which well-meaning persons could get caught is represented. Since the series is intended for instruction, however, the essential morality of the mainline evangelical traditions is reflected. The evangelical churches of this decade were confronted with social tasks that were different. Models for social change were based on individuals. This kind of modeling for social change followed the emulation of economic titans.

Uniquely, however, the material represented by the Sheldon corpus provides a picture of Victorian piety, with all its conflicts. The picture is certainly a middle-class picture, but the original audience was certainly a middle-class audience. As a type of social history, and certainly of social commentary, the writings provide a view of the culture of both the preacher and his congregation.

This paper has not been aimed at a detailed analysis of the issues treated in the series, although they have been mentioned. A more comprehensive analysis, however, would provide evidence for the concern that is reflected in the sermons. Alcohol and tobacco are both socially and religiously taboo. But, among the subjects treated by Sheldon, were you surprised to note questions concerning the professional role of women and the question of an integrated church membership? Incidentally, *Edward Blake* reflects some of the same campus tensions as those faced today: the dominant influence of intercollegiate athletics, the power of trustees, and faculty-student relationships.

Sheldon's twentieth-century corpus has not been examined in this writing. It follows, however, the same lines of his nineteenth-century works. His intense involvement in antialcohol movements continued. His mark was made by the end of the 1890s, and he spent the next four and a half decades being a spokesperson and elder statesman for prohibition and evangelical piety.

The one series of sermons, written on his front porch in the 100 degree heat of a Kansas summer, *In His Steps*, continues to be available in at least thirteen editions.[31] I have found it in use as parallel reading for a business ethics course in a Texas community college.

Tentatively, I would suggest that a review of Sheldon's corpus can provide some insight into the ideology of the present-day religious right. The distrust of plurality in both the piety of the 1890s and present-day religious conservatism is parallel. The piety of both is also grounded in the intense individualism of the personal religious experience and the sociocultural responsibilities of the redeemed individual. In the 1890s and 1980s, "What would Jesus do?" is a fundamental question.

For the social historian, this study is a beginning. To tackle the questions of social history that are relevant requires a complete reading of the *Topeka Daily Capital* and an awareness of the economic and social history of Topeka, Kansas, and the Midwest from about 1880 to 1940. For the theologian, the study is a beginning, because the essay does not treat in detail the religious questions (both theological and ethical) that are raised in the body of writings. Sheldon can be seen as one highly influenced by the teachings of the social gospel in the 1890s and as one who reflects one response to that emphasis in Protestant theology. For the book historian, this essay may be superficial, since it has not detailed the publishing history of Sheldon's work. For *In His Steps* this has already been done,[32] and for the others it is not that relevant. This has provided the opportunity, however, to place *In His Steps* into a broader context of Sheldon's body of work, so that it is not seen singularly.

But, as a type of literature, the Sheldon corpus should be examined as a phenomenon among religious novels. There is one distinction that must be maintained even in an examination of Sheldon's work as a novelist: the intent of the writer. Sheldon self-consciously used the serialized story form as a homiletic tool. His primary purpose was to instruct, to edify, and, in religious terms, to bring sinners under conviction. Thus, among collections of sermons, these novels are unique.

Appendix: Chronological List of Sheldon's Serial Sermons, 1891–1900

1891 *Richard Bruce or The Life That Now Is*. Chicago: Advance Publishing Co., 1898. © 1892. Congregational Sunday School and Publishing Society.

1892 *Robert Hardy's Seven Days: A Dream and Its Consequences*. Chicago: D. C. Cook, 1900.

1893 *The Twentieth Door*. Chicago: Advance Publishing Co., 1898. © 1893. Congregational Sunday School and Publishing Co.

1893 *The Crucifixion of Philip Strong*. Philadelphia: Henry Altemus Co., n.d.

1894 *John King's Question Class*. Chicago: Advance Publishing Co., 1899.

1895 *His Brother's Keeper, or Christian Stewardship*. Chicago: Advance Publishing Co., 1898. © 1896. Congregational Sunday School and Publishing Society.

1896 *In His Steps, Or What Would Jesus Do?* New York: Pyramid, 1960.

1897 *Malcolm Kirk: A Tale of Moral Heroism in Overcoming the World*. Chicago: The Church Press, 1898. © Frederick L. Chapman.

1897 *Lend a Hand*. Chicago: Fleming H. Revell, 1899.

1898 *The Redemption of Freetown*. Boston: United Society of Christian Endeavor, n.d.
1898 *The Miracle at Markam: How Twelve Churches Became One*. Chicago: The Church Press, 1899. © Frederick L. Chapman.
1898 *One of the Two*. Chicago: Fleming H. Revell, 1898.
1899 *For Christ and the Church*. Chicago: Fleming H. Revell, 1899.
1899–1900 *Edward Blake: College Student*. Chicago: Advance Publishing Co., 1900.

Notes

1. Charles M. Sheldon, *Charles M. Sheldon, His Life Story* (New York: George H. Doran, 1925).
2. *Topeka Daily Capital* (microfilm), issues cited. The Emporia State University Library, Emporia, Kansas, kindly loaned microfilm of this newspaper. See the following census data: Department of the Interior, Census Office, *Report of Manufacturing Industries in The United States at the Eleventh Census, 1880* (Washington, D.C.: Government Printing Office, 1895), 12: part II, 12–13, 584-587; *Report of the Population of the United States, Part I . . . 1895*, pp. 154, 458, 531,, 592-595, 798, 935; *Report of Farms and Homes: Proprietorship and Indebtedness . . . 1896*, p. 469; *Compendium of the Eleventh Census, 1890, Part I, Population . . . 1892*, pp. 156, 175, 549, 684–685, 819, 882; *Report on the Social Statistics of Cities, Part II, The Southern and the Western States . . . 1887*, pp. 766–768; *The Newspaper and Periodical Press, 1884*, pp. 249–250.
3. Ibid., 1 January 1890, pp. 1, 8.
4. Ibid., 1 June 1890, p. 16.
5. Ibid., 12 July 1890, p. 5.
6. Ibid., 17 July 1890, p. 1.
7. Ibid., 2 January 1891, p. 5.
8. Ibid., 9 January 1891, p. 1.
9. Ibid., 5 March 1891, p. Y.
10. Ibid., 5 April 1891, p. 4.
11. Ibid., 5 May 1891, section II, p. 3.
12. Sheldon, *His Life Story*, p. 15.
13. Ibid., pp. 195–197.
14. Ibid., pp. 197–198.
15. *The American Catalog, 1890–95* (New York: Peter Smith, 1941, reprint), p. 1248.
16. *The United States Catalog, Books in Print, 1902*, ed. Marvin E. Potter (Minneapolis: H. W. Wilson, 1903), p. 1725.
17. *The United States Catalog, Books in Print, 1912*, ed. Marvin E. Potter (Minneapolis and New York: H. W. Wilson, 1912), p. 2287.
18. *National Union Catalog, Pre-1956 Imprints* (London: Mansell, 1967–1980), 542: 585–590.
19. *Topeka Daily Capital*, 25 February 1946, p. 1.
20. Ibid., 4 October 1891, p. 4; 20 September 1891, p. 6.
21. C. M. Sheldon, *Robert Hardy's Seven Days: A Dream and Its Consequences* (Chicago: D. C. Cook, 1900), p. 54.
22. C. M. Sheldon. *The Twentieth Door* (Chicago: Advance Publishing, 1898), "Preface," n.p.

23. C. M. Sheldon, *The Crucifixion of Philip Strong* (Philadelphia: Henry Altemus, n.d.), p. 25—illustrations are dated "'98." This volume is #40 in Altemus's Illustrated Vademecum Series, which offered "The most popular works of standard authors carefully printed on fine paper, with illuminated titles and frontispiece. Full cloth, ornamented, boxes. Price 40 cents" (endpaper advertising). *In His Steps* and *Robert Hardy's Seven Days* were included in the 244 items in the Vademecum Series.

24. C. M. Sheldon, *One of the Two* (Chicago: Fleming J. Revell, 1898), pp. 49-50.

25. C. M. Sheldon. *Edward Blake: College Student* (Chicago: Advance Publishing, 1900), "Introduction," n.p.

26. Ibid., p. 58.

27. Ibid., p. 181.

28. Sheldon, *His Life Story*, pp. 97ff.

29. C. M. Sheldon, *In His Steps* (New York: Pyramid, 1960), front cover.

30. Frank Luther Mott, *Golden Multitudes: The Story of Best Sellers in the United States* (New York: Macmillan, 1947), p. 193.

31. *Books in Print 1984-85, Authors P-Z* (New York: R. R. Bowker, 1984), p. 4193.

32. Sheldon, *His Life Story*; and *The History of "In His Steps, or What Would Jesus Do?"* (Topeka, Kan.: Shawnee County Historical Society, n.d.).

Anne Wallace, Atlanta, 1900. Wallace did not fit the Grundy stereotype; she was a handsome woman. Daughter of one of the pioneer families of Atlanta, she received no formal library training. She was the first librarian in Atlanta, and perhaps in the South, to devote her energies to the larger picture of regional library development.
(Atlanta Public Library)

Atlanta's Female Librarians, 1883–1915

James V. Carmichael, Jr.

It is commonly assumed that female librarians at the turn of the century lacked autonomy, were paid less than their male contemporaries because the male establishment was exploiting them, and served in their librarian roles largely as cultural adornments. The evidence presented in this study suggests that in Atlanta, Georgia, at least, female librarians of the period dominated in library affairs; discrepancies in pay occurred along regional rather than gender lines; and Atlanta librarians and graduates of the Atlanta Library School seemed to move easily from librarianship into marriage without resort to feelings of guilt or "betrayal." Other distinguishing regional attitudes are noted in the correspondence of the School and serve as cautionary tales against wholesale revisionism.

The first female librarians (1883–1915) of the Young Men's Library Association of the City of Atlanta (YMLA) and the Carnegie Library of Atlanta, which grew out of the YMLA, resemble stereotypical southern upper-class women of the period more than they do the revisionist/feminist historians' descriptions of exploited female library workers.[1] The careers of these southern women demonstrate that, far from being timorous library ladies, they were progressive cultural and social leaders who for the most part were admired and even cherished by their library boards and their public. At least two of them enjoyed a considerable degree of professional renown. Paradoxically, they and the women they helped to train and school in library work were as likely to leave library work for marriage as they were to remain with it, yet they felt anything but betrayal of a "sacred trust" if they left their profession.[2] To a degree, they shared a sense of missionary enterprise with other librarians of their era, but the difference between them seemed to lie in the fact that the At-

James V. Carmichael, Jr., *is a doctoral candidate in librarianship, University of North Carolina at Chapel Hill.*

lanta librarians viewed the public library as a means to better southern conditions, rather than as an educational or cultural end in itself.

There were several reasons why Atlanta's women met so little resistance when they entered librarianship and why they became powerful leaders. Because the male population had been decimated during the Civil War, southern women of every class had already had exposure to many varieties of work, some in traditionally male occupations.[3] Library work was perceived as appropriate women's work in Atlanta in 1883, but not primarily for reasons of financial expedience. Nor was it only because the city had not yet produced any capable male librarians. Rather, in the years following the Civil War, the shortage of teachers had led southern states to accept females in an educational role. Georgia became the second southern state to found a state normal college in 1889.[4] There were other more fundamental reasons, however, why women met so little resistance in librarianship. Even before the war, southern women were extolled in political rhetoric as the crowning glory of the southern system, and their hard labor, personal sacrifice, and heroic effort during the war strengthened their image as the moral backbone of southern society. They thus quite naturally assumed the initiative in many phases of cultural development after the war.[5] Women were responsible, in fact, for raising the money for purchase of a lot for the first YMLA building in 1880.[6]

While the image of the southern lady demanded that she be strong, it also demanded that she be a belle.[7] The mystique of the southern belle required that she be adept in the "management" of men and that she rule by indirection, charm, and diplomacy while seeming to give credit to the men. The considerable administrative skills of the early librarians were softened by their charm and their deference to their boards—with one notable exception, Katherine H. Wooten. On the whole, the early librarians considered family background and connections, tact, charm, deportment, and the sympathetic understanding of southern problems and biases important to the southern librarian's career.

The career experiences of the early graduates (1906–1915) of the Carnegie Library School of Atlanta were not always so positive. In the less-developed areas of the South where some of them worked, male chauvinism, backward library practices, crude library facilities, and prejudice against public libraries provided obstacles. In addition, it was tacitly assumed that the graduates accepted the biracial system in the South, and those who did venture to other parts of the country sometimes expressed discomfort in racially integrated libraries. Also, the early graduates of the School were not always the intellectual equals of the first female librarians of Atlanta. The good example of the librarians who taught them usually fired the enthusiasm of even the dullest student, however, and, through contacts with the School and the alumnae association, a network of shared identity gradually evolved. In spite of individual differences, several characteristics distinguish both Atlanta's female librarians and their students as southern female librarians of this period.

"Acceptable Guardians . . ."

Callaham has traced the growth of the YMLA (1867–1902) from a struggling subscription library to a public library in the modern sense,[8] the first such building in the South to be built with Carnegie funds. From 1902 until 1905 the Carnegie Library had an informal training institute for new employees headed by Anne Wallace. From 1905 until 1930 the Carnegie Library housed the Carnegie Library School of Atlanta, the first southern library school, and until the 1930s the only accredited southern library school. From 1883, when the first female librarian was elected at the YMLA, until 1949 women ran the Atlanta library and, of course, also ran the school after it was founded. All of the school's pupils were female until 1930. Considering women's prominent role in library affairs, it is necessary to reiterate briefly how they came to occupy this position, and then to describe some common characteristics among them.

From 1867 until 1883 the YMLA employed six male librarians in succession, and none proved entirely satisfactory. Several of them were disabled Confederate veterans.[9] The eccentricities of one of them, Charles Herbst, included writing the names of delinquent members in the flyleaves of books.[10] The sixth male to be employed, Allie C. Billups, claimed that the demands of his office did not permit him time to collect members' dues, and he was finally dismissed on 23 February 1883 for "violating his duty in closing and leaving [the] library locked up without leave."[11]

Women had meanwhile gained a steady hold on library affairs. They had been granted membership in the YMLA in 1873, and by 1880 the board had granted life membership to a woman. The president of the YMLA, Julius Brown, publicly acknowledged the debt the YMLA owed to its female constituency when the cornerstone of its first building was laid in that same year: "Women's hands and women's smiles made the money with which these lots were bought,"[12] he said, referring to the numerous bazaars, concerts, and entertainments women had organized to raise the necessary money.[13] Meanwhile, in an effort to modernize the library, the board decided to compile a catalog of the YMLA's holdings with the assistance of Miss Fannie Wallace, who was elected assistant librarian when the incumbent, A. M. Greene, resigned in January 1883.[14] On the advice of notable public librarian William Frederick Poole, his protégée, Mary A. Beane of the Brookline, Massachusetts, Public Library, was also temporarily engaged to oversee the reorganization of the library.[15] When the board discharged Allie Billups as librarian, no suitable replacements applied for the position. On the recommendation of several of the board members, a female member, Lida A. Field, who was a native of Dahlonega, Georgia, and had taught for some time in Atlanta, was nominated and elected librarian by a vote of 11 to 2. The board expressed its confidence that she would make "an acceptable guardian of the library and a guide to the younger members."[16]

With the exception of Lida A. Field, who was librarian of the YMLA from 1883 to 1889, all of the first six female librarians were Atlantans with impeccable social credentials. Frances Alexander (Fannie) Wallace (1889–1892), Anne Nicholson Wallace (1892–1908), Julia Toombs Rankin (1908–1911), Katherine Hinton Wooten (1911–1914), and Delia Foreacre Sneed (1914–1915) were all daughters or granddaughters of pioneer stock. To claim that their families were antebellum aristocrats perhaps forces the issue; nevertheless, the fathers of the Wallaces and Sneed served the Confederate army with distinction,[17] while Rankin was the niece of Confederate statesman Robert M. Toombs.[18] Wooten's grandfather reportedly saved the Sacred Heart Church in Atlanta from Sherman's torch,[19] and he took great pride in being one of the disfranchised during Reconstruction.[20] The families of these women helped to carve a settlement from the wilderness in the antebellum years, and to rebuild Atlanta from the ashes after the war. Alexander M. Wallace was collector of customs under President Grover Cleveland; J. W. Rankin was a prominent merchant and druggist; Greenberry Foreacre, Sneed's father, was a railroad pioneer who settled in Atlanta in 1858.[21] Foreacre served as provost-marshal of Atlanta before the Union occupation.[22] The daughters of these prominent men had reason to be conscious of their southern heritage, and none more so than the Wallaces, whose half-brother, an editor, was shot and killed by a carpetbagger in 1867 for his published views.[23]

All of these early librarians were educated privately. Sneed received part of her education abroad. Only Rankin and Sneed had formal library training: Rankin received her certificate at the Pratt Institute in 1898, and Sneed graduated from there in 1905.[24] As a whole, the experience that the early librarians brought to their job was limited. Sneed worked for a year as secretary for the Georgia Library Commission in 1905–1906, while Rankin's only work outside the Atlanta library consisted of organizing the Birmingham Public Library in 1904.[25] None of the other librarians had ever worked in libraries other than the YMLA or the Carnegie. Professional qualifications, therefore, were not the primary consideration in the hiring of the early librarians. There was a benevolent provincialism in library affairs in the very early years, and it extended to hiring practices, where personal recommendations were often the only criteria for judging applicants for positions. This provincialism even assumed a somewhat nepotic flavor in the hiring of Anne Wallace, sister of Fannie, to be her assistant, and for a short while in 1883 their sister Minnie also worked in the YMLA with Fannie Wallace and Lida Field.[26]

In professional activities, however, the first female librarians were far from parochial. Anne Wallace became first vice-president of ALA in 1902, three years before the occupation of that position by a female was mandated by a special bylaw.[27] Ironically, she was the only southerner to hold an "executive" position (honorary or otherwise) in the national association until 1936. In other spheres of activity, Atlanta's female librarians were equally prominent. Sneed became president of the League of Library Commissioners in 1908. Anne Wallace, Rankin, and Sneed all served terms on the ALA Council. Wallace also addressed the ALA on southern library development at the Asheville Conference in 1907, while Wooten updated the same topic before the Washington, D.C., delegates in 1914.[28]

These early Atlanta librarians saw state and national activities as one of the hallmarks of their professional commitment. It is to the credit of Anne Wallace that she first persuaded the Atlanta library board to pay for the librarian's expenses to ALA conferences in 1896, long before such financial endorsement was common.[29] Rankin used the occasion of her summer vacation in Europe to attend the International Conference of Librarians in Brussels in 1910, but, of course, she paid her own expenses there.[30] The board, however, independently voted to grant Anne Wallace leave with pay when her doctor recommended a sea voyage for exhaustion in 1907.[31] These women were in the public eye on a regular basis in the women's section of the Atlanta newspapers, and they were heeded, indeed, pampered in some instances, by their boards. The Atlanta librarians were respected outside the South as well. Some measure of the esteem that Anne Wallace generally commanded may be gleaned from Andrew Carnegie's unusual wedding gift to her: a $5,000 bond.[32]

Though it is obvious that the early Atlanta librarians were committed to their work, four of the first six librarians—the Wallaces, Rankin, and Sneed—left librarianship for marriage apparently with few qualms of conscience. Sneed later claimed that she had only worked as a librarian until such time as her son should attain his majority.[33] During this era, of course, married women did not work, although widows like Sneed,

American Library Association Conference, Asheville, N.C., 1907: (left to right): Mr. Post, Mrs. Hopkins, Elfrida Everhart, Mr. Hopkins, Julia Toombs Rankin, and Anne Wallace. When Wallace left librarianship for marriage in 1908, Rankin succeeded her, but eventually she succumbed to matrimony, too. Of Atlanta's first six female librarians, four left the profession to be married.
(Faxon photo, ALA Archives)

Post Conference Excursion, ALA Conference, Asheville, N.C., 1907: Anne Wallace, driving, reins in hand. Wallace was the first woman licensed to drive an automobile in Georgia. According to R. R. Bowker, she also started a vogue for habitan *hats at the conferences.* (Faxon photo, ALA Archives)

and perhaps wives of very improvident husbands, were accepted in the workplace. The main motive for work seems to have been in nearly all cases financial rather than altruistic. When Anne Wallace's husband died suddenly in 1921, for example, she returned to library work as head of the struggling Drexel Library School in order that her son might finish his education.[34] Yet even Wallace, the prime mover in southern librarianship at the turn of the century, viewed her profession as part of the stuff of life rather than as a panacea for society's ills. When she was awarded an honorary doctorate by the University of Georgia in 1929 for her professional achievements, Wallace (now the widowed Mrs. Howland) told her students she would prefer to continue being addressed as Mrs. Howland. "Any person with sense who works hard can get a D-R before her name," she quipped, "but it takes a real woman to be a M-R-S!"[35]

A final distinguishing characteristic of Atlanta's early librarians was their progressive attitude toward disadvantaged populations. Anne Wallace set the precedent in this area with her distinctly sympathetic efforts on behalf of blacks. When the YMLA disbanded and turned over its stock to the new Carnegie Library of Atlanta—of which Anne Wallace had been "acclaimed" the head—she suggested saving the old YMLA shelving for a black library branch.[36] She also secured an agreement "through Mr. [Robert Curtis] Ogden of New York," president of the Conference for Education in the South, to educate any woman she might select in practical library work "when" a black branch was secured.[37] H. H. Proctor, the black Atlanta Congregationalist minister, petitioned the board for a black branch in 1904, and a special committee of the board, including Wallace, drew up a request for $10,000 from Carnegie.[38] Though Carnegie granted $30,000 for two branches in 1906,[39] only one was built—for whites. Not until 1921 could the city be convinced to appropriate money for maintenance of a black branch.

Julia Rankin began a pilot program for library services to the blind, and helped the Jewish women of the city to secure a depository at the Jewish Educational Alliance.[40] Kate Wooten opened depositories at factory sites and telephone exchanges.[41] Generally speaking, the service orientation of the early librarians was not diminished by local biases. Even though not much progress was made in special services for Jews, and none was made in services for blacks by the public library, the attitude of the librarians seems remarkable considering anti-Semitic sentiment in Atlanta, such as became evident in the famous Leo Frank trial in 1915,[42] and the deterioration of race relations, culminating in a dreadful riot in 1906, which affected all segments of Atlanta society from 1890 to 1908.[43]

The one sour note in this collective biography concerns the career of Katherine Hinton Wooten. Wooten became increasingly insistent in her demands for a pay raise from the city in 1914, and in spite of appeals from the board to the city on her behalf, the city refused to approve a raise. Then, in an unprecedented action, Wooten resigned, at the same time issuing a statement to the Atlanta papers outlining her complaints. Her successor, Delia Foreacre Sneed, who had been principal of the library school since 1908, later said that it had been evident from the beginning that events were "approaching a catastrophe of some kind."[44] It is difficult to determine whether the fact that Wooten was the only Catholic among the early librarians militated against her in subtle ways; certainly, she grew up in circumstances that were culturally distinct, if equally elevated, from the other librarians. More significantly, however, she had asked to be relieved of the dual responsibility of managing the school and the library.[45] Her negligence of the school may have aroused resentment from Sneed and others to whom the school, with its program of in-service training,[46] was an integral part of library operations.

Sneed wrote in 1915 that Wooten was "completely down and out as far as the library world is concerned, the city government, and her own trustees. . . . She furnished her own complete demolition in her last months here and her own worst enemy could not wish to see it completed further."[47] Though the circumstances of the Wooten case are obscured in the official records, it is evident from the confidential correspondence of the school that favoritism and jealousy played no small part in Wooten's downfall. The inappropriateness of her appointment of a new assistant librarian gave rise to Sneed's claim that Wooten was "injudiciously fond" of the girl, who was promoted beyond her capabilities.[48] The official report that Sneed made to the board in 1915 referred only to Wooten's negligence of book selection, a duty that Sneed felt was the primary work of a head librarian.[49] Obviously, other factors were involved in Wooten's disgrace. None of her actions, however, incensed Sneed more than her abrasive public posture with regard to her salary; the resulting embarrassment to the board had been "mortifying."[50]

The Wooten case demonstrates that there were limits to what a southern lady librarian could do to better her position in Atlanta in 1914. Above all, a southern lady librarian must always behave as a lady and retain a respectful attitude toward her board. She must accept disappointments gracefully. The aftermath of Wooten's actions was predictable. the enthusiastic, somewhat informal spirit of civic enterprise and cooperation that had characterized relations between the library and City Hall in the early years abated. From about 1915 forward, formal accountability was the keynote of library administration in Atlanta.

In several different respects, Atlanta's early female librarians conformed to societal expectations defined by regional values: the cult of the southern lady demanded that business acumen, political savoir faire, and cultural leadership be cloaked, or at least lightly veiled, in charm and deference to the male power structure; the primacy of marriage and the family, more intense in the South than elsewhere, urged them to forsake their career for the more basic work of raising a family; the myth of the southern belle, to which spinsterhood was anathema, exerted a similar influence; and the broad service philosophy of American public librarianship, while democratically correct, was transformed and modified by the librarians to suit the realities of local conditions.

After a woman was established as Atlanta's librarian in 1883, it was taken for granted that the librarianship would belong to a woman. The Carnegie Library School of Atlanta received no applications from males until 1930, and then probably only because the school had just moved to Emory University, and monies from the Rosenwald Fund had become available to urge more males into librarianship in the South. If inequalities existed between the salaries of male and female librarians, as Arthur Bostwick noted in his address to the 1909 graduating class of the library school, the news incited nothing more than "a cordial tea-time reception."[51]

That the head librarians of Atlanta were able to resign themselves to the lack of library services to blacks while publicly and in the classroom espousing a progressive social spirit may reflect their cognizance of the overriding paucity of library services to all segments of southern society during this period. Even the little steps that were taken by Anne Wallace and others toward changing the situation, while they may seem patronizing in retrospect, were unusual for that era. Atlanta itself, the breeding ground of New South progressivism, was an anomaly among the sleepier towns of Georgia like Augusta and Savannah. "I am not sure what the rest of the state thinks of Atlanta," wrote Sneed. "Those of us who live here have our dark moments of suspecting that Atlanta is sometimes ill spoken of by her elder sisters."[52] Nevertheless, the Atlanta spirit apparently did not encompass defiance of racial conventions, or the outright revolt of southern women who were the backbone, if not the *raison d'être*, of the southern system.

The Pioneer Graduates

One gauge of the influence of Atlanta's female librarians on southern librarianship lies in the careers of the graduates of the Carnegie Library School of Atlanta. A hitherto untapped documentary resource, the alumnae files of the school (now housed at Emory University), reveals that the school served as a virtual employment agency in its early years. The school exerted pressure, when necessary, on capricious employers. In many cases, the school engineered successive appointments throughout its graduates' careers. All of the librarians, and particularly Delia Foreacre Sneed, who was principal of the school from 1908 to 1914, negotiated salaries, smoothed over differences between graduates and employers, and always offered voluminous advice on the organization and administration of libraries.

For the purposes of this study, a 40 percent random sample of the graduates of the first ten years' classes (1906–1915) was taken from the Graduate Handbook of 1917, excluding the members of the classes of 1916 and 1917. The resulting sample, numbering 40, was distributed among the classes as follows: 1906, 5 graduates; 1907, 4; 1908, 1; 1909, 5; 1910, 4; 1911, 2; 1912, 6; 1913, 5; 1914, 3; 1915, 5.

The corresponding alumnae files of the Carnegie Library School of Atlanta were then pulled and carefully read to obtain the following information: (1) age when application to the school was made; (2) where the graduate was born, or her principal residence when applying to the school; (3) education; (4) previous work experience; (5) where the graduate worked: library, by type; (6) whether or not the graduate later married; if so, whether she returned to librarianship or not; (7) father's occupation, if known; (8) religion, if known; (9) whether or not the graduate was an ALA member in 1915; (10) whether or not the graduate was included in *Who's Who in Library Service* (1933); and (11) whether or not the graduate left the South during her career; if so, did she return? The results are summarized in table 1.

As might be expected, nearly all (38) of the sample graduates came from the South. Anne Wallace originally planned to have a representative from each of the southern states in the early classes,[53] but most applications came from Georgia, and particularly Atlanta, where word of the school and its work was spread through word of mouth or through lectures at the Girls' High School and at Agnes Scott Institute. Of the 40 graduates included in the sample, 11 had attended Girls' High. Another condition that favored the predominance of local girls was the reluctance of families or guardians to let their daughters or charges live alone in a strange city. The school anticipated this fear by keeping a list of boarding houses where the proprietor was "known."[54] The expense of travel and boarding was also a factor in limiting the geographic distribution of candidates.

"Southern conditions" demanded women of a certain social standing or breeding. At least until 1915, personal attributes of good breeding, tact, and appearance vied with performance on the entrance examination as the principal qualifying factor for admission. Although the father's occupation of only 12 of the sample graduates is known, they include the daughter of Clark Howell, the editor of the *Atlanta Constitution*, the daughter of the state chemist, and the daughter of a member of the State Board of

Laying of cornerstone, Carnegie Library of Atlanta, 9 September 1900. On a suggestion received from Melvil Dewey, Anne Wallace approached Andrew Carnegie for funds to endow a library school for the South. The school opened on the third floor of the Carnegie Library in 1905, with an optimal class size of twelve. The library also served as meeting place for the Georgia Library Association and carried out the early work of the (as yet unfunded) Georgia Library Commission. (Atlanta Public Library)

Table 1
Collective Profile, CLS Graduates, 1906–1915
N = 40
(40% Sample)

AGE	
18–20 yrs.	7
21–25 yrs.	16
26–30 yrs.	10
31–35 yrs.	6
36 or older	1
	40
(Avg. age = 24.35)	

GEOGRAPHIC DISTRIBUTION	
Georgia	16
Ga., Atlanta	10
Alabama	4
N.C.	4
Virginia	2
Bermuda	1
Florida	1
Indiana	1
Texas	1
	40

EDUCATION		
High School		
Public		28
Private		7
Tutor, etc.		5
		40
College		
None		10
Partial	1	
Certificate	22	
A.B.	4	
M.A. (not LS)	2	
M.L.S.	1	
	30	
		40

PREVIOUS EXPERIENCE	
Teaching	6
Lib. Asst. (LA)	9
Tutor	2
Writer	1
Librarian	1
Teaching; LA	2
Business; Teaching	2
Govt.; LA; Librarian	1
Bookstore; LA	1
Teaching; Librarian	1
	26
No Experience	14
	40

CAREER: LIBRARY TYPE	
Public	9
C.L. Atlanta	5
Academic	7
State Commission	1
State Librarian	1
State Archivist	1
Other State	1
Government	1
Army	1
Library School	2
School	1
Business	1
	31
Fired, quit LS	1
	32
No career; died, etc.	8
	40

MARRIAGE	
Married	19
Returned to career	(7)
Gave up career	12

LEFT SOUTH	
Left South	10
Returned	(5)
Stayed Away	5

INCLUDED IN WWLS (1933)	16
ALA MEMBER IN 1915	19

RELIGION	
Catholic	1
Protestant	
Baptist	3
Episcopal	7
Presbyterian	5
Methodist	3
Not Known	21
	40

Note: Excludes characteristic Father's Occupation, since so few are known.

Medical Examiners. There are also the daughters of two other doctors, two ministers, two merchants, a photographer, the niece of a professor in the state university, and the sister of the state entomologist. In addition, the sample includes the daughter of a First Family of Virginia (FFV).

The recommendations contained in the files reveal the kinds of qualities that were deemed desirable in applicants. These qualities included good "breeding," which in the South could simply mean being known by the person recommending the girl through family or other social connections. "[C]omes from a family of culture and refinement," said one such recommendation from Atlanta's prestigious Washington Seminary.[55] The later principal of the school, Susie Lee Crumley, recommended one graduate to the mayor of Shreveport in 1923 as "a Virginia lady of gentle birth and distinction of mind."[56] If not strictly exclusive, the school clearly recognized the advantages of being well born: "She comes of an excellent family, has been well educated, & has all the advantages of travel."[57]

Other recommendations strike a similar chord: "her mother is a woman of strong character."[58] "[S]he is one of the brightest girls I have ever met from one of our best families";[59] "recommendations on coming to us were of the very best, and from some of the most prominent people in Montgomery."[60] Physical attractiveness (and lacking that, physical stamina), bookishness, organizational ability, and, above all, tact were also considered desirable qualities, especially since, as Sneed said, "the idea in the library world is fixed that southern girls are more apt to have a pleasing personality . . ."[61]

The entrance examination was a preliminary, but not an absolutely definitive indicator of success. Depending on class size, makeup, and withdrawals, candidates were accepted with scores as high as 96/100 and as low as 56/100. The school was capable of defending physical infirmities of graduates, such as slight deafness, chronic fatigue, or the wearing of eyeglasses from the scrutiny of employers, once the girls had become alumnae. If not openly "elitist," a term that seems redundant when applied to a segregated society, the school certainly favored the girl who had "profited by the advantages of birth and education in a refined home."[62]

"Southern conditions" also embraced a wide variety of locales, physical facilities, and local situations that often demanded an uncommon degree of tolerance even from native southerners. In North Augusta, South Carolina, one library organizer had to contend with an eighty-seven-year-old YMCA librarian who was blind and opposed to the public library idea. She struggled for three years to convert him to modern library practice, and when he finally died and his position became available to her, the city proved equally recalcitrant in endorsing a public library.[63] From Cordele, Georgia, one graduate confirmed Sneed's apocryphal classroom vignette about "a certain library in South Ga. into which one made one's entrance by crawling over the desk. Well, we're the guilty party!"[64] In Talladega, Alabama, the library was "the special pet of some of the rich people there."[65] In the Quitman, Georgia, subscription library in 1909, the only encyclopedia was a Chamber's published in 1869.[66] The heat was a problem everywhere in the South; even in Atlanta's state-of-the-art building, summers were "hot as fire."[67]

The school was not provincial in its outlook, however, for, by 1911, fifteen graduates had gone to work with the New York Public Library and its branches and the school received "splendid reports of them."[68] One surviving graduate of the class of 1914 remembered that some of the "New York girls" lived in a boarding house bordering Central Park and that the establishment had staunchly maintained its identity as a "Southern home."[69] The reactions of the graduates who did venture out of the South provide a barometer of the range of southern attitudes on race, the North, and other cultural differences. Of the sampled graduates, ten left the South, and five eventually returned. More probably would have braved a job in the North or elsewhere had not such factors as fearful guardians or parents, dependent relatives, the cost of travel, and the higher cost of living outside of the South discouraged them.

The main disadvantage with living in New York, according to Wooten's report on the New York girls, was that "they [were] constantly broke as living is so high."[70] At least one graduate found it exciting to work in a children's room in a New York library because "the class of children we deal with is very different from those we come in contact with in Atlanta."[71] Indeed, northern conditions were so different that not all graduates felt entirely comfortable with the changes. One graduate working in Portland, Oregon, found that the class of people who came to the library were "very much the same as my own West Enders [in Birmingham, Alabama.]" In a more candid vein, she added that her customers included "some cunning Japanese and some little *darkies*. I am glad to say that only one darky has been in so far but that is enough for me." Ironically, this graduate was hired in Portland because it was taken for granted that she could tell "Uncle Remus stories." A visit to Chicago both delighted and shocked her, for at the Stanfield Park branch of the library, she found the second floor "full of dirty Jewish children, but what interested me most was the basement. It was full of mothers who were taking shower baths. Each woman was given a towel and a piece of soap . . . I could hardly tear myself away it was so much fun." She received a final shock in Chicago when she learned that Miss Bond, one of the assistants, who was "exceedingly nice and pleasant . . . was a Negro! I knew she was different but I had decided she was a Jew."[72]

The attitude of other graduates toward immigrants was as pronounced as the one quoted above, if more sanguine. One young lady relayed the news from Chapel Hill that her classmates in New York wrote "very enthusiastically about their foreign children, so I suppose they don't mind the dirty immigrant kisses of little Jacob Arenowitches or Isaac Schwartzes [*sic*] being planted on their 'neat' shirtwaists."[73]

Most of the graduates were mute on racial issues, however, if for no other reason than that discretion seemed advisable due to more racially progressive attitudes of librarians from other parts of the country. Lloyd Josselyn, in the Jacksonville, Florida public library, frankly warned one graduate that if "one does not really enjoy the work, be it waiting on the general public, cataloging uninteresting old volumes, or working with dirty bright little Jews, then I do not want such an assistant on the Library Staff."[74]

Sneed, then principal of the school, admitted in 1913 that the "New York Public Library . . . can make use of a number of assistants who are too young or too inexperienced to go to other places but who work well under direction."[75] Nevertheless, there were probably other factors than work experience to explain why more of them did not stay in more established, modern facilities in other regions. At least one such factor was prejudice against the North. "Mother has such a distaste for New York as a home for a young girl," wrote one alumna, declining a job offer in New York. She added, however, that she was strongly "tempted to join that crowd."[76] The school, which could be sympathetic to the graduate who wanted a "real" library, could also take the parents' side. As Sneed consoled one distressed family member, "I do not know why we would seem to feel that to be a few hundred miles away from home is less undesireable [*sic*] than several thousand, since in either case so far as protection is concerned a young woman is thoroughly thrown on her own resources, but somehow, I do feel that it would be better for Emily to be in the neighboring state of Texas."[77] It was not until the 1920s that the graduates, and women generally, traveled with more ease. By that time, one veteran of the early days of the New York girls could report from Long Island that she was "gasping for breath" since "nine tenths of the southern population known to me [is] in New York."[78]

One startling statistic that emerges from the sample is the number of librarians who married: 19, or 47.5 percent. Although Garrison reported that only 25 percent of the graduates of Smith, Wellesley, and Vassar who were between twenty-six and thirty-seven years of age in 1903 were married,[79] as compared to only 18 percent of the pre-1900 graduates of the University of Illinois and only 7.4 percent of women librarians in 1920, nearly 50 percent of this sample married. More than 30 percent never returned to librarianship.

Unlike Garrison's examples, the southern graduates who married did so with impunity, and even relief, as had the librarians at the Atlanta library. They left librarianship as had Anne Wallace, "radiantly happy," according to Julia Rankin, and with "about as much interest in library affairs as Mrs. Noah had."[80] Sneed reported in 1913 that the former Miss Wallace "looks well and happy and has forgotten all about libraries."[81] She wrote to another graduate that "we have had numberless changes since you were here but they have all been caused by matrimony and everyone who has left seems more than happy in their new life."[82]

Defection was not seen so much with disparagement as with indulgence. Given the opportunity to marry, southern women of this period seemed to feel that marriage, while not compatible with a career, was certainly a viable, perhaps an enviable, alternative to a life alone. "I am leading what most people consider a very humdrum life," wrote one young housewife, complacently. "I nurse the children myself."[83] Rankin expressed mock horror at one of the staff of the library who "has left us for a mere man . . . who she will take unto herself in July," but Rankin herself left the library to marry later that year.[84] To one librarian who seemed doubtful about her forthcoming marriage, Sneed ressured her that marriage "must be epidemic in the library world as we have nine marriages to our credit in less than a year. If you need any encouragement I will tell you that they all seem radiantly happy."[85] Rankin declared that "we have so many Library babies now that we feel quite as conversant with babies as with catalogues, and frankly the babies seem to be much more compensating."[86]

There may have been, and probably were, in the southern school at this time committed professionals who would not have given up their careers even had marriage been an alternative, but if so, they do not seem to have been noticeable as a group during this phase of southern librarianship. Like Anne Wallace Howland, most of the married women who returned to librarianship did so after the death of a spouse, when economic factors, rather than purely professional concerns, were again an issue in their lives.

One final point that bears examination is associational leadership. Two of the sample graduates held national offices, one as president of the Association of State Librarians and one as president of the Association of American Library Schools. Three held offices in their state associations, and one held office in the regional library association. Remembering that only one southerner after Wallace held an executive post in the ALA before 1936, it is perhaps surprising that so many graduates, 47.5 percent, or nearly half, had joined the ALA by 1915, particularly since, for many of them, there was "no hope of getting off [to ALA conferences] & besides its [*sic*] too expensive a trip for the short absence."[87] The regional underrepresentation in national leadership positions can be explained partially in terms of the South's voting strength (see table 2). Librarians of the thirteen Confederate states constituted only 6.77 percent of ALA membership in 1908 and only 9.97 percent by 1929. Only the Southwest and the Northwest had fewer librarians. Strangely, the South also had the largest proportion of librarians who were ALA members in 1908, 21.69 percent as compared to 15.95 percent in the Northeast, and nearly as many in 1929—39.40 percent as compared to the Northeast's 39.41 percent. Because conventions were usually held outside the South, fewer could attend ALA conferences, and thus southern librarians were less well known nationally than those from other regions. The low "return" on ALA membership in terms of leadership positions may have been one of many reasons, along with cultural, historical, political, and economic reasons already familiar to students of southern history, that southern librarians formed a regional association in 1920, in spite of the misapprehension of at least one national leader from Indiana, Mary Ellen Ahern, that "a regional body would weaken the national one."[88]

Conclusion

Although several tendencies characterize Atlanta's female librarians and the early graduates of their school, they were not radically different from their northern contemporaries. In fact, there were many similarities: most importantly, both constituted an educational, social, and cultural elite and were capable of patronizing or imposing their views on disadvantaged minorities. As noted above, however, elitism is redundant, perhaps irrelevant, in a segregated society. In general, the South was more homogenized ethnically than the North, and racial polarities were the basis of a legalized caste system. Within the proscriptive limits of this narrow system, even the smallest official gesture of minority recognition, like Anne Wallace's efforts to secure services for blacks, seems liberal, if not heroic. Considering the racial violence of the period during which she acted, and the discouragement northern philanthropists and educators were experiencing in Atlanta at the hands of the legislators,[89] her gestures of recognition were most courageous. The principal difference between the elites of the North and South was that the southern elite, through bitter experience, was aware of the region's peculiar difficulties, its poverty, its political turbulence, and the backward state of its ed-

Table 2
ALA Membership by States
1908 and 1929

Region[1]	Librarians[2]	ALA Mem.[3]	Percent Region's Total	Percent Total ALA Members
		1908		
West	620	105	16.93	5.93
Northwest	414	77	18.59	4.35
Middle States	2738	538	19.64	30.39
Northeast	5809	927	15.95	52.37
Southeast	466	98	21.03	5.53
Southwest	108	25	23.14	1.41
Total	10155	1770		
13 Confederate States	553	120	21.69	6.77
		1929		
West	4210	1106	26.27	9.99
Northwest	1561	565	36.19	5.10
Middle States	10705	3971	37.09	35.88
Northeast	10762	4242	39.41	38.33
Southeast	2200	902	41.00	8.15
Southwest	873	281	32.18	2.53
Total	30311	11067		
13 Confederate States	2802	1104	39.40	9.97

[1]Excluding the District of Columbia. Regional definitions from Howard W. Odum, *Southern Regions of the United States* (Chapel Hill: University of North Carolina Press, 1936), p. 286. Odum includes West Virginia in the northeastern states and Texas in the southwestern.

[2]Source: U.S. Bureau of Education, Bulletin No. 5, 1909; Louis R. Wilson, *The Geography of Reading* (Chicago: ALA and University of Chicago Press, 1938), p. 175.

[3]Source: *Bulletin of the American Library Association* 2 (July 1908): 49; *Bulletin of the American Library Association* 23 (September 1929): 731.

ucational resources. Changing laws had not brought racial equality; experimental farming had not broken the hold of King Cotton; nor would the public library or the schools transform overnight the South's largely illiterate population.[90]

The southern female librarians described in this paper had realistic expectations of their careers. For them, the profession of librarianship was not a panacea for society's ills, nor did it provide a forum for issues of sexual inequality. If males dominated positions of leadership in the library profession, they did so outside the South. Southern communities of this period simply could not garner the kind of financial support necessary to attract many male librarians, especially those from other parts of the country. Even if salaries had not been a stumbling block, however, regional attitudes on race probably would have been. There were exceptions, of course: Lloyd Josselyn at Jacksonville Public Library and Carl A. Milam at Birmingham Public Library, to name only two. Also, Louis Round Wilson at the University of North Carolina at Chapel Hill, a native southerner, was for many years the leading spokesman of southern librarianship and was president of ALA in 1936—but only after he had assumed the deanship of the University of Chicago's Library School. On the whole, however, librarianship in the South clearly belonged to women, and never more so than after formal training was institutionalized in Atlanta in 1905.

Atlanta's female librarians and the progeny of their school did, in fact, exert a great deal of power, however demurely they may have exercised it. Their power was not prescribed by their pay, since salaries were relatively low indicators of personal worth in a society still staggering from a paucity of all varieties of public institutions.

Notes

Abbreviations

AHS Atlanta Historical Society
Atlanta, Georgia

ALA American Library Association
(Archives, University of Illinois,
Champaign-Urbana, Illinois)

APL Atlanta Public Library
(Board of Trustees' Minutes,
Director's Office, Atlanta Public Library,
Atlanta, Georgia)

CLA Carnegie Library of Atlanta
(Scrapbooks, Atlanta Public Library,
Atlanta, Georgia)

CLSA Carnegie Library School of Atlanta Alumnae Files, Division of Librarianship, Emory University, Atlanta, Georgia

YMLA Young Men's Library Association of Atlanta (Archives, Special Collections, Atlanta Public Library, Atlanta, Georgia)

1. For example, Dee Garrison, *Apostles of Culture: The Public Librarian and American Society, 1876-1920* (New York: Free Press, 1979), esp. pp. 173-185.

2. Ibid., p. 176.

3. Anne F. Scott, *The Southern Lady: From Pedestal to Politics 1830-1930* (Chicago: University of Chicago Press, 1970), pp. 110-111.

4. A. D. Mayo, "Southern Women in the Recent Educational Movement in the South," U.S. Bureau of Education Circular of Information, no. 1 (Washington, D.C.: U.S. Government Printing Office, 1892), pp. 40-57.

5. Scott, *The Southern Lady*, pp. 134-163, esp. p. 152; John P. McDowell, *The Social Gospel of the South: The Women's Home Mission Movement in the Methodist Episcopal Church, South, 1886-1939* (Baton Rouge: Louisiana State University Press, 1982); Mrs. J. C. Croly, *The History of the Women's Club Movement in America* (New York: Henry G. Allen, 1898), pp. 357-369, esp. 358-359.

6. Mss. notes of president's speech, 28 June 1880, YMLA Minutes.

7. Anne G. Jones, *Tomorrow Is Another Day: The Woman Writer in the South, 1859-1936* (Baton Rouge: Louisiana State University Press, 1981), pp. 3-50; Catherine Clinton, *The Plantation Mistress* (New York: Pantheon, 1982), pp. 62-63, 178-179.

8. Betty E. Callaham, "The Carnegie Library School of Atlanta (1905-1925)," *Library Quarterly* 37 (April 1967): 149-179.

9. Ibid., p. 150.

10. *Atlanta: A City of the Modern South* (New York: Smith and Durrell, 1942), pp. 169-170; Franklin M. Garrett, *Atlanta and Environs: A Chronicle of Its People and Its Events* (New York: Lewis Historical Publishing, 1954), I: 761. Garrett includes a listing of all of the YMLA librarians.

11. YMLA Minutes, 23 February 1883.

12. Mss. notes of president's speech, 28 June 1880, YMLA Minutes.

13. Garrett, *Atlanta and Environs*, pp. 759-761.

14. YMLA Minutes, 19 February 1883.

15. Ibid.

16. YMLA Minutes, 3 April 1883.

17. George W. Clower, "Col. Alexander M. Wallace, 1822-1901: Pioneer Atlanta Citizen," *Atlanta Historical Bulletin* 12 (March 1967): 26; Delia F. Sneed, "Sketch of D. G. Foreacre" (manuscript), Greenberry J. Foreacre Papers AHS; Garrett, *Atlanta and Environs*, I: 486-488.

18. Obituary of Julia Rankin Foster (clipping), CLS Scrapbooks, vol. 7.

19. "Katherine Hinton Wooten," in "Trail of the Pioneers," pp. 197-198 (manuscript), Sarah Huff Collection, AHS.

20. Ibid.

21. Garrett, *Atlanta and Environs*, I: 486-488.

22. Ibid., p. 523.

23. Ibid., p. 824.

24. Pratt Institute, Graduates' Records.

25. Ibid.
26. YMLA Minutes, 2 May 1883.
27. Letter from Joel M. Lee to author, 10 October 1984.
28. Anne Wallace, "The Southern Library Movement," *ALA Bulletin* 1 (July 1907): 63-67; Katherine H. Wooten, "Library Development in the South," *ALA Bulletin* 8 (July 1914): 158-166.
29. Librarian's Report, 4 June 1901, YMLA Scrapbook.
30. Minutes, July through September, 1910, APL Minutes, vol. 3.
31. Minutes, 12 March 1907, APL Minutes, vol. 2.
32. *Atlanta Constitution*, 18 February 1908, p. 5.
33. Delia F. Sneed to Frances S. Bradley, 24 February 1915, CLSA Bradley file.
34. Letter from Wallace Howland to the author, 22 July 1984.
35. Telephone interview with Wallace Howland, 18 September 1984.
36. Librarian's Report, 1 October 1901, APL Minutes, vol. 1.
37. R. R. Bowker, "Women in the Library Profession," *Library Journal* 45 (1 July 1920): 590.
38. Minutes, 5 July and 2 August 1904, APL Minutes, vol. 1.
39. Minutes, 1 December 1906, APL Minutes, vol. 1.
40. Minutes, 8 August 1911, APL Minutes, vol. 3.
41. Carnegie Library of Atlanta, *Annual Report, 1912* (n.p.).
42. Leonard Dinnerstein, *The Leo Frank Case* (New York: Columbia University Press, 1968).
43. Glenn W. Rainey, "The Race Riot of 1906 in Atlanta" (master's thesis, Emory University, 1929); Horace C. Wingo, "Race Relations in Georgia, 1872-1908" (Ph.D. dissertation, University of Georgia, 1969).
44. Delia F. Sneed to Frances S. Bradley, 24 February 1915, CLSA Bradley file.
45. Julia T. Rankin to the Board of Trustees of the Carnegie Lbrary of Atlanta, 9 September 1911, APL Minutes, vol. 3.
46. Callaham, "The Carnegie Library School of Atlanta," pp. 152-153.
47. Delia F. Sneed to Frances S. Bradley, 23 March 1915, CLSA Bradley file.
48. Delia F. Sneed to Frances S. Bradley, 24 February 1915, CLSA Bradley file.
49. Librarian's Report, 8 December 1914, APL Minutes, vol. 4.
50. Delia F. Sneed to Frances S. Bradley, 24 February 1915, CLSA Bradley file.
51. Clipping, *Atlanta Journal*, 1 June 1909, CLS Scrapbooks, vol. 1.
52. Librarian's Report, 9 February 1915, APL Minutes, vol. 4.
53. Anne Wallace to Laura Elmore, 30 May 1905, CLSA Bibb file.
54. Katherine Wooten to Janet Berkeley, 28 August 1913, CLSA Berkeley file.
55. Recommendation from E. C. Weimar, 2 May 1913, CLSA Berkeley file.
56. Susie Lee Crumley to L. E. Thomas, 23 February 1913, CLSA Berkeley file.
57. Mrs. Frank O. Foster (Julia Rankin) to Delia F. Sneed, 14 May 1914, CLSA Chamberlin file.
58. Recommendation from Mrs. B. C. David (1909), CLSA Daniel file.
59. Recommendation from E. P. Martin (1914), CLSA Hendrick file.
60. Delia F. Sneed to S. E. Bradshaw, 29 June 1912, CLSA Pitcher file.
61. Delia F. Sneed to Ethel Pitcher, 29 April 1915, CLSA Pitcher file.
62. Recommendation, 26 May 1908, Ella May Thornton file.

63. CLSA Pauline Benson file.

64. Helen Brewer to Susie Lee Crumley, 30 March 1915, CLSA Brewer file.

65. Julia Rankin to Frances Archer, 11 April 1911, CLSA Archer file.

66. Ethel L. Daniel to Julia Rankin, 27 October 1909, CLSA Daniel file.

67. Julia Rankin to Katherine Seon, 14 August 1909, CLSA Seon file.

68. Julia Rankin to Pauline Benson, 5 June 1911, CLSA Benson file.

69. Interview with May (Smith) Rayle, 19 August 1983, Atlanta, Georgia.

70. Katherine Wooten to Ethel Pitcher, 30 October 1911, CLSA Pitcher file.

71. Katherine Seon to Julia Rankin, 2 September 1909, CLSA Seon file.

72. Louise Roberts to Susie Lee Crumley, 20 February 1916, CLSA Roberts file.

73. Annie C. Jungermann to Delia F. Sneed (20 November 1914), CLSA Rymer (i.e., Jungermann) file.

74. Lloyd W. Josselyn to Mabel Jones, 7 November 1913, CLSA Mabel Jones file.

75. Delia F. Sneed to R. P. Stephens, 6 May 1913, CLSA Mabel Jones file.

76. Randolph Archer to Julia Rankin (December 1910), CLSA Archer file.

77. Delia F. Sneed to Marion Weil, 20 March 1913, CLSA Kemp file.

78. Annie J. Rymer to Susie Lee Crumley, 23 August 1921, CLSA Rymer file.

79. Garrison, *Apostles of Culture*, p. 176.

80. Julia Rankin to Eva Wrigley, 28 October 1909, CLSA Wrigley file.

81. Delia F. Sneed to Pauline Benson, 16 September 1913, CLSA Benson file.

82. Delia F. Sneed to Nan Strudwick, 13 January 1913, CLSA Strudwick file.

83. Mattie Bibb to Julia Rankin, 12 May 1911, CLSA Bibb file.

84. Julia Rankin to Eva Wrigley, 5 June 1911, CLSA Wrigley file.

85. Delia F. Sneed to Maude Durlin, 18 March 1912, CLSA Kemp file.

86. Julia Rankin to Mrs. William Edmundson, 5 June 1911, CLSA Bibb file.

87. Randolph Archer to Julia Rankin (January 1911), CLSA Archer file.

88. Mary Edna Anders, *The Southeastern Library Association, 1920–1950* (Atlanta: SELA, 1956), p. 8.

89. Wingo, "Race Relations in Georgia," pp. 185–216.

90. C. Vann Woodward, *Origins of the New South, 1877–1913* (Baton Rouge: Louisiana State University Press, 1971), p. 400; George B. Tindall, *The Emergence of the New South, 1913–1945* (Baton Rouge: Louisiana State University Press, 1967), pp. 258–276.

Women and Libraries

Anne Firor Scott

One great gap in library history is created by the failure of historians, so far, to make a systematic analysis of the part played by women's associations in creating public libraries. Perhaps 75 percent of such libraries were initiated by women's groups, often originally for their own use. Close study of this phenomenon would reveal a good deal about the growth of self-education and adult education as significant aspects of American culture.

As all of you are well aware, there has been for some years now a growing interest in the history of libraries, including the history of American libraries. The people who write on the subject universally agree that understanding the history of libraries of various kinds helps us understand the social and cultural history of whatever time we choose to investigate. Many fascinating and learned articles and a few books have expanded on this theme, and from them we can learn a good deal about early social libraries, circulating libraries, Sunday school libraries, mechanics' or merchants' libraries, as well as about the growth of the great research libraries such as the Boston or New York public libraries or those connected with universities.[1]

As I undertook to prepare this, my first venture into library history, I searched the literature in vain for any analysis of what must be one of the most interesting strands of American library history—the part played by women's associations in creating many of our public libraries. In 1933 the American Library Association apparently announced that 75 percent of the public libraries then in existence owed their creation to women—yet, except for an old article by Mois Coit Tyler, none of the standard works in library history so much as mentions this fact.[2]

This is perhaps not the time and place to expand at length on the question of why historians notice some things about the past and not others—if the subject intrigues you, I could suggest the lead article in

Anne Firor Scott *is William K. Boyd professor, Department of History, Duke University.*

the June 1984 issue of the *Journal of American History*, "On Seeing and Not Seeing: A Case of Historical Invisibility," which deals with the long silence about the history of women's organizations in general.[3]

Here today, my purpose is to convince you that the role of women's clubs in creating public libraries deserves a high place on your agenda for research. I take as my text a few sentences from an article in the first issue of the *Journal of Library History*, in which Frank Woodford wrote: "No structure of a public type more closely touches and affects the lives of people, or exerts a more profound influence on the character of a community than does the public library . . ."; ". . . a history of a library reflects clearly the history of the community it serves and does it better than can the history of almost any other local institution."[4] If Woodford was right, and even allowing for a certain professional bias he certainly has a point, there is every reason to examine the history of the local public libraries in many towns and small cities in the United States.

Since all the basic research remains to be done, let me set a framework and suggest some of the lines of investigation, and urge those of you whose principal interest is in library history to take up the challenge of finding out something about that 75 percent of public libraries of which the ALA spoke in 1933. In trying to put the bits and pieces of what I know about women and libraries into context, I go back to the early days of North American settlement when the written word was not a very important part of most people's lives. Even for those who were literate, which might mean only that they could write their names and perhaps puzzle out some Bible verses, most of the important business of life was carried on orally. The folklore of the frontier tells us that most families who had any books at all had only three: the Bible, *Pilgrim's Progress*, and a book of sermons. From the beginning, of course, there were exceptions: New England ministers, Virginia gentlemen, and the occasional transplanted scholar imported books and read them. Such people were generally men.

There were literate women—a few—but they were far from typical. When the first colleges opened—Harvard, William and Mary, and Yale—they were for men only. The first governor of Massachusetts is often quoted on his diagnosis of the madness of a woman. It was caused, he said, by reading and writing books and doing other unwomanly things . . . He was only formulating what most people seemed to think: that "learning" was beyond the capacity of women's brains. But despite this widespread view, intellectual curiosity is not a sex-related characteristic, and there were always a few women who insisted on studying on their own, who reads the books in family libraries, who occasionally wrote books, and who spoke forcefully about their desire for a better education.

After the American Revolution the country embarked upon a busy program of college-building. There had been nine colleges in 1776; by 1860 thousands had been started, and a considerable number had survived. Any man who really wanted a collegiate education could get it, though the proportion of those who did so remained small. For women there was a parallel development: a considerable growth in the number of female seminaries, some of which tried to provide a curriculum exactly like that of the men's colleges, though most were careful not to stir up opposition by calling themselves colleges.[5] Soon graduates of these seminaries were turning up all over the country teaching in the common schools. Most of these women taught for a while, then married and devoted themselves to family life—but more and more they constituted a group of literate women who, having had a little education, often had a desire for more.

As early as 1800 the first women's voluntary associations had appeared in New England in the shape of benevolent societies, which were followed by missionary and Sunday school societies, maternal associations, temperance, education, and antislavery societies, and societies devoted to women's rights. During the Civil War women organized the work of the great Sanitary Commission, and in hundreds of northern and midwestern communities they worked, throughout the war, in what they called "a wider sphere of usefulness."

From the very beginning women's associations exhibited a strong tendency toward self-improvement. While they sewed for the poor, one member was designated to read aloud an "improving" book. Tiny benevolent societies formed lending libraries, first for their members and then, gradually, for the whole community. By the 1870s a perceptive observer would have noticed that the changes in women's literacy and educational opportunity were part of a whole complex of social and economic changes that were altering the face of the country.

As a result of immigration and natural increase, the population was growing rapidly; roads and canals, steamboats and railroads, the cheap printing press—all speeded communication and trade; factories were beginning to replace domestic production of textiles, shoes, and clothing. Towns grew. The number of women not completely engaged in domestic industry also grew, and the number who could afford domestic servants increased.[6] By the 1870s all of these changes had made possible a vast expansion in the number of women's associations, a phenomenon that was destined to have a profound effect on the life of many, probably most, American communities.

The history of this movement is important, but for our purposes I focus on one particular kind of association: the literary or culture club.

The earliest such clubs appeared before the Civil War among black women in Philadelphia, who felt a desperate need for education otherwise unavailable to them, and among a group of white women in Iowa.

After the war in one town and city after another, under an enormous variety of names, women organized groups for self-education. They set out to study history, art, philosophy, Shakespeare, and modern science. Many of them had been trained in the female seminaries to write papers using data drawn from books. In towns where there were public libraries, clubwomen began to form the most active group of patrons. But in the smaller cities and towns where no public library existed, other expedients had to be tried. Some clubs in New York state, for instance, ordered books by mail from the New York State Library. (That library was generous enough to lend books even to some clubwomen in Maine!) Others began to buy books and to establish reference shelves, for the use of their members, and these collections soon grew into community libraries. Some organizations existed for the express purpose of creating public libraries.[7]

The prototype may have been the Ladies Library Association of Ann Arbor, Michigan, where as early as 1866 thirty-five women joined together, taxed themselves, rented a room, chose books that members could use free, and any member of the community could borrow for ten cents. By the 1890s innumerable clubs were trying to create public libraries. To give some sense of how this movement could affect even a poor, rural state with a high rate of illiteracy, I turn to the 1902 and 1903 yearbooks of the Arkansas Federation of women's clubs.

The Women's Library Association of Arkadelphia with 65 members had a library of over 600 volumes; the Rainbow Book Club of Brinkley had 15 members and devoted itself exclusively to library work; a club in Conway with 30 members had a library department; the Woman's Book Club in Crawfordsville with 13 members had established a library; in El Dorado, the Self-Culture Club with 23 members was collecting a library; the Woman's Book Club of Harrison with 22 members was building a library; the Hot Springs Fortnightly Club with 37 members maintained a traveling library for the country schools; the Woman's Cooperative Club of Little Rock had founded a library . . . and so it went through Mena, Morrillton, Osceola, Van Buren, Warren, and Waldron. At least 14 libraries had been founded in one decade, and there were more to come. The Virginia Federation of Women's Clubs reported in the 1930s that, while there had been only 3 public libraries in Virginia when the first woman's club was organized, fifty years later, there were at least 60 that had been organized by women.[8] The reports compiled in 1898 by Jennie June Croly in her massive *History of the*

Woman's Club Movement show similar patterns all across the country. A dedicated quantifier could have some fun going through Croly's volume just to pull out and record the libraries that women founded.[9]

It was not a very big jump from founding small local libraries to lobbying in the legislature for library commissions and supporting taxes for public libraries. In Georgia the federation of women's clubs was, from the beginning, very strong on library work, especially on developing traveling libraries to reach the rural communities. The women also supported a bill to permit women to hold the office of state librarian. This was the first state office opened to women in Georgia. In other states many clubs, even in 1896, reported the creation of a public library as their principal reason for being.

Women's work for libraries was closely related to their work for public education. Very early in the life of many literary clubs, women began to look beyond their own education to that of children; in many communities, women's clubs were a major factor in the development of public schools. As they worked to improve the schools, one focus of activity was always the school library. The traveling library was a favorite cause: one Maine club reported "50 books in a strong box can be sent to any town or hamlet in the state when a number of responsible persons who are willing to use, care for, and pay transportation and such additional charges as may be deemed necessary write in and apply for same . . ."

It is not at all surprising, given this background, to discover that Sarah Byrd Askew, the "organizer and missionary" for the New Jersey Public Library Commission in 1905, who would later invent the bookmobile, had strong support in all her endeavors from the New Jersey Federation of Women's Clubs. If someone should investigate the passage in New Jersey in 1920 of a law authorizing the creation of county libraries, I would be willing to wager you will find that the principal support for the bill came from women's organizations.[10]

Nearly all of what I have said today I have dug up from the sources in the past six weeks. This is obviously the barest beginning—but it is enough to embolden me to offer some general propositions:

(1) That the history of public libraries as it has been written so far is incomplete, and that, when the part played by women's organizations in the creation of libraries across the country is adequately documented and published, the history will have to be rewritten.

(2) That if it is true that the history of libraries is a good window into changes in the culture, then the close study of the early days of many public libraries will throw new light on the tremendous social change represented by the education of women, the development of women's organizations, and then the movement of women into public political activity.

I hope that many of you who are interested in library history will give this matter some thought, and that some of you will take up the challenge to study with care the early beginnings of community public libraries.

Notes

1. Jesse Shera, "The Literature of American Library History," *Library Quarterly* 15 (January 1945); 1-24; Clarence E. Sherman, "The Changing Public Library," *Library Journal* 57 (15 June 1932): 563-567; Louis Shores, *Origins of the American College Library* (Nashville: George Peabody Library, 1934); John F. Lewis, *History of the Apprentices Library of Philadelphia 1820-1920* (Philadelphia: Historical Society of Pennsylvania, 1924); Robert D. Leigh, *The Public Library in the United States* (New York: Columbia University Press, 1950); Michael Harris (ed.), *Reader in American Library History* (Washington, D.C.: Microcard Editions, 1971); and issues 1-8 of the *Journal of Library History* are only a few of the secondary works. Primary sources are voluminous. Dee Garrison, *Apostles of Culture: The Public Librarian and American Society, 1876-1920* (New York: Free Press, 1979), though focused in part on women as librarians, seems unaware of the work of women in creating libraries.

2. Sophonisba P. Breckinridge, *Women in the Twentieth Century* (New York: McGraw Hill, 1933), p. 93.

3. *Journal of American History* 71/1 (June 1984): 7-21.

4. *Journal of Library History* 1/1 (1966): 34-41.

5. Anne F. Scott, "The Ever Widening Circle . . ." *History of Education Quarterly* 19 (Spring 1979): 3-25; Frederick Rudolph, *The American College* (New York: A. A. Knopf, 1962).

6. George R. Taylor, *The Transportation Revolution* (New York: Holt, Rinehart, 1951).

7. Jennie June Croly, *The History of the Woman's Club Movement in America* (New York: H. G. Allen and Co., 1898), covers reports from many states and contains hundreds of reports of the creation of libraries.

8. *Yearbooks* of the Arkansas Federation of Women's Clubs for 1902-1903; Etta Belle Walker Northington, *The Virginia Federation of Women's Clubs 1907-1957* (Richmond: The Federation, 1958), esp. pp. 123-127.

9. Croly, *History of the Woman's Club Movement*.

10. Edward James and Janet James (eds.), *Notable American Women* (Cambridge: Harvard University Press, 1971), I: 61-62.

Portrait of John Pintard, 1817, by John Trumbull.
(Courtesy of the New-York Historical Society)

Books, Power, and the Development of Libraries in the New Republic: The Prison and Other Journals of John Pintard of New York

Larry E. Sullivan

The eminent New Yorker John Pintard (1759–1844) was the driving force behind a multitude of cultural, social, political, reform, and library organizations of the first half of the nineteenth century. Pintard had very firm ideas on books, reading, and libraries, as well as on the important issues of his day. Throughout most of his life he recorded his thoughts on books in a series of journals and letters. A symptomatic reading of his writings on literature reveals the reading interests of the New York elite of his age and calls into question accepted notions of the reading habits of the nineteenth-century bourgeoisie. Pintard read both extensively and intensively, was fond of the novel and sympathetic fiction, avidly read newspapers and periodicals, but he also believed strongly in the moral qualities of literature. His basic conservatism manifested itself in his ideas on the utilitarianism of libraries and their role in the improvement and the uplifting of the "masses." Pintard's activities illustrate well the integral part of libraries in nineteenth-century power networks and in the growth of bourgeois culture.

> What happiness it is that I have a turn for books! How many, many hours of keen anguish have they beguiled! Possibly, had I not been blessed with this disposition, I might have fallen a dreadful sacrifice to intemperance. The cheerful glass has been too often resorted to, in cases like mine, to dissipate the clouds of adversity.[1]

John Pintard wrote these lines in 1793 at the age of thirty-four. They

Larry E. Sullivan *is professor and chief librarian, Herbert H. Lehman College of the City University of New York.*

reveal a strong belief in the moral qualities of literature, a belief that never wavered throughout his eighty-five years. To him, books and their repositories, the libraries, were utilitarian instruments for social and educational improvement and reform. Libraries fit within a network of power relationships along with prisons, schools, and voluntary charitable associations. They existed to make the world better, to provide examples and imitative ideals, to preserve society in the image of an educated middle class. Through the discursive practices of Pintard and other like-minded benevolent philanthropists who came to the fore after the American Revolution, we see played out a drama of subconscious mental violence on society through the advocacy of certain patterns of social and educational habits. These men believed firmly in a moral imperative for society, and they acted accordingly. Or as Pintard said less harshly: "It is a consolation that the promoters & friends of every good work pursue the silent tenor of their course, & it is a gratification that instead of relaxing, their efforts are invigorated and extended. . . . Some time will be required to perfect a system that cannot fail to improve the rising generation."[2]

Who was John Pintard, why is he important, and what do his thoughts and writings have to do with the history of books and libraries? Never a well-known politician, statesman, or president of voluntary societies or political parties, Pintard was nevertheless a highly significant person, because he performed the very important but less glamorous function of the organizer and secretary of a variety of organizations. He made them run on a day-to-day basis, and consequently he had tremendous influence on the direction of numerous social, political, and cultural societies in New York during the first half of the nineteenth century.

Born in 1759 and orphaned a year later, John Pintard was brought up by his paternal uncle, the New York merchant Lewis Pintard (1732–1818).[3] He received a classical education in Hempstead, Long Island, and was a member of the College of New Jersey's (later renamed Princeton) class of 1776. During the Revolution he served as assistant agent for American prisoners. Before the age of thirty he was well-established in the business, political, and social life of New York City. On 10 May 1787 he was appointed the first secretary of the Mutual Assurance Company of New York, which was the city's first fire insurance company. In 1789 he was elected assistant alderman of the second ward of the city and he represented New York in the fourteenth session of the State Assembly, January–March 1791. At the same time, the state of New Jersey selected him as one of five commissioners to erect bridges over the Hackensack and Passaic rivers.

Even this early in life he was very active in a variety of organizations: in 1790–1791 he was secretary of the New-York Manufacturing Society; first sagamore (and later grand sachem) of the Tammany Society; a trustee of the American Museum, the first museum in New York City; and senior warden of the Holland Lodge of Masons, among other offices. Later on he organized and became secretary of the New-York Historical Society; was clerk of the corporation of New York, and city inspector; organized New York's first savings bank in 1819 and was its chief officer from 1823 to 1841; helped found the General Theological Seminary and was a generous donor to its library; revived the Chamber of Commerce; promoted the Erie Canal; organized the Society for the Prevention of Pauperism and the House of Refuge and helped build their libraries; and actively supported Sailor's Snug Harbor, the Mercantile Library, and the American Bible Society and its library. It is an understatement to say that he was a busy and involved man. In 1817 he mentioned holding eleven positions in a variety of remunerative and nonremunerative posts.[4] And he counted among his friends mayor (later governor) De Witt Clinton, Elias Boudinot, president of the Continental Congress, many other prominent citizens (he even borrowed books on the French Revolution from Aaron Burr),[5] and most of the philanthropists of his day.

Until the second generation of the nineteenth century, there were few reformers dedicated to a single cause. Pintard and his colleagues were involved in a multiplicity of charitable, reform, and philanthropic organizations. They treated society as an organic unity, and their efforts comprised a network that treated all the ills of their time. In the 1830s and later we begin to see the domination of reformers committed to the eradication of one evil—the abolitionists, temperance advocates, and the like.[6] It is not my main purpose to explain why this phenomenon occurred when it did, but to examine how Pintard fit into his historical context, to analyze the relationships among the discursive units, or books, that Pintard read, and the libraries he created or promoted, and the part these institutions played within early-nineteenth-century power networks that fueled the charitable and moral actions.

I view Pintard's life as an archetypical text that when symptomatically read reveals the essential dynamics of contemporary social consciousness, a social consciousness that reached its heights during the years following the Revolution. Beginning in the 1830s it gradually declined until the 1850s, when various social and economic changes finally put an end to the cultural hegemony of the bourgeoisie educated in the traditional classical manner. It was then that the bourgeois city changed its character. Even though wealth remained concentrated in a few hands right up until the Civil War (and after), the bourgeoisie could no longer ignore the clear-cut social divisions in the country. It was then that the rhetoric of social dominance changed and the elite concerned with libraries and other institutions perhaps *consciously* fought to control the reading habits of the "lower classes."'[7] Pintard would never control, only "improve," because the later connotation of control did not fit within his mental constructs.

Ironically, this view of Pintard begins with his imprisonment in 1797. Pintard was intimately involved with the stock manipulations of New York financier William Duer to the extent that he cosigned almost one million dollars' worth of Duer's notes.[8] When Duer defaulted on his debts in 1792, Pintard was caught in the ensuing panic and removed himself to Newark, New Jersey, where he remained in exile for eight years. It was in Newark that he began diary writing, the first extant journal dating from 1793. In 1797 the courts finally caught up with him and placed him in debtor's prison, where he remained from March 1797 to August 1798. During this imprisonment he kept a highly detailed diary and what he termed his Journal of Studies, into which he continued making entries until 1803. These diaries are rare sources for the history of reading habits.[9]

We know reading tastes primarily through such archival material as probate inventories, circulating library readers' statistics, booksellers' records, and printers' daybooks, as well as printed book advertisements, library catalogues, and the like. Letters and memoirs are also most useful.[10] However, this evidence usually tells us what was available to read and not what was actually read. Of course, the knowledge that a book went through several editions and sold copies in the many thousands, or that a book circulated widely among numerous people, allows us to make the reasonable inference that the book was read. But although we can assume from this evidence that such and such books were read, we never have complete assurance.

Pintard's writings tell us explicitly what he read, not only what he bought. In fact, his diaries mention everything—the works he read, bought, what he thought about them, the weather on the day he read them, and every other type of occurrence he thought interesting, which included much. Most important are the Prison Reading Diary and the concurrent Journal of Studies. We have a gap in his reading documentation until 1816, when he began a long series of letters to his daughter, who had recently taken up residence in New Orleans.[11] This correspondence continued until 1833, when his daughter died. We know little of his reading activity between 1833 and his death in 1844. It is unlikely that he did much reading at the end of his life, however, because he became progressively blind during his last years. The letters, of course, are not as sytematic as the journals in mapping his reading habits, but they do provide us with valuable insights into his views and ideas concerning the moral utilitarianism of literature and libraries.

In the journals and letters Pintard made numerous comments on the value and merit, and meaning, of the books he read. Although Pintard was outstanding in the breadth of his activities and his writing, he was no exemplary literary critic. His comments are mundane and devoid of any penetrating insight. Because of this, however, I feel he is all the more important and representative of his world. His observations provide a special usefulness by their very lack of critical genius. So an examination of his views reveals the typical rather than the exceptional, and this is my very aim—to understand the "ideal type" of influential elite literary taste of the period and how it affected the origins and development of libraries and other institutions in the New York of the early Republic.

One other methodological point: to a certain extent I place Pintard's readings into approximate discursive groupings. I fully realize the limitations in categorization and do not stick to it as an iron rule.[12] I do this not to fit Pintard into my own schema but because he loosely categorized his reading in his course of study. He wrote of his "historical studies," his "*lectiones legales*," and the like.[13] Therefore, the groupings, by and large, are his and not mine.

John Pintard's reading habits do not fit neatly into any of our accepted notions of the history of reading. In him, we find an amalgam of extensive and intensive reading, but always with a utilitarian purpose. His reading methodology did not vary, whether he was studying novels, newspapers, history, theology, or moral philosophy.[14] If he had a reading problem, it is familiar to our own age; he could not keep up with the great number of books available. He realized and remarked on the common perception that it was an "age of lighter reading" but did not necessarily see that as a bad thing.[15] And he understood and took advantage of new technology in printing. To cite only one example, he actively used and advised publishers on the stereotyping of books in order to achieve a wider distribution.[16] He did not fit into the mold of the stern moralist who saw the fashion for sympathetic fiction and novel and newspaper reading as either a cause or a reflection of the downfall of civilization. He found a purpose in reading just about everything except for the obscene or immoral. And I would suggest that many of his colleagues shared his reading tastes, but were not as vocal as the anti-novel faction.[17] Perhaps a systematic study of books in will inventories of the period will bear this conjecture out.

Roughly speaking, the books Pintard mentioned in his various writings from 1793 to 1833 fall into the following groupings: literature, seventy-six titles; theology, seventy-eight titles; history, eighty-four titles; and law, thirteen titles. These are approximate figures because I have counted such works as Shakespeare's plays, essays by Addison, Steele, and Johnson, and numerous numbered sermons as single titles.[18] Therefore, if we wished to take quantification to its exact limit, we could easily multiply these figures many times.

In literature Pintard categorized novels, plays, poetry (little read, but often donated to libraries), and especially the semiformal familiar essay, which imparted his brand of moral philosophy and values. In Pintard's mental universe the novel was like an amusement center, existing for repose and to replenish energy for more serious pursuits. Listen to him in 1827 in his sixty-eighth year:

> I send for Darling the last Waverly, Tales of the Conangate, in the preface to which Scott avows himself the Author. The present work does not detract from the character of this wonderful prolix Genius. His stores of invention and mind appear inexhaustible. To me these works are most delectable, and always beguile after fatigue of dry reading and restore the tone and vigor of my mind. Old people in many particulars resemble the young, that of novel reading is one. Scott's are instructive as well as pleasing. They serve to relax and beguile the cares as well as the ennui of existence. . . . May I never do worse than read the standard English novels of the last and present age, but I am not discriminate in my reading, rather fastidious than otherwise. But wearied and worn down these works are greater restorative than a bottle or cards.[19]

It is evident that without books, Pintard probably would not have been sober enough to write his letters or diaries. In fact, the relationship between books and temperance was common at the time. The contemporary New York bookseller Hocquet Caritat advertised "The decrease in drunkenness in this country, is perhaps owing to the introduction of circulating libraries, which may be considered as temples erected by literature to attract the votaries of Bacchus."[20]

Pintard also shared the common or popular taste for the sympathetic novel. He remarked favorably on Henry Mackenzie's *Julia de Roubigne*, and he was fond of Sterne's *Sentimental Journey*. He found the Gothic novel to his liking and early on he read "Monk" Lewis and Ann Radcliffe's *The Italian*. Of the latter he could say, "Of all the flights of imagination since the days of Shakespeare, this novel exceeds everything I have ever perused. . . . I read it with a glow of sympathy from first to last."[21] He read *Peregrine Pickle, Tristram Shandy, The Fool of Quality*, and *Gil Blas* and looked with great pleasure on Cooper and Catherine Sedgwick. And late in his life he wrote of Washington Irving, "whose genius & writings have raised if not founded, in jealous old England, the literary character of our country, one whom his fellow citizens will delight to honour. Long may he live to enjoy and wear the laurels that encircle his brow.''[22]

It is worth noting that Pintard continually remarked on the growing economic success of writers such as Cooper, Sedgwick, and Irving.[23] He had more than a passing interest in book sales: he was in the trade at one time, and attempted to buy into John Ward Fenno's book business in 1801.[24] And if he wanted to make any money, which of necessity he did, he would have to know what would sell. Fenno turned Pintard down and died the following year. But we are fortunate to have Fenno's probate bookstore inventory and we can see the kind of books and business Pintard thought profitable.[25] In the inventory we find all the popular books of 1800, with novels next to Shakespeare, Edward Young's *Night Thoughts* (Pintard thought highly of it and once remarked on its popularity in France),[26] Milton, Dryden, 28 copies of *The Pleasure of Hope*, and 237 copies of *Bubble and Squeak*.

I emphasize his taste for novelistic literature because he did not fit the stereotype of the antinovel bourgeois. He had his thumb on the pulse of popular taste, tried to profit from it, and even shared in it to a certain extent. Pintard was also a trustee and generous donor to the first subscription library in New York City, the New York Society Library, also known as the City Library.[27] He provided this library, which is still in existence, with general literary works, and from the above evidence it is obvious he would not oppose the introduction of novels or romances, as long as there was some moral content.

Pintard also looked approvingly on newspaper reading, something his sterner contemporaries decried. In 1793 he wrote:

> It is astonishing what gratification a newspaper affords in a country retirement, secluded from the busy world. . . . The general circulation and reading of newspapers throughout the United States forms the striking feature in the American character. To this source may be traced that general information on all subjects which peculiarly distinguishes our citizens from the mass of the Old World. A newspaper comes to our fireside and its multifarious contents affords a something to gratify the curiosity of every description.[28]

Pintard's view of newspapers is not surprising. These periodicals, by and large, shared his conservative outlook on life and reflected the power relationship prevalent in New York City throughout the first half of the nineteenth century. Although the term ''aristocracy'' took on a negative connotation after the Revolution, and the nineteenth-century rhetoric glorified the ''common man,'' by no stretch of the imagination was New York (or anywhere else in the United States) democratic. New York City was governed by and for the rich, and most newspapers promoted the interests of the wealthy. It is demonstrably true that most city officials during this period catered to the rich, and that the wealthy totally dominated the city's influential voluntary associations.[29] As more of the rich withdrew from active politics, it was through the voluntary benevolent associations that they purveyed their social views and values. And it was in these organizations that Pintard and his kind were most active. On numerous occasions he remarked that his motives "arise from a sincere disposition to be useful in my day & generation and to apply the talents with which I am endowed for the Benefit of Society. . . ."[30] and "I must serve my fellow citizens in the silent walks of charity and benevolence."[31] Silent, but very effective.

Pintard's views on society were conservative and evangelistic. He did not trust the masses and was no democrat. In 1798 he wrote: "The Spirit of Democracy appears to me to be founded on jealousy and envy, the most malignant of passions of the human heart are usurping authority over every generous principle. The virtue, talents, and riches of every person distinguished for either is sufficient to render him an object of odium and distrust."[32] He voted against the 1821 constitution because of its suffrage provisions. He thought cities were cesspools of vice, and he could say about the common people that "like most Americans they are composed of malleable stuff, readily susceptible of polish but like most half educated people, I speak of the mass, more disposed to catch the vices than the virtue of refined society."[33]

His solution to ameliorating this vice-prone nature was education, and that meant books, reading, libraries, schools, benevolent associations, and ultimately prisons. Although he was not very active politically in the traditional sense, his life and writings constitute an organized strategy of particular political action—an effective discourse to instill virtue in that "malleable stuff" he called the "people." This course was his class's method to create a well-ordered public. Some of the "lower order" perceived, although dimly, this strategy and worked against it, but without great effect.[34] And Pintard was not ignorant of opposing radical philosophies. His tactic was to contain dissent by ignoring it. Oppression, he thought, would only make martyrs. This method is evident in his remarks on the freethinking feminist Frances Wright, her speeches, and her newspaper, the *Free Enquirer*: "Let her blow out I say. Opposition will only increase her dissolute followers. . . . Let her alone is my maxim & she will talk & write herself down."[35] And she did.

It is not surprising, therefore, that theology, history, and what he considered "serious" literature were the greatest influences on his thought and actions. In literature, Samuel Johnson was his constant companion. In 1793 he remarked:

> I feel myself more indebted to the writings of Johnson, and his minute biographer, Mr. Boswell, for many resolutions I have formed, to pursue a moral and religious course of conduct hereafter through life, than any other writer whatever. I purpose to read everything that has fallen from the pen of Johnson and have no doubt but that I shall be eminently enlightened and improved.[36]

It was then that Pintard also wrote that principles should be fixed "round which we may rally all our thoughts and steer our bark through life's tempestuous ocean."[37] Literature was to be his navigator and he set off with his Journal of Studies quoting Boswell's *Journal of a Tour to the Hebrides* on the importance of recording one's daily readings.[38]

Apparently Pintard did read everything Johnson wrote, and more than once. He studied the *Rambler* daily and went through the *Dictionary* systematically in 157 days, it requiring 9 minutes per page to absorb properly.[39] Late in his life, in 1833, he could still say about Johnson: "I feel more indebted to this eminent moralist than to any other English author."[40]

And what kind of values did Pintard find worthy in essayistic literature? Let us look at a few examples and see how the ideas highlighted in his journals and letters related to his social actions and his involvement in libraries. In March 1798, after reading Johnson on idleness, he resolved to "learn diligence." Then on 29 April 1798 he noted: "If wit or wisdom be the dean, if honesty, be the heart, INDUSTRY is the right hand of every vocation; without which the shrewdest insight and the best intention can execute nothing. A SLUGGARD is qualified for no office, no calling, no station among men, he is a mere nobody; taking up room, pestering and clogging the world."[41] Twenty years later he blamed the great increase of poverty and indigence in the city not only on the great wave of immigration but also on the newcomers' sloth and idleness. The solution was a benevolent society to study and alleviate the miseries of the poor, and eventually a library to enlighten them. In 1818 he said about the Society for the Prevention of Pauperism, of which he was a founder and manager (with Thomas Eddy and John Griscom): "The intention of this Society is not to afford alms but labour, so that there shall be no pretext for idleness, to give the means of occupation to the industrious, to educate their children & expel the drones from Society."[42] Quite evident in this passage is the natural relation between morality, industry, and education.

In order to prepare himself to improve the industry of the poor, he spent "his leisure hours," he wrote, "devoted to works on political economy, to enable him to discharge his duty with some degree of diligence."[43] He did not mention which books on political economy he read in 1818, but earlier he read Rumford's essays,[44] which I am sure included *On the Management of the Poor.* Listen to him on Patrick Colquhoun's *Treatise on the Police of the Metropolis*: "No work that has ever come under my inspection contains so much useful information, or evinces so much investigation of a very complicated subject. . . ."[45] Pintard wrote this before Colquhoun's influential *Treatise on Indigence*, which attributed the growth of the pauper element to "a general inattention to the religious education and moral habits of the children of the lower classes." But the British moralist had a decided effect on the founders of the Society for the Prevention of Pauperism, and for nearly two decades Colquhoun corresponded with Pintard's close colleague Thomas Eddy, supplying him with endless publications on the poor and dangerous classes.[46]

In 1819 Pintard put into action his plan to educate paupers and formed a library. Included we find all of Colquhoun's works, as well as those by Bentham, John Howard, Adam Smith, and numerous treatises on poverty, intemperance, and prison discipline.[47] It is significant that the Society for the Prevention of Pauperism undertook a study of the causes of poverty, issued a report on the findings, and then changed its name and became the Society for the Reformation of Juvenile Delinquents. Under the latter name it sponsored the House of Refuge, the first reform school in America.[48]

It is also no coincidence that the same men who were involved in eradicating pauperism and delinquency were also responsible for the establishment of Newgate Prison, the creation of the Mechanics and Apprentices Library, and the active Free School Society and its libraries.[49]

In the Free School Society, Pintard was especially fond of the highly regimented Lancastrian pedagogical method, which maintained order and discipline, and supposedly instilled proper moral values.[50] These reformative aims resembled those of the emerging prison system. And we should not be surprised to learn that not only did Pintard work actively in penal reform, but his few essays frequently dealt with prisons and penal discipline.[51] Therefore, I think it appropriate to suggest again his mental relationship among books, libraries, schools, prisons, and power.

It is along these same lines that he viewed the Mechanics and Apprentices Library, of which he was a founder. On the opening ceremony of the library in 1820, he remarked that "such a large collection of decent young apprentices added greatly to the impression of every mind that reflected on the importance of the institution and of the moral effects of which it will be productive on the rising generation. . . ."[52]

Although I have grouped Pintard's readings following his own organization, we must remember that they all form one construct. And its nucleus was religion. In 1793 he commented that "I have regularly devoted all the Sundays to Religious purposes and reading, a practice I sincerely mean invariably to pursue during the remainder of my life.''[53] He also could see the merits of new printing technology for religion, remarking in 1798 that ''Nothing can be more essential to the cause of religion in this country, than to promote a cheap edition of a book, which ought to be in every professing Christian's hands. . . .''[54] Pintard's theological readings not only helped him set his moral principles but also aided him in his benevolent and philanthropic work and in setting collection policies for theological libraries.

Religious reading in no way declined during the first half of the nineteenth century; if anything it increased. New York City, regardless of its reputation for sin and wickedness (probably because of this reputation), became a focal point for religious groups during the first part of the century. So many religious and missionary societies established bases there that, by 1830, the city was the foremost religious center in the nation.[55] During this era of the second great awakening, not only Pintard's class found serenity and guidence in religion; mechanics, artisans, and the like were also fond of spiritual reading and sermonizing. In fact, sermons were an increasingly popular literary as well as oratorical genre during this period, and rarely did an occasion end without a sermon.[56]

The number of religious works, including sermons, was large in any respectable library of the period. To take the most famous example, sermons outnumbered all other books in George Washington's library. Pintard made constant reference to his sermon reading, and he read and reread his favorite sermons throughout his life. For forty years he made repeated references to Isaac Barrow, Vicemus Knox, Jeremiah Seed, and others. He was absolutely effusive on Timothy Dwight and expressed admiration at the number of editions his work went through.[57]

Never devoid of the sentimental, Pintard shared the popular passion for the works of the Reverend Leigh Richmond, of which he was ''enraptured.'' He especially delighted in ''Miss Richmond's description of the last moments of her father,'' which, he remarked, ''so overpowered me that I was obliged to lay the book aside, and weep in silence under the cover of my shade. No Tragedy, however deeply pathetic, in my play reading days ever affected more intensely.'' This memoir was hugely successful, so much so that Pintard noted ''that several of our Evangelical Ministers have purchased from five to a dozen copies for circulation among their parishioners whose circumstances are too circumscribed to lay out even a dollar.''[58]

The Bible was the cornerstone of Pintard's religious reading. He read the Greek Testament over twenty times alone, and the whole Bible at least once a year throughout his life. He was an active promoter of the American Bible Society, which he considered the most important benevolent society ever established in the country. He was the founder of the Bible Society's library, set up other libraries in New York and New Haven, and could speak on the subject of collection building:

> When the business of the Trustees concluded, by permission I was allowed to address them on the propriety of making collections of books for the Theological Library, being you know quite in my way, and I promised to set an example. I have had an eye to this purpose for some years, and while I have gratified and improved myself by collecting and reading some very valuable ecclesiastical works, I shall be able, without feeling it, to place on the shelves books that I need not blush to offer, or the Seminary to accept, and I hope what I remarked made a suitable impression.[59]

I would like to emphasize again that here we see that Pintard viewed books and libraries as integral parts of the general missions of his organizations—to impose order and values on a multiplicity of publics. All of these educational institutions I have been discussing existed to consecrate the present social order; knowledge found in books was to be acquired, not criticized, and readers were only to understand the validity of the texts put before them. Improvement of the mind through the reception of accepted views and notions was the primary objective. There is no question that we are dealing with conservative political and ideological forces, The idea of "reform" in the title of some of these organizations meant primarily eradication of evil through the conservation of elitist values.

The study of history only reinforced Pintard's frame of reference and also led him to establish one of the great historical libraries of the country. His conception of history incorporated all of his other ideas about religion and moral and political philosophy. His view of history was patriotic, nationalistic, utilitarian, and intensely religious. His praise of Timothy Dwight, one of America's leading spokesmen for the Scottish "common sense" school of philosophy, was consistent with his outlook. Through the study of history Pintard saw the reality of God and the importance of high moral standards in society.

Because he saw the strong hand of Providence in history, he was extremely optimistic about America's future. At exactly the same time when disease, poverty, filth, overcrowding, and high mortality rates were becoming pervasive in New York City, Pintard could exclaim, "I am confirmed in my belief that the world is growing better. . . . This is indeed the Era of Great Good, throughout the whole world. I trust that our beloved country may compare zeal and effort with any other. Not a new institution is announced or an existing one reanimated, but that my heart dilates with overflowing and gratitude.''[60] Such a mental universe had no place for jeremiads about the doom of civilization, societal dislocation, the ranting about the introduction of cheap literature, or radical opinions about class divisions. If religion was the foundation of his bourgeois city, and moral philosophy and literature the walls, then history was surely the gateway.

To him, history was not antiquarian but highly utilitarian. Historical studies ''add greatly to my stock of useful information,''[61] he said. History teaches lessons, it embodies the moral imperative. Look at our past, how we became unique, follow our great leaders, and we will surely benefit. Can anyone receive an education without knowledge of it, especially of American history? ''It is worse than a sham,'' he exclaimed, ''it is gross, for an American who has any pretension to education to be ignorant of his own country.''[62]

When he was fourteen he read Rollins's *Ancient History* and wished he had read it earlier. Later he read Hume, Smollett, and Gordon's *History of the American Revolution* and shared the popular taste for biography (especially of Washington) and the historical works of Washington Irving. It comes as no surprise that he had a great liking for ecclesiastical history, and even pursued a two-year course of study on the Reformation and Counter-Reformation. The light side of history, voyages and travel literature, he treated like novels, to refresh and reinvigorate him for more serious study.

Pintard was never content just to read. He had to make use of his knowledge. And on the basis of his historical studies, he established one of the premier historical libraries in the country. As early as 1789 Pintard proposed a Society of Antiquaries to Jeremy Belknap of Boston. Then, in 1804, he, Mayor De Witt Clinton, Peter Stuyvesant, and several other notable New Yorkers, many connected with the other philanthropic activities already mentioned, met in Clinton's office and, according to the minutes of the meeting, ''agreed to form themselves into a society the principal design of which should be to collect and preserve whatever may relate to the natural, civil or ecclesiastical history of the United States in general and of this State in particular. . . .''[63] During the first years of the New-York Historical Society's existence, Pintard spent countless days organizing and raising funds and materials. He formulated a more detailed collection policy and appealed to the public in broadsides and newspapers to save valuable books and documents for the study of history, concluding that ''without the aid of original records and authentic documents, history will be nothing more than a well-combined series of conjectures and amusing fables.''[64] Well before others realized their value, Pintard exclaimed the usefulness of ephemera, newspapers, manuscripts, and similar materials. His own donations and constant efforts resulted in a magnificent library, and by 1816 he could write, "It is astonishing what a fund of Historical materials have been collected already . . . the collections made will prove a most important legacy to posterity."[65] And by 1849 the Society could boast that it had the best American history collection in the country.

The New-York Historical Society is only the largest and best known of the libraries Pintard either established or patronized. Most of these libraries still exist today. His library efforts, I must emphasize again, fit well within the general pattern of his other benevolent and charitable actions, actions obligatory to a man of his station. Libraries, in common with other institutions, were ways to structure and reinforce a mental and moral universe—the bourgeois city of the early nineteenth century. They were only one part in the general network of discursive practices that reinforced and strengthened a conservative ideology common to these philanthropists. To Pintard and his kind, the object of a library was no different from the aim and usefulness of a prison or a school. They fit well within the natural order of things.

Pintard embodied a type that was more prevalent than heretofore recognized. He was a figure who combined the old and the new in reading tastes. Perhaps we can call him a bridge from the eighteenth century to the world of pleasure-reading for amusement in the Victorian age. He could enjoy all kinds of literature and find some value in most. He read both extensively and intensively. And although his thoughts and actions form a pattern of political action for societal dominance, they were not consciously oppressive or demeaning.

It is not my intention to link Pintard with the later public library movement, its founders, and their ideas. However, I would like to suggest that a fundamental difference, or epistemological break, existed between their mental worlds. If the public library benefactors of the mid-nineteenth century, for instance, consciously used such genres as the novel as instruments of social control—as bait to bring in the lower classes and educate them—as some library historians have attempted to prove, this notion would have been foreign to Pintard.[66] I do not use the term "social control" in my description of Pintard, and his vocabulary would not have allowed it. Pintard would not have understood Matthew Arnold's view that the education of the working class is not to be conducted for its own benefit or spiritual condition, but solely for the preservation of the upper classes. Novels help lure them in, all the better to control or incorporate. Or as one recent critic expressed it, "If the masses are not thrown a few novels, they may react by throwing up a few barricades."[67] Pintard would be puzzled, but perhaps George Ticknor would smile and nod knowingly.

Notes

1. John Pintard, ms. Diary, Newark, New Jersey, 1 October–26 November 1793, 3 February–5 March 1794; entry for 13 November 1793. John Pintard Papers, New-York Historical Society, New York, New York. All of the manuscripts used in this paper reside in the Manuscripts Division of the New-York Historical Society and are cited courtesy of that institution.

2. Dorothy C. Barck (ed.), *Letters of John Pintard to His Daughter, Eliza Noel Pintard Davidson, 1816–1833*, 4 vols. (New York: New-York Historical Society, 1937–1940), 3 November 1830, III: 185 (hereafter cited as Pintard, *Letters*).

3. Pintard's life is detailed in David L. Sterling, "New York Patriarch: A Life of John Pintard, 1759–1844" (Ph.D. dissertation, New York University, 1958); also see Pintard's entry in the *Dictionary of American Biography*; Walter Barrett, *The Old Merchants of New York City* (New York: Doolady, 1870); and James G. Wilson, *The Memorial History of the City of New York* (New York: New York History Co., 1892–1893).

4. "Mama was counting up last night my several offices lucrative & honorable. . . . In all Eleven stations, the duties incident to the whole I severally & punctually discharge," Pintard, *Letters*, 2 January 1817, I: 47.

5. Ms. Diary, 12 November 1793. In Pintard's 1800–1801 Diary he mentioned that on 9 July 1801 he "dined tête-à-tête with Aaron Burr."

6. For interpretations of the many reform movements of the first half of the nineteenth century, see Charles C. Cole, *The Social Ideas of the Northern Evangelists, 1826–1860* (New York: Columbia University Press, 1954); Clifford E. Griffin, *Their Brothers' Keepers; Moral Stewardship in the United States, 1800–1865* (New Brunswick, N.J.: Rutgers University Press, 1960); Alice Felt Tyler, *Freedom's Ferment: Phases of American Social History from the Colonial Period to the Outbreak of the Civil War* (New York: Harper and Row, 1944); Ronald G. Walters, *American Reformers, 1815–1860* (New York: Hill and Wang, 1978); and the literature cited in these works.

7. For an excellent interpretation of the changes in class consciousness during this period, which culminated in the labor crisis of 1850, see Sean Wilentz, *Chants Democratic: New York City and the Rise of the American Working Class, 1788–1850* (New York: Oxford, 1984). For stimulating discussions on changes in thought and expression during the eighteenth and nineteenth centuries, see Michel Foucault, *The Order of Things* (New York: Pantheon, 1970), and *The Archeology of Knowledge* (New York: Pantheon, 1972), translations of *Les mots et les choses* (Paris: Gallimard, 1966) and *L'Archéologie du savoir* (Paris: Gallimard, 1969), respectively.

8. David L. Sterling, "William Duer, John Pintard, and the Panic of 1792," in Joseph Frese, S.J., and Jacob Judd (eds.), *Business Enterprise in Early New York* (Tarrytown, N.Y.: n.p., 1979), pp. 99–132.

9. John Pintard, ms. Reading Diary in Newark Prison, 1 January 1797–5 August 1798; ms. Journal of Studies, 1797–1804. The first part of the Reading Diary expands on the entries in the Journal of Studies. He divided the latter into columns so he could enter the number of minutes he spent each day on his regular readings.

10. For a discussion of sources of reading habits, see David D. Hall, "The Uses of Literacy in New England, 1600–1850," in William L. Joyce, David D. Hall, Richard D. Brown, and John B. Hench, *Printing and Society in Early America* (Worcester, Mass.: American Antiquarian Society, 1983), pp. 1–47; Robert

Darnton, "Reading, Writing, and Publishing in Eighteenth-Century France: A Case Study in the Sociology of Literature," *Daedalus* 100 (1971): 214–256; idem., "Readers Respond to Rousseau: The Fabrication of Romantic Sensibility," in *The Great Cat Massacre and Other Episodes in French Cultural History* (New York: Basic Books, 1978), pp. 215–263; Cynthia Z. Stiverson and Gregory A. Stiverson, "The Colonial Retail Book Trade: Availability and Affordability in Mid-Eighteenth Century Virginia," in Joyce et al., *Printing and Society in Early America*, pp. 132–173; and Larry E. Sullivan, "The Reading Habits of the Nineteenth-Century Baltimore Bourgeoisie: A Cross-Cultural Analysis," *Journal of Library History* 16 (Spring 1981): 227–240.

11. He kept a diary from 1806 to 1811, but it does not contain any reading entries. It is conceivable that he maintained a concurrent reading diary that is now lost. For instance, in addition to the Prison Diary and Journal of Studies, he had a diary from 1800 to 1801 that dealt mainly with his efforts to secure a position in the Jefferson administration.

12. See Darnton, "Reading, Writing, and Publishing in Eighteenth-Century France."

13. For instance, Diary, 1 October 1793: "I commenced a course of Law Reading with Mr. Boudinot, my friend, as also a general reading of Miscellaneous subjects, as occasion & inclination led. I purpose, however, to take up a regular series of historical reading, as soon as the weather grows cooler & I am done with the repairs of the place I am on, which are nearly completed." In his Journal of Studies he placed law books on a separate page labeled *Lectiones Legales*.

14. On the concept of a "reading revolution" (*Leserevolution*), or a shift from intensive to extensive reading that supposedly took place in the late eighteenth century, see Rolf Engelsing, *Der Burger als Leser: Lesergeschichte in Deutschland 1500–1800* (Stuttgart: Metzler, 1974); cf. Darnton, "Readers Respond to Rousseau," and Hall, "Uses of Literacy in New England."

15. Pintard, *Letters*, 27 January 1818, I: 107.

16. Ibid., 31 October 1831, III: 289, for one example among many.

17. On the low regard for novel-reading in the early nineteenth century, see James Hart, *The Popular Book* (New York: Oxford University Press, 1950); and Larry E. Sullivan, "Cheap Books and 19th Century Libraries," *A B Bookman's Weekly* (29 March 1981): 2410–2428.

18. I counted all the titles mentioned in his manuscript diaries and published letters. It must also be noted that he reread many of these titles throughout his life.

19. Pintard, *Letters*, 10 December 1827, II: 379–380. See also the entry for 22 June 1829, III: 82.

20. Quoted in Hart, *The Popular Book*, p. 54.

21. Prison Reading Diary, 13 October 1797.

22. Pintard, *Letters*, 22 May 1832, IV: 56.

23. Ibid., 14 June 1830, III: 156, for a comment on Sedgwick.

24. Journal of Studies, October 1801.

25. Ms. Inventory of the Estate of John Ward Fenno, 1802, New-York Historical Society.

26. "It is remarkable that of all the English Poets, the French prefer Young," Prison Reading Diary, 31 January 1797.

27. The New York Society Library was founded in 1754. See Austin Baxter Keep, *History of the New York Society Library* (New York: De Vinne Press, 1908).

28. Diary, 12 November 1793.

29. For penetrating insights into the social and economic life of New York City during the first half of the nineteenth century, see the following works by Edward Pessen: *Jacksonian America; Society, Personality, and Politics* (Homewood, Ill.: Dorsey Press, 1969); *Riches, Class, and Power before the Civil War* (Lexington, Mass.: D. C. Heath, 1973); "Political Democracy and the Distribution of Power in Antebellum New York City," in Irwin Yellowitz (ed.), *Essays in the History of New York City* (Port Washington, N.Y.: Kennikat Press, 1978), pp. 21–42. For benevolent societies, see Raymond A. Mohl, *Poverty in New York, 1783–1825* (New York: Oxford University Press, 1971); idem, "The Humane Society and Urban Reform in Early New York, 1787–1831," *New-York Historical Society Quarterly* 54 (January 1970): 30–52; Roy Lubove, "The New York Association for Improving the Condition of the Poor: The Formative Years," *New-York Historical Society Quarterly* 43 (July 1959): 307–327; Carl F. Kaestle, *Pillars of the Republic: Common Schools and American Society, 1780–1860* (New York: Hill and Wang, 1983); Carroll Smith Rosenberg, *Religion and the Rise of the American City: The New York City Mission Movement, 1812–1870* (Ithaca, N.Y.: Cornell University Press, 1971); Robert S. Pickett, *House of Refuge: Origins of Juvenile Reform in New York State, 1815–1857* (Syracuse, N.Y.: Syracuse University Press, 1969); M. J. Heale, "The New York Society for the Prevention of Pauperism, 1817–1823," *New-York Historical Society Quarterly* 55 (April 1971): 153–176; idem, "From City Fathers to Social Critics: Humanitarianism and Government in New York City, 1790–1869," *Journal of American History* 63 (June 1976): 21–46; and idem, "Humanitarianism in the Early Republic: The Moral Reformers of New York, 1776–1825," *Journal of American Studies* 2 (October 1968): 161–175.

30. Pintard, *Letters*, 2 December 1817, I: 94.

31. Ibid., 24 May 1833, II: 154.

32. Prison Reading Diary, 11 May 1798.

33. Pintard, *Letters*, 11 January 1822, II: 121.

34. Wilentz, *Chants Democratic*, pp. 145–216.

35. Pintard, *Letters*, 15 January 1829, III: 58. The most recent biography of Frances Wright is Celia Morris Eckhardt, *Fanny Wright: Rebel in America* (Cambridge, Mass.: Harvard University Press, 1984).

36. Diary, 3 October 1793.

37. Ibid.

38. Journal of Studies (p. 1): "Every man should keep minutes of whatever he reads. Every circumstance of his studies should be recorded; what books he has consulted; how much of them he has read; at what time; how often the same authors; and what opinions he formed of them, at different periods of his life."

39. Prison Reading Diary, 20 April 1798.

40. Pintard, *Letters*, 18 May 1833, IV: 150.

41. Prison Reading Diary, 29 April 1798.

42. Pintard, *Letters*, 26 October 1818, I: 151. On the SPP, see Mohl, *Poverty in New York*.

43. Pintard, *Letters*, 28 November 1818, I: 157.

44. Journal of Studies, 17 January 1799.

45. Prison Reading Diary, 10 February 1798.

46. Mohl, *Poverty in New York*, p. 253.

47. *The Second Annual Report of the Managers of the Society for the Prevention of Pauperism in the City of New York* . . . (New York: E. Conrad, 1820).

48. Concerning the House of Refuge, Pintard remarked: "Prevention is better than cure, and with perseverance we shall save numbers of little Devils from

becoming big ones'' (Pintard, *Letters*, 19 April 1826, II: 257). It is interesting to note that among reformative techniques at the House of Refuge, from 1826 to 1856, ''literary improvement,'' or instruction of the mind, was the most often mentioned (see Pickett, *House of Refuge*, p. 192).

49. See Arthur A. Ekirch, Jr., ''Thomas Eddy and the Beginnings of Prison Reform in New York,'' *New York History* 24 (July 1943): 376-391.

50. Kaestle, *Pillars of the Republic*, pp. 40-44.

51. For instance, in January 1826 he placed an article on the House of Refuge in Mordecai Noah's newspaper, the *Advocate*. There is also an unpublished essay on prison discipline in the Pintard Papers at the New-York Historical Society.

52. Pintard, *Letters*, 25 November 1820, I: 349-350.

53. Diary, 1 October 1793.

54. Prison Reading Diary, 29 July 1798.

55. Sidney I. Pomerantz, *New York: An American City, 1783-1803* (New York, 1938), p. 392; and Rosenberg, *Religion and the Rise of the American City*, pp. 45-51.

56. Wilentz, *Chants Democratic*, p. 77.

57. Pintard, *Letters*, 14 September 1831, III: 276.

58. Ibid., 18 March 1829, pp. 68-69.

59. Ibid., 12 September 1820, I: 323; also 6 November 1817, I: 90; 11 January 1822, II: 119-120; and Prison Reading Diary, January 1797. He could even read Locke's *Essay on Human Understanding* and remark that it ''serves to corroborate the Evidences in favor of Divine Rev. and the Xstian religion'' (Prison Reading Diary, 28 December 1798).

60. Pintard, *Letters*, 12 November 1825, II: 199; and 13 February 1826, II: 228.

61. Prison Reading Diary, 2 February 1797.

62. Pintard, *Letters*, 14 November 1831, III: 297-298.

63. For the New-York Historical Society, see R. W. G. Vail, *Knickerbocker Birthday* (New York: New-York Historical Society, 1954); and Pamela Spence Richards, *Scholars and Gentlemen: The Library of the New-York Historical Society, 1804-1982* (Hampden, Conn.: Archon Books, 1984).

64. ''To the Public,'' broadside, issued on 12 February 1805 and again on 15 September 1809; collections of the New-York Historical Society.

65. Pintard, *Letters*, 12 June 1816, I: 14.

66. For this interpretation of the public library movement, see Michael H. Harris, ''The Purpose of the American Public Library: A Revisionist Interpretation of History,'' *Library Journal* 98 (15 September 1973): 2509-2514; and idem, ''Public Libraries and the Decline of the Democratic Dogma,'' *Library Journal* 101 (1 November 1976): 2225-2230. For critiques of Harris's view, see Richard Harwell and Roger Michener, ''As Public as the Town Pump,'' *Library Journal* 99 (1 April 1974): 959-963; and Phyllis Dain, ''Ambivalence and Paradox: The Social Bonds of the Public Library,'' *Library Journal* 100 (1 February 1975): 261-266.

67. Terry Eagleton, *Literary Theory* (Minneapolis: University of Minnesota Press, 1983), p. 25.

Louis Round Wilson's *Geography of Reading*: An Inquiry into Its Origins, Development, and Impact

Robert Sidney Martin

The capstone of Louis Round Wilson's contributions to the library literature is *The Geography of Reading*, in which he correlated the distribution of libraries and library resources with other cultural facilities and social institutions. This topic was a central focus of Wilson's research for more than three decades. It originated in Wilson's perception of the scarcity of library resources in his native North Carolina, but the focus of his studies gradually broadened to encompass the entire nation. As his topic grew, he applied increasingly sophisticated research methodologies. In this he was profoundly affected by his close associations with Howard W. Odum, William S. Gray, and Douglas Waples. In many ways, *The Geography of Reading* represents a unique marriage of Odum's regionalism and Waples's mechanics. The origin and development of *The Geography of Reading* reveal Wilson's substantial abilities as a designer of research and provide an interesting insight into the Graduate Library School's "Spirit of Inquiry."

Louis Round Wilson is well known to students of American library history for many reasons. Foremost of these, of course, is the impact he had on the development of education for librarianship during his service as dean of the University of Chicago's Graduate Library School from 1932 to 1942. Before that, he had served as librarian at the University of North Carolina from 1901 to 1932, during which time the University's library emerged as the foremost in the South. He is also well known for his leadership in professional organizations, both regional and national. But whatever his claims to fame may be, it would be safe to say that he is *not* known for his research in librarianship. Indeed, he has been sharply criticized—even vilified—by some writers, who accuse him of subverting the great research promise of the GLS and transforming it into a mere school of administrative practice.[1] An examination of Wilson's

Robert Sidney Martin *is assistant director of University Libraries for Special Collections, Louisiana State University.*

publications, however, reveals that he made a number of important contributions to the literature that fully merit the appellation of "research." Among these, the foremost is *The Geography of Reading.*[2]

Published in 1938, when Wilson was sixty-two, *The Geography of Reading* represents the culmination of his lifelong investigation of regional variation in library resources. Wilson was convinced that libraries of all types were educational institutions and that they had an indispensable contribution to make to a democratic society. He was troubled by the fact that library resources were not evenly distributed across the nation, and particularly disturbed that his native South seemed to be the region least favored. He sought, therefore, to understand the causes and effects of this inequality in order to lay the groundwork for a systematic plan of improvement. It was a problem that fascinated, perplexed, and preoccupied him for his entire adult life, one to which he returned time and again to broaden his focus, deepen his analysis, and improve his methodology.

He first became aware of the problem as early as 1904.[3] By 1907 he had committed his initial thoughts on the subject to print in the form of an article entitled "The Growth of Libraries," published in Walter Hines Page's vehicle for progressive thought, *The World's Work.*[4] From this small beginning, Wilson's contributions to the library literature developed over the years. A glimpse at his bibliography indicates the number and range of his efforts in promoting library development. He wrote articles extolling the benefits of every type of library.[5] These papers and articles were in no way reporting the results of research; they were, instead, expressions of Wilson's library creed. Through them run the interwoven threads of his convictions that, in the Jeffersonian ideal, an educated citizenry is a prerequisite of a functioning democracy; that, accordingly, the education of the masses should be a primary concern for all; and that, fundamentally, libraries of all types are educational institutions, secondary in importance only to the school.

During this period Wilson's work fell under the influence of Eugene Cunningham Branson, who had come to the University of North Carolina from Georgia in 1914 to become the chairman of the new Department of Rural Economics. In this role, Branson was the dominant figure in social science, not only in North Carolina, but throughout much of the South. Branson was, above all, a publicist, and his work consisted primarily in attracting attention to a number of important social problems like farm tenancy and soil depletion. His purpose was to foment informed public discussion on the amelioration of these problems, and as a result, his publications remained largely descriptive accounts of his investigations.[6] The incarnation of Branson's approach to social science was *The University of North Carolina News Letter*, established immediately after his arrival in Chapel Hill in 1914. This organ at times enjoyed a circulation as high as 20,000 and was frequently excerpted in the press of the state. It achieved its purpose admirably, often exciting debate and controversy. Wilson worked closely with Branson, serving on the editorial board of the *News Letter*, and his own approach to studying social problems seems to have paralleled Branson's.[7]

Branson was soon eclipsed as an influence on Wilson by an important theoretician and practitioner of social science, Howard Washington Odum. Odum arrived in Chapel Hill in 1920 to head the University's new Department of Sociology and School of Public Welfare.[8] One authority has noted that "Odum's arrival in Chapel Hill resembled the onslaught of a cyclone."[9] He was a catalyst of social change, and he immediately set to work establishing mechanisms for investigating scientifically the myriad social problems of the South. Wilson and Odum came into frequent contact on the campus and eventually became close friends and supportive colleagues. There is no question that Wilson's own approach to research underwent a metamorphosis due to Odum's influence.

Wilson's latent interest in the regional variations in library resources was rekindled in 1921 when he attended the annual meeting of the American Library Association in Swampscott, Massachusetts. While in the Bay State he took a side trip to Salem, where he discovered, much to his astonishment, that this small city of 42,000 boasted library collections surpassing in number those of all the major North Carolina cities combined. His curiosity piqued, he investigated further and learned that, in every way, New England's library resources surpassed those of his native region manyfold. He returned home shaken and perplexed.[10]

Using the ready vehicle of the *News Letter*, Wilson immediately reported his experience to the state. In an article entitled simply "Better Libraries Needed," he underscored the disparity in library resources between New England and North Carolina. He pointed out the differences in attitude that this disparity revealed and stressed the injurious impact on the education of the citizenry that he felt was the inevitable result. The article, like all those in the *News Letter*, included some raw data to buttress the argument, but it was primarily a propaganda piece, a call to action.[11]

Wilson was not content to let the matter drop there, however. During the ensuing year he gathered what information he could, not only on the status of libraries in North Carolina, but also on other indicators of social well-being. In September and October 1922 he reported the findings of this investigation in a series of articles in the *News Letter*. Entitled "Does North Carolina Read?" the series documented just how poor the reading resources for North Carolina were. He also compared reading resources with other objects of public spending, demonstrating, for example, that there were almost exactly the same number of automobiles in North Carolina as there were books in its public libraries. "And there is not a farmer in the State," he wrote, "who does not consider his Ford an indispensable means to promote the welfare of his household and farm." Likewise, North Carolinians spent millions on good roads because "they are the solid realities over which an awakened State moves to a higher plane of civilization." North Carolinians were reluctant to spend money for books, Wilson thought, because they failed to see their practical utility. "So far, books remain in the luxury class. North Carolina, by and large, has not yet recognized them as tools to be utilized like automobiles and good roads in building a finer civilization." He went on to point out the practical value of books for lawyers, engineers, doctors, bankers, and merchants. Ultimately, he concluded, "books are tools for getting ahead."[12]

In the series, Wilson not only examined the status of libraries, but also delved into the number of newspaper and journal subscriptions and the availability of bookstores in the state. He pointed out that North Carolinians had purchased more books per capita in 1855 than in 1920. He demonstrated that North Carolina stood near the bottom of the ladder in per capita subscriptions to newspapers and popular magazines. He also made an important correlation: "counties which do not contain cities, with highly organized public libraries, book stores, and news stands, read far less than those that have these facilities."[13]

Wilson adopted a line of argument in this series that he was to follow in future publications. He cited Francis Bacon's dictum that "much reading maketh the full man" and, using this as a point of departure, noted the deleterious effect that the lack of reading resources had on the cultural and political health of North Carolina. If Bacon had been called upon to illustrate his dictum in terms of the modern North Carolina polity, Wilson claimed, "he probably would have said that reading on the part of the average voter would enable him, when he talked politics, to discuss the principles of public issues, rather than the personalities of candidates who happened to be running for office."[14] In short, Wilson's argument reduced to the tenets of the progressive educational creed, and his call for action was an extract from the standard progressive agenda of education, public health, good roads, and better government.

The articles were widely excerpted in the press of the state and caused not a little controversy. Many editors commented favorably and at length on Wilson's presentation of the situation.[15] A number of other writers picked up Wilson's theme and extended his arguments, applying them to their own localities.[16] Not all the reaction was favorable, however. A number of weeklies denied Wilson's claims, defended the cultural status of their towns, or editorially shrugged their shoulders.[17] Others objected to the whole idea of Wilson's study. "We Are Folks, Not Specimens" was the headline of one local editorial, which went on to complain that Wilson's articles were an example of "the latest statistical fad." North Carolinians were tired of being compared to Yankees; "we are just folks, good, bad, and indifferent."[18] One respondent offered suggestions on "How To Read Less, Yet Be Unashamed." Among her prescriptions: never read a book until you have wanted to for at least two months —better, two years.[19]

The series earned Wilson accolades from his friends and colleagues in the University, the state, and the profession. Branson wrote, "you have started something that is not likely to end for many years to come in North Carolina. Your message was great. . . ."[20] Wilson routinely sent copies of his work to colleagues for comment, and among those who responded to the series was William Warner Bishop, who agreed that the statistics were discouraging, but commended Wilson for doing "pioneer work," thereby "laying your successors under infinite obligation."[21] The series does indeed seem to have had a lasting impact on the course of library development, at least within the borders of North Carolina. The historian of the public library movement in the Southeast, Mary Edna Anders, credits Wilson with having laid the foundation for the eventual emergence of the North Carolina Citizen's Library Movement in 1927.[22]

Wilson continued his investigation into the problems he had explored in the series, but with an increasingly sociological, statistically oriented methodology. He continued to gather data from whatever sources he could. He wrote numerous letters to publishers concerning the circulation of their journals and other publications.[23] In 1923 he published an article in Odum's new vehicle for reporting social science research, the *Journal of Social Forces*. As always, his approach was action-oriented. He noted that his statistics were provided not simply to buttress his argument, but rather "for showing just what the situation is in the state in order that proper measures may be devised to change it for the better." After documenting the current status of libraries, much as he had done in the *News Letter* series, Wilson went on to discuss the causes for the lack of reading and reading resources in North Carolina. He enumerated the four factors that he considered paramount: that North Carolina was a rural, agricultural state, that books had been thought of largely in terms of culture and not as tools or means of promoting individual welfare; that publicity concerning books and libraries had been extremely limited; and that those whose duty it had been to teach others the use of books had not been trained in their use themselves.[24] Wilson then ventured to recommend three possible remedies for the situation: "That . . . public and school librarians stress the practical as well as the cultural value of books; that the State Department of Education, in cooperation with the schools and colleges, provide adequate training on the part of teachers in the use of books; and that the state commit itself unreservedly to a program of county-wide, tax-supported free libraries which, with adequate financial support, can insure proper administration and ample book resources for the entire citizenship.''[25]

Like the *News Letter* series, this article had an important impact. It brought the problem to the attention of the emerging coterie of sociologists in the South, and it established Wilson's reputation among them as an investigator of social problems. It was certainly, as Tauber has noted, ''one of the more important of Wilson's publications.''[26] Nevertheless, his method remained essentially descriptive, and his prose hortatory.

At this time Wilson began to broaden his focus from North Carolina to the entire South. In May 1924 he delivered the Visiting Exchange Lecture at the University of Virginia, where he took as his topic ''Print in the Service of the South.'' The title was ambiguous and misleading; by ''print,'' Wilson meant libraries, books, magazines, publishers, and bookstores, while by ''the South,'' he vaguely meant that section of the country south of Washington and east of Texas. In his lecture, Wilson demonstrated that the South was failing to make full use of the benefits of print, indicated some of the consequences of this failure, and suggested some ways for changing the situation. The lecture represented simply the extension of his previous arguments to the South as a whole.[27]

As Wilson was thus beginning to look at the problem beyond the borders of his own state, his approach to the subject was also undergoing some modification. One factor in this development was the establishment of the Institute for Research in Social Science at the University of North Carolina in September 1924. Growing out of the emerging consensus supporting an expanded role for government in addressing social problems, and funded by a Rockefeller grant, the Institute was founded with the purpose of fostering the cooperative study of social problems arising from conditions peculiar to the state and the region.[28] The research sponsored by the Institute was to be undertaken by the senior faculty of the University, and their personal research interests essentially determined its agenda. The actual work of the research projects, however, was in large part carried out by a team of graduate research assistants that the Institute's grant-funding enabled it to attract and support. The publications that resulted from these investigations ''put Chapel Hill on the map of American social science.''[29]

Both Wilson and Odum were on the Institute's Board of Governors, and hence among those who established its research agenda.[30] Wilson immediately saw that, with the assistance of the Institute, he could begin to undertake some serious research into the problem that had so long held his interest. He wasted little time in securing the backing of the Institute, and the assistance of one of the funded graduate students, in pursuing his quest.[31] Throughout the 1924–1925 academic year he directed a study by a graduate student, Orlando Stone, that formed the basis of Stone's thesis, "Reading Habits of North Carolinians as Indicated by Several Indices."[32] Stone ranked North Carolina in comparison to other states on a number of variables, including circulation of selected national magazines, daily newspapers, public libraries, and college libraries. He utilized fairly sophisticated statistical techniques in analyzing his data. Rank-order coefficients, for example, indicated strong correlations between reading and a number of desirable social traits.[33]

At about this time Wilson's long-simmering thoughts about his topic began to take on a more definite form. Having broadened his focus from North Carolina to the South as a whole, and deepened his analysis to employ some detailed statistical approaches, he prepared a draft of a single comprehensive report, incorporating all of his research to date. Entitled "Reading as a Southern Problem," this manuscript can be seen as the first tentative draft of the work that eventually became *The Geography of Reading.*[34]

In the foreword to this typescript, which ran to some seventy pages, Wilson set forth the objectives of his study. He noted that, although the South had made tremendous advances in agriculture, industry, transportation, public health, and general education, "it has failed to advance in anything like a comparable way in its provision of what, for lack of a more exact term, may be called the facilities or materials of reading." He proposed to document that claim, to point out the causes contributing to this failure, to indicate some of its consequences, and to suggest some remedies. His first task was to define "reading"

> as an inclusive term having to do with libraries, library schools, and library associations, with the publication and distribution of books, magazines, and newspapers, with bookstores and book review pages in Southern communities and Southern dailies, with radios, telephones, theaters, churches, and other agencies for the promotion of reading or conveying information other than that embraced within the curriculum of schools and colleges.[35]

Wilson also defined the area included in his study: "the South," for his purposes here, comprised Alabama, Florida, Georgia, Kentucky, Louisiana, Mississippi, North Carolina, South Carolina, Tennessee, Texas, and Virginia.

In a manner by now familiar, Wilson demonstrated the ways in which the South was deficient in the factors that he lumped under the rubric of "reading." The causes for this deficiency were the South's rural character, its paucity of resources to devote to "reading," its attitudes toward taxation and public education, and the large proportion of blacks in the population with the concomitant—and then unquestioned—necessity of providing for two parallel institutions of education. The effect of the deficiency was threefold: it cost the South numerous opportunities for material development; it meant a general lack of constructive and informed criticism of southern institutions and southern problems; and it resulted in a loss of intellectual freedom and a limitation on the free exchange of ideas. Wilson thought that efforts to resolve this problem would unquestionably take one of three lines: drawing upon the best experience gained from the library and allied institutions, modifying the attitudes of the people toward these institutions, or strengthening the agencies best-suited to promoting reading. Under this last heading, Wilson included appeals to the private foundations, the state governments, and the federal bureaucracy for financial support for the library associations, the libraries, and the universities.[36]

Wilson was still troubled, however, by the lack of any scientific data concerning the impact of reading on the individual. To confirm his perception of the state of knowledge, he wrote to a number of the leading investigators of reading, asking them if they knew of any studies relevant to the problem. Among these individuals were William S. Gray of the University of Chicago; E. L. Thorndike of Columbia University; W. W. Charters of the Carnegie Institute of Technology; and L. A. Williams of the University of California.[37] None of these illuminati were able to suggest any relevant research.

Wilson also wrote to his colleagues in the library profession, similarly asking for information. His letter to Sarah Bogle was typical:

> We are always speaking of the advantages of libraries, and of course their beneficial results are obvious, but I have been trying to get statistical data resulting from scientific tests. If this section of the country has only one-third of the facilities for reading that certain other sections have, I have an idea that the consequent failure on the part of school children . . . to measure up with the school children in other sections better provided for, should be capable of statistical demonstration.[38]

Although this quest for information was fruitless, it did have one beneficial result: it brought Wilson's work to the attention of William S. Gray, the dean of the University of Chicago's School of Education and perhaps the leading reading researcher in the country. At Gray's request, Wilson sent him a copy of his "Reading as a Southern Problem" and asked him for suggestions. He cautioned Gray that the manuscript was incomplete, and that he had had no opportunity to work on it in over a year. Wison was quite frank about his intent: "My principal objective," he wrote, "was to show the South that it did not possess more than one-fourth or one-third of the reading facilities enjoyed by the rest of the country."[39]

Gray was impressed with Wilson's work. "Your study is a most significant one," he wrote. He noted that it was of national, not merely regional, value, and he urged Wilson to expand his focus to the national level and to complete the work before the data grew obsolete. "There is immediate need for such a study to awaken the interest of leaders in many sections of the country to the reading problem," Gray noted.[40] Wilson thanked Gray for his kind remarks and helpful suggestions and gave him permission to use the data and tables from his work "in any way you see fit."[41] As a result, Wilson's findings are prominently featured in Gray's seminal work *The Reading Interests and Habits of Adults*, which was published the following year. He reproduced several tables from the "Does North Carolina Read?" series and summarized Wilson's "Reading as a Southern Problem" at some length. Terming it "a most valuable study," Gray observed that Wilson supplied "convincing evidence that the reading problem in any section of the country is intimately related to its history, the character of the population, its educational status, its wealth, its attitudes, beliefs, and ideals, and the social and economic forces that are at work."[42]

This was not the only national notice of Wilson's as yet unpublished research. Carl Milam brought it to the attention of Robert L. Duffus, who had been commissioned by the Carnegie Corporation to make a study of the publication and distribution of books. Duffus thought that the study was "extremely worthwhile," sought Wilson's permission to quote from it, and urged him to revise and publish the work.[43] Duffus gave Wilson's data and analysis prominent mention in his book—in a chapter titled "The Geography of Reading."[44]

Wilson was unable to follow the advice of both Gray and Duffus to move forward rapidly with the work. Pressured by other duties and activities, he was forced to allow his research to lie dormant for a number of years. Although he continued to use the work he had already done in many of his speeches and public statements, these were all based on old data.[45]

In 1932 Wilson left Chapel Hill to take up his new responsibilities as dean of the Graduate Library School at the University of Chicago. The shift from the library to the library school enabled him to devote considerably more time to his research and also provided a corps of eager graduate research assistants. At Chicago, he found himself in close proximity not only to Gray, but also to the man who was probably the foremost library researcher in reading, Douglas Waples, who was more familiar with the tools and techniques of social science research than Wilson, but who approached the subject from a completely different perspective and focused his inquiries on different aspects of the problem.[46] Although Wilson probably was influenced by his association with Waples and the other members of the Chicago faculty, the dominant influence on his research methodology was none other than his old friend Howard W. Odum. Odum had developed an entirely new approach to the investigation of social problems, an approach that became known as regionalism. Wilson continued to follow his own line of inquiry and began to apply to it Odum's emerging methodology.

Regionalism was the logical culmination of Odum's sociology; it was "a natural outgrowth of the whole direction of his work through *Social Forces*, the Institute for Research in Social Science," and his myriad other activities.[47] Regionalism is an elusive concept, one with important implications in literature, geography, history, political science, economics, sociology, and many other fields. "By regionalism," Odum wrote, "we mean a new American social economy and cultural determinism, as opposed to the early American sectionalism and geographic, economic determinism. . . . regionalism assumes first, last, and always a totality composed of several areal and cultural units, a great national unity and integrated culture in which each region exists as a region solely as a component unit in the whole."[48] Regionalism was a means of synthesizing all of the social sciences, and thereby viewing all of society whole, "not in bits and snatches from the viewpoint of some narrow specialty." But regionalism is also much more than that. "It is a program of action. It is an approach whereby the regions may be integrated into the national whole without losing their differentiation. It is a practical basis on which to pursue social planning."[49] One of the most important characteristics of regionalism is this orientation toward action. Regionalism "cried aloud for implementation in social action and social planning. For all the reactions the new discipline met in the region, Odum never concealed the fact that he was a sociologist and that certain social theories implied certain social action. In retrospect, regionalism represents the high point of Odum's achievement and influence."[50]

The development of Odum's theory and methodology of regionalism occurred mostly after 1930. It found its first full expression with the publication of *Southern Regions of the United States* in 1936.[51] In this work, "Odum achieved the synthesis of his mature thought in regional theory, Southern development, and a cultural-statistical approach to the analysis of regional divergence and national integration. . . . It became a basic book in courses and seminars, [and] had an important impact on policy and thought. . . ."[52]

Wilson maintained close contact with Odum's work for, although *Southern Regions* was not published until 1936, he drew heavily on it in his own 1934 study, *County Library Service in the South.* In 1929 the Julius Rosenwald Fund had provided money for a five-year program to establish, on a demonstration basis, countywide library service in selected southern communities. In 1934 the Graduate Library School was asked by the Rosenwald Fund to assess the success of this project. Wilson and his University of Chicago associate Edward A. Wight undertook this task and prepared a report on their findings.[53] The initial chapter of the report, giving the geographic and demographic background of the region under study, is clearly derived from, and explicitly credited to, Odum's work, which is cited as "in press." In fact, some of Odum's maps and tables actually appeared in the Wilson and Wight book before they appeared in Odum's own work. This makes unequivocally clear the intellectual genealogy of Wilson's own evolving perspective and method and demonstrates how far in advance of most library researchers he was in adopting an innovative methodology.

In many ways, *County Library Service in the South* can be seen as a dress rehearsal for the *Geography of Reading*. It addresses some of the same issues, utilizing some of the same data and methodology. Like Wilson's earlier work, it remained focused on only one region, but it is clear that Wilson was already broadening his attention to the entire nation.

In 1933, in an article reviewing recent advances in reading research, Wilson concluded with a call for more work and listed four general areas in which such research would probably be undertaken. First among these was "a kind of reading map or index or measuring stick . . . which will reveal quickly the general distribution of reading facilities and resources within the nation. . . ."[54] This is in essence a description of the project he planned to carry out. A year later, reporting on "Research in Progress in Library Science," he summarized the investigations then underway at GLS, among which were several reading studies by Waples, Leon Carnovsky, and E. W. McDiarmid. Prominently featured on the list was Wilson's own project.

> *A Study of the Distribution of Library Resources.* By Louis R. Wilson. In this study an attempt is being made to indicate the distribution, by state, and in some instances by counties and individual communities, of libraries, books, magazines, newspapers, and other means of conveying ideas. . . . The study is also concerned with the social and economic background of the various states and sections which promote or retard library development. . . .[55]

The work was concluded four years later and published as *The Geography of Reading*.

As already noted, *The Geography of Reading* constitutes the culmination of Wilson's lifelong attempt to get at the problem of regional variation in library resources. In it, he attempted to answer the questions that had preoccupied him for most of his career. *The Geography of Reading*, he wrote in his introduction, "is concerned primarily with the distribution of libraries in the United States and with problems associated with their use, support, and social significance." His purpose was "to answer, or to suggest the answers" to five questions:

> 1. What is the extent of inequality in access to libraries and library resources among the states and regions of the United States?
> 2. What relation does this inequality bear to variation in the distribution of social, educational, and cultural institutions and media for the communication of ideas in America?
> 3. Why does this disparity exist?
> 4. What is its significance? and
> 5. What can be done to increase library resources where they are comparatively slight or do not exist at all?[56]

This list is clearly an expanded version of the questions addressed a decade earlier in "Reading as a Southern Problem."

Wilson felt it necessary to explain his rather cryptic title. "A glance at the content of the volume," he wrote, "will show that it is not a geography. . . ." He continued, "Neither is it concerned with many of the aspects of reading with which the public usually associates the term. It is concerned with the geographical or spatial distribution of libraries, bookstores, magazines, newspapers, etc.; and maps are used extensively to present graphically the data concerning this distribution."[57]

The book is divided into four parts. In the first, he documented extensively the actual status of library resources across the country. He examined numerous variables reflecting the accessibility, size, financial support, and use of public, school, academic, and special libraries. In the second part he similarly examined "other facilities for education and communication," including bookstores and rental libraries, magazines and newspapers, telephones and radios, public schools, and agencies of adult education. In the third part he examined some of the causal factors underlying the regional disparities demonstrated in the first two parts, including geographic, demographic, and economic variables.

In each of these parts he followed a uniform method of presenting and analyzing his data. First, there was a table indicating the status of each state, in rank order, for the variable under discussion. These tables usually included the totals for each state, the data reduced to a per capita figure, and a standard score for each state. This "standard score" was defined as "the deviation of that state from the average of the forty-eight states, expressed in units of standard deviation."[58] This permitted the ready comparison of data from table to table.

Following the table, the per capita data were presented in map form, with the states divided into five intervals and each state shaded according to its interval membership. These maps provided a graphic depiction of the regional disparities that were the heart of Wilson's study. For each variable, the states were also divided into regions, following the six regions established by Odum in his *Southern Regions*, and the scores for each region were presented on a bar graph. In all, the book contains some 117 tables and 173 maps and graphs displaying the data collected.

Wilson lamented the fact that there was no central source of data concerning libraries and other cultural agencies that were the focus of his study. Instead, he was forced to gather his data from a wide range of sources, including statistics published by the American Library Association, the U.S. Office of Education, the various state agencies, and myriad commercial handbooks and directories.[59] As Stephen Karetzky notes in his survey of library-reading research, "Wilson discussed the limitations of his data honestly and sensibly, and his analysis of data was sophisticated."[60]

Perhaps the most sophisticated of his analyses was the creation of two indices of library development. The first of these, based on the ALA statistics published in 1935, was an index of public library development. It consisted of an adjusted mean of the standard scores of each state for the variables of percent of population served, per capita circulation, per capita expenditure, and volumes per capita. Wilson justified the use of these four variables because an extended study by one of his students at the Graduate Library School, G. Flint Purdy, had shown them to correlate more strongly with public library development than any other variables. The second index derived by Wilson was one to overall library development. It was drawn from the statistics published by the U.S. Office of Education in 1931, covering libraries of all types. It was also a weighted average, reflecting six different variables.[61]

In the fourth part of the book, Wilson summarized his conclusion and recommendations. He had clearly demonstrated that there was a distinct regional variation in the availability of reading resources. "A careful examination of the tables and maps—especially the maps," he wrote, ". . . will reveal a fairly definite library pattern for the nation." If one compared the maps of each of the many variables examined, "the fact begins to emerge . . . that there is a library map, or geography of reading, of the United States, which has fairly definite boundaries and characteristic features."[62] What's more, this regional variation in libraries was accompanied by similar regional variations in schools, adult education organizations, bookstores, magazines and newspapers, motion picture theaters, radios, and telephones. "Where library resources are abundant, these are abundant. In this sense," Wilson pointed out, ". . . the library becomes a ready index by which to measure the standard of living, or, as a sensitive thermometer, it serves to register the cultural temperature of many areas of America."[63]

Wilson also suggested a number of causes for the regional variation that he had documented. Those that were quantifiable he had indexed and correlated against libraries. The strongest of these was wealth, the simple ability of the region to pay for library service. Almost equally important—and related to wealth—was the degree of urbanization. But Wilson was quick to point out that there were other causes that he had not been able to quantify. Among these were the willingness of people to support essential institutions through taxation, the attitudes they held toward cooperative public ventures, and the strength of devotion to local rather than state or federal solutions to social problems.[64]

Wilson was unable to provide an answer to his fourth question, concerning the significance of the variations he had documented; there simply were not enough data. But he suggested various effects that an uneducated, illiterate, and unreading populace might have on the future of a democratic nation.[65]

Finally, Wilson listed his recommendations for rectifying the problem he had identified. First among these was more research. "One of the great limitations of librarianship today," he pointed out, "is that it lacks a fundamental body of data as well as of special studies which can be compared exactly and applied to the solution of the problems by which it is beset."[66] The most important aspect for future study, he thought, was to attempt to define the social significance of reading. Beyond this, Wilson made a number of constructive suggestions for future action by librarians. Finally, he called upon the states to assume the responsibility for the library as they had for the school, and he pointed out the crucial role the federal government had to play in the equalization of library resources.

> Variation in economic ability, the shift in the point at which taxes are collected, the trend of cities to recruit themselves from rural areas, the fact that the United States is a democracy and that its stability rests upon the intelligence and understanding of all its people—these facts lead to the conviction that if equalization of library resources is to be achieved, it can best be done through state and federal participation rather than complete dependence upon local support.[67]

Wilson's work was favorably received in the library world. Reviews in all the major journals acknowledged it as a landmark contribution. A. F. Kuhlman, director of the Joint University Libraries, in an extensive *Library Journal* notice, hailed it as "the most important book that has appeared in the field of American library literature. It stands forth as a landmark which should become the turning point in library development." Kuhlman's lengthy review summarized all of Wilson's data, commended the diligence of the work and the rigor of the methodology, and urged that it be read by all who were concerned with the role of libraries in American society.[68] Harry Miller Lydenberg's review in the *Library Quarterly* was much less effusive and much more evenhanded. Lydenberg was troubled by some of the statistical manipulations in the book, and he questioned a number of Wilson's assumptions, but he nevertheless acclaimed the work as "ideal in effort, overwhelming in statistical mass, objective in treatment, sweeping in deduction, and persuasive in recommendation." He was impressed by "the sheer weight and mass of the supporting apparatus and documentation." He concluded that "we have had many surveys of the American library scene, many statements of belief and conviction, but none come to mind so impressive in statistical buttress and support as we find here spread before us."[69] Indeed, the mass of statistical material in the book was not roundly applauded in some quarters. Lionel McColvin, writing in the *Library Association Record*, noted that the incredible detail "must rout at sight many would-be students" and admitted that "I, for one, would be happy to take much of the data for granted. . . ." He found the tables and maps "distracting and monotonous."[70] In general, however, the reviews were extremely favorable.[71]

Assessing the impact of a work like *The Geography of Reading* is difficult. The book was apparently ignored completely by geographers and other social scientists at the time of its publication; there were no reviews outside of the library and general reviewing media. And because of the ponderous nature of its argument and presentation, one may assume that it was a work that was but little read. It has certainly sunk slowly from sight and finds no place at all among the current reading of librarians, library educators, and library school students. That it no longer is highly esteemed by those now preoccupied with attempting to establish librarianship as a "scientific profession" cannot be denied. Houser and Schrader, for example, in discussing Wilson's publications, dismiss it merely as a work "about the 'geography of reading.'" Elsewhere they admit that the work is laudable "both in its substantive content and in the scientific research basis for its findings," but they incorrectly assert that it "stands apart from all of his other writings." They ultimately go so far as to claim that it was "the only contribution to scientific research in library science he produced. . . ."[72] These remarks are clearly inaccurate and unjustified.

That Wilson's work has virtually sunk into oblivion may be the result of a number of factors. To begin with, the data on which it was based aged rapidly, soon rendering it obsolete. Then, too, the difficulties Wilson faced in simply compiling his data and calculating his statistics are probably not fully appreciated in these days of centralized statistical reporting, national databases, and automated number-crunching. In addition, the title of the work is cryptic and not very descriptive of the content, while the text is almost impenetrable and filled with tables and statistics.

And yet, in an unusual way, the book has had a sort of staying power. From time to time it reemerges very briefly in the library literature, accompanied by a glowing reference and a plea that it soon be replicated. For example, in 1973 Carol Niemeyer noted the work in a review article and pointed out that it "warrants replication." Yet it seems significant that this was the only reference to the book in an entire issue of *Library Trends* devoted to "Research in the Fields of Reading and Communication."[73] George Bobinski placed the *Geography* on his 1979 list of "Notable Books in Library Science" and called for it to be updated.[74] Writing in 1974, geographer Wilbur Zelinsky, in what appears to be the sole mention of Wilson's work in the geographical literature, noted that *The Geography of Reading* remained, in spite of its vintage, the best general treatment of the sociology of reading.[75] As recently as 1984, Robert V. Williams pointed out that Wilson's was but one of two studies systematically exploring the relationships between libraries and the social settings in which they exist.[76]

Although it has yet to be completely updated, *The Geography of Reading* has been partially replicated by Wilson's one-time protégé, Robert Downs. First in 1957 and then again in 1975, Downs documented the status of American library resources, in the process paying tribute to Wilson's example.[77] And it appears that we may soon benefit from another partial replication of Wilson's work by Howard White, of the Drexel University College of Information Studies, who now is in the process of updating selected variables from the *Geography.*[78]

In spite of its relative obscurity, there are two specific ways in which the *Geography* has enjoyed an important influence. The first of these is in the area of federal aid to libraries. Following soon after the 1936 annual meeting of the American Library Association, at which Wilson, as president, set the agenda for a campaign to secure such federal aid, the *Geography* had a pronounced impact. As E. W. McDiarmid wrote, most of the federal aid programs to libraries came only after Wilson had "defined the population of non-library users as rural and indigent."[79] The other way in which the *Geography* was directly influential was in establishing the survey as a valid form of investigation of library problems. Guy R. Lyle designates the *Geography* as "a landmark survey," noting that it "has all the earmarks of a modern scientific educational survey."[80] Wilson himself soon became the preeminent library surveyor.[81]

Perhaps the most important contribution of Wilson's *Geography*, however, was in its methodology. In adopting Odum's regionalism as the basis for his approach to the problem, Wilson immediately cast his work into the mainstream of current social science. He also thereby struck out in a new direction in reading research. Up until then, that field had been dominated by William S. Gray, on the one hand, and Douglas Waples, on the other, both of whom focused their attention on the mechanics of reading rather than the availability of reading resources.[82] Waples himself, in his important book *Investigating Library Problems*, praised the *Geography* as an excellent example of quantitative analysis, particularly for its use of correlation statistics, which laid the foundation for the subsequent qualitative analysis.[83] Karetzky has pointed out that, although most library researchers agreed that reading was an important focus for their work, there was little agreement on the appropriate methodology to be used. "Most of them . . . felt cramped with the mechanistic, sociological approach Waples considered necessary. . . . Although others sometimes proposed valid alternatives, only Wilson actually developed his."[84] "To some extent, Wilson was the leader of his own reading research movement."[85]

Because *The Geography of Reading* is the culmination of a lifelong preoccupation with one important problem, it reveals many things about Wilson's attitudes and aptitudes. First of all, it unequivocally demonstrates that, far from having an antiresearch bias, he was a capable practitioner of social science, familiar with the most modern concepts and methods of his day. He was able to adapt those concepts and methods and bend them to the application of a problem that had preoccupied him for many years. It also demonstrates that, like Odum and many other socially minded individuals, Wilson viewed research pragmatically. For them, social research was an indispensable prelude to social action, enabling them to demonstrate to the public the existence and the causes of social problems, and lending credence to the programs for amelioration that they then suggested. Finally, it conclusively underscores the way in which, for Wilson, libraries were inextricably bound up in the fabric of society. One of the contributions of the work, according to Guy R. Lyle, was "its unequivocal demonstration that library problems do not exist in splendid isolation from one another or from other agencies of communication. Dr. Wilson showed that they are as interwoven as the strands in a spider's web."[86]

Notes

1. The strongest statement of this view is perhaps Lloyd J. Houser and Alvin M. Schrader, *The Search for a Scientific Profession: Library Science Education in the U.S. and Canada* (Metuchen, N.J.: Scarecrow Press, 1978). A more balanced interpretation of Wilson is found in John V. Richardson, *The Spirit of Inquiry: The Graduate Library School at Chicago, 1921–51* (Chicago: American Library Association, 1982).

2. Louis R. Wilson, *The Geography of Reading: A Study of the Distribution and Status of Libraries in the United States* (Chicago: University of Chicago Press, 1938).

3. Louis R. Wilson, "Louis Round Wilson, Librarian: A Biography," Louis Round Wilson Papers, Southern Historical Collection, Wilson Library, University of North Carolina at Chapel Hill, p. 155.

4. Louis R. Wilson, "The Growth of Libraries," *World's Work* 14 (June 1907): 8985–8986; reprinted in Maurice F. Tauber and Jerrold Orne (eds.), *Education and Libraries: Selected Papers by Louis Round Wilson* (New York: Shoe String Press, 1966), pp. 3–7.

5. See, for example, "The Public Library as an Educator," *Library Journal* 35 (1910): 6–10; "State Libraries: Their Improvement," *North Carolina Review*, 2 April 1911, p. 12; "A Constructive Library Platform for Southern Schools," *Library Journal* 37 (1912): 179–185.

6. Daniel Joseph Singal, *The War Within: From Victorian to Modernist Thought in the South, 1919–1945* (Chapel Hill: University of North Carolina Press, 1982), p. 120.

7. Louis Round Wilson, *The University of North Carolina, 1900–1930: The Making of a Modern University* (Chapel Hill: University of North Carolina Press, 1957), pp. 220, 464.

8. Ibid., pp. 445–448.

9. Singal, *War Within*, p. 120.

10. "Prefatory Note," dated 24 May 1967, in Louis R. Wilson, "Reading as a Southern Problem," typescript, 1926, Wilson Papers.

11. "Better Libraries Needed," *University of North Carolina News Letter*, 3 August 1921.

12. "Does North Carolina Read?" *University of North Carolina News Letter*, 3 August 1921.

13. "Does North Carolina Read?" *University of North Carolina News Letter*, 27 September 1922.

14. "Does North Carolina Read?" *University of North Caroline News Letter*, 20 September 1922.

15. See, for example, "Books and Motor Cars," *Greensboro Daily News*, 11 September 1922; "The Neglected Tool," *Asheville Citizen*, 18 September 1922. Many other editorials are found in Wilson Papers, II: 272–276.

16. See, for example, Ben Dixon MacNeill, "They Will Not Read and Can Not Write, These Tar Heels," *Raleigh News and Observer*, 17 September 1922.

17. For example, "Fayetteville Optimistic as to Reading in North Carolina," *Raleigh News and Observer*, 26 September 1922.

18. *Goldsboro News*, 26 September 1922.

19. Linda Whitaker Brame, "How to Read Less, Yet Be Unashamed," *Raleigh News and Observer*, 1 October 1922.

20. Branson to Wilson, 25 October 1922, Wilson Papers, II: 4.

21. Bishop to Wilson, 7 October 1922, Wilson Papers, II: 4.

22. Mary Edna Anders, "The Development of Library Service in the Southeastern States, 1895–1950" (D.L.S. dissertation, Columbia University, 1958), p. 71.

23. See, for example, Wilson to L. A. Weaver, 4 October 1922, and other letters in Wilson Papers, II: 4.

24. Ibid., p. 83.

25. Louis R. Wilson, "The Use of Books and Libraries in North Carolina," *Journal of Social Forces* 1 (1923): 79, 83, 85.

26. Maurice F. Tauber, *Louis Round Wilson: Librarian and Administrator* (New York: Columbia University Press, 1967), p. 187.

27. Wilson, "Print in the Service of the South," *Virginia Alumni Bulletin* 17 (July 1924), reprinted in Wilson, *Education and Libraries*, pp. 295–308.

28. Wilson, *University of North Carolina*, pp. 462–463.

29. Singal, *War Within*, p. 121.

30. Wilson, *University of North Carolina*, p. 466.

31. Wilson to IRSS Board (1924), Wilson Papers, III: 248.

32. Orlando Stone, "Reading Habits of North Carolinians as Indicated by Several Indices" (M.A. thesis, University of North Carolina, 1925); Louis R. Wilson, "Note . . . ," 23 May 1967, which is bound in with a copy of the thesis in the North Carolina Collection, Wilson Library, University of North Carolina (Cp 020.9 S87r).

33. Stone, "Reading Habits," pp. 50–62.

34. Wilson Papers, VI: 28.

35. Ibid., p. 3.

36. Ibid., pp. 44–46.

37. Wilson to Thorndike, Gray, Charters, and Williams, 14 September 1927, Wilson Papers, V: 528.

38. Wilson to Bogle, 15 September 1927, Wilson Papers, V: 528.

39. Wilson to Gray, 17 March 1928, Wilson Papers, V: 529.

40. Gray to Wilson, 18 May 1924 (i.e., 1928), Wilson Papers, V: 529.

41. Wilson to Gray, 22 May 1928; Wilson to Gray, 19 December 1928, Wilson Papers, V: 529.

42. William S. Gray and Ruth Munroe, *The Reading Interests and Habits of Adults: A Preliminary Report* (New York: Macmillan, 1929), pp. 23–26.

43. Duffus to Wilson, 23 November 1929; Duffus to Wilson, 4 December 1929, Wilson Papers, V: 529.

44. R. L. Duffus, *Books: Their Place in a Democracy* (New York: Houghton Mifflin, 1930), pp. 200–207.

45. See, for example, "Library Conditions and Objectives in the South," *University of North Carolina Extension Bulletin* 7 (1920): 54–61; "Libraries Will Promote State's New Awakening," *Raleigh News and Observer*, 28 July 1929.

46. See the review of Waples's contributions to reading research in Stephen Karetzky, *Reading Research and Librarianship: A History and Analysis* (Westport, Conn.: Greenwood Press, 1982).

47. George B. Tindall, "The Significance of Howard W. Odum to Southern History: A Preliminary Estimate," *Journal of Southern History* 24 (1958): 293.

48. "From Sections to Regions," *Saturday Review of Literature* 16 (12 June 1937): 5.

49. Tindall, "The Significance of Odum," p. 298.

50. Rupert B. Vance and Katherine Jocher, "Howard W. Odum," *Social Forces* 33 (1955): 207.

51. Chapel Hill: University of North Carolina Press, 1936.
52. Vance and Jocher, ''Odum,'' p. 207.
53. Louis R. Wilson and Edward A. Wight, *County Library Service in the South: A Study of the Rosenwald County Library Demonstration* (Chicago: University of Chicago Press, 1935).
54. ''The Reader Receives New Consideration,'' *Library Journal* 58 (1933): 357.
55. ''Research in Progress in Library Science,'' *Library Journal* 59 (1934): 340.
56. Wilson, *Geography*, p. 2.
57. Ibid., pp. 3–4.
58. Ibid., p. 7.
59. Ibid., esp. pp. 4–5.
60. Karetzky, *Reading Research*, p. 258.
61. Wilson, *Geography*, pp. 184–188.
62. Ibid., p. 87.
63. Ibid., p. 434.
64. Ibid., pp. 434–435.
65. Ibid., pp. 435–438.
66. Ibid., p. 438.
67. Ibid., p. 442.
68. A. F. Kuhlman, ''The Geography of Reading,'' *Library Journal* 63 (1 December 1938): 915–919.
69. *Library Quarterly* 8 (October 1938): 546–548.
70. *Library Association Record* 40 (October 1938): 541–542.
71. See Karetzky, *Reading Research*, pp. 268–272, for a discussion of some of the reviews.
72. Houser and Schrader, *Search*, pp. 60, 65.
73. Carol A. Niemeyer, ''Implications of Research in Reading and Communication,'' *Library Trends* 22 (October 1973): 221.
74. George S. Bobinski, ''Notable Books in Library Science: A Preliminary List,'' *Library Trends* 15 (July 1979): 64.
75. Wilbur Zelinsky, ''Selfward Bound? Personal Preference Patterns and the Changing Map of American Society,'' *Economic Geography* 50 (1974): 152.
76. Robert V. Williams, ''Theoretical Issues and Constructs Underlying the Study of Library Development,'' *Libri* 34 (1984): 10.
77. Robert B. Downs, ''Distribution of American Library Resources,'' *College and Research Libraries* 18 (May 1957): 183–189; and ''Library Resources in the United States,'' *College and Research Libraries* 35 (March 1975): 97–108.
78. *College of Information Studies Newsletter* (Drexel University), Fall 1984.
79. E. W. McDiarmid, *The Library Survey* (Chicago: American Library Association, 1940), p. 180.
80. Guy R. Lyle, ''The Evolution of the Library Survey,'' in Maurice F. Tauber and Irene Roemer Stephens (eds.), *Library Surveys* (New York: Columbia University Press, 1967), pp. 9–10.
81. See Tauber, *Louis Round Wilson*, pp. 216–235.
82. See Karetzky, *Reading Research.*
83. Douglas Waples, *Investigating Library Problems* (Chicago: University of Chicago Press, 1939), pp. 50, 56.
84. Karetzky, *Reading Research*, pp. 355–356.
85. Ibid., p. 272.
86. Lyle, ''Evolution of the Library Survey,'' p. 10.

The Historiography of Canadian Library History, or Mapping the Mind of the Canadian Past

Peter F. McNally

The study of Canadian library history is discussed in relation to a variety of factors. A statistical analysis of publications reveals that 1965 was an important watershed year and that significant variations can be observed between the shape of English- and French-language writings, and between both of them and those of the United States and Great Britain. Similarities and dissimilarities are noted between the general historiographical traditions of English and French Canada and their impact upon Canadian library history. The attitude of Canadian graduate library education toward library history is also noted.

This paper is an outgrowth of my current project to compile a comprehensive guide to Canadian library history. While a few selective guides have appeared concentrating upon either English- or French-language publications, no guide to the publications in both official languages has appeared to date.[1] Given this lack of a comprehensive guide, it will come as no surprise to learn that Canadian library history is virtually bereft as well of historiographical studies. Bibliography and historiography, as any librarian knows, are invariable bedmates.

As distinct from the literature on them, Canadian libraries have enjoyed a long and venerable history. There is evidence that personal collections were brought to Canada by the early French settlers of the sixteenth century. The Jesuit College and its library were established in Quebec City in 1635, which makes them the oldest institution of higher learning and the oldest nonpersonal library on the continent. Since then Canadian library development has been much slower than that in either the United States or Britain but still very interesting: in 1882 the province of Ontario passed the country's first free public library legislation and in 1901 formed the first library association; 1904 saw Canada's first library education program begin at McGill University, Montreal; in

Peter F. McNally *is associate professor of library science, McGill University.*

1916 the *Ontario Library Review*, the country's first library journal, appeared; the Canadian Library Association was formed in 1946; and the National Library of Canada was established in 1953. Today Canada has over 5,000 formal libraries covering the usual range of government, academic, school, public, and special libraries. There are seven university graduate library programs and eighteen at the collegiate technical level. Over a period of three hundred years, Canada has produced a large and flourishing library system through the endeavors of its people, who now number about twenty-five million, or one-tenth the population of the United States.[2]

What then of the historical study and appreciation of this centuries-old tradition? To this question, no straightforward answer is possible; rather, several levels of evaluation must be considered. A few of these evaluative levels are the macro-appreciation of the entire shape of Canadian library history; the micro-study of its individual parts, contributors, and titles; an understanding of English- and French-language traditions in the development of both our libraries and their historical study; investigation of how the study of Canadian library history relates to the study of Canadian history in general, both English and French; and finally, comparison of the Canadian library history traditions with those of the United States, Britain, and France. This paper does not even try to answer all of these questions, but attempts to point out some of the preliminary conclusions that have presented themselves to one investigator in this area.

To begin with, no appreciation of Canada, its library development, or historiographical tradition is possible without an awareness of the country's bilingual/bicultural nature. Approximately 25 percent of the population considers French to be its mother tongue and is concentrated mostly in the province of Quebec, with smaller communities of varying size and significance spread throughout the rest of the country. Also, there are about one million English-speaking people in the province of Quebec, mostly in the Montreal area.

A survey of the literature on Canadian library history I carried out during 1984/85 revealed the profiles illustrated in tables 1 and 2. I feel reasonably confident of having located the bulk of material that has appeared over the past twenty years since 1965, and rather less confident about the material prior to then. The bibliographical control of the earlier material, particularly of periodical literature, is very uneven and sometimes nonexistent. Even so, it seems likely that the bulk of the material and the most significant individual items have been identified and that the relative standing between language groups, between periods, and among the twelve categories employed should remain reasonably stable. The choice of 1965 as a demarcation date is partly arbitrary and partly purposeful. In 1965 Antonio Drolet published the most recent monographic survey history of Canadian libraries.[3] To distinguish between the items that appeared before and after the publication of his study seemed sensible.

Table 1
An Analysis of English-Canadian Library History

	Number of Items		
	To 1964	1965 to Date	Total
1. Public Libraries	47	93	140
2. General Topics	33	39	72
3. Academic Libraries	12	56	68
4. Specialized Libraries	13	35	48
5. Library Associations	17	24	41
6. National, Provincial, and Legislative Libraries	7	22	29
7. Biography	5	16	21
8. Library Education	2	18	20
9. Library Cooperation	2	13	15
10. Personal Libraries	1	10	11
11. Adult Education	1	8	9
12. School and Children's Libraries	0	8	8
TOTALS	140	342	482

A number of things become apparent upon studying these results—some readily, others less so. The total figure of 689 for books, theses, articles, essays, and pamphlets—in English and French, scholarly and nonscholarly—was much larger than anticipated. On the other hand, the number seems very small compared with the 3,260 items listed by Harris and Davis in their comprehensive 1978 guide to American library history (table 3),[4] and even smaller when compared with the 3,161 items published on British library history (table 4) between 1962 and 1980 and listed in Denis Keeling's exhaustive four-volume bibliography.[5] No comparable guide to French library history has as yet been located.

A number of other things will strike the observer. The English/French ratio of publication at 2.23:1 is much lower than the population ratio of 3:1 or the general publishing ratio of 4:1. As for the dividing date of 1965, it has proven to be even more significant than anticipated originally: 208

items through 1964, and 481 items, or more than double the number, since then. This suggests that Drolet's 1965 history is more of a watershed and more in need of updating than has previously been appreciated.

Table 2
An Analysis of French-Canadian Library History

	Number of Items		
	To 1964	1965 to Date	Total
1. Personal Libraries	19	25	44
2. Specialized Libraries	20	21	41
3. General Topics	8	23	31
4. National, Provincial, and Legislative Libraries	3	18	21
5. Academic Libraries	13	8	21
6. Library Education	1	14	15
7. Biography	1	12	13
8. Public Libraries	2	9	11
9. Library Associations	1	5	6
10. School and Children's Literature	0	4	4
11. Adult Education	0	0	0
12. Library Cooperation	0	0	0
TOTALS	68	139	207

Other quantitative comparisons between Anglophone and Francophone Canadian writings can best be made by including comparisons with American and British writings on library history. Even though the classification systems used by McNally, Harris/Davis, and Keeling for the publications from their three countries have certain variations, there is sufficient similarity to permit comparative analysis among tables 1, 2, 3, and 4. "Public Libraries" and "Academic Libraries" rank first and third with both English Canadians and Americans. By comparison, "Private Libraries" rank first with French Canadians and the British. These patterns may be purely coincidental, but they do suggest an initial interpretation: that English-Canadian librarianship, and hence its history, may be more closely allied to the American pattern, whereas the French-Canadian approach may be closer to the European models. On the other hand, "National, Provincial, and Legislative Libraries" place

Table 3
An Analysis by Subject of Michael H. Harris and Donald G. Davis,
American Library History: A Bibliography
(Austin: University of Texas Press, 1978)

	Number of Items
1. Public Libraries	667
2. Biographical	434
3. Academic Libraries	407
4. Special Libraries	348
5. Predecessors of the Public Library	277
6. Reading Tastes and Book Trade	227
7. Library Associations	162
8. Private Libraries	158
9. General Studies	136
10. Special Aspects	127
11. Historiography and Sources	93
12. Education for Librarianship	82
13. School Libraries	77
14. State Libraries	65
TOTAL	3260

sixth and fourth, respectively, among English and French Canadians, reflecting the fact that Canada has two national libraries and the importance of government in all aspects of Canadian library development. By comparison, ''State Libraries'' ranks last among Americans and ''National Libraries'' ranks ninth among the British. ''Biography'' ranks seventh among both English and French Canadians as opposed to second and third, respectively, among Americans and the British, which suggests a general lack of concern among Canadians for the contributions of their leaders and predecessors.

Other observations can be made showing that English- and French-Canadian library history are as equally divergent from one another as from American and British patterns. ''Public Libraries'' is the most obvious example, as they rank eighth among French Canadians but first with English Canadians and Americans, and second with the British. That public libraries have been relatively undeveloped in Quebec until recently must provide some of the explanation for this discrepancy. ''Personal Libraries'' provides the next most obvious discrepancy, rank-

Table 4
An Analysis by Subject of Denis F. Keeling,
British Library History: Bibliography, 1962–1980
(London: Library Association, 1972–1983)

	Number of Items
1. Private Libraries	611
2. Public Libraries	457
3. Librarians	377
4. Academic Libraries	360
5. Special Libraries	265
6. Ecclesiastical Libraries	209
7. Librarianship	207
8. Subscription Libraries	191
9. National Libraries	134
10. British Isles	123
11. Reading	82
12. Universal Libraries	66
13. Study of Library History	42
14. Mechanics' Institutes and Other Workers' Institutes	37
TOTAL	3161

ing only tenth among English Canadians, but first with French Canadians and the British, and even eighth with Americans. "Library Cooperation" and "Adult Education" were considered sufficiently significant topics among English Canadians to be granted their own headings and placed, respectively, ninth and eleventh. By comparison, neither topic rates its own section in either the American or British guides, although items on both topics can be found through the subject indexes; no items were found on either topic among French-Canadian publications. This latter fact may also be accounted for by Quebec's relative lack of public libraries.

In other words, when looked at in statistical profile, Canadian library history reveals similarities and dissimilarities not only between its English- and French-language schools but between them, singly and together, and British and American library history. Given that librarianship and the study of history are both culturally based activities, this pattern of similarity and dissimilarity should come as no surprise to anyone. Culture determines the development of libraries and their historical appreciation. And the historical interpretation of libraries, or anything else, must occur within the historiographical tradition developed by the culture in question. In the case of Canada, since the beginning of indigenous historical writing about 1800, two historiographical traditions have developed: the one English and the other French; if they share certain common elements, they also reveal fundamental variations. Canadian library history cannot help but have been influenced by the assumptions of these historiographical traditions.

The dominant themes of Canadian history have been survival and nation-building: how the people of the top half of the North American continent have managed to develop and grow as an independent nation, usually in cooperation but sometimes in conflict with the European-based empires of France and Britain and the imperial march of American manifest destiny; and how the divergent and at times centrifugal forces of Canadian regionalism and cultural/linguistic diversity—particularly English and French—have accommodated the twin demands of local autonomy and central authority.

Canadian English-language historical writing in the nineteenth century has been characterized as Whig history concerned with politics, nationalism, and progress, and with the spread of British and Protestant institutions throughout the Dominion.[6] Primary attention was paid to biography and the history of political institutions; little if any attention was paid to cultural history. Following upon the professionalization of history at the turn of the century and the teaching of Canadian history in the universities, there emerged during the interwar period a new school of historical interpretation, greatly influenced by social scientists and geographers, called the environmentalist or Laurentian school. Its adherents developed a unique interpretation of Canadian history based upon the premise that Canada existed not despite, but because of, its often difficult geography. Economic history flourished in this milieu but not cultural/intellectual history. Only since the 1960s has the orthodoxy of Laurentianism broken down sufficiently for divergent schools of historical thought to develop and permit the serious and coherent study of cultural and intellectual history in English Canada.

French-Canadian historical writing has from its beginnings displayed a verve and a sense of national purpose that have made it highly distinctive.[7] Its dominant theme "survivance," or survival, was first enunciated in Canada's first great work of historical analysis in either English or French, François-Xavier Garneau's *Histoire du Canada depuis la découverte jusqu'à nos jours* (1844–1852). Garneau, who was basically a conservative nationalist, was spurred into writing his history by the attack upon French Canadians, which he perceived in the famous Report on Canada prepared for the British government, after the Rebellion of 1837 in what are now Quebec and Ontario, by Lord Durham, who wrote: French Canadians "are a people with no history, and no literature." Garneau and indeed most French-Canadian historians who have followed him have been determined to prove Durham wrong. Garneau saw as the three major elements of French Canada's survival the French language, the code of civil law, and the Roman Catholic religion. For over a century, until well after World War II, variations of his conservative nationalism dominated French-Canadian historical writing. The Roman Catholic church identified itself closely with the survival school; indeed, there was scarcely a Francophone historian during this period who was not either a priest or trained by priests. As in English Canada, the focus of their work was upon biography and political history; cultural history received only somewhat more emphasis than in English Canada. Over the past thirty years, French-Canadian history has become secularized and reasonably freed from nationalist orthodoxy. Again as in English Canada, social/cultural/intellectual history has finally emerged as a viable scholarly pursuit.

Given this inhospitable milieu, it is easy to understand why Canadian library history has not produced a larger body of publications. The question then becomes: what of the quality and trends among these publications that have appeared? English- and French-Canadian schools, it will be appreciated, provide very different answers.

English-Canadian library history can be characterized as amateur histories written by librarians for other librarians, which emphasize internal institutional and administrative activities rather than the role of libraries within broader social, cultural, and intellectual contexts.[8] These studies reveal few identifiable research fronts with the exception of mechanics' institutes and adult education. The few major studies that have appeared stand frequently in isolation, unrelated to the larger number of minor studies on neighboring topics. By comparison, Canadian library history in French can be characterized as professional histories written by historians or librarians for either a general or a scholarly audience and developed within strong social, cultural, intellectual, and political contexts.[9] Institutional and administrative elements are largely ignored. Two aspects of this development are particularly notable: first, French-language work reveals the existence of a number of research fronts whose coherent growth is beginning to provide a clear picture of the historical development of Quebec libraries; and second, the study of Quebec libraries has attracted a number of professional historians, who have made notable contributions.

Two possible explanations may lie behind the contrasting characteristics displayed by the publications of the two language groups. French Canadians have adopted with enthusiasm the concept of "l'histoire d'imprimé,'' or the study of print culture as a unifying focus for study in this area. Historical bibliography, bibliographically based intellectual history, and the history of libraries are seen as facets of the same process. Publications in this area contain essays on topics as diverse as literacy and the analyses of wills to determine the numbers and types of books they list. By comparison, English Canadians have been little affected as yet by the developing study of print culture.

The other factor, which appears to affect mostly English Canada, has been the neglect of library history by our graduate library schools. The professionalization of history in this country since the turn of the century demands that academic, university-based research and publication provide the direction and standards for all historical scholarship. As tables 5 and 6 indicate, theses in Canadian library history are few and far between, particularly when compared with those in American library history.[10] It should also be mentioned that the majority of those in English, including all the doctoral dissertations, have been submitted to American universities. In their nearly fifteen years of existence, neither of the two

Table 5
An Analysis of Theses in the Field of Canadian Library History

	Number of Items		
	English	French	Total
1. Specialized Libraries	5	6	11
2. Public Libraries	4	1	5
3. Academic Libraries	4	1	5
4. Adult Education	3	0	3
5. General	2	1	3
6. National, Provincial, and Legislative Libraries	2	1	3
7. Personal Libraries	0	2	2
8. Library Education	0	1	1
9. Library Associations	0	0	0
10. Biography	0	0	0
11. Library Cooperation	0	0	0
12. School and Children's Libraries	0	0	0
TOTALS	20	13	33

Table 6
An Analysis by Subject of Michael H. Harris,
***A Guide to Research in American Library History*, 2nd ed.**
(Metuchen, N.J.: Scarecrow Press, 1974)

	Number of Items
1. Public Libraries	229
2. College and University Libraries	142
3. Biographies	65
4. Special Libraries	42
5. School Libraries	32
6. Other Predecessors of the Public Library	32
7. Types of Library Service	22
8. Library Associations	20
9. State Libraries	18
10. Library Education	18
11. Private Libraries and Reading Tastes in Early America	16
12. Studies of the Literature of American Librarianship	14
13. Miscellaneous	3
TOTAL	653

Canadian doctoral programs in library science has yet produced a graduate in library history, although they have recently admitted students to work in this area.

What of the future? Library history is an integral part of social/cultural/intellectual history, an area of traditional neglect within Canadian history that is finally receiving serious attention. While library history is of benefit to the library profession in understanding itself and developing its theoretical base, ghettoization as the plaything of the profession is no answer. Rather, Canadian library history needs to become a joint project of people from many subject areas, including librarianship, who will employ methodologies from a wide range of social science and humanistic disciplines in attempting to place libraries within their proper historical context while working toward the common goal of mapping the mind of the Canadian past.

Notes

1. Guides that have appeared to date are Claude Galarneau, ''Le livre ancien au Québec: Etat présent des recherches,'' *Revue Française d'Histoire du Livre*, nouvelle série, 16 (juillet-août-septembre 1977): 335–348; David Hayne, ''A Survey —Quebec Library History,'' *Canadian Library Journal* 38/6 (December 1981): 335–361; Yvan Lamonde, ''La recherche sur l'histoire de l'imprimé et du livre québécois,'' *Revue d'Histoire de l'Amérique Française* 28/3 (décembre 1974): 405–414; idem, ''La recherche récente en histoire de l'imprimé au Québec,'' in his *L'Imprimé au Québec: Aspects historiques (18e–20e siècles)* (Québec: Institut québécois de recherche sur la culture, 1983), pp. 11–24; Elizabeth Homer Morton, ''Library History of Canada: A Panoramic Survey,'' *Library History Review* 1/4 (December 1974): 65–98; 2/1 (March 1975): 82–106.

2. The following contain essays that are invaluable in understanding the Canadian library tradition: Georges Chartrand (ed.) *Livre, bibliothèque, et culture québécoise; Mélanges offerts à Edmond Desrochers s.j.*, 2 vols. (Montréal: ASTED, 1977); Allen Kent and Harold Lancour (ed.), *Encyclopedia of Library and Information Science* (New York: Dekker, 1968–); Loraine Spencer Garry (ed.), *Canadian Libraries in Their Changing Environment* (Toronto: Centre for Continuing Education, York University, 1978); Yvan Lamonde (ed.), *L'Imprimé au Québec: Aspects historiques (18e–20e siècles)* (Québec: Institut québécoise de recherche sur la culture, 1983); Peter F. McNally (ed.), ''Theme Issue on Canadian Library History,'' *Canadian Library Journal* 38/6 (December 1981); Bruce B. Peel (ed.), *Librarianship in Canada, 1946 to 1967: Essays in Honour of Elizabeth Homer Morton* (Ottawa: CLA, 1968).

3. Antonio Drolet, *Les bibliothèques canadiennes, 1604–1960* (Montréal: Cercle du livre de France, 1965).

4. Michael H. Harris and Donald G. Davis, Jr., *American Library History: A Bibliography* (Austin: University of Texas Press, 1978).

5. Denis F. Keeling, *British Library History: Bibliography, 1962–1980* (London: Library Association, 1972–1983).

6. The most accessible introductions are Kenneth Windsor, ''Historical Writings in Canada to 1920,'' vol. 1, chapter 13, pp. 222–264; William Kilbourn, ''Canadian History and Social Science (1920–1960); Pt. 1, The Writing of Canadian History,'' vol. 2, chapter 2, pp. 22–43; Michael S. Cross, ''Canadian History,'' vol. 3, chapter 4, pp. 63–68, all in Carl F. Klinck, *Literary History of Canada*, 2nd ed., 3 vols (Toronto: University of Toronto Press, 1976).

7. Accessible English-language accounts can be found in the relevant sections of Fernand Ouellet, ''Québec 1760–1867,'' vol. 1, pp. 45–77; and Ramsay Cook, ''French Canada,'' vol. 2, pp. 249–276, both in *A Reader's Guide to Canadian History*, 2 vols. (Toronto: University of Toronto Press, 1982).

8. These points are developed in more depth in a paper being considered for inclusion in an anthology to be published by the Canadian Library Association: Peter F. McNally, ''Canadian Library History in English, 1964–1984, A Survey and an Evaluation.''

9. These points are developed in more depth in a paper being considered for inclusion in an anthology to be published by the Canadian Library Association: Peter F. McNally, ''Canadian Library History in French, 1964–1984, A Survey and an Evaluation.''

10. Michael H. Harris, *A Guide to Research in American Library History*, 2nd ed. (Metuchen, N.J.: Scarecrow Press, 1974).

Two Centers of German Research Activities in Library History: Cologne and Wolfenbüttel

Paul Kaegbein

There are two German institutions today seriously concerned with library history—in Cologne, the University of Librarianship and Documentation as well as the Chair of Library Science at the University of Cologne; in Wolfenbüttel, the Round Table on Library History affiliated with the Duke August Library. For them, the achievements in library history research are characterized under general and methodological aspects. Single research results are mentioned and a selection of important examples in various fields of library history is given listing the completed research projects.

There is a German saying, which general experience confirms, that "A burnt child fears the fire." This is true also for historiography, especially in a country like Germany, which has suffered so much from its own contemporary history during the thirties and forties of this century. After the end of World War II, it was a relatively long time before historical research was widely undertaken again in Germany.

This can be seen, for instance, by glancing at Germany's historical bibliography. During the second half of the thirties, the renowned *Jahresberichte für deutsche Geschichte* (Annual Reports for German History) listed in its bibliography at least 2,500 items yearly, culminating with 3,000 in 1938.[1] Not until 1952 did volume 1 of the new series appear, covering 964 items published in 1949, increasing quickly during the next years to about the same figures as before the war.

A similar situation is visible as far as library history is concerned. Only gradually did the building up of learned journals and research centers devoted to this field take place in postwar Germany. One of the older institutions engaged in library history is the Library School of North Rhine Westphalia in Cologne, supplemented in this matter later by the Chair of Library Science at the University of Cologne. More

Paul Kaegbein *is professor of library science, University of Cologne.*

recently the Round Table on Library History at Wolfenbüttel can be regarded as another German center in this area. Both of them are addressed here in connection with the research results achieved.

Cologne

On the foundations of the earlier West German Library School in Cologne going back as far as 1928, the Library School of North Rhine Westphalia was established in 1949 as a central institution for the education of librarians of all levels,[2] under the direct supervision of the Ministry of Cultural Affairs of this German state. In 1981 it was transformed into an independent university of library and documentation science.[3]

The two-year postgraduate education of subject specialists at this institution ends with a state examination, a part of which is a written thesis. For the years 1949 to 1970 the titles of these 385 theses are listed in a classified bibliography,[4] and for the years 1971 to 1984 another 541 items can be found in specific lists.[5] From the examinations in spring 1985 six other titles can be added. All of them, with only very few exceptions, are available in machine-typed form through the library of the university mentioned above;[6] besides, a lot of them are published elsewhere as monographs or as articles in learned journals—sometimes in a shortened version or with a different title.[7]

According to the judgment of unbiased experts, these theses can be regarded as an important contribution to German library literature.[8] Most of them deal, of course, with questions of practical library work from the methodological or theoretical point of view. But a considerable proportion of the theses are devoted to library history, in an increasing number: in the first period from 1949 to 1970, at least 53 items are oriented toward this area, whereas between 1971 and 1984, at least 95 titles can be found. This is an increase from about two to three papers on library history yearly, during the first period of 22 years to about seven papers during the last 14 years or, in comparison with the whole number of theses, an increase from about 13.7 percent in the first period to about 18.5 percent in the second period—not including the history of the book, of printing, and of publishing. Quite obviously there is an ascending tendency, as the figures from the last years show.

If one considers that the candidates are allowed to propose the topics of their examination theses, the conclusion can be drawn that recent years show some increase in interest in history. This corresponds to the general trend toward neo-historicism that has recently emerged in Germany. Nevertheless, in the context of library education curricula, interest in library history should not be overestimated, as the percentage mentioned above proves. Of course, the character of such examination

Table 1

	Library History Titles	Total No. of Theses
1980	6	35
1981	9	30
1982	12	37
1983	7	34
1984	14	29

theses is different. While some give only state-of-the-art reports on earlier research results, others rely on printed materials and unpublished sources, representing in this way valuable research themselves.

Looking into the contents of the theses characterized here, I would like to make some general introductory statements. Although most of the papers are specific in content, one can find among them several of more general character. Besides the great number addressing German library history, there are also some dealing with foreign libraries. The historical development of single libraries is often compared with their present situation in the theses, thus providing details for future studies of the modern period.

In selecting the relevant titles from the lists mentioned above, not only book history and history of printing and publishing have been omitted, but also, with few exceptions, theses concerned with the history of very specific collections in libraries. But included were titles about the historical development of specific parts of librarianship like catalogues, classifications, buildings, and so on. Library history is not mentioned as a specific group by either the classified bibliography or the lists referred to above, which are arranged alphabetically by the author. Thus, it might be valuable to group here the broad field of library history theses.

Antique and medieval library history are covered by few but important titles. The implication of the results of excavations in the Near East for libraries and archives has been analyzed by Hans-Peter Adler according to modern criteria of library science.[9] Our knowledge about libraries in ancient Egypt, formerly based mainly on Fritz Milkau's publication,[10] has been enlarged substantially by Günter Burkard, who first presented a methodological basis for the treatment of archaeologic or epigraphic findings and then applied it to individual sites, where in fifteen cases the existence of libraries could be identified positively or at least with a very high probability.[11] For the history of libraries in Alexandria during the Greek period in Egypt, a report on German research results between

1955 and 1971 has been delivered by Maria-Luise von Graberg.[12] The situation of libraries in ancient Rome has also been investigated recently.[13]

General library history in the Middle Ages and the early modern period is only covered by two theses, one of them describing information about libraries in the writings of Hieronymus,[14] and the other one interpreting library journeys in Germany during the eighteenth century.[15] It is understandable that more attention is given generally to the history of libraries during the last two centuries.

The prehistory of public libraries in Germany marked by the development of reading societies has received greater interest in recent years. Experts in social history as well as in the history of literature are looking at this phenomenon in connection with the spreading of research in reading and reader studies. Among the Cologne examination theses, besides an early publication on medical reading societies,[16] different kinds of reading societies have been described in three towns: Hanover, Helmstedt, and Mannheim.[17] Other theses investigated libraries of workers' organizations in the nineteenth and twentieth centuries and the attitudes of these organizations toward education and libraries.[18]

Examples for specific periods in the history of German public libraries are the thesis by Sabine Zehrer on Friedrich von Raumer and the Anglo-American prototype for the formation of public libraries in Berlin;[19] an investigation about the so-called Richtungsstreit (struggle of tendencies) by Tibor Süle;[20] and the study by Jutta Sywottek about the political coordination of public libraries in the Third Reich.[21] The important change in lending procedures from counter to open access is described by Regine Glötzel,[22] and the cooperative acquisition program in North Rhine Westphalia by Ulrich Moeske.[23]

Special questions in the area of academic and research libraries are investigated by Ingrid Holtgrewe and Engelbert Plassmann, who specifically focus on users' legislation.[24] Nikolaus Scholl, Nikolaus Strelczyk, and Verena von Grote deal with the image of the librarian profession and women in libraries.[25] Ursula Renner-Henke looks at the librarian as reflected in German fiction;[26] Manfred Pape investigates the historical development of the question of closed or open access;[27] and Jutta Fielitz deals with the history of information services.[28]

It is not possible to mention here all the individual libraries whose history has been described in the theses; only some examples for various categories can be given. The libraries of the monasteries and churches of Cologne, Wimpfen, and Spandau near Berlin have been investigated on the strength of their holdings.[29] Older administrative libraries have been described in the towns of Hanover, Cologne, Schwäbisch Hall, and Lüneburg,[30] and newer city libraries in Cologne, Wuppertal, and Göttingen.[31] For regional libraries and their predecessors, the libraries of ruling nobilities, especially the cases of Wolfenbüttel,[32] Oldenburg,[33] Neustrelitz,[34] Speyer,[35] and Karlsruhe,[36] should be named. Skipping over numerous other libraries, including special libraries, two very exceptional examples have to be mentioned. In the state of Baden-Württemberg, in which the consciousness of historical tradition is very much alive, the histories of two university libraries, Freiburg[37] and Tübingen,[38] have been covered almost completely from the eighteenth to the twentieth century. In both cases, the history of their older buildings also has been treated.[39]

As the titles of the studies of these two libraries show in detail, library history in these cases is regarded foremost as administrative history, arranged according to the years of directorate of the chief librarians and underlining their specific ideas and treatment of library policy. As far as chief librarians can be regarded as important to library history, this seems to be legitimate to a certain extent. It is especially justifiable in the case of Georg Leyh, whose eminence in German librarianship has already been the subject of the well-known studies by Marta Dosa.[40] Generally, all of these specific theses based on archival materials may be considered components for a still missing comprehensive history of these old university libraries.

A similar situation obtains for the oldest German university, Heidelberg. An important part of the history of its library in the nineteenth century is described by Hellmut Vogeler,[41] while the old library building is the topic of another thesis.[42] General questions of the building history of European libraries have been discussed by Barbara Schneider-Esslinger,[43] and the history of the development of the reading room, with its reference collections, by Günter Baron.[44]

There are many contributions to the history of catalogs and cataloging. Worth mentioning here are studies on the development of union catalogs in the United States since 1935,[45] on Panizzi's rules for the alphabetic catalog,[46] and on Cutter's "Expansive Classification."[47] There are twenty other theses about libraries in foreign countries, mainly European. The Soviet Union leads with four studies of a more general nature that discuss the development of library services,[48] of library historiography,[49] and of library science.[50] For Denmark,[51] the United Kingdom,[52] Spain,[53] and France,[54] two titles each can be listed.

All of these theses and many more on libraries in other countries are noteworthy contributions to international librarianship. Of particular interest is Matthias Buschkühl's history of the famous Library of the Trinity College in Dublin,[55] based on archival sources, and that of the University and National Library in Strassburg, 1871–1944, which has been presented by Peter Borchardt.[56] He describes the destiny of this library during the periods of German and French rule over Alsace, focusing especially, on the basis of unpublished materials, on its fate during World War II.

Library journals are the subjects of some other theses,[57] among which one about the *Library Quarterly* should be mentioned.[58] Another very interesting topic is the attention that German libraries and librarianship have received from professional journals abroad,[59] and from newspapers. As far as the latter are concerned, Michael Knoche has shown in his thesis that reports about libraries in newspapers deal mostly with aspects other than the central area of the librarian's work.[60] Library stocks and outstanding examples of books, together with questions of their conservation, are much more interesting to journalists than problems of library use.

It is very informative to pursue the history of literary taste in studies on commercial lending libraries and reading societies in Germany in the last two centuries. Such studies combine research in book and library history with questions of the reception of literary works from the sociological point of view,[61] and thus offer a broader context for the examination of the history of the book as a cultural phenomenon.[62] A good example of this approach is the recent paper of Reinhard Ligocki on the development of the German commercial lending library in the nineteenth century.[63] Summarizing the results of earlier studies, he considers in detail the interconnections between the development of these institutions and the mass production of popular pulp fiction in periods when books were relatively expensive. Two examples reveal the broad influence that commercial lending libraries in Germany must have had in the past. The so-called Beygang-Museum in Leipzig (1794–1819) offered in 1799 about 70,000 volumes to the inhabitants of that town. One century later, at the end of the 1890s, the reading circles of Borstell and Reimarus in Berlin held a stock of about 600,000 volumes of fiction and other publications in numerous copies and also subscriptions to 190 journals, managed altogether by 74 staff members.

Turning now from the broad variety of themes covered by the theses of the University of Library and Documentation Science in Cologne to the study of library science at the University of Cologne, we see that this curriculum as well includes library history as one of five subtopics that are part of the final examination for the master's degree. The lectures in German library history given here during the last years by Wolfgang Schmitz formed the basis for a recent book on this theme.[64] It follows some other German publications on library history by Karl-Heinz Weimann (1975),[65] Ladislaus Buzás (1975–1978),[66] Joris Vorstius and Siegfried Joost (last edition 1980),[67] and Wolfgang Thauer and Peter Vodosek (1978).[68] The new direction of Schmitz's work, however, is to examine library history from the point of view of literary tradition, thus following an interdisciplinary method. More than other comprehensive works in this field, Schmitz's study concentrates on the role of library catalogs as important sources of library collections, especially for the Middle Ages and the early centuries of modern times. Of special value for experts in Germanic studies will be Schmitz's index of important older manuscripts arranged according to their preservation in German libraries. This book can be regarded as an excellent example of the important results growing out of the German tradition in combining academic teaching and research at university level.

Another activity of the Chair of Library Science in the field of library history should not be neglected. In 1977 a new primary journal on research and practice in libraries was founded and in 1985 is in its ninth volume.[69] It is intended mainly as a publication for longer research papers.[70] Among them a number of articles important for library history can be traced, some of which have already been mentioned above.

Illuminating library historiography in Great Britain after World War II is a review of literature given by R. Paul Sturges in 1980.[71] Two research papers of Manfred Komorowski deal with modern German library history in the Eastern region,[72] and two other papers address the development of classification in the University Library of Tübingen and in German public libraries.[73]

Here it has to be mentioned that historical themes are not only included in the postgraduate theses mentioned at the beginning of this survey, but also can be found among those presented in connection with the examinations for the diploma degree for public librarianship at the library schools in Berlin, Hamburg, Cologne, and Stuttgart. Into this category fall, besides the last paper mentioned, two others published in *Bibliothek*. One of them is concerned with the development of reading rooms in German public libraries;[74] the other one gives a comparative analysis of the changing opinions of leading German political figures as well as of librarians about the position of the public library during the period 1949–1977.[75]

Last but not least in this series, two articles must be named that illustrate the history of librarianship in connection with social development and library policies. Peter Vodosek has investigated the development of librarianship as a female vocation,[76] describing in particular the history of the Association of Women Working in Libraries, founded in 1907 in Berlin. Together with the above-mentioned paper of Verena von Grote,[77] it is one of the very few German interpretations of this area. Walter Hofmann's papers, which are preserved today in Stuttgart, allowed Engelbrecht Boese to study in his Stuttgart diploma thesis the "Institute for the Study of Readers and the Written Word," which signified the climax in Hofmann's library career in the years 1926–1937.[78]

Of course, a number of contributions published in the journal *Bibliothek* do not originate in Cologne, but they are worth mentioning here in connection with the efforts of the Chair of Library Science in Cologne to make them easily available to experts in library history.

Wolfenbüttel

In the Federal Republic of Germany another focal point in library history is in Wolfenbüttel. The Duke August Library at Wolfenbüttel, founded in 1573, with its unique collections originating mainly from the seventeenth and eighteenth centuries, has developed into a world-renowned research institute for this period by annexing to the library a lot of adjacent resources and facilities. The comprehensive holdings of manuscripts and rare books, together with recent literature relevant to the period, allow the intensive study of European, but also of early American, history and letters.

This has been acknowledged by the foundation of the American Friends of the Herzog August Library, Inc.[79] The purpose of this nonprofit organization is to support American scholars in all fields to work at the Library at Wolfenbüttel by providing fellowships and research grants. A new magazine called the *American Wolfenbutteliana*, to be published twice a year, will keep readers informed about American-German cultural exchange and the special activities at the Wolfenbüttel library.

These activities include several Round Tables established as research centers for specific areas: the Lessing Academy (founded in 1971), the International Round Table on Baroque Literature (founded in 1972), the German Society for the Study of the Eighteenth Century, and the Wolfenbüttel Round Table on the History of the Book (both founded in 1975), the Wolfenbüttel Round Table for Renaissance Studies (founded in 1976), and the Wolfenbüttel Round Table on Library History (founded in 1979 by separating itself organizationally from the Round Table on the History of the Book).

Before the founding of the Round Table on Library History, questions in this area have been addressed by the Round Table on the History of the Book; an example was the latter's fourth convention in 1979, which dealt with German books and libraries in the seventeenth century.[80] Also, a seminar on continuing education for librarians on "Library History as a Learned Discipline" can be seen as a forerunner of the Round Table on Library History.[81]

This Round Table has the task of investigating the holdings of all kinds of libraries and their usage by readers, of revealing the archival sources for library history and describing the development of individual types of libraries, of library administration and library building and also of their politico-cultural functions during history. The Wolfenbüttel Round Table works closely with its sister Round Table on the History of the Book, for instance, in organizing the annual spring conventions whose topics alternate yearly between these two associations. Only those devoted to library history are mentioned. They have proved an important achievement for library history in Germany. The first annual convention in April 1980 treated "Libraries in the Social and Cultural Change of the Nineteenth Century." Two years later "Buildings for Libraries" was the theme for the second convention, while in 1984 questions of "State Initiative and Library Development since Enlightenment" were discussed.

The proceedings of the first meeting have been published,[82] and those of the third meeting are also available recently at the book market.[83] Unfortunately, until now, the numerous illustrations that accompanied the papers of the second convention prevented the publication of a proceedings volume. This is especially lamentable, since one of those papers, prepared by Donald E. Oehlerts, dealt with public library buildings in the United States between 1850 and 1917, and two others with the architecture of the reading room of the British Museum (by Ian Willison), and with the library buildings of Sir Christopher Wren in their connections with library history (by Peter Hoare). Only some of those papers have in the meantime been published elsewhere: for instance, a study by Engelbrecht Boese on Walter Hofmann's concept of building libraries.[84]

Thus, the library historian is dependent on the reports about this meeting that have been published in professional journals; the most informative of such reports is the one by Angela Karasch.[85] It is not possible to go through all the papers devoted to questions of library buildings in detail here, but an exception must be made in the case of the study by Hanns Michael Crass of Henri Labrouste, his library buildings in Paris, and their influence in Germany. Some years ago, Crass published his Cologne doctoral dissertation as a handsome volume on library buildings in Germany during the nineteenth century; this is easily accessible to English-language readers through its extensive abstract in English.[86]

For the other conventions of 1980[87] and 1984,[88] reports can also be consulted. As the proceedings of the first meeting have been available for some years, only the last meeting is discussed here in detail. As with the earlier conventions, the international participation was very significant. Speakers from Austria, Denmark, Hungary, and the United Kingdom reported about the historical relationships of their governments with library development.

One of the papers was that of Peter Borchardt about German library politics in Alsace, using the example of the University and National Library in Strassburg.[89] Paul Sturges explained British library legislation during the second half of the nineteenth century in connection with the movement for better industrial and handicraft education. Herta Gregor investigated Czech library legislation for public libraries between the two world wars, which has been regarded as exemplary for other countries too. Similarly, the library legislation in Denmark influenced at least some developments in other countries, as Preben Kirkegaard showed in his lecture. The connections between the Hungarian government and the church libraries were delineated for the period after World War II. Two complementary lectures of Peter Vodosek and Michael Knoche gave several examples of the various beginnings of the public library movement in Germany. The Austrian library reformation at the end of the eighteenth century, vital to the development of the university libraries of that country, was interpreted by Walter Pongratz.

The next biannual convention of the Wolfenbüttel Round Table on Library History, scheduled for spring 1986, will deal with the topic "Libraries and Enlightenment." Besides these conventions, the Round Table arranges seminars each fall. The first, which took place in January 1980, discussed library history especially as the history of library collections. The proceedings of this seminar have been published recently.[90] The increasing relevance of the reception of books as an important part of the modern history of literature is dealt with from the point of view of building up library stocks.

Other seminars were devoted to "Reformation and Municipal Libraries" (autumn 1983) and to "Private Libraries in Early Modern Times: Problems of Their Study" (autumn 1984), and are being planned on "The History of Music Collections in Libraries" (for autumn 1985), "Handwritten and Printed Library Catalogs as Sources for Library History," and "Iconography of Libraries."

The Round Tables on the History of the Book and on Library History cooperate with the Duke August Library in editing the periodical *Wolfenbütteler Notizen zur Buchgeschichte.* Here articles on library history are also published. Especially noteworthy is a research report on medieval library history in Germany by Werner Arnold,[91] which is very informative regarding recent results in this area. Volumes 1 to 8 (1983) of this periodical contained a current bibliography of the history of the book in German-speaking countries, with an extensive chapter on libraries and library history. These lists have been replaced in recent years by an independently published bibliography.[92] In the future, closer contacts are also foreseen with the IFLA Round Table on Library History, in this way complementing the good relations of the Wolfenbüttel Round Table on Library History with foreign groups engaged in this field.

Summing up, research in library history in the Federal Republic of Germany has developed more strongly during the last years than in earlier decades. The two centers delineated in this report will continue their work in library history and so contribute considerably to the further development of the discipline. Library history in general is not an isolated field in which only the respective country is interested. The interconnections between library developments in various countries as a general cultural phenomenon can often be made clear, and many specific situations form building-stones for a more comprehensive library history. One must hope, therefore, that in the future as well, German research results in this field will continue to be internationally available for the benefit of the worldwide community of scholars in library history.[93]

Notes

1. *Jahresberichte für deutsche Geschichte* (last volume published: 15/16, pt. 1: 1939/40, Leipzig: Koehler, 1942; new series 1: 1949- , Berlin: Akademie-Verlag, 1952-).

2. An overview on the German system of library education is given by Paul Kaegbein and Diann Rusch, "Library and Information Science Education in West Germany," *Journal of Education for Librarianship* 22 (1981/82): 154–172.

3. See Paul Kaegbein, "The German University of Library and Documentation Science," *International Library Review* 14 (1982): 343-344.

4. Ingeborg Konze and Ludwig Sickmann, *Verzeichnis der beim Bibliothekar-Lehrinstitut des Landes Nordrhein-Westfalen 1949–1970 angefertigten Hausarbeiten für den höheren Dienst an wissenschaftlichen Bibliotheken* (Köln: Greven 1971), Bibliographische Hefte, 6. A continuation for the years 1971–1985 is being prepared.

5. Vgl. Verband der Bibliotheken des Landes Nordrhein-Westfalen, *Mitteilungsblatt*, new series 21 (1971): 141–142; 22 (1972): 61–62, 267–268; 23 (1973): 50–51, 274–275; 24 (1974): 76–77, 170–171; 25 (1975): 42–43, 257; 26 (1976): 46–48, 217–218; 27 (1977): 64–66, 274–275; 28 (1978): 130–133; 29 (1979): 58–59, 185; 30 (1980): 77–80; 31 (1981): 103–106, 180–181; 32 (1982): 63, 175–176; 33 (1983): 49–50, 305–306; 34 (1984): 82–83, 150–151, 465.

6. Address: Fachhochschule für Bibliotheks- und Dokumentationswesen in Köln. Fachhochschulbibliothek. 1, Claudiusstrasse, D-5000 Cologne 1.

7. In such a case only this published version is cited in the following notes.

8. Werner Krieg in his preface to the bibliography cited in note 4, p. vi.

9. Hans-Peter Adler, "Beobachtungen zu Bibliotheken und Archiven des alten Vorderasiens: Moderne bibliothekarische Kriterien, angewendet auf die Ergebnisse der Ausgrabungen" (1972).

10. Fritz Milkau, "Der Alte Vorderorient," Neu bearbeitet von Josef Schawe, in *Handbuch der Bibliothekswissenschaft*, 2nd ed., vol. 3: *Geschichte der Bibliotheken* (Wiesbaden: Harrassowitz, 1955), pt. 1, pp. 4–17.

11. Günter Burkard, "Bibliotheken im alten Agypten," *Bibliothek* 4 (1980): 79–115.

12. Maria-Luise von Graberg, "Neueste deutsche Forschung zur Geschichte der Bibliotheken Alexandreia's (1955–1971), Ein Bericht," *Libri* 24 (1974): 277–301.

13. Rudolf Fehrle, "Das Bibliothekswesen im alten Rom: Voraussetzungen, Bedingungen, Anfänge" (1984), prepared for publication as a monograph.

14. Heinz Martin Werhahn, "Bibliotheksnachrichten bei Hieronymus" (1953).

15. Peter Jörg Becker, "Bibliotheksreisen in Deutschland im 18. Jahrhundert," *Archiv für Geschichte des Buchwesens* 21 (1980): cols. 1361–1534; English summary in cols. 1532–1534.

16. Gunter Mann, *Die medizinischen Lesegesellschaften in Deutschland* (Köln: Greven, 1956), Arbeiten aus dem Bibliothekar-Lehrinstitut des Landes Nordrhein-Westfalen, 11.

17. Hella Schwemer, "Grosse Lesegesellschaft und Societätsbibliothek: Ein Beitrag zur Geschichte des öffentlichen Bibliothekswesens in Hannover" (1982); Hermann Staub, "Die Akademische Lesegesellschaft zu Helmstedt von 1789 bis 1810, Zugleich ein Beitrag zur Geschichte der Universitätsbibliothek Helmstedt" (1983); Ilse Makowski, "Emanzipation oder 'Harmonie': Zur Geschichte der gleichnamigen Mannheimer Lesegesellschaft in der ersten Hälfte des 19. Jarhhunderts" (1984).

18. Benedikte Winterstein, "Beiträge zur Entwicklung der deutschen Arbeiterbibliotheken 1890–1933" (1974); Heinz-Dieter Stege, "Bildung und Bibliothek in Konzeptionen der deutschen Arbeiterbildungsvereine zwischen 1830 und 1868" (1983).

19. Sabine Zehrer, "Friedrich von Raumer und die Entstehung der Berliner Volksbibliotheken nach anglo-amerikanischem Vorbild" (1975).

20. Tibor Süle, *Bücherei und Ideologie: Politische Aspekte im "Richtungsstreit" deutscher Volksbibliothekare 1910–1930* (Köln: Greven, 1972), Arbeiten aus dem Bibliothekar-Lehrinstitut des Landes Nordrhein-Westfalen, 42.

21. Jutta Sywottek, "Die Gleichschaltung der deutschen Volksbüchereien 1933 bis 1937," *Archiv für Geschichte des Buchwesens* 24 (1983): cols. 385–536. Compare also for complementing the topic of libraries in the Third Reich some recent American research papers by Pamela Spence Richards, "Aryan Librarianship," *Journal of Library History* 19 (1984): 231–258, and "German Libraries and Technical Information in Nazi Germany," *Library Quarterly* 55 (1985): 151–173.

22. Regine Glötzel, "Von der Theke zur Freihand: Zur Entwicklungsgeschichte der Ausleihverfahren öffentlicher Bibliotheken in Deutschland" (1976).

23. Ulrich Moeske, "Das kommunale Sondersammelgebietsprogramm im Lande Nordrhein-Westfalen: Entstehung und Erfahrungen 1956 bis 1976, dargestellt an Hand der Literatur und unveröffentlichten Materials" (1977).

24. Ingrid Holtgrewe, "Die Entwicklung des Benutzungsrechts der öffentlichen wissenschaftlichen Bibliotheken seit Anfang des 19. Jahrhunderts" (1968); Engelbert Plassmann, "Geschichtliche Grundlagen des Benutzungsrechts der deutschen Bibliotheken: Vorstellungen der Bibliothekare und Normen der Benutzungsordnungen von der Mitte des 18. bis zur Mitte des 19. Jahrhunderts," *Bibliothek und Wissenschaft* 8 (1972): 142–200.

25. Nikolaus Scholl, "Bibliothekar und Wissenschaft: Studien zur Geschichte des bibliothekarischen Berufs," *Bibliothek und Wissenschaft* 1 (1964): 142–200; Nikolaus Strelczyk, "Studien zur Entwicklung von Berufsbild und Berufsausbildung wissenschaftlicher Bibliothekare in Deutschland" (1971); Verena von Grote, "Die Anfänge der Beschäftigung von Frauen als Berufsbibliothekarinnen im deutschen Bibliotheksdienst (1895–1921)" (1981).

26. Ursula Renner-Henke, "Der Bibliothekar in der deutschsprachigen Schönen Literatur des 19. und 20. Jahrhunderts" (1982).

27. Manfred Pape, "Freihand- oder Magazinbibliothek: Zur Geschichte der Kritik an deutschen wissenschaftlichen Bibliotheken seit Georg Leyh, Mit einem Überblick über ihre bibliotheksgeschichtlichen Voraussetzungen" (1981).

28. Jutta Fielitz, "Zur Geschichte des Auskunftsdienstes an wissenschaftlichen Bibliotheken in Deutschland" (1983).

29. Hans-Hermann Röhrig, "Bibliotheca Conventus Coloniensis Camelitarum Discalceatorum (CCCD)," *Jahrbuch des Kölnischen Geschichtsvereins* 36/37 (1962): 173–223; Kurt Hans Staub, "Die Bibliothek der Dominikaner zu Wimpfen am Neckar und ihre Handschriften," *Durch der Jahrhunderte Strom* (Frankfurt am Main: Klostermann, 1967), pp. 179–185; Eckhard Plümacher, "Die Bibliothek der St. Nikolai-Kirche in Spandau. Ein Beitrag zur Geschichte des kirchlichen bibliothekswesens in Brandenburg vom 16. bis zum 18. Jahrhundert," *Jahrbuch für Berlin-Brandenburgische Kirchengeschichte* 46 (1971): 35–101.

30. Jürgen Busch, "Die Ratsbibliothek in Hannover," *Hannoversche Geschichtsblätter*, new series 10 (1957): 169–234; Hans Dehnhard, "Die Kölner Ratsbibliothek im 17. und 18. Jahrhundert" (1963); Karl Konrad Finke, "Die ehemalige Ratsbibliothek in Schwäbisch Hall und ihre juristischen Bestände aus dem 16. Jahrhundert" (1967); Avelke Dähn, "Geschichte der Lüneburger Ratsbücherei" (1977).

31. Brigitte Garbe, "Öffentliche Bibliotheken in Köln von der Franzosenzeit bis zur Gründung der Kölner Stadtbibliothek: Die Entwicklung von Syndikats-, Wallraff- und Gymnasialbibliothek 1794 bis 1885" (1977); Brigitte Robenek, *Geschichte der Stadtbücherei Köln von den Anfängen im Jahre 1890 bis zum Ende des Zweiten Weltkrieges* (Köln: Greven, 1983), Kölner Arbeiten zum Bibliotheks- und Dokumentationswesen, 3; Jutta Römer, "Die Stadtbibliothek grossstädtischen Bibliothekssystem" (1982); Ulrich Hunger, *Geschichte der Göttinger Stadtbibliothek von 1934 bis 1961* (Herzberg: Bautz, 1985), Arbeiten zur Geschichte des Buchwesens in Deutschland, 11.

32. Helmar Härtel, "Herzog August und sein Bücheragent Johann Georg Anckel: Studien zum Erwerbungsvorgang," *Wolfenbütteler Beiträge* 3 (1978): 235–282; Georg Ruppelt, *Von der herzoglichen Bibliothek zur Herzog August Bibliothek: Geschichte der Wolfenbütteler Bibliothek von 1920 bis 1949* (Göttingen: Bautz, 1980), Arbeiten zur Geschichte des Buchwesens in Deutschland, 4; Ingrid Recker-Kotulla, "Die Herzog August Bibliothek in Wolfenbüttel: Gebäude und Aufstellung der Bestände in historischer Sicht" (1981).

33. Renate Hobelmann-v. Busch, "Die Baugeschichte der grossherzoglichen öffentlichen Bibliothek in Oldenburg," *Oldenburger Jahrbuch* 78/79 (1978/79): 29–82; Klaus-Peter Müller, "Die Landesbibliothek Oldenburg von der Jahrhundertwende bis 1945" (1984).

34. Horst Börjesson, "Die Landesbibliothek Neustrelitz" (1976).

35. Rudolf Jung, "Die Gründung der Pfälzischen Landesbibliothek und ihre Entwicklung bis zum Jahre 1945," in *Die Pfälzische Landesbiblothek 1921–1971* (Speyer: Pfälzische Landesbibliothek, 1971), pp. 9–79.

36. Ulrich Weber, *Wilhelm Brambach und die Reorganisation der Grossherzoglich Badischen Hof- und Landesbibliothek in Karlsruhe (1872–1904)* (Köln: Bibliothekar-Lehrinstitut des Landes Nordrhein-Westfalen, 1954), Arbeiten aus dem Bibliothekar-Lehrinstitut des Landes Nordrhein-Westfalen, 3.

37. Peter Schmidt, "Die Universitätsbibliothek Freiburg 1744–1795" (1984); Elmar Mittler, *Die Universitätsbibliothek Freiburg i.Br 1795–1823: Personal, Verwaltung, Übernahme der säkulasierten Bibliotheken* (Freiburg, München: Alber, 1971), Beiträge zur Freiburger Wissenschafts- und Universitätsgeschichte, 35; Johannes Günther, "Die Universitätsbibliothek Freiburg i. Br. 1823–1849: Die Verwaltung der Universitätsbibliothek Freiburg im Breisgau von der Ernennung Eisengreins zum 'ersten Bibliothekar' als Nachfolger Baggatis (1823) bis zum Tode

des Oberbibliothekars Amann (1849)," *Bibliothek und Wissenschaft* 9 (1975): 37–133; Gerhard Stamm, "Die Universitätsbibliothek Freiburg vom Dienstantritt Heinrich Josef Wetzers (1850) bis zur Auflösung der Bibliothekskommission (1888): Reformen und Reformpläne, Grundzüge der Verwaltung" (1969); Ingo Toussaint, *Die Universitätsbibliothek Freiburg im Dritten Reich*, 2nd ed. (Munich, New York, London, Paris: Saur, 1984).

38. Gerd Brinkhus, "Die Bücherstiftung Konrad Hagers für die Universität Tübingen im Jahre 1539: Eine Studie sum ältesten erhaltenen Bestand der Tübinger Universitätsbibliothek," *Bibliothek und Wissenschaft* 14 (1980): 1–109; Werner Paul Sohnle, *Gelehrtenwirtschaft hinter Schloss und Riegel: Die Universitätsbibliothek Tübingen am Anfang des 19. Jahrhunderts (1798–1836)* (Tübingen: Mohr, 1976), Contubernium, 9; Peter Michael Ehrle, *Robert von Mohl als Leiter der Tübinger Universitätsbibliothek (1836–1844)* (Tübingen: Mohr, 1975), Contubernium, 10; Harald Weigel, "Adelbert Keller und Johannes Fallati als Leiter der Tübinger Universitätsbibliothek (1844–1855)" (1985); Ludger Syré, "Die Universitätsbibliothek Tübingen unter ihrem Direktor Karl Geiger (1895–1920)" (1985); Hannsjörg Kowark, *Georg Leyh und die Universitätsbibliothek Tübingen (1921–1947)* (Tübingen: Mohr, 1981), Contubernium, 19; Hartmut Zillmann, "Bibliothekar im totalitären Staat: Die Erwerbungen ausländischer Literatur der Universitätsbibliothek Tübingen im Dritten Reich" (1984).

39. Angela Karasch, "Der Carl-Schäfer-Bau der Universitätsbibliothek Freiburg (1895–1903)" (1982); Ralf Wildermuth, "Der Bonatzbau der Universitätsbibliothek Tübingen bis zur Einweihung im Jahre 1912" (1984).

40. Marta Leszlei Dosa, *Scholarship, Libraries, Politics in the Life and Work of Georg Leyh* (Ann Arbor, Mich.: University Microfilms, 1973); Marta L. Dosa, *Libraries in the Political Scene: Georg Leyh and German Librarianship, 1933–1953* (Westport, Conn.: Greenwood Press, 1974).

41. Hellmut Vogeler, "Johann Christian Felix Bähr als Oberbibliothekar der Universitätsbibliothek Heidelberg (1832–1872)," *Bibliothek und Wissenschaft* 7 (1970): 40–137.

42. Reinhard Tiesbrummel, "Das Gebäude der Universitätsbibliothek Heidelberg: Seine Baugeschichte in den Jahren 1901 bis 1905" (1978).

43. Barbara Schneider-Esslinger, "Tendenzen des Bibliotheksbaus der 20er und 30er Jahre in Europa" (1984).

44. Günter Baron, "Die Entstehung der Lesesaalhandbibliothek in den deutschen Universalbibliotheken im 19. Jahrhundert" (1966).

45. Marlene Mies, "Zentralkataloge in den Vereinigten Staaten von Nordamerika: Ihre Entwicklung seit 1935" (1951).

46. Gerd Schmidt, "Panizzis Regeln für den alphabetischen Katalog. Zur Entstehungsgeschichte der 91 'Rules for the Compilation of the Catalogue,'" in *Bibliothekswissenschaft, Musikbibliothek, Soziale Bibliotheksarbeit* (Wiesbaden: Harrassowitz, 1982), pp. 71–76.

47. Bernhard Adams, "Charles Ammi Cutters 'Expansive Classification': Eine kritische Darstellung" (1965).

48. Beate Gresser, "Entwicklungen im sowjetischen Bibliothekswesen auf dem Gebiet der lokalen und regionalen Bestandsvermittlung seit 1945, Dargestellt an Hand sowjetischer Fachliteratur" (1981).

49. Irmgard Wille, "Buch- und bibliotheksgeschichtliche Themen in der russischen und jugoslavischen Fachliteratur seit 1950" (1964); Mechthild Golczewski, "Die Darstellung der russischen Bibliotheksgeschichte in der sowjetischen Bibliothekswissenschaft nach dem Zweiten Weltkrieg," *Bibliothek* 7 (1983): 32–59.

50. Gerd Wilbert, "Die Bibliothekswissenschaft in der Sowjetunion: Zentrale Probleme im Spiegel der Diskussion des letzten Jahrzehnts," *Bibliothek* 7 (1983): 5-26.

51. Richard Gerecke, "Danmarks Biblioteksforening 1919-1978" (1979); Christian Andersen, "Die Staatsbibliothek in Aarhus seit ihrer Gründung im Jahre 1902" (1980).

52. Hermann Koch, "Geschichte und Entwicklung der Bibliotheken des British Council, Dargestellt anhand einiger Beispiele" (1975); Robert Klitzke, "Zur Gründungsgeschichte der British Library" (1980).

53. Renate García y Más, *Die Biblioteca Nacional in Madrid* (Berlin: Colloquium-Verlag, 1975), Biblioteca- Ibero-Americana, 20; Arturo Quintana Font, "Die Bibliothek der Benediktinerabtei Montserrat" (1976).

54. Hermann Bode, "Nachrichten über Pariser Bibliotheken: Aus einem Reisetagebuch des Johann Friedrich Armand von Uffenbach" (1961); Holle Ganzer, "Das Interesse der französischen Enzyklopädisten am Buch-, Verlags- und Bibliothekswesen" (1979).

55. Matthias Buschkühl, "Die Bibliothek des Trinity College in Dublin" (1981).

56. Peter Borchardt, "Die deutsche Bibliothekspolitik im Elsass: Zur Geschichte der Universitäts- und Landesbibliothek Strassburg 1871-1944," in *Staatliche Initiative und Bibliotheksentwicklung seit der Aufklärung*, ed. Paul Kaegbein and Peter Vodosek (Wiesbaden: Harrassowitz, 1985) pp. 155-213.

57. Karl Nolden, "Das Serapeum 1840-1870" (1959); Stefan Ertz, "Julius Petzholdt's 'Anzeiger' 1841-1886" (1967); Horst Röhling, "Slavische bibliothekarische Fachzeitschriften und ihre Berücksichtigung in 'Library Science Abstracts,'" in Röhling, *Slavica-biblioteca-ecclesia orientalis* (Frankfurt am Main, Bern, Cirencester/UK: Lang, 1981), pp. 9-26.

58. Gernot Gabel, "Die amerikanische bibliothekswissenschaftliche Zeitschrift Library Quarterly: Eine Darstellung und Analyse vor dem Hintergrund der Bibliothekarausbildung in den Vereinigten Staaten" (1976).

59. Dieter Henning, "Dreissig Jahre deutschen Buch- und Bibliothekswesens (1903-1933) im Spiegel niederländischer und skandinavischer Fachzeitschriften" (1960); Clemens Hying, "Das deutsche Bibliothekswesen nach 1945 in amerikanischer Sicht" (1968).

60. Michael Knoche, "Wissenschaftliche Bibliotheken im Spiegel der deutschen Tagespresse," *Bibliothek* 5 (1981): 207-219.

61. Rolf Engelsing, "Der Bürger als Leser: Die Bildung der protestantischen Bevölkerung Deutschlands im 17. und 18. Jahrhundert am Beispiel Bremens," *Archiv für Geschichte des Buchwesens* 3 (1960): 205-368.

62. Some theoretical and methodological aspects in this field have been discussed by Gabriela Žibritová in her paper "Metodologické problémy výskumu dejín knižnej kultúry," *Zborník filozofickej fakulty univerzity Komenského, Informatika* 1 (1973): 163-175 (summary pp. 174-175: methodological problems in historical research of book culture).

63. Reinhard Ligocki, "Zur Entwicklung der deutschen Leihbibliothek im 19. Jahrhundert" (1984).

64. Wolfgang Schmitz, *Deutsche Bibliotheksgeschichte* (Bern, Frankfurt am Main, New York: Lang, 1984), Germanistische Lehrbuchsammlung, 52. A review will appear in the *International Journal of Reviews in Library and Information Science* 2 (1985/86).

65. Karl-Heinz Weimann, *Bibliotheksgeschichte* (München: Verlag Dokumentation, 1975).

66. Ladislaus Buzás, *Deutsche Bibliotheksgeschichte des Mittelalters* (Wiesbaden: Reichert, 1975), Elemente des Buch- und Bibliothekswesens, 1; *Deutsche Bibliotheksgeschichte der Neuzeit (1500–1800)* (1976), Elemente des Buch- und Bibliothekswesens, 2; *Deutsche Bibliotheksgeschichte der Neuesten Zeit (1800–1945)* (1978), Elemente des Buch- und Bibliothekswesens, 3. This work will be published in English translation: Ladislaus Buzás, *A History of German Libraries, 1800–1945*, trans. William Douglas Boyd with the assistance of Irmgard H. Wolfe (Jefferson, N.C.: McFarland, 1985).

67. Joris Vorstius and Siegfried Joost, *Grundzüge der Bibliotheksgeschichte*, 8th ed. (Wiesbaden: Harrassowitz, 1980).

68. Wolfgang Thauer and Peter Vodosek, *Geschichte der Öffentlichen Bücherei in Deutschland* (Wiesbaden: Harassowitz, 1978).

69. *Bibliothek: Forschung und Praxis*, ed. Paul Kaegbein, Hans Joachim Kuhlmann, Elmar Mittler, and Josef Tiwisina (München, New York, London, Paris: Saur, 1977–), with English abstracts for all articles, three numbers per year with annual index; five-year index 1977–1981 appeared in 1982.

70. An overview about research work and other articles on public libraries published here is given by Paul Kaegbein, "Das Öffentliche Bibliothekswesen als Forschungsbereich, Dargestellt am Beispiel der Zeitschrift 'Bibliothek,'" *Verband der Bibliotheken des Landes Nordrhein-Westfalen: Mitteilungsblatt*, new series 34 (1984): 270–276.

71. R. Paul Sturges, "Die bibliotheksgeschichtliche Literatur in Grossbritannien: Forschungsbericht," *Bibliothek* 4 (1980): 155–162.

72. Manfred Komorowski, "Das Schicksal der Staats- und Universitätsbibliothek Königsberg," *Bibliothek* 4 (1980): 139–154; Manfred Komorowski, "Die wissenschaftlichen Bibliotheken im Generalgouvernement Polen (1940–1945)," *Bibliothek* 7 (1983): 69–75.

73. Walter Gebhardt, "Zur Geschichte der Sachkatalogisierung an der Universitätsbibliothek Tübingen 1817 bis 1861," *Bibliothek* 6 (1982): 74–88; Dirk Klotz, "Die Entwicklung der Sacherschliessung in deutschen öffentlichen Bibliotheken von 1900 bis 1945," *Bibliothek* 1 (1977): 71–93.

74. Gerhard Thorn, "Die Entwicklung des Lesesaals in öffentlichen Bibliotheken: Von der Lesehalle zum Informationszentrum," *Bibliothek* 4 (1980): 116–138.

75. Brigitte Braun, "Öffentliche Bibliothek und kommunale Kulturpolitik in der Bundesrepublik Deutschland: Vergleichende Analyse der Auffassung von Kulturpolitikern und Bibliothekaren," *Bibliothek* 2 (1978): 77–111.

76. Peter Vodosek, "Zur Entwicklung des bibliothekarischen Berufs als Frauenberuf," *Bibliothek* 5 (1981): 231–244.

77. See note 25 above.

78. Engelbrecht Boese, "Walter Hofmanns 'Institut für Leser- und Schrifttumskunde' 1926–1937," *Bibliothek* 5 (1981): 3–23.

79. Further information can be received by contacting: The American Friends of the Herzog August Library, Inc., Executive Office: Gunnar A. Kaldewey, 1014 Fifth Avenue, New York, NY 10028.

80. *Bücher und Bibliotheken im 17. Jahrhundert in Deutschland: Vorträge des 4. Jahrestreffens des Wolfenbütteler Arbeitskreises für Geschichte des Buchwesens, 22. bis 24. Mai 1979*, ed. Paul Raabe (Hamburg: Hauswedell, 1980), Wolfenbütteler Schriften zur Geschichte des Buchwesens, 6.

81. *Bibliotheksgeschichte als wissenschaftliche Disziplin: Beiträge zur Theorie und Praxis, 7. Fortbildingsseminar für Bibliothekare 23. bis 25. Januar 1979*, ed. Peter Vodosek

(Hamburg: Hauswedell, 1980), Wolfenbütteler Schriften zur Geschichte des Buchwesens, 7. Principal questions of library history, also in connection with its teaching, that can not be dealt with in this paper have been discussed by the lecturer at the Library School in Cologne. Tibor Süle (see note 20) in his studies "Geschichte und Bibliotheksgeschichte," *Verband der Bibliotheken des Landes Nordrhein-Westfalen: Mitteilungsblatt*, n.s. 24 (1974): 212–222, and "Geschichte in der bibliothekarischen Ausbildung," in *Bibliothekarische Ausbildung in Theorie und Praxis* (Köln: Greven, 1975), pp. 145–160.

82. *Bibliotheken im gesellschaftlichen und kulturellen Wandel des 19. Jahrhunderts*, ed. Gerhard Liebers and Peter Vodosek (Hamburg: Hauswedell, 1982), Wolfenbütteler Schriften zur Geschichte des Buchwesens, 8.

83. *Staatliche Initiative und Bibliotheksentwicklung seit der Aufklärung*, ed. Paul Kaegbein and Peter Vodosek, Wolfenbütteler Schriften zur Geschichte des Buchwesens, 12 (Wiesbaden: Harrassowitz, 1985).

84. Engelbrecht Boese, "Büchereibau bei Walter Hofmann," *Bibliothek* 8 (1984): 123–128.

85. Angela Karasch, "Bauten für Bücher: Zweites Jahrestreffen des Wolfenbütteler Arbeitskreises für Bibliotheksgeschichte," *Bibliothek* 6 (1982): 244–248. Another report by Horst Röhling can be found in *Verband der Bibliotheken des Landes Nordrhein-Westfalen: Mitteilungsblatt*, new series 32 (1982): 284–287.

86. Hanns Michael Crass, *Bibliotheksbauten des 19. Jahrhunderts in Deutschland: Kunsthistorische und architektonische Gesichtspunkte und Materialien*, with an English summary: "Library Buildings in Germany during the 19th Century" (München: Verlag Dokumentation, 1976) (English summary on pp. 129–150).

87. Horst Röhling, "Erstes Jahrestreffen des Wolfenbütteler Arbeitskreises für Bibliotheksgeschichte," *Verband der Bibliotheken des Landes Nordrhein-Westfalen: Mitteilungsblatt*, new series 30 (1980): 378–382; Werner Arnold, "Bibliotheken im gesellschaftlichen und kulturellen Wandel des 19. Jahrhunderts: Erstes Jahrestreffen des Wolfenbütteler Arbeitskreises für Bibliotheksgeschichte," *Zeitschrift für Bibliothekswesen und Bibliographie* 27 (1980): 462–464; Hellmut Vogeler, "Erstes Jahrestreffen des Wolfenbütteler Arbeitskreises für Bibliotheksgeschichte," *Bibliothek* 4 (1980): 164–165.

88. Michael Knoche, "Staatliche Initiative und Bibliotheksentwicklung seit der Aufklärung: Drittes Jahrestreffen des Wolfenbütteler Arbeitskreises für Bibliotheksgeschichte vom 14. bis zum 16. Mai 1984," *Bibliothek* 8 (1984): 249–251; Horst Röhling, "Drittes Jahrestreffen des Wolfenbütteler Arbeitskreises für Bibliotheksgeschichte," *Verband der Bibliotheken des Landes Nordrhein-Westfalen: Mitteilungsblatt*, new series 34 (1984): 317–320; Werner Arnold, "Staatliche Initiative und Bibliotheksentwicklung seit der Aufklärung: Drittes Jahrestreffen des Wolfenbütteler Arbeitskreises für Bibliotheksgeschichte vom 14. bis 16. Mai 1984 in der Herzog August Bibliothek Wolfenbüttel," *Buch und Bibliothek* 36 (1984): 610–612, and *Wolfenbütteler Bibliotheks-Informationen* 9 (1984): 18–19.

89. See note 56 above.

90. *Bibliothek und Buchbestand im Wandel der Zeit*, ed. Franz A. Bienert and Karl-Heinz Weimann (Wiesbaden: Harrassowitz, 1984), Buchwissenschaftliche Beiträge aus dem Deutschen Bucharchiv, 8.

91. Werner Arnold, "Mittelalterliche Bibliotheksgeschichte in Deutschland," *Wolfenbütteler Notizen zur Buchgeschichte* 9 (1984): 58–76.

92. *Bibliographie der Buch- und Bibliotheksgeschichte* (*BBB*), worked out by Horst Meyer, vol. 1: 1980/81– (Bad Iburg: Meyer, 1982–).

93. An example of successful cooperation within this community may be seen in the fact that Pamela Spence Richards agreed to look through this paper not only from the linguistic point of view but also with her skilled professional eye. The author owes her much gratitude for both aspects.

Index

Eugene B. Jackson and Ruth L. Jackson

NOTE

This Index is in two sections: SUBJECT AND TITLE INDEX, p. 474, and AUTHOR INDEX, p. 490. In the first one, the terms are selected from previous *JLH* Indexes, LIBRARY LITERATURE, and *LIBRARIES & CULTURE*, Proceedings of Library History Seminar VI, Austin, TX, 19-22 March 1980. Entries are arranged letter-by-letter. Acronyms appear at the head of the letter involved. As there are no multiple authors, the entries in the AUTHOR INDEX are a simple rearrangement of the names in the Table of Contents.

One would hope that by the time Seminar VIII appears that its Indexes would be a resort of machineable typesetting tapes rather than the traditional methods used to this point. In the meantime, comments on *JLH* indexes should be sent to the Editor.

SUBJECT AND TITLE INDEX

AUTHOR INDEX